TRAVELER'S GUIDE TO THE
GREAT ART TREASURES
OF EUROPE

Traveler's Guide to the
Great Art Treasures
of Europe

DAVID LAWRENCE MORTON

G.K. HALL & CO.

BOSTON

Acknowledgments

The author wishes to thank the Irish Tourist Board, Aer Lingus Irish Airlines, the National Tourist Office of Spain, and Iberia Airlines for their kind cooperation.

Traveler's Guide to the Great Art Treasures of Europe

Copyright 1987 by David L. Morton

Book design and production by John Amburg
Copyediting supervised by Michael Sims

Library of Congress Cataloging-in-Publication Data

Morton, David Lawrence.
  Traveler's guide to the great art treasures of Europe.

  Includes index.
  1. Art—Europe—Guide-books. I. Title.
N6750.M67 1987   709′.4   87-8460
ISBN 0-8161-8733-9
ISBN 0-8161-8931-5 (pbk.)

For Suzanne, my wife,
who persuaded and inspired me
to write this book.

Contents

——— *France* ———

Netherlands

Portugal

Spain

To the Reader

For many years now, ever since I have been visiting Europe, I have observed travelers exhausted by the prospect of so many great works of art and frustrated by their inability to remember enough about them to fully appreciate what they were seeing. Yet, this is to be expected. It is exceedingly difficult to recall what one read years ago in a college text book, or even recently in one of those large "coffee-table" art books, when you are standing in a crowd of museum spectators far from home, surrounded by hundreds of works of art.

This book is meant to relieve that difficulty by simply pointing out the greatest works of art that are worthy of your attention, and discussing, in a short text, their importance in the history of art, the artists who created them and their overall meaning. It is hoped that the book will prevent the physical and mental fatigue that comes from not knowing about what you are looking at, or even *what* to look at.

I have arranged the book geographically by country. Cities are listed alphabetically within each country; museums, buildings and monuments are listed alphabetically within each city; and the artists whose works are discussed are listed alphabetically within each museum.

I have also provided a useful glossary of terms relating to painting, sculpture and architecture, and an index which lists cities and their principal museums, buildings and monuments, as well as artists, with the names and locations of their works.

You will find an asterisk (*) after the names of many of the major artists throughout the book. This refers to the existence of a short general text, or at least some additional useful information about the artist, usually placed before the discussion of one of the artist's major works in the country of his birth. The list of artists and their works in the Index contains a corresponding asterisk directing the reader to the page that contains this general information.

In most cases, I have given the room numbers, or the names of the rooms in museums and palaces, for each work of art, but these will not always be accurate. (Occasionally, works are moved within a museum, or away on loan, or removed for restoration; in some cases the works have been removed while the museum is being renovated.) Similarly, the hours of admission given for the places covered in the book are subject to change.

In the large museums (National Gallery and Tate Gallery in London; Louvre in Paris, Royal Museum of Fine Arts in Antwerp, Royal Belgian Museums of Fine Arts in Brussels, Rijksmuseum in Amsterdam, Uffizi Gallery in Florence, Alte Pinakothek in Munich, Prado in Madrid, and Kunsthistorisches in Vienna), where I have included a discussion of many works of art, a room-by-room index, keyed to the names of the artists whose works are discussed, is provided at the beginning of the section covering the museum. That means, as you visit the various rooms of these museums, you have the opportunity of quickly noting if a room you have entered has any works that are discussed. If it does, you need only to turn to the name of the artist, listed alphabetically, to find the text.

The works of art that I have singled out for discussion do not reflect my own personal preferences. Most of them are, by time and authority, the greatest works of art in Europe called to your attention without regard for a specific itinerary, though some of them have found their way into the book also because they are representative of a country's national art. There are still others, of course, that I have not included, or have relegated to a brief mention. This was done to give you an idea of the collection of a museum or palace, or to call your attention, once again, to a country's national art, or just because you should know that they are there. I wish I could have discussed every great work of art in Europe, but there are too many of them. No one book that the traveler could comfortably carry with him could be big enough for that.

David Lawrence Morton

Austria

While this section on Austria is devoted mainly to the European paintings that occupy the picture gallery of the famed Kunsthistorisches Museum in Vienna—as one of Europe's truly great collections it cannot be overemphasized—the abundance of the baroque style will probably capture most of your attention in Austria.

The baroque, which provided Austria with its greatest achievement in art, was developed in Italy and France and got to Austria somewhat late. Austrian artists accepted it as their own and created a distinct Austrian style, more cheerful and light than Roman high baroque and French formalism. It provided Austria with an outpouring of artistic energy that found its expression in architecture and interior decoration. Architects, painters, and sculptors, often working together, created an atmosphere of gilded saints and cherubs, soaring twisted columns and painted heavens on ceilings, that make it possible in Austria for even the most casual traveler to enter the dreamworld of the baroque. You will see it everywhere, especially in churches, abbeys, and palaces, so grand and delightful that you may never tire of it.

Also of particular interest is Vienna of the fin-de-siècle. There was an astonishing outpouring of creative activity during that time, when the painter Gustav Klimt was the leader of the Vienna Secession—the revolt against academic art—that contained the germs of this century's most important artistic and intellectual movements. His art and the art of his contemporary Egon Schiele—well displayed in Vienna—has in recent years experienced a vogue in Europe. In 1985 a Schiele painting was sold at Sotheby's in London for a record $2.7 million.

Melk

Located fifty-five miles west of Vienna, on the Danube

BENEDICTINE MONASTERY

Hours: Open daily 9AM–12 noon and 2–5PM; guided tours, Apr. and May, 9–11:30AM and 1–4PM (till 5PM in summer), otherwise 11AM–2PM. Admission fee.

Abbey Church

This splendid baroque church was designed by **Jakob Prandtauer** (1660–1726) in 1702 and completed in 1738, after his death. It is surrounded by the abbey buildings, but dominates the group with the symmetrical towers of its west front and its great octagonal dome. If you look at the buildings from various locations—especially from the river—you will see that the group succeeds in forming a unified, harmonious design. The interior of the church is lavishly decorated with gold ornaments, marble, and paintings by Rottmayr, Troger, and Fanti.

Marble Hall and Library

Flanking the forecourt are the marble hall and library, also by Prandtauer. The former contains frescoes by **Paul Trogir** (1698–1762), a major figure in the development of Austrian rococo ceiling decorations. His allegorical painting on the ceiling—*Reason Guiding Humanity from the Darkness of Obscurity Toward the Light of Civilization and Culture*—is a notable example. The library also has a marvelous ceiling painting by Trogir, and 1,800 manuscripts dating from the ninth century onward.

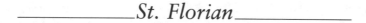

St. Florian

Located on the Danube, west of Melk, eight miles southeast of Linz

MONASTERY

Hours: Open May–Sept., daily, guided tours 10AM, 11AM, 2PM, 3PM, and 4PM; Easter to end of Apr. and Oct., daily, guided tours 11AM and 3PM; Nov.–Easter, one may see only the church. Admission fee.

Altdorfer, Albrecht (ca. 1480–1538), German

The treasure of this baroque abbey is the **Altdorfer Gallery**. Like Dürer, Grünewald, and Cranach, the other great Northern artists of the early sixteenth century, Albrecht Altdorfer was uniquely German in his intense interest in nature and in the emotional expressiveness of the human figure. His work shows the heights achieved by the Danube style, considered a forerunner of eighteenth-century Romanticism.

At St. Florian the Altdorfer collection comprises the remains of two folding altarpieces dedicated respectively to St. Sebastian and St. Florian. These colorful panels combine landscape effects with a bold use of architecture to produce a heightened dramatic effect. The night landscapes of the panels called *Christ on the Mount of Olives* and *The Seizure of Christ* are breathtaking.

Also at St. Florian, see the **grand staircase** leading to the imperial apartments, extending two stories with balustrades adorned with statues and walls and ceilings covered with frescoes and stucco.

Salzburg

There are two important baroque churches in Salzburg built by the master architect of the baroque in Austria, **Fischer von Erlach** (1656–1723).

The **Dreifaltigkeitskirche** (Holy Trinity, 1694), located on the east bank of the river on Markplatz, is Fischer's prelude to his Vienna masterpiece, the Karlskirche (St. Charles's Church). Its grand plan is essentially the same, though on a smaller scale, and like the Vienna church its dome frescoes are by Rottmayr (1700). The **Kollegienkirche** (College Church, 1694–1707), on the Universitatsplatz, built for the Benedictine University, is similar to the Dreifaltigkeitskirche but taller. Note the rich baroque altar with the stucco composition behind and above it culminating in billowing clouds, symbolic of clouds of incense. In both of these churches Fischer merges architecture, sculpture, and painting to produce a baroque effect, carrying it further than it had gone in Italy. Only in Vienna does Fischer's work reach greater heights.

An earlier structure shows that while Austrian artists were learning to master the baroque style, Italian artists took their place. The **Cathedral** (1614–28), located on the Domplatz, is an example, having been built by Santino Solari of Como, and is the first Italian church north of the Alps. The design of its facade, Roman baroque, is carried inside, with noble proportions based on the Latin cross plan.

Adjoining the cathedral is the **Residenz,** the former residence of the archbishops, whose richly decorated state rooms can be visited daily from June 1–Sept. 30, 10 and 11AM and 2, 3, and 4PM; Oct.–May, 10 and 11AM and 2 and 3PM; on Sat., Sun., and holidays at 10 and 11AM; admission fee. The **gallery** within (second floor) contains 200 paintings, including Rembrandt, Titian, and Brueghel. It is open daily 10AM–5PM; admission fee.

In the **Mirabell Palace** and gardens (free admission), on Mirabell Platz, among additions made by **Lucas von Hildebrandt** (1668–1745) is a beautiful **staircase** (1726) ornamented by vases and putti in the baroque style. The medieval **Hohensalzburg Fortress** is perched on a hill atop the city and can be seen from everywhere. The central keep of the castle dates from the twelfth century, but the rest of it, including the walls, were added or restored through the seventeenth century. Most notable in its interior is its great hall and Golden Room (both dating from the early sixteenth century). These are richly decorated and have some extraordinary metal and ceramic stoves for which Austria is famous. Guided tours of the fortress are conducted every fifteen minutes from May to Sept., 9AM–5:30PM; every thirty minutes from Oct. to Apr., 9:30AM–3:30PM; admission fee.

_____ *Vienna* _____

Museums

AKADEMIE DER BILDENDEN KÜNSTE

Schillerplatz 3

Hours: Open Tues., Thurs., Fri., 10AM–2PM; Wed., 10AM–1PM and 3–6PM; Sat., Sun., 9AM–1PM. Admission fee.

This art school, founded in 1692, has a gallery of old master paintings that include *Crowning of the Virgin*, by Dieric Bouts (ca. 1415/20–75); *Tarquin and Lucretia*, by Titian (ca. 1487–1576); *Lucretia*, by Lucas Cranach the Elder (1472–1553); a *Crucifixion*, by Memling (ca. 1433–94); *Portrait of a Woman*, by Rembrandt (1606–69); *Orithyus Kidnapped by Borée* and fourteen oil sketches by Rubens (1577–1640); plus paintings by Guardí, Lorrain, and others.

The triptych of the **Last Judgment**, by **Hieronymus Bosch** (ca. 1450–1516), is the museum's most famous masterpiece. On the left-hand panel Bosch tells the story of the Fall of Man beginning in the Garden of Eden. On the right-hand panel he describes the tortures of Hell. The center panel is the Last Judgment, which Bosch expresses with a human theme. We see a typical Boschian landscape filled with the tortures of the most imaginative kind, often being carried out with complicated implements and machines.

ALBERTINA MUSEUM

Augustinerstrasse 1

Hours: Open Mon., Tues., Thurs., Fri., 10AM–4PM; Wed., 10AM–8PM ; Sat., Sun., 10AM–1PM; closed Sun. in July and Aug. Admission fee.

This museum, near the Hofburg, has an unrivaled collection of 40,000 drawings, sketches, and watercolors, and more than one million etchings, engravings, and prints. While all of the great masters from the Middle Ages to the twentieth century are represented, the treasures of the collection are the **Dürers**. These include such marvels of draftsmanship as his silverpoint *Self-portrait at Thirteen*, exquisite watercolors like *Young Here* and *The Great Piece of Turf*, and detailed preparatory studies for paintings, such as **Praying Hands**.

Only a fraction of the collection at the Albertina is on display at one time, but there is a room where selections from the stock may be studied on request.

KUNSTHISTORISCHES MUSEUM

Burgring 5, Maria-Theresien Platz

Hours: Open Tues.–Fri., 10AM–6PM; Sat., Sun., 9AM–6PM. Admission fee.

Picture Gallery

The picture gallery of the Kunsthistorisches Museum, with its rich array of works from every period and school of European painting, is one of Europe's most distinguished collections. Largely the work of the Hapsburg family, who assembled it over a period of four hundred years, the collection was first housed in Vienna in the Stallburg wing of the Imperial Palace until it was moved by Maria Theresa into the Upper Belvedere Palace. There, in 1781, the public was first allowed access to the collection, and in 1783 the first catalog appeared. As a result of the Napoleonic Wars many works were removed to France as spoils of war, but in 1815 most were returned to Vienna. In 1891, the gallery was transferred from the Upper Belvedere to the Kunsthistorisches Museum, which Emperor Franz Josef I had built to unite the entire Hapsburg art collection. At present about 800 pictures are displayed—about a tenth of the total.

Index to the Rooms of the Kunsthistorisches Picture Gallery

Artists mentioned below have works referred to in the text that follows. These works are listed under the names of the artists, arranged alphabetically.

Room 2   Tintoretto
Room 5   Caravaggio
Room 8   van Eyck, van der Weyden, van der Goes
Room 10   Bruegel
Room 13   Rubens

Cabinet 1   Mantegna, Giorgione
Cabinet 2   Titian
Cabinet 6   Raphael
Cabinet 8   Correggio
Cabinet 11 Velázquez
Cabinet 15 Dürer
Cabinet 16 Cranach, Altdorfer
Cabinet 18 Holbein
Cabinet 20 Rubens
Cabinet 23 Rembrandt
Cabinet 24 Steen, Vermeer

Altdorfer, Albrecht (ca. 1480–1538), German

The Resurrection (ca. 1518): cabinet 16
This panel and *The Entombment,* in the same room, are a continuation of the Altdorfer altarpieces at the Monastery of St. Florian. *The Entombment*

was sold to the Vienna gallery by the monastery in 1923 and *The Resurrection* in 1930. Like the remaining panels at St. Florian, they represent the finest achievement of the Danube School of painting.

Note, in *The Resurrection,* how Altdorfer has used the dawn setting to heighten the dramatic effect of the risen Christ, shown as a luminous apparition glowing with an inner light. The rising sun in back of Christ and the moonlight still penetrating the clouds add to the supernatural brightness.

Bruegel, Pieter, the Elder (ca. 1525–69), Flemish
The Pieter Bruegel collection is the finest and largest in the world. Apart from the four mentioned below, the others also deserve attention.

Christ Carrying the Cross (1564): room 10
Looking at this painting one is caught up in a typical Bruegelian crowd— over 500 figures have been counted. The mannerist composition places the figure of Christ, being led to the Hill of Calvary for his execution, in the background, and places less important figures in the foreground. This gives Bruegel room to display the callousness of the common man witnessing the tragedy of Christianity without realizing what it means to him and to mankind. Nobody in the cavorting crowd even notices Mary and the small group of mourners that surround her, visible in the lower right hand corner.

The Peasant Wedding (1567/68): room 10
The significance of this painting lies in the contribution it made to artistic realism in European painting. Prior to *The Peasant Wedding,* which depicts the most straightforward rendering of everyday life painted in the sixteenth century, few artists thought of painting such a subject. It was not until the seventeenth-century Dutch genre scenes of Steen, or the nineteenth century in France with painters like Courbet, that there was a serious attempt to portray the common man.

Like other Bruegel paintings, *The Peasant Wedding* is full of symbolic comment, which has given rise to a debate concerning the meaning of the picture and the correctness of the title. That a wedding feast is taking place cannot be doubted. The composition of the picture draws our eye from the right shoe of the servant dressed in blue in the foreground, upward between the red cap of the servant and the red cap of the figure passing plates, to the lady, or bride, sitting under a primitive crown. The bride's parents are probably seated at her left occupying a place of honor. The groom, who, some critics say, is not even in the picture, may be the figure leaning back from the table raising his jug for more drink, or he may be the man at the head of the table serving, since it was the custom for a bridegroom to serve the bride at a banquet in the house of the bride's parents.

Of greater interest, though, is the satirical content of the scene. This is a wedding feast, a sacred rite, but it is dominated by gluttony. Everyone at the table, except the bride, her parents, and the two guests at the extreme left end of the table care only about the food and wine. Is this callousness what the Franciscan monk is complaining about to the bearded gentleman, or burgomaster, seated at the extreme right in the picture?

Hunters in the Snow (1565): room 10

This painting is one of the five surviving paintings done by Bruegel as a series of months—*The Gloomy Day* and *The Return of the Herd* in the Vienna gallery (Room 10) are two more, and *The Harvesters* in the Metropolitan Museum of Art in New York and *The Hay Harvest* in the National Gallery in Prague are the other two. While all of them are linked to the medieval tradition, which treats the life of man in terms of his dependence upon the changing seasons, they are high points of European art because for the first time a major artist has painted landscapes without biblical scenes.

In *Hunters in the Snow*, winter is shown as the time of year when the peasant can relax from his struggle with the soil. The peace of the scene is brought out by the firm, taut composition of verticals, horizontals, and diagonals. There is even a sense of security for the viewer of the picture who, by following the pictorial route laid down by the artist, is prevented from getting lost among the details. The uninterrupted diagonal procession of the hunters and their dogs, accented by the tall trees, penetrates into the middle ground, leading the eye along the edge of the frozen ponds to the distant Alpine summits. These are reminiscent of the mountain drawings Bruegel brought back from his journey to Italy and published as a series of engravings in 1560. This diagonal movement is repeated along the row of houses and, against the steel-blue sky, the gray-green ice and the white snow, everything combines to produce a single magnificent effect. That is what is most remarkable about *Hunters in the Snow*—it conveys to us in a hauntingly precise way the brooding winter world of northern Europe and the dark figures of the people who inhabited it.

The Tower of Babel (1663): room 10

The story of the *Tower of Babel* relates how King Nimrod, shown in the lower left corner, ordered a tower built to reach heaven, and how God punished him for his presumptuousness by making his workers speak in a confusion of languages so that the job could not be completed. As a symbol of human arrogance and pride, it was enormously popular. Bruegel painted it three times.

Bruegel's visit to the Colosseum in Rome seems to have inspired him in the incompleteness of the structure. The Romanesque and Gothic elements, such as the massive buttresses, are intended to produce an archaic effect. Though there is a sense of credibility to the enormous size of the tower, because Breugel has painted details of the city lying below it, one senses the folly of the project, and that it is doomed to failure.

Caravaggio* (1573–1610), Italian

The Madonna of the Rosaries (ca. 1606): room 5

Even though Caravaggio's work was sometimes rejected as too realistic, it was right for its time. The revolution of religious thought demanded art that appealed to the emotions. Caravaggio's painting is quite different from the religious works that came immediately before it in Italy. His characters drawn from everyday life, the dramatic lighting, and the composition that creates a surge of movement, all involve the spectator in the scene as never before.

Caravaggio's work had an important effect on seventeenth-century artists. There can be no greater tribute paid to Caravaggio than the fact that *The Madonna of the Rosaries* was purchased by Rubens, Jan Bruegel the Elder, and Hendrik van Balen, all Flemish painters of note, and that it was presented by them to the Dominican church at Antwerp.

Correggio (ca. 1489/94–1534), North Italian

Jupiter and Io (early 1530s): cabinet 8

In Correggio's treatment of the story Ovid tells of Jupiter's love for the nymph Io, we have an example of the Leonardoesque sfumato (light and dark) combined with a Venetian sense of color and texture. We also have one of the most daring pictures ever painted in Italian art up to that time. The artist's interpretation shows Jupiter, who has transformed himself into a cloud to spread darkness over the countryside to prevent the nymph's flight, engulfing Io's nude body with his amorphous hand, and Io swooning in his cloudlike embrace. It is clear that Correggio is depicting Io at the moment of sexual climax in a glorification of the female figure. There are many erotic paintings in the history of art; this one by Correggio is as vivid as any.

The Vienna gallery also has Correggio's *The Rape of Ganymede* (cabinet 8), which forms a counterpoint to *Jupiter and Io*.

Cranach, Lucas, the Elder (1472–1553), German

The Crucifixion (1500–1503): cabinet 16

This painting is one of Cranach's earliest known works and a fine example of the Danube School of painting. We see Golgotha surrounded by steep cliffs and wild trees. There is an agitated feeling, where the falling light paints long shadows on the ground and makes the colors glow as though by some inner source. Even the crosses have expressive value. That of the good thief on the left rises from the group of holy mourners and consists of a straight, almost black tree trunk. To the right, rising above the group of executioners, the cross of the bad thief is yellowish white and curved like the rogue nailed to it—an image of impenitent pride. Christ's Cross, however, is different. Taller and thinner, its bark has been partly stripped as though it, too, has been injured.

Dürer, Albrecht* (1471–1528), German

The Adoration of the Trinity (1511): cabinet 15

While Dürer was an artist who bridged the gap between the Middle Ages and the Renaissance, this painting is one of Dürer's more medieval works, though it has a sense of unity modern for its subject matter. It shows the three levels of the Gothic Augustinian conception of the universe. On the highest level of the heavens God is supporting the Cross of the crucified Christ, with the dove of the Holy Ghost fluttering overhead. This level dominates the composition. On the middle level, to the left, the Virgin leads a multitude of female saints, and to the right John the Baptist is seen with men of the Old Testament—Moses, David, and the prophets. On the lower level, on a cloud floating above a landscape, are those in adoration—clerics to the left, laics to the right. Dürer himself occupies a small place in the right-hand corner on the earth below.

In a more modern looking work, *The Madonna with the Slice of Pear,* from 1512 (cabinet 15), shows that Dürer's work in Germany was influenced by the Renaissance. The Christ Child has acquired a grandeur that is Michelangelesque; the Virgin's head is among the loveliest painted in the late Gothic period. See also Dürer's portraits: *Emperor Maximillian I* (1519), *Johann Kleberger* (1526), and *Portrait of a Young Girl* (1505).

Eyck, Jan van* (ca. 1390–1441), Flemish

Cardinal Niccolo Albergati (1430s): room 8
This picture, with its luminous detail and polished finish, typical of van Eyck paintings, was probably done at the behest of Duke Philip the Good of Burgundy, to whom Jan was court painter. The cardinal, on a diplomatic visit from Rome to the Burgundian court, probably could not have gotten his portrait painted in Italy by a first-rate artist, because Italian masters during van Eyck's time rarely painted portraits other than donors on religious works; regular portraits were left to minor artists. But eight of Jan van Eyck's surviving paintings are simple portrait heads.

Giorgione* (ca. 1477–1510), Venetian

The Three Philosophers (ca. 1506): cabinet 1
This painting is typical of Giorgione's subjective art. No one seems to know who the figures in *The Three Philosophers* represent. They have been interpreted as the three Magi who meet each year at a small cave to await the appearance of the star announcing the Messiah; or as the three ages of human learning (antiquity, the Middle Ages, and the Renaissance); or as the three phases of Aristotelianism (Pythagoras, Ptolemy, and Archimedes); or even the young Marcus Aurelius being instructed by two philosophers on Caelian Hill. However, the mood of dreamy devotion to beauty, humanity, and nature that Giorgione conveys is not dependent upon a subject.

Goes, Hugo van der* (ca. 1440–82), Flemish

The Fall of Man (ca. 1470): room 8
This early panel is the left half of a diptych. With its companion, a *Lamentation,* it shows the fall and redemption of man.

In the *Fall of Man* Hugo has painted with Eyckian realism. But unlike van Eyck, whose landscapes continue infinitely into the distance, here the natural surroundings are precisely delineated. The two figures, which have a surface reality that makes them not nude but naked, have been placed in the foreground, with Eve, who has the leading role, at the center. The drama of the Fall is suggested by the eloquent decline in stature of the figures, from the tall, calm, upright Adam, via the slightly restless Eve, to the small ugly serpent with a woman's head.

Holbein, Hans, the Younger (1497–1543), German

Jane Seymour (1536/37): cabinet 18

Jane Seymour, the third wife of Henry VIII, has been described by her contemporaries as pale, of medium height, and not particularly beautiful. This description of her and her motto, "Bound to obey and to serve," have been captured by Holbein in her portrait painted in 1537 shortly before she died in childbirth.

Mantegna, Andrea (1431–1506), Italian

St. Sebastian (1459/60): cabinet 1

According to legend, St. Sebastian was a high officer in the Roman army, but fell into disgrace for helping Christian prisoners and for revealing that he too was a Christian. The emperor handed him over to his Numidian archers, who tied him to a column in the Colosseum and shot arrows into him.

As a subject for a painting, St. Sebastian fitted in perfectly with Mantegna's interest in antiquity, in which he was regarded an expert. Yet, while the setting interested him (Mantegna signed his name to this picture in Greek), it is obvious the pagan world he depicts in ruins is more symbolic of his religious feelings as a Christian.

Raphael* (1483–1520), Florentine

The Madonna in the Meadow (1505): cabinet 6

In this painting and in other paintings of the Madonna executed by Raphael in Florence early in his career, in which the Virgin and the infants St. John and Christ are shown in the open air set against a peaceful landscape, Raphael developed a personal style, obtaining a harmonious clarity of form and balance of forces within a self-contained composition.

The three figures are enclosed within an almost equilateral triangle, the basis for the stable composition which expresses the psychological bond between them. It is one of the most peaceful figurative arrangements ever created in European painting. Nothing disturbs the serenity of the scene. Only St. John's staff in the form of a cross hints at the future.

Rembrandt* (1606–69), Dutch

Self-portraits (three): cabinet 23

Rembrandt painted over one hundred self-portraits during his lifetime. He is the only artist who turned self-portraiture into biography, as an examination of three self-portraits in the Vienna gallery shows. The three follow one another from 1652 to 1658. While they constitute only a part of Rembrandt's life, it was a period when the artist was having financial problems that led to his bankruptcy.

In the **Large Self-portrait,** dated 1652, Rembrandt presents himself in a defiant near-frontal pose, showing self-assurance, spirit, and vital energy. Three years later, in **Self-portrait with Gold Chain** (1655), Rembrandt is now turned slightly toward the right. He wears a dark barret, a fur coat, and a gold chain. The greater part of his face is wrapped in soft half-shadow and, owing to the turned-up collar and the attitude of the head, the impression here is no longer one of self-confidence. Finally, in the *Small Self-portrait,* painted last (between 1656 and 1658), Rembrandt's financial problems are now bearing down upon him. Everything is concentrated on the head; the portion of the figure represented is more narrowly confined than in the other two self-portraits. In this painting we cannot fail to miss Rembrandt's inward unrest, which shows up in his quivering face that reveals anxiety and bewilderment.

Rubens, Peter Paul* (1577–1640), Flemish

Helena Fourment in a Fur Coat: cabinet 20
This painting is Rubens's portrait of his second wife, his most tender compliment to the woman who filled the last ten years of his life with happiness. We see her half nude with her face turned toward the painter and her body twisted in a way that seems as though she has been surprised while dressing. In his will Rubens ordered that this painting, which he called *The Little Fur,* should not be sold.

Self-portrait: cabinet 20
Rubens's self-portrait, painted a few years before his death, is a picture of a still-handsome man happy to lead a quiet life at home after a distinguished career as a statesman and artist.

Steen, Jan* (1626–79), Dutch

The World Upside-Down (1663): cabinet 24
Here is Jan Steen at his best: the finest painter of genre scenes (paintings of everyday life) in seventeenth-century Holland. He enjoys showing us a drunken household surrounded by its own litter, but he is also interested in the play of light and color around his subjects, and has given us a composition that is a work of genius.

Notice the way Steen guides us from one figure to another, starting first with the girl who directs her empty smile at us. She leads us to the drunken cavalier, whose leg is resting on her knee and to whom she is offering a glass of wine. The cavalier shows no interest in her and is looking at the old maid behind him whose apron he clutches with his left hand, causing roses she is carrying to fall to the floor. A pig who has wandered into the house smells them inquisitively (a reference to the proverb, "Only a fool throws roses to pigs"). The old maid pays no attention to the cavalier and continues to lecture the man reading. No doubt his book is open for the benefit of the duck on his shoulder, a symbol of corruption and ruin. And so it goes. The duck is turned toward the violinist, who is looking toward the sleeping matron, who in turn leads to the naughty children who spread more disorder with their mischief. All around is a movement of the eye from object to object, but to prevent the picture from breaking up into its elements the artist has stabilized his composition by creating symmetries around the central couple, which embrace not only the main figures but also details, such as the broken crocks and half-eaten scraps on the floor.

No doubt every character and object refers to an old Dutch proverb and has some definite meaning. Steen himself could not refrain from inscribing his work with a moralizing text; on a slate lying on the stairs are the words, "When you lead the sweet life be prudent."

Tintoretto* (1518–94), Venetian

Susanna and the Elders (1552–54): room 2
Tintoretto has chosen the tense moment when Susanna, bathing alone in what she thinks is the privacy of her garden, is being spied upon by two lustful elders (judges) who were given permission by Susanna's rich husband to use the garden to settle people's law suits. In the background, behind the elder who peers around the rose hedge, there is sexual implication unmistakable in the stag and the female deer at the water's edge. Farther away the silhouette of Venice is visible, glittering in the sunlight. The other elder, an upright figure, is standing at the far end of the rose hedge, which links the two evildoers. Susanna, unaware of her fate, appears cut off in the foreground of the picture with no way of escape. Her almost life-size figure, painted with delicate modeling and flesh tints, makes her one of the most magnificent of Tintoretto's nudes.

Titian* (ca. 1487–1576), Venetian

The Gypsy Madonna (1510): cabinet 2
This early Titian shows a close dependence on Giovanni Bellini, in whose studio Titian spent his apprenticeship. It has Bellini's Venetian concern with color, texture, and surface pattern, and a composition similar to Bellini's *Young Woman with a Mirror* (cabinet 1). However, there are differences that indicate the coming Titianesque style. The oval face of the Madonna, especially her lips, have a new fullness, and her well-rounded form and earthy fleshtones harmonize with the rich colors of her costume and the background drapery. It is the colors that are most different; with Titian's emerging imagination and technique, they have not only become sensuous but also the principal element in building forms.

Though Titian's idea of womanhood was still to emerge over the coming years, replacing Bellini's quiet, sweet Madonnas with figures more fleshy and real, the *Gypsy Madonna* is an indication of things to come.

Velázquez, Diego* (1599–1660), Spanish

Philip IV of Spain (1660): cabinet 11
During Philip's inept rein he brought Spain to bankruptcy, drained the nobles and the church of their wealth, and reduced the masses to poverty. The king's pallid face and tired eyes testify to his feeling of gloom. No matter how much Philip blamed himself for Spain's misfortunes, Velázquez seemed not to have blamed him at all. There was probably no closer relationship between a monarch and an artist than that between Philip IV and Velázquez. Owing to that, Velázquez has painted Philip with the feeling of a friend who understood the weakness of the king and felt sorry for him.

The Infanta Margarita Theresa in Pink (1654): cabinet 11
Princess Margarita was the daughter of Philip IV and Mariana of Austria,
Philip's second wife and daughter of Emperor Ferdinand III. At fifteen Margarita married her uncle, Emperor Leopold I, but she died in Vienna at
twenty-two. Even though Velázquez appears to be interested in the floral
beauty of Margarita's dress, he has painted her in the innocence of childhood, with a plump face that glows in the soft light. It is the most delicately
colored of Velázquez's paintings and is considered the artist's most exquisite
infanta portrait.

This painting and others painted by Velázquez appealed to the impressionists. This can be understood in the color and light brought out with
blobs of color in which the brush stroke is visible. Two hundred years later
Monet and his friends used the same technique of brushwork.

The Infante Philip Prosper (1659): cabinet 11
The melancholy portrait of Philip IV's little son, Philip Prosper, on whom
rested the hopes for the continuation of the Hapsburg line in Spain, was
painted when the prince was two years old. Two years later the child was
dead.

When Philip Prosper was born in 1657 he was described as a lovely
baby, but he turned out sickly. Velázquez shows him wearing charms to
ward off the evil eye, guard him against disease, and protect him from witchcraft. As though he had a premonition of the child's approaching death,
Velázquez has painted a picture of a lonely child with an empty space behind
him that adds to the melancholy.

Vermeer, Jan* (1632–75), Dutch

The Artist in His Studio (1660–72): cabinet 24
This painting is considered Vermeer's masterpiece. The bright light from behind the curtain, the air and space throughout the composition that, typical
of Vermeer, is somewhat geometrical, and the pure color all delight the eye.
So does the curious pose of the artist and his model.

There is a debate as to the meaning of the picture. One interpretation
holds that the artist's model represents Fame, Victory, or Clio, the muse of
history. In this context, the map on the wall tells of the glory of the Netherlands that in the seventeenth century was rich, powerful, and the home of
art. Fame, wearing a laurel wreath, has taken up her residence there. However, others feel that the painting is Vermeer's own homage to art, painted
for himself. With this in mind, the painter at his easel symbolizes the world
of man, and the model, standing in full light, the artistic sense of expression.
All this vague symbolism, along with the clear light, beauty of color, and
spatial structure, add to the captivating quality of the picture.

Weyden, Rogier van der* (ca. 1399–1464), Flemish

Altarpiece with the Crucifixion and Two Donors (ca. 1440): room 8
This work, dating from the time Rogier was the city painter at Brussels, was
probably conceived as a fixed altarpiece, since the lateral panels are too nar-

row to cover the central panel completely, and the three panels are firmly bound together by a broad hilly landscape that continues behind the frames. Furthermore, this unified effect is emphasized in the arrangement of the blue-black mourning angels and the figures below. Though differentiated from the other figures, the Magdalena, with her jar of ointment, and St. Veronica, holding the Sudarium, link up with the central panel in the same plane as the two male figures at the front of the Cross. It is unique to find the donor couple introduced into the main scene on an almost equal footing with the holy figures. However, they have been kept apart from the Cross by the crack in the ground which separates them from the Virgin.

Sculpture

On the ground floor area, below the picture gallery, there is a distinguished collection of Greek, Roman, and Egyptian sculpture and decorative arts. Among this collection are portions of the *Parthenon frieze;* a tinted marble *Bust of a Woman* by **Francesco Laurana** (ca. 1430–ca. 1502), that has a masklike beauty and lifelike color which compensates for Laurana's frozen style; a lovely gilded and painted lindenwood *Madonna,* by **Tilman Riemenschneider** (ca. 1460–1531), probably not painted by the German master, who preferred to leave his wood carvings uncolored; and some marvelous high Renaissance pieces: *Venus Felix,* by **Antico** (ca. 1460–1528), a bronze statuette with gilded hair and drapery, silver inlaid eyes, and a base inset with nine silver coins; **Giovanni Bologna's** (Giambologna, 1529–1608) *Astronomy,* a gilded bronze statuette from the master of the small bronze figure; and the most famous piece in the collection, the gold *Salt cellar* made for Francis I by the Florentine goldsmith, **Benvenuto Cellini** (1500–71).

Buildings

THE BELVEDERE

There is one entrance at Rennweg 6 (Lower Belvedere) and another entrance, at the other end of the Belvedere, at Prinz Eugenstrasse 27 (Upper Belvedere)

Hours: Open (including both palaces and three museums) Tues.–Sat., 10AM–4PM; Sun. 9AM–1PM; closed public holidays. Admission free.

Two magnificent palaces separated by twenty-six acres of formal gardens make up the baroque world of the Belvedere. Both buildings, the Lower and the Upper Belvedere, were built by Prince Eugene of Savoy, the general who defeated the Turks in 1683 at the gates of Vienna and ultimately drove them from Europe. It was these victories that ushered in the exuberant Age of the Baroque. The dangers that had so long threatened the empire were at last banished, and palaces instead of fortified castles could be built.

Prince Eugene employed as principal architect **Lukas von Hildebrandt** 1668–1745), who had the perfect background for such an undertaking. He had grown up in Italy, where he was a pupil of Carlo Fontana and an admirer of Palladio. As a result, his work on the Belvedere shows a blend of Teutonic solidity and Mediterranean caprice.

The **Lower Belvedere,** the more Mediterranean-like of the two palaces, completed in 1716, is largely single-storied and simple, with deep horizontal lines. Inside, however, the decoration is ornate, with deep-red marble flooring and columns. Its finest room, the so-called Marble Hall, has ceiling pictures by Altomonte.

The **Upper Belvedere,** which was intended for ceremonial functions rather than as a residence, was completed in 1721–22 and is the pinnacle of Hildebrandt's creation. The building is in seven sections, three-storied at the center and two-storied at the flanks, where the four corners are each rounded off with an eight-sided cupola. While it is massively overbearing in comparison to the Mediterranean-style Lower Belvedere, the fine baroque interior is a blend of Italian gaiety mixed with Austrian design. Notice the center double staircase in white marble with rounded cherubs supporting wrought iron lanterns, and its finest room, the **Marble Hall,** twice the size of the Marble Hall of the Lower Belvedere. Though somewhat heavy in its decoration, it succeeds in maintaining a certain lightness due to the height of the room, which runs right through the central tract of the palace.

The Hapsburgs bought the palaces in 1752 after Prince Eugene's cousin and heiress, Princess Viktoria von Sachsen-Hildburghhausen, had squandered his fortune in only sixteen years. The imperial art collections were housed in the palaces from 1781 to 1891. Then, until 1914, the Upper Belvedere was the residence of the Austrian heir to the throne, Archduke Franz Ferdinand (assassinated in Sarajevo in 1914). Since the end of the monarchy the Belvedere has housed museums devoted to Austrian art from the baroque to the modern. The art may be seen in reverse chronological order by starting at the Upper Belvedere, on a hill overlooking Vienna.

Gallery of the Nineteenth and Twentieth Centuries—Upper Belvedere

This is the state collection of modern Austrian art, starting with neoclassicist painting and including Austrian sculpture. On the first floor of the west wing is the great historical painting by Hans Makart (1840–84), *The Entry of Charles V into Antwerp.* A superior painter, Makart enjoyed great fame in Vienna during his time. His work reflects the spirit of nineteenth-century Vienna—a love of festive pomp and an extravagant, dreamlike decoration.

The **second floor** displays the works of **Gustav Klimt** (1862–1918) and **Egon Schiele** (1890–1918), two leading artists of the Jugendstil—the name used in German-speaking countries for art nouveau. Klimt, also the last great social portrait painter of the time—see the portrait of *Sonja Knips* (1898)—founded the Vienna Secession movement which expressed the new art's revolt against the aesthetic reveries of nineteenth-century art. He is best known today for the mosaiclike landscapes he did after 1903 and his ornamented figure painting that link the subject with the surfaces surrounding it. See Klimt's **Judith with the Head of Holofernes,** still somewhat in the manner of the late-nineteenth century society portraits; *The Kiss,* his most famous painting; landscapes, such as *Mohnwiese;* and the large *Beethoven Frieze,* painted in 1902 for a Secession show celebrating Beethoven. With these and other works, Klimt became one of the most important influences in the development of modern European painting.

Egon Schiele, a pupil of Klimt's, was also associated with the Vienna Secession. But as a young man, like Oscar Kokoschka (1886–1980), whose work you can also see here, he produced work more expressive of the doubts of the troubled time before World War I. His constant searching and questioning himself is reflected in his art, which often shows a predilection for the weak and the self-destructive. See his Klimt-like *Sunflowers,* in which he makes a start in free abstract painting; the linear *Wife of the Artist;* the searching, *Artist's Family;* and the morbid *Death and Girl.* Schiele and his wife died of influenza in 1918. If he had lived he may have become one of the leading painters of the first half of the twentieth century.

Museum of Austrian Medieval Art—Lower Belvedere

Located in the former Orangery, this repository of Austrian medieval art contains work primarily of the fifteenth century. It was only in this later period that art became widespread in Austria. Its collection of winged altars and painted and carved tableaus, which once served as devotional pieces in Austrian churches, is a marvelous display of medieval supernaturalism.

Museum of Austrian Baroque Art—Lower Belvedere

This collection, devoted to the most productive period of Austrian art, from 1680 to 1790, traces the development of Austrian painting from baroque to rococo. There are excellent works by the leading painters of the time: Martino Altomonte (1657–1745), Paul Trogir (1698–1762), and Johann Rottmayr (1654–1730), with other artists whose aim was to create a heavenly world by picturesque illusion. There is also the most comprehensive collection of works by Austria's two great sculptors: Raphael Donner (1693–1741) and Franz Xavier Messerschmidt (1736–83).

THE HOFBURG (ROYAL PALACE)

This is a large complex of buildings located between the Volksgarten and the Burggarten, and between the Michaelerplatz and the Burgring

The Hofburg today contains many of the city's most important cultural entities: the Austrian National Library, the Spanish Riding School, the Albertina Museum, the collections of court porcelain and silver, the imperial apartments, and the imperial treasury.

The most notable parts of this complex were built in the early eighteenth century from plans by **Johann Bernhard Fischer von Erlach** (1656–1723), the official architect of the imperial court of Vienna. After his death, his son, Josef Emmanuel Fischer von Erlach (1693–1742), carried out his designs and added to them.

The von Erlach's finest work at the Hofburg is the **National Library** (facing the Josefsplatz) completed in 1735 and considered one of the greatest achievements of Austrian baroque, though it is also a display of the coming neoclassicism in architecture; looking at its facades you can see its decoration is less dramatic and overwhelming than if it had been done in the basic baroque style.

Another important building from this period is the **Imperial Chancery** (facing Michaelerplatz) also completed by Joseph Emanuel Fischer von Erlach (1729), but entirely his own. While it may lack his father's original and imaginative touch, it is still an excellent design and carries further the neoclassic development.

See also the most recent addition to the Hofburg called **Neue Hofburg** (between the Burggarten and the Heldenplatz) built between 1881 and 1908 during the reign of Franz Josef. Though less important architecturally than the older parts of the Hofburg, the Neue Hofburg is nevertheless an imposing building with a facade of sweeping colonades in the solid nineteenth-century style.

KARLSKIRCHE (ST. CHARLES'S CHURCH)

Karlsplatz

This church was built as the result of a vow made by Charles VI during a plague in 1713. It was designed by **Fischer von Erlach** (1656–1723) and built between 1716 and 1737, being completed after Fisher's death by his son. It is considered von Erlach's most important work.

True to the baroque, which did not bind the artist to rules, the structure contains contrasting architectural styles, combined to present a dramatic effect. In front is a Roman portico with six Corinthian columns flanked by two tall Trajan Columns, modeled after those in Rome, but drawn from the idea of the minaret. Each column is ornamented with spiral relief carvings illustrating the life of St. Charles Borromeo, symbolizing the victory of faith over disease.

While the facade of the church is broad, the great green **baroque dome**, which rises behind it to a height of 230 feet, is the overpowering element in the design. It emphasizes the core of the building, which is in the shape of an enormous oval drum and dome intersected by a Greek cross.

Inside the decoration is somewhat somber. Most attention is drawn to the interior of the oval dome, decorated with frescoes by Johann Rottmayr (1654–1730).

The Karlskirche, as prominent as it is, stands isolated in the history of architecture; outside of Fischer's own work it has neither antecedents nor successors. It is an original masterpiece, Fischer's best work, and a marvelous display of Austrian baroque monumentality.

SCHÖNBRUNN PALACE

Located at the end of Mariahilferstrasse

Hours: Open for conducted tours of State Apartments Oct.–Apr., daily, 9AM–12 noon and 1–4PM; May–Sept., daily, 9AM–12 noon and 1–5PM; June–Aug., Wed., Thurs., Sat., 7–9:15PM; July and Aug. conducted tours with concert, Wed., Sat., 7–9:15PM. Admission fee.

Schönbrunn Palace, like Versailles, is one of Europe's great palaces. There is a domestic aura about the place, even though it is untenanted. Its low, sprawling layout, its wings thrust forward to embrace the entrance and beckon the visitor toward it, and the warmth radiating from the famous Schönbrunn yellow of its facade give this effect.

Its history goes back to 1682, when Emperor Leopold decided to construct a summer residence that would be the talk of Europe and the envy of her courts. He selected **Fischer von Erlach** (1656–1723), the master of Austrian baroque, to create the plan. Von Erlach did this on a scale too grand even for an emperor. A second plan was more manageable for the Hapsburgs and work began in 1696. The three-storied structure was completed in 1713, and final alterations were carried out in 1749.

The interior of the palace is far more elaborate than its exterior. Its showpiece, the **Great Gallery**, 140 feet in length and splendid in white and gold with a richly inlaid wooden floor, is one of the most sumptuous baroque interiors in Europe. Almost equally impressive are the **Million Room**, so named because it was supposed to have cost one million thalers to decorate with pure gold; the **Gobelin Salon**, with enormous tapestries; the enchanting **Hall of Mirrors**, where musical history was made by a four-year-old boy from Salzburg named Mozart playing the harpsichord before the astonished empress and her guests; and other interiors shown on the palace tour (a total of forty-five of the 1,441 rooms that make up the palace are shown).

ST. STEPHEN'S CATHEDRAL

Stephensplatz

Hours: Open (guided tours of the interior), Mon.–Sat., 10:30AM and 3PM; Sun. and holidays, 3PM; also May–Oct. evening tours, Sat., Sun., and holidays, 7PM. Admission fee.

This cathedral is Vienna's great medieval monument and one of the largest in Central Europe. It was founded in 1137, but its present form dates from the fourteenth century.

Its main **exterior** characteristics are its huge southern tower rising 446 feet, and its steeply pitched patterned roof of glazed tiles. The tower was completed in 1433 and work commenced on an additional northern tower in 1450, but in 1511, when the work was half completed, it was stopped and never resumed. In 1579 the unfinished tower was topped by a cupola. As it is, there is a satisfying balance between the huge bulk of the roof and the soaring single tower.

The most celebrated work of art in the dark, medieval **interior** (nave) is the late Gothic sandstone pulpit (1510–15) in which its designer, Anton Pilgram, included his own portrait. He peers out of a window below the steps, humbly subordinate to the busts of the four fathers of the church that surge out from the elaborate tracery. Also of interest is the red marble tomb of Emperor Friedrich III (d. 1493), in the Apostles' choir, illustrating the struggle between good and evil, and, in the left apsidial chapel, the carved wooden, painted, and gilded Wiener Neustadt altarpiece dating from 1447.

Belgium

Belgium is the contributor of one of Europe's most important periods of painting, the Flemish School from the fifteenth to the seventeenth century. It gave us some of the greatest masters in the history of art: Jan van Eyck (ca. 1390–1441); Rogier van der Weyden (ca. 1399–1464); Hans Memling (ca. 1433–94); Pieter Bruegel the Elder (ca. 1525–69); Peter Paul Rubens (1577–1640); Anthony van Dyck (1599–1641); Jacob Jordaens (1593–1678); and many others. It also gave Europe the technique of oil painting, which turned painters away from the more limited medium of tempera. Tempera did not allow color tones on the panel to be smoothly blended, making it difficult to achieve clear three-dimensional effects. The oil technique made possible a high degree of reality through its wide range of color, luminosity, and polish. In this sense we have the Flemish masters to thank for showing the way to modern art.

Some Flemish masterpieces of painting are on display in almost every capital city of Europe, for Flemish paintings were a favorite of many royal collectors. But most of the work still remains in Belgium. Most are to be seen in the Belgian art cities of Antwerp, Bruges, Brussels, and Ghent.

Also on display is Gothic, Renaissance, and Baroque architecture that includes religious buildings as well as civil structures: guild halls, belfries, and town halls, many on town squares where their beauty is enhanced by those open spaces.

Antwerp

Museums

MAYER VAN DEN BERGH MUSEUM

Lange Gasthuisstraat, 19

Hours: Open Tues.–Sun., 10AM–5PM; closed Mon. (except Easter Mon., Whitmonday, Mon. after the second Sun. in August), Jan. 1 and 2, May 1, Ascension Day, Nov. 1 and 2, Dec. 25 and 26. Admission fee.

Fritz Mayer van den Bergh became a passionate art collector at the age of twenty thanks to the wealth of his parents. After his death in 1901, at forty-three, his mother housed his collection in a sixteenth-century mansion where it remains today.

The collection is diverse, with examples of fourteenth- and fifteenth-century sculptures in wood, stone, alabaster, and ivory, collections of coins, textiles, and plaquettes, and a variety of crafts: pottery, porcelein, precious metals, enamels, paintings on glass, copper, and bronze, furniture, and other objects. Its most famous treasures, however, are its paintings: two by Pieter Bruegel the Elder, and three early Flemish panels.

Bruegel, Pieter, The Elder (ca. 1525–69), Flemish

Mad Meg (Dulle Griet) (ca. 1561): room 9
There are many interpretations of this picture, more closely related to the work of Hieronymus Bosch than other Bruegel paintings. Paintings such as *Mad Meg* were ordered during the sixteenth century in Flanders by intellectuals who wished to see certain moralizing symbolism, unknown to us today, expressed in art for the edification of their circle of humanist friends.

A giant, witchlike woman rushes headlong with sword in hand to challenge the seemingly impotent one-eyed monster of hell and lesser demons. Carrying a collection of loot, with the blank stare of a fanatic, she may be greed personified, a symbol of madness, the image of a shrew, or possibly an allusion to foreign domination, a contemporary issue in the Low Countries. There are Flemish proverbs that refer to "raiding hell" or "going to hell with sword in hand," but what Bruegel's picture actually means is not clear.

The museum's second painting by Bruegel is the *Series of Twelve Proverbs,* twelve medallion paintings each illustrating a popular Flemish proverb. They were mounted on a single panel in the seventeenth century and each parable was given an inscription.

The Nativity, St. Christopher, and *The Resurrection* (three panels, ca. 1400); room 6, displayed in a glass enclosed cabinet in middle of room
These three small early Flemish painted panels, *The Nativity* on the left, *St. Christopher* on the right, and *The Resurrection* on the back of the right-hand panel, are characteristic of the work produced before the van Eycks. They were once part of a polyptych (the other parts are in Baltimore) that was thought to have been painted by Melchior Broederlam (died after 1410), a Flemish primitive who worked around Ypres. Today they are believed to have been painted by an unknown artist living in the Netherlands between the Maas and Rhine rivers ("Nederlands Maaslands-Rijs"), since it was discovered that the iconography of St. Joseph on *The Nativity* panel—he is seen cutting up his hose to wrap the Child in swaddling-clothes—is closely connected to Aachen Cathedral where those hose are venerated and have been the most valuable relics in its treasury since the Middle Ages.

See also, in **room 4,** *The Calvary Triptych,* by **Quinten Massys** (1466–1530). The six carved angels surrounding it are excellent examples of Brabant wood carving of the middle fifteenth century. Massys is the Antwerp master who helped bring the Renaissance style to the Low Countries. Notice the sense of movement in the figures and the interest in depicting a landscape in depth.

In **room 7** see the large *Peasant Interior,* by **Pieter Aertsen** (1508–75), a Dutchman who became a master painter at Antwerp. He is best known for his genre scenes and still lifes, usually of fruits, vegetables, and food of all kind heaped to overflowing. This scene represents the January 6 Feast of Epiphany. Seventeenth-century painters in the Low Countries learned from Aertsen, and even Velázquez in Spain, who painted kitchen scenes early in his career, was influenced by him. There is also a large portrait of *Francesco I de Medici,* grand duke of Tuscany, by Bronzino (1503–72), who was the official portraitist to the Florentine ducal court; *St. Mary Magdalene,* by Jan Gossaert (ca. 1478–ca. 1536), whose paintings done in the Italian style made him one of the leading painters of sixteenth-century Antwerp and the *Landscape with St. Christopher* by **Jan Mostaert** (ca. 1475–1555/56). Coming more than 100 years after the small *St. Christopher* panel in room 6, it has the same iconographic detail but is a larger painting with more animation and emotional content. Notice the look of puzzlement on Christopher, who wonders why the child on his shoulders is so heavy (i.e., Christopher does not know he is carrying Christ, who has the weight of the world on his shoulders).

ROYAL MUSEUM OF FINE ARTS

Leopold de Waelplaats, 1–9

Hours: Open Tues.–Sun., 10AM–5PM; closed Mon., Jan. 1, May 1, Ascension Day, and Dec. 1. Admission fee.

This museum has one of the best collections of Flemish painting in Europe. There are over 22,000 pictures by old masters and modern artists, and although the emphasis is on Flemish artists—the museum prides itself on its collection of paintings by Rubens, its native son—the major foreign schools are well represented. The collection encompasses a survey of five centuries of European painting.

Apart from its twenty-four paintings by Rubens, there are also paintings by van Eyck, van der Weyden, Memling, Massys (five paintings), van Dyck (ten paintings), and Jordaens (eighteen paintings). An entire room is devoted to James Ensor, Belgium's modern artist considered a precursor to twentieth-century expressionists.

Index to the Rooms of the Royal Museum

Artists mentioned below have works referred to in the text that follows. Works are listed under the names of the artists, which are arranged alphabetically.

Ground Floor: Nineteenth and Twentieth Centuries

(The rooms on this floor are regularly reorganized for temporary exhibitions.)

Room 8   Delvaux, Magritte
Room 19   Ensor

First Floor: Old Masters, Fourteenth–Seventeenth Centuries

Room H   van Dyck, Jordaens
Room I   Rubens
Room K   van Dyck
Room Q   Antonello da Messina, van Eyck, van der Weyden
Room R   Massys, Memling
Room S   Fouquet

Antonello da Messina (ca. 1430–79), Italian

Crucifixion (1475): room Q
Although this masterpiece of the Italian quattrocento was painted in Venice in 1475 by an Italian master from Sicily, it is filled with the characteristics of the Flemish school; there is a vigorous realism in the smallest details. Antonello, who came into contact with the Flemish style in Naples, may have introduced the Flemish oil medium into Italy. The new medium, which gave colors strength and luminosity and made possible the fusion of one color into another, replaced the old tempera method and became the Venetian style. Though spending only about one year in Venice, Antonello was the only major painter of the fifteenth century born south of Rome who had great influence in Venice.

Delvaux, Paul (b. 1897), Belgian

Pink Bows: room 8
The first surrealist painter is popularly considered to be the fifteenth-century Flemish master, Hieronymos Bosch (ca. 1450–1516). In our own time, as though to keep the tradition going, some of the best surrealists have been Belgian, among them René Magritte (1898–1967) and Paul Delvaux.

Pink Bows is an example of the naturalistic surrealism of Paul Delvaux's best work, done between 1936 and 1942. In his dreamworld of nude, sleepwalking women in a scene of classical buildings with skeletons and rocks flung about the landscape, Delvaux deals with the theme of love via the Freudian world of the subconscious. Are we being enticed by the female figure, symbolizing the gift of love all tied up in a pink bow, to enter the sad world behind her? Is the female figure certain we will fall into the trap and tie ourselves to love by picking up the pink bow? Is love and life itself a fraud that becomes clear only when we are alone with our surrealistic dreams? It may be impossible to read these or any other thoughts into Delvaux's images, since they may be uncontrolled by conscious reason. Delvaux has said, "A painting isn't made to be explained. It's made to be looked at. People can read into it what they like."

Dyck, Anthony van (1599–1641), Flemish
Van Dyck and Rubens were the only Flemish baroque artists recognized as great masters. For a time van Dyck, the younger of the two, worked with Rubens as an assistant, but his fame spread rapidly and he was able to establish himself at an early age. He is best known today for his portraiture—see *Portrait of Cornelis de Wael* (room H)—but he was also a prolific painter of religious subjects. The Antwerp museum has two examples of this work.

The Crucifixion: room K
This painting of the Crucifixion is memorable for two reasons. First, nothing is seen of the surroundings of the scene; we are shown only the solitary figure of Christ on the Cross set against a dark sky with storm clouds. (The account of the Crucifixion tells of three hours of darkness over the land followed by an earthquake after the death of Christ.) Second, Jesus is meant to be near death, but we are not shown any of the painful details, as many Italian baroque paintings would have included. There is an indication of the victory instead of the suffering of the Crucifixion, accented by Jesus looking upward toward Heaven. This mode of expression was also employed by Rubens in his Crucifixion paintings.

Descent from the Cross: room H
The triangular composition of this painting is typically baroque, as is the dramatic lighting, which makes the scene appear as though it were being acted out on a stage. Christ's head is being supported by Mary, His mother. Mary Magdalene, her costume and hair in disorder, has stooped to kiss Christ's lifeless hand, and St. John approaches with a mantle. Van Dyck has modified the baroque style in containing the action, with a restraint of movement characteristic of many of his religious paintings. This helps give the painting the soft van Dyck touch, which is also present in his portraiture.

Ensor, James (1860–1949), Belgian
James Ensor, along with his contemporaries van Gogh, Gauguin, and Edvard Munch, succeeded in overcoming the superficial style and formal restraints of the time to create an art that was a precursor of twentieth-century expressionism and surrealism.

The Entry of Christ into Brussels: room 19
This is Ensor's satirical idea of the kind of welcome Jesus Christ might receive if he rode into a modern metropolis on Palm Sunday. It is difficult to make out the small figure of Christ mounted on a donkey; he is positioned in the center of the middle ground behind the red banner, "Vive La Sociale" (long live the socialist state), which is Ensor's expression of disgust with modern society, whose members would probably turn the event into a socialist holiday. His huge canvas (nine by twelve feet) is filled with soldiers, the town magistrate, bands, and delegations of workers and citizens waving banners proclaiming their special interests. Toward the front we see that their

faces are not faces at all but grotesque, leering masks, among them the prominent death's head with top hat in the left foreground next to the young worker shown in profile. In Ensor's iconography the mask hides nothing, it reveals everything. It is as hideous as the personality behind it that in thought and deed perpetuates all manner of evil.

Ensor painted *The Entry of Christ into Brussels* as an indictment of modern society and of contemporary art. He was only twenty-eight at the time and had experienced continued rejection of his paintings at the art exhibitions in Brussels. His art, far ahead of its time, had to wait for society to catch up to it. It was not until 1929, forty-one years after it was painted, that *The Entry of Christ into Brussels* was exhibited. Ensor, a fatalist, never thought his art would transform European sensibilities. *The Entry of Christ into Brussels* came to be viewed by Ensor as an expression of his independence and probably his superiority. He remained attached to it always. He sold it only on the condition that he retain possession of it for life. It hung on his studio wall until his death in 1949.

Intrigue (1890): room 19

This painting represents Ensor's sarcastic comment on the marriage of his sister to a Chinese art dealer living in Berlin, whom she left after one year to live in Ostende with her daughter.

Masks dominate the picture. The irony of Ensor's masks is that they may not be masks at all. In Ensor's art, as already mentioned in *The Entry of Christ into Brussels,* the real mask may be a person's unmasked face, which may not reveal the true personality. The eyes peering out from under Ensor's masks can be sarcastic, bright, dull, idiotic, or threatening. Using the mask, Ensor has given us the range of human personality. There is also a plastic quality in the masks that allows him to use all types of colors and shapes, including those not used in faithfully reproducing a human head. This way Ensor can paint freely, completely covering the canvas and giving full expression to his imagination and sense of color.

A number of other paintings by Ensor here are different from the two discussed above. Among them are *Afternoon in Ostende* (1881), an example from Ensor's "dark period," and *Woman Eating Oysters* (1882), a picture linking Ensor with impressionism. (Both paintings are in room 19.)

Eyck, Jan van* (ca. 1390–1441), Flemish

Madonna of the Fountain (1439): room Q

This small panel is typically Eyckian in its rendering of detail and in its interest in plants and flowers. It is different from van Eyck's other paintings of the Virgin in that the informal atmosphere he usually creates is lost by positioning the Virgin in front of a luxuriant silk tapestry upheld by angels rather than against a domestic background.

Van Eyck has marked this panel with his motto, *Als ick Kan* (As I can), interpreted to mean that van Eyck lived in a period not concerned by notions of genius, when art was considered merely a craft. Nevertheless, an artist of the genius of van Eyck, court painter to John of Bavaria and Philip the

Good, must have been admired widely. His *Als ick Kan* may be one of the greatest understatements in the history of art.

St. Barbara: room Q
The story of St. Barbara was popular during the fifteenth century. Barbara's father, a pagan nobleman, had a tower built with the intention of shutting up his daughter away from suitors. Barbara persuaded the workmen to make three windows symbolizing the Trinity instead of the intended two. Her father was so incensed at learning of his daughter's espousal of Christianity that he had her killed.

This unfinished panel of St. Barbara, drawn with a brush on a white ground, is dated 1437. The composition showing St. Barbara in front of a Gothic tower is of interest because when depicting a saint, fifteenth-century artists usually showed a standing figure holding objects symbolizing their attributes or relegated these objects to minor positions in the foreground. There are many paintings of St. Barbara holding a miniature tower in her hand; in this picture St. Barbara has a prayer book in one hand (symbolizing the word of God), and a peacock feather in the other hand (symbolizing her immortality). But here van Eyck has chosen to make the tower dominate the picture, possibly searching for a new and more expressive way of depicting St. Barbara, or simply wanting to show his skill in drawing a Gothic tower. A fold in the ground divides the picture to separate the tower from the figure of St. Barbara.

Fouquet, Jean (ca. 1425–77/81), French

Virgin and Child (Madonna of Étienne Chevalier): room S
This Madonna, the right-hand panel of a diptych (the left-hand panel representing the donor, Étienne Chevalier, is in the Berlin Museum), has often been called a portrait of Agnes Sorel, mistress of King Charles VII of France. It represents a blend of Flemish reality with early Italian Renaissance elements. Fouquet had made a trip to Italy in 1445 where he learned the theory of perspective and gained a feeling for the monumental. This is evident in the Madonna. Though Northern in style, it has the Italian influence of statuesque solidity combined with undeniable sensuality not present in fifteenth-century Flemish art.

Jordaens, Jacob (1593–1678), Flemish

Family Concert ("The Old Sing, the Young Chirp") (1638): room H
Jordaens was a contemporary of Rubens and van Dyck. The three are usually mentioned as dominating the artistic scene in Flanders in the seventeenth-century. After the death of Rubens, who was seventeen years his senior, Jordaens was regarded as the leading painter in Antwerp. Even today he is a kind of people's choice because of paintings like *Family Concert* with a bourgeois character. There are about twelve versions of this painting, based on an old Flemish saying, "The old sing, the young chirp." Painted in contrasts of light and shade that set out his figures in strong relief, it is an intimate scene with a sense of joy in it.

Magritte, René (1898–1967), Belgian

Revenge (Vengeance): room 8
Magritte has made a painting within a painting, which shows a room where two clouds float in front of a painting on an easel. The world of the interior and the exterior are fused. The clouds cast a shadow on the wall, like the canvas and easel.

This picture may be Magritte's revenge on nature, in the logic that the clouds are not real clouds but a picture of clouds. As a painting its reality is different from real clouds.

Massys, Quentin (1466–1530) Flemish

Deposition from the Cross: room R
This large central panel of Massys's triptych is a scene of the Deposition painted in the early sixteenth century (1508–11). The emphasis on the figures is representative of the high Renaissance style in painting being introduced into Antwerp. Realistic elements are in keeping with the Flemish style. Massys's desire to unite both styles—the traditional with the Renaissance—places him between two ages; in the Low Countries he represents a bridge between Rogier van der Weyden and Rubens.

In the same room there is *St. Mary Magdalene* by Massys in which he portrays the saint as a young Flemish girl.

Memling, Hans (ca. 1433–94), Flemish

Man with a Coin (Portrait of John of Candida) (1478): room S
Memling may have worked in Rogier van der Weyden's studio. His work is reflective of the master's style, but his figures are softer than Rogier's. His portrait of John of Candida (or it may be a numismatist displaying a piece from his collection) shows his typical style, with the figure bathed in subtle light to create a calm atmosphere. The parklike landscape in the background adds to the toned-down effect.

Though Memling was the leading painter of Bruges, he was soon forgotten after his death, and was downgraded to a minor place in early Flemish painting. He was rediscovered by the Victorians who admired his "sweet primitive" work. Today he holds a place as a typical Flemish primitive.

The museum has Memling's *Music Making Angels,* room S. These are three panels that once decorated the organs in the Church of Santa Maria at Najera, Spain, burial place of the kings of Castile. Its display of fifteenth-century musical instruments is of interest to music lovers.

Rubens, Peter Paul (1577–1640), Flemish
The character of early seventeenth-century Flemish painting was embodied in the work of Peter Paul Rubens, the great baroque painter of the north. His studio in Antwerp was like a picture factory in order to keep up with the commissions awarded to him by royalty, the clergy, and the wealthy. At one time he had two hundred painters and students in his employ, and he made two fortunes during his career of about thirty years in Flanders. His paintings are rich in color, robust, sensuous, theatrical, imaginative in com-

position, and, in his best work, improvisational, as though the colors flow spontaneously from his brush.

Two paintings of the twenty-four Rubens works that can be seen in the museum are examples of the best of his mature period.

Adoration of the Magi: room I
This huge painting was done in thirteen days (1624), a very short time for a painting of this size. It is also one of Rubens's masterpieces. Its composition has descending diagonals on the left and rising ones on the right surround the Moorish king. The column behind the Virgin, the roof above her, and the pilaster on the left in the background all provide a framework to support the delicate figures of the Virgin and Child, balancing them against the surging, masculine Magi and their retinues. The effect of chiaroscuro accentuates the sculptural roundness of every figure and the sweep of the garments.

Christ on the Cross ("Le Coup de Lance"): room I
This altarpiece, completed in 1620, is like *The Adoration of the Magi*, from Rubens mature phase (1620–28). Light colors dominate the picture, made dramatic by the dark sky. The composition is based on baroque elements of horizontals, interlocking diagonals, and receding lines leading the eye in a circular route from the centurion's thrusting lance, over to the thieves writhing on their crosses, down the right side of the painting via the vertical cross and the legs of the thief to the mourners below, and back to the centurion via the outstretched arms of Mary Magdalene. The bright light on Mary Magdalene and her position below Christ is significant in baroque art. As the image of the penitent Christian, she is a figure that the Counter-Reformation Catholic church wished to emphasize.

Weyden, Rogier van der (ca. 1399–1464), Flemish
Jan van Eyck and Rogier van der Weyden were masters of the Flemish style, but van Eyck had few pupils, and therefore less personal influence on the Flemish School, than van der Weyden. Rogier can be credited with spreading the Flemish style throughout Europe.

Beginning to paint a few years after van Eyck, Rogier had learned much about the depiction of reality from his predecessor, but he was not simply concerned with details. Outward appearance concerned him less than the inner feelings of humans, and his figures predominate. He achieves a balance between the feelings of his figures in real experience and the Gothic symbolism of the religious conventions of the fifteenth century. This fusion of the actual and the spiritual world is actually very modern, a kind of abstract emotionalism that gives the Flemish style a special dimension.

Altar of the Seven Sacraments (ca. 1434): room Q
This triptych is notable for its central panel that shows the Eucharist celebrated in the choir behind a Calvary. Under Rogier's hand the Christ on the Cross, above the weeping group of St. John and the three women, expresses religious feeling as a human emotion, elevating the brutal reality of physical suffering to a spiritual level. His four figures are vigorously outlined, with white headdresses against the silvery pillars of the church. The lateral panels,

painted in a different style, show scenes of baptism, confirmation, confession, ordination, marriage, and extreme unction.

Portrait of Philippe de Croy: room Q

Rogier may have been one of the first Flemish masters to visit Italy. His contact with the Italian Renaissance seemed to soften and humanize his Flemish mysticism. This is evident in portraits done during his last phase. This portrait of Philippe de Croy (ca. 1460), with delicate flesh tones and elegant modeling of the hands, is an expression of human feelings. It comes from a diptych that on the left had a *Virgin and Child,* now disappeared.

RUBENS HOUSE

9–11 Wapper

Hours: Open daily 10AM–5PM; closed Jan. 1 and 2, May 1, Ascension Day, Nov. 1 and 2, and Dec. 25 and 26. Admission fee.

Rubens lived in this mansion from 1615 until his death, twenty-five years later. In the **studio** (off the entrance hall) he produced most of his paintings. At thirty-one feet by twenty-six feet wide with ceilings twenty feet high, it is justly called the "Great Studio." Its tall windows allowed light to enter the room where Rubens and his associates, at one time including Anthony van Dyck, worked on as many as three paintings at once.

Though the house is not exactly the way it looked when Rubens lived there, it gives an idea of the splendid style in which the master, diplomat, and patrician lived. The **portico** that borders one side of the inner court and connects the studio with the residence is in an imposing baroque style incorporating elements of both northern and southern Renaissance styles. It can be seen in such works by Rubens as the cycle of paintings in the Louvre depicting the life of Marie de' Medici. The quotations from the Roman poet Juvenal, that Rubens had stone masons inscribe on the keystones of the side arches, leave no doubt about his intellectual humanism and stoicism. The left-hand inscription reads, "Leave it to the gods to give what is fit and useful for us; man is dearer to them, than to himself." The other reads, "One must pray for a sane spirit in a healthy body, for a courageous soul, which is not afraid of death, which is free of wrath and desires nothing."

After passing through the portico one enters the **garden,** similar in design and plantings to the time Rubens and his wife strolled in it away from the noise of the city and the busy studio. Dominating its design is the **pavilion,** also seen in Rubens's paintings. To Rubens it represented a pagan country temple. It contains figures of Hercules, Bacchus, holding a bunch of grapes, and a modern Venus, which takes the place of an original statue of Ceres, now lost.

Back inside the house, there is a *Self-portrait* in the dining room done prior to Rubens's second marriage in 1630 to Hélène Fourment. It is the most valuable painting in the house, though during Rubens's life the house contained his personal collection of many of his own paintings and about 300 old masters, including Jan van Eyck, Hugo van der Goes, Quentin Massys, Pieter Bruegel the Elder, Titian, Veronese, Raphael, and others. We know that to be true from the inventory of Rubens's estate done at his death in 1640. Unfortunately, these riches were sold and dispersed by Rubens's heirs.

Buildings

CATHEDRAL OF NOTRE DAME

Groenplaats, 21

Hours: Open Mon.–Fri., 12 noon–5PM; Sat., 12 noon–3PM; 1–4PM. Admission fee.

Antwerp Cathedral, begun in 1352 and completed in 1584, is an example of late Gothic design with northern French influence. This can be seen in the facade, where much of the sculpture was removed during the Reformation, and in the chevet, transept portals, and triple aisles. The graceful, well-proportioned 404-foot high spire, dominating the skyline of the city, is also French in design.

The interior, the largest in Belgium (its size is not immediately apparent because the space is broken up by side aisles and columns), is virtually a museum because of its three paintings by Rubens. (While the cathedral is being restored, works of art are not in their permanent places. The cathedral supplies you with a plan listing and numbering the works, which are easy to find.)

Rubens, Peter Paul* (1577–1640), Flemish

Descent from the Cross: south transept (temporarily in nave)
The triptych showing the *Descent from the Cross*, completed by Rubens in 1611–12, is from Rubens's classical period. Here the coloring is lighter and the Italian influence, while evident in the treatment of the figures, less accentuated. The composition is well controlled, with sweeping curves that lead the eye into the center. Cold, limpid light is focused on Christ and spreads throughout the picture. When this painting was displayed in Antwerp it was recognized as a triumph of color, form, and design, and established Rubens as the foremost painter of religious subjects of his time.

The other two paintings in the cathedral are *The Assumption of the Virgin* (1626; temporarily located in the nave to the left of *Descent from the Cross*), an example of Rubens's fully developed baroque art, and *The Raising of the Cross* (1610; temporarily located in Rubens atelier in the first chapel of the north aisle), which shows Italian influence in the Michelangelesque modeling of the figures.

TOWN HALL

Grote Market

Hours: Open Tues. and Sat., 8:30AM–3PM. Free admission.

The Antwerp Town Hall is the outstanding Flemish building of the sixteenth century (1561–66), the structure that was the start of a native style in the Flemish regions. Its architect, Cornelis Floris (ca. 1514–75), was the son of a stonemason and resident of Antwerp.

Unlike Italian Renaissance work, the building shows nothing of French style either. In France a building with such a centerpiece would have corner pavilions to balance it. Yet the centerpiece at Antwerp contrasts well with the horizontal lines of the side portions, in a design indigenous to Belgium. It is related to Belgium's medieval belfries, but with a difference: in the belfries the vertical emphasis of the center dominates the whole. In the Town Hall it is the facade, with its elaborate detail and substantial dimensions, that impresses most, making the center almost trivial in comparison. There is not a better example of Flemish mannerism in Belgium; it inspired the design of similar structures in Germany and Holland.

The Grote Market (Main Square) has sixteenth-century **guild houses**, partially restored to their original splendor. They are fine additions to the setting of the Town Hall.

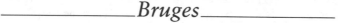

Bruges

Museums

GROENINGE MUSEUM (CITY MUSEUM OF FINE ARTS)

Dijver, 12

Hours: Open Mar.–Sept., daily 9:30AM–12 noon and 1:45–6PM; Oct.–Feb., Wed.–Mon., 10AM–12 noon and 1:45–5PM; closed Jan. 1, Nov. 1 and 11, and Dec. 25 and 26.

This museum was founded in 1716 by a group of artists and art lovers who hoped to make a collection of works by contemporary artists, but unexpectedly acquired some of the finest fifteenth-century Flemish paintings. This happened in the nineteenth-century when the museum was the recipient of a series of works taken from Belgian churches and institutions in Bruges by the French armies in 1794, but returned to Belgium after the defeat of Napoleon.

Today the collection is best known for its fifteenth- and sixteenth-century Flemish art, with emphasis on the Bruges school. There is also a modern section that traces the development of Brabant Fauvism, Flemish expressionism, and surrealism in Belgium. The museum's building, located in a cobblestone courtyard behind the church of Notre Dame, was built in 1920–

30, but expanded and modernized in 1982–83. Its design and construction resembles a simple convent, and its interior Gallery of Flemish primitives reminds one of a row of chapels.

Note: The following is a description of the most important rooms in the museum. Artists are not listed alphabetically.

Room 1: This first room of the Gallery of Flemish primitives contains the works of the most important Flemish artist, Jan van Eyck.

Eyck, Jan van* (ca. 1390–1441), Flemish

The Madonna of Canon van der Paele: (1436): room 1
In this painting, a traditional scene of a donor being presented to the Madonna by his patron saint, we see the exact drawing of reality, which Jan van Eyck was so famous for, from wrinkles to armor hinges. The minuteness of the finish is extraordinary and the portrait of the donor, Canon van der Paele, is an objective rendering of a human face.

St. George, the donor's patron saint, is introducing him to the Madonna, seated on a throne in the choir of a Romanesque church. On the left is the patron saint of Bruges, St. Donatian (this panel was painted for the Church of St. Donatian in Bruges, which no longer exists), who is holding his attribute, a wheel with five lighted candles. (According to legend, in order to find the saint's body at the bottom of a river, a wheel with five lighted candles on it was floated down the river and stopped over the spot where the saint lay.) The Canon van der Paele is gazing into space away from the Madonna and Child, unaware that their eyes are on him. By this device van Eyck makes the scene a vision in the spiritual eye of the canon, who is absorbed in contemplation, rather than to suggest the scene in actually taking place.

The museum also has the last of van Eyck's eight surviving portraits, **Margaret van Eyck** (room 1), of the artist's wife, done when she was thirty-three (1439). An example of Jan's late work, it shows a tendency to greater realism. Features are individualized and no effort to soften the severity of the gaze is made. Considering that this painting was made before the middle of the fifteenth century, when painting was medieval, you can see that the work of Jan van Eyck represented a new style of painting in Europe.

Room 2: Petrus Christus (ca. 1415/20–ca. 1473), whose works here were acquired by the museum in 1965 and 1983, was a master at Bruges in 1444. His style shows the influence of van Eyck and he may have been an apprentice of van Eyck. At his best, his work is characterized by a quiet mystery and a refined elegance, which is seen in his works displayed here: the two signed and dated panels (Christus's works number only about twenty-two, of which ten are signed and seven dated), *The Annunciation* and *The Nativity,* were painted in 1452 and probably were part of a triptych or polyptich; and the left panel of a small triptych showing *Isabel of Portugal with St. Elizabeth,* possibly commissioned by Isabel of Portugal when she entered a convent in 1457. St. Elizabeth of Hungary (1207–31), shown in a nun's habit, married Ludwig of Thuringia, who died six years later. She entered the Franciscan Order and devoted the remainder of her short life to the care of the sick. Her triple crown, an allusion to her royal birth, is also symbolic of her three states: virgin, wife, and widow.

Other masterpieces in room 2 are by the Ghent painter Hugo van der Goes and the Bruges master Hans Memling.

Goes, Hugo van der (ca. 1440–82), Flemish

Hugo van der Goes came after Jan van Eyck, but he was not content to follow the style established by his predecessor. He deliberately set out to reinterpret traditional themes and may have become mentally deranged in an attempt to surpass van Eyck's *Adoration of the Lamb* in Ghent. We know that Hugo had moods of depression when he feared for the salvation of his soul, and would repeat that he was eternally damned. He entered a monastery after 1475 and died there in 1482.

The Death of the Virgin (1481): room 2

This painting is one of van der Goes's last works, and it reveals the tortured state of his mind. The cold blue tones and the extreme precision of the drawing of the faces and hands create a mood of utter desolation and sorrow. The upper portion, showing the apparition of Christ in a blaze of light, does not strike the violent contrast we are accustomed to seeing in paintings showing Heaven and earth. In the faces of the apostles, characterized as common people, grief is shown not in calm piety but in self-accusation and repentance in their agony over the death of the Virgin.

Memling, Hans (ca. 1433–94), Flemish

St. Maurus, St. Christopher and St. Giles (Moreel Triptych): room 2

As seen in the Hospital of St. John in Bruges and in the museum in Brussels, some of Memling's paintings are associated with the Moreel family. Willem Moreel was the burgomaster in Bruges and this triptych (1484) was painted for the altar of a chapel built by the Moreels to serve as the family burial place in the thirteenth-century Church of St. James in Bruges.

The **center panel** shows St. Christopher, who was the patron saint of travelers (he was removed from the Catholic church calendar in 1969 because of his doubtful historicity), with the infant Jesus on his back; St. Maurus, the Benedictine teacher with open book in hand; and St. Giles, the patron saint of beggars and cripples, protecting a doe. The three figures are juxtaposed without any link between them, but the black shapes of the two saints are carried over into the dark coloring of the water as they stand out against the brown rocks. The red robe worn by St. Christopher enriches the dark tones of black, brown, and green in the painting and pulls the composition together.

In the **two side panels**, showing the large family of Willem Moreel (five sons and eleven daughters), not all of the likenesses are individualized. The ones that conform to a standard pattern may have been added later as the family increased. The large figure with a helmet is Guillaume de Maleval, the founder of the Eremitic Order. His presence at the side of the donor is perhaps explained by Moreel's Savoyard origins.

Room 3: During the fifteenth-century, especially its last quarter, an enormous number of paintings was produced in Bruges by a great many lesser artists. Many show the influence of Rogier van der Weyden, but without his poetic genius, which enabled him to express the inner feelings of humans balanced within the fifteenth-century world of Gothic symbolism and mystery. Two such artists, whose names we do not know, are displayed in this room: the **Master of the Lucy Legend,** whose *St. Nicholas* (1486–93), part of a side panel of a triptych, is painted with infinite detail and shows a magnificent background cityscape of Bruges; and the **Master of the Ursula Legend,** represented by a series of panels from two wings of an altarpiece (before 1482) showing the *Legend of St. Ursula* (for the story of St. Ursula see Memling Museum).

Room 4 contains the work of Gerard David, the last great painter in Bruges who carries the Flemish tradition into the early sixteenth-century. There are also fine examples of painting from one of his disciples, **Adriaan Isenbrandt** (ca. 1490–1551): *Portrait of Paulus de Nigro* (1518) and the *Triptych of Madonna and Child, St. John, and St. Jerome.*

David, Gerard (ca. 1460–1523), Flemish

The Baptism of Christ (Altarpiece of Jean des Trompes): room 4
Though born in Holland, David lived for twenty years in Bruges, where he became the leading painter. He was not an innovator, working in the tradition of fifteenth-century Flemish painting. In David's time Bruges was losing its leadership to rising Antwerp, where Massys, his contemporary, was uniting traditional style with the Renaissance spirit.

The triptych was executed between 1502 and 1507 for the donors Jean des Trompes and his family. In the fifteenth-century tradition there is an abundance of detail and a landscape that extends all the way across the triptych. The immobility of the figures, typical of David's style, is softened by the colors and the folds of the robes.

On the **left panel** we see the donor and his son Philippe with St. John the Evangelist. On the **right panel** is the donor's first wife, with Elizabeth, her patron saint behind her, and her four daughters. (On the reverse of the wings, right side, is a painting of the donor's second wife and daughter with St. Mary Magdalene and, on the left side, Mary and the Christ Child.) In the **central panel** three incidents from the life of St. John the Baptist are taking place. On the left St. John is preaching in the desert; in the center foreground we see the baptism of Christ; and on the right the scene of *Ecce Agnus Dei* in which St. John is pointing to Jesus and saying, "There is the Lamb of God" (Fourth Gospel 1:36).

"Examples of Justice" Panels (Arrest of Sisamnes and Judgment of Cambyses): room 4
These two large panels were ordered by the magistrates court in Bruges and

are earlier works (1498) than the *Baptism of Christ* triptych. The story is taken from Herodotus (5:25) in which Cambyses, king of the Medes and the Persians (sixth century B.C.), punished a dishonest judge by having him flayed alive. It was not unusual for this scene to be hung in courts of law during David's time as a warning to corrupt judges.

In the **first panel** we see King Cambyses and his assistants making a surprise visit to Sisamne, the corrupt judge, whose arm is gripped by one of the king's escorts as he listens aghast to a recital of his misdeeds. In the background Sisamnes is shown in front of his house receiving a bribe from one of the parties to a lawsuit. The **second panel,** one of the most gory in European art, shows Sisamnes being skinned alive in the presence of the king and his court. On the right, in the background, the victim's son has taken his father's place on the seat of justice, which has been upholstered with his father's skin. Herodotus makes the scene clear by saying in his text, "Bade him never forget in what way his seat was cushioned."

The figure of the corrupt judge is supposed to be a likeness of Pieter Lanchals, the treasurer to Maximilian I of Austria, who was executed as a conspirator for opposing Bruges's imprisoning of Maximilian in 1488. It is sometimes claimed that the panels were commissioned in memory of the unjust execution of Lanchals. In the Church of Notre Dame in Bruges, the Lanchals Chapel has a monument to Pieter Lanchals.

Room 5: The evidence is not conclusive that the triptych of *The Last Judgment* in this room is by **Hieronymus Bosch*** (ca. 1450–1516), though many critics consider it from the hand of the great master. Still, it serves as an excellent example of the fantastic Boschian style, probably dating from the early sixteenth century.

Room 6: In sixteenth-century Bruges the new spirit of the Renaissance was reflected in painting by Italianate figures reminiscent of Leonardo and Raphael, such as *Holy Family with St. Elizabeth and St. John,* by **Cornelis van Cleve** (1520–?) and *Madonna and Child,* by **Jan van Hemessen** (1519–after 1563); large panorama scenes with dramatic content, as in the *Crucifixion,* by **Jan Provoost** (1465–1529); and a new imaginative iconography considered more modern for the time, seen in Jan Provoost's *Last Judgment* (1525), commissioned for the City Hall of Bruges. Much of its elaborate frame, probably designed by the architect and painter Lanceloot Blondeel (1498–1561), is original. At the top there is the symbolic relationship between Jesus and Mary, whose exposed breast is meant to emphasize her role as the mother of Christ. Below there is the Italian feature of the saved being transported across the water to their reward in heaven, contrasted with the traditional Flemish scene of the doomed below in a Boschian hell that includes corrupt friars and nuns.

Room 7: The Bruges master whose work epitomizes the transition to the Renaissance is Pieter Pourbus, little known outside Flanders. He is the most accomplished painter in Bruges in the second half of the sixteenth century and is today one of the most admired painters in Bruges whose works adorn many churches.

Pourbus, Pieter (1524–84), Flemish

Jan van Eyerwerve and Jacquemyne Buuck (two paintings): room 7
Pourbus's portraits of wealthy citizens of Bruges are painted in a refined and humanistic style. In these wedding portraits, painted separately to preserve the identities of the bride and groom, the paintings share a common source of light from the left side, which lights up the faces and hands of the subjects who are seen in the same room with a window that overlooks the Kraanplaats. The groom is characterized as a strong figure by the technique of shining light on only one side of his face, and posing him with hands on hips and arms thrust forward, as if he wants to resist our scrutiny. The bride, with light falling on her whole face and hands clasped, appears softer, with a feminine grace expected of a lady of high position; the dog at her side is symbolic of her unquestioned fidelity. The view from the window, half of which is seen in each picture, is a source of personal identity. The bride and groom may own some of the buildings seen, and the huge crane used for lifting heavy objects, like the wine barrels set in rows in the street, may allude to the groom being in the wine trade. Both paintings have putti carrying individual family emblems, and are signed by the artist under the windows and dated above (1551), as if they were official marriage documents.

See also Pourbus's *Last Judgment* (1551), painted with Italian classical perfection, no doubt an imitation of Michelangelo's *Last Judgment* in the Sistine Chapel in Rome (painted ten years earlier). Though the *Last Judgment* and the wedding portraits are the earliest dated works of Pieter Pourbus, they are masterpieces he never surpassed.

Room 8: The museum has a rich collection of the works of Jacob van Oost (1601–71) who dominated painting in Bruges in the seventeenth century, as Pieter Pourbus did in the sixteenth century. The few years he spent in Italy influenced his painting, such as his *St. Martin* and *The Crowning with Thorns*, where the light of Caravaggio adds to the drama of both scenes. His portraits, which represent his best work, owe a great deal to his fellow countryman Anthony van Dyck. They have a similar softness and faithful rendering of facial expressions. The group portrait of a *Bruges Family* (1645), considered his masterpiece, shows his joy of painting his subjects, who are depicted as happy, bright people enjoying their success and position in society.

The museum's eighteenth- and nineteenth-century works are not distinguished. The collection of twentieth-century Belgian paintings, **room 13,** is excellent, however, with fine examples of the postimpressionist school known as **Brabant fauvism**—see the works of Rik Wouters (1882–1916), Jean Brusselmans (1884–1953), Louis Thévenet (1874–1930), and Edgard Tytgat (1879–1957); **Flemish expressionism** and the art colonies at Sint-Martens-Latem—see the works of George Minne (1866–1941), Gustave Van de Woestyne (1881–1947), Constant Permeke (1886–1952), and Gustave de

Smet (1877–1943); and **surrealism** in Belgium—see the works of René Magritte (1898–1967) and Paul Delvaux (1897). For a discussion of Modernism in Belgium, 1880–1960, see Royal Belgian Museums of Fine Arts, Museum of Modern Art, Brussels.

MEMLING MUSEUM (HOSPITAL OF ST. JOHN)

Mariastraat, 38 (across from the church of Notre Dame)

Hours: Open Mar.–Sept., daily 9:30AM–12 noon and 1:45–6PM; Oct.–Feb., Wed.–Mon., 10AM–12 noon and 2–5PM; closed Jan. 1, Nov. 1 and 11, and Dec. 25 and 26. Admission fee.

This museum contains the richest collection of paintings by Hans Memling, one of Bruges's best resident painters of the fifteenth century. It is located in the former St. John's Hospital, which, dating back to the thirteenth century, was one of the oldest hospitals in Europe. Lying beside one of the canals of Bruges, it also contains an old pharmacy, installed in 1643, which may be visited.

Memling, Hans (ca. 1433–94), Flemish

Triptych of St. John the Baptist and St. John the Evangelist (Mystic Marriage of St. Catherine) (1479)
This altarpiece was painted for the hospital chapel. The **central panel** is divided by pillars into narrow scenes from the lives of the two patron saints of the hospital, St. John the Baptist, with the lamb of God, and St. John the Evangelist, holding the chalice. (John was made to drink from a chalice poisoned with a snake as a test of his faith; he survived unharmed. In medieval times the chalice stood for Christian faith, the snake for Satan.) In the center, the Virgin holds the Child who places the ring on the finger of the richly clothed St. Catherine, whose attributes, the wheel and the sword, lie in front of her. (A wheel with iron spikes was devised to torture her, but a thunderbolt from heaven destroyed it before it could harm her; she was, instead, beheaded with a sword.) St. Catherine represents the contemplative side of the religious life of the sisters of the hospital. St. Barbara, sitting across from her with her attribute, the tower, represents their active life. The four saints are positioned at the angles of a parallelogram with the Virgin placed at the intersection of the diagonals on the central axis.

The **left wing** of the triptych shows the gruesome scene of the beheading of St. John the Baptist. A passive-looking Salome is handed the severed head on a plate from the executioner. The **right wing** of the triptych, showing St. John the Evangelist writing the Book of Revelation on the Isle of Patmos, is one of the most delicate of Memling's works. There is a landscape showing a wrecked ship and the four horsemen of the apocalyse. The horseman, representing death, is menacing a group of men attempting to hide in caves. At the top is St. John's apocalyptic vision of Christ enthroned with the lamb giving him the scroll containing the secrets of men's destiny.

Shrine of St. Ursula (before 1489)
This famous portable shrine, in the shape of the central nave of a Gothic church, is a masterpiece of woodcarving, with panels painted with Eyckian detail showing scenes from the St. Ursula legend. The story, popular during the Middle Ages, tells of the martyrdom of Ursula, a beautiful princess from Brittany, who consents to marry the son of a pagan English king if he converts to Christianity and accompanies her on a pilgrimage to Rome attended by 11,000 English virgins. They travel to Rome where the prince is baptized. On their return journey they arrive at Cologne when the city is being beseiged by Huns who kill the prince; they also kill the virgins after unsuccessfully attempting to rape them. Ursula is killed by an arrow when she refuses to become the bride of the barbarian king.

Starting from the **first panel on the right-hand long side**, we see Ursula, accompanied by the virgins (mercifully reduced to 11), landing at Cologne on her trip up the Rhine. She is greeted by Queen Sigillinde of Cologne. The city is shown behind the town gate with architectural detail. Notice, above on the right, in a room of the castle whose front wall has been removed—as if it was a stage set of a medieval mystery play—an angel warning Ursula that she will suffer martyrdom.

The **second panel** shows the arrival of Ursula in Basel, where the sails of the boats are being lowered. To the right we see the ladies, with skirts pulled above their ankles, starting up the road leading over the Alps to Rome.

On the **third panel** Ursula is being greeted in Rome by Pope Cyriacus. The prince is seen clothed in red, at the lower left. In the church, on the right, pilgrims are being baptized. Further inside, in the north aisle, Ursula is receiving Communion, while, to the left, the prince is making his confession before baptism.

On the **fourth panel of the other long side**, the return journey is shown at Basle where the group is starting down the Rhine. The pope and his entourage are accompanying them, and pilgrims leaving the city also intend to join.

The fifth and sixth panels, painted as one, show the martyrdom in Cologne. On the **fifth panel** the defenseless group is being attacked in their boats by soldiers. In the upper right a soldier has driven his sword into the heart of the prince who is being supported by Ursula. On the **sixth panel,** which has a glorious example of a military tent of the period, Ursula is seen refusing the turbaned figure offering himself to her. Resigned to her fate, she passively awaits the arrow aimed at her by the archer. Notice that the armor of the soldiers reflect the surroundings, a quality of painting established in Flanders by van Eyck.

On one end of the shrine is a painting of the *Virgin and Child* with two donors. On the other end is *St. Ursula* with her attribute, the arrow, protecting her companions with her mantle.

The museum also displays Memling's famous *Diptych of Martin van-Nieuwenhove* (1487), which has the portrait of the donor at the age of twenty-three (he became burgomaster of Bruges) shown praying to the Virgin and Child; the so called *Sambetha Sibyl* (1480), probably a likeness of Maria Moreel, one of the daughters of Willem Moreel, who can be seen in the right-hand panel of the *Moreel Altarpiece* that her father commissioned from Memling (Groeninge Museum, Bruges); the steely grey *Descent from the Cross* (1480), a triptych made for Adrien Reyens, the father superior of the hospital (although it may remind you of Rogier van der Weyden, it lacks the expressiveness of the master and is less skillful in technique); and the triptych of the *Adoration of the Magi* (1479), sometimes called the *Floreins Triptych*, after Friar Jan Floreins who became governor of the hospital, which is a version of Memling's earlier *Adoration of the Magi* (1470) now in the Prado in Madrid (the man looking at the scene through an opening in the wall appears in the same position in the Madrid painting).

Buildings

MARKT (MARKETPLACE)

This great square in the center of the city was the main marketplace in the Middle Ages and until recently still served as an outdoor market on Saturday mornings. It is dominated by the enormous thirteenth-century **Halles** (covered market hall) with its fourteenth- and fifteenth-century **belfry**. It was reconstructed a number of times; while the four corner turrets date from 1395, the octagonal part above is from 1482–87. At one time the belfry was topped by a spire, but it was destroyed by lightning in 1741 and never rebuilt. The height of the structure (you can climb to the top—365 steps) is 279 feet and, since it also contains a carillon, it is heard as well as seen throughout the city.

BURG (CITY HALL SQUARE)

This smaller square, only a short walk from the Markt, is the site of the oldest **town hall** in Belgium, dating from 1376. It is a building reflecting the city's importance when it was a member of the Hanseatic League, with a facade decorated with statues and bas-reliefs representing scenes from the Bible and history. (The present pieces are restorations, the originals having been destroyed during the French invasions of 1792.) Inside is a Gothic hall with an early fifteenth-century oak roof and walls covered with late nineteenth-century paintings depicting the history of Bruges and Flanders. (*Hours:* open Mar.–Sept., daily 9:30AM–noon and 2–6PM; Oct.–Feb., Sun.–Mon. 10AM–noon and 1:45–5PM; closed Jan. 1; admission fee.)

To the right of the Town Hall is the **Chapel of the Holy Blood**, a building dedicated to displaying the relic of some drops of the blood of Christ acquired by the town during the Second Crusade (1147). The building is a curious mixture of Romanesque, Gothic, and Renaissance construction and consists of two chapels built one upon another. The lower chapel dates from the twelfth century and is heavy, dark and Romanesque; the Gothic upper chapel was added in the fifteenth and sixteenth centuries and houses the relic. Its facade shows the influence of Renaissance design. (*Hours:* open Oct.–Mar., Thurs.–Tues. 10AM–noon and 2–4PM, Wed. 10AM–noon; Apr.– Sept., daily 9:30AM–noon and 2–6PM; The relic is offered for veneration Fri. 8:30–11:45AM and 3–4PM; admission fee to museum on upper level.)

To the left of the Town Hall, with a street running beneath it, is the little *Greffe* (Recorder's House). It is a richly decorated early sixteenth-century Renaissance building. To its left is the *Palace of Justice* (eighteenth century) which contains, in the magistrates chamber, an excellent Renaissance fireplace of oak and black marble decorated with an alabaster frieze showing the story of Susanna and the Elders in four scenes. **First panel:** Susanna, the wife of a prosperous Jew living in Babylon, is spied upon by two elders while bathing in her garden. They threaten that unless she give herself to them both they will swear they saw her in the act of adultery with a young man, a crime punishable by death. Susanna refuses and cries for help. **Second panel:** Susanna is before the court where young Daniel, cross-examining the elders, proves her innocence. **Third panel:** The elders are sentenced to death. **Fourth panel:** The elders are stoned to death. Susanna in Hebrew means lily, a symbol of purity. Her story is depicted in Christian art from the earliest times through the Renaissance, when it was used by artists as an opportunity to depict female nudity. (*Hours:* open Apr.–Sept., daily 10AM–noon and 2–5:30PM; Oct.–Mar., daily 2–4PM; admission fee.)

CHURCH OF NOTRE DAME

Mariastraat (across from St. John's Hospital and Memling Museum)

Hours: Open Mon.–Sat., 9–11:30AM and 2:30–6PM; Sun., 2:30–6PM. Free admission.

This large Gothic church was built between the thirteenth and fifteenth centuries and has a grandiose brick tower (375 feet high) reinforced by tapering buttresses. It is known for the works of art in its interior. In the choir and east end (admission fee) there are the richly decorated **tombs of Mary of Burgundy** (1498–1502, late Gothic) **and her father Charles the Bold** (1558, Renaissance), excavated Burgundian tombs with wall frescoes, and a collection of Flemish paintings.

Charles the Bold (1433–77) was the last of the great Burgundian princes to favor Bruges, occasionally making the city the site of his glittering court. He married Margaret of York in 1468, sister of Edward IV of England, in this church. The wedding was one of the most lavish occasions ever held in Bruges. Charles loved pomp and ceremony, but he loved war even more. He devoted his life to eliminating French and German influence from his lands and suffered an early death fighting the French near Nancy. He left no son, but his daughter Mary, one of the greatest hieresses of all time, married Maximillian I of the Holy Roman Empire. When Mary died in 1482 at the age of twenty-five, as a result of a riding accident during a hunt, Maximillian obtained the Netherlands and Upper Burgundy. That is how the Low Countries became part of the vast Hapsburg empire.

The best of the paintings are from the Bruges School in the sixteenth century. First there is a triptych whose central panel is a moving *Transfiguration* (ca. 1520) by Gerard David (ca. 1460–1523). Its side panels (1573), however, are by Pieter Pourbus (1524–84), one of the painters who continued the tradition of the Bruges school after the death of Gerard David and the rise of the new center of art in Antwerp. There are other altarpieces by Pieter Pourbus, including a *Last Supper* (1562), and *The Seven Sorrows of the Virgin*, by Adriaan Isenbrandt (ca. 1490–1551), another disciple of Gerard David. There is also a large altarpiece showing *The Passion of Christ*, by Bernaert van Orley (ca. 1492–1541), the painter who dominated the school of painting at Brussels during the first half of the sixteenth century. All these works are examples of the Flemish schools adopting the humanism of the Renaissance and the Italian styles that had become dominant in Europe. The greatest art treasure of the church, a small statue by Michelangelo, is the best example of Italianism making its way into the great cities of northern Europe.

Michelangelo* (1475–1564), Florentine

Virgin and Child (Bruges Madonna): chapel at east end of south side of nave
This small marble group is one of the few works by Michelangelo that can be seen outside of Italy, having been bought in Florence in 1506 by a Bruges merchant. It was executed in 1503–4 after the more famous *Pietà* (1498–99/1500) in St. Peter's in Rome, and it reflects the more sober classicism of the high Renaissance style. The figures here are densely massed into a compact group, as opposed to the more loosely arranged composition in Rome. The forms are fuller and stronger, and the face of the Virgin is broader, less polished. The idealized elegance of the *Pietà* in Rome has given way to more natural representations.

Brussels

Museums

ROYAL BELGIAN MUSEUMS OF FINE ARTS

Rue de la Régence 3; Regentschapstraat 3

Hours: Open Tues.–Sun., 10AM–5PM; closed Jan. 1, May 1, Nov. 1 and 11, Dec. 25. Free admission.

This new museum complex was officially inaugurated in 1984 after several years of renovating the **Museum of Ancient Art** and the construction of a new **Museum of Modern Art**. The result combines both museums in what is one of the finest facilities for viewing art in all Europe.

Note: The entire collection has been color coded. Visit the museum according to the following chronological order.

Old Building

Circuit Blue	Fifteenth and sixteenth centuries
Circuit Brown	Seventeenth and eighteenth centuries
Circuit Yellow	Nineteenth century

New Building

Circuit Green	Twentieth century

Index to the Collection of Flemish Paintings in the Old Building

Artists mentioned below have works referred to in the text that follows. Works are listed under the names of the artists, which are arranged alphabetically.

Circuit Blue: Fifteenth- and Sixteenth-Century Paintings

Room 11	van der Weyden
Room 12	van der Goes
Room 13	Bouts
Room 14	Memling
Room 21	Gerard David
Room 22	Massys
Room 25	Gossaert
Room 31	Bruegel

Circuit Brown: Seventeenth- and Eighteenth-Century Paintings

Balcony, left side of entrance	van Dyck
Balcony, far end side	Jordaens
Room 62	Rubens

Circuit Yellow: Nineteenth-Century Paintings

Room 69	Jacques-Louis David

Bouts, Dieric (ca. 1415/20–1475), Flemish

The Emperor Otto's Justice (two panels): room 13, circuit blue
Dieric Bouts, a contemporary of Rogier van der Weyden, shows some of Rogier's dramatic tension in his work, created by accenting the flow of movement through the limbs of the figures. Dieric followed the Flemish tradition in his introduction of portraits into his work. The two panels that make up *The Emperor Otto's Justice* contain a series of portraits that probably represent the governors of Louvain, who commissioned the paintings for the town hall as a reminder to the magistrates to render justice.

Both panels depict an incident from the court of Otto III (980–1002), the Holy Roman Emperor. Otto's wife had made advances to a German count, who rejected her. In revenge, she falsely accused the count of besmirching her honor, to have him condemned to death by the emperor. As the count walks to his execution he pleads with his wife to prove his innocence. The **first panel, Execution of the Innocent,** shows three stages in the drama: the count being led to his execution; his widow receiving his severed head from a soldier; and the empress in the background telling lies into her husband's ear. The count's widow, in order to prove the innocence of her husband, undergoes an ordeal by fire (the medieval practice to establish innocence). This results in the emperor atoning for his wrong judgment by sentencing his own wife to be burned at the stake. In the **second panel, Trial by Fire,** we see the widow holding a red-hot iron without ill effect, while in the background the empress is being burned to death.

It is believed that the first panel, *Execution of the Innocent,* was left unfinished at Dieric's death and later filled in by another painter. In the lower half of the panel, the figure of a man standing at the edge of the painting on the left, and the drapery of the countess, appear certainly not to have been painted by the hand of Dieric Bouts. The second panel was painted entirely by Bouts between 1471 and 1473.

Bruegel, Pieter, the Elder (ca. 1525–69), Flemish

Landscape with the Fall of Icarus: room 31, circuit blue
Painting in the Netherlands during Bruegel's time (mid-sixteenth century) was becoming specialized into separate subject matters. While this turn to specialization became pronounced only during the Golden Age of painting in seventeenth-century Holland, in the work of Pieter Bruegel we have a painter of genre scenes a century earlier, as well as a great landscape painter. An example is *The Fall of Icarus,* showing land, sea, a setting sun, and the vague presence of a town. Bruegel had made the standard trip to Italy and was dazzled by the Italian countryside and the Alps. The scene in *The Fall of Icarus* may have been based on the landscape he saw near Messina.

At the same time, Bruegel has illustrated here a story from Ovid's Metamorphoses describing how Icarus escaped from his imprisonment on the Isle of Crete by using a pair of wings, attached to his shoulders with wax, to fly away. Icarus ignores the warning of Daedalus, who constructed the wings, and flies too high. The sun melts the wax and we see, in Bruegel's painting, the legs of Icarus as he disappears into the sea. Icarus has been punished for his overambitiousness, but the more fitting punishment is that his fall is not even noticed. Life and the continuum of the natural cycle goes on; no plough stops for a dying man. Bruegel is telling us that the hero is not Icarus, who flew too high, but the simple ploughman or the fisherman who ploddingly goes about his work.

This picture is the only one Bruegel ever did on a mythological subject. Other masterpieces by Bruegel in the collection are on religious subjects: *Fall of the Rebel Angels, Adoration of the Magi,* and *Census at Bethlehem* (all in room 31).

David, Gerard (ca. 1460–1523), Flemish

The Madonna with the Milk Soup: room 21, circuit blue
Gerard David is the heir to Memling and the last great painter of the Bruges
School. His charming small painting of the Madonna feeding the Child, is
one of many versions of the scene that he painted. In this one, as in the
others elsewhere, he depicts a synthesized landscape but has included a bourgeois interior with still-life elements in great detail. It is more of a genre
scene than a religious painting, and shows the direction Flemish painting was
to take in the sixteenth century. The museum's painting of David's *Adoration of the Magi* (room 21) is more in keeping with the art of the Middle
Ages.

David, Jacques-Louis* (1748–1825), French

Death of Marat (1793); room 69, circuit yellow
Jean Paul Marat was one of the leading fanatics of the French Revolution,
the darling of the mob, who repeatedly called for, and got, thousands of
heads to roll on the guillotine. One of those he accused of treason was the
lover of Charlotte Corday, a beautiful young revolutionary. Determined to
avenge her lover's death, she obtained an interview with Marat on the pre-
text of disclosing a Girondists' plot and plunged a dagger into his chest. Six
days later she went to the guillotine without remorse, confident she had rid
France of its worst enemy. Those who praised her heroism were also arrested
and guillotined. David, the official painter of the revolution, when learning
of the assassination of his friend Marat, whom he had seen the day before
the murder, was shocked out of his academic ivory tower long enough to
paint a realistic picture. He puts us directly in touch with the scene where
we see Marat stabbed to death in his bathtub—Marat was known to bathe
daily seeking relief from the sores of his venereal disease that covered his
body, which David conveniently leaves out of his painting. The trompe l'oeil
papers and wooden box evoke the power of realism, and the contrast of light
and shade enforces the impression of tragedy.

Dyck, Anthony van* (1599–1641), Flemish

Portrait of Genoese Lady and her Daughter: balcony, left side of entrance,
circuit brown
Van Dyck cornered the market, one might say, on society portraiture. He
had an uncanny insight into human personality and could size up character
at a glance. During his long stay in Italy, which lasted to the end of 1627,
he became portraitist to many of the Italian nobility. The portraits of his
monumental Genoese period, which this painting represents, achieve a certain grandeur. In this one color is the major element of the composition. The
dark background against which he sets the voluminous dark dress of the
mother (probably the Marquess Spinola) is balanced by the splash of van
Dyck red above her head and the silvery gray dress of her daughter.
   There is a series of van Dyck portraits in the Brussels Museum, among
which are some of his best works: *Portrait of François Duquesnoy* (1622–

23), the Flemish sculptor living in Rome. He holds a satyr's head as a symbol of his profession and looks directly at us, confident in his own talent; and *Portrait of Alexander della Faille* (ca. 1629), the Flemish mathematician, Jesuit, and advisor to Philip IV of Spain, whose face reflects his intelligence, and whose pose, with the instruments of his profession, reflects his dignified position in society.

Goes, Hugo van der* (ca. 1440–82), Flemish

The Virgin and Child, St. Anne and a Franciscan Friar: room 12, circuit blue

Hugo van der Goes kept to subjects favored by his predecessors, but deliberately set out to reinterpret them. The pyramidal structure of the central group, the Madonna with St. Anne holding the Child, is a bold innovation for its time and succeeds in achieving a sense of monumentality. Hugo's need to be innovative makes his compositions bold and new. Even the Franciscan friar, the donor, on his knees and seemingly a part of the holy scene, is innovative. His solid form on the right, turned inward at an angle, balances the larger central group. The sense of monumentality, the expressiveness of the hands (often found in Hugo's work), and the limpid coloring of pale blues make this painting a moving work.

Gossaert, Jan, also called Mabuse (ca. 1478–ca. 1536), Flemish

Venus and Cupid (1521): room 25, circuit blue

Jan Gossaert is a Flemish painter who early in the sixteenth century turned to Italy for inspiration. He journeyed there (1508–10) as part of Philip of Burgundy's diplomatic mission to Pope Julius II. In Rome he made drawings for Philip of the antiquities of the city. Gossaert evidently fell completely under the Italian spell. He became the first Flemish mannerist of the Italian School, introducing pagan figures like Venus into sixteenth-century Flemish painting. Small panels, such as this *Venus and Cupid,* dealing with mythological subjects set against classical backgrounds, made him famous. There isn't a bit of religious feeling in his *Venus and Cupid,* which shows a naked Venus holding Cupid's hand while stepping on his foot so that he will leave her alone. Its sensual and profane references made Gossaert's art refreshingly different from earlier traditions.

Jordaens, Jacob (1593–1678), Flemish

The King Drinks (1630s): balcony, far end side, circuit brown

This painting is probably the most popular in Belgium. Every Belgian knows the story it depicts from Flemish folklore. On Twelfth Night (celebrated January 5, the eve of Epiphany) a family feast takes place. Each guest receives a piece from a cake containing a single bean. The person who gets the bean is proclaimed king for the night. A paper crown is placed on his head and he appoints a wine server, a jester, and a musician, and may indulge in any whim. It is a noisy, happy party with much food, drink, smoke, and gaiety, as the picture shows. Jordaens delighted in painting feasts with a robust exuberance; he painted this scene several times.

Susanna and the Elders (1630–35): balcony, far end side, circuit brown
The story of Susanna and the elders is an often-painted theme. In the Old
Testament story, Susanna, wife of a wealthy man, is desired by two elders
who try to seduce her as she bathes in her garden. The naked woman tries
to protect herself from the old men, who plead for her favors. They threaten
that unless she gives herself to them, they will swear they caught her in an
act of adultery, a crime punishable by death. The sumptuous peacock is the
attribute of Juno, protectress of women, and looks away from Susanna in
her plight, focusing instead on Cupid. The dog is the symbol of Susanna's
fidelity.

Massys, Quentin (1466–1530), Flemish

The St. Anne Triptych: room 22, circuit blue
In this triptych, commissioned in 1507 and completed in 1509, Massys again
shows his feeling for Renaissance art. His work is still Flemish but it does
not depend on the art of van Eyck or Rogier. It may have been inspired by
Leonardo da Vinci (1452–1519). The arrangement of the figures in Massys'
central panel reminds one of the composition in Leonardo's *Last Supper*
(Santa Maria delle Grazie, Milan) where the figures also appear in three triangular schemas.

In the **central panel,** Massys has created a composition of mild forms
(the four men seem more feminine than masculine) with a structure based on
the sculptural aspects of the human body. There is a Renaissance instinct
that Massys has for the human figure. There is nothing of the fifteenth-
century Flemish tautness and thinness about them. His landscape in the
background is never allowed to penetrate the interior scene, and material objects do not interest him, as they did his fifteenth-century predecessors.
Massys's major concern is with depicting the holy families with a quiet dignity. This he does in front of an airy, symmetrical Brunelleschian portico,
where even the children look serious beyond their ages. The only relief from
this attitude of imposing dignity is the little child in the left-hand corner who
is reading a book upside down. Massys has clearly been touched by the spirit
of the Renaissance.

Memling, Hans (ca. 1433–94), Flemish

Portrait of Barbara Van Vlaedenberghe and *Portrait of Willem Moreel* (two
panels): room 14, circuit blue
The quiet mood Memling captures in his paintings of the Virgin and in his
portraits seems to have appealed to his contemporaries. In Bruges, where he
spent most of his life, his talent as a painter to nobility and to merchants
made him a citizen of substance. In 1480 town records show he was among
those who paid the highest taxes.

The portraits of *Willem Moreel,* the burgomaster of Bruges, and *Barbara Van Vlaedenberghe,* Moreel's wife (obviously these panels were once
part of a triptych), are among the most distinctive portraits Memling executed. They show that Memling did not try to flatter his sitters. His quiet,
formal style, which always depicted his subjects at half-length in prayerful

contemplation, may have toned down anything offensive in his sitter's physical appearance, but did not get in the way of his rendering them as individual characters.

Rubens, Peter Paul* (1577–1640), Flemish

The Martyrdom of St. Lievin (1635) and *The Way to Calvary* (1637) (two paintings): room 62, circuit brown
These paintings are two outstanding examples from among many Rubens did late in his career that deal with the death and torture of religious figures. Yet, in spite of their depiction of terrible suffering, they are always presented with glittering magnificence.

In *The Martyrdom of St. Lievin,* where one of the saint's executioners has torn out his tongue and is feeding it to a dog, while another is holding him by the beard and is about to brand him with a hot iron, the whirlwind of shapes and colors almost makes one forget the horror of the event. Similarly, in *The Way to Calvary,* where Christ has fallen beneath the Cross in pain, the horror of the scene is countered by the beauty of Veronica who is wiping His brow. The exciting color and harmony of movement in these paintings, set within compositions that are almost wide open on all sides, make these scenes of horror beautiful works of art.

Weyden, Rogier van der* (ca. 1399–1464), Flemish

There is a courtly air to Rogier's portraits, which are usually shown at half-length, with the figures clasping or crossing hands, or holding an arrow. Rogier outlines his sitters' features, bringing out the smallest details. Whatever Rogier can see, as revealed by direct light shining on his subjects, he shows to us. His portraits are definitely more alive than those of van Eyck, or the Flemish portrait painters of the fifteenth century who came after him.

Man with the Arrow (1456): room 11, circuit blue
This man is wearing the chain of the Golden Fleece, indicating that he is a nobleman. While there has been considerable speculation as to his identity, he is considered today to be the Portuguese nephew of Philip the Good, Jan van Coimbra. The clearly drawn features reveal an attractive face with a touch of melancholy that to us, today, perhaps indicates that he is already aware that his life will not be a long one.

Portrait of Laurent Froimont: room 11, circuit blue
This portrait formed part of a diptych, now dispersed, and is dated between 1456 and 1460. The face is honest, serious, and young, but at the same time mature. Everything has been painted with intense accuracy, and the delicacy of the flesh tones brings out the volume and structure of the elegant head. There is an aristocratic dignity about this subject that goes well with the motto written on the background: "As Reason Teaches."

Modernism in Belgium, 1880–1960

Note: This description of modern Belgian art is meant to guide you through the museum's collection of late nineteenth- and twentieth-century art. See the collection of nineteenth-century paintings (circuit yellow), displayed in the old building, before moving to the new building, which is devoted to twentieth-century art (circuit green). The following artists and their locations in the museum can be referred to in the text below:

Old Building: Circuit Yellow

Room 80 Jacob Smits
Room 81 Jacob Smits, Fernand Khnopff
Room 88 Henri Evenpoel
Room 89 Gustave van de Woestyne

New Building: Circuit Green

First floor James Ensor; Henry van de Velde, Théo van Rysselberghe, Jean Brusselmans, Rik Wouters, Edgard Tytgat
Second floor Constant Permeke, Gustave de Smet, Frits van den Berghe, René Magritte, Paul Delvaux
Third floor Pierre Alechinsky

Belgium's contribution to modern art has been substantial, but apart from the recognition given to some of her exceptional painters, namely James Ensor and René Magritte, many outstanding Belgian artists are not known outside Belgium. This is perhaps because of the vast fame achieved after 1900 by certain French artists (van Gogh, Gauguin, and others), because of the provincial nature of the Flemish expressionists, and because the hoarding of their works in their homeland made them difficult to see abroad.

James Ensor (1860–1949)—circuit green—belongs to the generation that included such artists as van Gogh, Seurat, Munch, and Hodler. Their art was not so much postimpressionist as antiimpressionist in technique and expression. Like these artists, but working apart from them, Ensor found and used new symbols to express new feelings, initiating the nonrepresentational painting that came to dominate twentieth-century art. More than any painter, his art is associated with masks. The mask, used instead of the human face, gave Ensor the liberty to distort for effect, giving full vent to his social criticism by revealing everything in the mask that the unmasked face hides. The plastic quality of the mask also allowed Ensor to use all types of color and shape, completely covering his canvases if he wished. Thus Ensor's work is a direct precursor of twentieth-century expressionism, where the end to be expressed takes precedence over the technique.

The accomplishments of James Ensor were unsurpassed and unique, but there were other figures of the Belgian avant-garde. In 1883 a group of artists who called themselves **Les Vingt** (The twenty) was founded in Brussels as a protest against academic realistic art then dominating the official Salon. **Théo van Ruysselberghe** (1862–1926) and **Henry van de Velde** (1863–1957)—both circuit green—were members of the group who expressed themselves in the new stylistic development called pointillism—the French pointilist, Georges Seurat, was hailed as a god in Brussels at the same time he was still a controversial figure in Paris. Others in the group, not receptive to outside influences, were symbolists who adopted their own psychoanalytic-romantic style based on occult mystification. This is reflected in the work of **Fernand Khnopff** (1858—1921) who produced the strange painting *The Caress* (1896)—room 81, circuit yellow—in which the body of a leopard has the head of a woman. Another gifted painter at this time, **Henri Evenpoel** (1872–99)—room 88, circuit yellow—used a bright palette and themes from everyday life to bring him close to the French Nabis. His premature death at the age of twenty-seven deprives us of knowing how far his considerable talent would have taken him.

Flemish expressionism appeared at the beginning of the twentieth century when a group of artists settled in the village of Sint-Martens-Latem on the Lys, not far from Ghent. Their separatism indicated a rejection of the cultural and spiritual environment of Brussels, already a leading center of Art Nouveau and the avant-garde artists of Les Vingt and its successor after 1894, La Libre Esthétique. In the simple atmosphere of the Flemish countryside, the art colony at Sint-Martens-Latem worked within a religious-pastoral-proletarian symbolism. Among those who first evolved in that direction was the older **Jacob Smits** (1855–1928)—rooms 80–81, circuit **yellow**—and **Gustave van de Woestyne** (1881–1947)—room 89, circuit yellow. Woestyne was one of the first painters to settle at Sint-Martens-Latem in 1899. His early work shows idyllic landscapes, and portraits and peasant heads.

The simplicity of the art produced at Sint-Martens-Latem did not last. The artists who made up the second Latem group (from 1910, but maturing only after World War I) were less melancholy and more interested in vigorous pictorial structure: **Gustave de Smet** (1877–1943), **Frits van den Berghe** (1883–1939); and **Constant Permeke** (1886–1952)—all circuit green. De Smet's calm pictures of rural life are geometrically drawn and broadly painted, somewhat like the work of the early German expressionists. Frits van den Berghe, at first a painter of peasant scenes, after 1927 turned to masks and spectral figures, like James Ensor before him, to express what he considered the emotional restlessness of modern life. Constant Permeke, the leading figure of Flemish expressionism, painted people close to the earth; workers of the land and fishermen of the sea. To express such simple people his draftsmanship was simple—basic massive forms able to resist the forces of nature—and his colors dense, mainly thickly applied yellows and browns.

An expressionist development with a fauvist touch, originating simultaneously with Flemish expressionism, flourished mainly around Brussels and was known as **Brabant fauvism**. The style is illustrated by the works of **Jean Brusselmans** (1884–1953), **Edgard Tytgat** (1879–1957), and **Rik Wouters** (1882–1916)—all circuit green. Brusselmans's fauvism matured into a constructivist expressionism that emphasized the creation of forms but never lost touch with nature and reality. Tytgat's narrative, highly individual style has forms that are naively simplified. Rik Wouters, who died before he could fully develop his exceptional talent, is considered an authentic Belgian fauvist, which means his colors are muted and not as aggressive as proper French fauvists.

Surrealism was born in Paris, like a phoenix rising from the earlier Dada movement, but no other trend in modern Belgian art gained as much international notoriety. Its leading figures in Belgium, **René Magritte** (1898–1967) and **Paul Delvaux** (b. 1897)—circuit green—are photographic surrealists (every object in their pictures is painted with photographic realism even though such objects may never have existed) who marry the unreal with the real. The museum's collection of Paul Delvaux's work is particularly outstanding showing that artists fascination with the female figure, skeletons, and trains.

Abstract expressionism developed in New York, but was taken up extensively in Europe after World War II. A vigorous expression of it was in the international group called Cobra (from the initial letters of Copenhagen, Brussels, and Amsterdam). The painters of this group were all different, but adhered to the principal of complete freedom of abstract expressive forms. **Piere Alechinsky** (b. 1927)—circuit green—a leading Belgian member of Cobra, paints controlled canvases, particularly in his earlier works of the 1950s, with tightly woven structures. His vision, like that of every abstractionist, is personal, but his sense of controlled energy gives the viewer confidence in his art and the feeling that anything is possible.

Among the Belgian art in the modern museum—circuit green—are fine examples of their well-known foreign contemporaries: Marc Chagall, Giorgio de Chirico, Salvador Dali, Max Ernst, Paul Gauguin, Oskar Kokoschka, Fernand Léger, Henri Matisse, Jean Metzinger, Emil Nolde, Francis Picabia, and others.

Buildings

GRAND PLACE (MAIN SQUARE)

The magnificent Grand Place, in the center of old Brussels, dates back to the twelfth century when the land it occupies was drained and used as a marketplace. It has also served as the site of medieval tournaments, and it is believed that Philip the Good, the Duke of Burgundy and ruler of the Low Countries, may have taken part in some of them.

The square is dominated by the **Hotel de Ville** (Town Hall) built in the flamboyant Gothic style (1402–50). It is unique in Europe as a high point of civic architecture in the fifteenth century, when wealthy merchants in the Low Countries were independent and—more so than in other countries—had the confidence and public spirit to devote some of their wealth to the building of trade and town halls. Its lofty central spire, which rises to a height of 312 feet, is a marvel of airy stonework and is topped by a statue of St. Michael (patron saint of Brussels).

Opposite the Hotel de Ville is the **Maison du Roi** (King's House). It was built in 1515–23 in the Gothic style and rebuilt in the 1870s. It features a flamboyant portico across its full width, surmounted by a delicate loggia of similar style and a central tower with a bulb-shaped cupola. For a long time it housed government officials. Today it is the site of the Communal Museum, which displays works of art devoted to the history of Brussels.

The beautiful **guild houses** surrounding the Grand Place on all sides date from the eighteenth century. Earlier buildings were largely destroyed in 1695 by a French army under the command of Marshal de Villeroy who savagely bombarded the city. The rebuilding of these magnificent structures took place on the same medieval sites they always occupied, so that the baroque buildings you see today are just as narrow and high as before. Each one is different from the rest, yet all of them form a homogeneous unit and blend well with the two larger Gothic structures nearby.

To enjoy the magnificence of the Grand Place it should be visited during the daytime, and again at night, when an extraordinary illumination lights up the gilded facades of the buildings. Its reputation as Europe's most splendid town square is well deserved.

ST. GUDULE (CATHEDRAL OF ST. MICHEL)

Place St. Gudule

This Gothic cathedral, dedicated to two saints, occupies the top of a hill and is the national church of Belgium. It can be traced back to 1226, the date of the construction of its choir, which makes it the earliest Gothic work to be found in Belgium. Its twin western towers and the portico below are northern French, but its interior is of the classic Belgian pattern drawn from both French and German design, with large cylindrical columns dividing the nave (1425–75) and choir from the aisles. The huge interior columns support statues of the apostles, but the most notable features of the interior decoration are sixteenth- and seventeenth-century stained glass windows in the transepts and choir, and a baroque pulpit (1699) made by Hendrik Frans Verbruggen (ca. 1655–1724). His scene of the *Expulsion from Paradise* at the base of the pulpit is sculptured with an unrestrained naturalism: a marvelous example of Flemish baroque.

Ghent

MUSEUM OF FINE ARTS AND MUSEUM OF CONTEMPORARY ART

De Liemaerckereplein, 3, in the Citadel Park

Hours: Open Tues.–Sat., 9AM–12:30PM and 1:30–5:30PM; Sun. and holidays, 1:30–5:20PM. Admission fee.

This museum, located in a lovely park, has a fine collection of late nineteenth- and twentieth-century Belgian painting. For a chronological review of this art and its achievements, refer to the section **Modernism in Belgium, 1880–1960** in the Royal Belgian Museum of Fine Arts, Museum of Modern Art, Brussels.

The following artists have works displayed in the museum (rooms D, E, and F) and are mentioned in the section on modern Belgium art above: James Ensor (1860–1949), Théo van Rysselberghe (1862–1926), Henri Evenpoel (1872–99), Gustave van de Woestyne (1881–1947), Gustave de Smet (1877–1943), Frits van den Berghe (1883–1939), Constant Permeke (1886–1952), Jean Brusselmans (1884–1953), Edgard Tytgat (1879–1957), Rik Wouters (1882–1916), and René Magritte (1898–1967).

Apart from the fine collection of nineteenth- and twentieth-century Belgian paintings, the museum is still best known for *The Mad Killer* (1822) by Théodore Géricault (1791–1824), which is from a series of paintings of lunatics done by Géricault in the last years of his short life, among his finest works (room 13); and two paintings by Bosch.

Bosch, Hieronymous* (ca. 1450–1516), Flemish

St. Jerome: ground floor, room 3
Bosch's "abstract" art has always appealed to our interest in the world of dreams, so it is not surprising that Bosch is popularly considered a unique eccentric. But rather than look for an explanation of Bosch's art within a hallucinatory world of the subconscious, you would be on firmer ground considering that Bosch, a prominent and wealthy citizen of Hertogenbosch, put a puritanical emphasis on hard work, and had a hatred of the physical sins: gluttony and lechery. Bosch was really less of a psychoanalyst than a revivalist.

In Bosch's depiction of St. Jerome he shows us a man of powerful intellect who has thrown away his book (on the ground in the right-hand corner) and is prostrate in the desert embracing a crucifix. All sorts of objects are strewn around the scene, each one with a particular meaning: there is the red cardinal's robe and hat, an indication of Jerome's future reward for his devotion to Christ, even though St. Jerome lived during a time when the office of cardinal did not exist in the church; a toylike lion is seen lapping water, a reference to the fable of Jerome pulling a thorn from the paw of the lion which thereafter made him a devoted friend; the hollow tree is reminiscent of bygone temptation; the owl, sitting on one of its branches, is the bird of darkness, or of heresy; the disorder of the rocks, which seem to be transformed into shapes resembling the Tables of the Law, may indicate the misuse of the law; and the skull twined over with wild vines is a symbol of the emptiness of the world.

Though this painting is not filled with the devil scenes that Bosch is so famous for, it nevertheless has the Boschian sermon directed at the conscience of the world's sinners.

Christ Carrying the Cross: ground floor, room 3
This painting is one of Bosch's last works (Bosch never dated his paintings), where he focuses on the weak, good figure at the center, crushed by evil toughness all around. Hence Christ is shown without any distance between Him and man. He is pressed against evil humanity with eyes closed, dreaming the nightmare the painting depicts. One of the executioners has seized the Cross with both hands and is sadistically pressing it down on Christ's

shoulder. The face of Veronica has been transformed into a waxen figure turned away from Christ. In the lower right corner the henchmen are exulting with sadistic glee over the bad thief who scowls back at them, while in the upper right the good thief is being admonished with evil fanaticism by a Dominican.

ST. BAVO CATHEDRAL

St. Baafsplein

Hours for visiting the *Adoration of the Lamb:* Open Apr.–Sept., Mon–Sat., 9:30AM–12 noon and 2–6PM, Sun. and holidays, 1–6PM; Oct–Mar., Mon.–Sat., 10:30AM–12 noon and 2:30–4PM, Sun. and holidays, 2–5PM. Admission fee.

This Gothic cathedral had its start as a twelfth-century Romanesque church (only the central part of the Romanesque crypt survives), and was completed in its present form in the sixteenth century. Its single western tower and spire, which rises to a height of 269 feet, is reminiscent of the German style, and its richly decorated interior has many works of art including paintings (Joos van Ghent's *Calvary Triptych* is in the north transept, Rubens's *Conversion of St. Bavo* is in the tenth chapel) and sculptures (Laurent Delvaux's oak and marble pulpit is in the nave). Yet all of St. Bavo's treasures and even the cathedral itself do not equal one of its works of art: Van Eyck's *Adoration of the Lamb.*

Eyck, Jan van (ca. 1390–1441), Flemish
The Flemish Renaissance School of painting in the fifteenth century differed from the Italian School in that it was concerned with the smallest details of nature and of everyday material things. Its use of the oil technique gave its works a luminous quality that was considered new during its time. That Jan van Eyck was a dominant figure in the emergence of this school, which was highly thought of in Italy and elsewhere, is well known, but the popular idea that this style began with him out of nothing is ridiculous. There were many other artists who were busy preparing the way for van Eyck, such as the Limbourg brothers whose illuminated manuscript, *The Very Rich Hours,* shows the pleasure of specific detail; Claus Sluter, whose sculpture at the Chartreuse de Champmol in Burgundy shows that a naturalistic figure could be psychologically profound; and Melchior Broederlam, whose late fourteenth-century panels focused on the dignity of human action in the world. The oil technique was not van Eyck's invention, but his fame throughout Europe helped to spread the use of that medium, especially in Italy. This seeks to put Jan van Eyck in correct perspective but is not meant to detract from his overall achievements. He remains one of the great geniuses in the history of Western painting, whose skill articulated early Renaissance art in northern Europe.

As for his origins, most evidence points to him coming from Maseyck, a town near Maestricht in the Meuse area: he left a legacy to an institution in Maseyck, his daughter Liévine entered a convent there in 1450, and a document deriving from Philip the Good (1435 or 1436) refers to him as "Johannes van Tricht," that is, Jan van Maestricht. We know for certain that he had a brother, Lambert, employed by Philip the Good (1431), and he may have had a brother, Hubert, who was a painter and gave him his training, though there is controversy as to whether Hubert ever existed.

Jan's name appears for the first time in 1422 at the Hague, where he was in the employ of John of Bavaria. When his patron died in 1425, Jan obtained a similar position with Philip the Good at Bruges. From that time on he worked and lived largely in Bruges and Tournai, except for some secret diplomatic missions he undertook for Philip in 1426–28 and 1436. He bought a house in Bruges in January, 1432, and finished the *Adoration of the Lamb* on May 6 of that year. Thereafter, between 1432 and 1439, he signed nine paintings, but there are others which are obviously by him. He died in Bruges on July 9, 1441.

The Adoration of the Lamb (1432): sixth chapel of the ambulatory
The theme of the inner panels of the unfolded polyptych is the glorification of Christ. The lamb, which the figures in the lower panels face, is the symbol of Christ in his sacrificial role. Man's disobedience to God, as indicated by the outer upper left and right panels of Adam and Eve, has been atoned for by Christ.

Start with the **center panel in the lower zone**. Here we see a red altar (red is the color of the Passion—the suffering and death of Christ on the Cross) covered with a white cloth (white is the color of purity) on which stands a lamb from whose breast blood flows into a chalice (the symbol of the Redemption). The lamb should not be compared to its role as a sacrificial animal in non-Christian rites. Here we see it standing, not crouching like an immolated victim. As depicted by van Eyck, it is an object of eternal life that is no longer suffering, even though its blood is flowing into the chalice. On the upper part of the red altar is written, "Behold the Lamb of God which taketh away the sin of the world." The two red pendants hanging from the antependium (the decoration on the front of the altar) have embroidered inscriptions that read, "Jesus, the Way, the Truth and the Life." There are two angels before the altar worshipping the lamb. Four angels behind it carry the instruments of the Passion: the cross to which Jesus was nailed, the lance which was thrust into his heart, the sponge from which He was given vinegar to drink, and the column of the flagellation. On either side are four adoring angels. In the center foreground is a fountain with water flowing from two vases held by an angel and gargoyles attached to the column. It is symbolic of spiritual life and salvation and it overflows its basin and runs out into a rivulet toward us, the viewers of the polyptych. The figures in the left foreground are prophets (Old Testament patriarchs) and Gentiles. The Gentiles dressed in exotic costumes may represent ancient philosophers and even Vergil, who according to popular belief in the Middle Ages predicted the coming of Christ. This group symbolizes all those who have believed in one personal God and lived according to His natural law. According to Catholic teaching they are deserving of and will be admitted to eternal bliss. The figures in the right foreground, headed by kneeling, unkempt men, with popes, bishops, priests, and civilians all dressed in red, are those who have made public confession of faith in the church. Some of them are easily identifiable, such as St. Peter with his book (the gospel) accompanied by St. Paul. Behind St. Peter is St. Stephen, the deacon, the first martyr who was stoned to death. He carries stones, his special attribute, in a fold of his dalmatic. St. Lievin, the patron saint of Ghent, is shown behind him holding his tongue with pincers. In the middle distance, on the left and on the right, are saints: men on the left, women on the right. They are all carrying palms in their hands, a symbol of the Christian's victory over death. Some of the objects the women carry enable us to identify them: St. Agnes with the lamb, St. Barbara with the tower, St. Dorothy with the bouquet of roses and apples, and St. Ursula with the arrow. Above, in the center, is the dove, the symbol of the Holy Ghost. Its rays of light are being shed on all those who have come to give thanks and praise to God.

On the left wing nearest the central panel are the Knights of Christ. There is some disagreement as to the identity of these personages, but they probably represent princes who took part in the crusades to the Holy Land, still fresh in the minds of people in the fifteenth century. On the wing to the left are the Just Judges (this is a copy; the original was stolen in 1934 and never recovered), and here too there is controversy as to the identity of the figures. Some scholars see portraits of Jan and Hubert van Eyck in this panel.

On the wing of the first right-hand panel are the Holy Hermits. In back of them, emerging from behind a rock, are two female saints, St. Mary Magdalene with her jar of ointment and St. Mary the Egyptian who is often shown as her companion. On the panel to the extreme right are the Holy Pilgrims being led by St. Christopher, the giant.

In the upper zone is Christ in the center panel. His depiction as a commanding, enthroned figure, and the three vaulted arches above his head (which have the inscription, "God the all powerful in His divine majesty, the first of all, the best because of His goodness and loving kindness, the most generous rewarder in His infinite bounty") cause people to think he may be God the Father rather than Christ. The inscription could be applied to God, and we are used to seeing Christ represented in this period as a less regal and formal figure. But the representation of the pelican feeding its young with its blood (the symbol of the sacrifice of Christ on the Cross to redeem mankind) with the name "Jesus Christ" on the curtain in the background, and the presence of the Virgin and St. John the Baptist in the two side panels (they are never depicted with God the Father, but very often with God the Son) mean that the center figure can only be Christ.

The Virgin is shown as a beautiful young woman meditating on the text of a book. She is seated wearing her blue robe and mantle (blue pigments were the most expensive and usually used for the Virgin) and behind her crown are stars, often shown with her in early Renaissance art.

The figure of John the Baptist is shown pointing toward Christ, recalling the moment when John pointed out the "Lamb of God." He holds a book open at the passage from the prophet Isaiah that tells of John the Baptist as the precursor of Christ.

The **panels of singing angels** are of secondary importance, but their depiction in realistic detail is a source of delight, especially to musicians and music lovers.

The **panels of Adam and Eve**, at the opposite ends of the upper zone, appear to be real portraits. Note how Adam's foot looks as if it were stepping out of the frame, and how Eve's belly is emphasized according to the fashion of the day. The realistic detail of these panels has offended people through the centuries. During the prudish nineteenth century they were sold to the Belgian government (to be displayed at the Royal Museum in Brussels) and replaced here with clothed copies.

In the Ghent altarpiece, Jan van Eyck carried to fruition some new features of painting that, because of the fame of the altarpiece from its inception, helped to spread the new style throughout Europe and established him as the foremost master of Flemish painting. While Jan portrays the essence of the Christian faith during a time when nothing was more important to society, he also intensely represents nature. Every detail is individualized to do justice to the whole of creation. This is no more evident than in the panels of Adam and Eve. Earlier paintings never showed nudes so true to nature in every detail, and even though these figures are representations without backgrounds of the Garden of Eden we sense that they have the Renaissance awareness of their place in the total environment. Adam seems to gaze out upon the world, simple and frank. Eve's gaze is turned thoughtfully inward with a peculiar inner strength. We clearly realize that she has precipitated the action.

We also see that Jan van Eyck has provided us with a homogeneous spatial image in his landscape setting on the panels in the lower zone. Until the Ghent altarpiece, nowhere had an artist cared so much about portraying realistic depth. Jan's individualization of the figures, during a time when most other artists never used real models for the faces they painted, humanized the work. Great crowds visited it when it was first placed in the cathedral, just as they do today, and it became popular from the start.

CASTLE OF THE COUNTS ('S GRAVENSTEEN)

Geldmuntstraat

Hours: Open Apr.–Sept., daily 9AM–5:15PM; Oct.–Mar., daily 9AM–3:15PM. Admission fee.

When Philip of Alsace, count of Flanders, returned from the Holy Land in 1180, he found it necessary to build this castle to control the proud, unruly burghers of Ghent, who had built fortified towers in the city. The site had probably been used earlier as a Viking fortress. When Philip built there it already had had a ring wall since 1000.

The oldest surviving part of the castle is the twelfth-century keep (center building) containing a great hall used by the counts for ceremonial meetings, rather than as a residence. Notice the perimeter walls that make use of the bartizan, or projecting turret, to increase the flanking power of the castle. It is a splendid example of a medieval castle, and its display of instruments of torture in room 17 adds to the atmosphere.

Other civic buildings in Ghent of interest are the town **belfry** and the **Cloth Hall,** both of which stand on the St. Baafsplein across from St. Bavo Cathedral. Also, the display of old **guild houses** on the Graslei is a glorious sight, though they are best seen from the other side of the Leie, from the Koornlei. These lovely buildings date from the twelfth to the seventeenth century and reflect Romanesque, Gothic, and Renaissance styles.

Britain

This island serves as one of the greatest storehouses of Western art to be found anywhere in the world. More of the architectural past survives in Britain than anywhere else, much of it in lovely surroundings: great country houses in scenic parks and magnificent cathedrals surrounded by green lawns. Painting has also played an important role, though it was not until as late as the eighteenth century that England herself achieved greatness in this art. When it came, it lasted about one hundred years, from 1750 to 1850, because of a number of gifted individuals: William Hogarth (1697–1764), a genre painter, who devoted himself to social commentary; Thomas Gainsborough (1727–88) and Joshua Reynolds (1723–92), portrait painters who could depict their subjects not only with elegance but also with soul; Gainsborough, also a landscapist, who made a contribution that inspired John Constable (1776–1837), who liberated the art of landscape painting and gave it a new vitality; and finally J. M. W. Turner (1775–1851), one of the geniuses of Western art, whose work was a predecessor of twentieth-century expressionism.

Yet the art you can see in Britain today goes far beyond that of the English School because the English were also the greatest collectors of foreign art that the world had ever seen. Their enlightened connoisseurship has made Britain, especially London, a showplace of art where you can see masterpieces from classic Greek sculpture to modern art. As a bonus, this bonanza of art is displayed in some of the finest museums in the world.

Country Houses in Britain

No architecture in Europe is more pleasurable to visit than English country houses. Officially referred to as "historic houses," many of them have treasures of silver, armor, tapestries, paintings, sculptures, and furniture. Most are surrounded by gardens and parks, sometimes designed by experts, like Capability Brown (1715–73) and Humphry Repton (1752–1818), which enhance their beauty and make it possible to view them from every angle.

What follows is a list of some of the outstanding country houses in Britain that are open to the public. A short description of each will be found listed alphabetically by location in the main section on Britain. There are, of course, others as imposing and artistically important. One of the joys of visiting Britain is discovering these places, which you can do by using *Historic Houses and Gardens*, published by the National Trust and the National Trust of Scotland. It is available for a fee from British Tourist Authority offices in New York, Chicago, Los Angeles, and Dallas.

Blenheim Palace, Oxfordshire
Blickling Hall, Norfolk
Castle Howard, Yorkshire
Chatsworth, Derbyshire
Haddon Hall, Derbyshire
Hardwick Hall, Derbyshire
Hatfield House, Hertfordshire
Holkham Hall, Norfolk
Kedleston Hall, Derbyshire
Knole, Kent
Longleat House, Wiltshire
Montacute House, Somerset
Oxburgh Hall, Norfolk
Penshurst Place, Kent
Petworth House, Sussex
Warwick Castle, Warwickshire
Wilton House, Wiltshire
Woburn Abbey, Bedfordshire

Bath

Though the Romans visited Bath to take the warm mineral waters (you can still see the Roman lead-lined pool, original paving stones, and other objects dating back to 54 A.D.), the city today is the result of enlightened town planning done in the eighteenth century.

Bath had remained a small town, mostly known in the Middle Ages as a center for the cloth trade, until the value of its mineral waters was popularized about 1720. This brought royal patronage and the town became a summer resort attracting the famous, the titled, and the wealthy of England. To this day it is known for descriptions of its social life made by some of Britain's greatest authors—Fielding, Smollet, Sheridan, Austen, and Thackeray. Everyone who was anyone visited Bath. Beau Nash (1674–1762) presided over its social life from the Grand Pump Room, overlooking the Roman Bath, in an atmosphere that rivaled the royal court.

It was also in the eighteenth century that an experiment in town planning became a model for other towns all over Britain. Before Bath was redesigned, buildings had been planned individually or in groups of twos or threes, but between 1750 and 1800 houses were designed by street, incorporating architectural elements into a unified whole. Such a construction was the **Royal Crescent** (1765–75), which forms an enormous arc on the edge of the crown of a hill around a great lawn. It provides a view of the city for its thirty houses whose facades (which collectively have one hundred and fourteen Ionic columns) are almost unchanged from the day they were built. It is a fine example of terrace architecture. A Georgian house with authentic nineteenth-century funiture is maintained as a museum at no. 1 Royal Crescent (open Tues.–Sat., 11AM–5PM, and Sun., 2–5PM; admission fee). Other terraces and crescents in the city are Landsdown Crescent (1789–93) and Camden Crescent (1788).

Earlier construction in Bath is seen in **Queen Square** (1728–35), designed in the Palladian manner; and the **Circus,** completed in the 1760s, with three crescents of rows of town houses with various stone ornaments. Plaques mark the houses where Gainsborough, Pitt, and Clive of India lived. No street enters the Circus opposite another, assuring unity of design; no matter where one enters, one faces a facade.

Other sights are the Grand Pump Room and Pulteney Bridge, an English version of the Ponte Vecchio. The **Pump Room** was rebuilt between 1786 and 1788 as a place for visitors to take the curative waters. It still serves this purpose. One may have tea or coffee at a table in the vast palm-decked room, with its Corinthian columns, and go back to the time of Beau Nash in the 1730s and 1740s. Beyond the Pump Room doorway lie the remnants of the Roman baths.

The exterior of the Pump Room is built in three blocks. At either end are colonnades in the Ionic order, each with a pediment in which the tympanum is decorated with female sphinxes. The central block, which is the Pump Room itself, has a colonnade in the Corinthian order raised above street level.

Pulteney Bridge (1769–74), with shops on both of its sides, is the work of Robert Adam (1728–92). It is actually only a small part of an intended estate for William Pulteney, never carried out.

Bedfordshire

WOBURN ABBEY

In Woburn, eight and one half miles northwest of Dunstable on A50

Hours: Open Apr.–Oct., Mon.–Sat., 11AM–5:45PM, Sun., 11AM–6:15PM; Feb., Mar., Nov., daily 1–4:45PM; closed Dec., Jan. Admission fee.

Until 1945 this great eighteenth-century mansion in a 3,000-acre park designed by Humphrey Repton was a private house seldom entered by anyone outside the duke of Bedford's family and friends. Yet today Woburn Abbey is one of the most-visited country houses in Britain. From an artistic point of view, its main attraction is fourteen state apartments decorated with eighteenth-century French and English furniture, a fabulous Sèvres dinner service, presented to the fourth duke by Louis XVI, and a rich collection of old master paintings (Rembrandt, van Dyck, Cuyp, Teniers, Reynolds, Gainsborough, Velázquez, Holbein, and others), including a well-known group of Venetian views by **Canaletto** (additional admission fee). In the eighteenth century Englishmen of wealth and noble birth did not consider their education complete before taking the Grand Tour. They flocked to Venice, which catered to their taste for gaiety, entertainment, and culture. Antonio Canale, called Canaletto (1697–1768), was one of their favorite painters. His paintings of pageants and city views were bought as souvenirs and hung in Britain's country homes and town houses. The superior collection here is a fine example of Canaletto's skill. The architecture is always scrupulously rendered and flooded with the light of high noon.

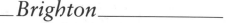

Brighton

ROYAL PAVILION

In the center of Brighton (Old Steine)

Hours: Open June–Sept., daily 10AM–6:30PM; Oct.–May, 10AM–5PM. Admission fee.

Only the Prince Regent of England (later George IV) could have built such a fantastic structure. The Royal Pavilion is a delight to the eye from a period in English history (1788–1823) when a "prince of pleasure" presided over a profligate society.

George Augustus Frederick (1762–1830), the Prince of Wales (the prince regent [1811–20] and then George IV [1820–30]), was a spoiled child when he visited Brighton at the age of twenty-one, in 1783, searching for a cure for swollen glands in his neck. He fell in love with the seaside, and, starting from a farmhouse on the site of the present building, he began building projects that resulted in the Royal Pavilion.

The first building, known as the Marine Pavilion, designed by Henry Holland and completed in 1787, was a Palladian house with a shallow central dome. Additions were made to it between 1801 and 1803. Then the prince redesigned the interior in a Chinese style bringing back a taste for *chinoiserie* popular in the early eighteenth century. In 1808, when the royal stables at Brighton were completed in a Moslem Indian style, with an eighty-foot cupola, the prince changed his taste from Chinese to Indian. This brought on the final version of the Royal Pavilion undertaken by **John Nash** (1752–1835), whose work includes the planning of Regent's Park, St. James's Park, Regent Street, and Trafalgar Square in London. He started work on the Royal Pavilion in 1815, and it led to the Indian-influenced style that you see today with its onion dome over the saloon and smaller domes on each side, flanked by two other domes (one over a banqueting room, the other over a music room). The **banqueting room** resembles the tent of an Oriental potentate. There are chandeliers (weighing over a ton), great mirrors, and Oriental decoration. The **kitchen,** finished in 1816, has cast iron palm-tree columns supporting the roof that are decorated with leaves of sheet bronze. There are more than 500 pieces of copperware and other cooking equipment.

The prince spent most of his time at Brighton. His brother, William IV, also spent time at Brighton, but Queen Victoria abandoned it in 1845 and took with her most of its furniture. In 1850 the city of Brighton acquired it and in the twentieth century most of the furniture was returned, so the Royal Pavilion appears as it did when the prince regent lived here.

Cambridge

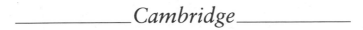

It is a joy to wander through the courtyards and lawns of the colleges that comprise Cambridge University. Their buildings reflect styles of every period in Britain from the medieval to the present. Because of their location, surrounding the town and bordered by lawns and the Cam River, they have always been everyone's idea of what a great university should look like.

FITZWILLIAM MUSEUM

Trumpington Street

Hours: Open Tues.–Sat., 10AM–5PM, Sun., 2–5PM; closed Dec. 25, Boxing Day, and Good Friday. Free admission.

This university museum, housed in a splendid nineteenth-century classical building, was founded in 1816 by the generosity of a former undergraduate, Richard, 7th Vicount Fitzwilliam of Merrion, and today has a varied collection of paintings, sculptures, and objets d'art. It was one of the first museums to display quality instead of quantity, breaking with the tradition of filling every inch of wall space with paintings. Its warm wall fabrics of red and gold, period furniture along its walls, and rich carpets you can walk on, create a homey feeling as if one were a guest in a great country residence.

Start by ascending the double Victorian staircase in the magnificent entrance hall. **Room 3**, the large room in front of you, has British paintings from the seventeenth and eighteenth centuries, including portraits by van Dyck, Lely, Reynolds, and Gainsborough. Most interesting are paintings by **Hogarth** (1697–1764): *A Musical Party*, three portraits, and a set of paintings on a sexual theme, *Indiscretion—Before and After,* done in the French eighteenth-century fashion, but with Hogarth's own English earthy interpretation. *Before*, in the French style, shows a man making advances to a somewhat coy woman. *After,* showing the lusty aftermath, goes further than the French rococo *galanteries.*

Before leaving room 3 climb the spiral staircase to the **balcony** of small paintings that runs round the entire room. It is a wonderful way to get a close look at old master paintings as though they were in your own home. You will find delightful small eighteenth-century paintings by Lancret, the imitator of Watteau; a Poussin *Italian Landscape;* oil sketches by Constable;

Blake's *Ugolino and his Sons in Prison; The Bride of Bethehem,* by William Holman Hunt, the Pre-Raphaelite Victorian artist; and small sixteenth-century Flemish and seventeenth-century Dutch paintings.

Rooms 1 and 2, to the right, contain nineteenth- and twentieth-century British paintings: three oils by Turner; Pre-Raphaelite paintings by Ford Madox Brown and studies and drawings by Rossetti; and fine examples of paintings by W. R. Sickert, Harold Gilman, and Stanley Spencer, and portraits by Augustus John. From Jacob Epstein (1880–1959) there is a sculptured head of *Albert Einstein.*

Rooms 4 and 5, to the left, display French paintings. Among those in **room 4** are paintings by Claude, Delacroix, Corot, Courbet, and a late **Poussin** (1594–1665), *Rebecca and Eliezer at the Well,* formerly in the collection of the art historian Anthony Blunt. **Room 5** has a small but fine collection of impressionist paintings: landscapes and country people by Pissaro; a bronze *Head of Coco,* by Renoir; examples of Georges Seurat's pointilliste method; and works by Monet, Degas, and Cézanne.

From room 4 there is an entrance into **room 6 (Upper Marlay)** filled with early Italian paintings. Here are three magnificent panels (ca. 1320), *St. Geminianus, St. Michael,* and *St. Augustine,* by **Simone Martini** (ca. 1284–1344), the Sienese master. These panels belonged to a polyptych that was probably in an Augustinian convent at San Gimignano. From Florence there is a small *Virgin and Child Enthroned* (ca. 1400) by Lorenzo Monaco (ca. 1372–1422/4), one of his earliest known works; a *Madonna and Child with St. George and St. John the Baptist,* by Filippo Lippi (ca. 1406–69); and two predella panels by **Domenico Veneziano** (ca. 1400–61): *The Annunciation,* which communicates a symmetrical, harmonious, ideal world in an enclosed garden (symbol of the Virgin) with a closed gate (symbol of the Immaculate Conception); and the *Miracle of St. Zenobius,* which shows us a dramatic scene from the real world of the streets of Florence where St. Zenobius, bishop of Florence, has restored the life of a child run over by an ox-cart.

Room 7, with its high Renaissance Venetian paintings, contains the greatest treasures of the Fitzwilliam. There are sensuous scenes of *Venus and Cupid,* by **Palma Vecchio** (ca. 1485–1528) and **Titian** (ca. 1487–1576). From Titian there is also a dramatic *Tarquin and Lucretia* showing the virtuous Lucretia raped by Sextus, son of the tyrant Tarquin, while her servant is helpless and blindfolded to the left. The luxurious *Hermes, Herse and Aglauros,* by **Veronese** (1528–88), tells the story of how Aglauros, envious of Hermes' (Mercury) love for her beautiful sister Herse, tries to prevent Hermes from entering Herse's chamber and is turned to black stone (the color of her thoughts) by Hermes. We see Herse awaiting her lover Hermes unconcerned with the fate of her sister.

The far end of room 7 leads to **room 8,** devoted to Flemish and Spanish paintings. Among these is a village scene by Pieter Brueghel the Younger; seven *Designs for the Eucharist Series of Tapestries,* by Rubens (1577–1640), and his exciting *Death of Hippolytus;* and religious scenes by Esteban Murillo.

At the other end of room 7 is the **Broughton Flower Paintings room** which leads into the **Dutch room** devoted to seventeenth-century painting. Fine examples of this Golden Age of art are seen in portraits by Barent Fabritius, Gerrit Dou, and Frans Hals; landscapes by Hobbema and Jacob and Salomon Ruisdael; an Italianized *Sunset after Rain*, by Cuyp (1620–91); and an unconventional *Interior, with a Painter and His Wife* by Steen (1626–79).

The remainder of the museum, reached from the Octagon off room 8, is devoted to twentieth-century art, which is a constantly changing exhibition.

KING'S COLLEGE CHAPEL

King's College, north side of the Great Court

Hours: Open in term, Mon.–Sat., 9:30AM–3:45PM; Sun., 2–3PM and 4:30–5:45PM; outside term, Mon.–Sat., 9:30AM–5PM, Sun., 10:30AM–5PM. Free admission.

This aisleless and towerless chapel, nearly as large as a cathedral, is the architectural gem of Cambridge. Begun in 1446 and completed in 1515, it is the finest result of experience gained in over three hundred years of Gothic building. Such decorations as the woodwork of the screen, the choir stalls, and the stained glass are sixteenth century. It is important for representing the last phase of Gothic in England, perpendicular Gothic, the most English of Gothic forms. Its predominant characteristic is slenderness and delicacy of design in both exterior and interior. Vertical lines replace the flowing geometric shapes of traditional Gothic. A large proportion of the direct lines of the tracery intersect at right angles giving the name of perpendicular to the style. The shafts on either side of the interior lead the eye up eighty feet to the roof, which is supported by a display of intricate **fan vaulting,** the finest in England. Here too are stained glass windows that have a high proportion of their original glazing and convey a true idea of the color and glow that worshippers in the early sixteenth century enjoyed. Today this glass, covering over 10,000 square feet, is the largest, most complete, collection of stained glass windows in the world. The glowing altarpiece, Rubens's *Adoration of the Magi*, which stands under the east window, is a recent addition, a gift to the college in 1959.

TRINITY COLLEGE LIBRARY

Trinity College, Neville's Court

Hours: Open Mon.–Fri., 1–4PM. Free admission.

Trinity College, founded by King Henry VIII in 1546, is the largest of the colleges at Cambridge. Entering the college from Trinity Street, you will pass into Great Court, with its elaborate Renaissance fountain built in 1602. It is the largest college court in Britain. A flight of steps on the west side leads through to the second smaller court, Neville's Court, named after the builder of the Great Court. Here, on the west side, is the Trinity College Library, one of Sir Christopher Wren's masterpieces built in 1676–84.

Wren (1632–1723) employed a serene Roman design of superimposed Doric and Ionic colonnades featuring eleven continuous bays. Only four statues on the parapet, placed over the four center columns, relieve the design. A curiosity is the level of the library floor, which was dictated by the level of the adjoining buildings. This forced Wren to build his floor at the springing of the arches in the ground floor arcade, making the cartouche-enriched tympana solid and thus the arches false. Wren justified this design by saying he saw it successfully employed on the Continent. The interior, which you can visit on weekday afternoons, has book cases carved by Grinling Gibbons.

Leave Neville's Court passing through the south entrance into New Court, where the west entrance will lead to the college grounds. From here you will see that Wren modified his design on the river side. The classical orders are omitted, the upper windows are slightly recessed, and two great portals have been introduced.

Coming between Wren's early, somewhat busy, buildings and his later complex designs, the Trinity College Library is Wren's simplest work.

Canterbury

CANTERBURY CATHEDRAL

Hours: Open all hours. Free admission.

Canterbury is the original seat of the Church of England. Its Christian origins go back to the sixth century when St. Augustine, the founder of the Christian church in England, built the first of his abbeys here. The cathedral itself originated in the eleventh century, and by the twelfth century had been twice rebuilt because of fires that destroyed large parts of it. During the fourteenth century it was completely rebuilt again in the Gothic style, retaining its Norman remains (parts of the original Norman cathedral can be seen in the crypt). Canterbury Cathedral is today representative of a collection of styles favored during various periods of its long construction (1070–1508), with perpendicular Gothic, that last phase of Gothic that is native to England and emphasizes height, predominant.

Exterior

The roads dropping down from the hills that surround Canterbury afford some of the best views of the cathedral. Three towers rise above the rooftops of the city. The great **central tower** (235 feet high) is ornate in design with large windows and decorative turrets. Known as "Bell Harry Tower," it is among the best examples of fifteenth-century church towers in England. The tallest aisle windows in England in the south side of the nave are evidence of the perpendicular style in full development, which is carried over into the windows of the western transepts.

Interior
Nave: The piers have three vaulting shafts rising unbroken from the floor to the vaults, which though simple in design are decorative enough to hold the eye to the entire ceiling. The main source of light is from the aisle windows, which give the interior a unity of space characteristic of buildings from this period (late fourteenth century).

Central Tower: The crossing between the nave and the choir affords the best views in the cathedral. A decorative network of stone girders helps support the great central tower. Look up to see the delicate fan vaulting of its interior. Also, while standing under the crossing, look toward the north and south transepts for a view of the great perpendicular windows.

North Transept: Just left of the central tower (facing the apse) is the spot where, on December 29, 1170, Thomas à Becket was murdered, to become a celebrated martyr. Becket, the one-time friend of Henry II, had been struggling with the king since his appointment as archbishop of Canterbury. In one of Henry's notorious rages he cried out, "Is there no one who will rid me of this low-born priest?" Some of his knights hacked Becket to pieces before the altar of St. Benedict. The incident was seen as Henry II's assertion of the authority of the crown over the clergy. Becket's fame as a martyr spread and the king was so humiliated he had to do penance by walking barefoot through the streets of Canterbury and submitting to a scourging at Becket's tomb. Becket became a saint and his shrine at Canterbury Cathedral was one of the most popular places of pilgrimage in the Middle Ages. We have an account by Chaucer, in his *Canterbury Tales*, of a typical journey to Becket's shrine. The enormous income the cathedral derived from the pilgrims helped to finance the construction of the building. But in 1538 the cathedral's good fortune came to an end when Henry VIII seized the shrine and its gold and jewels—twenty-six cartloads of it. Nothing of these riches remains in Canterbury today.

Crypt: The western portion of the crypt has the original Norman (Romanesque) carved capitals and ornamented pillars. The windows, however, are fifteenth-century additions. Do not fail to see the undercroft of the southeastern transept, a Huguenot chapel used by French Protestants since 1568; and the lower chapel of St. Gabriel, with thirteenth-century mural paintings.

Choir: The design of the choir has arcades and an upper structure that is clearly French Gothic. It was started by a Frenchman, William of Sens, a master mason, who worked on Sens Cathedral in France. Four years after he started the work, however, he fell from the scaffolding and was crippled. His place was taken by "William the Englishman," who completed it in 1184. The result is a compromise between French design and the instincts of the native craftsmen, such as the lavish use of dark marble for detached carving.

The woodwork of the seventeenth-century stalls are attributed to Grinling Gibbons (1648–1721); in the aisles there is thirteenth-century glass; and in one of the obliquely placed Norman chapels (St. Andrews) there is a surviving mid-twelfth-century wall painting of *St. Paul and the Viper at Malta.*

Trinity Chapel: This is east of the choir behind the high altar where it once contained the body of St. Thomas à Becket encased in a gold-plated shrine adorned with precious jewels, such as the *Régale de France,* a famous ruby, donated by Louis VII in 1179. It was all dismantled by Henry VIII in 1538 and its contents confiscated. Henry had the ruby mounted as a ring. Today you can see only the marble surface where the pilgrims prayed, deeply indented by their knees. On one side of Becket's shrine is the tomb of Edward the Black Prince (d. 1376), with a gilt bronze effigy; on the other side are the tomb of Henry IV (d. 1413), the usurper of Edward's son, Richard II; and the tomb of Henry II's second wife, Joan of Navarre.

Becket's Crown (the Corona): Opposite Trinity Chapel is the circular chapel called the Corona, dating from construction made by "William the Englishman," but the design probably from William of Sens. It has a mixture of round and pointed arches and is typical of the period of transition from Romanesque to Gothic, and of the English custom of salvaging from the past by building around older work. This chapel used to contain a piece of Becket's skull (the piece his assassins cut off when they murdered him in the cathedral), and still contains the archaic stone chair, of Saxon origin, on which the primates of England are enthroned.

_____Derbyshire_____

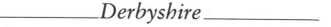

CHATSWORTH

Bakewell, one half mile east of village of Edensor on A623, four miles east of Bakewell, ten miles west of Chesterfield

Hours: Open Apr.–Oct., Tues.–Sun., 11:30AM–4:30PM. Admission fee.

Dignity and stateliness are words that best describe Chatsworth, the house of the dukes of Devonshire. While it was rebuilt at the beginning of the eighteenth century, after the Glorious Revolution of 1688 with the aristocracy at the height of its power, its history goes back to the time of Elizabeth Cavendish, "Bess of Hardwick," who persuaded the first of her four husbands to purchase the site in 1549. Her mania for building resulted in a structure even larger than the one you see today, but it was entirely replaced. The present Chatsworth was built by the first duke between 1687 and 1707, and additions were made by the sixth duke between 1820 and 1830.

Individual rooms have been criticized as unworthy of a great house, but overall the house is grand, with an excellent collection of art: Poussin's *Landscape with Settlers Hunting, A View of Tivoli,* attributed to Salvator

Rosa, Veronese's *Adoration of the Magi,* paintings by Claude, van Dyck, Reynolds, and Sargent, and the works of a contemporary British artist, Lucian Freud. The state drawing room is decorated with tapestries (ca. 1635) after cartoons by Raphael; the great dining room, added in the nineteenth century, has an adjoining sculpture gallery, with classical-style works, for strolling after dinner. Another nineteenth-century addition to the house is the library, formerly the long gallery, containing part of the famous Chatsworth collection of books and manuscripts. It is a magnificent room with a lived-in feeling created by the warm color and texture of the bookcases, the furniture, and the exquisitely bound volumes.

Equal to the fine interior are the magnificent grounds and formal gardens laid out by Joseph Paxton (1801–65) in 1826. Paxton was also the designer of the Crystal Palace for the Great Exhibition in 1851 in Hyde Park. At Chatsworth he built a number of glass structures, forerunners in design of the Crystal Palace, but only one remains—the hillside arboretum, a series of eleven glass enclosures against a stone wall. The central entrance has a fantail design over the door, and inside are rare plants that Paxton planted in 1850 and that are still flourishing today.

Paxton built the famous water cascade that descends from a rock formation and appears like a waterfall, and the Emperor Fountain, which throws its water 290 feet into the air.

In 1843, Queen Victoria and Prince Albert were guests of the duke. Paxton illuminated the gardens, conservatories, waterfalls, and fountains with 12,000 multicolored lights. The next morning, when guests awoke early to see how Paxton had accomplished his magic, not a trace of the evening's illumination could be found. Paxton's men had worked through the night restoring the grounds to their natural peaceful beauty.

HADDON HALL

Bakewell, two miles southeast of Bakewell and six and one-half miles north of Matlock on the Buxton-Matlock road (A6)

Hours: Open Apr.–Sept., Mon.–Sat., 11AM–6PM, Sun., 2–6PM. Admission fee.

Haddon, on a hill overlooking the river Wye, is a complete example of an English manor house surviving from the Middle Ages; its oldest part dates back to the thirteenth century. None of it is less than four hundred years old, although it was extensively restored in the early part of the twentieth century. Notice that its hall, with kitchens and buttery, divides one court from another. A large **banqueting hall** with windows on both sides, a fifteenth-century tapestry, and a fireplace was the center of the house in medieval times. The house also contains an English long hall, constructed in 1611 (109 feet by eighteen feet), paneled in oak and carved walnut in the spirit of the Renaissance. The terraced gardens retain their Elizabethan style and display roses, the flower of Haddon.

HARDWICK HALL

Two miles south of Chesterfield, Mansfield road (A617)

Hours: Open Apr.–Oct., Mon., Wed., Thurs., Sat., Sun., 1–5:30PM.

Hardwick recalls the old rhyme, "Hardwick Hall, more glass than wall." The **west front** has fifty large windows with small panes of leaded glass. One can imagine the builder, "Bess of Hardwick," supervising construction (1591–97) so as to be certain there was more glass than stone.

"Bess of Hardwick" (Elizabeth Cavendish, countess of Shrewsbury) was born in the old manor house at Hardwick in 1520, the daughter of a country squire. She was married at the age of twelve to a neighbor's son, aged fourteen, who died a few months after, leaving her a large amount of property. She was married again, at the age of twenty-seven, to Sir William Cavendish. Together they were the builders of the original Chatsworth, a larger structure than the present-day Chatsworth. Her second husband died in 1557; the third and fourth husbands also died, leaving her enormous wealth—the richest woman in England, after the queen.

Bess's last husband, the sixth earl of Shrewsbury, had been appointed jailer to Mary Queen of Scots, who was put into his custody for fifteen years and lived in his country houses. The earl succumbed to Mary's charms, and Bess refused to speak to her husband during the last years of his life. During that time she indulged herself in her passion for building. She rebuilt her ancestral home at Hardwick and when the earl died (when she was seventy), she began the construction of Hardwick Hall. She was clearly the designer of the house, although she probably had professional help. She was a meticulous worker who threw herself into the project. Hardwick Hall is one of the finest pieces of Elizabethan domestic architecture in the perpendicular style. It has a wide, dramatic staircase built lengthwise through the house, a rectangular **high chamber** containing Brussels tapestries and classical decorations, and an Elizabethan **long gallery,** 165 feet by twenty-two feet (second in length only to that of Montacute House), with lavender Flemish tapestries. A portrait of "Bess of Hardwick" hangs in the long gallery, and her initials are carved into the stone on top of the four square towers of the west front.

KEDLESTON HALL

Four and one-half miles northwest of Derby on Derby-Hulland road via the Derby Ring road Queensway

Hours: Open Sundays from last Sun. in Apr. to last Sun. in Sept.; also Easter Sun., Mon., and Tues., and bank holiday Mondays and Tuesdays. Admission fee.

This large Palladian mansion (started 1758) is the work of **Robert Adam** (1728–92), the architect and designer. Other architects had started Kedleston, but Adam's work (1760) on the south front and on most of the interior, including the marble hall with its twenty Corinthian columns, overshadows everything else and points to his versatility and the craftsmanship of the painters, stuccoists, and carvers who worked for him.

The **marble hall** is situated on the *piano nobile* and is based on the Roman atrium. Its alcoves contain statues and its walls monochrome panels depicting scenes from Homer. The two chimney-pieces with stucco relief figures were also designed by Adam as was the gilded organ in the adjoining music room, and some of the furniture. Even the great park has something by Adam: the stone bridge with its three segmented arches and elegant balustrade is his. Kedleston's collection of paintings is by Reynolds, van Dyck, Veronese, and other old masters.

Durham

DURHAM CATHEDRAL

Hours: Open all hours. Free admission.

This cathedral, perched castlelike on a hill in the center of a peninsula surrounded by the river Wear, commands one of the most beautiful settings of any cathedral in England. Along with its neighbors, fortified monastery buildings (today a college), it was to be a bulwark against the warlike Scotch, as well as a bishop's see. Its nave, which has been little altered, was finished in 1133 and is a complete example of the Anglo-Norman style. It is the largest Romanesque building in Europe, and the earliest surviving example in England of a rib-vaulted church with transverse arches, probably the earliest high-vault pointed arches anywhere, structural elements that led to the Gothic pointed arch.

The origins of the cathedral go back to the seventh century and St. Cuthbert, the bishop of Lindisfarne. In 687, Cuthbert asked to be buried in the cathedral at Lindisfarne and to have his remains stay with it should it be moved later. St. Cuthbert's tomb remained in place until 875 when, in the face of the Norse invasions, the monks abandoned the island, and with them went the bones of St. Cuthbert. It was not until 995 that the monks arrived at Durham, where the foundations of the cathedral were laid in 1091. The nave was finished in 1133. Over the short period of forty years the cathedral was roofed and the piers were strengthened by arches and flying buttresses. Built after the first wave of Norman construction, it benefited from improved engineering techniques. Its walls (about seven feet thick) and its piers are massive. The twin western towers are also Norman to the level of the nave clerestory. The remaining parts are from the early English period (simple Gothic) and go well with the 218-foot central tower, a fifteenth-century construction.

The **interior** of the cathedral has piers decorated with carved ornament alternating with clustered piers that are unornamented. Beyond the choir is the Gothic Chapel of the Nine Altars. It was added in the thirteenth century to replace the original Norman apses and blends with the Norman character of the cathedral. Of special interest is the galilee (a place in a church less sacred than the rest, in France usually the narthex or entrance), here used as a **lady chapel**. It is unusual to find a lady chapel at the west end of a church. This location is attributed to St. Cuthbert's desire to keep women as far away from the high altar as possible. A cross embedded in the floor at the far end of the nave marks the spot beyond which ladies could not go.

Across the Palace Green, next to the Library, is **Durham Castle,** founded by William the Conqueror in 1072. Never conquered by the Scots, it is unique among England's northern strongholds, and in excellent condition. Today it is used by Durham University, but you can, and should, visit it. (Hours: July–Sept., 10AM–12 noon and 2–4:30PM on weekdays, 2–4:30PM Sun. During the academic year, Mon., Wed., and Sat., 2–4PM. Admission fee.) Its outstanding features are the kitchen, Tunstall's Gallery, and Constables' Hall.

The kitchen, with huge fireplaces, dates from the fifteenth century, but some parts may be 300 years older. Tunstall's Gallery, a sixteenth-century construction, contains a chapel with fine woodwork. A late twelfth-century **doorway,** leading to the State Rooms (not on display), is designed in the ornate Romanesque manner, the best of its kind in England. On the floor above, Constables' Hall is a good example of apartments built in great Norman castles. Details of leaf-carving and uninterrupted roll-moldings around the doors are exceptional.

Edinburgh

Edinburgh is a combination of an Old Town, medieval in origin, and an eighteenth-century New Town separated from each other by the celebrated Royal Mile. At the east end of Royal Mile is Holyrood House, a late fifteenth-century palace that served as the home of Scotland's kings and queens. At the west end is Edinburgh Castle, set high on a ridge in the Old Town and visible from all parts of the city. As a natural fortress, it served as the site of the earliest settlements in Edinburgh. In the second half of the eighteenth century, the Old Town, with its jumble of winding narrow streets, became intolerably overcrowded and the New Town was planned. Princess Street, George Street, Queen Street, and elegant squares and crescents, such as Charlotte Square, Randolph Crescent, Ainslie Place, and Moray Place, are examples of Georgian architecture and eighteenth-century town planning. If Edinburgh had paid more attention to the genius of Robert Adam the results would have been better. Adam tried to spread calm horizontals over broad surfaces of the New Town. He designed all the buildings for Charlotte Square, but only the north side was built to his specifications. The reserved horizontal calm of his design at the Register House was thwarted by the nineteenth-century builders who put up two high buildings ruining the view of Adam's scheme and, at the university, completed after Adam's death, an inappropriate high dome and pediments were put on the buildings destroying Adam's emphasis on horizontal surfaces. The classical tradition survived longer in Scotland than in southern England. Adam's horizontals never had a chance in a city that thought in terms of perpendiculars.

NATIONAL GALLERY OF SCOTLAND

The Mound, just off Princess Street

Hours: Open Mon.–Sat., 10AM–5PM, Sun., 2–5PM. Free admission.

This museum, sometimes described as "the most enjoyable small picture gallery in Europe," has a fine collection of works by some of the most famous European old masters from the fourteenth century to 1900.

Starting in **room 7**, at the opposite end of the building from the main entrance, there is an impressive display of Italian paintings. An early triptych from Florence with the *Crucifixion*, by Bernardo Daddi (ca. 1290–1350), shows concern with solid underlying forms derived from Giotto, Daddi's teacher. A *Madonna and Child*, by **Lorenzo Monaco** (ca. 1372–1422/4), a Sienese painter who settled in Florence, combines Sienese line and spirituality with Giottoesque amplitude of form. The Madonna seated on the lion-headed throne of Solomon signifies the passing of authority from the Old Testament to the New Testament. Another interesting fifteenth-century work (1470–80) is the *Ruskin Madonna,* by **Verrocchio** (1435–88), so called because it once belonged to John Ruskin, the English critic and author. It illustrates how Verrocchio, goldsmith, sculptor, and teacher to the young Leonardo da Vinci, translated his sculptural style into painting. There are two paintings by **Raphael** (1483–1520), *The Bridgewater Madonna* and *The Holy Family with a Palm Tree,* both done in Florence about 1507 before he left for Rome. They have the Florentine influence of Fra Bartolommeo's pyramidal grouping, Michelangelo's compactness, and Leonardo's curvilinear softness, showing Raphael, a genius, could learn from genius.

Room 8 contains several works by **Titian** (ca. 1487–1576): the early *Three Ages of Man* (ca. 1515–20), painted in his romantic-Giorgionesque style; *Madonna and Child with St. John and a Donor,* in which his art is now free from the static and contemplative vision of Giorgione; and great pagan mythologies of his mature period, *Diana and Actaeon* and *Diana and Callisto,* both painted for Philip II of Spain about 1560. They add vibrant color and light to the Renaissance ideals of form and space.

The small **room 9** is devoted to the *Trinity Panels,* by **Hugo van der Goes** (ca. 1440–82), the Flemish master who followed the example of Jan van Eyck's realism and precision of draftsmanship. These two wings, which may have been organ shutters or parts of an altarpiece whose central panel was destroyed during the Reformation, were commissioned in about 1478 by Sir Edward Bonkill, first provost of the Collegiate Church of the Holy Trinity in Edinburgh where they once hung. Bonkill's image as donor appears on the reverse of one of the wings. His connections in Bruges, where his brother was a naturalized citizen, enabled him to get one of the great Flemish artists of the time to create a work of art for his church in Scotland. The heads of the royal family of Scotland (James III and his queen, Margaret of Denmark) were painted in by a local artist after the panels arrived in Edinburgh.

Italian paintings are continued in **room 10** along with the display of Spanish works, most notable of which are *Fabula*, an illuminated allegorical night scene by El Greco (1541–1614), and *Old Woman Cooking Eggs*, by **Velázquez** (1599–1660), his first masterpiece done when he was nineteen years old. It derives from the Sivillian *bodegón* or kitchen scene, popular at the time, in which ordinary people are shown with objects used for the preparation of food. But Velázquez's painting also shows genius in its attention to detail and the quiet contemplative mood it catches in the woman and in the boy.

Room 11 has sixteenth-century Northern paintings. From France there is a portrait of *Madame de Canaples*, by Jean Clouet, court painter to Francis I; from Germany *Venus and Cupid*, by Lucas Cranach, and *Allegory of the Old and New Testaments*, by Hans Holbein; and from Flanders *The Three Legends of St. Nicholas*, by Gerard David—the last panel shows the saint bringing three boys back to life who were salted down as meat during a famine—and a *Portrait of a Notary*, by Quentin Massys.

Room 12 follows with seventeenth-century works by Rubens, portraits by van Dyck, including a large group of *The Lomellini Family*, and an early painting by **Vermeer** (1632–75), *Christ in the House of Martha and Mary* (ca. 1654), one of the few religious paintings the Dutch master painted. Its broad brush strokes, rich colors, and dominance of the figures are uncharacteristic Italian baroque elements for a Vermeer, which attest to its early date (only two Vermeers of the less than forty extant are dated). Vermeer is thought never to have traveled in Italy, but he could have studied Italian paintings, which were plentiful in the Netherlands during his time. At the turn of the century this painting was sold in Bristol for 8 English pounds, before cleaning in 1901 revealed Vermeer's signature. Its value today would conservatively be placed in the millions.

Room 13 has paintings by seventeenth-century artists associated with Rome. These include Poussin, Claude, Reni, and Paul Bril. *Il Contento*, an interesting painting by Adam Elsheimer (1578–1610), the German painter and engraver who went to Rome in 1600 and remained the rest of his life, tells the story of how Jupiter sent Mercury down to Earth to abduct the god Content, whom the people loved too much, and leave instead the female figure of Discontent.

Room 14, one flight up, contains paintings from the reserve collection. **Room 15**, on the ground floor, has eighteenth- and nineteenth-century Scottish paintings, among which are works by the well-known Allan Ramsay and Sir David Wilkie.

Room 16 is devoted to paintings of Holland in the seventeenth century, its Golden Age. Shown are fine examples of landscapes by Jacob Ruisdael, Cuyp, and Hobbema; genre scenes by Steen, Terborch, and Dou; a wonderful *Interior of the Grote Kerk at Haarlem,* by Pieter Saenredam; and paintings by Rembrandt (1606–69): *Young Woman with Flowers in her Hair* (1634), a *Self-portrait* at the age of fifty-one, and *Woman in Bed,* once thought to be a portrait of Rembrandt's mistress, Hendrickje Stoffels, but considered today to be the biblical scene of Sarah on her wedding night watching as her husband Tobias successfully exorcizes the devil, who has already caused the death of her seven previous husbands, before they could consummate their marriage.

Room 17 is the start of eighteenth-century painting, among which the elegant *Finding of Moses* by G. B. Tiepolo (1696–1770), a typical Venetian work, whose decorative composition shows the influence of Veronese, is the finest. Room 18, with works by Gainsborough, Constable, Bonington, and Cotman, show eighteenth-century British paintings.

On the first floor, five rooms are reserved for the French school between the seventeenth and nineteenth centuries. From the seventeenth century there are *The Seven Sacraments* (1644–48) by **Poussin** (1594–1665), the second time he painted this series. Poussin, a Frenchman who lived in Rome, has drawn from the classical sources he knows so well. His carefully balanced compositions and regard for realistic detail are testaments to his being at his greatest powers. Paintings by Watteau, Boucher, Greuze, Lancret, and Chardin demonstrate eighteenth-century French painting. The nineteenth century in France is shown by the works of the famous impressionists: Degas, Renoir, Pissarro, and Monet. The postimpressionist collection is even finer with works by Cézanne, van Gogh, Gauguin, and Seurat.

The museum's newest galleries, located in the basement, display the works of Scottish artists. Apart from Allan Ramsay, Henry Raeburn, and David Wilkie, their names are not well known outside of Britain, but the range of their art is great and, especially in the nineteenth century, their style sophisticated.

SCOTTISH NATIONAL GALLERY OF MODERN ART

Belford Road

Hours: Open Mon.–Sat., 10AM–5PM, Sun., 2–5PM. Free admission.

This collection, a continuation of that of the National Gallery of Scotland, covers the most significant artistic activity of the twentieth century. Only post–World War II American painting is lacking, but there is a good collection of British painting and sculpture from this period with special emphasis on Scottish work.

You will see cubist still lifes by Braque and Picasso; works by the leading German expressionists, Jawlensky, Nolde, and Kirchner, who led Germany into the modern movement; the interesting Ferdinand Hodler, a leading figure in modern Swiss painting, represented by *Lake Thun,* one of a series of landscapes he painted of the Bernese Oberland region of Switzerland; works by Russian painters who lived in France, Mikhail Larionov and his wife, Natalia Goncharova, both known for the set designs they did for Diaghilev's Ballets Russes; Magritte's *Black Flag* and Max Ernst's *Great Lover,* surrealist works by two leading figures of the movement that grew out of the negative attitudes of the earlier Dada movement; works by Matisse, *The Painting Lesson* and *Head of a Woman;* Vuillard's *Corner of the Studio* and *Candlestick;* Bonnard's *Lane at Vernonnet;* Utrillo's *La Place du Tertre;* and others by some of the best-known artists of the twentieth century: Derain, Klee, Permeke, Schwitters, Kokoschka, Miró, Man Ray, Mondrian, Léger, and Jean Dubuffet.

The museum's growing collection of sculpture include works by Moore, Hepworth, Epstein, Giacometti, Marini, Lipchitz, and others. A sculpture garden is being developed in the museum's extensive grounds.

SCOTTISH NATIONAL PORTRAIT GALLERY

Queen Street

Hours: Open Mon.–Sat., 10AM–5PM, Sun., 2–5PM. Free admission.

Situated in the same neo-Gothic red stone building as the National Museum of Antiquities, the Portrait Gallery holds a collection of over 2,000 portraits of the main figures in Scottish history since the mid-sixteenth century. Men and women in all fields of human endeavor are shown—politicians, musicians, soldiers, scientists, artists, philosophers—in paintings and sculptures that were acquired not for their artistic excellence but for their historical significance. Nevertheless, the collection contains works by leading artists including van Dyck, Lely, Reynolds, Raeburn, Epstein, and Rodin.

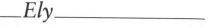

Ely

ELY CATHEDRAL

Hours: Open all hours. Free admission.

The flat East Anglian countryside surrounding the little city of Ely is dominated by this great cathedral, which has one of the longest naves in England (537 feet). It grew out of a Benedictine abbey established by Queen Etheldreda of Northumbria in 673, and was an Anglo-Saxon stronghold that did not surrender to William the Conqueror until 1071. When the first Norman abbot was appointed by the Conqueror in 1083 he began to enlarge the existing church and by 1180 the nave was completed. In the early thirteenth century the beautiful galilee porch, projecting from the west wall, was finished and the choir lengthened, but much of the new choir was destroyed when the central tower, built just before 1100, fell in 1322. The fourteenth-century tower you see today, in the shape of an octagonal lantern, is the crowning glory of the cathedral and one of the wonders of English cathedral architecture. Its rib vaulting above the octagon, and the lantern that it supports, are both made of wood faced with lead.

Before visiting the interior, notice on the **west front** the contrast between the Romanesque main structure and the Gothic style of the projecting galilee porch with its three pointed windows. This facade could have been better had the northwest tower been completed, but it was abandoned, leaving the west front with only the southwest tower.

Inside, the long **nave** seems very high because of its comparative narrowness. There is also a feeling of disproportion in the massive walls, strong arches, and many shafts supporting only a canted wooden ceiling. At the crossing, the great **Octagon**, the only Gothic dome in existence, may be the most beautiful example of Gothic architecture. Stand under it and look up to see the glowing eight-pointed star that gives a sensation of space and light. Since it would have been impossible to carry out such an undertaking in stone, the complicated vaulting is made of wood. All England was searched for the appropriate timber, the vertical pieces being eight oak beams, each about sixty-three feet long and three feet thick.

Also, visit the **Lady Chapel** (1321–53) at Ely, a separate building cornering the north transept. It was built as an aisleless hall and even now, after the destruction of its statues, remains one of the richest and most graceful interiors of its period.

_____ Hertfordshire _____

HATFIELD HOUSE

In Hatfield opposite station, twenty-one miles north of London

Hours: Open Mar.–early Oct., Tues.–Sat., noon–5PM, Sun., 2–5:30PM. Admission fee.

Hatfield House was built (1608–12) by Robert Cecil, the first earl of Salisbury and chief minister to the crown. As a Jacobean house it is less elaborate than Elizabethan houses, with smaller windows, built of brick instead of stone, with a horizontal roof-line. It has a **marble hall** rising to a height of two floors that, with its carved screen, minstrels' gallery, bay window, and huge fireplace, could be found in a Tudor house. There is a **long gallery**, 180 feet by twenty feet, and a **great staircase** with elaborately carved woodwork that shows the influence of the Italian Renaissance. True to its Jacobean style, really a continuation of the Elizabethan style with the addition of foreign influence, the house has the work of craftsmen from Italy, France, and Flanders. Its ornamentations become a version of Italian mannerism, which at its best is crisp and delightful, and at its worst, such as in the strapwork of the ceilings and the caryatids that extend from walls, is grotesque.

In its large park are the remains of an oak tree under which, it is said,

Princess Elizabeth was sitting when she was told of her accession to the throne of England as Elizabeth I.

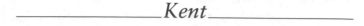

Kent

KNOLE

At the Tonbridge end of Sevenoaks east of A225

Hours: Open Apr.–Sept., Wed.–Sat., 11AM–5PM, Sun., 2–5PM; Oct.–Nov., Wed.–Sat., 11AM–4PM, Sun., 2–4PM. Admission fee.

Knole is one of England's largest stately homes, with a collection of furniture and decorations worth viewing for its own sake: 365 rooms, fifty-two stairways, and seven courtyards, giving it the name "Calendar House." Its layout leads from court to court and divides the house into separate areas, each with its own character.

The oldest part of Knole is fifteenth century, when it first served as a palace for archbishops of Canterbury (1456–86). It came into the possession of Henry VIII and then Elizabeth I, who in 1566 gave it to her cousin Thomas Sackville. It has remained for more than four hundred years in the Sackville family, which has improved it over the centuries. There is a large collection of portraits, some by van Dyck, Gainsborough, Kneller, and Romney, and a room devoted to Reynolds's portraits of famous figures of his time: Dr. Johnson, Oliver Goldsmith, and the actor David Garrick. The tapestries and furniture, many already antique when they first entered Knole, and other decorations, such as the silver work in the king's bedroom, are exceptional. Its park of over one thousand acres has deer that roam freely.

PENSHURST PLACE

Tunbridge Wells, in Penshurst Village seven miles south of Seven Oaks

Hours: Open Apr.–Oct., Tues.–Sun., 12:30–5:30PM (open bank holiday Mondays); Nov.–Mar., Sun. 12:30–5:30PM. Admission fee.

Penshurst Place is known for its medieval architecture and as the birthplace of Sir Philip Sidney (1554–86), who owned it for a short time before his death from wounds received at the Battle of Zutphen. The heart of the building is the fourteenth-century **great hall** (ca. 1340), still intact, with a low dais at one end, a gallery supported by a screen at the other, huge decorated Gothic windows on either side, windows up in the gables, a fine chestnut timber roof, and a brick-tiled floor. It has no fireplace, only an open hearth in the middle of the floor. Smoke flowed freely upward to escape from the roof by a louver. In medieval times the whole family would assemble here daily; the two trestle tables that served them can be seen. Additions to the house were built from the great hall, thereby preserving it. By 1607, with the completion of the Elizabethan-Jacobean **long gallery,** running the length of the upper story of the southern wing, containing portraits of the Sidney family, Penshurst was complete. The park, of which there are views from the long gallery, has a lake, lovely paths, and fine plantings.

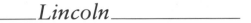

Lincoln

LINCOLN CATHEDRAL

Hours: Open all hours. Required donation.

After the Norman Conquest a new church was built on the hill on which Lincoln Cathedral now stands (it has been the site of a settlement since prehistoric times). Of this original fortresslike construction, dating from 1072–90, only a small part still remains. On April 15, 1185, an earthquake damaged the building so severely that all but the west front had to be taken down. New construction, culminating in the present cathedral, was begun 1192 and continued until 1280 with the completion of the Angel Choir.

Starting at the **exterior** of the west front you notice a screening wall with three large cavities that rise over Norman doors flanked by recessed niches of earlier Romanesque work. Observe the late Romanesque carvings of beasts amid trailing foliage that contrast sharply with the fourteenth-century frieze. The cathedral is immense (57,000 square feet), with two pairs of transepts, clustering chapels and porches, and a chapter house with radiating buttresses. Its original central tower, built about 1200, collapsed forty years later. The present one was built 1306–11 and once had a high spire (destroyed in 1548). The two west towers were probably built about 1400 and they too once had wooden high spires (removed in 1807). As they exist today, the three towers make up a harmonious group that convey an impression of dignified strength.

On entering the nave from the main west door, one is impressed by the spaciousness of the Gothic **interior,** compared with heavier Norman interiors, even though the vault is low. This defect is accentuated by the fact that the piers are slender and widely spaced. Walk to the crossing of the central tower with its 130-foot vault. To the north is the rose window called "The Dean's Eye," and to the south, at the end of the transept, is the window called "The Bishop's Eye," a circular kaleidoscope of colored glass. Both transepts have eastern aisles, each divided into three small chapels. Also of note is the stone screen of the choir, an early fourteenth-century work flanked by thirteenth-century aisle doorways sculptured in arch-molds and capitals, and the **Angel Choir** (1265–1320), at the east end. The ornamentation here is richer than anything in the nave, and its giant window, which measures fifty-nine by twenty-nine feet, is a remarkable technical achievement. Its glass, dating from 1855, lends nothing to its beauty, but its carvings of angels in the spandrels of the main arcade, that give the choir its name, consist of many accomplished pieces (they were executed by more than one artist).

You should also visit the **chapter house** of the cathedral, originally the administrative offices. Every cathedral had one, usually rectangular; this one is the first of the polygonal chapter houses, and it set a fashion peculiar to England.

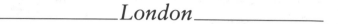

London

Museums

BRITISH MUSEUM

Great Russell Square

Hours: Open Mon.–Sat., 10AM–5PM, Sun., 2:30–6PM. Free admission.

This famous museum has a varied collection encompassing almost everything except easel paintings: prints and drawings, manuscripts, sculpture, china, glass, jewels, and ethnological collections. It grew out of the collection of Sir Hans Sloane, who at ninety-two had assembled mineral specimens, corals, vegetable specimens, insects, shells, birds, mathematical instruments, coins and medals, manuscripts, and other objects amounting in all to 53,000 items. The British government's purchases of the Sloane collection and others were housed in Montague House in Bloomsbury, which, as the British Museum, was opened free to the public in 1759.

The Elgin Marbles (477–33 B.C.): Greek: ground floor, room 8
Among the museum's treasures are sculptures from the Parthenon on the Acropolis of Athens. These are in the west wing in the **Department of Greek and Roman Antiquities' Duveen Gallery.** Popularly called the Elgin Marbles, they were brought to England in 1812 by Lord Elgin and consist of three kinds of sculptures: Metopes, square panels four feet three inches square, that formed a decorative band in high relief that encircled the outside of the temple just below the cornice; the frieze, a continuous band in low relief that originally ran all around the cella wall inside the colonnade of the Parthenon; and the figures in the round that stood in the east and west pediments at each end of the roof.

Metopes (north end of hall—to right on entering): These were in place on the Parthenon by 438 B.C. by which time the building was roofed. The best preserved examples deal with the struggles of centaurs (half man and half horse) and Lapiths (a Greek tribe living in Thessaly). According to legend, the centaurs were invited to the wedding of Pirithous, king of the Lapiths, and there got drunk, attacked their hosts, and attempted to rape their wives. We see them doing battle within compositions that capture the violence and intensity of a split-second of combat. Notice the metope depicting a centaur attempting to carry off a Lapith woman. He is holding her tightly about the waist so that her tunic, which falls in graceful folds, has slipped from her shoulder exposing her breast. The theme of the struggle between Lapiths and centaurs was a favorite in Greece, symbolizing the struggle of intellectual power and beauty against brute strength.

The east pediment figures (north end of hall): In this pediment, which depicts the birth of Athena, the central figures were destroyed but the sculptures in the left and right ends are largely preserved.

The figure of *Dionysus* (D), the second to last figure in the left corner, and the only pediment figure with its head, is the god of wine and revelry. His strong, well-modeled body is firmly defined without much detail in order to avoid a lifeless generalization of the figure. The areas of this statue not seen after it was placed in the pediment are as carefully modeled as those in full view.

The figures of *Demeter* (E) and *Persephone* (F), seated figures next to *Dionysus,* and *Eileithyia (or Iris)*—she may be *Hebe,* a cup bearer of Zeus (G), the standing figure next to them—portray a sense of life and space. The sculptor has made the drapery of the standing *Eileithyia* express her action. As the goddess of birth she hurries toward *Demeter* to give news of the birth of Athena. The flowing curves of her costume express her haste, while at the same time she is still looking behind her, witnessing the scene that has just taken place.

On the far right of the pediment, in the *three goddesses* group (K, L, and M), *Aphrodite,* the goddess of love, is reclining on the bosom of her mother, *Dione,* and is a balancing figure to the reclining *Dionysus* on the left side. Both women wear a thin Ionian tunic with deep pleats across the knees. Suited to her character as the goddess of desire, Aphrodite's tunic has slipped from her right shoulder and only the curve of her breast keeps it from falling further. To the right of these two figures is *Leto (or Hestia).* This group represents the most impressive ensemble on the eastern pediment. In the far right of the pediment is *Selene's Horse* (O), depicted with compelling realism.

The Frieze (large central room): This measures three feet, three inches high, and originally ran 525 feet around the cella. It illustrates the Panathenaic procession, the celebration that took place every four years on the day of Athena's birth. On the last day of the festival an embroidered robe was carried from the lower city to the Acropolis and placed on a wooden statue of the goddess. It was escorted by thousands of citizens, and this spectacle is immortalized on the frieze carved in low relief.

The figures, mounted or on foot, fill, but do not crowd, the frieze. They vary in pose and include handsome youths, beautiful maidens, magistrates, and sacrificial animals. Horses are emphasized because the Greeks considered the horse a sacred animal, the one they imagined that dead souls came back to, and votive offerings of horses were made to Athena. Obvious is the individuality of various citizens, especially the spirited young mounted

Athenians. They show a sense of religious devotion on their faces radiating the human qualities that are a striking feature of the work.

To treat without monotony a band of sculpture so long and narrow called for a man of genius, which was found in **Phidias**, a friend of Pericles and chief sculptor for the work at the Acropolis. Phidias also made the ivory-and-gold statue of Athena that stood in the cella of the Parthenon, and another bronze statue of Athena that stood on the Acropolis facing the Propylaea. Neither has survived. Naturally the sculptures on the Acropolis had to be executed by many different hands, which is why the quality differs. Only certain pieces are by Phidias himself, but all are considered to be in the "Phidian style."

The west pediment figure (south end of hall—to left on entering): This is the figure of *Cephissus* (A), located in the extreme left-hand corner of the pediment, probably representing the River Cephissus. He is the embodiment of the fifth-century Greek ideal—virile, supple, and well proportioned.

Outside the Duveen Gallery, to your right, proceed to the **Room of the Harpy Tomb (no. 5)**, which shows the development of Greek art from about 500 to 440 B.C. Here are the four carved marble slabs of the *Harpy Tomb* (ca. 480 B.C.) which, while archaic and clumsy, began to point to a new naturalism that flowered a hundred years later in the masterpieces of Greece's Golden Age; and the *Strangford Apollo* (490 B.C.), a statue that marks the end of a long series of Kouros figures (statues of naked young men) started about 600 B.C. This one, in a vital style, with a face that has the expression the older figures never had, shows an agreeable sense of balance in its composition by the transfer of its weight to one leg.

Return to the entrance of the Duveen Gallery walking north to the **Room of the Caryatid (no. 9)** and other remains from the Temple of Erechtheum (409 B.C.) on the Acropolis. The **priestess (caryatid)**, both column and woman, was one of a row of female figures supporting the roof of the Erechtheum. Notice how the straight folds of the right leg, which is braced to take the weight, resembles the flutes of the column we would expect to see in such a position.

Continue through room 10 to the **Mausoleum Room (no. 12)**. Here are the various pieces from the Mausoleum of Halicarnassus, a building known in its time as one of the seven wonders of the world. The excellent statue mistakenly known as *King Mausoleus of Pargamum* (fourth century B.C.), after whom "mausoleum" is named, is heavily robed and powerfully individualistic. The subject's un-Hellenic features and wild hair are faithfully rendered by the sculptor. The **three friezes** in high relief illustrate a chariot race, the Battle of Centaurs and Lapiths and the struggle of the Greeks and Amazons. Comparing them with the figures of the Parthenon frieze, the characters in the Mausoleum are rendered in bolder relief and are more widely spaced, creating an emphasis on each individual figure. The violence of the action, in which the fighters attack and withdraw, permits the use of the diagonal line and allows for the disposal of the drapery of many of the Amazons, so that they are seen virtually in the nude.

At the foot of the stairs at the entrance to the **Hellenistic Room (no. 13)** is another notable sculpture, the *Demeter of Cnidos* (fourth century), which was unearthed in 1858. The head was detachable and was found separate from the rest of the body, with less damage. Thus the contrast that you see between the head and body was not originally intended. Judging from the appearance of the body, especially the heavy and naturalistic folds on her breast, this excellent statue is by an accomplished artist, representative of the "Phydian style."

A visit to the museum's **Department of Manuscripts,** ground floor, should include a look at the *Lindisfarne Gospels* (698 A.D.), room 30, an illuminated manuscript made in the monastery of Lindisfarne in Northumbria. As in the *Book of Kells* in Ireland, it has stylized Celtic elements, though the colors are more restrained than in the Irish manuscript. Two discoveries just before and during World War II are of great significance: the **Mildenhall Treasure,** room 40 (located in the **Department of Prehistoric and Romano-British Antiquities,** upper floor), which consists of thirty-four pieces of silverware, possibly made in Rome during the fourth century; and the early seventh-century **Sutton Hoo ship burial** objects, room 41 (located in the **Department of Medieval and Later Antiquities,** upper floor), which include gold jewelry and sword fittings. Both treasures give an intimate look at ancient times and are also marvelous works of art.

COURTAULD INSTITUE GALLERIES

Woburn Square, part of the University of London

Hours: Open Mon.–Sat., 10AM–5PM, Sun., 2–5PM. Admission fee.

The Courtauld Institute of Art is for London what the Ashmolean and Fitzwilliam museums have long been for Oxford and Cambridge. It was founded in 1931 by Samuel Courtauld, the textile industrialist, and Viscount Lee of Fareham, who gave their collections to the museum. With additional bequests the museum became a gallery of early Italian paintings and other old masters shown in rooms decorated with period furniture and carpets. Also displayed is the collection of paintings by masters of impressionism and post-impressionism, brought together by Courtauld. (At the end of 1986 the gallery is expected to move into its new home at Somerset House in the Strand, once the home of the Royal Academy.)

The most famous of the Courtauld paintings are *A Bar at the Folies-Bergere,* by **Manet** (1832–83), which shows a barmaid against a mirror reflecting a crowd of figures seen as shifting points of light; *The Theatre Box* or *"La Loge,"* by **Renoir** (1841–1919), showing a beautiful woman in a work in which the artist uses much black, yet which he called "queen of colors"; *A Young Woman Seated at a Powder-Table,* by **Seurat** (1859–91), a carnivallike picture depicting the artist's mistress, that once showed Seurat's own face in the mirror on the wall, which was later painted out and replaced by a pot of flowers; and *Nevermore* and *"Te Rerioa"—The Dream,* two paintings by **Gauguin** (1848–1903) that express his feelings for a primitive life and also display his discrepancies in scale and his linear treatment of figures.

Among the other paintings in the impressionist and postimpressionist collection are works by Degas, Sisley, Pissarro, Signac, van Gogh (including a self-portrait showing his bandaged ear), Monet, and Modigliani, and a group of very fine Cézannes: *Still-life with Plaster Cast,* an excellent *Montagne Sainte Victoire,* and *Lake of Annecy,* one of his few landscapes not painted in Provence.

NATIONAL GALLERY

Trafalgar Square

Hours: Open Mon.–Sat., 10AM–6PM, Sun., 2–6PM. Free admission.

The National Gallery of London, although only half as large as the collection of the Louvre in Paris, houses one of the most comprehensive collections of European paintings.

The collection had a difficult start. Sir Joshua Reynolds, first president of the Royal Academy, made the original proposal for the establishment of a gallery in 1768, but no action was taken. In 1777, the collection of the late prime minister Sir Robert Walpole was offered for sale and a proposal that the nation purchase it was rejected. The Walpole paintings were bought by Catherine the Great of Russia, and today form part of the collection of the Hermitage in Leningrad.

Creation of a museum was authorized in 1824 and thirty-eight works from the collection of John Julius Angerstein were purchased, including the six paintings of Hogarth's series, *Marriage à la Mode,* and five canvases by Claude Lorrain. The gallery opened in the Augerstein House at 100 Pall Mall, and later, in 1838, Queen Victoria inaugurated its present building on Trafalgar Square. The Gallery grew rapidly and by 1855 had become a major institution. Its collection continues to grow, thanks to government assistance in preventing great art works from being exported. For an example, a law allowing taxpayers to remit paintings instead of cash has brought to the museum Memling's *Donne Triptych,* among other treasures.

Index to the rooms of the National Gallery

Artists mentioned below have works referred to in the text that follows. You will find these works listed under the names of the artists, arranged alphabetically.

Room 10	Antonello da Messina, Bellini
Room 20	Rubens
Room 22	Rubens
Room 23	Dürer
Room 24	van Eyck, Master of Flémalle, Memling, van der Weyden
Room 25	Bruegel, Holbein
Room 26	Rembrandt
Room 27	Hobbema, Rembrandt
Room 28	Vermeer
Room 29	Caravaggio
Room 30	Moroni
Room 37	Constable, Turner
Room 38	Gainsborough, Reynolds
Room 39	Gainsborough, Hogarth
Room 41	Velázquez
Room 43	Ingres
Room 44	Manet
Room 45	Cézanne, Seurat, van Gogh

Antonello da Messina (ca. 1430–79), Italian

St. Jerome in his Study: room 10
The importance of Antonello in the development of Italian and especially Venetian painting cannot be overstated. As his name indicates, he was born in Sicily, but his early training in Naples, under the artistic influence of the Burgundian and Spanish court, brought him in contact with the Flemish style. During Antonello's sojourn in Milan he met Petrus Christus, the great Flemish master, an important influence in his mastery of the oil medium and of the Flemish skill in detail. Antonello eventually came to Venice, where his method of painting with oil, in which colors can be fused one into another, soon replaced the tempera method and became the basis for the Venetian School, which dominated painting in Europe during the sixteenth century.

St. Jerome in his Study is an early painting by Antonello (possibly as early as 1450) that is so much in the Flemish style that it was once attributed to Jan van Eyck. We are admitted to the saint's study through a framing arch, typical of Spanish Gothic forms used in Sicily. The arch also seems to create depth and to detach St. Jerome from the viewer. The Flemish sense of detail is seen in the tiny objects in the room and in the rich majolica floor. Almost every object has a Gothic religious meaning, such as the peacock in the foreground which, from the belief that its flesh never decayed, symbolizes immortality and Christ's resurrection. Light, which comes from everywhere, is the unifying force. It adds to the cool stillness of the scene and the expression of space, which is enhanced by the view of the placid landscape in the background. Everything is balanced in the Northern manner.

Notice the lion prowling quietly on the right side of the room. According to legend, Jerome pulled a thorn from the paw of the lion which thereafter became his loyal friend.

Portrait of a Man (ca. 1475–79): room 10
Antonello was one of the finest portraitists of his time. This head, which has the Flemish minuteness of detail down to individual hairs, is modeled in striking light. The eyes, which look directly at us, create close contact with the viewer. We may be looking at Antonello himself, because an inscription on the back dating from the seventeenth century suggests it is a self-portrait.

Bellini, Giovanni* (ca. 1430–1516)

The Madonna of the Meadow: room 10
The city of Venice rarely produced religious painters, but Giovanni Bellini was an exception; he is well known for his Madonna paintings. This one, completed about 1505 at the end of his career, is different from his earlier, larger hieratic Virgin and Child altarpieces. The Renaissance idea of the Madonna was humble, or what is called the Madonna of Humility, in which the Virgin is seen seated on the floor. Medieval theology regarded humility as the root from which all the virtues grew (thus Christ grew from the Virgin). The depiction of placid scenes of the Virgin seated, her hands in prayer with the Child asleep on her lap in an attitude similar to that of the dead Christ in a *Pietà*, appealed to the poetic sense of the Renaissance humanists.

Here the Madonna is seated on the ground in a pyramidal form that anticipates Raphael. Even her sweetness and humility are Raphaelesque. Behind her is a pastoral landscape with a walled city and a cowherd asleep against a fence. The scene is illuminated by light that softens the outline of the Madonna and harmonizes the dark blue of her cloak with the azure of the sky. With such a painting as this, Bellini passes the Venetian heritage of rich color and the unifying presence of light on to succeeding generations of artists.

The Doge Leonardo Loredan: room 10
That Bellini was the leading portraitist of Venice is attested to by this painting from about 1501–2. It shows the doge Leonardo Loredan who led Venice from 1501 to 1521. Bellini painted the doge's portrait at the start of his rule when he was sixty-five. Although it is conceived as a marble bust standing against a clear blue background with the figure looking straight ahead in a formal pose, which leaves no doubt about his authority, Bellini's soft brushwork makes it certain that we are looking at a real person. This doge is a most artistocratic figure.

Bronzino, Il (1503–72), Italian

An Allegory (ca. 1546): room 8
The Reformation hardly affected artists in Italy, but it provided an unsettling atmosphere that led, with Michelangelo's example, to a revolt against the accepted standards of high Renaissance art. We call this revolt mannerism, and of the young artists who subscribed to it, Il Bronzino was probably the most talented. His *Allegory* is in step with the mannerists' desire to show the human figure in new ways, twisting it into seemingly impossible poses. The mannerists did not believe in fixed ideas in art—a modern attitude.

With the changing religious currents there also came a questioning of everyday life. In *An Allegory* (the picture has in the past been called *Venus, Cupid, Folly, and Time* and *Venus Disarming Cupid*) the sin of luxury is treated in an astonishing mannerist way. We see a bald winged man, at the top right, representing Time, who, with Truth, at the top left, has unveiled a scene of incest and sexual indulgence that is symbolic of the moral dilemma of the day. A grown-up Cupid is caressing his mother, Venus, who is gently disarming him by removing his arrow with her right hand while holding a golden apple in her left—awarded to her in the past for her beauty by Paris, but now out of shape and, in fact, rotten. Shamelessly, a putto on the right, above the mask of Fraud, prepares to throw roses at them. At the left Envy tears her hair, and a mannerist monster in the background, with the face of a girl, body of a serpent, and claws of a lion, is offering a honeycomb in one hand and the sting of her tail in the other.

Bruegel, Pieter, the Elder (ca. 1525–69), Flemish

The Adoration of the Magi: room 25
This large picture is not typical of Bruegel's most famous work. Missing is Bruegel's use of the scene to denounce human folly. Here he is simply showing us the story of the three kings offering gifts to the child who is sitting on the Virgin's lap in what could be viewed as a Michelangesque pose. This is not to say that this picture has been influenced by the Italian School. On the contrary, the man with the arrow in his hat is clearly Bosch-like (see Bosch's *Christ Mocked* in the National Gallery, room 24), and we have seen the faces of the soldiers and the bystanders before in Bruegel's many peasant scenes. Finally, in the figure of the young man who is gossiping in the ear of Joseph (the husband of the Virgin) about Mary's purity, we find that Bruegel has found room to depict a scene of human sinfulness which the malicious tattletale represents.

The painting is a concert of color that radiates from the blue figure of the Virgin to the surrounding figures in a harmony of earth colors. The composition is also brilliant, with crossed diagonals centering on the Christ Child and the movement of the figures directed toward the Virgin and child.

Caravaggio* (1573–1610), Italian

Supper at Emmaus (ca. 1602): room 29
This secularization of the story of two disciples who meet Christ after the resurrection, sit down to supper with Him at Emmaus, but do not recognize Him until He takes the bread, says a blessing, offers it to them and then vanishes, is typical of Caravaggio's revolutionary art. It had an influence on some of the greatest masters of the sixteenth and seventeenth centuries, especially Spanish and Dutch painters. The introduction of genre into religious scenes, where the beardless Christ has the features of a common street person in sixteenth-century Rome, and the other figures look like the peasants they really were, was new to painting. So was the dramatic light and dark that projected forms violently to the viewer. The basket of fruit at the edge

of the table also shows what a superb painter of still life Caravaggio was. The depiction of common figures and the dramatic lighting serve to involve the viewer in the painting as never before. It was an advance of truth and everyday realities that was fully appreciated later by artists and the public alike.

Cézanne, Paul* (1839–1906), French

Les Grandes Baigneuses (The Large Bathers) (ca. 1895): room 45
Cézanne was concerned with form modeled in color, rather than in light and shade, as the old masters had done. His *Bathers,* one of a number of works he did between 1895 and 1906, is typical of this point of view, and represents his most abstract style. He simplifies forms, which successfully convey to the viewer the female body in simple strokes that are at one with the equally simple bending trees of the landscape. Such forms, combined with the strong light of the Mediterranean, create a pictorial quality that communicates essentials. Compared to photographlike paintings, still popular during Cézanne's time, his art makes an intellectual approach more powerful in its pictorial possibilities with more to say and more for us to think about.

Constable, John (1776–1837), English

The Hay Wain (1821): room 37
In the early part of the nineteenth century the romantic painters of Europe were far ahead of the English in rejecting the neoclassic doctrine, but it remained for John Constable to effect the revolution in landscape painting. When *The Hay Wain* was exhibited at the Paris Salon of 1824 it won the gold medal. Delacroix, who was captured by it, repainted his own *Massacre of Scio. The Hay Wain* is Constable's best known work, with all the qualities that made Constable, if not wholly recognized in his own county, at least appreciated on the Continent. As a nature scene from Constable's own Suffolk countryside, it conveys the sense of intimacy Constable felt for nature. Its composition does not seem to be based on a deliberate scheme. The house and the trees on the left have been placed there because that is where they actually were. The color has a freshness and a variety of tone new for Constable's time, achieved by placing certain spots of color side by side to reinforce each other, such as the reds and greens—an example of early impressionism in England. *The Hay Wain* and other paintings by Constable, instead of idealized landscapes in the manner of Poussin and Claude done in a studio as settings for some moment of classical or religious drama, had an effect on the French Barbizon School of 1820–50. Constable's oil sketches, done out-of-doors, like the unfinished *Weymouth Bay* (room 37) of 1816, where light is a dominant element that brings out forms in the landscape, had an even greater effect. The intangible qualities of light, sky, and atmosphere that Constable recorded on his canvas make *Weymouth Bay* and others like it (visit the Victoria and Albert Museum to see Constable's oil sketches) forerunners of the impressionists that succeeded him.

Dürer, Albrecht* (1471–1528), German

The Painter's Father (1497): room 23
This is the more mature of the two portraits Dürer made of his father, a goldsmith of Nuremberg. The writings of the artist tell us how much he admired his father, and this painting of him is one of the most sympathetic of all Dürer's works. True to his style, Dürer portrays his father with a tremendous intensity, filled with the wisdom and reserve of old age. The pattern of light that circles him leads to the head and the penetrating stare, worthy of the psychological drama of Dürer's finest portraits. Its pyramidal composition shows Italian influence, and its luminosity is inherited from the Flemish style.

Eyck, Jan van* (ca. 1390–1441), Flemish

The Wedding Portrait of Giovanni Arnolfini: room 24
The double portrait of Giovanni Arnolfini, a wealthy merchant from Lucca living in Bruges, who was also councillor to Philip the Good, and his wife Giovanna Cenani, the daughter of another merchant of Lucca, is the only double portrait and the only full length portrait of its epoch. Yet it is also something more—an actual marriage contract in pictorial form. We see a marriage scene complete with two witnesses standing where we are standing, whose faces are reflected in the mirror in the background. The inscriptions on the wall, "Jan van Eyck was here, 1434," in legal script, suggests Jan being one of the figures in the mirror and thus a witness who has signed and dated his name as if the picture were a legal document.

The two figures are shown standing in a room filled with ornaments that have symbolic meaning. Notice the single candle burning, even though it is daytime. Apart from representing the all-seeing eye of God, a candle was carried in wedding processions. A burning candle was also required at the taking of an oath; that an oath is being taken is evident by the position of the couple's hands. Giovanni Arnolfini grasps his bride's hand in his left hand, and raises his right hand to place it on hers, a symbol of their fidelity. Consummation necessary to complete the marriage is represented by the fact that the scene is in the bridal chamber. Other symbolic elements are the discarded shoes, referring to the biblical command, "Put off thy shoes from off thy feet, for the place whereon thou standest is holy ground"; the bride's little dog, representing fidelity; the apples near the window reminding us of the fall of man in the Garden of Eden and of original sin; and the round mirror, embellished with scenes of the Passion, symbolizing purity, as does the necklace to the right of it. The aspergillum hanging over the back of the armchair has presumably been used to sprinkle the room with holy water; and the figure of St. Margaret, the patron saint of childbirth during van Eck's time (in 1969 she was removed from the church calendar) is an obvious symbol, sculptored into the top of the chair.

Though Jan van Eyck depicts these objects with accuracy, in order to tell a story and to enliven his pictures, his main reason for using them is to present the world as a wonderful, interesting place. It is this Renaissance spirit that places his paintings in the forefront of the history of art in western Europe.

The museum also has one of Jan van Eyck's great portraits, *Man in a Turban* (room 24). It is from 1433, about the same time as the *Wedding Portrait of Giovanni Arnolfini*, and it is also a first; we know of no other portrait before this in which the gaze of the subject is directed straight at the spectator, as if the sitter were looking straight into a mirror. This has led to the theory that it may be Jan van Eyck's self-portrait. But the sitter looks too old to be the painter and may actually be the father of his wife, Margaret van Eyck (her portrait is in the Groeninge Museum in Bruges).

Gainsborough, Thomas (1727–88), English

Gainsborough is one of the great figures in English painting, who, with Reynolds (1723–92) and Hogarth (1697–1764), helped English painting achieve European rank. Yet Gainsborough's art is in contrast to these two. Reynolds and Hogarth were Londoners; Gainsborough was, by birth and affection, a countryman. He was closer to Reynolds, whose art, like his own, was essentially aristocratic, as opposed to Hogarth who, as a man of the people, painted in realistic terms. But there are also meaningful differences between Gainsborough and Reynolds. Reynolds looked for inspiration to Italy, where he had spent some years, while Gainsborough never left England, and was not interested in Reynolds's intellectual approach to painting. Self-taught, Gainsborough painted with a free style and trusted his own instincts, which served him well. However, this is not to say that Gainsborough was unfamiliar with the great masters. He studied the Dutch painters of the seventeenth century, especially the landscapists, and he even undertook the restoration of paintings by Ruisdael and others. While his success came from fashionable portraits of the wealthy in England, he was also a fine landscapist: see *The Watering Place* in room 38. In it Gainsborough depicts a believable Arcadia that no city person could have painted. Gainsborough loved the East Anglia countryside where he grew up, and the Lake Country. He came close, in his mature style, to the landscape masterpieces that Constable (1776–1837) would later paint.

The Painter's Daughters with a Cat: room 39

Gainsborough painted his children a number of times. This unfinished double portrait was done when Gainsborough moved to Bath (1759–60) to paint society portraits at that fashionable watering place. Only the two heads are finished. They are in full color, with glowing flesh and penetrating brown eyes. The rest of the painting is made deliberately imprecise in rapid strokes on an ocher ground. This spontaneity of style and his sympathy for the attitudes of children allow him to capture his daughters without artificiality. The little girls are painted for their own sake.

The Morning Walk: room 38

This wedding portrait is typical of the work that made Gainsborough famous. The figures seem to be a part of the background, rendered with the same transparencies—especially in the young lady. It is dated 1785, near the end of Gainsborough's life, when his portraiture reached heights of dignity and grace.

Mrs. Siddons: room 38
This work is of the same year as *The Morning Walk* and is probably Gainsborough's most famous portrait. It shows the actress, Mrs. Sarah Siddons, in a rich dress with ribbons, plumed hat, and fur muff, in a harmony of cold blue and black tones offset by the warmth of a large red curtain. The striking quality is in the delicately modeled features of Mrs. Siddons, with her somewhat nervous expression emphasized by a black hat and the red background.

Gogh, Vincent van* (1853–90), Dutch

Sunflowers (August 1888): room 45
When Vincent van Gogh left Paris and moved to Arles in the south of France he discovered color as if it had never been known before. Even the impressionists, whom he had left behind in Paris, had never been so impressed with color as Vincent was during the spring of 1888 when the sun of Provence flooded into his art. He perceived yellow as the color of pure light and love and painted a series of panels of sunflowers for his room. After the dull grays of his native Holland and the muted tones of Paris, sunflowers were a revelation to him. But his works were not appreciated by either critics or the public during his lifetime. He had so much warmth and love for humanity to give through his painting, but he lived less than two more years after painting these sunflowers, taking his own life in July, 1890.

The Chair and the Pipe (van Gogh's Chair): room 45
This painting, done in Arles in December, 1888, and January, 1889, seems casual, but van Gogh planned his paintings carefully. There is a complex system of intersecting lines and parallels. The yellowish line on the door that ends in a right angle is connected to the leg of the chair. The yellow lines of the floor correspond to the rungs of the chair, and the crossing lines of the seat are as much a part of the floor as they are of the chair.

The visual qualities of color are also intricately worked out. The yellow of the chair is carried over into the brownish-red of the floor and into the blue-green of the door. Similarly, the blue-green of the door reappears in blue outlines of the yellow rungs and legs of the chair, and the brown tones of the floor are again seen in the contours of the chair.

The painting also may have a symbolic quality. Van Gogh painted it as one of a pair. The other, called *Gauguin's Chair*, in the Van Gogh Museum in Amsterdam, seems a portrait of Gauguin as this chair is a portrait of van Gogh. Gauguin's chair, illuminated by gas light, is the more sophisticated in design, with armrests and curved legs. Its seat holds two books. Van Gogh's chair, by contrast, reflects the light of the sun, and its design and workmanship is rough. The artist's pipe and tobacco pouch, lying on its seat, tell of Vincent's loneliness. Earlier, when his father died, Vincent had painted a still life of the old man's pipe and pouch. In a letter written to his brother Theo he once referred to *The Empty Chair*, an old graphic that was supposed to represent the death of Charles Dickens, an author Vincent loved to read.

Hobbema, Meindert (1638–1709), Dutch

The Avenue, Middelharnis: room 27
The sentimental landscapes of Hobbema had an enormous appeal and influence on artists in France and England in the eighteenth and nineteenth centuries. This one (there are eight other landscapes by Hobbema in the National Gallery) has been a favorite from the day it came to the museum in 1871.

Hobbema had been trained by the Dutch landscapist Jacob van Ruisdael, but after painting wooded landscapes, and finding life financially difficult, he married at the age of thirty and obtained a position with the city of Amsterdam as official wine gauger. He did not paint again until twenty years later when he completed *The Avenue, Middelharnis*. Possibly because it was a commission, he abandoned his wooded landscape and instead painted an open panorama.

The foreshadowed road on a wide flat surface carries our eye into the depth of the picture. We focus our attention on the distance, especially the church of Middelharnis with its bulbous tower (today the church is still there minus the bulbous part of the tower). The tall trees not only mark the perspective of the road, but also carry our interest to the spaciousness of the sky. The work did not change Hobbema's standing as an artist; his art was never appreciated until the nineteenth century, and he died poor.

Hogarth, William (1697–1764), English
With Hogarth, starting in the 1730s, British painting began to achieve importance and evolved over the work of Reynolds and Gainsborough (portraits) and Constable (landscapes), into a school of European rank.

Hogarth's contribution was in genre painting, which he described as "modern moral subjects . . . similar to representations on the stage." These he produced in series somewhat like the chapters of a novel. They were more realistic, or brutal, than the famous genre scenes that Steen painted in the previous century in Holland. Hogarth's vivid narratives were intended to be engraved and the reproductions sold to the public. They met with a great deal of financial success.

Biting satire and vivid narrative do not alone make great paintings, but Hogarth was an excellent draftsman with a feeling for space and for coordinating figures within it. He was also somewhat of an impressionist. His *Shrimp Girl* (room 39) shows he is capable of setting line aside to concentrate on light and color, a technique reminiscent of the Barbizon painters two hundred years later.

The Marriage Contract (Marriage à la mode series, 1744): room 39
In this painting, the first of six in the series, Hogarth's critical eye is focused on young wastrels of the nobility who marry wealthy women of a lower class for their money. The scene is set as if it were on a stage. The bride and the groom have their backs to each other. The young nobleman is admiring him-

self in the mirror while his bride-to-be twirls her ring on her handkerchief as she receives the attentions of a clerk. A gouty lord points to his family tree as he receives a cash settlement and mortgage on his estate. This can be seen through the windows, partly finished. The father of the bride, a merchant, inspects the marriage contract with the same absence of emotion he might feel in concluding a business arrangement. Two chained dogs, like the bride and the groom, ignore each other. They make a parallel with the young couple. The other five paintings continue the narrative, which becomes a tragedy. There is the boredom of the couple after marriage; the gaiety of the household, the husband's venereal disease which takes him to the quack doctor, the infidelity of the wife leading to a duel in which the husband is killed, and finally the suicide of the wife when she reads of the execution of her lover.

Hogarth shows in his paintings his objection to the popular attitude that English painters were inferior to others, while the public would accept anything originating on the Continent. He has grotesque art objects cluttering the mantelpiece of the young couple's home, demonstrating their poor taste. A hideous rococo clock and mediocre Dutch paintings adorn the walls of the wife's father's house.

Hogarth's pictures are not moralistic because the culprits—the parents of the young couple—do not bear the brunt of the tragedy. The consequences of wrongdoing fall directly on the couple. Hogarth seems to feel they deserve their fate by their stupid attitude.

Holbein, Hans, the Younger (1497–1543), German

The Ambassadors (1533): room 25
The two men in this picture are French ambassadors to England in 1533; the mathematical and astronomical devices show they are intellectuals. The distorted skull, emblem of one ambassador, breaks the perspective that the geometric pattern of the floor defines. It is a mannerist device that may stand for a warning against pride in learning.

Holbein's typical portraits, such as the painting of the sixteen-year-old *Christina of Denmark* (in the same room), done in 1538 when Henry VIII planned to marry her, show that he rarely painted such a wealth of objects in detail as he did in *The Ambassadors*. It is likely that when Holbein painted *The Ambassadors* he was trying to display his skills in order to obtain the position of court painter to Henry VIII, and it seems to have worked. Shortly thereafter he began his series of English court portraits, for which he is famous and of which *Christina of Denmark* is an example.

Ingres, Jean-Dominique (1780–1867), French

Madame Moitessier Seated (1856): room 43
Over his long career Ingres was the leading figure of the Academy in France, which laid down the rules for the official art during the nineteenth century. Those rules insisted upon a high degree of draftsmanship, of which this portrait is an example. While Mme Moitessier is almost photographically perfect, she is also painted with an aesthetic vision. Her pose is taken from a

classical figure in a painting from Herculaneum, which Ingres knew from his eighteen years in Italy. He gives her a psychological mystery by casting her reflection in a mirror in the background.

Leonardo da Vinci* (1452–1519), Florentine

Virgin of the Rocks: room 8
Leonardo painted two versions of this picture; the other, in the Louvre, is earlier (1483) and is entirely by Leonardo, whereas this one dates from about 1506 and shows extensive passages of pupils' work. As in the Louvre painting, the landscape of brown stalactite rocks in the background holds our attention. With their floral forms they are an expression of Leonardo's scientific interests, but also give a dark background against which figures stand out with a soft chiaroscuro that gives them a fifteenth-century religious delicacy. The background also creates a contrast between a barren world without Christian grace and another with Christian love, exemplified by the holy figures in the foreground.

Cartoon of the Virgin and Child with St. Anne and St. John (1499–1500): room 7
Unlike the Virgin of the Rocks at the National Gallery, in Leonardo's early style, this cartoon (a preparatory drawing on paper for a painting) is from Leonardo's mature period. In it Leonardo has worked out a vertical classical composition of a closely knit group with a greater dense of mass than in the Virgin of the Rocks. When Leonardo painted a Virgin and St. Anne picture ten years later, today in the Louvre, he changed the composition to a pyramidal design, but it has the same two women you see here, who look about the same age, though they are supposed to be mother and daughter. Sigmund Freud in 1910 explained they represent the two women in Leonardo's early life: one was his real mother, a young peasant girl, the other his loving stepmother, the wife of his father. The curious smiles on their faces make us think of the enigmatic smile of the Mona Lisa.

Manet, Édouard (1832–83), French

The Waitress (ca. 1878): room 44
Manet started out as a realist but he went on to become the pioneer of a new generation of painters called impressionists. They went beyond realism in their attempt to record not only the way a scene looked, but also their perception of it at a given moment. The Waitress gives a fleeting impression of a waitress in a Paris café as she is about to serve beer to her patrons. The short brush strokes convey the elements of light and atmosphere. There is no need to look at the canvas carefully; detail has been ignored in favor of a momentary impression translated to the way we really see things and assimilated into instant meaning by our brain. (This painting is part of a larger painting called At the Café. Another part of it is in the Reinhart collection in Wintherthur, Switzerland.)

Master of Flémalle, known as Robert Campin (ca. 1378–1444), Flemish

The Virgin and Child before a Firescreen: room 24
There has been much controversy as to the identity of the Master of Flémalle, and he is generally thought to be the Tournai painter Robert Campin,
whose work the younger Jan van Eyck probably saw and learned from when
he visited Tournai as envoy of the duke of Burgundy. Campin's concern with
depicting actual people and objects as participants in the holy mysteries place
his work outside the international Gothic style and makes him an important
innovator of the Flemish School.

This painting of the Virgin and Child, dated about 1420, shows the Virgin as a simple Flemish girl in a cozy domestic interior with an open window
looking out on an ordinary street. Rather than paint a gilded Gothic halo
around her head, Campin has contrived one out of the wickerwork firescreen
behind her, a modern idea for its time, although other objects, treated with
minute realism, still carry Gothic religious significance. The chalice at the
Virgin's left arm is obviously a reference to Christ's Passion. The open book
refers to the Virgin being the mother of wisdom. The sculptured lions on the
wooden bench are symbols of the Resurrection. Even the Virgin's position,
seated on the floor, refers to the Madonna of Humility. Medieval theology
regarded humility as the source from which all other virtues grew, an idea
appropriate to the Virgin from whom Christ grew.

Memling, Hans (ca. 1433–94), Flemish

The Donne Triptych: room 24
This triptych has a charm that few paintings of the fifteenth-century Flemish
School can match. One reason is that Sir John Donne and his wife and
daughter are shown with the Madonna, Child and Sts. Catherine and Barbara in the central panel. Another reason is Memling's down-to-earth style
that presents the Madonna as a girlish figure, the Child as an animated baby,
and the two Saints John as attractive young men.

The painting is significant because it helps establish Memling's date of
birth. Considering that the triptych was probably painted in 1468 when the
wedding of Charles the Bold to Margaret of York was being celebrated at
Bruges, Memling's adopted home town, and that on this occasion distinguished Englishmen visited the city, it can be assumed that Sir John Donne
was present for the occasion. It is also reasonable to assume that the man
standing behind the pillar near St. John the Baptist is a self-portrait of the
artist. If we note that Memling looks in his early thirties, we can infer that
he was born about 1433.

Moroni, Giambattista (ca. 1520/25–78), Italian

The Tailor: room 30
Giambattista Moroni spent almost his entire career in Bergamo, the town of
his birth. Many of his altarpieces painted for provincial towns in the area
have survived, but he is best known as a gifted portraitist who earned the
admiration of the great Titian, who advised the people of Bergamo to have
portraits painted by Moroni rather than Venetian artists. Perhaps Moroni's

talent came out in portraiture because, as Bernard Berenson suggests, he lacked inventiveness and needed a living model. Certainly his religious paintings are commonplace. Yet once Moroni had a model he could bring out their individual characteristics whether they were tailors, lawyers, soldiers, local squires, or anyone else. He brings them to us with a photographic quality and never allows his colors to get in the way of his draftsmanship. They are a harmony of reserved tones heightened with sparkling light and fused with a neutral background. The restraint of color and facial expressions gave a delicate melancholy to his subjects.

Piero della Francesca* (ca. 1416–92), Umbrian, under Florentine influence

The Baptism of Christ (ca. 1442): room 4

This work is possibly one of the first commissions Piero received when he returned from Florence in 1442. He does not imitate Masaccio or Veneziano, already having his own powerful style. His Christ and St. John the Baptist, in the center, are people from everyday life, but they show Piero's idea of human grandeur. There is also Piero's relationship of forms. Vertical elements, such as the solidity of Christ's legs, are carried over into the white tree-trunk, and the horizontal elements are expressed in the white dove (Holy Spirit) above Christ's head, almost indistinguishable from the white clouds beyond. Similarly, the curve of the body of the man undressing is reflected in the bend of the river. Piero's colors are remarkably preserved, giving us a chance to see how pale and cool they are without being cold.

The priests' images, reflected in the water, resemble Greek prelates whom Piero might have seen in 1439 when the Council of Ferrara met in Florence. Such hats are still worn by Greek Orthodox priests. Here the figures are supposed to represent the guardians of Old Testament law receding into the background, in favor of the New Testament, represented by the baptism of Christ.

The Nativity (ca. 1475): room 4

This is a late work done when Piero was thought to be losing interest in painting (by 1480 he ceased to paint altogether) and there is evidence that it was done for himself, perhaps as an experiment. It is a work of refinement in which Pietro's creative talent reaches a high note before it dies away.

Here the influence of Flemish painting has finally gotten to Piero. He reacts to the Flemish example iconographically by painting the Christ Child lying on the ground, similar to the way Hugo van der Goes painted Him in his famous *Portinari Altarpiece,* which caused a sensation in Florence in 1475. Exposure to the Flemish style has also given his painting additional subtlety: compare the feet and ankles of the angels in *The Nativity* with those of the nearby *Baptism of Christ* and you find a more expressive outline unlike the solid effect of the earlier painting. Something similar has taken place in the depiction of the Madonna, transformed from the plain, solid figure of Piero's earlier work into a beautiful young lady. While Piero's sense of perspective is still alive, so that the solid wall of the shed beckons us into the landscape, the landscape itself has undergone a change. The background in *The Baptism* was done with a free brush, almost impressionistic, but in *The Nativity* the background is carefully drawn with every round tree and bush carefully articulated.

Why did Piero depart from his original style at such a late date? Perhaps he felt he was losing his genius and he needed a new stimulus.

Raphael* (1483–1520), Florentine, born in Umbria

Allegory, The Ansidei Madonna, and *Portrait of Pope Julius II:* room 8
In keeping with the National Gallery's reputation of having a comprehensive collection of European paintings, three paintings by Raphael, covering his early period (ca. 1500), his middle Florentine period (1504–8), and his Roman period (1509–20) respectively, provide an opportunity to observe the growth of his art from its provincial beginnings in Umbria to its ultimate achievement at the Vatican.

First, there is the very early *Allegory* (ca. 1500), displayed with the cartoon—sometimes called *Dream of a Knight,* but probably *Dream of Scipio.* The youth in armor lies asleep on his shield while two goddesses stand over him with the gifts of valor (sword), wisdom (book), and love (flower), the attributes necessary for the Renaissance idea of the universal man. Raphael, only seventeen at the time, has handled the balance and symmetry of the picture somewhat crudely.

Raphael's altarpiece, *The Ansidei Madonna,* which he started in Florence in about 1504, shows a difference four years can make in the life of a genius. The work shows how quickly Raphael learned from the Florentine masters. Only the face of John the Baptist shows any connection with the Umbrian School. Much of the rest is Florentine, influenced by such as Luca Signorelli and Fra Bartolomeo. The Florentine monumentality of the throne and the bold steps in front of it dominate the picture and show Raphael's talent peaking at an early age (he is only about twenty-one).

The *Portrait of Pope Julius II* (1511–12) represents Raphael's mature period. This is the Renaissance pope who was the patron of Michelangelo and employed Raphael as decorator of the papal apartments. Seated in contemplation, the pope is painted in rich color worthy of the Venetian School and with striking realism. The pope is seen as a doer of great deeds whose time is drawing to a close.

Rembrandt* (1606–69), Dutch

A Woman Bathing in a Stream (1655): room 26
After the death of his wife Saskia, in 1642, Rembrandt remained a widower with one son until Hendrickje Stoffels, a daughter of a soldier, joined his household about 1645. She was a great companion to Rembrandt, and they remained together until her death in 1664. They never married; a second marriage would have deprived Rembrandt of the income from his first wife's estate.

This painting of Hendrickje is his most personal picture of her, although it is little more than a sketch in oils. Rembrandt probably painted it for himself, never intending it to be sold. He shows Hendrickje bathing in a stream, absorbed in the coolness of the water. By giving Hendrickje a monumentality of form Rembrandt also gives her a tranquil appearance. Here is the same kind of heroic truth that Rembrandt put into his great half-length portraits.

The National Gallery has one of the finest collections of Rembrandt masterpieces, including, in room 26, his famous *Woman Taken in Adultery, Self-portraits,* and portraits of his young wife *Saskia van Ulenborch* and his mistress *Hendrickje Stoffels.* Room 27 has portraits of various other people, such as *Jacob Trip* and *Margaretha de Geer.*

Reynolds, Sir Joshua (1723–92), English

Lord Heathfield, Governor of Gibraltar (1787): room 38
While Sir Joshua Reynolds is considered the most academic painter England ever produced (he was the first president of the Royal Academy), he is regarded as one of the great English painters of portraits. He completed more excellent portraits during his lifetime than anyone else. The *Portrait of Lord Heathfield* depicts the general who withstood the siege of Gibraltar by the French and Spanish in 1779. The key in the general's hand symbolizes his tenacious control of Gibraltar, and his tanned face conveys an energy that assures us England could not be in better hands. A good deal of Reynolds's academism came from his study of the old masters in Italy; the color and light in this portrait seem to come directly from the Venetians.

Rubens, Peter Paul* (1577–1640), Flemish
Rubens has always had a place of importance in the National Gallery. England played a part in his career, when he first went to England in 1629, sent by Philip IV on a diplomatic mission. He was welcomed at the court of Charles I, where he became popular and was given a knighthood and a commission to decorate the ceiling of Inigo Jones's new Palladian palace of Whitehall.

"Le Chapeau de Paille" (Portrait of Susanna Fourment) (ca. 1622): room 22
Rubens's letters mention his admiration for Helena Fourment, his second wife, whom he married when she was sixteen and he was fifty-two. His canvases show her in various settings, including mythologies that celebrate her nude beauty. This painting, incorrectly called *"Le Chapeau de Paille"* ("The Straw Hat"), a name that has stuck despite the black felt hat the subject is wearing, is of *Susanna Fourment,* Helena's' older sister, who often posed as a model for Rubens. Layers of paint have been applied with a transparent effect to bring out her pearly skin, delicate and white at her neck and her breasts. Even the black hat and dress bring out the alluring quality of her milky flesh. There is something coy, yet relaxed and self-assured, about her candid gaze. It holds the spectator's attention as she probably was successful in holding Rubens's.

Rubens painted this portrait about eight years before he married Susanna's younger sister, at a time when Susanna had just married her second husband. It probably represents a wedding portrait; the forefinger of her right hand almost certainly has a wedding ring on it.

The Judgment of Paris (ca. 1631/33): room 20
This is the story of the pastoral beauty contest presided over by Paris to choose the most beautiful goddess in the world. He holds the golden apple that he will present to the winner, Venus, and thus start the strife that Eris, shown in the mirror on the left, has planned. At the side of Paris is Mercury, the messenger who has delivered the three goddesses to Paris: Minerva, Venus, and Juno. The three nude female figures are three studies (front, side, and back) of Rubens's young wife Helena Fourment. It is the artist's delight in painting the female nude, and Helena in particular, that makes this painting so brilliant. Rubens painted the scene again, also using his wife as the model, some years later for Philip IV of Spain (see the Prado, Madrid).

The Castle of Steen (1636): room 22
In 1635, when he was fifty-eight, Rubens retired to a country house he bought in the parish of Steen, near Malines, about a half day's journey from Antwerp. It was a Renaissance chateau, which still exists, with a garden, orchard, drawbridge and moat, lake, farmhouse, stables, and outbuildings. He added to it by purchasing surrounding farmlands. He even assumed the title Lord of Steen, which he held as his favorite honor.

This picture seems to show that Rubens, free from the affairs of the courts, found joy in the countryside—the peace he sacrificed during his younger days. He has painted a landscape not merely as a setting for a religious or mythological scene. It is now a celebration of the countryside for its own sake. The colors of autumn are everywhere, a sportsman with his dog is stalking partridges in the sun, cattle are grazing in the meadow, and a cart laden with farm produce is setting out for market. It is probably close to the life Rubens led at Steen.

Seurat, Georges-Pierre (1859–91), French

Bathers, Asnières (1883/84): room 45
Seurat's style is sometimes called neoimpressionism, but it is quite different from the impressionists who came twenty years before him. Seurat wanted a systematic method that avoided the accidental arrangements of the impressionists. Form was important, which he created with simplified outlines holding a geometrical mass. His method, pointillism, reduced colors to primary values, then arranged the colors on the canvas painstakingly in tiny dots to mingle and create a whole range of secondary colors. The *Bathers, Asnières* is Seurat's first large work done in this style before he perfected it. He reworked parts of the painting to make the colors sharper.

Tintoretto* (1518–94), Venetian

The Origin of the Milky Way (1577): room 9
Though Tintoretto was largely a painter of religious scenes, in this canvas he paints Michelangelesque human figures floating in space and a Titianesque golden nude. He proves himself a master at depicting a legend from antiquity in the spirit of Veronese, his contemporary.

According to the legend, Hercules was the offspring of Jupiter and the mortal woman Alcmen of Thebes, who had left him outside the city to die because she feared the anger of Juno, wife of Jupiter. But Jupiter interceded and, wishing to immortalize the mortal Hercules, guided him to drink Juno's milk. We are brought into the story at the moment the child has been placed at the breast of Juno, who awakens in anger, spilling her milk into the sky—thus the origin of the milky way—and to earth below to form white lilies (the bottom part of this painting has been cut off but showed white lilies growing). The black eagle with a thunderbolt in his claws is symbolic of Jupiter, and the peacocks are Juno's attribute. The three putti carry objects that emphasize the story: the net refers to deceit, and the flaming torch and bow and arrow to eroticism.

St. George and the Dragon (1550): room 9

This early work of Tintoretto has less of his chiaroscuro and more of the luminous coloring of Titian. Its composition, set within a landscape of windswept trees, with the story unfolding in depth, is typical of Tintoretto's mannerist style.

Titian* (ca. 1487–1576), Venetian

Bacchus and Ariadne: room 9

In this scene we see Bacchus arriving in his chariot, pulled by two cheetahs, to rescue Ariadne, the daughter of King Minos of Crete. She has been abandoned by Theseus on the island of Naxos. Bacchus has taken her jeweled crown and thrown it into the sky to become a constellation, visible in the upper left corner. His drunken followers are seen on the right: a satyr entwined with snakes, another with the hindquarter of a goat, a small reveler pulling the head of a slaughtered calf, and others engaged in pagan antics.

This painting is one of three that Titian was commissioned to do for Alfonso d'Este at the Ferarra court in 1516. They were intended to adorn an alabaster pleasure chamber, thus their paganistic themes. The Worship of Venus (1518) and Bacchanal (1520) are in the Prado, and Bacchus and Ariadne (1523) is the third of the series. In keeping with their earthy quality, all are colorful, with red and blue dominant. From this painting a sense of movement and action became a model for future baroque painters.

Of the many paintings by Titian in the National Gallery, The Vendramin Family, from about 1547 (room 9), is a group portrait of exceptional quality, especially in the depiction of the children; and the early Portrait of a Man, from about 1511–12 (room 9), is an example of Titian's breaking away from the influence of Giorgione with a new energy.

Turner, Joseph Mallord William* (1775–1851), English

The Fighting Téméraire (1839): room 37

The Téméraire, a British sailing ship with ninety-eight guns, was launched in 1798 and played an important role at the Battle of Trafalgar in 1805. It was a reminder of Britain's glorious past. This painting, showing it being towed to be broken up into scrap, evoked feelings of nostalgic patriotism in the hearts of Englishmen. There is a sense of melancholy in the end of the old and the beginning of the new, with the ugly modern boat belching out hot steam, set against the beautiful battleship. Turner especially liked this painting, refused to sell it, and referred to it as "my darling." The steam, reddish from the fire below in the tugboat, is echoed in the red clouds and in the red reflection of the sun on the water. Red was a symbol of destruction in Turner's art. The setting sun is an obvious symbol.

Rain, Steam and Speed—The Great Western Railway (1844): room 37
This is Turner's view of a train rushing over a bridge in rain and fog. Turner loved trains. His locomotive bears down upon us in a torrent of black and red, a dynamic force that we can almost feel. Thackeray wrote that "the world has never seen anything like this picture." It was a work of art detached from the eighteenth and even the nineteenth century, the impressionists not excepted. Such abstraction of light and atmosphere was not to be seen again until the twentieth century.

Uccello, Paolo (ca. 1397–1475), Florentine

St. George and the Dragon (1456): room 2
This little gem of a painting, which shows Uccello's dreamlike imagination, tells the story, from the *Golden Legend* (thirteenth century), in which St. George kills a dragon to rescue a princess offered to it as a sacrifice to keep it away from a city. Do not be misled by seeing the princess holding the dragon on a leash, as if it were her pet, because the legend says the dragon became subdued when leashed with the princess's girdle, enabling St. George to kill it. It was a story popular during the Gothic Age. Uccello's picture, in tempera on canvas, is rare for its day, as most paintings were done on wood panel. Religious expression is subordinated to his desire to create fantastic forms with a sense of perspective. Notice that the diagonal arrangement of the figures, which connect with each other (by St. George's thrusting lance, by the leash connecting the princess to the dragon and by the princess's body), leads the eye to the distant mountains, expressing a sense of depth.

Uccello's interest in perspective was an all-consuming fascination with him—he is considered an early Renaissance painter despite the Gothic scene of *St. George and the Dragon*. His **Battle of San Romano** (ca. 1450) in the National Gallery (room 2), is an example of his ability using the then new technique of foreshortening and perspective recession. He made three paintings on the subject for the Medici palace in Florence, depicting a battle of 1422 between Florentines and Sienese. The other two are in the Louvre in Paris and the Uffizi in Florence. (See Uccello in the Uffizi, Florence.)

Velázquez, Diego* (1599–1660), Spanish

The Toilet of Venus ("The Rokeby Venus") (ca. 1640s): room 41
The nude was not accepted as a fitting subject for Spanish artists during Velázquez's time. Velázquez painted at least five of them during his career and this is the only one to survive.

Velázquez had seen the paintings of nudes by the Italian Renaissance artists at the Hapsburg court in Spain and many more on visits to Italy. Titian's paintings of nudes, showing a reclining Venus, and Venus admiring herself in a mirror attended by Cupid, seem the obvious inspiration for the *Rokeby Venus*. Velázquez has used Titian's themes but turns his model's back to us, hoping his picture will fit into the conservative Spanish tradition. Unlike the uninhibited Italian pictures that show us all, Velázquez's nude's reflection in the mirror shows us less than we should logically see.

The composition of curves, starting with Venus's foot and traveling along her body in harmony with the lines of the bedsheets, is continued in the sweep of the curtain. The vertical lines of Cupid and of the mirror balance this gentle flowing movement while reminding us of it by the undulating textured pink ribbon hanging over the Cupid's arm and the top of the mirror's frame.

In the same room is a portrait of Velázquez's patron *Philip IV*. Although history has labeled Philip a religious fanatic, he owned many paintings of nudes, but they were not by Spanish artists.

Vermeer, Jan* (1632–75), Dutch

Lady Standing at the Virginal and Lady Seated at the Virginal: room 28
Both of these paintings are from Vermeer's final period (ca. 1670) and have meaning when viewed together. In both there is a picture within a picture. They take up much of the background space and the figure's head is joined to them. In the *Lady Standing at the Virginal* the picture on the wall is of Cupid holding up a tablet inscribed with the number one, while he steps upon other tablets numbering two through ten. This motif is traced to a contemporary engraving published in Antwerp extolling fidelity to one lover as opposed to the love of many. The lady standing at the virginal represents a faithful woman. In the *Lady Seated at the Virginal* the background picture is a version of *The Procuress*, by Dirck van Baburen (1622, now in the Museum of Fine Arts, Boston), suggesting the young lady is not as innocent as she looks. The viola beside the virginal may be symbolic of the lady's intention to play a duet—in the erotic sense. The compositions of these works have been questioned: the *Lady Seated at the Virginal* seems crowded, while the *Lady Standing at the Virginal* has heavy rectangles—formed by the instrument, the chair, and the pictures on the wall—that seem meaningless. The black edges of the virginal's lid and the nearly straight lines of the lady's arms seem awkward.

Weyden, Rogier van der* (ca. 1399–1464), Flemish

Portait of a Lady: room 24
The figure depicted here is nameless but represents one of the few portraits of women by Rogier van der Weyden. Like most of his portraits, she looks away from the spectator with an impersonal gaze. Little of her personality is revealed; there is little more than a pious, nunlike quality about her, even though the rings on her fingers show married status. It is the design of the picture, rather than the sitter, that makes the impression, skillfully constructed with her half-length figure forming a pyramid, accented by the smaller, more solid pyramid of her hands.

NATIONAL PORTRAIT GALLERY

St. Martin's Place

Hours: Open Mon.–Fri., 10AM–5PM, Sat., 10AM–6PM, Sun., 2–6PM. Free admission.

This gallery has an enormous collection of paintings, drawings, and sculptures of Britain's famous men and women from every walk of life. It is behind the National Gallery. A good likeness of a subject, rather than artistic merit, is of paramount importance in the overall aim here, but many of the sitters were painted by celebrated artists. Earliest portraits are of the Tudor period, from which there is a chronological progression to the present, giving us the full sweep of British history through art.

THE QUEEN'S GALLERY, BUCKINGHAM PALACE

Entrance in Buckingham Palace Road

Hours: Open Tues. –Sun. (and Bank holidays), 11AM–5PM; Sun. 2–5PM; closed Mon.

In the former chapel of Buckingham Palace, damaged during the last war, works from the royal collections are exhibited and changed about twice each year. There are paintings, sculptures, furniture, miniatures, and a variety of other treasures usually displayed along with the objects they are surrounded with in Buckingham Palace and Windsor Castle. This unique museum gives you the opportunity to see splendid works of art that are generally not on public display.

SIR JOHN SOANE'S MUSEUM

13 Lincoln's Inn Fields

Hours: Open Tues.–Sat., 10AM–5PM. Free admission.

This museum contains the art collection of the architect Sir John Soane, builder of the Bank of England and the houses at 12, 13, and 14 Lincoln's Inn Fields where he lived. He lived until 1837, to the age of eighty-four, and amassed a vast number of antiques and paintings—from the sarcophagus of Seti I, in the basement, to Hogarth—and managed to squeeze it all into his house.

The Picture Room (ground floor), where walls have hinged panels to contain extra layers of paintings, has Hogarth's series *The Rake's Progress* (eight paintings), and *The Election* series (four paintings). There is also a haunting painting called *The Italian Count,* by Henry Fuseli (1741–1825), which has the fearful imagery for which Fuseli is famous.

Hogarth, William* (1697–1764), English

The Rake's Progress
This series of eight pictures from 1733 makes a narrative of the career of Tom Rakewell, who inherits his father's money, has a fashionable life surrounded by music, falls into debauchery in the Rose Tavern, is arrested for debt, makes a marriage of convenience to a rich old woman, and ends up a gambler in prison for debt, and, finally, in the madhouse. In the caricatures, such as in *The Levee* (the second painting), the foolishness of the rake is seen on his face as he stands among parasites and ruffians. The tavern scene called *The Orgy* (the third painting) is one of Hogarth's masterpieces, purposely top-heavy in composition and high-keyed in color to add to the garishness of the scene. The rake is seen with a foot upon the table as he slides off the lap of a girl who has already relieved him of his watch. Another girl standing on a chair is trying to set fire to a map of the world. Portraits of Roman emperors on the wall have been disfigured, except for one, that of Nero. Our eye is drawn around the table to the girl undressing, then back to the rake.

These eight paintings had the effect of entertaining rather than sermonizing, and prints were made from engravings of each scene that sold well throughout the eighteenth century in England and on the Continent.

In the other series of four large paintings called *The Election* (1754–57) Hogarth satirizes the corruption of the politics of his day. These also tell a story. The scenes seem overcrowded, but the drawing is vigorous.

TATE GALLERY

Millbank

Hours: Open Mon.–Sat., 10AM–6PM, Sun., 2–6PM. Free admission.

The Tate, the largest public gallery in Britain, owes its existence to the simple sugar lump. That product was invented by Henry Tate, a grocer's boy in the north of England. With the fortune he made from "Tate's sugar cubes" he began buying contemporary art.

Tate's collection of sixty-five paintings and two sculptures he offered as a gift to the nation in 1890 with the proviso that the government provide a site where he could build a gallery of modern art. This site was that of the old Millbank Prison, then being demolished. Seven years later Britain had its Tate Gallery.

At first the Tate was intended only as a collection of contemporary British painting, as an annex to the National Gallery. But the Tate grew rapidly and today it has become a national collection of British art from all periods—from the sixteenth century up to about 1900. Every great British painter is included, with particular emphasis on Hogarth, Blake, the Pre-Raphaelites, and Turner, whose profusion of paintings at the Tate is a special joy.

Apart from the British collection, what is called the modern collection consists of works by British artists born after 1850 and foreign works from the impressionists onwards. Such artists as Cézanne, Gauguin, van Gogh, Picasso, and others are well represented here, as well as the schools of futurism, surrealism, abstract expressionism, pop, minimal, and conceptual art.

New galleries built with a contribution from the Calouste Gulbenkian Foundation opened in 1979 and doubled the space, so more of the Tate's 4,000 paintings can be shown at one time.

Index to the Rooms of the Tate Gallery

Artists mentioned below have works referred to in the text that follows. You will find these works listed under the names of the artists, arranged alphabetically.

Room 2	Hogarth
Room 3	Hogarth
Room 4	Gainsborough
Room 5	Wright of Derby
Room 7	Blake
Room 9	Turner (until completion of Clove Gallery)
Room 15	Brown, Hunt, Millais, Rossetti
Room 17	Whistler
Room 61	Spencer

British Paintings at the Tate

Blake, William (1757–1827), British

God Creating Adam (1795): room 7
During the second half of the eighteenth century there was a reaction against conformity of classicism called romanticism, which focused on emotion rather than reason, on the subjective rather than the objective, on the mystical rather than the measurable. Romanticism experimented with color and new modes of expression. William Blake fitted in well with this romantic approach to art, a mystic who painted purely from his imagination. He considered his own visions clearer than any observation he could make from nature. Though not appreciated during his life—he made a living by producing illuminated books—he never wavered in his artistic philosophy.

Blake's *God Creating Adam,* a color print finished in water color, draws from Michelangelo's Sistine Chapel frescoes and the Gothic effigies of Westminster Abbey where, as a boy, he had made drawings of various monuments for a London printer. His work is nevertheless original in spirit. God, set against a huge sun with rays of blue and purple, touches Adam, entwined in the coils of a serpent, which shall bring about his fall. This poetic expression of the creation is not the equal in technical mastery of Michelangelo's in the Sistine ceiling, but it showed a poetic imagination long suppressed in English painting.

In Blake's series of monotypes, such as the Tate's *Newton* (room 7), Blake expresses the evil power of the measuring mind, and in *Nebuchadnezzar* (room 7) he shows materialistic man reduced to an animal.

Brown, Ford Madox (1821–93), English

Christ Washing St. Peter's Feet (1852): room 15
In response to the frivolousness of English painting during his time, after his exposure in Rome to a group of German painters who called themselves the Nazarenes, Ford Madox Brown cultivated an archaic manner in his painting with a view toward depicting nature in a new and more honest way. The Nazarenes were drawing inspiration from medieval works. His *Christ Washing St. Peter's Feet*, where we see Christ engaged in a humble act, shocked the public. It was too realistic. The veins on Peter's feet and Christ's hands stand out sharply. The scene is heightened by Judas in the background, seen with his bag of silver as he bends over to replace his sandal. The classical composition is set off by the coloring and play of light on the brass bowl and white tablecloth, a characteristic of the Pre-Raphaelites. Brown never joined the Pre-Raphaelite brotherhood but had been a source of inspiration to Dante Gabriel Rossetti, one of the founders of the movement.

Brown's *Carrying Corn* (1854) (room 15), unlike *Christ Washing St. Peter's Feet*, a painting worked out over a long period of time, predates impressionism by twenty years, and captures a landscape under a moment of sunlight.

Gainsborough, Thomas* (1727–88), English

The Market Cart (1786): room 4
While known as a society portraitist, Gainsborough made a contribution to the art of landscape painting which, like *The Market Cart*, he painted for himself. Landscapes were an outlet for Gainsborough to vent his need for expression and his virtuosity with a brush. He was a countryman with a romantic interest in nature, as *The Market Cart* shows, which is not to say he was a realistic painter. *The Market Cart* is less a specific scene than a generalized setting. Its conventional blue hill and far reaching distance show that Gainsborough was under the influence of Claude Lorrain, the traditional landscapist then admired by the British. Still, Gainsborough's painting is fresh and alive with a sense of color and movement. The cart seems to issue forth out of the landscape with its load of red carrots, carried over into the reddish glow of a tree trunk. It has come to a clearing with a waterhole where a man is gathering wood. The movement of the wagon seems quite visible as the dog moves along beside the horse with a brisk step. This was Gainsborough's Arcadia. Constable, in the next century, admired Gainsborough, and wrote: "I fancy I see Gainsborough in every hedge and hollow tree."

Hogarth, William* (1697–1764), English

The Graham Children (1742): room 3
True to his dramatic sense, Hogarth has painted the four children of Daniel Graham, the apothecary to Chelsea Hospital, as if they were on a stage as the curtain goes up on a performance. The brother plays the bird-organ, his sister in the center dances, and the older sister holds the baby's hand. There is also a remarkable portrait of a cat.

Hogarth seemed to enjoy portraiture when not beholden to a patron's dictates. The study he did of his own *Servants* (ca. 1750–55) (room 3) shows originality and character without caricature.

O the Roast Beef of Old England: ("Calais Gate"): room 2
This is one of the most popular pictures Hogarth ever painted. Its origin goes back to a trip the artist made to France in 1748. Hogarth was not a traveler—he never made the usual artist's trip to Italy—and he had a dislike for the French. In 1743 he did visit Paris where he found a squalor that suggested the Middle Ages and a kind of Gallic insolence. Nevertheless, he made a second trip, and as he was waiting at Calais for the boat back to England, he amused himself by walking around the town and sketching the English Gate, a relic of a previous English occupation. A soldier arrested him as a spy and he had to prove to a magistrate that he was an artist. He was hustled off to England on the next boat and was reminded that in wartime he would have been hanged. *"Calais Gate"* (1748) takes revenge on the French.

First, Hogarth shows himself in the scene sketching the gate just as he is about to be arrested. The skinny, ragged soldiers, with their bowls of soup, represent the empty glory of France. Huddled in a corner is a Jacobite supporter of the exiled branch of the house of Stuart, who in 1745 were eliminated as a political force by Bonnie Prince Charlie. He laments his fate. Nearby are fishwives symbolizing the three witches in Shakespeare's *Macbeth*. In the middle of the painting a servant is staggering under the weight of an enormous sirloin of beef imported from England for the Lion d'Argent, the English inn, as a fat friar lays a finger on it, licking his lips. A Catholic procession is seen through the gate.

For Hogarth the sirloin of beef represented the superiority of England and of English liberty, as opposed to French oppression represented by the Catholic church. The sharp spikes on the porticullis of the English Gate are a reminder to the French of what they were in store for if they chose to make war with the British.

Hunt, William Holman (1827–1910), English

Claudio and Isabella: room 15
Hunt was one of three painters who formed the Pre-Raphaelite brotherhood in 1848, and it was he who remained most faithful to its principles (see Rossetti). He wrote a book about the movement, *Pre-Raphaelitism and the Pre-Raphaelite Brotherhood*, published in 1905. His *Claudio and Isabella*, painted in 1850, during the height of the movement, is one of a number of scenes he painted from Shakespeare. This one is from *Measure for Measure;* its theme is a sense of sin and sexual guilt. In it Claudio pleads with his sister, Isabella, to give up her virginity to save his life. He says, "Death is a fearful thing" and Isabella answers, "And a shamed life is hateful." The curve of Claudio's belt of chain is carried over into the curve of Isabella's sleeve; his pulling the chain on his leg is a sign of his wondering if his sister is correct. There is a silhouetting of their heads against the light of the prison window—Hunt used a real prison window, with live models in front of it, to study the play of light.

The Tate also displays Hunt's *Our English Coasts* (room 15), sometimes called *Strayed Sheep*, painted in 1852. It is a moralizing picture that refers to the exodus of Englishmen to America and the colonies to escape poor conditions at home. Apart from its symbolism, it is also a show of sunlight upon land and water in the realistic style of the Pre-Raphaelites.

Millais, Sir John Everette (1829–96), English

Christ in the House of His Parents (1850): room 15

Millais was one of the three young painters who founded the secret society called the Pre-Raphaelite Brotherhood (they signed their work "PRB" instead of using their names). His *Christ in the House of His Parents* was one of the first Pre-Raphaelite pictures shown. In its concern with medieval symbolism and in its detail it is typical of the movement in its purest form. The small boy, Christ, has hurt His hand and has come to His mother for consolation. He has dripped blood from the hand onto His foot, a portent of wounds to come on the cross. Another boy represents John the Baptist, and has water to bathe the Child's wound, symbolic of the water he will use to baptize Christ. The sheep are looking for their shepherd; the dove of peace sits on a rung of the ladder.

When the painting was first exhibited it caused a scandal. Its realism was criticized as vulgar. Dickens thought it hideous. No one appreciated that everything was copied from real life. Millais had studied a carpenter's shop; the model was a real carpenter. Composition was carefully worked out: a curve is formed by the heads of John, Joseph, Elizabeth and the assistant carpenter. Vivid colors were achieved by painting over a prepared white ground. Ruskin came to the defense of the Pre-Raphaelites and said they were "laying in our England the foundations of a school of art nobler than the world had seen for three hundred years."

In Millais's *Ophelia* (1852) (room 15), the model is Elizabeth Siddal, favorite model of the Pre-Raphaelites and future wife of Dante Gabriel Rossetti (see Rossetti, below). Here is further developed the technique of painting over a wet white ground into which colors were worked.

These two paintings by Millais are his only genuinely Pre-Raphaelite works. Later Millais slipped to the level of genre painting and was knighted and elected president of the Royal Academy.

Pre-Raphaelite Movement

Rossetti, Dante Gabriel (1828–82), English

In 1830 Constable had predicted, "In twenty years there will be no English art." By the 1840s English art had reached a low point. The direction provided by Constable and Turner might have led to impressionism but no one followed them. Then, in 1848, the creation of the Pre-Raphaelite movement proved Constable's prediction inaccurate. As a form of protest against mediocrity it emphasized the Gothic and what its founders—Dante Gabriel Rossetti, William Holman Hunt (1827–1910), and John Everett Millais (1829–96)—considered pure forms of art. They went back for inspiration to the early fifteenth century before the time of Raphael. Their interest in the

Gothic led to precision of detail and a devotion to figure subjects with a narrative content. Above all, the Pre-Raphaelites' concern was escaping the ugly realities of industrialized English society into a dreamlike world anchored by religion and legend.

The Girlhood of Virgin Mary (1849): room 15

This painting, a fine example of Pre-Raphaelite art, is filled with medieval symbolism that is unexpected in nineteenth-century English painting. The Virgin is being taught by her mother, Anne, to sew priests' vestments. An angel is placing white lilies, symbolic of her virginity, on a stack of books, representing the virtues. On the floor the palm and thorn branches prefigure the seven joys and sorrows of the Virgin. In the background, on the decorated altar, from the left arc various objects: a vase, meaning the Virgin is the vessel of Christ's Incarnation, which is placed next to a vine, carefully tended to by the Virgin's father, Joachim, referring to the coming of Christ; the rose is a reference to the Virgin as sinless, a rose without thorns; the lamp is an emblem of piety; Christ's seamless red tunic, beneath a cross-shaped trellis, is a reference to the crucifixion; and perched above all this is a white dove, symbolic of the Holy Ghost. The building in the distance may be the synagogue, marking the end of the Old Law and the beginning of the reign of the New Law, or it may refer to the coming Presentation in the Temple.

Beata Beatrix: room 15

This is a portrait of Rossetti's wife and model, Elizabeth Siddal, known as Lizzy. She had been a shop assistant at a milliner's in Cranbourn Street when she was discovered by the Pre-Raphaelites in the spring of 1850. Thereafter she became their favorite model (she is Millais's *Ophelia*, see above), but Rossetti took possession of her and they started living together in 1852. He taught her to draw and encouraged her in writing verse (Rossetti was himself a poet). Their relationship was doomed to failure; Lizzy was frigid and full of mysterious mental and physical ailments. Nevertheless, Rossetti continued the relationship, even after he fell in love with Jane Burden, a beautiful brunette who appears in many of his paintings, also modeling for William Morris. Morris married Jane in 1859, and Rossetti married Lizzy, but her fits of depression worsened. In 1862 Lizzy died from an overdose of opium.

Rossetti threw manuscripts of his poems into Lizzy's grave, moved out of his studio, and took a house is Chelsea. There he painted the *Beata Beatrix* in 1863. It is supposedly a picture of Dante's Beatrice (Rossetti had already painted many scenes from Dante's *Vita Nuova*, which he himself had translated into English), but is actually Rossetti's memorial to his wife. It shows Beatrice at the moment of her death, but she is shown not as a dead woman but as a woman in ecstasy. She leans forward with her head tipped back, her eyes shut, and her lips parted as if straining toward a revelation. A bird drops a poppy into her hands (the symbol of sleep and death, and the source of opium that killed Lizzy). The pale red of the bird of death is the same as that of the figure in the background who represents Love.

Ten years later Rossetti tried to take his own life the same way Lizzy had taken hers, but failed. Although he lived another ten years he was by then a drug-addicted recluse.

Spencer, Sir Stanley (1891–1959), English

The Resurrection, Cookham (1923–27): room 61

The popularity of Stanley Spencer is growing, likely owing to his realistic style. His depiction of village life, which sometimes takes on a folkloric quality, and his religious narratives that remind one of the Pre-Raphaelites, are also sources of his popularity. He was exposed to the entire modern movement (he first exhibited at the second postimpressionist exhibition organized by Roger Fry in 1912), but had the confidence to ignore the avant-garde. Most of his life he stayed in the village of Cookham, on the Thames, where he was born. A museum there in a chapel where he attended Sunday School is devoted to his works. The large canvas of *The Resurrection, Cookham* (nine by eighteen feet), the earliest of three Resurrections he was to paint, is set in the churchyard of Cookham beside the Thames, which can be seen in the background. The unstable perspective, for which Spencer is known, induces the viewer to examine the entire surface, exploring differing depths and angles as one would look at a cubist painting. All those people clambering out of their graves to join Christ, who is seen in the center with little children, was actually a part of Spencer's vision of a simple faith. That faith seems present even in his so-called "sex-pictures"—the realistic nudes modeled by his wife, Patricia Preece. These pictures, such as the famous *Leg of Mutton Nude* or *Double Nude Portrait: The Artist and His Second Wife* (1936), once considered too shocking to display in the Tate, are now part of its permanent exhibit. They are not the memorials to married love they may seem to be; rather they reflect the frustration and despair that resulted from the second Mrs. Spencer destroying the artist's first marriage, taking whatever money he had, and abandoning him on their honeymoon.

Turner, Joseph Mallord William (1775–1851), English

In his mature period Turner was painting works perhaps a hundred years ahead of his time. Though he was not unsuccessful during his lifetime, it has only been in the twentieth century that he has been fully appreciated. Part of his work was done in a fashionable style, and he accumulated a fortune and a very large personal collection of paintings. Turner was the son of a London barber who had a shop in Maiden Lane, and had no education except art lessons at the age of thirteen. He had his own studio at the age of eighteen, and at twenty-seven was made a member of the Royal Academy.

What makes Turner important in the history of art is that he produced paintings that represented the forces of nature—storms, rain, sunlight—and the forces of technology, such as steam and speed, that have no actual form. He could show the way these things look to us and the way we feel about them by changing them into pure color. He liberated color when it was considered improper, or too sensual. This release of color became a later phenomenon during the nineteenth century and led to modern art. But the greatness of Turner is not that he was an early impressionist, though the impressionists of the nineteenth century considered him their predecessor. He was more like our twentieth-century expressionists who use color to communicate.

Snow Storm (1842): room 9

In order to observe a storm at sea, Turner had sailors lash him to the mast of a ship for four hours during a fierce nighttime snowstorm off the coast of Harwich. He was sixty years old at the time, and said later that he was pessimistic about his survival. The result was a painting that depicts his most famous vortex scene. Turner had used the vortex in previous pictures as a symbol of humanity doomed to senseless life that ultimately sucked man into his fate. Yet *Snow Storm* is more than a pessimistic statement, as it expresses the force of a storm at sea. The natural forces his brush records on the canvas are a poetic expression of a reality—the way he felt the night he experienced this terrible storm.

Peace: Burial at Sea (1842): room 9

This picture was painted in commemoration of the death of Sir David Wilkie, Turner's fellow member of the Royal Academy, who died at sea on a return voyage from the Middle East, June 1, 1841. Turner was in his midsixties and had been a member of the Royal Academy for almost forty years. Wilkie was one of a number of Turner's fellow Academicians who had recently died; it seems the picture Turner painted was as much a mirror of his growing loneliness as it was the mourning of the death of a man.

It is a nocturne in dark and light. Under a rising moon emitting a cold white light, a dark, phantomlike ship, its black reflection on the water and its black smoke drifting into the night air—as if the soul of its victim were floating away—holds a funeral at sea, lighted by red torches that cut through the blackness. Design and composition seem to be secondary, while color, low-keyed as it is, is used to convey emotions and meaning. The suggestion of the white Rock of Gibraltar at the horizon is shown because Turner thought that Wilkie had been buried near there. Actually, he was buried off the coast of Malta.

Whistler, James McNeill (1834–1903), English/American

The Little White Girl ("Symphony in White No. 11"): room 17

Whistler was born in Lowell, Massachusetts, but spent most of his life in England. He was a free spirit and once claimed he had been born in Russia.

The girl dressed in white in this painting is Joanna Hefferman ("Jo"), for ten years his model, mistress, and housekeeper. Although she was voluptuous, as seen in the way Gustave Courbet, an early friend of Whistler's, painted her when Whistler first took her to Paris in 1861, she is shown here as a somewhat fragile beauty in the style of the Pre-Raphaelites by whom Whistler was influenced in the 1860s. The painting also shows Whistler's fascination with Oriental design in the Japanese fan Joanna holds, whose blue is carried over into the Chinese blue-and-white porcelain on the mantelpiece, and into the spray of blossoms at the right.

Wright of Derby, Joseph (1734–97), English

An Experiment on a Bird in the Air-pump (1768): room 5
When Reynolds and Gainsborough were painting portraits of the fashionable in London, the industrial revolution was underway in northern England and Scotland, and a provincial artist from Derby, Joseph Wright, was depicting it on canvas. It was a period of experiment and scientific inquiry, and the heroes of this new age were of the middle class. Wright's genre scenes depicted scientific investigation. He became known for his ability to portray candlelight, associated with study.

This painting, in a realistic style, is one of his best known, showing a family gathered around a table to view an experiment with an air pump. The result will be the death of the little girl's pet bird, but the father explains that it is in the interest of science. A scientist in the background has a determined stare and another man is in deep thought, wondering if experiments of this kind, and what they could lead to, will do good for mankind. The answer to the man's contemplation is still not clear, but on the basis of our experience of the past two hundred years we know that it led us to the moon, prophetically shown through the window.

Modern Foreign Painting at the Tate
Note: The Tate's collection of modern foreign paintings (rooms 27–48) is in a constant state of change. Only an indication of the most important artists and their works can be given.

The collection, the most comprehensive in Britain, begins with a display of impressionist and postimpressionist works. Paintings include Gauguin's *Faa Iheihe* from 1898, which means *Decoration* and is an allegory of life and death; Toulouse-Lautrec's *The Two Friends;* Degas's *Woman at her Toilet,* several Cézannes, including the *Gardener* and *The Avenue at the Jas de Bouffan;* the Nabis painters, Bonnard and Vuillard, with *Interior at Antibes, Bathing Woman from the Back,* and *Le Table,* by Bonnard, and *The Red Roof* and *Girl in an Interior,* by Vuillard, all early works; Utrillo's *La Porte St. Martin* from 1911, as well as a number of his other works; and Rouault's *Aunt Sallies,* an excellent example by this French expressionist whose art is mainly religious.

Matisse is represented by his *Arbre près de l'etang de Trivaux,* one of the landscapes he made in 1916 and 1917 around the little pond of Trivaux, his *Nude Study in Blue* (1900), *Standing Nude* (1907), *The Inattentive Reader* (1919), *Reading Woman with a Parasol* (1921), and a *Portrait of Andre Derain.* Derain is also represented with his *Portrait of Matisse* and his outstanding example of fauvism, *The Pool of London* (1906).

Some of Picasso's work from various phases is also in the Tate. The famous *Femme en Chemise* of 1905 is an early Blue Period painting. The *Seated Nude* of 1909 and *Guitar, Glass and Bottle* of 1912 are examples of his analytical cubism. His *Seated Woman* of 1923 is a striking example of the neoclassicism he produced between 1920 and 1924, but *The Three Dancers* (1925), *Seated Woman with a Hat, Dora Maas Seated,* and *Nude Woman in a Red Armchair* are rejections of this style. Georges Braque's still life of 1927, *Guitare et Pichet,* and Juan Girs's *The Sunblind* of 1914 are also here.

Outstanding examples of German expressionism are seen in Kirchner's *Bathers at Moritzburg* (1910–20), Schmidt-Rottluff's *Two Women* (1912) and Nolde's *The Sea B* (1930). Seen also are Munch's *Sick Child* (1907), one of a series he did based on the death of his sister, Permeke's *Harvest* (ca. 1924–25), an example of provincial Belgian expressionism, paintings by Kokoschka, including *Polperro, Cornwall* (1939), and the fascinating *Suicide* (1916) by George Grosz and *Carnival* (1920) by Max Beckmann, two German artists whose work is full of satirical ideas and symbols directed against middle-class values of twentieth-century materialism.

There are popular paintings by Marc Chagall, *The Poet Reclining* and *Bouquet with Flying Lovers;* the Italian futurist Giacomo Bella, *Abstract Speed—The Car Has Passed* (1913); and surrealists: Max Ernst's *Forest and Dove* (1927), Magritte's *Man with a Newspaper* (1928), and Paul Delvaux's *Venus Asleep* (1944).

Sculpture at the Tate
The Tate displays the greatest collection of modern sculpture in Britain and one of the finest collections in the world. The exhibition of sculpture is constantly changing. The following are some of the outstanding works that may be seen in the modern section of the museum (rooms 27–48): Rodin's *St. John the Baptist Preaching* (1879–80), *The Muse* (1896), *The Age of Bronze* (1875–77), and *Cybèle* (1904–5); Degas's *The Little Dancer Aged Fourteen* (1880–81); Renoir's *Venus Vietrix* (1914) and *La Laveuse* (1917–18); Maillol's *Torso of the Monument to Blanqui* (1905–6); Matisse's series of reliefs, of which *The Back I* (1910–12) is outstanding; Modigliani's *Head* (1913); Brancusi's *Study for Mlle Pogany* (1919–20); Picasso's *Le Coq* (1932); Marini's *Cavaliere* (1947); Giacometti's *Man Pointing* (1947); Manzu's *The Cardinal* (1947–48); and Butler's *Girl* (1953–54).

Of special interest are the sculptures of Jacob Epstein (1880–1959) and Henry Moore (1898–1986), both English artists (Epstein was born in New York of Russian/Polish parents but lived his life in England). Although Epstein's large-scale sculpture was at first not appreciated, often criticized for being deliberately brutal, his smaller works modeled in bronze won immediate acclaim. Of the smaller pieces, *Jacob Kramer,* the painter of Leeds, from 1921, is outstanding. Of the monumental bronzes *The Visitation* (1926) is one of his best.

Henry Moore gives a massive nobility to his figures. *Family Group* (1949) seems to be peopled from a prehistoric world—Moore's early work was influenced by the sculptures of ancient Mexico. Later in his career Moore was to pierce his swelling shapes with holes to emphasize the relationship between man and nature.

VICTORIA AND ALBERT MUSEUM

South Kensington, main entrance on Cromwell Road

Hours: Open Mon.–Thurs. and Sat., 10AM–5:50PM, Sun., 2:30–5:50PM. Free admission.

In 1851 a huge exhibition hall was built in Hyde park, the Crystal Palace, to show the world how art could apply to industry. When the exhibition ended the Crystal Palace was moved to Sydenham (a short distance away), but some objects were kept to begin a new museum in South Kensington that became the Victoria and Albert Museum. The spirit of confidence that built the Crystal Palace was transferred in part to the Victoria and Albert, so it seemed natural that it would come to hold one of the largest collections of art in the world. Inside the enormous neo-Renaissance exterior you will find a cornucopia of treasures. A printed floor plan is one of the best of its kind anywhere.

Here is a route you can follow to see some of the museum's greatest paintings and sculptures. Enter at the main entrance on the Cromwell Road. Get the plan of the museum at the information desk in front of you. Return to the main entrance and turn right, going down the steps to the **Continental Primary Collection 1600–1800** (blue section on your plan), to see the superb Jones Collection of eighteenth-century French painting, sculpture, and objets d'art. Its second room has a bust of *Voltaire* at eighty-four by **Houdon** (1741–1828), an example of Houdon's practice to sell replicas of the heads of his large statues; the museum's *Voltaire* is a copy from the head of a full-size statue that stands in the foyer of the Comedie Française in Paris. Across from him is Houdon's *Benjamin Franklin,* who was able to put into action in America what Voltaire was only able to write about. Further into the gallery you will find, in a glass case, the terra cotta group *Cupid and Psyche,* by **Claude Michel** (1738–1814), known as Clodion. This statue, with its soft and delicate modeling of the figures, is an excellent example of the slightly idealized eroticism in which this sculptor excelled, a technique that made him famous (and copied) until well into the nineteenth century. In the same room there is a painting of *Madame de Pompadour,* by **François Boucher** (1703–70), hanging over a commode veneered with panels of Japanese lacquer. Madame de Pompadour was the mistress to Louis XV and, to Boucher, one of the best patrons any artist ever had. Through her influence Boucher was appointed *Peintre du Roi* in 1765. This painting is one of eight known portraits that Boucher painted of his illustrious patron.

Return to the entrance level and proceed left to the **Gallery of the Raphael Cartoons** (green section on your plan).

Raphael* (1483–1520), Florentine, born in Umbria

Raphael Cartoons (series of seven): room 48
These tapestry cartoons (full-size working designs) painted on paper by Raphael, are part of a set of New Testament scenes (only seven of ten have

survived) commissioned by Pope Leo X in 1515 for tapestries planned for the Sistine Chapel in the Vatican. That they have survived is astonishing. When they were painted they were sent to a tapestry workshop in Brussels; there they would have been cut into strips for the weavers. In 1516–19 a set of tapestries—now in the Vatican Museum—was made from the cartoons by Pieter van Aelst of Brussels. Later, as unrivaled models of classic Renaissance composition and of excellence in drawing the figure in action, they were used for many other sets of tapestries until they became known in almost every country in Europe. In 1623 Prince Charles, later Charles I of England, purchased the cartoons in Genoa. Toward the end of the seventeenth century the strips of the cartoons were put together and treated as paintings. They hung at Hampton Court, in 1699, in frames designed by Wren; later they were hung in Buckingham Palace by George III in their present frames.

The sequence of subjects, which deal with the dynamic history of the early church, is as follows: *The Miraculous Draught of Fishes, Christ's Charge to St. Peter, The Healing of the Lame Man by St. Peter and St. John at the Beautiful Gate,* and *The Death of Ananias.* These four are on one wall. On the opposite wall are scenes from the life of St. Paul: *The Blinding of Elymas, The Sacrifice of Lystra,* and *St. Paul Preaching at Athens.* Raphael has chosen the climactic point of action in each scene and exploits it fully to illustrate the power of the Apostles and the glory of the church. In *The Miraculous Draught of Fishes,* where Christ has told Peter and his companions to lower their nets and, to their astonishment, the nets come up full of fish, the moment illustrated is Christ saying to Peter, kneeling before him, with Andrew, his hands outspread in amazement, behind him, "from now on you will be catching men." In *Christ's Charge to St. Peter,* a cartoon that is less sophisticated than the others, and may have been prepared as early as 1512—there is a conflict between the tightly composed group of figures and the vast expanse of landscape in which they are placed—Christ is saying, "You are Peter, the Rock; and on this rock I will build my church. . . . I will give you the keys to the Kingdom of Heaven." This episode was regarded by the church as the prototype of the sacrament of Holy Orders. The moment of depiction in *The Healing of the Lame Man by St. Peter and St. Paul at the Beautiful Gate* is the point at which St. Peter fastens his eyes on the lame beggar and takes his arm, which had been outstretched for alms, lifting him to his feet, and in the *Death of Ananias,* St. Peter has already given Ananias a tongue lashing for keeping for himself half of the money for the poor, and Ananias falls dying to the ground.

On the opposite wall, *The Blinding of Elymas* is shown as St. Paul strikes blind the sorceror of the Roman governor's court for trying to prevent him and Barnabas from speaking. In *The Sacrifice at Lystra,* where Raphael shows us the main elements of the narrative compressed on a single stage, we see, on the left, St. Paul in rent cloths in the act of healing a cripple and preparing to go down among the pagan populace who, believing he and Barnabas are Mercury (whose statue we see in the distance) and Jupiter, are preparing to make a sacrifice of an ox. Finally, in *St. Paul Preaching at Athens,* the intensity of the dramatization is seen in the rapt attention of the

Athenians. From a spatial point of view this cartoon is the most impressive. The foreground is cut off and the eye is led diagonally across the platform by the raised hands of Denis the Areopagite to the standing St. Paul, and diagonally across the middle ground by the raised arms of St. Paul. In the background we see a statue of Mars in front of a pagan temple on Mars's hill (in Greek: Areopagus).

The cartoons are also admired for their landscapes and architectural settings. In *Christ's Charge to St. Peter* we see a typical Italian hill town ablaze beside the sea of Galilee, and in *The Miraculous Draught of Fishes* not only are we treated to another hill town by the Sea of Galilee, but also still lifes of fish in the boats, and the birds in the water and over the lake. The cartoons bring the development of landscape painting a step closer to when it becomes an independent art in the seventeenth century.

The architectural elements in the cartoons are no less interesting. Notice the detail that Raphael paints into the streets of Lystra and Athens; and the columns in *The Healing of the Lame Man at the Beautiful Gate* are similar to those in St. Peter's in Rome, thought during Raphael's time to be columns from the Temple of Jerusalem. In the next century Bernini used the same models for the canopy over the high altar in St. Peter's basilica. Before leaving room 48 see **Neptune and a Triton,** by **Bernini** (1598–1680), which had a profound influence on baroque sculpture throughout Europe.

Leaving room 48, walk back to the area of the information desk and proceed, to your left, down the steps into **room 43** to see the **Soissons Diptych.** This late thirteenth-century French ivory diptych, formerly in the Cathedral Treasury of Soissons, typifies the Gothic style: an increased realism, a flowering line, delicate and elegant extension, and a tendency to view the world in microcosm.

Now proceed counterclockwise around the garden. **Room 16** has a marble bust of the famous doctor of medicine, *Giovanni di Antonio Chellini,* by **Antonio Rossellino** (1427–79), which, though 322 years earlier than the Houdon *Voltaire,* also shows a smiling sitter at the age of eighty-four. Donatello, Chellini's patient, gave him the beautiful bronze roundel seen close by, *Virgin and Child with four Angels,* known today as the **Chellini tondo.** Other pieces by **Donatello** (1386–1466) here are the bronze relief, *The Lamentation over the Dead Christ,* and the marble relief, *The Dead Christ tended by Angels,* both with the great depth of feeling that is characteristic of Donatello's work. Another marble relief, *The Ascension,* is one of Donatello's finest reliefs, showing Christ giving the keys to St. Peter. It is a practically colorless painting. It exemplifies the narrative genius of Donatello, which made him one of the greatest Italian sculptors of the fifteenth century.

Continue around the garden through the corridor of rooms devoted to the Italian Renaissance where you will see fine examples of sculpture in wood, bronze, terracotta, and marble, and exquisite objets d'art. In **room 14** there are enameled terracotta sculptures from the Della Robbia family of Florence, a fine *Meleager* made for the Gonzaga court by Antico (ca. 1460–1528) in **room 12,** and, in **room 18,** one of the most appealing little statues in the museum, *The Virgin with the Laughing Child.* It was probably designed as a sketch-model for a marble sculpture—the one you see here is a terracotta piece—and it was long attributed to Leonardo da Vinci, but it seems to be the work of the much-admired Florentine **Antonio Rosselino** (1427–79). It is one of the most memorable representations of the Virgin and Child to be seen anywhere in Europe.

Turn the corner into **room 21.** Here is the large marble group *Samson Slaying a Philistine* commissioned by Francesco de' Medici (1565–68) from the popular mannerist sculptor **Giovanni Bologna** (1529–1608). It is an excellent example of the artist's preoccupation with movement in sculpture and the only one of its kind that can be seen outside of Florence.

Now you are ready to visit the V&A's new **Henry Cole Wing** (pink section on your plan). It is easily reached from room 21 by going down the stairs in front of you, turning right, and straight ahead to the entrance and elevators that take you to six levels containing prints, photographs, watercolors, European old master paintings (1700–1900), and British paintings (1700–1900), most notable of which is the greatest collection of **John Constable** (1776–1837) oil sketches on **level 6.**

These sketches, which today we would call finished paintings, loom large in the history of European landscape painting and were a direct influence on nineteenth-century French impressionism. Working outdoors, usually in his native Suffolk countryside, Constable painted directly from nature. Even though he would later make a "finished" version of the painting in his studio for the public, the sketches are among Constable's most important works of art. You can see, on one wall, his *Salisbury Cathedral from the Bishop's Grounds* (1823) with its scattering of white dots over the canvas, called "Constable snow," to achieve a granular effect that depicted the shimmer of light upon things, just as the impressionists would later do, and the *Full-scale Study for "The Leaping Horse,"* made for the painting of 1825 that today hangs in the Royal Academy, showing Constable at the height of his powers and more dynamic in composition than his famous **Hay Wain** sketch next to it. These sketches, and many more like them in this great collection, are Constable's true originals and what he called "my own pictures." Actually, his finished pictures are the copies he made for the public.

THE WALLACE COLLECTION

Hertford House, Manchester Square

Hours: Open Mon.–Sat., 10AM–5PM, Sun., 2–5PM. Free admission.

The museum at Hertford House is an expression of the connoisseurship in which the British excelled during the nineteenth century. The quality of its art objects is outstanding, and its surroundings in an eighteenth-century mansion in the heart of London make it a pleasure to visit.

The collection was largely put together between 1800 and 1890 by the third marquess of Hertford (considered to have been the original for Thack-

eray's *Vanity Fair*), and the fourth marquess, with his illegitimate son, Sir
Richard Wallace (1818–90). It was bequeathed to the nation by Lady Wallace in 1897, according to the wishes of her late husband. Hertford House
was purchased by the government to ensure the collection would remain in
its original setting, and it was opened to the public in 1900.

While the art treasures at Hertford House include furniture, china, bric-
a-brac, sculpture, and armor, it is best known for its excellent collection of
paintings, especially those of the eighteenth-century French school—the
strongest collection in London.

Room 1, on the ground floor, has a famous portrait of the *Countess of
Blessington,* by **Sir Thomas Lawrence** (1769–1830), one of the leading portraitists of eighteenth-century England and successor to the American Benjamin West as president of the Royal Academy. Countess Blessington, an Irish
woman born in 1789, was well known during her day as an author, a great
beauty, and a lady of society who gave extravagant parties at her London
home. She had been married in Ireland at an early age, but left her husband
because of his brutality and later became the mistress to an English army
officer. After the death of her husband she married the earl of Blessington,
who paid her lover £10,000 for the loss of his paramour. After the death of
the earl, she became the lifelong companion to Count Gabriel d'Orsay,
whom she had met in Paris in 1822, probably the year Lawrence painted her
portrait and the year she made her debut as an author. The following year
she met Lord Byron at Genoa and had a great success with her *Journal of
Conversations with Lord Byron*. She wrote numerous novels in the 1830s
and 1840s that were widely read. She died in Paris in 1849, bankrupt in spite
of the substantial income earned from her literary career.

The remaining rooms on the ground floor stress objets d'art and armor.
In **room 2** there are paintings by Murillo and Rubens, and a striking *River
Scene with a View of Dordrecht* (ca. 1647) by Cuyp; **room 3** has a bronze
bust by Germain Pilon (1530–90), of *Charles IX of France,* the weak king
whose reign was filled with religious civil war between Catholics and Hu-
guenots (French Calvinists); and **room 10** has paintings by Richard Bonington (1802–28), the English painter who spent the greater part of his short
working life in France, where he may have been as influential as Constable
in introducing the English landscape technique into French romantic painting. He exhibited in the same now-famous salon that contained Constable's
Hay Wain and Delacroix's *Massacre at Chios*.

The greatest treasures of the Wallace Collection are located on the first
floor, which is reached by ascending the **grand staircase,** itself a work of art.
Its wrought iron and bronze **balustrade** (1733–41) was made for the stairs
leading to Louis XV's library in the old Palais Mazarin, now the Bibliothèque nationale in Paris. Sold as scrap in the mid-nineteenth century, it is
now thought to be the finest example of French metalwork of the period to
have survived. Surrounding the staircase are paintings by **François Boucher**
(1703–70), who exemplifies the rococo of the Ancien Régime in France. The
powdered pinks and blues, and compositions with swirling movement, are

typical of his work and show the rococo to be a development of the baroque, but in a lighter vein.

Room 13 has a display of Venetian scenes by **Canaletto** (1697–1768) and **Francesco Guardi** (1712–93), artists who specialized in cityscapes of Venice and were popular with the British aristocracy who took the Grand Tour of the Continent in the eighteenth century. They bought Canalettos and Guardis as souvenirs—as we would buy picture postcards today. Both artists are distinguished by their careful observation of architecture and use of alternating shadows and glittering surfaces to give a realistic view of Venice with a romantic spirit, admired by tourists. In Guardi's *San Giorgio Maggiore* the angular buildings are reflected in the lagoon beneath pink clouds, and the colors of the water and the boats add to the dreaminess of the lagoon and convey a much-admired rococo view of Venice.

Room 14 has more paintings by Canaletto. Then there is seventeenth-century Flemish and Dutch art in rooms 15–18: room 15 has a group of oil sketches by Rubens and a Rembrandt self-portrait. **Room 16** has an early Rembrandt, *The Good Samaritan* (1630), and interior domestic scenes by Nicolas Maes, Pieter de Hoogh, Metsu, and Steen's splendid *Harpsichord Lesson* (1660s). **Room 17** is devoted to Dutch landscapes and seascapes, the finest of which are Hobbema's *Watermill*, Wouwermans's *Horse Fair*, and seven seascapes by **Willem van de Velde the Younger,** who lived for a time in Greenwich as court painter to King Charles II. As one of the great draftsmen of Holland, he drew every detail with precision for art-loving collectors interested in the sea and ships, which played an important role in the history and everyday life of Britain. **Room 18** has Dutch art influenced by the Italianite taste of the Utrecht School. The most notable of these are the paintings of Aelbert Cuyp, whose *Avenue at Meerdervoort,* which shows Dordrecht in the distance, is a fine example of this style.

Room 19, the largest room at Hertford House, was built by Wallace (1872–73) over the former coach house and stables to house what he considered his finest paintings. Here is *Perseus and Andromeda,* by **Titian** (ca. 1487–1576), painted in 1554 for Philip II of Spain, one of seven paintings Titian did on themes from the works of Ovid. In this one we see Andromeda chained to a rock as a sacrifice to a seamonster. Perseus, flying overhead, falls in love with her and, with sword in hand, comes to her rescue by slaying the monster.

The **Poussin** (1594–1665), *Dance to the Music of Time* (ca. 1639–40), was done at the height of Poussin's fame, just before he left Rome for France at the invitation of Richelieu. The figures represent (left to right): Pleasure, Poverty, Riches, and Work, bounded by the limits of life. On the left is past and future; in the sky Aurora leads Helios, the sun god, into the heavens.

The two magnificent portraits by **van Dyck** (1599–1641), *Philippe le Roy* and his wife *Marie de Raet,* were painted in Antwerp just before van Dyck settled in England in 1632. They are splendid examples of his delicate color and faithful rendering of facial expressions. It is this talent that earned him the position of chief painter to Charles I of England. The *Rainbow*

Landscape was painted by **Rubens** (1577–1640) about 1636 in his late years when the countryside around his house, Het Steen, which he had little time to enjoy during his busy life, took on greater meaning. It is a companion piece to his *Castle of Steen* in the National Gallery.

The *Lady with a Fan,* by Velázquez (1599–1660), shows one of the painter's few sitters who was not a member of the court, thought by some to be a member of his family. Its date is also a mystery; it may be from 1632–35, 1638–39, 1648, or later. It also has a mysterious red dot of paint below the white bow of the dress.

The five English portraits are by Reynolds, Gainsborough, Lawrence, and Romney. *Nelly O'Brien* (ca. 1763), by **Reynolds** (1723–92), is a portrait of the celebrated courtesan, and **Mrs. Robinson** is painted by Reynolds, Gainsborough, and Romney (three portraits). Mary Robinson was a famous actress whom the Prince of Wales (later George IV) saw playing the role of Perdita in Garrick's production of Shakespeare's *Winter's Tale.* She became one of the early mistresses of the prince who maintained her in luxury for three years. The portrait by **Gainsborough** (1727–88) was done for the Prince of Wales in 1781 during the height of his romance with Mary Robinson, when he was only nineteen.

There are two superb Dutch portraits in the gallery. One by **Rembrandt** (1606–69) is of his son *Titus* painted around 1656 at the age of sixteen; he died in 1668 at twenty-eight. The masterful play of light on the boy's wonderful hat, half of his face, and slightly over his right shoulder, is part of the effect of chiaroscuro that makes this painting extraordinary. The second portrait, *The Laughing Cavalier* (1624) by **Frans Hals** (1580–1666), is easily the most famous painting in the Wallace Collection. It was misnamed in the nineteenth century; the man (we know he is twenty-six from the inscription in the upper right corner) has more of a suppressed smile than a laugh. The detail of the embroidered sleeve, with bees, winged arrows, flames, and flaming cornucopias, may be related to an amorous emblem giving us the clue that the man's smile expresses self-satisfaction.

Room 20 has a collection of French nineteenth-century paintings from 1820–60, such as would have been seen in the official annual salons in which the academies wielded tremendous power. While few of these works are new and original for their time, many are not mere "machine," as they were called by the irreverent artists of the period. *An Artist Showing His Work,* by Meissonier (1815–91), is of interest, and *Venus and Adonis,* by Prud'hon (1758–1823), a work of cool eroticism with a seductive light that typifies Prud'hon's use of soft chiaroscuro, is a fine example of the work that earned him the reputation as "the French Correggio."

From **room 21** through 25 there is the finest collection of French eighteenth-century paintings and furniture to be seen anywhere in Britain. The art of Watteau, Boucher, and Fragonard are well represented here with work that epitomizes the revolt of the new age against the formality and heaviness of the long reign of Louis XIV, who died in 1715.

This new, less pretentious, age moved out of the Hall of Mirrors into the salons and boudoirs of some of the most engaging and powerful women ever to take their place in European society. They set a standard of manners and morals that catered to enlightened people of wealth and position who craved freedom and license in life—as well as in art—and to a great extent achieved them. This new pleasure-seeking age was able to set aside the rules and order of the seventeenth century and lead a more enlightened life based on a delicate balance of sensibilities and good taste.

In painting, the art of the new age is best expressed by the fêtes galantes of **Antoine Watteau** (1684–1721), as seen in *Les Champs Elysées* (ca. 1718) and *A Halt during the Chase* (1720), **room 21**. The *fêtes galantes*—loosely translated into English as "gay parties" based upon ritualistic courtly love— was a dreamworld of Watteau's poetic imagination. They usually take place out of doors in a parklike setting. There may be some pretty children and some animals, sometimes music is being played, as in *The Music Party* (ca. 1716), **room 21**, but the main characters are always ladies and gentlemen dressed in gay costumes that sparkle like jewels with flashes of green, blue, yellow, and lavender in place of the somber browns of the previous age.

After Watteau's early death, **Boucher** (1703–70) became the heir to the rococo. As the favorite painter of Madame de Pompadour, who was the favorite mistress of Louis XV—her portrait by Boucher is in **room 22**—he painted idyllic landscapes and playful mythologies that have the softness of the boudoir for which they were meant.

By the second half of the century a reaction had already set in against excessive artificiality and fashionable charm. **Jean Honoré Fragonard** (1732– 1806) who could, and did, paint any subject with technical and poetic virtuosity—fêtes galantes, scenes of family life, landscapes, pastorals, religious scenes—seemed to prolong the spirit of the rococo. Before the condemnation of the Revolution finished him as an artist and cut his pension by two thirds, he earned a good living catering to the amorous whims of his clients and produced a number of masterpieces. Such is *The Swing* (1766) in **room 21**. It was ordered by a lovesick young nobleman who wanted a painting of his mistress soaring high on a swing pushed by a bishop while he lay at her feet swooning at the spectacle of her flying skirts. But Fragonard's swift brush, fresh color, and artistic technique raises a trivial theme into a painting of distinction. The motion of the swing and the flight of the pink slipper, which the young woman kicks off, is the summation of Fragonard's life and style, and of an age of pleasure that finally was brought down from the heights by the Revolution.

THE WELLINGTON MUSEUM

Apsley House, Hyde Park Corner

Hours: Open Mon.–Sat., 10PM–6PM, Sun., 2:30–6PM. Free admission.

The original house on this site was built by Robert Adam for Baron Apsley, hence its name, Apsley House, but the house here now was reconstructed for the first duke of Wellington in 1828 by the architect Benjamin Wyatt. It was given to the nation by the Wellington family in 1947 and opened to the public in 1952.

While a good part of its collection is devoted to paintings of Wellington's military and public career, there is also a collection of old master paintings, many of which are outstanding. Some 160 paintings of the collection had been captured by the duke from Joseph Bonaparte's carriage when he was fleeing after the Battle of Vittoria in 1813 during the Peninsula War. Though Wellington offered to return these to the king of Spain the latter insisted that he keep them as honorable spoils of war.

At the **entrance hall,** above the sales counter, see the painting *His Last Return from Duty* (1853), by James W. Glass (1825–57), a touching picture of the duke on his brown horse leaving Whitehall for the last time as commander in chief. The two old-age pensioners who, no doubt, have fought under the duke in his great military campaigns, salute him with the left hand (the practice of saluting on the opposite side of an approaching officer was ended in 1918).

The **staircase vestibule** is dominated by the larger-than-life marble nude statue of *Napoleon,* by Canova (1757–1822). Canova had made a plaster bust of Napoleon and used an antique nude figure in the Uffizi Gallery in Florence. He completed the statue in 1811 and set it up in the Louvre, but Napoleon disliked it and it was stored until 1816 when the British government bought it and presented it to the duke of Wellington, Napoleon's rival, who had defeated him only one year earlier. The winged figure of Victory, standing on a globe held by Napoleon, seems as if it has flown from Napoleon to the duke.

Ascend the staircase to the **Piccadilly Drawing Room** (first room to the left). Here are some fine seventeenth-century paintings: *Judith Slaying Holofernes* (ca. 1603) by **Adam Elsheimer** (1578–1610), the German painter who lived in Rome and experimented with Caravaggesque lighting effects. He was particularly good at painting night scenes where the lighting comes from a single source, like this one where a large candle lights up the murder scene. Elsheimer's influence on the development of chiaroscuro was great. Claude Lorraine and certain Italian artists learned from him, as well as Rembrandt in Holland and the German romantics in the nineteenth century; *The Milkwoman* and *The Eavesdropper,* by Nicolaes Maes (1634–93), one of the painters who studied with Rembrandt. He is a master of these quiet domestic scenes, but seems never to have learned Rembrandt's subtle use of color or deep sense of humanity for his subjects; *A Musical Party* (ca. 1675), by **Pieter de Hooch** (1629–ca. 1683), shows that this artist could populate his interiors with people but care more about the setting. Notice the open window giving out onto a forestlike park. It is typical of de Hooch to combine interiors with outdoor spaces. What seems to be a gathering of perfect ladies and gentlemen may be participants in a house of ill repute; *The Smokers* (ca. 1635–38) is by **Adriaen Brouwer** (1605–38), the Flemish painter of small works limited to a few subjects, who painted smokers a number of times (the smoke probably symbolizes the transitory nature of human life). There is also a number of superb paintings by Steen, the master of the genre scene.

Steen, Jan* (1626–79), Dutch

The Physician's Visit: Piccadilly Drawing Room
Another title for this painting is *The Lovesick Maiden.* Typically, Steen provides clues to the nature of the maiden's ailment; which is explained by the
painting on the wall of Venus and Adonis—Cupid's arrow made Venus fall
helplessly in love with Adonis, who left her to hunt wild boar despite her
pleading with him not to go. The child playing with arrows on the floor is
the maiden's Cupid, and from the look on his face we can see he has done
his work. The dog symbolizes animal nature. Other items in the room contain sexual imagery, such as the canopied bed and candlestick in the background.

The Dissolute Household: Waterloo Gallery
This is a scene Steen loved to depict. Like *The Physician's Visit* he painted
it many times and like that picture it may be called by another name, *The
Five Senses.* All of the senses are displayed among three generations of a family and their pets. Steen himself is seen smoking a long clay pipe, which may
refer to the sense of smell. The glass of wine being offered to him by the girl,
who does not mind his leg resting on her thigh, refers to taste, as does the
food on the table. Touch is expressed by the mischievous monkey and dog,
and the child picking the pocket of the sleeping woman. For hearing there is
the man playing a violin and a clock with a bell ringer. The neighbor peering
out of the window in the adjacent house, like the flames in the fireplace and
the picture on the wall, is an allusion to sight. Steen is telling us that giving
oneself wholly to the senses results in a dissolute household, symbolized especially by the objects strewn on the floor: playing cards, a scoreboard, and
oyster shells—all symbolizing vices.

The other two paintings by Steen in the **Waterloo Gallery, A Wedding
Party** and *The Egg Dance,* are equally as fine. Displayed here also are paintings by **Velázquez** (1599–1660), outstanding of which is *The Waterseller* (ca.
1619), painted by Velázquez in his youth when he was still in Seville. His
instinct for optical realism, which in this still life with people shows us every
detail down to the drops of water on the water-seller's jugs, remained one
of his lifelong strengths as an artist. Finally, there is *The Agony in the Garden* (ca. 1525), a jewel of a painting by **Correggio** (ca. 1489/94–1534), the
northern Italian painter who carries the influence of Leonardo further into
the sixteenth century. We see Christ on the Mount of Olives—after the Last
Supper, before the Crucifixion—struggling with his two natures: the human
that feared torture and death, and the divine, aided by the angel, that gave
him strength. Correggio's delicacy of color and dazzling radiance of light
makes the mystery of the scene convincing.

Buildings

London is one of the oldest cities in Europe but compared to Rome or Paris
has fewer buildings of great architectural importance. With a few exceptions,
its prominent buildings are more valued historically than architecturally—

Buckingham Palace, for example, where John Nash was called upon, in 1825, to transform old Buckingham House into a palace suitable for a royal residence. His design was never carried out; the king died and the patronage was taken away from Nash. The building that finally resulted was not satisfactory and was rebuilt in 1913.

A pleasing architectural characteristic of London is the square. Squares originated with Covent Garden (1630) in the reign of Charles I. Many of London's other squares are almost as old, even those in Mayfair, but fine houses were not built around them until the eighteenth century by Georgian architects. Hanover Square (1720) has a few remaining original houses on its west side, as does Berkeley Square (1730s). Unfortunately almost nothing of the original architecture remains in Grosvenor Square (1725). These squares, and others, have trees and lawns, which are a refreshing sight in a city as crowded as London.

HOUSES OF PARLIAMENT

Entrance: Old Palace Yard

Hours for Houses of Parliament and Westminster Hall: Open Sat. 10AM–5PM and at various other times provided neither house is sitting.

The Houses of Parliament, with Westminster Hall, St. Stephen's Hall and Chapel, and adjoining courtyards and offices make up Westminster Palace. The entire complex, with the exception of Westminster Hall and the crypt of St. Stephen's Chapel, are nineteenth-century (1836–88) neo-Gothic buildings but, unlike many other Gothic revival constructions of the period, they are designs worthy of the "mother of parliaments."

Before the nineteenth-century construction there had always been the Palace of Westminster, a royal residence until Henry VIII seized Whitehall in 1529. Thereafter the House of Commons sat at the palace from 1547 until it burned in 1834. New construction was ordered in the Gothic style because of the proximity of Westminster Abbey. **Sir Charles Barry** (1795–1860) won the competition for the work, which was completed after his death by his son. In 1852 Parliament began sitting in the new building and continued to do so until 1941, when German bombs destroyed the House of Commons. Reconstruction of it was completed in 1950.

Of the three towers in this complex the largest is **Victoria Tower**, rising 336 feet. It is a fine example of the Perpendicular Gothic character of the building and has intricate carvings and four octagonal corner turrets that rise to the height of the tower. The **Clock Tower**, 320-feet high, is best known because it houses Big Ben. The **Central Tower**, capped by a lantern, rises 300 feet above the central hall of the building, which is octagonal in plan and has a lofty vault decorated by over 200 bosses.

Westminster Hall, constructed in the last years of the fourteenth century, the finest sight at Westminster, is where the high courts of England sat from the latter half of the thirteenth century until 1825. Sir Thomas More,

Guy Fawkes, and Charles II were tried in it, and after the Restoration the exhumed head of Oliver Cromwell was placed on the roof and remained there for twenty-three years. The hall is architecturally outstanding for its hammerbeam roof, which extends over twelve bays, each about twenty feet in span. (Westminster Hall is permanantly closed to the public, but you can see a part of it if you visit the Stranger's Gallery when the House of Commons is sitting.)

ST. PAUL'S CATHEDRAL

St. Paul's Church Yard

Hours: Open daily 8AM–6PM (to 5PM in winter). Crypt and galleries open Mon.–Fri., 11AM–4:15PM (to 3:15 in winter). Guided tours Mon.–Sat., 11AM and 2PM. Admission fee for tours and to some areas.

This is the building most closely associated with the career of **Sir Christopher Wren** (1632–1723). He was a man of genius—a mathematician, astronomer, inventor—but he changed careers in mid-stream to become England's most brilliant and prolific architect, rebuilding much of the city of London after the great fire of 1666 and, with it, St. Paul's Cathedral.

The cathedral had deteriorated over the centuries and had been propped up previously by Inigo Jones, but the great fire took such a toll that it was decided to raze the ancient structure and to start anew. Though Wren could not get the church commissioners to approve anything but a Gothic layout, he built a classical design. Only the two bell towers at the west end and the semicircular bays that protrude from the facade of the transept arm are in the baroque style. Its distinctive external silhouette is the result of its huge **cupola,** a synthesis of the ideas of Bramante and Michelangelo, made up of an inner and an outer dome so as to lower the inner part of the dome to harmonize with the inner vaults. It rises from a rotunda of pillars until it culminates in a little pillared lantern, golden ball, and cross. Its decorated colonnade around the drum is thought to be more than Wren wished. He probably would have preferred a simple row of gigantic columns clear to the pediment.

The **interior** of the cathedral is light and airy, owing to the replacement of the old stained glass windows with clear glass after they were blown out by a bomb in 1941. The finest craftsmen worked on St. Paul's during its thirty-five years of construction (1675–1710). Decoration includes frescoes by Thornhill on the inner surface of the dome (again against Wren's wishes), woodcarvings by Gibbons, and ironwork by Tijon. In 1958, in the Jesus Chapel, directly behind the high altar, a memorial was installed for the 28,000 American servicemen who were killed while based on British soil. A high altar of marble with a wood canopy of oak was also installed in memory of over 300,000 Commonwealth citizens who lost their lives in both world wars. It replaced the original reredos destroyed in 1941. The **crypt** is the largest in Europe and holds the tombs of many of Britain's great personages, including, appropiately enough, Sir Christopher Wren.

A flight of 143 steps leads up to the galleries that contain Wren's plans for St. Paul's. Another 116 steps lead up to the Whispering Gallery, which runs round the dome. Its extraordinary acoustics enable you to hear a whisper across the other side of the dome as though it was spoken next to you. The view upward is of the Pauline frescoes of James Thornhill. Another 117 steps lead up to the Stone Gallery round the outside of the dome, and 166 more steps lead to the Golden Gallery. Both offer unforgettable views of London.

St. Paul's is England's great monument to classic design, London's famous landmark, and perhaps Wren's greatest single achievement. It may lack the splendor of the Italian baroque or the religious sense of the Gothic, but a building possessing a dome to rival the dome of St. Peter's in Rome is one of the great architectural achievements of all time.

THE TOWER OF LONDON

Tower Hill

Hours: Open Mar.–Oct., Mon.–Sat., 9:30AM–5PM, Sun., 2–5PM; Nov.–Feb., Mon.–Sat., 9:30AM–4PM. Admission fee.

The colorful and bloody history of the Tower of London, site of the crown jewels, usually takes precedence over its architecture, but the fortress-palace known as the **White Tower,** whose construction was begun by William the Conqueror in 1070 and completed in 1097, is a fine example of the "hall-keep" English castle that may owe its design to the fortified palaces of late-Carolingian northern France. That it was a palace as well as a castle can be seen in its **St. John's Chapel** on the third floor, the oldest church in London. A superb example of early Norman architecture, it remains in near-perfect condition, with its nave, narrow aisles, and ambulatory encircling the apsidal end. Here the royal family conducted religious services undisturbed by the rest of the palace. The Tower is built of Kentish rag stone and at one time was whitewashed. While it appears square it is of an irregular shape with fifteen-foot walls, ninety feet high. When built it was not only as a royal residence and fort but also as a proof to the people that William was there to stay.

WESTMINSTER ABBEY

Broad Sanctuary

Hours: Open Mon.–Fri., 9AM–4:45PM, Sat., 9AM–2PM and 3:45–5:45PM. Admission fee to Royal Chapels, except Wed., 6–8PM, when there is free admission and photography allowed.

This great church occupies a site where the Saxons maintained an abbey. That structure was enlarged in the days of Edward the Confessor (d. 1066), and when William the Conqueror chose it for the scene of his coronation, in 1066, it and its successor became the place where every British monarch has been crowned, except Edward V (1470–83) and Edward VIII who was king in 1936 but abdicated. The church here now was started by Henry III (1207–72) in 1245. Subsequent building and rebuilding maintained its original early English Gothic style, which, in the height of its vault and chevet, the arrangement of its radiating chapels, the use of bar window-tracery, which removes the appearance of solid stone in the window area, and its lavish decorations, such as the naturalistic foliage carving, shows a French influence, probably from the cathedrals of Reims and Amiens. The two baroque towers that flank the main entrance were done by Hawksmoor in 1739.

The abbey is cluttered with tombs, monuments, and cenotaphs of little artistic value but of historic interest. Of architectural interest is the **Henry VII Chapel** (1503–19) at the east end of the abbey. It replaced the former lady chapel and is like a separate church. Its nave has aisles at each side and there are radiating chapels all around its apsidal east end. The elaborate fan vaults are great feats of engineering.

Next to the church are **cloisters** that date back to the thirteenth and fourteenth centuries, and a thirteenth-century **chapter house**, octagonal with a fan vault ceiling supported by a single central pier. It shows the enthusiasm the Westminster masons had for French bar window-tracery. The chapter house windows are far more expansive than those in the church. They give the appearance of a space almost entirely surrounded by glass threaded together with stone tracery. The House of Commons sat here until 1547 when it moved into Westminster Palace.

WHITEHALL PALACE, THE BANQUETING HOUSE

Whitehall

Hours: Open Tues.–Sat., 10AM–5PM, Sun., 2–5PM. Admission fee.

The original Whitehall Palace, expanded and embellished by Cardinal Wolsey and seized by Henry VIII, was destroyed by fire in 1698. Only the **Banqueting House**, built by **Inigo Jones** (1573–1652) in 1619–22 to replace an earlier structure that had also burnt down, remains. It is considered to be the finest work of Inigo Jones in the Palladian style and remains much as Jones left it. The exterior facade has two orders, the lower in Ionic and the upper in Corinthian, with a balustrade crowning the top of the building. It may have influenced Wren in his design of St. Paul's cathedral.

Inside, the **Double Cube Hall**, designed as a banquet hall, is 110 feet in length, 55 feet wide, and 55 feet in height. Its notable feature is the ceiling painting, *The Apotheosis of James I,* by **Rubens** (1577–1640). Its nine panels are best viewed from the south end of the hall (at the throne). There is an argument whether they have been placed the way Rubens intended. He received the commission to paint them in 1629 from Charles I when visiting London as a painter-diplomat for the court of Spain. He then painted them in Antwerp and sent them to England for installation. They do not belong to Rubens's greatest works, but in England they are one of the finest ceiling paintings in the country.

London Environs

DULWICH COLLEGE PICTURE GALLERY

Dulwich, College Road, S.E. 21

Hours: Open Tues.–Sat., 10AM–5PM., Sun., 2–5PM. Admission fee.

This pleasant museum, in a south-eastern suburb of London, forms part of Alleyn's College of God's Gift, founded by the actor Edward Alleyn in 1619. Alleyn left the school twenty-eight pictures, none of inspiring value; later donors gave the masterpieces we now see here.

Room 1 contains nineteenth-century English family portraits, some by Gainsborough. The best of the English school of portraiture, however, is in **room 2**, *Mrs. Siddons as the Tragic Muse,* by **Reynolds** (1723–92). It was a famous painting during its time because the subject, England's leading actress for thirty years, earned fame and fortune for her portrayal of Lady Macbeth. The painting of her in the gallery is a replica Reynolds did in 1789 of the original portrait now in the United States.

Another English lady, *Venetia Stanley,* who lived 100 years earlier than Mrs. Siddons, is portrayed on her deathbed by **Sir Anthony van Dyck** (1599–1641) in **room 3**. She was the much-loved wife of Sir Kenelm Digby, the author, diplomat, and naval commander. Van Dyck has used the more refined lighter colors of his last period to show her as she lay two days after her premature death in 1633. Only the red rose of Venus is an addition to the scene to symbolize Lady Digby's beauty in life and, in reference to the pricking of its thorns, the wounds of love suffered by her husband.

The museum is rich in paintings by **Murillo** (1618–82), the Spanish painter from Seville who was famous for his religious scenes. Today his genre paintings, depicting street people of Andalusia, are considered his finest work. Compare the realism and tender poetry of his *Flower Girl* in **room III,** one of the best Murillos in the Dulwich, and his *Two Peasant Boys* and *Two Peasant Boys and a Negro Boy* in **room 5,** with the overdone religious sentiment of his *Madonna of the Rosary* in **room 4.**

Poussin, Nicolas* (1594–1665), French

Triumph of David: room 4
This painting is an example of Poussin's early style, painted in two stages (before 1628 and after 1631); there is a marked difference in style between the center group of women and children and the group of women on the left. Though the subject is from the Bible, Poussin, a classicist living in Rome, seems more concerned with showing us a procession of happy people celebrating a great event, similar to those he saw on classical sarcophagi. Poussin gets our attention with the fragment of pilaster in the lower left foreground and then directs our eye diagonally first to the severed head of Goliath, as pained and as human as any ever painted, and then to a group of shadowy figures in the right background, one of whom may be Saul. King Saul was jealous of David's youth and military success and eventually tried to kill him. The fragment of pilaster, so simple, so injured, so immobile, has the quality of affecting the mood of celebration with a sense of something fearful and foreboding. And, if we see David's triumphal entry into Jerusalem as a prefiguration of Christ's final entry into Jerusalem, as was the custom of the early Christian church, found first in Christian art of the fourth century on sarcophagi from the Roman catacombs, the fragment of pilaster takes on even further meaning.

Room 6 is devoted to the works of **Aelbert Cuyp** (1620–91), the seventeenth-century Dutch landscapist strongly influenced by the Italianized taste of the Utrecht School. Most of his work depicts grazing animals in placid landscapes of meadows and riversides often bathed in warm light. His late *Road near a River* (ca. 1660) is particularly fine.

Room 7 continues with small seventeenth-century Dutch and Flemish paintings. **Room 8** has oil sketches by Rubens (1577–1640) that are interesting in showing his manner of working. Here too is the rococo painting, *Le Bal Champêtre* by Watteau (1684–1721), of which Constable wrote to his biographer, "[it] seems as if painted in honey; so mellow, so tender, so soft, and so delicious. . . ." Also there are works of the Italian School shown in this room, the most notable of which are *Portrait of a Young Man,* by Piero di Cosimo (1462–1521), and two small predella panels by **Raphael** (1483–1520), *St. Francis of Assisi* and *St. Francis of Padua* (ca. 1504–5). The main panel of the altarpiece they came from is in New York's Metropolitan Museum of Art.

Rooms 9 and 10 are largely devoted to seventeenth- and eighteenth-century British portraits. **Room 11** displays more of the gallery's superb seventeenth-century Dutch collection, in particular two paintings by **Rembrandt** (1606–69): *Girl Leaning on a Window-Sill* (1645), one of the most appealing portraits Rembrandt ever did, if, in fact, it is not a genre scene; and *Portrait of a Young Man* (1663), once thought to be Rembrandt's son Titus. Both paintings show Rembrandt as a master of portraiture who has the talent to bring out the inner character of people. He makes us see his subjects as he sees them, more seeing through them than looking at them.

HAMPTON COURT PALACE

Hampton Court, 10 miles west of London

Hours: Open May–Sept., Mon.–Sat., 9:30AM–6PM, Sun., 11AM–6PM; Mar., Apr., and Oct., Mon.–Sat., 9:30AM–5PM, Sun., 2–5PM; Nov.–Feb., Mon.–Sat., 9:30AM–4PM, Sun., 2–4PM. Admission fee.

This massive palace on the Thames is a combination of the Tudor and the classical seventeenth-century English styles. It was started by Cardinal Wolsey in 1514, but when he fell from grace in 1529 the palace was turned over to Henry VIII. He lived there with a number of his queens, enlarged it, and built state apartments (now lost) and his famous **Tudor great hall** (1535), the model for hundreds of similar galleries. Its high timber ceiling is splendidly carved and arched for a cathedrallike effect. The **Royal Chapel,** also begun by Wolsey, has a fan-vaulted ceiling with carved and gilded pendants. Although the English were aware of the Renaissance design popular across the channel in Europe, they preferred their own Tudor style in this period.

The Henry VIII Tudor part of the palace is formed around the base court and the clock court. Adjoining them is Sir Christopher Wren's late seventeenth-century addition built for William and Mary after the Revolution of 1688. **Wren** (1632–1722) worked here from 1689 to 1701, yet only a fraction of his overall design remains. Originally he wanted to pull down the old Tudor palace, leaving only the great hall, and replace it with two great courts at right angles to each other, but William III insisted that Wren enlarge the existing palace. The huge addition, despite its different style, harmonizes well with the older structure. Wren's facades avoid monotony by the use of three kinds of brick and a Portland stone that give color and texture.

The interiors of the palace have ceilings painted by Verrio (d. 1707), original fireplaces by Gibbons (1648–1721), and **state rooms** that contain paintings of the royal collection. Some of these were owned by Henry VIII and Charles I. After the execution of Charles I, the contents of the royal palaces were sold by the Parliament and dispersed throughout Europe. The sale of the treasures in Hampton Court and the Whitehall Palace was conducted over three years. At Whitehall there was a gallery that included twenty-eight canvases by Titian, nine by Raphael, four by Correggio, and seven by Rubens. It is said that the Puritans destroyed pictures of Christ and the Virgin Mary, but some, considered immodest, were hidden away. Thus some were forgotten and saved. *Adam and Eve,* by Mabuse, today in the king's dressing room at Hampton Court, is one of those. About 500 paintings are displayed in the state rooms built for William and Mary by Wren.

In the **first presence chamber** is a large equestrian portrait of William III painted by Sir Godfrey Kneller (1646–1723). The **second presence chamber** has a number of Venetian works: *Jacopo Sannazaro,* by Titian (1477/89–1576); *Esther and Ahasuerus,* by Tintoretto (1518–94); *Shepherd with a Pipe,* by Giorgione (1477/78–1510); and *The Concert,* in the past attributed to Giorgione and to Lotto, but now thought to be by Giovanni Bellini (ca. 1430–1516).

The collection of Venetian paintings continues in the **audience chamber**, with works by Tintoretto: *Apollo and the Nine Muses, A Knight of Malta, Portrait of a Dominican,* and *Portrait of a Man;* portraits by Lotto and Parmigianino; and *The Marriage of St. Catherine,* by Veronese (1528–88).

There are also Italian paintings in the **king's drawing room**. Here are *Lucretia,* by Titian, *Head of an Old Man,* by Lotto (ca. 1480–1556), *Portrait of a Venetian Senator,* by Tintoretto, *St. Catherine* and *Virgin and Child,* by Correggio (1489/94–1534), both of which belonged to Charles I, and a *Virgin and Child,* by Andrea del Sarto (1486–1531), among others. The ceilings of William III's bedroom and dressing room are by Verrio and in the **king's dressing room** there is one of the few religious paintings, *Noli me Tangere,* by Holbein (1497–1543), and *Adam and Eve,* by Mabuse, also known as Jan Gossaert (ca. 1478–ca. 1536). Both of these paintings were in the collection of Henry VIII. In the **king's writing closet** there is an excellent portrait of *Isabella d'Este,* by Giulio Romano (1492/99–1546), and other mannerist paintings.

In **Queen Mary's closet** two paintings by Lucas Cranach (1472–1553) are noteworthy: *The Judgment of Paris* and *Adam and Eve.* The **queen's bedroom** contains a *Diana* by the French seventeenth-century painter Simon Vouet (1590–1649), and *An Allegory of Truth and Time,* by Annibale Carracci (1560–1609).

The **Prince of Wales' presence chamber** has an outstanding collection of Italian primitives. Here is a triptych by Duccio (ca. 1255–ca. 1318) showing *The Crucifixion, The Annunciation,* and *The Virgin and Christ Enthroned;* a center panel, *Virgin and Child* of an altarpiece by Gentile da Fabriano (ca. 1370–1428); a little panel of *St. Peter,* by Fra Angelico (ca. 1400–1455); a lovely *Marriage of the Virgin,* by Bernardo Daddi (born ca. 1390); and a *Portrait of a Man,* by Giovanni Bellini.

In the **cartoon gallery**, designed by Wren to display the Raphael cartoons that are now in the Victoria and Albert Museum, hang seven tapestries made from the original cartoons. (See Victoria and Albert Museum, London.)

The **communication gallery**, linking the king's and the queen's state apartments, has the series called "Windsor Beauties"—portraits of ladies from the court of Charles II—by Sir Peter Lely (1618–80), that Pepys called "good, but not like."

Lower Orangery

This building, on the river side of the grounds, displays the nine **Mantegna Cartoons** (full-size working designs for tapestries painted in tempera on canvas). They illustrate *The Triumph of Caesar* and though they have been much restored the genius of Andrea Mantegna (1431–1506), a master of the Renaissance idea of mass and perspective, is evident. Side by side they form an eighty-eight-foot long frieze depicting a procession of characters of ancient Rome. There are soldiers, slaves, musicians, beggars, various animals, and others escorting Caesar, riding in glory on a chariot. The work was sold by the Gonzaga family, for whom Mantegna was court painter, to Charles I.

THE IVEAGH BEQUEST

Hampstead
Kenwood House, N.W. 3

Hours: Open daily Apr.–Sept., 10AM–7PM; Oct.–Mar., daily 10AM–5PM, or dusk. Admission fee.

Kenwood House, on seventy-four acres in Hampstead Heath (only eight miles from the center of London), has a rich collection of paintings and is an example of a great home of a gentleman of the eighteenth century. It was left to the city of London by Lord Iveagh in 1927.

In 1767 the house on the site was remodeled by **Robert Adam** (1728–92), who added a **library** on the east side that is today one of the finest Adam rooms in Britain. It was intended as "a room for receiving people," as Adam tells us. Its gilt decorations and Italianate ceiling paintings by Antonio Zucchi (1726–95), do not disturb the intimacy of the room.

Of the many English paintings, there is the portrait of *Mary Countess Howe,* by **Gainsborough** (1727–88) and his *Two Shepherd Boys with Dogs Fighting* (both in the Orangery) and a landscape, *Going to Market* (Lord Mansfield's dressing room). There are other portraits by Reynolds, Romney, Lawrence, and Raeburn. It is the **Dutch paintings** (dining room) that are the most famous. Of these, two are masterpieces of the seventeenth-century Golden Age: a *Self-portrait* by **Rembrandt** (1606–69), painted about 1663, an example of Rembrandt's most mature work; and the very pleasant work, **The Guitar Player,** by **Vermeer** (1632–75). It appears not to have suffered from its temporary theft in 1974. There is also *The Man with a Cane,* by **Franz Hals** (ca. 1580–1666), and others by Cuyp, Bol, Weenix, Wynants, Williem van der Velde, Jan van der Cappelle, and van Ostade.

ROYAL NAVAL COLLEGE

Greenwich, six miles east of central London on the Thames

Hours: Open for Painted Hall and Chapel, Fri.–Wed., 2:30–5PM. Free admission.

The palace at Greenwich was a favorite residence of the Tudor sovereigns. Henry VIII and his two daughters, Mary and Elizabeth, were born there; Henry married twice there and signed Anne Boleyn's death warrant there. But under Cromwell the palace fell into disuse, and after one large block was constructed in 1665, during the reign of Charles II, the enterprise was allowed to lapse. Later, with the accession of William and Mary, the site became a naval hospital. **Christopher Wren** (1632–1723) was in charge of the project, and most of the buildings seen today at Greenwich are his, though Vanbrugh and Hawksmoor carried out part of the plan.

Seen from the river, the extravagant size of Wren's twin colonnaded buildings, terminating in the great domes over the chapel and Painted Hall, are a splendid baroque vista. But it is the elegant little **Queen's House,** linked to two buildings by classical colonnades, that is the most interesting. James I had **Inigo Jones** (1573–1652) build it in 1617 for his queen, Anne of Austria. It was the first Palladian building in England and, in contrast to the great houses that came before it—Hatfield, Knole, Hardwick, and others—it was a house designed for a family, not a medieval court. It became the pattern in succeeding ages for all the great houses of England. It is too small to serve as a focal point at Greenwich and would have been pulled down when Greenwich Palace was rebuilt had it not been for Queen Mary, wife of William III of Orange. Though she never lived in it, she insisted it be left undisturbed with a view down to the Thames.

A noted artistic element of Greenwich is the ceiling painting done between 1707 and 1726 by **Sir Thomas Thornhill** (1675–1734) in the dining hall—today's **Painted Hall,** which Kenneth Clark has called "one of the finest rooms in England." It is in the tradition of the Italian high baroque and of its kind, it has no equal in Britain.

In 1873 the hospital was closed and the buildings turned into the Royal Naval College. The Queen's House and the two buildings connected to it contain the National Maritime Museum, showing paintings dealing with England's maritime history back to the seventeenth century. There are works by some of England's noted painters, by Dutch masters, and by two Americans, Benjamin West and John Singleton Copley.

WINDSOR CASTLE

Windsor, 23 miles west of London

Hours: Castle grounds open May–Aug., daily 10AM–7:15PM; Mar., Apr., Sept., Oct., daily 10AM–5:15PM; Nov.–Feb., 10AM–4:15PM. State apartments open May–Oct., Mon.–Sat., 10:30AM–5PM, Sun., 10:30AM–1:30PM; Nov.–Mar., Mon.–Sat., 10:30AM–3PM; Apr., Mon.–Sat., 10:30AM–5PM, closed when queen is in official residence, approximately end of May through June. Call 95-68286. Admission fee.

Windsor is Europe's largest inhabited castle and has been a royal fortress and residence for more than eight centuries. It was started by William the Conqueror about 1070 and, in 1110, made into a royal residence by Henry I. Of these early buildings nothing remains. Its **Round Tower** was the original keep but was enlarged in the nineteenth century. Succeeding monarchs, from Henry II onward, added construction.

Its most notable feature, **St. George's Chapel,** was begun in 1472 by Edward IV, and completed by Henry VIII in 1528. Henry VIII is the first of many English monarchs to be buried there, including all those since George III (d. 1820). The chapel has a simple rectangular shape with many large windows and fan vaults that roof the building. The English Gothic building balances mass and form harmoniously and has a reserved grandeur that is characteristically British.

North of the Round Tower are the **State apartments** that contain lavishly furnished rooms and an art collection. The **king's dining room** has woodcarving by Gibbons and several portraits of royal personages, and one called *The Chinese Convert*, by Sir Godfrey Kneller (1646–1723). The **king's drawing room** contains a masterpiece by van Dyck (1599–1641), *St. Martin Dividing his Cloak with a Beggar*, painted when van Dyck was twenty-two; and a good example of a religious work by Rubens (1577–1640), *Holy Family*. In the **king's state bedchamber** is a portrait by Gainsborough and a Canaletto, among other paintings.

In the small **king's dressing room** are to be found the greatest number of masterpieces. Here is the *Portrait of a Man Holding a Volume of Petrarch* by the Frenchman Jean Clouet (1486–ca. 1540), painter to Francis I; a Dürer (1471–1528), *Portrait of a Man;* a *Portrait of a Man* by the Fleming, Hans Memling (1435–94); two portraits of people from the court of Henry VIII by Holbein (1497–1543); a self-portrait by Rubens painted in 1623, and his *Portrait of a Young Lady* and a *Portrait of van Dyck;* by van Dyck there is a triple portrait of *Charles I* intended for the use of the sculptor Bernini in making a bust of the king. There is a portrait by Andrea del Sarto (1486–1531) of his wife; and three portraits by Rembrandt (1606–69), a *Self-portrait* done in middle age, *Portrait of a Young Man in a Turban* dated 1631, and a *Portrait of his Mother* dated about 1629.

In the **king's closet,** apart from the landscape, *The Rape of Europa,* by Claude Lorrain (1600–1682), a portrait of *David Garrick in the Part of Kitely,* by Reynolds (1723–92) and *Garrick and his Wife,* by Hogarth (1697–1764), there is an extraordinary collection of the works of the Venetian painter Canaletto (1697–1768).

In the **queen's drawing room** are a number of portraits by van Dyck that include a portrait of Charles I, two portraits of his queen, Henrietta Maria, a group portrait of his five children, and portraits of his courtiers.

In the **queen's ballroom** are more of the royal collection's Canalettos, a portrait of a daughter of George III by the American, John Singleton Copley (1738–1815), and portraits by Copley's countryman, Benjamin West (1738–1820), who spent fifty years of his life in England.

The **queen's present chamber** and the **queen's guard chamber** have collections of busts, including those of *Handel, Philip II of Spain,* the *Duke of Alva, Wellington,* and *Winston Churchill.*

St. George's Hall has a large display of busts and portraits of Stuart and Hanoverian monarchs, all members of the Order of the Garter, and the **Waterloo Chamber** has a collection of portraits by Sir Thomas Lawrence (1769–1830) depicting people who contributed to the defeat of Napoleon: the pope, monarchs, and generals—*Pope Pius VII, Prince Metternich, Wellington,* and others.

The most important collection at Windsor is probably the *old master drawings* in the **royal library.** There are drawings and sketches by Leonardo da Vinci, Michelangelo, Raphael, and Holbein, among many.

_____*Norfolk*_____

BLICKLING HALL

One and one-half miles northwest of Aylsham on north side of B1354 (fifteen miles north of Norwich on A140)

Hours: Open Apr.–Oct., Tues.–Wed., Fri.–Sun., 2–6PM. Admission fee.

Blickling Hall, one of the finest Jacobean houses in England (1616–27), has romantic bay windows, towers capped by ogival cupolas, and a turret with an open-topped lantern. Robert Lyminge, the architect, also worked on Hatfield House; but at Blickling he had a freer hand, with the result that this building is less severe. For a great Jacobean house it is fanciful, and, while it certainly owes something to Flemish, French, and Italian influences, it is still mainly English in design and feeling. It also has a good example of the **long gallery** (120 feet by twenty feet), including an elaborate plaster ceiling and an immense library. There is an oaken double stairway with carved newels, balisters, and rails, and a collection of paintings, tapestries, and furniture. The gardens are of the eighteenth century.

HOLKHAM HALL

Two miles west of Wells, south of Wells-Hunstanton road (A149)

Hours: Open June, Sept., Sun., Mon., Thurs., 1:30–5PM; July, Aug., Mon., Wed., Thurs., 1:30–5PM. Admission fee.

This Palladian house is an example of the work of **William Kent** (1685–1748), the great architect of the Palladian School in England and protégé of Lord Burlington, whose patronage he enjoyed for thirty years. Kent started the house in 1734 for Thomas Cook, earl of Leicester, who, after returning from the grand tour in 1718, decided to rebuild his family home into a Roman palace. Holkham Hall is devoted to the idea of classical purity, an eighteenth-century concern, and is quite un-English. Its **marble entrance hall,** rising almost to the full height of the house, with Ionic columns of Derbyshire alabaster, is based on the design of a Roman basilica. Yet the **long library,** a room that owes most of its color to the calf bindings of Lord Leicester's editions of the classics, is not oppressive, and the **sculpture gallery** also seems habitable. It is a house of distinction, a memorial to the Palladian age, which is exactly what its builders intended it to be. Its collection of portraits by Lely, Kneller, Gainsborough, and van Dyck, landscapes by Claude and Poussin, and the most famous painting in the house, Rubens's *Return from Egypt,* go well with the house, as do its formal grounds, laid out by Capability Brown.

OXBURGH HALL

Seven miles southwest of Swaffham on the south side of Stoke Ferry road

Hours: Open Apr.–early Oct., Tues.–Thurs., Sat., Sun. (and bank holiday Mondays), 2–6PM. Admission fee.

Here is an example of Norfolk brickwork in a picturesque building surrounded by a moat. Although it seems to be a fortress, a close look shows it to be a work of architectural elegance. It was started by Sir Edward Bedingfeld in 1482 and has been occupied by the Bedingfelds for five hundred years. Its least altered part is its most striking feature, the **great tower**, formed by two octagonal turrets joined by a curtain wall. Through this archway Henry VII passed in 1497. Oxburgh has preserved the room in which he slept as the **king's room** on the central floor of the tower. Next door to it is a room that contains bedhangings and coverlets embroidered by Mary Queen of Scots and Bess of Hardwick.

In 1775 the Tudor hall and great chamber opposite the gateway were pulled down, but five southeast and southwest towers were built to fill the gap, and external corridors added around the inside of the courtyard during the nineteenth century. Three times Oxburgh came close to perishing: once, after the Civil War, when Cromwell's soldiers ransacked it and left it burning (the Bedingfelds are Catholic); next, in the eighteenth century, when the family could not afford to keep it up; and last, in 1951, when it was threatened by residential development.

Oxford

Oxford, unlike Cambridge, is an industrial city, but the many colleges of its ancient university present an array of architecture that make it one of the most beautiful cities in Europe. To see the university's thirty-four colleges and numerous buildings a student guide may be hired. (Apply at the Information Center, St. Aldates.) If you are going alone, start at Carfax, a downtown intersection where four main streets meet. Carfax is derived from the Norman French "quatre voies." At the corner stands the fourteenth-century **St. Martin's Tower**; its top may date back to Saxon times.

A block south, on St. Aldate's Street, is **Christ Church College**, the largest of Oxford's colleges, founded by Cardinal Wolsey in 1525. It has the celebrated **Tom Tower** over the main gate, built by Wren in 1682, containing the giant Tom, a seven-ton bell that traditionally rings 101 times each night over the **Tom Quad**, largest in Oxford, over one hundred yards square. In the southeast angle of Tom Quad, a large archway and staircase with fantracery leads up to the **Great Hall** (115 feet long, forty feet wide, and fifty feet high) with an elaborate hammer-beam roof. It houses a great collection of portraits, including one of Wolsey.

Back on the Quad is the entrance to **Christ Church Cathedral,** which serves as both chapel for the college and cathedral of Oxford (open daily 11AM–5PM). It was completed in 1180. Its irregular appearance is due to Wolsey having removed three western bays of its nave to build the great quadrangle. However, its Norman character remains intact, and it has one of the earliest examples of an early English spire, rising 144 feet. The high point of the interior is the late perpendicular vaulting (1478–1503) in its choir, which shows the structural transition to fan vaulting.

On the south side of the Quad is an extension to the college, Canterbury Quadrangle. Here is the **Christ Church Picture Gallery** (open Mon.–Sun. 10:30AM–1PM and 2–4PM). It has a large collection of paintings and drawings. Among the paintings *Virgin and Saints,* by Piero della Francesca, *Jacob and Rachel,* by Hugo van der Goes, and Annibale Carracci's *Butcher's Shop* (probably showing the artist's family) are most notable.

Walk back along the eastern side of Tom Quad and turn right into Peckwater Quad. Canterbury Quadrangle, the smallest in Oxford, lies ahead. Through the college's back gate, on Merton Street, is Oriel College, Corpus Christi College, and **Merton College.** Merton's Mob Quad is Oxford's oldest surviving quadrangle. Its beautiful **thirteenth-century chapel** has some of the oldest stained glass in England, and its T-shaped plan, the result of its uncompleted nave, which stopped short at the transepts, set the pattern for other college chapels.

After leaving the college, walk on Merton Street turning left up to **High Street,** which Sir Nikolaus Pevsner, the architectural historian, described as one of the world's great streets. In front of you is **Queen's College,** which Pevsner considered the finest piece of classical architecture in Oxford. Its library has elegant rococo plasterwork and decorative bookcases, and its chapel a coved ceiling and superb scenes.

Return to the High Street, where, from the corner of Queen's Lane, you will have the finest view of the grand curve of High Street. Further down the High is **Magdalen College,** which has a great Gothic bell-tower, finished in 1509. Its position beside the river and bridge is the best situation in Oxford.

Returning to High Street, walk up Queen's Lane to **New College.** (Built between 1379 and 1382, it is hardly new.) Its T-shaped medieval chapel is the largest in Oxford and has stained glass in its west end designed by Reynolds, the eighteenth-century painter. An El Greco painting of *St. James* is also on view, as is a fine collection of brasses.

As you come back out the main gate of New College, continue on New College Lane to Broad Street. The **Bodleian Library** comes into view on the left. It is one of the greatest and earliest public libraries in Europe; its oldest part, an early fifteenth-century building (Divinity School), has an elaborately vaulted and arched **stone roof.** Across from the Bodleian is Christopher Wren's first experiment in architecture, the semicircular **Sheldonian Theatre** completed in 1669. The Sheldonian is a product of the moment when Wren, then professor of astronomy at the university, was slowly shifting his attention from science to architecture. Its roof, which spans an area of seventy by eighty feet without visible supports, is an ingenious piece of timber engineering, but its architecture is awkward. The facade, featuring a rusticated podium supporting an insufficient story that looks merely like an enlarged attic, shows little design experience.

Across from the Bodleian Library is the circular **Radcliffe Camera** built by James Gibbs (1682–1754) in 1737–48 as a library. Its huge dome has the verticality of Michelangelo's St. Peter's and its drum, supported on curved buttresses, recalls Longhena's Santa Maria della Salute in Venice. Set on an open piazza, this baroque building is perhaps Gibbs's finest work. Continuing toward the High Street, **St. Mary's Church's fourteenth-century** spire rises 188 feet and is one of the most richly decorated in England.

ASHMOLEAN MUSEUM

Beaumont Street, off St. Giles Street

Hours: Open Tues.–Sat., 10AM–4PM, Sun., 2–4PM. Free admission.

This is the oldest public museum in Britain, having been opened to the public in 1683. Among its many treasures is a display of statues and fragments from *Sir Arthur Evans' excavations at Knossos in Crete* (Arthur Evans room no. 13, first floor) and a collection of Anglo-Saxon antiquities that includes the famous *Alfred Jewel* (medieval room no. 4, ground floor), made for Alfred the Great who died in 899. It bears the inscription, "Alfred had me made," and is decorated in gold with cloisonné. There is also a collection of paintings representing many European schools from early Italian to twentieth-century English painting.

Among the Italian paintings are two from the fifteenth century (both in the Fortnum Gallery, room no. 21, first floor): *The Hunt,* by Paolo Uccello (ca. 1397–1475), painted after 1460, and *A Forest Fire,* by Piero di Cosimo (1462–1521), painted about 1487. *The Hunt* is one of Uccello's romantic works, showing the artist's delight in perspective. *A Forest Fire* is based on a pagan mythological theme that gives the painting a surreal, dreamlike atmosphere; notice that one of the animals that turns toward the viewer has a human face.

Two French paintings from the seventeenth century (both in the Weldon Gallery, room no. 25, first floor) are by artists who spent most of their careers in Italy and are among the museum's greatest treasures: *The Exposition of Moses,* by Nicolas Poussin (1594–1665), painted in 1654, and *Ascanius Shooting the Stag of Sylvia,* by Claude Lorrain (1600–1682), painted in 1682. *The Exposition of Moses* is a Biblical subject mixed with mythology. Like other paintings by Poussin, its composition leads the eye to every part of the canvas as one follows its figures. Its spirit has the ordered classicism that made Poussin the first internationally famous French artist. *Ascanius shooting the Stag of Sylvia* derives from Virgil's epic poem, the *Aeneid,* and shows Ascanius, son of Aeneas, the Trojan prince, about to shoot the pet stag of Sylvia, daughter of Tyrrhus, the keeper of King Latinus's herds in

Latium. This starts a war between Latinus and Aeneas. The result is the acquisition of land that will later become the territory of Rome. The picture is typical of Claude's hazy, harmonious countrysides.

The small Combe room (no. 26, first floor) contains a collection of Pre-Raphaelite paintings by Holman Hunt, Millais, and others.

Many of the colleges that make up Oxford also contain fine works of art, but these are not generally open to the public. An appointment to see them must be made in advance.

Oxfordshire

BLENHEIM PALACE

At the southwest end of Woodstock, eight miles north of Oxford

Hours: Open Mar. 23–Oct. 31, daily 11AM–6PM. Admission fee.

This vast baroque country palace was given by Queen Anne to John Churchill, the first duke of Marlborough (1650–1722) in recognition of his military victories over the French at the Battle of Blenheim, August 13, 1704, where the defeat of Louis XIV was believed to have saved England forever

from French imperialist designs. When the gift was made the palace had not yet been built. The queen conferred the royal manor of Woodstock on the duke and his heirs forever, and Parliament voted a sum of £500,000 for the construction of the buildings. The duke chose **John Vanbrugh (1664–1726)** as the architect over the obvious choice of Sir Christopher Wren, the queen's favorite, and the choice of the duke's wife, Sarah Jennings, duchess of Marlborough. Although the queen was pleased with Vanbrugh's plan, the duchess never modified her dislike of it. She battled with Vanbrugh and after twenty years actually barred him from the house.

The duchess had her own idea as to what Blenheim should look like. She wanted a comfortable country home and anticipated the possibility of falling from royal favor, which actually happened (Blenheim was finished at the Marlboroughs' own expense). Vanbrugh felt Blenheim should be grandiose, with no expense spared.

So Blenheim was built to Vanbrugh's plans, and its great scale (its roof covers three acres) has been a main object of criticism. Some have called it a massive heap of stone, barbaric, even absurd. But others have praised it. Sir John Soane wrote, "This work alone may be said to stamp Vanbrugh the Shakespeare of architects." Sacheverell Sitwell called it "one of the most extraordinary feats of architecture."

Criticism probably can be made of the exterior: the columned portico is too high for its width, and above the pediment are clumsy pillars and broken arches. At the four corners of the building are towers of horrendous design.

Whatever you may think of Blenheim, you will be impressed by its tapestries, its huge library, its great organ, its paintings, and its magnificent sunken Italian gardens, water gardens, and artificial lake. Blenheim also had a part in the life of Winston Churchill and his mother, Jennie Jerome, a rich American from Brooklyn, New York. She married Lord Randolph Churchill, the brother of the then duke of Marlborough, and gave birth to Winston on November 10, 1874, in a little room that you can visit here. Blenheim had another American woman in its history; the wife of Winston Churchill's cousin George, the ninth duke, was Consuelo Vanderbilt, daughter of William Kissem Vanderbilt, a grandson of Cornelius Vanderbilt.

Salisbury

SALISBURY CATHEDRAL

Hours: Open all hours. Admission fee to visit Chapter House and Close.

Salisbury has the distinction of being the only English Cathedral built all of a single period (pure early English, or Gothic), over a short time (thirty-eight years, 1220–58), and on land that had been unencumbered by previous architecture. The original cathedral had been built a few miles away at Old Sarum.

The cathedral's beauty is mostly due to its lofty **spire** (ca. 1320), built about a century later than the rest of the cathedral. It does not depart from the original conception. The tallest medieval spire in England (404 feet), it is the subject of many of John Constable's paintings and drawings.

The plan is simplicity itself. The choir, nave, and transepts are of identical height. Even the much lower Lady Chapel at the east end (now the Trinity Chapel), has aisles the same height as the nave. Every one of these members are straight sided and right angled. All are given equal stress. Only the screenlike **west front**, the last part of the cathedral to be constructed (1258), seems out of proportion with the rest of the building and is a haphazard patchwork of forms, with niches now filled with modern statues.

The decoration in the interior is plain, even cold. The Purbeck stone is artificially darkened with varnish, there is a minimum of foliate carving, most of the interior screens and other decorations were destroyed, and its old glass was smashed and removed. In the **Trinity Chapel,** where new stained glass was installed in 1980, the effect is of a rebirth of this old part of the cathedral (1221). Forming the "Prisoners of Conscience Window," panels of colored glass, most in blue, made in Chartres, France, bring light and color to a part of the cathedral that was lacking in decoration.

Salisbury also has the oldest (1263–84) and largest **cloister** of any English cathedral (the library above it houses one of the four original copies of the Magna Carta). Its four spacious walks are vaulted with plain, simple quadripartite vaults, and give the effect of great breadth and spaciousness, opening upon an open court in which today grow two magnificent cedars.

The lovely **chapter house** is octagonal in shape with admirable space, thanks to the slender delicacy of the central pier and the large windows, which almost fill the wall. The carvings around the base of the pier, and the sculpture depicting sixty little scenes of the Old Testament in the spandrels of the wall arcade, are fine examples of this late thirteenth-century work.

For those who have seen the Gothic cathedrals of France, such as Amiens, founded in the same year as Salisbury, a visit here permits comparisons between French and English design. Salisbury has the typical long, narrow English nave, while French designs reduce the proportion of length to width by as much as half. The east end of Salisbury is square, while in France the east end is usually rounded; the Salisbury west front is a screen meant to hide the structure, while in France the outer facade reveals the construction of the building. Salisbury sits on a broad green lawn, while French cathedrals usually have city houses built right up against their walls.

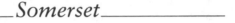

Somerset

MONTACUTE HOUSE

In Montacute village four miles west of Yeovil on north side of A3088

Hours: Open Apr.–Oct., Mon., Wed.–Sun., 12:30–6PM.

This house, a survivor from the Elizabethan period, was built between 1588 and 1601 and in spite of an addition to its west front in 1785, its Elizabethan character remains.

The original builder, whose family occupied the house until 1915, was Edward Phelips, the speaker of the House of Commons in 1604 and prosecutor at the trial of Guy Fawkes in 1606. The architect was William Arnold.

The beautiful **east front,** originally the front entrance but now the rear, gives on a grassy forecourt closed on three sides by a balustrade that matches the one on the roof. The house appears somewhat restrained in spite of the great detail that has gone into it, largely because it is made of local Ham stone, of a warm ochre with rich texture. (The same stone is used inside the house.) **Domed pavilions** at each end of the garden are purely decorative masterpieces of design.

The **west side** of the house, now its front entrance, was added in the eighteenth century from another house being demolished, and it fits in perfectly. Apart from the Renaissance detail it brought to the west front the addition also had the effect of modernizing the interior with corridors that added privacy to the bedrooms. Previously, a bedroom could be entered only by passing through another.

The **interior,** little altered except for the addition of those corridors, has large windows, some filled with armorial bearings of colored glass, paneling in the library, and a long gallery at the top of the house (172 by twenty feet) with small rooms off of it and a collection of portraits on its walls. A ground hall has a classical stone screen.

Sussex

PETWORTH HOUSE

West Sussex, Petworth, five and one-half miles east of Midhurst, in center of Petworth

Hours: Open Apr.–Oct., Tues.–Sun., 2–6PM. Admission fee.

This late seventeenth-century house, partly French in design, sits at the gates of the village of Petworth. It seems too narrow a house for its height and length (320 feet) and its rooms, though luxurious, seem to have been laid out without any plan. But the house, within a magnificent 2,000-acre park surrounded by a thirteen-mile wall, is a joy to visit for its collection of **paintings** and **wood carvings**. One resident, the third earl of Egremont, was a patron of the arts whose favorite guest was Turner. Shown here are Turner's painting of the great park (after viewing it look out the window and compare the view) and other paintings by van Dyck, Reynolds (who also spent time at Petworth), Claude Lorraine, and other old masters.

Petworth's most famous room is the **Grinling Gibbons Room,** named after a sculptor who decorated it in a naturalistic style. Gibbons (1648–1721) did much work in other country houses and in many public buildings, including St. Paul's Cathedral in London. His exquisite carvings do appear ill placed in this long room, for when seen from one end they seem only a bulky mass.

The house also has a medieval **chapel** with early English arcades and seventeenth- and eighteenth-century gilded woodwork placed against thirteenth-century stone.

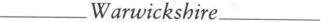

Warwickshire

WARWICK CASTLE

In the center of Warwick, just north of Stratford-upon-Avon

Hours: Open Mar.–Oct., daily 10AM–5:30PM; Nov.–Feb., 10AM–4:30PM. Admission fee.

The castle at Warwick, beside the river Avon, has origins that go back to William the Conqueror. It is a Norman shell-keep castle, but none of its present buildings is from before the fourteenth century. It is a rather good example of a late fourteenth- and early fifteenth-century external fortress combined with comfortable apartments that were extensively altered during the eighteenth century. The most outstanding room in the apartments is the **great hall** (330 feet in length), which holds a collection of arms and armor, as well as a good collection of paintings: portraits by Rubens (Loyola), van Dyck (Charles I, Stafford, and Prince Rupert), Cranach (Sibylla of Cleves),

Holbein, and Lely. Above a white marble fireplace in the state dining room is Rubens's picture of two lions, which are said to have killed their keeper while the artist was at work. In the greenhouse is the famous **Warwick Vase** (five and one-half feet high) found in Hadrian's villa at Tivoli, Italy, by Sir William Hamilton. It is believed to be a Roman work of Hadrian's time (early second century A.D.), though others attribute it to the workshop of Lysippus (late fourth century B.C., Greek).

From the grounds of the castle there is a view of the two late fourteenth-century **towers** at either end of the east wall. Each contains many tiers of well-lighted rooms with fireplaces, latrines, and bedrooms. They are self-contained units; one has a prison on its lower level.

Wells

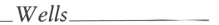

WELLS CATHEDRAL

Open all hours. Voluntary donations asked.

One of the smallest cathedrals in England, Wells is also one of the most beautiful. It was built over a long period, starting in 1186 and ending in the fifteenth century, but presents a remarkable unity of Gothic design. Its importance is due not only to fine architectural elements, but also to the medieval environment that surrounds it—cloisters, chapter house, chapter library, bishop's palace, the houses of the dean, archdeacon, and chancellor, and the vicar's close (two rows of buildings dating from 1348 facing one another). Collectively, they form one of the most complete medieval domestic ranges in England.

The conspicuous feature of the cathedral is the **west front** (1239), a giant screen displaying 300 of an original 400 statues, 150 of which are life-size or larger. This array of church sculpture extends 147 feet across the facade, enveloping the sides of the two towers. This panoply of saints, priests, kings, nobles, ladies, and other characters would have been greater in medieval times, enriched with metal ornament and resplendent with gilt and color. Also, the **central tower** is treated with commendable detail.

The **nave** has ten bays, is of modest height, and is unique in that the shafts terminate above the triforium openings that form a continuous arcade, affording no indication of the bay structure. Its effect is one of solidity without heaviness. The sculpture on some of the capitals, showing scenes from everyday life, add to the character of the work. Also unique to the west country masons are the scissor-shaped girders bracing three sides of the crossing supporting the central tower. They were constructed in 1320 to strengthen the structure.

On the east end there is a polygonal **lady chapel** done in the decorated style, one of the small architectural masterpieces of English Gothic. Its tall windows are filled with fragments of fourteenth-century glass that gives a timeless quality to the space.

From the north choir aisle a passage leads to the undercroft and up a footworn stairway to the **chapter house**, lighted by eight traceried windows. It has a central pier that sprouts thirty-two closely packed ribs studded with carved bosses.

_____Wiltshire_____

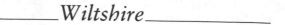

LONGLEAT HOUSE

Four miles southeast of Warminster, four and one-half miles southeast of Frome on A362 (between Bath and Salisbury)

Hours: Open Apr.–Oct., daily 10AM–6PM; Nov.–Mar., daily 10AM–4PM.

Longleat is one of the most visited houses in England, distinguished for its four palatial facades, which have a coherence of design that surpasses much other Elizabethan architecture. All three classical orders are represented in pilaster form, one to each story: Doric below, Ionic in the middle, and Corinthian at the top. With its many windows the building has a glitter from a distance. The house, bordered by trees, is seen amid carefully tended lawns. Below it a chain of lakes is formed from the watercourse (or leat) from which the house gets its name.

It took thirty years to build Longleat, between 1550 and 1580—it burned for four hours in 1567, when almost completed. Its builder was Sir John Thynne, whose family has lived at Longleat since his death in 1580. The design is his own. Unlike other houses of the period, this has two inner courtyards that serve as light wells; every main room faces the park. Almost the entire interior was transformed in the nineteenth century so it is not possible today to see the earlier ones. But the plain rooms on the top floor, where Thomas Ken (1637–1711), bishop of Bath and Wells, lived with his collection of books as the guest of the owners of Longleat, are still there, including his library. The rest of the house is luxuriously furnished and has Italianized decoration done in 1860 by Italian craftsmen brought in by the fourth marquess. Capability Brown laid out the gardens in 1757 and remodeled the 800-acre park, which is itself comparable to a work of art.

WILTON HOUSE

In town of Wilton, two and one-half miles west of Salisbury on Exeter road (A30)

Hours: Open Apr.–early Oct., Tues.–Sat., 11AM–6PM, Sun. 1–6PM. Admission fee.

King Alfred founded an abbey in the ninth century on the site of Wilton House. When the abbey was dissolved in 1544 the land was given to William Herbert, first earl of Pembroke (1507–70), by Henry VIII. It has since remained in the Herbert family.

The first earl built a Tudor house on the site, but what is visible today is largely the result of Inigo Jones's work after a fire in 1647 destroyed a large part of the building. The central tower part of the east front is all that survives of the original. Jones (1573–1652) rebuilt the whole garden front with an exterior that has a great Venetian window flanked by sculptured figures. Behind this facade are seven rooms of which two state rooms are famous. These are the **double cube room,** measuring sixty by thirty by thirty feet, and the **single cube room,** measuring thirty by thirty feet. Both are French in character and are lavishly decorated. The double cube room is hung with portraits by van Dyck, between which are carved oak decorated drops of fruit and flowers. The chimney-pieces of Italian marble fit well into rooms of such great proportions.

Wilton also has one of the finest art collections of any English country house—classical sculpture, furniture by Kent and Chippendale, and paintings by Rembrandt, Rubens, van Dyck, Tintoretto, and Richard Wilson. The house has always been associated with artists. Philip Sidney, brother-in-law of the second earl, wrote his *Arcadia* at Wilton, and Edmund Spenser, Philip Marlowe, John Donne, and Ben Jonson visited here. There is some evidence that Shakespeare's *As You Like It* was first performed at Wilton, with Shakespeare himself as part of the cast.

The 800-acre park was laid out by Capability Brown, but in 1736 the earl of Pembroke, called the "Architect Earl," added a **Palladian bridge** that became almost as famous as the house itself. Winston Churchill once set up his easel in the garden and tried to capture its beauty.

_____Winchester_____

WINCHESTER CATHEDRAL

Hours: Open all hours. Free admission.

Winchester has the largest nave of any medieval church in the world (526 feet) in one of the finest representations of the perpendicular style in England.

Winchester was the capital of the kings of Wessex in the seventh century. The bishop's see founded here became so important that Egbert, first king of England, chose it as the scene of his coronation in 827. Had the Anglo-Saxons perpetuated themselves, Winchester, would probably have become the center of British government; this cathedral would have been the coronation church. The Conqueror did consider it his second capital, and the Normans built a large abbey on the site. Subsequent building that went on as late as 1493 changed it from a Norman structure to a great Gothic cathedral as it increased its size. In the seventeenth century it was damaged during the Civil War when Parliamentary troops stabled their horses in the great nave and peasants, looting its treasure, smashed its stained glass windows. By 1652 it was in such a bad state that thought was given to tearing it down.

It is only in the twentieth century that extensive restoration of the foundations has been carried out.

The brilliance of the Gothic nave was achieved by recasing the original Norman core, now hidden or combined with Gothic elements; similarly, its tall vaulting shafts were added to bring the interior into the Gothic style in 1405. In the **transepts** one can still see the Norman work, in contrast to the more ornate converted nave. A curious feature is their aisles, continuous with those on the eastern and western sides, forming a succession of small groined chapels.

The **lady chapel** at the east end is an early perpendicular Gothic work dating from the late twelfth century. Elaborate arcading and paneling still appears in its first bay, and its recently restored woodwork is from the fifteenth century. On the north, the **Chapel of the Guardian Angels** has roof paintings and a bronze effigy of the duke of Portland by Lessueur.

The Norman **crypt** houses a twelfth-century library containing over 4,000 volumes and some illuminated manuscripts of good quality. Of greater interest, however, is that the crypt shows the ground plan of the original Norman structure that once stood above it.

York

YORK MINSTER

Hours: Open all hours. Central tower open Apr.–Sept., Mon.–Sat., 10:30AM–7PM; Oct.–Mar., Mon.–Sat., 10:30AM–3:30PM. Admission fee. Chapter house open May–Oct., Mon.–Sat., 10AM–7PM. Admission fee.

York has long been an archbishopric, ranking immediately after Canterbury, which explains why York Minster grew into the largest church in England, with architectural features impressive for their richness and ambitious for their scale.

The cathedral here now is the fourth church that has stood upon a site dating back to 627. It is the immediate successor of a Norman structure built in the twelfth century, of which the piers of its crossing still form the core of the piers of the central tower. The Norman church had a nave as wide as the present one but with narrower aisles.

Exterior
The oldest part of the present minster, except for the Norman crypt below ground, is the **south transept**, built between 1227 and about 1241. Its size dictated the proportions of the rest of the cathedral. The **north transept** is impressive. Completed in 1255, it has the tallest lancet design in England— above the famous Five Sisters (windows five feet wide by fifty-three feet high) are five graduated lancets in the gable.

The fourteenth-century **west front**, the most elaborate, is a striking feature. Its proportions and workmanship, combined with its two fifteenth-century towers, make a powerful Gothic impression. Its big central window is a rare example of flowing tracery. The **central tower,** also from the fifteenth century, is the largest in England.

Interior

The **nave,** the highest and broadest in England, an imposing example of the decorated style, was begun in 1291 and finished about 1345. The architecture of the cathedral, however, has often been criticized as another English Gothic building too broad for its height, with dull geometrical and decorated tracery in its windows. The exception is at the west end, in the large beautiful "Heart of Yorkshire" window. Shafts that rise from the floor support nothing more than a wooden roof. The nave, choir, and transepts were never completed with a stone vault. In 1840 a fire destroyed the original magnificent choir stalls.

The fourteenth-century **lady chapel** at the east end is perpendicular in character, with decorated elements. Its main feature is its enormous window containing the greatest mass of fifteenth-century glass in Europe. The glass of York Minster is its chief glory, in its fourteenth-century window in the chapter house, in the magnificence of the west window, and in the window in the north transept called the **Five Sisters,** set with sea-green thirteenth-century *grisaille* glass, some original.

There are finer cathedrals in Britain and elsewhere, but that will not prevent you from being enchanted with its great size, its sparkling windows, and its fine quality of workmanship. It is very much in league with the greatest medieval cathedrals of Britain and the Continent.

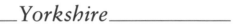

————————Yorkshire————————

CASTLE HOWARD

North Yorkshire, fifteen miles northeast of York, three miles off A64

Hours: Open Apr.–Sept., Tues.–Sun., 1–6PM; Oct., Wed., Sat.–Sun., 2–5PM. Admission fee.

Castle Howard, like Blenheim and Chatsworth, was built during the eighteenth century (1700–1737) when aristocratic families had the wealth to undertake such projects. Castle Howard was the first architectural commission that **John Vanbrugh** (1664–1726) had been given. He had been a soldier and a successful playwright, as well as a man-about-town and a member of the influential Kit Kat Club, and he knew Lord Carlisle, who wanted to built the greatest country house in England. Vanbrugh impressed Lord Carlisle so much with some sketches that he received the commission. Vanbrugh hired **Nicholas Hawksmoor** (1661–1736), Wren's chief assistant, and formed a partnership. Vanbrugh did the designing and Hawksmoor the technical work. Together they built Castle Howard into this baroque palace, and put the first **dome** on a private house in England. It is best seen above the long facade of the south front that faces the garden, where it sits back from the facade. It covers the **great wall,** with its square floor plan and Corinthian pilasters under the arches that support the dome.

Though the rooms in this house are small (except the long gallery), they glitter with old master paintings, statuary, tapestries, antique furniture, and priceless porcelain. Their size has an advantage in not smothering your senses.

The estate is also notable for its 1,000-acre park with lakes, a bridge, a mausoleum, and Vanbrugh's graceful **Temple of the Four Winds.**

France

The art treasures of France not only reflect the artistic history of France, but also are a major part of Western culture. France became the art center of the world in the twelfth and thirteenth centuries with the development of Gothic architecture, the most original of art styles since that of the Greeks. Except for the period between the fourteenth and seventeenth centuries, when the center of Western culture shifted again to Italy, France has maintained its position as the art center of Europe.

Before the Gothic style, great Romanesque churches were built in France in the eleventh century along the pilgrimage routes leading to Rome and to Santiago de Compostela. Based largely on the early Christian basilica, they took a multitude of French Romanesque forms. What was most original about them was sculptural art with a new dramatic expressiveness, a rediscovery of sculpture in the round.

The Gothic style in the twelfth and thirteenth centuries began in the Ile de France and spread throughout Europe. It was a climax of medieval art brought about by growth of towns that led to a demand for extraordinary churches that soared to great heights and were embellished with flamboyant decoration. The engineering and artistic genius needed to create such an architecture—pointed cross vaults formed by intersecting circles of equal diameter, and flying buttresses used to support walls with vast stained glass windows—was present in France. It also led to the creation of some of the most enlightened sculptural figures as seen at the cathedrals of Chartres, Paris, Reims, and Amiens. French Gothic architecture and sculpture set a style in Europe that reigned supreme into the fifteenth century.

The Gothic style was later supplanted by Renaissance architecture, applied in France by native artists who developed it into French forms. Many of the beautiful châteaux of France are the result of this sixteenth-century building activity. Baroque, essentially a royal art, played an important part in France's development. The French refined it and built such glorious edifices as the palace of Versailles, which was copied throughout all of Europe. French baroque evolved into French rococo, an ornamental style but lighter and more elegant than the weighty baroque. Later the neoclassicism of the late eighteenth and nineteenth centuries, which played a role in all the arts in France, also influenced the development of art in the rest of Europe.

Painters of importance had been busy in France during the centuries of artistic development, but perhaps the most original contribution France made in painting belongs to the impressionists of the nineteenth century. Impressionism had been influenced by some contemporary English landscapes, but when it blossomed in France it was totally French. It brought the artist out of doors to paint what he saw and to reproduce differences in color in varying sources of light. Realism, not abstraction, was the impressionist's objective. Scenes before thought unworthy of painting—rain, fog, snow—became subject matter. Light became the dominant principle, conveyed to the spectator by the division of tone and the use of shimmering spots of color. The technique led eventually to modern art.

The display of art is another contribution France has made to the history of Western culture and, more exactly, to the history of art museums. Paris has been the starting point for many of the museums that house the art collections of Europe. Nowhere else has the concept of a great art collection, owned by the state, and put on display for the enjoyment of the public, taken root more firmly than in France. The Louvre was created to serve that purpose. Though a large part of its collection was made by military conquest, the Louvre established the concept of a great national gallery intended not only for the French but for all people. If a catastrophe hit Paris, one would expect the French to rebuild the Louvre first.

Albi

STE-CÉCILE CATHEDRAL

This unusual cathedral is a fortress as well as a church. It reflects the turbulent history of Albi, where in the thirteenth century heretics condemned the Church of Rome as the devil itself. The Albigensian heresy was suppressed in 1244, but the newly appointed bishop of Albi felt so insecure that he built the cathedral (started in 1272) not only for religion but also for protection. The great **western tower**, rising to a height of three hundred feet, is worthy of a medieval castle, with enormous round corner turrets and no windows on its lower levels. It is surmounted by a majestic Gothic octagon supported by flying buttresses and pierced by pointed windows. The vertical red brick walls of the cathedral rise from ground to cornice and are more than eight feet thick and one hundred feet high, and the small, narrow lower windows are placed at a height of twenty-four feet. It is a structure from which to fight off an enemy. The severity of the exterior is somewhat relieved by the south entrance, constructed between 1519 and 1535 (the cathedral was not completed until the sixteenth century), which has an ornate stone porch.

The **interior** is a wide nave with no aisles or transepts. Twenty-nine chapels encircle it, between the enormous buttress walls. It has an elaborate rood screen, or jube, which lies across the entire nave in the choir and is the best preserved of its kind in France. It was built in the flamboyant style around 1500, covered with curving tracery and statues in niches. There is also an enormous **Last Judgment** painted on the west wall, but it is badly mutilated. Italian artists painted the rest of the wall and the vaults with Renaissance frescoes that are among the few to have survived in France.

TOULOUSE-LAUTREC MUSEUM

Place de l'Archeveché

Hours: Open July–Sept., daily 9AM–12 noon and 2–6PM; Oct.–June, Wed.–Mon., 10AM–12 noon and 2–5PM. Admission fee.

Toulouse-Lautrec, Henri de (1864–1901), French
Although Toulouse-Lautrec is associated with fin de siècle Paris, this display of his art in a provincial museum in the south of France is here because the artist was born in Albi. At his death at the age of thirty-seven his mother presented all the paintings left in his studio to his friend Maurice Joyant, who sought to establish a Toulouse-Lautrec museum. It opened in 1922 at the former archbishop's palace (Le Palais de la Berbic), and has the largest extant group of paintings, drawings, prints, and posters by Toulouse-Lautrec, as well as Joyant's collection of paintings by Gauguin, Vuillard, Bonnard, Matisse, Dufy, Rouault, and Vlaminck, and sculptures by Maillol and Rodin.

Henri de Toulouse-Lautrec was the son of Count Alphonse de Toulouse-Lautrec-Maufra and thus descended from the counts of Toulouse. He was a delicate child, and two accidents as a boy left him a dwarf. The museum has a full-length portrait of him by Vuillard that shows him as a small, unattractive man. While his physical deformity came early in life his talent also came early. He studied painting in Paris and settled in Montmartre in the 1880s, where he painted the scenes he is known for: dance halls, cabarets, brothels, and the people in them. He identified with his subjects and was not the caricaturist he is sometimes mistakenly thought to be. Nor was he a satirist. He did have a gift for penetrating the human soul with an incisiveness that was profoundly honest. Nothing of a subject's personality escaped him.

The Salon in the Rue des Moulin (1894)
Lautrec's deformity probably caused him to avoid the society into which he had been born and to seek friends among social outcasts. Among these were the prostitutes of Paris. This canvas shows a brothel, with prostitutes on sofas; though they are scattered about the room, their indifference draws them together. One figure stands out, the madame's assistant, sitting erect with folded hands. Her features are more clearly defined than those of the others. Her curious remoteness sets the tone of this picture in which Lautrec never moralizes, criticizes, or dramatizes. His toned-down colors of mauve

and pink evoke a calm atmosphere. He is simply telling us that the salon is a way of life that exists—the oldest profession—and that there is no need to think of it as shocking or offensive.

A number of other pictures by Lautrec include *The English Girl at the Star, Le Havre* (1889); *Study for the Poster "Moulin Rouge"* (1891); *Head of an Englishman at the Moulin Rouge* (1892); *Yvette Guilbert* (1894); *Portrait of Dr. Tapié de Céleyran* (1894); *Chocolat, Dancing* (1896); *Woman Combing Her Hair* (1896); and *La Modiste* (1900).

_____Amiens_____

CATHEDRAL OF NOTRE DAME

Hours: Open daily 7:30AM–12 noon and 2–7PM.

This largest cathedral in France has a unity of style because it was built over a comparatively short period of time (1220–88). Its design and workmanship make it the classic French Gothic cathedral—an example of the high point of the Gothic style. It is also one of the most intelligently built because its builders could learn from the cathedrals already started at Chartres, Beauvais, and Reims. From Chartres they learned to make use of buttresses and ribbed vaulting to support aisles that provided huge windows opening onto the nave; from Beauvais they learned the sky was not the limit so made their choir lower than the one that toppled at Beauvais; and from Reims they learned to reduce thicknesses of walls and pillars to let more light into the nave.

The Latin cross plan at Amiens is simple, with short transepts that do not extend much beyond the nave, a magnificent curved apse at the east end that contains seven chapels, and a western facade inspired by Notre Dame at Paris. This simplicity is carried out on a massive scale. The cathedral measures 456 feet in length, 102 feet in width inside, and the roof of the nave rises to 145 feet. Such dimensions give a sense of grandeur, but it is the overall design and execution of detail that make the cathedral a great work of art. For example, the three-stage elevation of the **nave,** which has a fusion of triforium and clerestory into one unit, is harmoniously proportioned, a perfection of vertical movement in stone. Yet, without the narrow band of carved foliage below the low triforium arcade, which counters the soaring vertical lines of the wall by its horizontal presence, the interior would appear to rise uncontrollably upward. The superstructure of the **east end** is more brilliant. Here the exterior wall of the triforium is glazed so that colors are seen through the inner tracery, converting it into a zone of light. With clerestory and triforium glazed, and moldings connecting the two, the choir becomes a two-story elevation with much of its surface devoted to detail. This treatment of the surface, with the conversion of triforium and clerestory to a display of glass, makes a new kind of Gothic called Rayonnant.

Sculptures are everywhere; two prominent pieces should be noted. On the west front is the large statue of Christ, called *Le Beau Dieu d'Amiens,* on the pillar dividing the central portal. It is probably the finest medieval statue (thirteenth century) of the blessing Christ to have survived. It shows Christ holding the Gospel in His left hand with His right blessing the faithful who enter the cathedral. While a symbol of spiritual power, the figure has a compassionate look. The Byzantine characteristics of such statues during the Dark Ages have been abandoned here in a style that is purely French. In its time it was unconventional, for Christ is shown as a teacher, healer, and bestower of spiritual blessings, as He was on earth, instead of the judge and the vengeful conqueror of the Byzantine conception. Similarly, the thirteenth-century *Virgin and Child* (La Vièrge Dorée) on the facade of the south transept portal is a humanized work, graceful in the French style. This Virgin is a prototype of the many Madonnas that were to spread throughout Europe during the next four centuries.

The sixteenth-century (1508–22) **choir stalls** are the most complete set of their kind, with 4,700 figures making up a flamboyant decoration encompassing, in the Gothic tradition, an array of religious and profane themes that relates the whole story of life from creation through the two Testaments. The figures are probably the work of Flemish woodcarvers.

The **Musée de Picardie,** 48 Rue de la République (open Tues.–Fri. 10AM–12:30PM and 2–6PM, Sat. 10AM–6PM, Sun. 10AM–noon and 2–6PM; free admission) has a collection of eighteenth-century French paintings outstanding of which is a *Self-portrait* by Maurice Quentin de la Tour (1704–88), the famous French pastelist, and the *Laundresses* by Fragonard (1732–1806). Nineteenth-century paintings include some by Géricault, Delacroix, and Gauguin and there are twentieth-century paintings by Bonnard and Matisse. Flemish, Dutch, and Spanish old masters are also in the collection with landscapes by Jan van Goyen (1596–1656), *Portrait of Professor Langelius* by Frans Hals (ca. 1580–1666), *Portrait of a Man* by El Greco (1541–1614), and *The Miracle of St. Donatus* by Murillo (1618–82).

Arles

Note: All sites open daily 9 AM–12 noon and 2 PM–6 or 7PM. An all-inclusive ticket is available at any museum or monument.

Arles and its neighbors Nîmes and Orange were places of importance during Roman times. While the Roman remains at Arles are only fragments, an idea of the city's former splendor can be had at the great **Arena,** which has a Doric base and a Corinthian upper story (its third story is missing). It is one of the largest Roman arenas in France and at one time seated about 26,000 people. In the Middle Ages it became a place of refuge for the population of Arles; an entire city was housed within its walls. In the nineteenth century it was cleared and restored. Next to it are remains of a **Roman theater** built during the reign of Augustus. It served as a quarry for centuries.

The city also had a palace built by Constantine, now disappeared except for a small portion of its baths.

The **Museum of Pagan Art** (Musée Lapidaire Paien) in the seventeenth-century church of St. Anne on the Place de la République displays various finds excavated in the area, including objects from the Alyscamps, a vast necropolis during Roman times and a burial place during the Middle Ages. The sculptures found there from the Christian period are displayed in the **Museum of Christian Art** (Musée d'Art Chrétien) in the seventeenth-century Jesuit church on Rue Balze, west of the Place de la Cour.

CHURCH OF ST. TRÔPHIME

This typical Provençal church, once a cathedral, is austere with an interior that has a plain lofty aisle covered with a barrel vault. But its fine cloister and porch at the west front do make St. Trophime a jewel among the Romanesque churches of Provence.

In the **cloister**, delicate twin columns with carved capitals support the round arches of the arcades. The corners have massive rectangular piers with figures of saints and apostles that take the weight of the vault. All of the statues, high reliefs, and foliage capitals here are typical of the Romanesque style.

The **porch** on the west front seems to have been based on a Roman triumphal arch. It has a rich display of figures with a bold tympanum and lintel showing *Christ in Majesty* and the apostles, planned on the same lines as the tympanum of the west door at Chartres. An elaborate frieze with many small figures covers the cornice and runs around the portal. Statues of the apostles flank the central doorway arch, and the inner sides of the deep door jambs rest on carved figures of lions. While there is something Oriental in the repose and blank expressions of these figures, the classic Roman tradition is seen in the severity of horizontal lines and square niches.

The Romanesque style of Provence is thought possibly to be a forerunner of the greater Romanesque period of Europe and perhaps the inspiration for the west portal of Chartres. This theory is based on the fact that there are more classical monuments surviving in Provence than in any other part of France, so many classical examples were available to the artists of medieval Provence. Nevertheless, no building survives in Provence that can be dated between the classical period and the eleventh century (the cloisters and the west front of St. Trophime are not earlier than 1165–1200). This suggests the Romanesque style in Provence came at the end of the Romanesque period in Europe—not at its beginning.

Nineteen kilometers from Arles is the **town of St. Gilles.** There the old church, begun in 1116, has a west front consisting of three heavily sculptured doors linked by a colonnade. Classical influences are seen in the larger figures of the facade. As one of the last expressions of Romanesque art, they could be considered southern versions (though not precursors) of the west portal at Chartres.

Autun

Autun was built on the Via Agrippina, one of the main Roman roads through Gaul, by Emperor Augustus. It was a thriving town in the time of Christ, with an amphitheater larger than those at Arles and Nîmes—in fact, second in size to the Colosseum at Rome. Little remains of it except two Roman gates (Porte St. André and Porte St. Arroux) and the ruins of a square tower thought to have been part of a temple of Janus. The city declined rapidly after the Roman era, recovering only with the arrival of the dukes of Burgundy who, in the twelfth century, started the cathedral.

CATHEDRAL OF ST. LAZARE

Place du Terreau

This church was begun in 1120 to accommodate pilgrims who flocked to Autun to pray at the site of the remains of St. Lazarus, who, it was believed, came to France with Mary and Martha, and died in Autun. It was completed in a short time (consecrated by Pope Innocent II in 1132). The interior is barrel-vaulted with transverse arches, and its east end has three apses. Though flamboyant Gothic chapels were built by Cardinal Rolin in the fifteenth century (he also built the Gothic central spire), this is a good example of Burgundian Romanesque, showing influence of ancient Rome in its classically fluted pilasters and piers, and in the design of its pointed arches. Those pointed arches might lead to the idea that Autun Cathedral is a transition from Romanesque to Gothic, but it is only a coincidence that pointed arches were being experimented with in Burgundy in the twelfth century. They were inspired by Roman art and are not a part of the new Gothic style that came from Paris.

    Memorable at Autun are works of Romanesque sculpture on the capitals of many columns. These functional elements are decorated with scenes from the Old and New Testaments and with imaginary demons, including a menagerie of Romanesque beasts. Many of the capitals are copies of originals on display in the cathedral's Capitulary Hall and in the nearby **Musée Rolin**, 15 rue des Banes (open Wed.–Mon. 9:30AM–noon and 2–6:30PM, till 4PM Oct.–Mar.; admission fee). This museum has a figure of _Eve_ by **Gislebertus** found in a wall of the cathedral in 1866. Though only one half of a relief (the other half is lost), it is a masterpiece of expressionist art in which, at the moment before the fall, Eve gestures to Adam using the powers of her feminine appeal. There is also a good collection of paintings by French and Flemish primitives, including a _Nativity with Cardinal Rolin_ (ca. 1481–83) by the Master of Moulins (active 1480–99). This panel, influenced by Hugo van der Goes, is the earliest work ascribed to this fifteenth-century French master, whose name is unknown.

Gislebertus (active ca. 1125–ca. 1140), French

The Last Judgment (1135): Tympanum and lintel of west portal facade

It is rare that we have the signature of a medieval artist. Gislebertus, however, signed his name to his work on the tympanum and lintel of this west portal. His elongated sculptured figures in the style of the Burgundian school have the dramatic qualities of scenes from a medieval miracle play, from which he may have drawn inspiration. Every figure in his work expresses anxiety, bliss, or despair. Everyone is in motion. A large figure of Christ fills the center of the tympanum. He sits on a throne between emblems of the sun and moon with hands outspread in judgment. On the lintel below the tympanum are the faithful who will gain a heavenly reward. They are separated from the damned by an angel with a sword. Two colossal hands reach down to seize one of the damned, a probable reference to the burial prayer "Deliver me, O Lord, from eternal death, from the hand of hell, and from the jaw of the lion." Other figures are a woman whose breasts are being devoured by a snake—she represents lust—and a drunkard beating an empty barrel. These expressionistic works conveyed visions to a public that probably believed in them.

Bayeux

CENTRE GUILLAUME LE CONQUÉRANT

Rue de Nesmond

Hours: Open June–Sept., daily 9AM–7PM; Oct.–Mar. 15, daily 9:30AM–12:30PM and 2–6:30PM; Mar. 16–May, daily 9AM–12:30PM and 2–6:30PM. Admission fee.

Bayeux Tapestry (eleventh century)

This early narrative tapestry, which hung in the nave of the cathedral until the Revolution, depicts scenes of an invasion that took place more than eight hundred years ago: the 1066 invasion of England by William the Conqueror. He had a doubtful claim to the Anglo-Saxon throne, vacated by the death of Edward the Confessor, who left no heir. Landing at Pevensey with a Norman army of adventurers and land-hungry vassals, William killed King Harold, Edward's successor, at the Battle of Hastings. It took only five years more for the Normans to subdue the entire English kingdom.

Much of our knowledge of William's conquest comes from this tapestry, commissioned shortly after the conquest by William's half-brother, Odon, bishop of Bayeux and builder of the cathedral. French legend holds that Queen Mathilda, William's wife, took part in sewing on it to while away the long hours of her husband's absence—in France it is called "Queen Mathilda's Tapestry." The truth is that it was done by a school of Saxon weavers.

It is a kind of cartoon strip, 215 feet long by twenty inches wide, giving a detailed description of the events of 1066 in fifty-eight panels embroidered of coarse red, yellow, blue, and green wool on linen. We not only see historical events of the time but also get a detailed look at medieval society, its customs, costumes, tools, ships, weapons, even hair styles (the Saxons have long hair while the Normans are skinheads). An English-language narrative is available on rented tape recorders on the premises.

The nearby **Cathedral of Notre Dame**, though rebuilt a number of times, preserves its original Romanesque design in its crypt, nave arcades, lower parts of its lantern crossing, and west towers. Especially noteworthy are the columns and capitals of the nave, the Romanesque decorations, the Gothic clear story, the vaulting, and the various tracery.

Beauvais

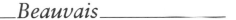

CATHEDRAL

The Cathedral of St. Pierre at Beauvais is only half a cathedral. It contains no nave, only a choir and transepts—where the nave should be is the tenth-century church of Basse-Oeuvre. But even in its truncated state it represents the high Gothic style in one of its finest forms.

Begun in 1225, at a time when religious feelings ran so high that it was common for a city to devote almost all of its energy and wealth to the building of an enormous, richly decorated church, the cathedral was hoped by its builders to surpass every known church in height and beauty. They raised the choir (completed in 1272) to a height of 158 feet, but the skill of the architects did not match their artistic daring. Pillars were placed too far apart to support such a height; there was not strength enough in the lower aisles to support the upper arcades, and the columns of the flying buttresses were too light. The result was that the vaulting crumbled and the roof fell in on November 29, 1284. It took forty years to rebuild. The Hundred Years War put an end to further construction until 1500, when the transepts were begun, to be completed in 1555. Instead of building a nave, the builders decided to put up the highest Gothic dome in the world, to outdo the one rising over St. Peter's in Rome. They built their spire 492 feet above the cathedral pavement, forty feet higher than the dome of St. Peter's. On Ascension Day 1573, five years later, just after the clergy and the congregation had left the church and were in a procession in another part of the city, the great dome of Beauvais crashed to the ground. The damage to the choir was repaired, but that put an end to further building at Beauvais.

While Beauvais has had its structural failures, it is nevertheless an artistic success in its suspended vaulting, towering arcades, and flying buttresses. Its decoration is brilliantly divided into broad masses, as its large size dictates, but shows fine detail in its architectural elements. It is a product of imaginative genius that has no imitators, because it showed Gothic builders just how high and how far they could ever hope to go. After Beauvais, Gothic buildings tended toward a reduced monumentality. Attention moved toward achieving a higher degree of sophistication.

Bourges

CATHEDRAL OF ST. ÉTIENNE

Hours: Open daily 7AM–12 noon and 2–6:30PM. Admission fee to crypt.

This Gothic cathedral, built between 1195 and 1275, is designed on a different pattern from most other cathedrals of its time, which take their inspiration from the model of Chartres. At Bourges the differences start with the facade of its west front, with five great portals instead of the usual three. These open onto one nave with double instead of single aisles. There are no transepts or galleries, and there is a crypt unusually large for a Gothic church, built above ground level and pierced by large windows. The unique design of this cathedral is not its only attribute; it has excellent sculpture on its front facade, the best stained glass in France after Chartres, and its interior is a creation of great beauty, light and airy.

St. Étienne is not without its drawbacks. Its west front facade has been criticized for being too wide for the proportions of the building, for having a jumbled appearance, and for having two towers that seem too low. The long outline of its facades has been considered monotonous and in need of something to break it up, such as transepts or a tall tower.

West Front Facade

As you face the facade, the five recessed portals have sculptures that represent: *The Last Judgment* in the center portal, flanked by portals depicting the lives of *St. Guillaume* and the *Virgin*, on the left; and *St. Étienne* and *St. Ursin* (the first bishop of Bourges), on the right.

The Last Judgment (ca. 1275): tympanum of center portal

This depiction of the Last Judgment displays a taste for movement and detail that for its time was new to Gothic art. Starting from the lowest band, we see nude figures rising from their graves on Judgment Day. While nudes rarely appear in medieval art, the license to depict them here derives from the Bible. They are depicted with attention given to anatomical truth and in a variety of poses that show an awareness of the human body, all in a state of glorious youth. The medieval spectator was taught that one would arise on the Day of Judgment at the age of thirty-three, the age Christ triumphed over death, whatever one's actual age might be. In the second band we see Archangel Michael with spread wings holding the scales with which he weighs man's good and evil deeds. He shelters a soul, represented by a child, from a leering demon. To the archangel's right the saved are being ushered into Paradise, led by St. Peter holding a key, where Abraham, seated upon a throne, awaits them. One figure is a king, probably St. Louis of France, who had recently died. To the left of the archangel the damned are taken over by an assortment of demons to be pushed or thrown into the flame-spewing mouth of Hell. The grotesque heads carved on the demons' bellies are symbolic of the evil of putting one's soul in the service of the lower appetites. Presiding at the top is a remote seated Christ with hands outstretched, as though appealing to the living rather than the dead. At His sides are the Virgin and St. John. Above, the sun and the moon are shown being carried away by angels, since this light cannot compete with the radiance of Christ.

Early twelfth-century Romanesque sculptures on the two lateral portals (north and south sides) were probably taken from the previous church on the site. Finely pleated drapery clings to the columnar figures; the barbaric decorations of animal and vegetable motifs are characteristic of the Romanesque School.

Interior

The great nave gives an uncluttered atmosphere as it flows into the choir without transepts branching off at either side. The double aisles continue around the apse as a double ambulatory, and with the height of the nave rising 125 feet, give an open, monumental effect that is the epitome of Gothic design. The two outer aisles being built lower than the inner ones permits three rows of windows instead of only two.

With such attention paid to light, Bourges has a great amount of **stained glass,** of which the finest specimens are thirteenth-century windows in the choir and the apsidal chapels. One depicts the *Apocalypse* (south side of the choir). The risen Christ is seen here as a judge bearing a two-edged sword between His teeth. The number 7 takes on symbolic importance; Christ holds seven stars in His left hand, a reference to the stars that fell in the Apocalypse. In His right hand is a book with seven seals, referring to the seven sacraments, and at His sides are seven candles that refer to the seven churches of Asia. The fifteenth-century glass in the **Chapel of Jacques Coeur** (the last chapel on the north side of the choir, or twelfth chapel) is in contrast to the older thirteenth-century glass. After two hundred years the figures shown seem to have more volume than in the thirteenth-century glass. Renaissance painting had changed the depiction of flat surfaces to the illusion of three-dimensional bodies.

THE HOUSE OF JACQUES COEUR

Rue Jacques Coeur

Hours: Open Easter–Oct., Wed.–Mon., 9–11:15AM and 2–5:15PM; Nov.–Easter, Wed.–Mon., 10–11:15AM and 2–4:15PM. Admission fee.

This elegant Gothic house, built between 1443 and 1451 by Jacques Coeur, a merchant and finance minister to Charles VII, is probably the finest surviving example of the late medieval French town house. It reflects the confidence in peace that had come to France at the close of the Hundred Years War; though built around a courtyard, it is without provisions for defense. Windows of considerable size appear in the outer wall. In Gothic construction, symmetry was not important, as it was to become later in Renaissance architecture. Because of the dominant role of religion in medieval life, there are many architectural elements taken from church construction: the emphasis on verticality, cathedrallike flamboyant tracery, and sculpture over the tympana of each doorway. The house is ahead of its time in its layout, which shows a concern for easy circulation and in its provision for running water— even the Renaissance palaces that came after it did not have that convenience.

Jacques Coeur lived in the house only about two years. He had put his fortune at the service of the king during the Hundred Years War, which made the victories of Joan of Arc possible and saved France from English domination, but he was nevertheless falsely accused of poisoning the king's mistress, Agnes Sorel, and sentenced to jail in 1452 by judges who owed him money. He eventually escaped and went to Rome to serve the pope in the Near East.

There are other old buildings in Bourges. The **Hôtel de Ville,** just south of the cathedral, was formerly the archibishop's palace in the seventeenth century. It has gardens designed by Le Nôtre (1613–1700) that provide a view of the eastern end of the cathedral. There is the **Hôtel Cujas** at 6 Rue des Arènes, an early Renaissance house built by a Florentine merchant in 1515. Today it serves as the **Musée de Berry,** holding a collection of pre-Roman and Roman artifacts, and paintings of mostly French origin. There is the **Hôtel Lallemant,** at 6 Rue Bourbonnoux, built between 1487 and 1518, an early French Renaissance dwelling with furniture, tapestries, and objets d'art from the sixteenth to the nineteenth century. Both museums are open 10AM–noon and 2–6PM; closed Tues. Single admission fees or all-inclusive admission fee for the House of Jacques Coeur and the two museums.

_____ Carcassonne _____

Carcassonne has famed medieval **walls** to walk all over or view from a distance—they are illuminated at night. Though criticized for overzealous restoration done in the nineteenth century by the architect Viollet-le-Duc (1814–79), Carcassonne gives the best idea in Europe of a fortified medieval town.

The history of Carcassonne goes back to the time of Julius Caesar and the Visigoths, who came after the Romans (fifth to eighth centuries). Fragments of the walls the Visigoths built can be seen worked into the newer construction. During the Albigensian crusades in the early thirteenth century, Carcassonne was a battleground when captured by Simon de Montfort, the soldier who defended the church against heretics and slaughtered thousands of people throughout Provence. In 1218, when Montfort was besieging the city of Beaucaire, he was killed by a stone thrown down at him from a church. His body was taken for burial to Carcassonne's Cathedral of St. Nazaire (his monument is in the south transept, but his body was reinterred elsewhere). The fortifications were strengthened in that century; and as late as the seventeenth century the town still served as a stronghold, in the war between France and Spain. But when peace came in 1659 the city was left to deteriorate, and it came close to being demolished during the nineteenth century when Viollet-le-Duc carried out his restorations.

There are two castellated walls, one inside the other, that encircle the town. They incorporate fifty-four towers dating mostly from the thirteenth century. Passage into the town was through two castlelike gates—the Porte Narbonnaire on the east side and the Porte d'Aude overlooking the lower town. There is also a citadel, built about 1130–50, without a donjon, in a rectangular plan round an open courtyard. Its gatehouse contained two portcullises (an iron grating made to slide down over the entrance) each operated from a different floor to avoid treachery. (A traitor could open one but still not open the castle to attackers.) The main defensive plan of the city is obvious: should an attacker break through the first line of walls, he would be exposed to fire from the second wall. Should he break through the second wall, he would finally have to take each of the towers, designed for independent defense. (The citadel and inner walls are open Apr.–Sept. 9AM–noon and 2–6:30PM; Oct.–Mar. 10AM–noon and 2–5PM; admission fee.)

CATHEDRAL OF ST. NAZAIRE

Within the walls of the upper city is the much restored thirteenth century cathedral, a mixture of the Romanesque (see the portal on the north side and the barred vaults of the nave) and the Gothic, with excellent stained glass. It incorporates Gothic Parisian features such as tracery in the windows of the apse and transepts. Like the apostles at the Sainte-Chapelle in Paris, statues covered by canopies stand on the corbels of the two piers flanking the entrance to the choir. The unknown Gothic architect, who skillfully fitted his Gothic choir and transepts into the 150-year-old Romanesque nave, gave the cathedral a pleasing synthesis of past and present.

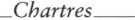

_____ _Chartres_ _____

CATHEDRAL OF NOTRE DAME

Hours: Open daily 7AM–7PM.

Built primarily between 1194 and 1260, this cathedral is of the greatest importance in the history of architecture, sculpture, and the art of stained glass. It stands on a site revered as a place of pilgrimage in pagan times when a druidical cult worshipped a statue of a virgin adjoining a sacred well into which Christian martyrs of Chartres are said to have been thrown. The identification of Chartres with the Virgin, even though originally pagan, may have been the reason Charles the Bold, in about 876, transferred to Chartres, from the treasury at Aix-la-Chapelle, the "Virgin's Veil," or _Sancta Camisia,_ said to have been worn by the Virgin at the birth of Christ. This relic had been given to Charles's grandfather, Charlemagne, by the emperor of Constantinople. But even before it came to Chartres churches had been built on the site, probably since the mid-fourth century. A basilica that had been built after 1020 burned to the ground in 1194, with the exception of the west towers, the facade between them and the crypt. The cathedral was rebuilt by

1220 in the short time of a generation, a feat that has gone down in history as one of the greatest cooperative efforts of mankind. It was done by offerings of funds and labor that poured into Chartres from all over France as well as from England.

With the rebuilding of the cathedral, new techniques in Gothic architecture were applied at Chartres. For the first time a massive cathedral went from the four-stage early Gothic elevation to a three-stage high Gothic construction of nave arcade, triforium passage, and clerestory window, doing away with tribune galleries. Bold flying buttresses in double tiers became the basic factor in the design, eliminating the wall from a structural point of view and thus enabling the clerestory windows to be made larger. The cathedral became a structure for the display of glass and allowed the builders to create a dramatic impression of height. In the Middle Ages this was an expression of civic prestige and spiritual feeling.

Exterior

West Front Facade (ca. 1150–70)

Two nonmatching **towers** dominate the facade. The taller one, on the north side, is probably older but there is some controversy about that. It is crowned by a thirteenth-century stage surmounted by a flamboyant spire, constructed between 1507 and 1513, 374 feet tall. The southern tower, shorter by twenty-six feet, dates from 1145–70 and has been called one of the greatest architectural achievements of the Middle Ages. Its simplicity and exquisite proportions, which show a powerful upward movement, make it one of the finest church spires.

Between the two towers are three portals, shallow in comparison to similar portals elsewhere. Above them are three lancet windows that resemble those of the early English style. Higher is a rose window spreading its tracery in all directions. The highest story between the towers is screened by an arcade over which rises a gable point. This arcade breaks the abruptness with which the pointed roof rises between the two spires. While the facade is plain in comparison with those at Reims and Amiens, what makes it important is its medieval statuary.

Sculpture on the West Front Facade

The sculptures on the west facade show transition from Romanesque to Gothic and must be dated close to 1150. They have the Romanesque emphasis of line exemplified in the columnar figures—Old Testament figures, the precursors of Christ—with their folded drapery in the Burgundian tradition. Though these figures stay within the columns from which they are inseparable, they are less severe than the Romanesque types from which they sprang. Their faces are humanized, possibly being portraits. While not fully Gothic, they point the way to emancipation from the earlier Romanesque.

The theme of the portals was well established in the twelfth century. In the tympanum of the central portal is the usual figure of Christ of the Apocalypse enthroned and surrounded by winged creatures symbolizing the four evangelists (Matthew, a man; John, an eagle; Luke, an ox; and Mark, a lion). Above are the twenty-four elders described in the Book of Revelation as seated around the throne, and below are the twelve apostles. In the left portal is Christ's Ascension into heaven and in the right portal the Nativity or Incarnation. The Old and New Testaments come together; Christ's divinity is established.

Sculpture on the Facade of the North and South Transepts (1224–50)

The facades of the north and south transepts have unique wheel-shaped flying buttresses outside the apse. The north transept facade is dedicated to the Virgin and characters of the Old Testament who preceded Christ. The facade of the south transept is devoted to the New Testament, with a *Last Judgment* in the central doorway. These figures, sculpted one hundred years after the figures on the west front facade, are expressions of a new naturalism that overtook the late Gothic style. The limitation of the statues to the column width no longer holds; figures are lifted from the background and stand almost clear of the wall. Relief carvings are worked more in the round. This tendency to freedom also brought a new concern with realism and drama, but without the deformations of the Romanesque style. It resulted in a new feeling of humanism divorced from the Romanesque-Byzantine tradition. In the north and south transept figures at Chartres we have our most perfect expression of Gothic sculpture.

Interior

Compared with the richly decorated exterior, the interior may at first appear chaste and dark, unless seen on a sunny day, when the kaleidoscopic stained glass will glow. The nave is one of the widest in France (forty-five feet), while its width is enhanced by the greater breadth of the choir, with its double ambulatory, and by the strong arms of the transepts, which extend the cathedral's width by an additional bay on each side.

An example of one of the cathedral's many fine architectural details is the form of the **piers of the nave** which reveal a subtle alternation in design. Where one pier is composed of an octagonal core with four round shafts engaged upon it, its neighbors reverse the scheme, having a circular core with four octagonal shafts. This design creates a fluctuation of patterns of shade—a change from a smooth transition of light to shade in the rounded surfaces, to the sharper breaks afforded by the octagonal form. Sophisticated touches of design like this, with the overall grandeur of columns, piers, and vaultings, create a fine example of the mature Gothic. At its best, as at Chartres, it is a combination of the subtle and the powerful—an expression in space and materials of the hearts and minds of those who built it.

Stained Glass (twelfth and thirteenth centuries)

One of the chief glories of Chartres Cathedral is its 130 stained glass windows, virtually all original. In early Gothic France stained glass replaced frescoed murals as the main decorative element in cathedrals. People marveled at the windows' resemblance to jewels, and found symbolic meaning in sunlight as the illuminator of Christ's dwelling on earth—divine light uniting Heaven and the church in the body of Christ. The windows also served an instructive purpose because few people could read, so stories depicted in the windows, lit up by the divine light of God, were convincing to the medieval worshipper.

The **oldest windows** are three on the west front above the portals and below the thirteenth-century rose window. Having escaped the great fire of 1194, these date from the late 1140s and are the finest that have come down to us. The window on the right depicts a *Tree of Jesse* (a genealogical tree showing Christ's ancestry starting with Jesse, the father of David); on the left side is the *Passion, Crucifixion and Redemption;* and in the center are scenes from the childhood and ministry of Christ, from the *Annunciation to the Entry into Jerusalem.* The predominant color is blue, which transmits the most light (red allows the least). The choice of colors is largely determined by the location of the glass; on the north side of the cathedral the color tends to be blue, while red appears on the south.

Other windows at Chartres are almost all from the thirteenth century. Of these the three **rose windows** dominate. The earliest, on the west front, depicts the *Last Judgment.* The rose window of the south transept shows Christ in Majesty surrounded by evangelists and angels. Here use of reds make the colors rich. The north rose, the latest of the three, depicts the Virgin and the Christ Child surrounded by doves of the Holy Spirit, angels, the twelve kings of Judah, who were Mary's ancestors, and twelve minor prophets. This rose and the window below it have more blue glass and show the most developed tracery.

Small **medallion windows** in the aisles and ambulatory were donated by various guild corporations of Chartres: carpenters, wheelwrights, wine merchants, clothiers, bakers, and blacksmiths, among others. They show the enthusiasm concentrated at Chartres by every branch of society and remind us of the unity of medieval society in the all-encompassing church.

Colmar

UNTERLINDEN MUSEUM

Place d'Unterlinden

Hours: Open Apr.–Oct., daily 9AM–12 noon and 2–6PM; Nov.–Mar., Wed.–Mon., 9AM–12 noon and 2–5PM; closed Jan. 1, Nov. 1, and Dec. 25. Admission fee.

This museum was originally a Dominican convent built in 1232 near a chapel dedicated to "St. John under the lime tree," hence its name, St. John unter der Linde. It displays a collection of Alsatian primitives, such as the *Altarpiece of Jean d'Orlier* by Martin Schongauer (ca. 1450–91). His *Virgin with the Rose Bush* is in the choir of the fourteenth-century church of St. Martin on Place des Dominicains in Colmar (open Apr.–Oct. daily 10AM–6PM; closed Nov.–Mar.; admission fee). Other objects are overshadowed by Grunewald's *Isenheim Altarpiece.*

Grünewald, Matthias (ca. 1460–1528) German

Isenheim Altarpiece (1510–15): room 5

Seeing this German work is an art experience in itself. Placed in the choir of the convent chapel, it overpowers the museum. Its most celebrated panels are those of the Crucifixion in a furious realistic style showing the agony as it had never been shown before. Its figure of Christ, set against a forbidding background, hangs from the Cross in a decomposing pale green and yellow, studded with thorns, a body as tortured as you will ever see painted. To add to the tragedy, no words seem to come from Christ's half open mouth; there is an expression of a centuries-old voiceless cry against man's fate. It is a depiction of suffering that only the late Gothic world of Germany could have produced.

This sublime Crucifixion, with its mystical atmosphere, is popular today, 465 years after it was completed. It seems to bridge the gap between the medieval and the modern, combining a realistic rendering of natural objects with the internal world of the mind.

Other panels of the altarpiece depict the Annunciation, concert of angels, Nativity, Resurrection, St. Anthony and St. Paul in the desert, and the Temptation of St. Anthony.

_____Loire Valley_____

Châteaux

Dictionaries define *château* as a "French castle" but it is far from a medieval fortress built for defense. There were such forts on the Loire in the Hundred Years War (1337–1453), but when peace returned to France in the sixteenth century, at the time of the Italian Renaissance, the châteaux we know today were built. Some do have architectural elements that could serve defensively, but they all have in common a country setting, an estate built on a grand scale and a building meant as a residence of comfort and elegance.

The châteaux discussed below—Azay-le-Rideau, Blois, Chambord, and Chenonceau—were, except Blois, built between 1508 and 1550. None was fortified. They were planned for luxury living and to make a good impression. A list of other châteaux is provided below, many as noteworthy as the four singled out here for special attention.

AZAY-LE-RIDEAU

Indre-et-Loire

Hours: Open Palm Sun.–Sept., daily 9AM–12 noon and 2–6:30PM; Oct.–Palm Sun., daily 9AM–12 noon and 2–4:30PM. Admission fee. Sound and Light show May, June, and July at 10:30PM; Aug. and Sept. at 10PM.

Surrounded by old trees in a green meadow on the Indre River a few miles from its junction with the Loire, the water forming a natural moat on one side of the house, Azay-le-Rideau was completed in 1524 by Gilles Bertelot, Louis XII's minister of finance. His wealth aroused the suspicions of the court and led to his self-exile from France, shortly after his fairytale château was completed, to avoid being hanged. The château became a possession of the crown. Today it is kept by the Académie des Beaux-Arts, which has turned it into a museum of Renaissance furniture and wall decorations.

The château is built on an *L*-shaped plan and is not large for châteaux in France. While there is a sense of the medieval in its corner turrets and machicolations, these are merely decorative, serving to enliven the appearance of the facade. The refined Renaissance style pervades the structure, which has large windows, lovely wall articulations, high-pitched slate roofs, pepper-pot turrets, and high pinnacled gables.

The front portico frames the double-arched windows of the great staircase. Its facade is rich with columns, pilasters, and sculptured niches that culminate in a monumental gable. The straight double staircase inside has vaulting embellished with large panels ornamented with medallions. A straight staircase with sculptured decoration above it eventually became an indispensable refinement for great houses built everywhere on the Continent.

BLOIS

Loir-et-Cher

Hours: Open Mar. 16–Sept. 30, daily 9AM–12 noon and 2–6:30PM; Oct. 1–Jan. 31, daily 9AM–12 noon and 2–5PM; Feb. 1–Mar. 15, daily 9AM–12 noon and 2–5:30PM. Admission fee. Sound and Light show Mar. 20–Oct. 20, in English at 10:30PM.

The oldest part of this château dates from the thirteenth century and can be seen in the Salle des États, or main hall, in the northwest wing, which served as the seat of the States General in the late sixteenth century. When Louis XII ascended the throne he favored Blois as a royal residence. He built a new east wing and rebuilt the west wing. The east wing, named for the king, has a profusion of gables and pinnacles in the flamboyant Gothic style, with only a slight influence of the Italian Renaissance worked into it. When Francis I, who also favored Blois, became king, he built the **north wing** (1515) in an Italianate design that shows how much the style of architecture had changed in only a short span of time. Indeed, it shows a determination to break completely with Gothic tradition and embrace the Italian Renaissance style. Loggias opening toward the city are worthy of any building in Italy. In its **inner court**, in a turret that stands out from the facade, is an openwork staircase with octagonal tiers that is classical in appearance and decoration. Thus Blois shows a transition from the Gothic of the older part to the classic of the Francis I wing.

In the small rooms of Blois great events took place. Catherine de Médicis kept poison hidden in compartments of her famous room, that has 237 carved wooden panels. She died there in 1589. In the royal suite of Henri III is the king's study and bedroom, scene of the murder of the Duc de Guise on December 23, 1588. (Henri assassinated the duke for challenging the crown by forming his Holy League.) Blois was also where Queen Marie de Médicis, kept under surveillance in 1617, despite her corpulence escaped on a dark winter's night by climbing a ladder and sliding down a hillside.

CHAMBORD

Loir-et-Cher

Hours: Open Apr.–Sept., daily 9–11:45AM and 2–6:30PM; Oct.–Mar., Wed.–Mon. 9–11:45AM and 2–4 or 5PM. Admission fee. Sound and Light show June and July at 10 and 11PM; Aug. at 9:30 and 10:30PM; Sept. at 9 and 10PM.

This huge château—400 rooms, seventy staircases, 365 chimneys, set in a 15,000-acre park with the longest wall in France—is Francis I's great Italian palace up to its third-floor roof. Beyond that it is inventive French with turrets, towers, chimneys, pinnacles, and belvederes. A central lantern in a cupola rises 100 feet.

The building of Chambord began in 1519 when Francis I approved plans drawn up by his Italian architects, of whom Domenico da Cortona was the most prominent. It is thought possible that Leonardo da Vinci, then in France, had a hand in it. At first it looks like the royal Renaissance palace it was intended to be, with its large, numerous windows and symmetrical design. The irregularity of French Gothic is gone, but something of the old military stronghold lingers on at Chambord in its central cubiform block with its inner and outer courts, its great donjons at the corners, and, once, a moat that is now filled in.

There is an Italian Renaissance arrangement of the rooms into apartments, but the openwork central staircase, with twin spiral flights allowing those descending to be unseen by those ascending, is a French idea.

CHENONCEAUX

Indre-et-Loire

Hours: Open Mar. 16–Sept. 15, daily 9AM–7PM; Sept. 16–Oct. 31, daily 9AM–6PM; Nov., daily 9AM–5PM; Dec. 1–Jan. 31, daily 9AM–12 noon and 2–4PM; Feb.–Mar. 15, daily 9AM–12 noon and 2–5PM. Admission fee. Sound and Light show Apr. 1–Sept. 30 at 10PM.

Chenonceaux, begun in 1515, is built on the foundation of an old mill that stood on the granite bed of the river Cher. Its builder was Thomas Bohier, a minister to the French kings. He probably used Italian architects at Chenonceaux for the Gothic architects of France could never have achieved an aristocratic grace at the time. The setting of the château is its main feature, since much of its detail was lost to nineteenth-century restorers. Its straight staircase, however, is original and, like the one at Azay-le-Rideau, is Italian in inspiration.

Women have figured prominently in the history of Chenonceaux, the first being Catherine Biçonnet, wife of the original builder, who supervised construction. Then came Diane de Poitiers, mistress of Henri II, whose topless portraits you can see elsewhere in France. She received the château as a gift from Henri and lived at Chenonceaux from 1547 to 1559. Its setting was perfect for carrying on her love affair with Henri, which continued to his death in a jousting accident. After that, Henri's wife, Catherine de Médicis, lost no time in evicting Diane de Poitiers (Diane was given the gloomy château of Chaumont) and built the bridgelike part of the château that extends over the river to the left bank. She used this addition for parties where nude nymphs floated in the water beneath the château and Italian fireworks were fired off. Catherine left Chenonceaux to her daughter-in-law, Louise de Lorraine, who accepted it as a widow, following the assassination of Henry III. She had the château painted in black, its ceilings decorated with skulls, bones, and gravedigger's tools to reflect her mourning.

Frivolity returned to Chenonceaux when Gabrielle d'Estreés, mistress of Henri IV (also known for her topless portrait, at the Louvre), moved into the château. Her union with Henri IV resulted in a bastard son, the Duc de Vendôme who, with his descendants, owned Chenonceaux for over a century. In the eighteenth century the château was owned by Claude Dupin, a wealthy tax collector, whose wife's salon at Chenonceaux was visited by many well-known personalities. Later, while a widow at Chenonceaux during the Revolution, she and the château were left undisturbed. During the next century restorations were carried out at Chenonceaux at the direction of a Mme Pelouze, who held festivities at the château that almost surpassed those three hundred years earlier of Catherine de Médicis.

Other Châteaux of the Loire Valley

Hours: The châteaux listed below are generally open late spring through early autumn, daily 9AM–12 noon and 2–5 or 6PM. All charge an admission fee.

AMBOISE

Indre-et-Loire

Only about one third of the original fifteenth- and sixteenth- century château remains. Its flamboyant Gothic Chapel of Saint-Hubert holds the supposed remains of Leonardo da Vinci who died at Clos-Lucé, his residence nearby. (There is a sound and light show.)

AZAY-LE-FERRON

Indre

A mixture of architectural styles from the fifteenth to the nineteenth century, this château is visited for its lovely park and collection of Empire and Restoration furniture.

CHAUMONT-SUR-LOIRE

Loire-et-Cher

A fortresslike château that Catherine de Médicis vengefully made Diane de Poitiers accept in exchange for the lovely Chenonceaux. It has magnificent low round towers on three of its exterior corners. The interior should be seen for its staircase towers, furniture, and decorative elements. (There is flood-lighting.)

CHERVERNY

Loir-et-Cher

This seventeenth-century château in the classical French early baroque style is lived in by the same family that built it. It has its original Louis XIII furnishings. In its royal chamber every inch of wall and ceiling is covered with various decoration. (There is a sound and light show.)

LANGEAIS

Indre-et-Loire

Here is a house built in a short space of time, between 1465 and 1469, in the style of a medieval fortress. Having been barely altered since the fifteenth century, and containing a collection of period furnishings, it offers an authentic look at how a lord lived in France in the time of Louis XI.

LOCHES

Indre-et-Loire

The Romanesque keep of this imposing château, which dates back to the eleventh century, is of interest, as are the dungeons that once held the duke of Milan, Ludovico Sforza (Il Moro). In contrast to them are fourteenth- and fifteenth-century royal apartments that offer views of the town below. See, in the town, the Church of Saint Ours, which has twelfth-century pyramid vaulting unique in France.

LUDE

Sarthe

This château is a combination of fifteenth-century defensive architecture in its angle towers, Renaissance decoration added in the sixteenth century, and Louis XIV architecture in the wing overlooking the Loire. Its interior has a collection of period furniture. (There is a sound and light show.)

MONTGEOFFROY

Maine-et-Loire

This late eighteenth-century château, built in a short time in the classical style, is still in the family that originally inhabited it and it retains its original Louis XVI furniture and collection of paintings. Everything here survived the Revolution. (There is floodlighting.)

SAUMUR

Maine-et-Loire

This château, with four corner towers, dominates the town from a hilltop. It was built in the fourteenth century, but has Renaissance features from the sixteenth century. Its interior contains two museums: one houses a collection of furniture, ceramics, and tapestries; the second is an equestrian museum. (There is floodlighting.)

SULLY-SUR-LOIRE

Loiret

This late-fourteenth-century chateau (the living quarters were added in the sixteenth and seventeenth centuries, and one facade was rebuilt in the eighteenth century), has a square keep, round towers at its corners and a location on an island in the Loire. A medieval fortress, its most illustrious occupant was the Duc de Sully (1560–1641), Henri IV's finance minister. (There is floodlighting.)

USSÉ

Indre-et-Loire

This fifteenth-century château between the banks of the Indre and the forest of Chinon has picturesque fortified towers and turrets that give it a feudal appearance. A close look reveals some Renaissance decorative elements, such as those in its sixteenth-century chapel, and a seventeenth-century baroque main facade facing the park. (There is floodlighting.)

VALENÇAY

Indre

Here is an example of a mid-sixteenth-century Renaissance château (the wing set at a right angle to the main building is from the eighteenth century). At one time it was owned by Talleyrand, some of whose furniture is preserved here, including a table used at the Congress of Vienna. (There is a sound and light show.)

VILLANDRY

Indre-et-Loire

The fame of this plain fourteenth- and fifteenth-century château rests on its Renaissance gardens, the most ambitious in the Loire Valley. Its fourteenth-century tower, at the southern end of its west front, is part of the original château.

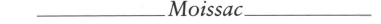

Moissac

CHURCH OF ST. PIERRE

Hours for cloister: Open daily 9AM–12 noon and 2–6PM; closed Dec. 25 and Jan. 1. Admission fee.

This church, rebuilt many times, is of importance for its south porch, its cloister, and its Romanesque sculpture.

In the eleventh-century Moissac was affiliated with the powerful monastery of Cluny and was thus favored by popes and kings for two centuries. At its height it had a community of a thousand monks and property throughout southern France. Moissac was one of the churches on the pilgrimage route to Santiago de Compostela in Spain, so received thousands of pilgrims and the economic benefits from them. This explains the richness of the sculpture here.

Sculpture on the South Porch (ca. 1110–20)
The sculpture on this porch is one of the great examples of Romanesque art. Its composition culminates in the tympanum showing the *Christ of the Apocalypse* (The Second Coming of Christ) surrounded by the symbols of the evangelists (Matthew, a man; John, an eagle; Luke, an ox; and Mark, a lion), angels and an extraordinary group of elders, many sitting cross-legged in animated positions looking up at Christ. Their small scale contrasts with the crowned, bearded figure of Christ who dominates the scene. The sculptor has not cut deeply into the stone but Christ's figure manages some mass, conveyed to us by the garment pressed in folds against His figure, with edges ending in a zigzag so that the surfaces create the effect.

The intensity of feeling is carried over into bas-reliefs on the side walls, which support the vault of the porch. These are later in date than the tympanum, probably carved when the tympanum was moved from its original site on the west side to the south door.

This sculpture played a role in the revival of monumental sculpture in France after the Dark Ages. It has been suggested that Romanesque sculpture started here, at Moissac, its motifs taken from illuminated manuscripts regularly reproduced. (The iconographical theme of the tympanum seems to be derived from an eighth-century Spanish manuscript.) The theory is that with the revival of art in Europe, designs from illuminated manuscripts were simply transferred to stone, at first in the bas-relief of the tympanum at Moissac, and later as statuary. While manuscripts clearly did play a role in the revival of sculpture in Europe, it cannot be safely assumed that Moissac was the beginning of the revival of art in France. It is more likely that art was revived in many different places. The great schools of the north (Cluny, the Abbot Sugar in Paris and Dijon) likely had a greater influence. The debt owed by France to Italy is also clear. There was a constant movement of clergy between the northern French cities and Italy, which probably resulted in Burgundy becoming the distribution center of Romanesque art in France. What we know of the sculptures in Cluny in the twelfth-century (but later destroyed) supports this theory. While Moissac was an important source of Romanesque art, it was probably not the first.

Cloister (1100–1110)

While the south porch is majestic, the cloister is enchanting with a beauty in arabesques and pagan designs that recalls Arab Spain. Only in the capitals and bas-reliefs of the corners is there traditional Christian iconography.

The apostles depicted on the corners, where the pier is conceived as a stele and the standing figure is confined within the framework of the arched niche, are vigorous in style but primitive in execution, a bit out of place among the fantastic animals and arabesques of the arcades.

_____Mont St. Michel_____

MONASTERY

Hours: Open May 15–Sept. 15, daily 9–11:30 AM and 1:30–6PM; Sept. 16–May 14, daily 9–11:30AM and 1:30–4PM. Tours in English are given daily, except Fri., at 10:30AM, 11:30AM, 1PM, 2:30PM, and 4:30PM. Admission fee.

This Benedictine monastery is famous for its precipitous site 250 feet high atop a pointed rock lying one and a half miles off the coast of Normandy. A causeway, built in 1879, connects it to the mainland. It was a monastery as early as the eighth century, and Benedictine monks built its twelfth-century abbey. In the thirteenth century, under the direction of King Philippe-Auguste, the huge building on the north side of the rock, known as La Merveille (The marvel), was built as a refectory and later a residence for knights stationed on the Mount.

At the end of the town's only street is the entrance of the abbey, where conducted tours begin. Visitors ascend to the **Church** (ninety steps) which retains part of its Romanesque nave and has a taller Gothic choir, both much restored in the eighteenth and nineteenth centuries. The **cloister,** part of the upper story of La Merveille, has a double arcade with two overlapping rows of pointed arches and carved foliage designs in its spandrels. Lying below, **La Merveille** is an example of thirteenth-century domestic architecture in three floors, each divided into two large halls. The guests' hall (salles des hôtes) has quadripartite rib vaults with small bosses, and the knights' hall (salle des chevaliers), on the same floor, may have served as the monk's scriptorium, but after 1469 was used as a dormitory for the knights garrisoned on the Mount.

One may descend from the top using the steps that run along the fifteenth-century ramparts that border the sea. Sensational views of the construction of Mont St. Michel can be had.

Nîmes

Nîmes became an important Roman city during the reign of the Emperor Augustus (27 B.C.–A.D. 14) because of its strategic position on the road between Italy and Spain. The remains of its Roman past survive mainly in its arena, in better condition than the one at Arles, and in its Maison Carrée, the best-preserved Roman temple in the world. An admission ticket purchased at any one of Nîmes's monuments will admit you to all of them. The monuments are open June–Sept., 9AM–12 noon and 2–7PM (till 5PM off season). The arena stays open June–Aug., 8:30AM–7:30PM; and July–Aug. for the Maison Carrée. Closed Tuesdays off season.

ARENA (ca. 30 B.C.)

The arena, or amphitheater, is an original Roman construction. Roman architecture grew from Roman needs and the arena played a role in providing entertainment for the masses. Every important town of ancient Rome had an arena. The one here, still in use, can seat 21,000 spectators. Like similar structures, its plan is oval with rising tiers of seats constructed around an elliptical area, the highest seats being about seventy feet above the ground. Its exterior wall, still in good condition, is built in two stories and uses the Doric order in both stages.

MAISON CARRÉE (ca. 16 B.C.)

Unlike the arena, which owes little to previous Greek forms, the Maison Carrée is a combination of forms derived from Greek and Etruscan architecture.

The Etruscans had a civilization while Rome was still a small city-state. Their temples, of wood and terra cotta on a raised platform with a sanctuary, or cella, that extended the width of the structure, were known to the Romans and were copied by them. The rectangular Maison Carrée follows the Etruscan, rather than the Greek, plan. Its cella runs the width of the building and rests on a pedestal, and does not conform to the style of Greek temples, which have free-standing colonnades and a continuous porch that may be approached on all sides. Although some of the colonnade remains in the Maison Carrée, much of it consists of engaged columns (columns attached to the wall instead of standing free of it). This shows the Romans used columns less as structural members than for decoration. It is likely that if those columns were removed the walls and roof of the building would still stand, but no column of a Greek temple could be taken away without causing the structure to collapse. To find Greek influence in this little Roman temple you must look at its proportions and its fine detail, especially in the entablature with carved modillions and scroll design in the frieze. Much of the rest of it is Etruscan.

PONT-DU-GARD (19 B.C.–18 B.C.)

Twenty-three kilometers northeast of Nîmes

This fine Roman aqueduct, a short section of the original that was twenty-five miles long, testifies to the engineering genius and practical character of the Romans. Solidly built, it consists of two tiers of arches, each about sixty-five feet high, and an upper tier of smaller arches twenty-eight feet high, which contains the water carrying section. Less a work of art than a feat of engineering, it does express a stark beauty.

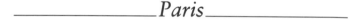

_____Paris_____

Museums

MUSÉE DE CLUNY

6 place Paul-Painlevé, 5ᵉ (reached from the boulevard St. Michel via the rue du Sommerard)

Metro: Cluny or St. Michel

Hours: Open Wed.–Mon. 9:45AM–12:30PM and 2–5:15PM; closed holidays. Admission fee.

The building housing this medieval collection is itself a work of art and has an interesting history. Before it became the residence of the monks of Cluny, it was known as the Palais des Thermes from the third-century Gallo-Roman building that used to stand here. Part of that structure remains and has Roman baths, sculptures, and reliefs. The palace dates back to the fifteenth century and is one of the few medieval buildings existing in Paris, an example of the late medieval French town house, or hotel, built by merchants or churchmen. The building was the residence of the rich abbots of the monastery of Cluny-en-Bourgogne. Its plan is the classic pattern built around a courtyard. It has six staircases, one in a tower projecting from the facade, and finialed dormers and window tracery in the flamboyant style.

The sister of Henry VIII of England, Mary Tudor, known in France as Marie d'Angleterre, stayed at Cluny in 1515. She had come to England at the age of sixteen to marry Louis XII, the fifty-year-old king. Louis died three months after the wedding and Marie d'Angleterre was installed at Cluny by Francis I, the new king. He was prepared to maintain Mary in a style a royal widow deserved, but feared she might produce royal offspring. With his position as the inheritor of the Valois-Angoulême throne thus in jeopardy, he kept a watchful eye on the young widow. One night he surprised Mary in the company of the Duke of Suffolk. He forced the two to marry and sent them off to England. The room next to the chapel on the first floor is named after Marie d'Angleterre. It is called the Chamber of the White Queen, for in medieval times white was the color of mourning.

The museum's collection has objects in the spirit of Mary Tudor's time. Furniture, ivories, metalwork, enamels, miniatures, and tools of crafts are displayed. The collection of fifteenth- and sixteenth-century tapestries, among which is the series known as the *Lady with the Unicorn,* is renowned.

Lady with the Unicorn series (late fifteenth century–early sixteenth century): first floor, room 11
Though its meaning is obscure, this series of tapestries is a work of great beauty and design. It was once thought it may have been meant to celebrate a wedding, but the presence of only one coat of arms on the flags suggests they were made for a man. In the nineteenth century, each of the six pieces (starting from the tapestry on the right side of the room) received the names *Sight, Music* (Hearing), *My Only Desires, Taste, Smell,* and *Touch.* In the first two and last three tapestries there is a reference to the senses. The third tapestry, called *My Only Desires,* showing the lady putting her jewels back in the jewel box, refers to her surrender to the senses. Every tapestry has the lady and her supporters, the unicorn and the lion, woven into the motifs. While the lion has often been a symbol of ferocity, here it may refer to the Resurrection, because the medieval world believed that when lion cubs were born they lay dead for three days until the father lion breathed life into them. The unicorn, in spite of its phallic overtones, is a symbol of female chastity, since a medieval bestiary based on the Greek *Physiologus* of the fifth century reads, "And thus did our Lord Jesus Christ, who is a unicorn spiritually, descend into the womb of the Virgin."

Whatever the meaning, *The Lady with the Unicorn* tapestries are among the most graceful and seductive works of art from the Gothic world of chivalry, fantasy, and romance.

MUSÉE JACQUEMART-ANDRÉ

158, Boulevard Haussman, 8ᵉ

Métro: Miromesnil or St. Philippe-du-Roule

Hours: Open Wed.–Sun., 1:30–5:30PM; closed holidays. Admission fee.

This museum is the result of a nineteenth-century couple's dedication to art. He was Edouard André, the son of a banker; she was Nélie Jacquemart, a fashionable portrait painter. They were married in 1881 and built a private collection which they installed in their residence on the Boulevard Haussman. After Edouard André died in 1894, Mme André continued a private Italian museum on the first floor of her home. At her death, in 1912, she bequeathed her home, her collection, and her fortune to the Institute of France, which turned her residence and art objects into a small museum.

Note: Paintings are frequently moved about the museum and some may not be displayed. The resident guard, Mr. Francois Duhamel, who speaks English, may be able to assist you if you cannot find the works of art mentioned below.

Room 1 has the *Portrait of François Gillequin* by Jean Baptiste Perronneau (1715–83), an eighteenth-century French painter who is recognized today as one of France's best portraitists. Room 4, whose ceiling is by Tiepolo, has Frans Hals's *Portrait of a Man* and Rembrandt's *Supper-at-Emmaus,* one of several paintings Rembrandt did on this subject (see Rembrandt, *Supper at Emmaus,* Louvre, Paris). Room 6, whose ceiling is also by Tiepolo, has a portrait of a child, *Small Boy Playing with a Cat,* by François-Hubert Drouais (1727–75), one of the most popular portraitists during his day who studied under Francois Boucher and succeeded him as court painter to Louis XV; and a small oval-shaped painting, a delightful rococo scene, *The Model's Debut,* by Fragonard (1732–1806). This picture shows a young woman exposing a young model's breasts for the approval of an artist, who attempts to raise the shyly resisting model's skirt with his painter's stick. It is a scene typical of pre-Revolutionary France. Room 7 (Great Hall), has *The Ambassador of Hippolyta, Queen of the Amazons, to the Court of Thesus, King of Athens,* by Carpaccio (ca. 1465–ca. 1525), which is a pageant of Venetian courtly life at the close of the eighteenth century; and the bronze plaquette by Donatello (1386–1466), *Martyrdom of St. Sebastian,* which exploits pictorial possibilities in bas-relief and has the heroic conception of the figure, a departure from the rather elegant style of Donatello's time.

Along the stairs leading up to the first floor are three frescoes by Tiepolo that once decorated the Villa Contarini in Venice, and in room 9 *St. George Slaying the Dragon* (1440–50) by Uccello (ca. 1397–1475), possibly the finest painting in the collection. It tells the story of St. George rescuing a princess who was being offered to a dragon as a sacrifice so it would stop molesting the city behind the walls seen in the distance. While the subject matter and the arrangement of the figures, seen in profile, are Gothic, Uccello's life-long interest in perspective recession, which he uses to show us the neatly mapped-out fields and city in the background, makes this a Renaissance work of art that was actually modern for its time.

MUSÉE DU JEU DE PAUME

Place de la Concorde, l^e

Metro: Concorde

Hours: Open Wed.–Mon., 9:45AM–5:15PM; closed holidays. Admission fee.

The Louvre, needing space for its impressionist and postimpressionist paint-ings, found it in the Jeu de Paume. The building, on the northwest corner of the Tuileries, was originally a place for playing "jeu de paume," a kind of indoor tennis. As one of the most heavily visited museums in the world, the Jeu de Paume usually has a line of ticket buyers extending into the Tuileries. Crowds are so large and space so restricted that it is difficult to see the paint-ings. This problem should be solved when the collection is moved in 1986 to a permanent home along with other nineteenth-century art to the new **Musée d'Orsay** across the Seine. The old Gare d'Orsay, the Belle Epoque railroad station on the left bank, is being made into a new museum. It will be one of the largest museums in the world devoted exclusively to nineteenth-century art.

Impressionism
Though impressionism relates to our own time it was a product of the nine-teenth century. Its roots go back to the French Revolution at the end of the eighteenth century. It was a time when modern art was just about to de-velop. The traditional art patron and the artist were becoming separated be-cause of social, economic, and political changes. Patronage from the church and the nobility was ending, along with the demand for paintings with reli-gious and mythological themes. Official academies, echoing the desires of a new middle class with political and economic power, laid down rules for art-ists based on a revival of classicism. While many artists went along, some imaginative artists struck out on their own to experiment with new styles and techniques.

The first artists to challenge the academies were independent painters who made up the romantic movement. Though their art was later absorbed by the academies, who expanded their point of view regarding neoclassicism to include it, the romantics encouraged individualism and an interest in the common man and in nature. By the middle of the nineteenth century this led to realism, a style associated with Gustave Courbet (1819–77) in France, a reaction against both romanticism and neoclassicism. It was concerned with scientific observation and social problems, both highlighted by the industrial revolution. From this interest in visual reality, the next step led to impres-sionism.

The goal of the impressionists was to bring realism further so as to reproduce what the eye really sees in nature, what is visually assimilated by the mind. In order to do this, impressionists developed a technique of painting whereby the smoothness of application of paint to a canvas was abandoned in favor of open brush strokes using primary colors applied directly to the canvas. The idea was that varying sources of light could change the color of objects and therefore one's impression of what one sees. Impressionists applied colors that would blend not on the canvas but in the viewer's eyes. Painters also worked out-of-doors and included subjects in their paintings previously considered unpaintable—rain, fog, and snow, for example. As the movement progressed, impressionists developed individual styles that led to refinements of the technique. In the nineteenth century, there was a reaction against it, called postimpressionism. Major figures in that movement were Cézanne (1839–1906), van Gogh (1853–90), and Gauguin (1848–1903), from whom stem the modern expressionist movements in our own century. These artists reconsidered structural problems and decorative possibilities, and explored new uses of color, which led to the first expressive distortion, or abstraction—a new way to look at art.

French influence in this progression of nineteenth-century art was paramount. Until the Musée Gare d'Orsay is opened, nowhere else is it as concentrated and as accomplished as it is at the Jeu de Paume.

Note: Room locations have not been given for the Jeu de Paume collection of paintings discussed below, as they are expected to be moved to the new Musée Gare d'Orsay after this guide goes to press.

Cézanne, Paul (1839–1906) French
Cezanne's art evolved until in his late work he was expressing the structural nature of a pictorial statement over the decorative qualities. He had been unable to identify with the lack of form and composition in impressionism and had no use for the storytelling content of some impressionist art. Like modern artists who came after him and learned from him, he saw his paintings as arrangements of forms, color, and texture rather than as subjects with emotional meaning. Cézanne started out as an impressionist but became a postimpressionist along with Gauguin, van Gogh, and Seurat. This is seen in his still lifes. Fruit becomes spheres and other geometric forms. In his *Card Players,* one of his few genrelike paintings, it is a statement of form based on color and composition. Similarly, in his landscapes, such as *L'Estaque,* he expresses the scene in cubistlike planes, each with its pattern of color, to create a sense of depth.

Through his artistic imagination Cézanne encouraged us to see the world as he did, transforming everyday objects into ideal forms in an ideal space. This gave cubists and others the courage to look at the world more creatively and to express what they saw without constraints.

Degas, Edgar (1834–1917), French
Degas was one of the leading members of the impressionist movement and an organizer of many of the group's exhibitions, but he was an impressionist

with a difference. He had been trained in the old master tradition of fine drawing and as a result his figures have line and a solidity elsewhere missing from impressionist painting.

Degas expressed movement in his figures while remaining within the impressionist style. His ballet scenes, paintings of women working, women at their toilet, and horse racing, record spontaneous movement in figures who do not seem to know they are being observed. They hold little interest for Degas as events but exist for him only to display movement.

Degas's interest in photography is seen in paintings such as his famous *The Absinthe* (ca. 1877). He places his figures off center, as one would photograph a scene, and snaps the picture, so to speak, from below. As an admirer of the old masters he also pays attention to composition. Notice in *The Absinthe* how he directs the eye toward the people at the table and beyond by the slanting lines of the table edges, which we follow from the foreground into the depths.

Gauguin, Paul (1848–1903), French

The museum does not have many masterpieces by Gauguin because France ignored him as an artist during his lifetime. However, *Tahitian Women* (1891), *The White Horse* (1898), and *And the Gold of Their Bodies* (1901) are all examples of his late style in Tahiti where he went to escape civilization in a protest against materialism.

The primitive life Gauguin admired is reflected in his style of flat forms that emphasize color. He makes no attempt to render his pictures realistically, as the impressionists do; his linear style and areas of flat color, like stained glass, can be considered expressionistic. Gauguin's figures become a symbolic part of nature, what Gauguin felt was part of the overall scheme of the uncorrupted world where people could go without clothes as in the Garden of Eden. In *The White Horse* the naked people ride unsaddled horses as though they were at one with animals: in *And the Gold of Their Bodies* the two naked women, who sit on the ground with their backs forming part of the flat background, are integrated into the setting; and in *Tahitian Women*, though the figures are clothed, their solid forms become part of the flat pattern in being viewed from above. The figures seem tied to the earth with solid weightiness, to be a living part of the earth.

Gauguin is one of the postimpressionists who link nineteenth-century impressionism to twentieth-century expressionism.

Gogh, Vincent van* (1853–90), Dutch

The museum has some of the paintings van Gogh produced during his last phase when he was under Dr. Gachet's care at Auvers, including *The Church at Auvers,* a *Portrait of Dr. Gachet, Cottages at Cordeville,* and the last *Self-portrait.* All date from June, 1890, less than one month before Vincent, despairing of a cure for his mental illness, committed suicide.

The Church at Auvers and *Cottages at Cordeville,* with their swirling brush strokes, thick impasto, and dynamic compositions, reflect the painter's tortured mind. The same restlessness can be seen in the blue background of the *Self-portrait,* where pulsing forms are carried over into the figure. It has been supposed that this self-portrait was done while Vincent was in a psychotic state, but it is clear that he still had control of his artistic talents. The modeling of the head and coloring of blues and greens combined with the red of the beard show it. The same is true of the *Church at Auvers,* with its cobalt blue sky (blue meant infinity to van Gogh) and the green tones of the church and the ground, with a touch of red on its roof (green and red in Vincent's words stood for "the terrible passion of humanity"). Dr. Gachet appears in his portrait to be as confused about Vincent's ailment as Vincent was. The compassionate doctor, with his sympathy for the afflicted, has the look of a worried man who knows his own impotence in helping the mentally ill.

Manet, Édouard (1832–83), French
Though considered a realist in his time, Manet broke with the past to become one of the first truly modern painters. He is the first leader of the impressionists, but his work remains more traditional than that of the other impressionists. Unlike Courbet and other realists, he was not concerned with subject matter as much as he was with the technical aspects of light and color. Shown are **Luncheon on the Grass** and **Olympia**. These two paintings, both of 1863, display figures illuminated against dark backgrounds. (After 1865, Manet's work changes to the impressionist technique of depicting light more forcefully by applying paint in patches on light backgrounds.)

Luncheon on the Grass was taken from Giorgione's allegorical *Fête Champêtre* at the Louvre, but the public was scandalized to see a nude woman with two fully dressed men. Its mythological theme did nothing to abate the negative criticism. With *Olympia,* a pose taken from Titian's *Venus of Urbino* and reminiscent of Goya's *Naked Maja,* the public saw a prostitute painted against hard colors that emphasized the starkness of her life. No one, except some fellow artists, noticed that Manet was showing in these paintings that when light falls evenly on forms with only slight shadows, the forms become visually flattened. In 1863 Manet was painting as he observed light in nature.

Monet, Claude (1840–1926), French
Monet was the true impressionist. He believed in the goals of the movement and remained loyal to it to the end, even though his work became more abstract as he experimented with technique. As a landscapist he rendered subtle changes in weather conditions on various subjects—water lilies, haystacks, bright fields of flowers—important to him only as an end to his main purpose. Thus he painted the same scene many times to record the various effects of light, color, and atmosphere within a few hours' time. Monet's series of **Rouen Cathedral** (1894) is an example of that technique. The cathedral is not so much the subject as is the changing light on its facade, which Monet renders in his impressionistic broken color technique. When viewed from a distance the colors seem to blend together.

Monet's *Nymphéas* (Waterlilies) are murals at the nearby **Musée de l'Orangerie** across the gardens from the Musée du Jeu de Paume on the Place de la Concorde. There are also more than eighty paintings and drawings by Monet at the Musée Marmottan at 2 Rue Louis-Bailly.

Pissarro, Camille (1830–1903), French
Pissarro, older than the other impressionists, was a pioneer of the movement. Born on the island of St. Thomas in the Caribbean of a merchant family, Pissarro went to school in Paris but did not settle there until 1855. His career as a painter was a struggle against poverty and failure. In spite of a lack of critical approval he was admired by artists of his time, who looked to him as a leader and a teacher; Cézanne called himself the "pupil of Pissarro." He is credited with playing a role in all of the avantgarde movements of the nineteenth century in France, including postimpressionism. Although he is known for painting many cityscapes (Paris, Rouen, London) set in all kinds of weather, he is also known for country landscapes which, like Cézanne's work, often show a building up of the planes of a picture. His interpretation of country people caused Degas to refer to Pissarro's peasant women as "angels who go to the market."

Renoir, Pierre Auguste (1841–1919), French
More than the other impressionists, Renoir's work maintains a link with the great tradition of French painting exemplified by Delacroix, Fragonard, and Boucher. His use of the broken color technique makes him an impressionist, as in his *Moulin de la Galette* of 1876, a study of the effects of sunlight filtering through leafy trees upon people dancing and making merry. It is also typical of Renoir in showing us the happy side of life.

But Renoir was less absorbed by problems of atmosphere and light than he was with the human figure and specifically Parisian womanhood—dressed and undressed. In his depiction of the nude woman, his favorite theme, he is compared to Rubens. See his *Nude in the Sunlight* from 1876 and paintings of Gabrielle, whom Renoir hired as a nurse for his children.

Rousseau, Henri "Le Douanier" (1844–1910), French
Rousseau was no impressionist, although he was a contemporary of the impressionists and the postimpressionists. He was friendly with Pissarro, Seurat, and Gauguin, and was called a "naive" artist, self-taught and unconcerned with the problems of the main movements in painting—impressionism, fauvism, and cubism. As his name "Le Douanier" suggests, he was a customs official, his employment for fifteen years (until 1885). He started to paint only for pleasure. His imagination led to him painting dreamlike scenes. There is the exotic in some of his paintings, such as the *Snake Charmer* (1907). After 1885, when he began to paint full time, he maintained his style—a fresh mixture of naiveté, innocence, and wisdom. He influenced other "naive" artists, especially in America, and gave modern painters a certain simplicity to build upon.

Seurat, George-Pierre (1859–91), French
Seurat is referred to as a neo-impressionist because he rebelled against the impressionists' spontaneous manner to focus on spectrum analysis. He applied pointlike spots of color to his canvas in a systematic manner. These

dots approximate those of the spectrum and are blended by the spectator at a distance from the canvas into the colors intended. A major work, *The Circus,* of 1891, left unfinished because of the death of the artist at the age of thirty-two, demonstrates this method, called pointillism.

MUSÉE DU LOUVRE

Palais du Louvre, 1ᵉ, Main entrance, Porte Denon

Metro: Louvre, Palais-Royal

Hours: Open Wed.–Mon., 9:45AM–6:30PM; closed holidays. Admission fee (free admission on Sundays).

Note: All departments and rooms of the Louvre are open, "in principle," only Monday and Wednesday. On other days departments and rooms are closed on a rotating basis.

Thursday	Oriental antiquities—complete department
	Objets d'art—complete department
	Paintings—small room (north and south)
	Sculptures—Flora Pavilion and Wing
Friday	Egyptian antiquities—complete department
	Oriental antiquities—complete department
	Greek and Roman antiquities—Campana Gallery (ceramics)
	Paintings—rooms on second floor (nineteenth century)
Saturday	Greek and Roman antiquities—Court of the Sphinx and Campana Gallery (ceramics)
	Oriental antiquities—complete department
	Objets d'art—complete department
	Paintings—small rooms (north and south), Flora Wing and Zenith Gallery
Sunday	Greek and Roman antiquities—Campana Gallery (ceramics) and Room of Bronzes
	Oriental antiquities—complete department
	Objets d'art—complete department
	Paintings—small rooms (north and south), rooms on second floor (nineteenth century)
	Sculptures—Flora Pavilion and Wing

Note: The Louvre is undergoing extensive reorganization. Some works of art may have been moved since this guide went to press or are temporarily not on display.

The Louvre is probably the world's greatest art museum, having the largest collection of works of art, more than two hundred thousand, among them numerous masterpieces. It occupies the largest palace in the world. Though it was not the first public museum—the Ashmolean at Oxford, the Vatican

Museum, the British Museum, and the Charleston Museum in the United States all preceded it—it inspired the creation of many of Europe's other museums.

This house of art got its start from the collection of the kings of France, of whom Francis I (1515–47) was the first important collector. While fighting wars in Italy he fell in love with Italian art and invited Leonardo da Vinci, Rosso Fiorentino, and Benvenuto Cellini to his court at Fontainebleau. The patronage the king provided established the School of Fontainebleau. Italian works, including the *Mona Lisa,* became the nucleus of what became the national museums of France.

In the reign of Henry IV (1553–1610), during expansion of the palace of the Louvre (it had been under construction, on and off, since 1190), the arts in France had their most important patron. The king invited hundreds of artists to take up residence in the Louvre.

Royal art collecting on a large scale continued in the period Louis XIV (1643–1715) lived at the Louvre (Versailles did not become his official residence until 1678). With the encouragement of his minister, Cardinal Mazarin, Louis bought most of the paintings of the Gonzagas of Mantua; part of the collection of Charles I, king of England; and other collections. When Louis came to the throne there were two hundred paintings in the royal collection, while at the end of his reign there were two thousand.

But the palace of the Louvre itself fell upon hard times when Versailles overshadowed it. In the last fifteen years of his reign Louis XIV visited Paris only four times, and no longer stayed at the Louvre, which was falling into a bad state of repair. In 1749 Voltaire complained about it to Louis XV, but nothing was done, and there was talk of demolishing it.

The idea of making the Louvre a museum developed in the middle of the eighteenth century, encouraged by the success of a public exhibition of paintings at the Luxembourg Palace in 1750. It did not happen, however, until after the Revolution. The Musée du Louvre was inaugurated in 1793, and the painter of the Revolution, Jacques-Louis David (1748–1825), was appointed its first president. Revolutionary forces had seized art works from convents, churches, châteaux, and royal palaces to be put on public display. Art was no longer only for the privileged classes.

When Napoleon took power he changed the name to Musée Napoleon and brought to it collections confiscated from the capitals of his new European empire. He also parceled out works of art to provincial cities, where he ordered museums to be established, and influenced his relatives on the various thrones of Europe in founding national museums elsewhere. The Prado in Madrid, the Rijksmuseum in Amsterdam, and the Academy Gallery in Venice owe their existence to Napoleon.

Eventually art treasures were sent back from France to these national museums. Mass restitution took place after Napoleon's defeat at Waterloo, when five thousand works of art left the Louvre to return to their rightful owners. About one hundred paintings were never returned, including the Italian primitives Cimabue, Giotto, and Fra Angelico, considered of little value. Enough paintings still remained to cover the walls of the Louvre. In the nineteenth and twentieth centuries, additional works were obtained by purchase and gift, and construction of the Louvre was resumed. Today the Louvre is undergoing major reorganization and expansion. Sections of the palace never before opened to the public are being restored and used to display works of art from the Louvre's unseen collection. A much-needed new entrance is being built in the Cour Napoleon, the great, three-sided inner court of the Louvre. This construction, a sixty-foot-high glass pyramid designed by the architect I. M. Pei, has caused great controversy in Paris and beyond. But other parts of the renovation of the new Grand Louvre, as it is now referred to by its directors, are certain to be popular. The long-lost gardens designed by Le Nôtre at the end of the Cour Napoleon are being restored and the heavily trafficked street dividing the Tuileries from the Louvre will be put below ground.

SUGGESTED TOUR OF THE LOUVRE: WESTERN SCULPTURE AND PAINTING

Greek and Roman Sculpture

Starting at the Port Denon entrance to the Louvre (facing the outdoor Court of the Carrousel), walk left through the long Galerie Daru, around the staircase containing the *Nike of Samothrace,* through the Rotonde, to the rooms of the **Pavillion des Arts** and **Salle des Cariatides** to see the Greek and Roman sculpture. Return to the staircase and ascend to the first floor to see the *Nike of Samothrace.*

Paintings

Walk behind the *Nike of Samothrace,* through the Salle des Bijoux, into the **Salle des Sept Cheminées** to see seventeenth-century Italian paintings. Return to the *Nike of Samothrace.* Facing the *Nike,* proceed to your right, through the Salle Duchatel, to the **Salon Carré** facing the Seine. Here are fifteenth- and sixteenth-century French paintings.

The Salon Carré leads to the Grande Galerie, but before seeing the French paintings there turn right into the **Salle des Sept Metres**, which displays Dutch paintings.

Return to the **Grande Galerie** to proceed down its first part. Then enter the **Mollien Wing,** which is perpendicular to the Grande Galerie, where the French collection continues with eighteenth-century paintings. The Mollien Wing ends at the cafeteria, where you may want to rest. In the rooms to the right of the cafeteria—**Salle Mollien** and **Salle Daru**—are French nineteenth-century paintings.

Return to the Salle Denon, the room between the Salle Daru and Salle Mollien. Here is the entrance to the **Salle des Etats,** which holds the finest collection of sixteenth-century Italian paintings outside Italy.

Exit the Salle des Etats back into the **Grande Galerie** and continue with its second part, which starts after the entrance to the Mollien Wing, which you already went through. Paintings of the Italian School are displayed to the end of the Grande Galerie.

Now enter the **Salle van Dyck** and the **Galerie Medicis,** the great hall entered from the Salle van Dyck, to see paintings by Rubens. The Galerie Medicis is bordered on both of its sides, lengthwise, by small rooms (*cabinets*). On the side of the Seine there are fifteenth- and sixteenth-century Flemish and German paintings. The cabinets along the Tuileries have sixteenth- and seventeenth-century Flemish and Dutch paintings.

Continue into the **Flore Wing** to see Italian and Spanish paintings. Walk through the entire length of the Flore Wing to the stairway leading down to the ground floor.

Sculpture

On the ground floor—**Pavillon de Flore** and **Pavillion des Etats**—is the Louvre's collection of European sculpture. Signs lead to Michelangelo's *Slaves.*

Index to the Rooms of Paintings in the Louvre

Artists mentioned below have works referred to in the text that follows. You will find these works listed under the names of the artists arranged alphabetically.

Salle des Sept Cheminées	Caravaggio
Salon Carré	Clouet, Fouquet, School of Avignon, School of Fontainbleau
Salle de Sept Metres	Rembrandt
Grande Gallerie (first part)	Claude, Fragonard, La Tour, Poussin, Watteau
Mollien Wing	Boucher, Chardin
Salle Mollien	David, Ingres
Salle Daru	Courbet, Delacroix
Salle des Etats	Giorgione, Leonardo da Vinci, Raphael, Titian, Veronese
Grande Galerie (second part)	Angelico, Antonello da Messina, Ghirlandaio, Mantegna
Salle van Dyck	Rubens
Galerie Medicis	Rubens
Cabinets on the Seine	Dürer, van Eyck, Holbein, Massys, Memling, van der Weyden
Cabinets on the Tuileries	Vermeer
Flore Wing	Caravaggio

Paintings

Angelico, Fra (ca. 1400–55), Florentine

Coronation of the Virgin (1435): Grande Galerie (second part), third left bay
Fra Angelico was a Dominican monk whose outlook on life was rooted in

the Middle Ages, but whose artistic sense was that of the early Renaissance. This painting, the predella of which consists of six panels representing scenes from the life of St. Dominic grouped around a picture of Christ with the Virgin and St. John, comes from the church of San Domenico in Fiesole. Despite its early date and the Gothic spirit of the rich throne, Renaissance elements are pronounced, making this painting a transitional work. There is a Renaissance suggestion of depth shown by the receding floor tiles, which get smaller and smaller. There are two sets of perspective, one for the throne and one for the floor in the foreground, done to heighten the hierarchical distance between angels and saints on the one hand, and Christ and the Virgin on the other. There is a blue background to suggest sky instead of the old gold background, and there are saints and martyrs in the foreground who have weight and mass.

Antonello da Messina (ca. 1430–79), Italian

Portrait of a Man ("Il Condottiere") (1475): Grande Galerie (second part), fourth left bay
In Antonello da Messina we have an Italian painter from Sicily who came in contact with the Flemish style and the use of the oil medium and introduced it to his fellow Italian painters in Venice. For this reason he has a place in the history of art, and he was also a superb portraitist, as demonstrated by this painting of a man, usually referred to as *Il Condottiere* because of his proud military stance.

Antonello taught the Venetians how to use oils, to model a subject's head in striking light so as to bring out details of the flesh and the glitter of the eyes, but he also learned from them a sense of monumentality, as seen in the figure of *Il Condottiere*.

Boucher, François (1703–70), French

Diana Resting after Her Bath (1742): Mollien Wing, room 2, south wall
Boucher's work is typical of the rococo, the leading style during the reign of Louis XV (1715–74). He was the favorite painter of Madame Pompadour, the king's mistress, who took drawing lessons from him. His paintings reflect the attitude of the French court in the eighteenth century. They are seductively pretty with a softness of pinks and blues. Many of his paintings, such as this one, are based on mythological scenes which no doubt were acted out by the society for which he painted. Here we see Diana, the Greek goddess, and one of her companions, relaxing in seductive nakedness after her bath. It is the kind of painting that a sophisticated clientele could appreciate, and also recalls the tradition of grace and elegance of the School of Fontainebleau, of which *Diana the Huntress*, here in the Louvre, is mentioned below.

Caravaggio* (1573–1610), Italian

Death of the Virgin (1605–6) Salle des Sept Cheminées (Room of the Seven Chimneys)
Caravaggio was a realist in Italian painting whose work had an effect on

artists well into the seventeenth century. He is credited with leading art away from the high Renaissance academic style.

The *Death of the Virgin* may be the last work that Caravaggio painted in Rome before he fled in 1606 to avoid arrest for murder. Like many of his other works, it was controversial; he painted it for a church in Trastevere and gossip spread that he had used a drowned prostitute, pulled out of the river, as a model for the Virgin. The Virgin was shown swollen, with bare legs, and the apostles as an assorted lot drawn from the streets of Rome, dressed in ordinary clothing.

Caravaggio's naturalism depicted real people instead of idealized religious types. The church rejected the painting as indecorous, though other painters admired it as Caravaggio's best work. Rubens bought it for the duke of Mantua, with whom it remained until it was sold to Charles I of England in 1627. From there it went to Louis XIV of France.

The Fortune Teller, an early work of Caravaggio, that probably dates from 1589, is also in the Louvre (Flore Wing, left of entrance). It shows that Caravaggio could paint masterpieces on subjects from everyday life. When he did get church commissions he peopled his pictures with the same kind of genre characters.

Chardin, Jean Baptiste Siméon (1699–1779), French

Back from the Market (1739): Mollien Wing, room 1
Chardin, a man of the people and a self-taught artist, stressed the virtue in the characters in his paintings, as opposed to the rococo style of using make-believe court gaiety and stylized love. No one could confuse Chardin's characters with the beautiful people in Watteau's *fêtes champêtres* or Fragonard's mythological scenes.

Chardin's colors are different from the glittering tones of the rococo artists, with a limited range. He is famous for saying: "One uses color, but one paints from the heart." In *Back from the Market* or *The Provider,* as it is also called, colors are as Chardin sees them in life: cool, fresh whites, rich browns, and the appropriate blue to bring out the coarse, proper material worn by a woman. There is shown a seventeenth-century Dutch bourgeois interest in the still life; inanimate objects in Chardin's pictures often have an importance equal to that of his living figures. The arrangement of objects and people on the canvas, and their relationship to one another was most important.

Claude Lorrain (1600–82), French

A Seaport at Sunset (ca. 1639): Grande Galerie (first part), fifth right bay
Though born in France, Claude Lorrain spent most of his entire working life in Italy. This Italianate painting of a seaport shows his talent, which ranks him as one of the best landscapists of the seventeenth century. His later work, taken from his travels in the Campania region of Italy, is even more Italian in character.

Claude had a genius for depicting light. He explored the painterly qualities of a setting sun; in this seaport scene it gilds everything: water, buildings, and figures. His composition is balanced and includes weblike patterns in the riggings of the ships anchored in the harbor. Claude does not treat us to a real scene from life: the harbor, buildings, ships, and people are seen in the picture as though on a stage. Claude's aim seems to be only to show the dynamic qualities of the setting sun. Yet everything looks real enough to be convincing.

Clouet, Jean (ca. 1475–ca. 1540), French

Portrait of Francis I (ca. 1524): Salon Carré
Portraits were a large part of Renaissance painting and played a greater role in the north than in Italy. Jean Clouet may have been a native of the Netherlands, but we know him as a member of the court of France. This painting of the king of France, protector of Leonardo da Vinci and one of the builders of the Louvre, seems as much drawn as painted. The fashion was first to draw the subject in pencil and then to finish the picture in the studio. The finished product here reveals that technique. Much attention is paid to the depiction of the king's clothing and jewelry, which shows Clouet was within the northern Gothic tradition, but he did not completely ignore the new Italian style, seen in the position he has given the king's hands and the large folds of drapery enveloping his arms.

Courbet, Gustave (1819–77), French

After the Revolution of 1848 realism in painting accompanied the industrial revolution, which brought a growing interest in the physical nature of things. Courbet is one of the first artists in Europe who could be called a realist. His attitude was summed up in his statement: "Show me an angel and I'll paint one." His is an art that played a large part in turning many people away from classical artificiality and romantic exaggeration. His approach was an inspiration to the young impressionists whose aim was to paint what they saw outdoors in the real world.

Funeral at Ornans (1849): Salle Daru
This large painting shows Courbet's grandfather's funeral at Ornans, the artist's hometown in the Franche-Comté region of France. Such realism shocked a French public unaccustomed to seeing a peasant funeral given such importance. The stark cliffs of the landscape consolidate the alignment of the mourners, holding them in a design centered on the open grave. There is no drama or romanticism. It is simply a country funeral shown the way it really looks: dark, almost colorless, with some of the mourners showing indifference.

The Artist's Studio (1855): Salle Daru
This painting and the *Funeral at Ornans* were rejected by the International Exhibition in Paris in 1855. Courbet then displayed it with forty-three of his other paintings at his own *pavillion* in a show called "Le Réalisme." The composition of this work is one of a classical triptych. Courbet shows him-

self as an artist painting a landscape in which are a nude symbolizing Truth and a child symbolic of Innocence. On the right are the blessed people: those who believe in the artist's ideas and support his art. They are portraits of some of Courbet's friends. Two lovers embracing near the window represent free love. Elsewhere he depicts people who, he says, "live on death" outside the world of art, prisoners of their passions and material needs: the poacher, the hunter, the prostitute, the merchant, the worker, the poor Irish woman suckling her child while squatting on the floor dressed in rags, the priest, and Courbet's idea of the Jew.

David, Jacques-Louis (1748–1825), French

The end of the eighteenth century in France saw a return to classical art which since the time of Poussin and Claude Lorrain had been out of fashion. The frivolous rococo had been associated with the nobility; the bourgeois revolution replaced it by a revived classicism, considered a moral renewal and a symbol of the later Napoleonic Empire.

Jacques-Louis David was the leader of the classicist movement. He was a Jacobin, a spokesman for the Revolution who voted for the death of Louis XVI, and a supporter of Napoleon when he came to power. When the Bourbons regained the throne of France he fled to Brussels where he lived out his life in exile.

During the height of David's influence in Paris he reorganized the old Academy as the Institut de France and endowed it with the idea that art had to be noble and public. Subject matter was largely taken from Greek or Roman antiquity and the emphasis was on accurate drawing, not on color. In spite of avant-garde movements in France academic art styles as laid down by David continued to be followed through the nineteenth century, making it difficult for realists and impressionists to win official approval.

The Oath of Horatii (1785): Salle Mollien

The subject of this painting is from a story of ancient Rome in which three brothers swear an oath of patriotism before their father, who holds their swords aloft to sanctify the event. The soldiers' sisters are weeping because the brothers are about to fight in a battle against their husbands. It was painted for Louis XVI, but its message was meant to encourage patriotism and stimulate the French to fight for liberty, equality, and brotherhood.

David painted the *Oath of Horatii* in Rome and used simple Doric pillars as background to emphasize the simplicity, strength, and devotion to duty popularly associated with republican Rome. The center of the composition is the open hand of the father. An open hand is the trade mark of David, probably learned from his study of Caravaggio in Rome. As socially and politically enlightened as David was, he lived at a time when women's rights were not an issue. The women are shown in an eighteenth-century style with soft lines, passive and incapable of heroic action. In David's mind, the revolution, if it were to come, had to rely on the determined action of men associated with the great events of history.

The Lichtors Bringing to Brutus the Bodies of His Sons (1789):
Salle Mollien
Here again an appeal is made to patriotic virtue. Brutus had condemned his
sons to death for conspiring to restore the monarchy. Painted during a time
of revolution, it created popular excitement and was a great propaganda success. Again, the motif is Roman: the figure of Brutus, shown in shadow, is
taken from a statue in the Capitoline; the furniture is copied from antique
specimens uncovered at Herculanium and Pompeii; and the swooning daughter held by her mother is shown in the manner of a dying Niobe.

Portrait of Madame Récamier (1800): Salle Mollien
Though David's feelings were with the republican virtues, as exemplified by
the men in his paintings, he had compassion for women. When depicting
femininity he may be at his best, such as in the *Portrait of Madame Récamier*. Bareheaded and barefooted, her lithe body emphasized by the slender
lamp, she is a symbol of grace and feminine beauty.

Delacroix, Eugène (1799–1863), French
Romanticism in France came later than it did in Spain and England because
of the presence of the powerful French Academy, which was formed to protect neoclassicism. Leader of the romantic rebels was Delacroix, whose concern was individual freedom. This led him to support the underdog. His
Massacre of Scios (1824) depicts the slaughter of innocent Greeks by Turks
on the Island of Scios. His *Liberty Leading the People* (1831) celebrates the
Revolution of 1830. Both paintings demonstrate his feelings for the oppressed. He also had a desire to express his imagination through color,
which neoclassical art did not emphasize. Delacroix put his love for color to
use at the expense of his draftsmanship, after travels in Algeria and Morocco
where he admired Moorish civilization's exotic qualities.

With Delacroix and other romantics we have a return to an emotional
expression in art, like that of the earlier baroque. There came an individual
approach to experimentation with color that led to the impressionists and,
later, to modern art.

The Death of Sardanapalus (1827): Salle Daru
Delacroix referred to this painting as his *Massacre No. 2*, the first being his
Massacre at Scios. He took the subject from Byron's 1821 tragedy about the
Assyrian ruler Sardanapalus who, when faced with his death by invading ar-
mies, ordered his wives, servants, and treasures destroyed to prevent them
from falling into the hands of his enemies.

The theme of Sardanapalus permitted Delacroix to follow his fondest
desires in painting: an exotic Oriental scene, action with violence, a dramatic, emotional subject, contrasts of light and shade, and sumptuousness of
color. This painting created a scandal not only by its subject matter but also
in breaking neoclassical rules of harmony, proportion, and draftsmanship.

See also in this gallery *Massacre at Scios, Liberty Leading the People,*
Delacroix's *Self-portrait* at thirty-seven, and *Algerian Women.*

Dürer, Albrecht* (1471–1528), German

Self-portrait (1493): Cabinets on the Seine, seventh cabinet
Dürer's art stands between the late Gothic style and the Renaissance. There is a northern medieval concern for detail, exemplified by the sprig of thistle in Dürer's hand, a plant symbolizing conjugal fidelity and here announcing Dürer's own impending marriage in Nuremburg in 1494.

Typical of Dürer's portraits is the direct contact between the figure and the spectator. This is something Dürer happily maintained in his art even after he was influenced by the Italian Renaissance.

Eyck, Jan van* (ca. 1390–1441), Flemish

The Madonna of Chancellor Rolin (ca. 1436): Cabinets on the Seine, first cabinet
The face and attitude of Rolin, the duke of Burgundy's powerful chancellor, reflect a strong personality with an air of self-importance. In defiance of the custom of the time, van Eyck shows the minister on the same scale and space as the Madonna, without a saint to perform an introduction. Without a counterbalancing third figure it was not practical to place the Madonna in the middle, as Jan does in other Madonna and donor paintings (the Madonna and child in the middle with the donor and saint on either side). The artist fills the empty space with a landscape as a symbol of creation. The Christ child's head is silhouetted against the landscape, His creation, whereas the heads of the Madonna and the chancellor stand out against neutral surfaces.

The Madonna as the Queen of Heaven is emphasized by an angel holding a crown above her head. Capital reliefs above the chancellor's head show scenes from Genesis symbolizing the entry of sin into the world of man. The Christ child is blessing the chancellor with one hand and in the other hand holding a globe bearing a cross characterizing Him as the creator of the world.

Fouquet, Jean (ca. 1425–77/81), French

Portrait of Charles VII (ca. 1444): Salon Carré
Jean Fouquet was not only a panel painter but also a book illustrator. He painted this portrait of Charles VII, whom Joan of Arc put on the French throne, early in his career before he visited Italy in 1447. Its absence of background, the frontal presentation, and the symmetrical curtains are Gothic in spirit and show no trace of Renaissance influence. After Charles died in 1461 Fouquet went on to serve Louis XI as the first painter to the French court.

Fragonard, Jean-Honoré (1732–1806), French

The Bathers (before 1765): Grande Galerie (first part), eighth right bay
Fragonard is the last of the great rococo painters of the eighteenth century, following in the tradition of Boucher and Watteau. He often concentrated on erotic subjects. In *The Bathers* each figure presents some attractive aspect

of the female body. Although Fragonard's art could sometimes degenerate into ribaldry, he understood color and exploited the possibilities of light and shade. His figures float on his canvas with a grace found in a Tiepolo ceiling. He could raise a trivial theme into a painting of distinction.

The Revolution changed the style of art, and Fragonard's popularity declined rapidly. He died forgotten and in poverty.

Géricault, Théodore (1791–1824), French

The Raft of the Medusa (1819): Salle Daru
Géricault's technique was conservative, but he had enough of the romantic spirit to be classified a romantic painter who revolted in the neoclassic ranks of the French Academy. His *Raft of the Medusa* was the painting that made him famous, since its subject was taken from a contemporary incident depicted in realistic terms.

The *Medusa* was a French frigate which left Le Havre on July 2, 1816, bound for Senegal, with a captain, a reinstated emigre, who had not commanded a ship for twenty-five years. The ship may have been unseaworthy. It was wrecked off the coast of Africa, and the officers and passengers took the lifeboats, leaving the crew of one hundred and fifty with a raft without water or provisions. After twelve days adrift the raft was spotted and the fifteen survivors rescued. Accounts of the catastrophe were suppressed by the government, but Géricault got an account of the story from survivors and painted this picture from it. He was so enthusiastic about it that he built a replica of the raft in his studio and visited a local hospital to sketch the dying and the dead. He chose to depict the raft at the moment when its survivors sight the rescue ship.

When it was exhibited at the 1819 Salon the Academy condemned it because it criticized the government, though it contains neoclassic elements: an emphasis on the figure, the prevailing brown, the classic pyramidal composition with a baroque diagonal that brings the eye from the foreground scene of despair upward to the black man and promise of salvation. The only romantic element about it is its dramatic quality.

Ghirlandaio, Domenico (1449–94), Florentine

Portrait of an Old Man and a Little Boy (ca. 1480): Grande Galerie (second part), fifth right bay
Ghirlandaio ran a busy studio in Florence with his brother David, a brother-in-law, Bastiano Mainardi, and a group of pupils. With many commissions for frescoes and altarpieces in churches and other buildings, they painted in the popular taste of the period.

Here is a portrait of one of Ghirlandaio's customers, shown with a deformed nose in an honesty of representation. We see the small Flemish-like details of the figures, whose bright colors set them off against the darker background, and also get a keen sense of the old man's gentle character and of the loving admiration in the child. The old man loses his ugliness as we see him through the eyes of the child rather than our own.

Giorgione* (ca. 1477–1510), Venetian

Concert Champêtre (after 1506): Salle des États
Typical of Giorgione's art, this scene shows no obvious narrative. His aim is
to convey mood. Giorgione's imagination led him to express intangible feelings convincingly on canvas. His was the ability to express man and nature
unified into a poetic whole.

We see two men absorbed in the sounds of a lute one of them is playing
(Giorgione was known for his ability to play the lute). They pay no attention
to the two nude women, one about to play her recorder as the other pours
water into a well. There is a theme of music and poetry by which figures and
even the surrounding landscape seem spellbound. Nothing else matters, not
even the nudity of the women. The mood is developed by the use of earth
colors, shadow (there is more shadow than light), and the lack of definite
line.

These techniques of Giorgione influenced art into the nineteenth century. Manet's *Luncheon on the Grass* (Musée du Jeu de Paume, Paris) was
modeled after it. But Manet's painting created a scandal when it was exhibited at the Salon of 1863. No one saw anything poetic about it—only a nude
woman in the presence of two fully clothed men.

Holbein, Hans, the Younger (1497–1543), German

Portrait of Erasmus (ca. 1523): Cabinets on the Seine, seventh cabinet
Holbein knew Erasmus when the humanist Dutch scholar was living in Basel
and the artist had not yet abandoned his native city for England. Holbein
painted three portraits of him; this one is considered the best. It was Erasmus
who gave Holbein a letter of introduction to Sir Thomas More in England,
which led to Holbein's becoming a painter of portraits for the court of
Henry VIII. The *Portrait of Anne of Cleves* in the Louvre (same cabinet), one
of Henry's wives, is one of the many portraits of nobility that Holbein executed while in England.

In the *Portrait of Erasmus* we see the subject in profile, looking down
at his writing desk in a calm portrayal with balanced light and dark areas.
The brocaded wall hanging and the pilaster in the background not only give
warmth to his pallid face, but their verticals also give liveliness to the contours of his profile. Holbein has succeeded in capturing the character of a
thinker known for peace and intelligent restraint.

Ingres, Jean Dominique (1780–1867), French

Odalisque (1814): Salle Mollien
Ingres distorted the human figure for the sake of creating an abstract perfection of linear beauty. A master of drawing and pupil of David, Ingres used
little color in carrying on the neoclassical tradition.

The *Odalisque* represents Ingres's style at its most refined and accomplished. The figure may be an odalisque (a concubine in a harem), or Venus,
or a number of other representations. She is not individualized, although ev-

ery part of her body seems accurate. Only her exquisitely beautiful outline is important. She is merely an excuse for Ingres to display his powers of draftsmanship.

La Tour, Georges (1593–1652), French

Saint Mary Magdalene with a Candle (1630–35): Grande Galerie (first part), third left bay

It is not certain where La Tour came in contact with Caravaggio's style. There is no proof of his making a trip to Italy, although he may have come in contact with Caravaggio's followers in Holland. In any case he is the outstanding Caravaggist of seventeenth-century France who depicts country folk in the roles of biblical characters. Little is known of his early career. He lived in the provinces, although his art appealed to patrons such as Louis XIII. He paints night scenes illuminated by candlelight, which gives his figures a spirituality, although the scenes are right out of daily life. His Mary Magdalene is not so much a depiction of Mary Magdalene contemplating her repentance as it is that of a repentant woman painted as Mary Magdalene.

A similar painting is La Tour's *Saint Joseph the Carpenter* (ca. 1645), which looks like a scene from daily life, but whose divine light, illuminating the face of the child Jesus, expresses a higher life.

Leonardo da Vinci* (1452–1519), Florentine

Mona Lisa (1503–6): Salle des États

The *Mona Lisa* is unquestionably the most famous painting in the world. Transcending the various styles of painting over the last four hundred years, it has always been popular, sought after, copied, even stolen. Those who had it never thought of giving it up. Leonardo himself, after taking three years to paint it, seems not to have wanted to part with it. He took it with him to France where he went to live in the service of Francis I. He had painted the *Mona Lisa* (Mona is short for Madonna) while in Florence, a commission from the Marquis del Giocondo (hence its other name, *La Gioconda*). He wanted a portrait of his wife, then about twenty-four. At Leonardo's death the painting went to Francis I and remained at Fontainebleau up to 1625. When Charles I of England sent his emissary, the duke of Buckingham, to the French court to seek the hand of Henrietta of France, sister of the French king, the duke also made it known that Charles wanted the *Mona Lisa*. The king sent his sister to Charles, but kept the *Mona Lisa*. In 1800 Napoleon hung the painting in his room in the Tuileries, and it was later exhibited in the Musée Napoleon (the present-day Louvre). From there it was stolen in 1911 by an Italian workman, then found two years later in Florence. It was exhibited at the Uffizi, then in Rome and Milan before being returned to the Louvre in 1913.

As Leonardo worked on the *Mona Lisa* it seems to have absorbed him as more than the portrait of a woman, as a concept of the enigma of life. The Mona Lisa's haunting smile can be seen as the mystery of the soul. The misty landscape, in which there is no human being, animal, building, farm, field, or even tree, but only roads and a bridge, may represent an infinite universe.

Leonardo believed the blurring of the definition of facial details and of landscape background reinforced their psychological qualities, giving them new depth of meaning. His *sfumato*, smoky tones of light and dark, creates a hazy effect that gives a compelling reality to the expression and mood of the *Mona Lisa*. Her eyes stare directly at us and seem to change if we look long enough.

Virgin of the Rocks (begun 1483): Salle des États

To the left of the *Mona Lisa* is Leonardo's ideal madonna type in the *Virgin of the Rocks*. She is more beautiful than the *Mona Lisa*, with modeled features, soft cheeks, and a small chin to convey shyness and modesty, emphasized by her downcast eyes and the slight smile. Her head forms the apex of Leonardo's pyramidal composition, which he also uses in the *Mona Lisa* and in the *Virgin and St. Anne* (also on the same wall) to give a classical grandeur to the picture. His skill is such that he avoids static qualities of such massive arrangement by giving various figures twisted poses and gestures that emphasize movement. The misty, dark background of the rocks is a typical Leonardesque wilderness stretching to infinite distances, devoid of human habitation. A religious interpretation would call attention to their representing a dark mortality upon which the divine light of God enters through the Virgin Mary and Christ. The painting shows his work in chiaroscuro, or shading of light and dark, while drawing mass instead of line and adding tones of golden light to figures set against the darkness. With Leonardo's foreshortening of figures, such as in the Madonna's hand extended with light shining only on her fingertips, they are both animated and tied together in a related group.

There is less intellectuality in the *Madonna of the Rocks* than in, say, the *Mona Lisa* or the *Last Supper* in Milan, but it does fulfill Leonardo's aim in painting: to create on a flat surface form the eye interprets as three dimensional. He does it by emphasizing composition and mass instead of color.

Virgin and St. Anne (ca. 1508–10): Salle des États

This is one of the paintings, along with the *Mona Lisa* and the *St. John the Baptist* (displayed together at the Louvre), that Leonardo took with him to France and kept for himself. If the *Mona Lisa* is the quintessential portrait of the high Renaissance, the *Virgin and St. Anne* is the high Renaissance itself, the culmination of the pyramidal design that began before Leonardo.

St. Anne's feet point left while her hips are frontal and her head faces slightly to the right. The axis of her body is turned in an angle of ninety degrees, creating a torsion called *contrapposto* which produces tension and gives balanced movement to the entire composition. Raphael used the technique in his Virgin and Child paintings; other masters of sixteenth-century painting also followed Leonardo's geometric forms of complicated intertwining figures in a pyramidal whole.

Leonardo has abandoned slenderness in his figures in the *Virgin and St. Anne* for greater mass. In so doing he also set another cornerstone of high Renaissance art.

As innovative as the composition is in the *Virgin and St. Anne,* the landscape, a trademark of Leonardo, is also noteworthy. His hazy light, or *sfumato,* makes it seem blurred. The tree in the middle distance possibly refers to the cross, positioned as it is above the lamb, which symbolizes Christ's Passion. Its height exceeds that of the peaks in the distance, and its calm contrasts with their sense of turmoil. In such a religious painting the landscape evidently symbolizes the barrenness and chaos of earthly life as opposed to the harmonious love of Christ, the Madonna, and St. Anne in the foreground.

Mantegna, Andrea (1431–1506), Italian

The Crucifixion: Grande Galerie (second part), fourth left bay
This is the central panel from the predella of the San Zeno altarpiece in Verona executed by Mantegna in 1456–59. At a young age Mantegna had already mastered the technique of perspective. He used it to dramatize his paintings, both religious and secular. The steep perspective he attempts here starts with the two soldiers, mostly hidden by the frame in the foreground, and follows the paving stones receding into the background, which our eye follows via the curved lines moving inward on the ground. Every detail is accounted for, including minimal vegetation in this rocky landscape. The artist's knowledge of Roman antiquity is revealed in the accuracy of detail in clothing and equipment of the Roman soldiers.

The composition is built around the crucified Christ, whose body stands out against the cold blue sky. His hands, stretched to the sides, and His head repeat the form of the horizontal clouds. The crosses of the two thieves are turned inward to emphasize Christ's position in the center. The huge rocks repeat the verticality of the Crucifixion. It is a tragic, intense, emotional, and even majestic scene.

Massys, Quentin (1466–1530), Flemish

The Money Changer and His Wife (1514): Cabinets on the Seine, third cabinet
Massys, trained in the style of Dieric Bouts, was heir to medieval traditions, but formed a bridge between fifteenth-century realism, religious in outlook, and the secular realism of the sixteenth century. It is entirely fitting that Rubens once owned this painting, because Massys stood closer to Rubens than to van Eyck or Rogier van der Weyden. Massys behaved like a Renaissance artist rather than a medieval craftsman, taking no role in the local guild but building a great house that was the talk of Antwerp. About a century later, Rubens emulated his way of living (see Rubens House, Antwerp).

The Money Changer and His Wife focuses on two ordinary people in the new secular Renaissance spirit of sixteenth-century Antwerp. Nevertheless, the painting has a moralizing theme. Fascinated with the gold her husband is weighing, the wife turns away from the pious book she is reading, opened at a picture of the Virgin. The small mirror, showing the image of an anxious customer calling on the money changer, also reveals an open window, reflective of outside influences and the influx of wealth into Antwerp, which is depreciating religious values. Massys is not necessarily against this change in society; he simply presents it to us, as if to say "Think about it, it may not be a bad thing."

Memling, Hans (ca. 1433–94), Flemish

The Mystic Marriage of St. Catherine (ca. 1470): Cabinets on the Seine, second cabinet
Memling was fond of painting a religious story that included a group of saints. In this one he depicts a story popular during the Middle Ages in which we see the Virgin in her traditional blue robe in a solemn pose, typical of Memling's style. The child she is holding is placing a mystic ring on St. Catherine's finger, a symbol of spiritual betrothal to God.

Catherine dates back to fourth-century Alexandria. Her crown indicates noble birth, while her open book recalls her being the patron saint of education (she was renowned for her learning and wisdom). The wheel at her feet is symbolic of her martyrdom by the Roman emperor Maxentius, who had her bound to an instrument of torture consisting of four wheels studded with iron spikes. When a thunderbolt destroyed it before it could harm her, she was instead beheaded. (In 1969 she was removed from the Catholic church calendar because of her uncertain historicity.)

The other saints shown are St. Agnes with her lamb, portrayed with her because of the similarity of her name to the Latin *agnus*, "lamb" (actually her name comes from the Greek word for "chaste"); St. Cecilia, patron saint of music; St. Lucy, holding a dish that contains two eyes, given to her for her name, which means "light" (she is invoked for cures of diseases of the eye); St. Margaret, the patron saint of childbirth, with her special attribute, the dragon; and St. Barbara, sitting to the left of a Gothic tower her father had built to lock her away from suitors.

The same cabinet contains Memling's *Portrait of an Old Woman,* an example of the artist's skill at portraiture. Its soft light, characteristic of Memling's portraits, lends a degree of sympathy to the figure.

Poussin, Nicolas (1594–1665), French

By the time Louis XIV took the throne of France (1643), the classic period of French art was already under way. This period also saw the establishment of the Academy of Painters and Sculptors (in 1648) under royal protection. Its aim was to regularize art. Nicolas Poussin, who reached maturity before the Academy had gained its full power and spent his working career in Italy, was nevertheless an artist who painted as the spirit of France dictated. He is a classicist in subject matter and style, which he takes from Raphael, Titian, and Carracci. That does not make him less of a French painter; his work has a French logic, clarity, and controlled emotion.

The Triumph of Flora (ca. 1627–28): Grande Galerie (first part), second left bay above

This is an early work whose subject matter, in the Renaissance tradition, depicts an apotheosis of Flora, or Springtime. We see the goddess led on a golden chariot by cupids lent by Venus for the occasion. The procession sweeps from the right to the left across the picture, balanced by the static couple reclining in the foreground. The blue background and the trees echo the arrangement of the figures.

While the fluidity of the painting reminds one of the early baroque, in comparison with works in that Italian style, Poussin's *Triumph of Flora* is more reserved and carefully worked out.

Orpheus and Eurydice (1650s): Grande Galerie (first part), second left bay

This painting is from Poussin's mature period, when his skill at evoking an imaginative world of the past was at its height. The painting relates the story of the wedding of Orpheus and Eurydice from Ovid's *Metamorphoses*. Hymeneus, the god of weddings, was summoned, but came reluctantly and did not bring his customary good luck. His wedding torch sputtered, making the cloud of smoke billowing over the castle in the background (Rome's Castel Sant'Angelo) where the wedding had taken place—a bad omen, which brought tears to the eyes of the guests. Then Eurydice was bitten by a snake and died. We see her sinking to the ground after being bitten by the snake. Only a fisherman seems to have noticed what has happened. Orpheus is playing his lyre, listened to by two maidens. On the placid lake, naked figures are enjoying the sunny day.

The contrast of a tragedy in a lovely setting is the subject of the work. Poussin leads our eye from foreground to the distant hills in the background. He seems to say that nature is indifferent to the death of a beautiful young girl just married to her lover. He calls our attention to man's small place in nature's scheme.

Whether or not you agree with Poussin's philosophical statement, you may admire his technique, with horizontal, vertical, and diagonal lines organized throughout into a structure that achieves a grand atmosphere.

Raphael* (1483–1520), Florentine, born in Umbria

La Belle Jardinière (1507–8): Salle des États

This painting may be compared with Leonardo's *Virgin of the Rocks* and *Virgin and Child with St. Anne* in the same room. The paintings by Leonardo are done in a pyramidal form that was copied by Raphael. The cartoon, now lost, of Leonardo's *Virgin and Child with St. Anne* had been displayed in Florence in 1501, and Florentine painters were familiar with it. The plants and grasses are also borrowed from Leonardo, but Raphael synthesizes the older master's artistic elements into something all his own. Raphael's painting lacks the mystery of Leonardo's painting, and is less an intellectual problem in design. He is more interested in depicting the natural grace and tender feelings of the Madonna, whom he sets against an airy, familiar landscape, instead of Leonardo's fantastic background.

This is probably the last of the Madonna series that Raphael painted in Florence. Later in Rome he continued to find in the Madonna a vehicle for his Christian humanism. He never abandoned Leonardo's classical pyramidal arrangements.

Portrait of Baldassare Castiglione (ca. 1515): Salle des États
Raphael is so famous for his Madonnas and his frescoes in the Vatican that it is sometimes forgotten he was a great portraitist. This portrait is one of a number he did in Rome at the height of his career. In its balance and composure it is not far from the style of his earlier Florentine Madonnas. Count Castiglione, author of the *Book of the Courtier,* exemplified the ideal educated gentlemen of the high Renaissance. The monochromatic scheme and *Mona Lisa*-like form goes well with Castiglione's elegant sobriety.

Rembrandt* (1606–69), Dutch

Supper at Emmaus (1648): Salle des Sept Metres
Rembrandt painted several versions of the *Supper at Emmaus* (see Musée Jacquemart-André). It was a favorite theme of the sixteenth-century Venetian School, but this version may be the most sublime rendering of the scene ever painted.

The picture refers to the story of two disciples traveling to Emmaus, a village near Jerusalem. They meet Christ, though they do not recognize Him as the Savior. But when Christ blesses the bread of the evening meal, they recognize the true identity of their companion, who then disappears.

While Rembrandt depicts the moment the pilgrims recognize Christ, he does not show them drawing back in wonder, which is the way the scene was usually depicted by Italian artists, who employed aggressive stagelike effects to heighten the drama. Instead, Rembrandt gives a subdued sense of emotion to draw us into the sacred mood of the scene. We focus on Christ, who is slightly larger in scale than the pilgrims and is emphasized by the open space behind Him, symbolic of His spirituality. The light radiates from Christ, reflecting the white tablecloth, illuminating the faces and the hands of the pilgrims, and permeating the surrounding darkness with a warm, mysterious glow.

Some critics have seen a reflection of Rembrandt's Mennonite faith in this painting, which in Rembrandt's time was a liberal Protestant sect based on individual relationship of a man with God and with his fellowmen.

Bathsheba (1654): Salle des Sept Metres
Rembrandt's sense of humanity is reflected in the Louvre's *Bathsheba.* The model is Hendriekje Stoffels, Rembrandt's common-law wife. Rembrandt makes no attempt to show her as an ideal beauty; she is shown in heavy solid proportions. Rembrandt focuses on her warm and sympathetic character. He models her flesh with unsurpassed honesty, since to Rembrandt she is a person with no shortcomings of character to be covered up. We cannot look at her as the classical idea of the nude, but we can still admire her for her character and for the love Rembrandt felt for her.

The Slaughtered Ox (1655): Salle des Sept Metres
This painting of a slaughtered ox has been called a perfect example of "art for art's sake," a painting without a subject matter that anticipates modern concepts of art where the meaning is in organization of form and color, and in the vigor of the brush stroke. But other viewers feel a sense of compassion or even horror for the flayed beast, seeing it as almost as tragic a scene as those of the Crucifixions Rembrandt was etching when he painted this one. It probably has no equal until the coming of Goya.

Rubens, Peter Paul* (1577–1640), Flemish

La Kermesse (Country Fair) (1636): Salle van Dyck
When Rubens retired to the country château he bought in 1635, he became a landscape painter for his own enjoyment. He had always painted landscapes as backgrounds for his religious and mythological scenes; now he painted them for the joy of it. It was a period when, though growing old and suffering from gout, he had found the peace his earlier existence as famous artist and diplomat had denied him. *La Kermesse* is one of Rubens's happiest paintings, in sharp contrast to scenes he painted earlier that were inspired by courtly etiquette. Never before had he shown such merry peasants, here celebrating a country fair with bacchanal abandon. As the sun goes down they are still dancing and eating, and drunken passions are becoming very much in evidence.

Rubens displays masterful integration of composition, color, and movement. There is no central focal point. Figures seem to move from the lower left corner into the distant fields at the upper right, then back to the lower left. The dark tree at the center of the picture provides a vertical axis that is counterbalanced by the horizontal line of dancers below. The dark colors in the lower right-hand corner balance the tones of the crowd of people at the lower left-hand corner. The spectator's eye is pulled from one pulsating group to another by alternating shades of dark and light.

Helène Fourment and her Two Children: Salle van Dyck
About one year after Rubens painted *La Kermesse* he painted this portrait of Helène Fourment, his young wife, and two of his children: his son Frans, wearing a black felt hat with feathers, and his daughter Clara Johanna. Helène Fourment and the children (there were four besides the two shown here, and a fifth born after Rubens died) helped to make Rubens's country estate and his mansion in Antwerp a happy household. There is a touch of maternal gravity in the expression of Helène. Her hands have the enveloping touch of a mother, and the curves of her face and bosom express her motherly tenderness and the love and admiration Rubens had for her.

Paintings illustrating the *Life of Marie de Medici:* Medici gallery
In 1622, when Rubens was at the height of his powers, he was summoned to Paris by Marie de Medici, the queen mother, who was established in the Palace of the Luxembourg. To complete the decoration of the palace she commissioned twenty-two canvases depicting her own life, as well as a second gallery of the life of Henri IV. This task was undertaken by Rubens and

completed in four years, in time for the marriage of the sister of Louis XIII to Charles I of England.

In order to enliven the story of Marie de Medici's life, Rubens improvised scenes that intermingled allegory and reality. Gods and goddesses are everywhere: the Fates predicting Marie's fame; the Graces presiding over her education; the Virtues supporting her beneficent sway; Minerva prompting Henri IV to fall in love with Marie's picture; Minerva sustaining Marie in exile.

This was merely decorative painting with little depth. But it is also decorative painting at its best and it is impossible not to admire its grand scope, its remarkable unity, and the skill and imagination that carried it out.

School of Avignon (end of fifteenth century), French

Pietà (ca. 1460): Salon Carré
The School of Avignon refers to paintings created in Provence during the fourteenth and fifteenth centuries. The artistic activity came with the transferring of the papacy to Avignon in the fourteenth century (1309–67), making the city a new Rome. Though the papacy was returned to Rome, the school of art it inspired remained, under King René of Anjou, and many of its works have come down to us intact.

While there is no denying foreign influence in the painting from Avignon—the linear treatment of figures, the gold background, and the simplicity of design are Italo-Byzantine characteristics—this *Pietà*, which is the finest specimen from the period, is French and done by a Frenchman, though we are not certain of his name (it has been attributed to Enguerrand Quarton). Nor do we know the name of the white-robed donor kneeling and looking grave. An evocation of sorrow is expressed by the curving sweep of Christ's body toward which bend the figures of St. John and the Magdalene, and the strong vertical of the Virgin in the center, who dominates the composition.

School of Fontainebleau (sixteenth century), French

Diana the Huntress (ca. 1550): Salon Carré
The French invasions of Italy in the early sixteenth century resulted in the introduction of the Italian Renaissance into France. Francis I (reigned 1515–47), who resumed the Italian wars when he took the throne, acquired the best talents from Italy for France. He succeeded in attracting Andrea del Sarto and Leonardo da Vinci, who lived out the remainder of his life in France, dying at Amboise in 1519. King Francis used many Italian artists to turn the hunting lodge at Fontainebleau into a palace in 1530, and the Italian style displaced the French Gothic. The Renaissance had arrived in France.

Diana the Huntress, by an unknown artist, is a typical example of the school, which shows elongated limbs in the mannerist style. It may be a portrait of Diane de Poitiers, Henri II's mistress. Here we see her acting the part of a mythological character with whom she shares her name and a love of hunting. Her nudity is only partial in this picture; the gallery at her château had more sensual portraits of her without clothing, bedecked in her fabulous jewelry. A central effect of the introduction of Italian mannerism into France was its reduction of religious themes in favor of motifs allowing portrayals of realistic nudity. This interest in the erotic gave rise to the "bath theme," an excellent example of which is the Louvre's *Duchesse de Villers and Gabrielle d'Estrées* (shown in the same gallery to the left of *Diana the Huntress*). Here the erotic nature of the school is seen in a portrait of Gabrielle d'Estrées, the mistress of Henri IV (the replacemnt of Diane de Poitiers), who shares her bath with her sister, the Duchesse de Villers. It has been suggested that the duchesse's gesture at her sister's breast indicates that Gabrielle is soon to have the kings' child, the bastard Duc de Vendôme, while the ring may hint at a desire for marriage.

Titian* (ca. 1487–1576), Venetian

Crowning with Thorns: Salles des États
Once an altarpiece in a chapel of Santa Maria delle Grazie in Milan, the church whose refectory is famous for Leonardo's *Last Supper*, this picture dates from around 1542 and is one of Titian's mannerist paintings in which he relies more on form than is usual for him. Its sculptural sharpness is emphasized in the figure of Christ, seen in the attitude of Laocoön, and in his tormentors, who are shown with exaggerated muscles. Painted on panel instead of canvas, the work shows a smoothness of surface that heightens the sculptural effect.

At the end of Titian's career he painted this scene again using the same composition, but that is where the similarity ends. This realistic work in the Louvre is moving by way of its harmony of line and richness of color. The later work (see *Crowning with Thorns*, Bavarian State Art Gallery, Munich) moves one even more with a spirituality expressed in color and light created from an impressionistic brushstroke.

Madonna with a Rabbit: Salle des États
This painting has always been popular, with its pastoral setting and rich Venetian color. It is an example of Titian's early work, dating from 1530, in which the influence of Bellini and Giorgione, Titian's former masters, lingers. The dreamy atmosphere of the painting is owed to Giorgione, and there is a Bellinian Madonna. It was executed on commission for Federigo Gonzaga, whose portrait may appear in the man in the right middle ground. The pensive young face of the Madonna is thought to be a portrait of Titian's young wife, Cecilia, who died the year this picture was painted. The figure on the left, holding the Christ Child, is St. Catherine, appearing in a rich Venetian dress, as she often does in sixteenth-century paintings. (She was removed from the Catholic church calendar in 1969 because of her uncertain historicity.) The rabbit held by the Virgin symbolizes the Incarnation. Rabbits, without the presence of the Virgin, would normally indicate fecundity, and x-rays have shown that Titian originally painted many rabbits into the landscape. He removed them, no doubt, because of some remark made to him about the inappropriateness of their presence in this scene.

Man with a Glove: Salle des États
Portraiture played a major role in Titian's career. It was responsible for the
success he had as the official court painter to Charles V and Philip II. This
early portrait (ca. 1520–23) is among the best of the more than two hundred
he executed during his lifetime. We are not certain of the identity of the sitter, but he is likely a nobleman acting as ambassador in Venice for an Italian
court, possibly representing the duke of Mantua.

There is psychological penetration in the intense expression. His dignity
and reserve are believable, achieved by intensifying key details with light: the
white cuffs and the short collar from which his head seems to sprout like a
flower, his penetrating eyes and the still life of his gloves. There is a subtlety
in the relationship of these details and in the dark tonality of the figure
emerging from an almost equally dark background. The technique of high-
lighting casual elements such as the gloves set a pattern of inspiration for
such masters as Velázquez, van Dyck, and Rembrandt.

Vermeer, Jan* 1632–75), Dutch

The Lacemaker (ca. 1665): Cabinets on the Tuileries, second cabinet
This painting by Vermeer is the only one by the great Dutch master that one
can see in all of France (Vermeer's *Astronomer* is in the private collection of
Baron Édouard de Rothschild, Paris). Vermeer was not appreciated until two
hundred years after his death; there are only thirty-nine of his paintings extant.

The *Lacemaker* is one of those glowing paintings of a single female figure that Vermeer painted in the decade 1658–68. In all of them his ladies
are immersed in some activity, such as this lacemaker, absorbed in an occupation of domesticity. That is the simple subject of the picture. Its greatness
lies in the freshness and harmony of its color—especially the blues and yellows—the simplicity of its composition, and the excellence of its execution.
It captures a moment of reality with exceptional sensitivity.

Veronese, Paolo* (1528–88), Venetian

The Marriage at Cana: Salle des États
Veronese painted many feast scenes, but this one, thirty-two feet long, with
132 figures, is the largest of them all. It was ordered by the Benedictines of
San Giorgio in Venice for their refectory and delivered in 1563.

The subject, which records Christ's first miracle, performed at a wedding feast at the village of Cana in Galilee, in which He changed water into
wine, was earlier left out of monastic painting possibly because of its theme
of marriage, but by the fifteenth century it became a popular subject, along
with *The Last Supper,* for refectories.

Veronese was a master at painting theatrical banquet scenes with rich
architectural backgrounds and brocaded costumes, and he loved to add exotic looking characters like the ones he often saw in Venice. He had little
religious feeling, and you have to look twice to see Christ (in the center with
a halo). No one appears very impressed with Christ's miracle, which is God's
first manifestation of Christ's miraculous powers. Some of the men at the

table are more interested in the women, and the eating has reached a point of gluttony. Notice the woman picking her teeth (at the end of the table).

Veronese has included some important personages in his picture: the musicians are recognizable as portraits of the painter Jacopo Bassano with a viol, Veronese himself with a viola da braccia, and Titian with a bass viol.

Watteau, Antoine (1684–1721), French

Watteau is an eighteenth-century painter who expressed the ideals of the Old Regime in France before the Revolution. His paintings are full of the illusions of a world of beauty with charming variations on the theme of young couples held in the suspense of restrained love. He came from the Flemish region of northern France and was heir to the baroque style of Rubens. He tempered that sensuous style with the elegant imagery the age demanded, and took rococo painting to its greatest heights.

Pilgrimage to Cythera (1717): Grande Galerie (first part), tribune, right wall
This small canvas was intended for a small, intimate room. Many of Watteau's paintings are smaller than this one. It depicts ladies and gentlemen dressed in the fashion of the French court taking part in a scene in a theatrical production, Dancourt's *Les Trois Cousines,* first produced in Paris in 1700. The people are about to depart from Cythera, the Island of Love, so there is an undercurrent of eroticism in the scene. On the right is a statue of Venus decorated with floral offerings. A young man below it is whispering into the ear of his lady friend. Next to them another young man is helping his lady to her feet, while a third young man is preparing to descend the hill to the waiting boat, his arm round his female companion, who, before following him, takes a last look backward. Winged cupids hover over the crowd. The colors are sophisticated, and the costumes sparkle like jewels. An atmosphere of Italy is visible in the distant mountains shaded by a blue haze that reminds one of Leonardo's landscapes in the *Mona Lisa* and *The Virgin and St. Anne.*

Gilles (ca. 1720): Grande Galerie (first part), tribune, left wall
Watteau painted a number of pictures dealing with the theater. This one is of Gilles, an actor in Italian comedy, who at first looks stiff and lifeless. This is appropriate because Gilles has just abandoned reality and is about to enter the world of make-believe; in a moment his static appearance will be translated into action, as he becomes one of the characters in Watteau's unreal world of *fêtes galantes* and *fêtes champêtres.* A tinge of melancholy pervades the picture—present in many of Watteau's paintings, including the *Pilgrimage to Cythera.* It may have originated in the fact Watteau had tuberculosis and was aware that he would not live a long life. Perhaps the premonition of an early death played a part in his dreamy paintings.

Weyden, Rogier van der* (ca. 1399–1464), Flemish

The Braque Tryptych: Cabinets on the Seine, first cabinet
Jehan Braque married Catherine de Brabant in 1451, when she was nineteen,

and died the next year. From the presence of a skull on the outside of one wing of this tryptych, it is believed that the widow commissioned this work in memory of her husband. Rogier executed it in 1452 at about the time he returned from Italy. While the Italian School had only a slight influence on his style, in this altarpiece the Italian feeling for form is evident.

We see a gallery of half-length figures representing, in the center, a somber Christ with John the Evangelist and the Virgin at his sides, and on the wings John the Baptist and Mary Magdalene. The focus is on the faces, which look to have been painted from life, especially the Magdalene, who is dressed in contemporary attire.

Sculpture

Note: Greek and Roman sculpture is located on the ground floor, southwest corner of the Cour Carrée, in rooms of the Pavillion des Arts and Salle des Cariatides. Their traditional room locations are given, but reconstruction of the Louvre has caused the moving about of some works of art. When this book went to press the Venus *de Milo and the* Rampin Head *were temporarily placed in the Salle des Cariatides.*

The following works are not listed alphabetically.

Nike of Samothrace or *"Winged Victory"* (ca. 200 B.C.), Greek: at top of staircase east of Porte Denon
The artist who carved this magnificent Hellenistic statue is not known, but recent discoveries make it likely he came from Rhodes, famous during the Hellenistic period for its sculpture. It is thought to have been made to commemorate a naval victory of Rhodes over Antiochus III of Syria early in the second century B.C. The forward movement of the figure, countered by the majestic sweep of the wings, the lightness of the drapery ruffled by the wind (the goddess was placed on the prow of a ship), and the weight distributed equally on both legs with the right leg placed forward for better balance, shows technical and aesthetic mastery and makes this statue one of the great artistic achievements of the Hellenistic age.

Venus de Milo, no. 399 (second century B.C.), Greek: Pavillon des Arts, Salle de la Venus de Milo
Until this original Greek statue was found on the island of Melos in 1820, the image of the Greek Aphrodite was known only from Roman copies. It became world famous and is one of the best-known Greek statues.

The artist who carved the *Venus* is unknown. The small head and the twisted pose suggest Lysippus, but there is also a reflection of Praxiteles in the soft modeling of the flesh. A feature of the *Venus* is the head, in excellent preservation, which shows what is considered the ideal classical face. The arms were lost; this has given rise to speculation regarding their original gestures. Possibly the right hand held up the drapery and the left an apple, symbol of Melos.

No matter what the statue may have looked like with arms, it keeps the qualities that make it a great work of art. It has an Olympian calm with no exaggeration or unbalanced emphasis that lends a dignity in the classical tradition. Physical beauty in the *Venus de Milo* has been sublimated to a universal aesthetic that has the power to communicate with us today as effectively as it did to the ancient Greeks.

Rampin Head, no. 701 (mid-sixth century B.C.), Greek: Pavillon des Arts, Salle Archaique
Only the head of this figure is authentic. The torso is a plaster cast of the marble original now in the Acropolis Museum in Athens. It was probably part of a pair of horsemen representing Castor and Pollux, the sons of Zeus and Leda. Few archaic pieces of Greek sculpture are rendered with such dignity and feeling. The refinement is expressed in the strong lines of the face and the treatment of the hair and beard. It represents an advance in Attic sculpture; the turning of the head to the right is the first example where frontality has been abandoned for a more expressive approach.

Maidens from the Parthenon Frieze, no. 738 (442–38 B.C.), Greek: Pavillon des Arts, Salle du Parthenon
This is part of the sculptural decoration of the Parthenon frieze by Phidias. Most of the frieze is at the British Museum in London. The fragment here shows maidens taking part in the Panathenaic procession in Athens, held every four years to honor the goddess Athene. The two alternating male figures are probably marshalls of the procession. The ensemble of figures is arranged to suggest animation, achieved not only by their placement but also by the modeling of the draperies.

Hera of Samos, no. 686 (ca. 570 B.C.), Greek: Pavillon des Arts, Salle Archaique
This early piece of Ionian sculpture is typical of the many female statues in cylindrical form made on the island of Samos before 550 B.C. This one is Hera, wife of Zeus and patron of married couples. The missing arm was raised to the breast in an attempt at naturalism, as are the toes, showing a departure from Oriental influence.

The "Athena Medici," no. 3070 (ca. 450–20 B.C.), Greek: Pavillon des Arts, Salles de Phidias & de Polyclète
This is a Roman copy of a lost Greek original attributed to Phidias. It once stood in the garden of the Villa Medici in Rome and was brought to Paris by Ingres. The goddess is heavily draped and has a military cloak thrown over her shoulders, but a finer tunic is revealed by the opening of the drapery on her right side. Such work represents the high point of Greek art and was copied many times.

Michelangelo* (1475–1564), Florentine

Dying Slave (Bound Slave) (ca. 1513): ground floor, Pavillon des États, Michelangelo room, no. 9
This work and the *Rebellious Slave* in the same room are among the many statues meant for the tomb of Pope Julius II. The project plagued Michelan-

gelo for much of his career and came to nothing. The sculptures provide an opportunity to see Michelangelo's genius in creating movement within the medium of stone. His twisting *contrapposto* conveys the struggle of the bound slave; you can almost feel the slave's struggle within your own body. There are many interpretations of the *Dying Slave,* some complex. It can mean many things to different people. For some it represents man's soul enslaved by his animal nature. In the unfinished marble behind the slave there is an ape—a hint of the subhuman tendencies in mankind.

MUSÉE MARMOTTAN

2 rue Louis-Boilly, 16ᵉ

Métro: La Muette

Hours: Open Tues.–Sun., 10AM–6PM. Admission fee.

The Marmottan Museum, pleasantly situated between the Bois de Boulogne and the Ranelagh Gardens, is the result of the collecting efforts of an industrialist, Jules Marmottan, and his son Paul, an author and art historian. The son entrusted it to the Institute of France in 1932. It consists of an impressive collection of furniture, objets d'art, and paintings of the First Empire. There is a portrait by François Gérard (1770–1837) of *Desirée Clary,* whom Napoleon courted before she married Marshall Bernadotte in 1798 and ultimately became queen of Sweden (room 2, to the right of the entrance). There are paintings by Louis Boilly (1761–1845) that display everyday life from the reign of Louis XVI to that of Louis-Philippe, and there are primitives and tapestries of the fifteenth and sixteenth centuries.

The museum is most celebrated for its collection of impressionist works, largely those of Claude Monet (1840–1926), whose son bequeathed the museum more than 130 paintings and drawings of his father's works. The museum has built a special basement gallery to display the works. Also shown are works of Jongkind, Renoir, Morisot, and others. (For a discussion of impressionism, see Musée du Jeu de Paume, and Monet's *Waterlillies* at the Orangerie.)

Among paintings by Claude Monet are more than thirty paintings of his home at Giverny (many of them Nymphéas paintings), *Cathedral of Rouen, London, Parliament,* and his view of the harbor at Le Havre called *Impression, Sunrise* of 1872 (stolen in 1985 and not recovered at the time this guide went to press), the painting that is credited with giving the movement its name. It goes back to the famous exhibition held in 1874 at the studios of Nader, the photographer, by thirty painters who banded together to show their works, one of which was Monet's *Impression, Sunrise.* A reporter used the title sarcastically to criticize the group's work. He called them mere "impressionists" rather than painters. The artists accepted the term as their own.

MUSÉE MUNICIPAL D'ART MODERNE (MUSÉE D'ART MODERNE DE LA VILLE DE PARIS)

11 avenue du Président Wilson, 16e.

Metro: Alma-Marceau Iéna

Hours: Open Tues.–Sun., 10AM–5:30PM (Wed. until 8:30PM). Free admission to the permanent collection.

Owned by the city of Paris, this museum occupies the left wing of the Palais de Tokyo, the structure built for the World Exhibition of 1937. It opened its doors to the public in 1961, specializing in the works of twentieth-century artists, both French and foreign.

The Palais de Tokyo used to have another modern collection, that of the Musée National d'Art Moderne, in the opposite side of the building at 13 avenue du Président Wilson. That collection has been moved to the Pompidou Center at Beaubourg. The facility here, now called the Musée de l'Art et d'Essai, is devoted to special exhibitions. Parisians generally refer to both museums simply as the Palais de Tokyo.

The Musée Municipal d'Art Moderne got its start from a large donation of twentieth-century art: eighty Rouaults, 110 Gromaires, twenty-three Maria Blanchards, eighteen Dufys, thirteen Buffets. With it the museum took its place along with other twentieth-century art collections the city of Paris owned.

Of the many works of art that are outstanding see, on the **upper level,** one of the largest murals ever created, *La Fée Electricité* (filling one large room), which **Raoul Dufy** (1877–1953) painted for the Palace of Electricity at the 1937 International Exposition in Paris. It shows the history of electricity with the names of the contributors to its development starting with Archimedes and ending with Edison; and on the **lower level:** *The Street,* by Marc Chagall (1887–1985); *The Drunken Woman, Portrait of Vaux,* and *Girl,* by Georges Rouault (1871–1958); *The Dance,* by Matisse (1869–1954); *Evocation,* by Picasso (1881–1973); *San Francisco* and *Man Sharpening Scythe,* by Marcel Gromaire (1892–1971): *The Blue Bird,* by Jean Metzinger (1883–1957); *The River, Three People Sitting on the Grass,* and *Barges Tied-up at Camaret,* by André Derain (1880–1954); *Temple of Beauty,* by Pascin (1885–1930); *Woman with Blue Dress,* by Chaim Soutine (1894–1943); *La Fère en Tardenois,* by Utrillo (1883–1955); and full-length portraits by Modigliani (1884–1920), *Woman with a Fan* and *Woman with Blue Eyes.*

MUSÉE NATIONAL D'ART MODERNE AT THE GEORGES POMPIDOU NATIONAL CENTER FOR ART AND CULTURE

Plateau Beaubourg, 4ᵉ

Metro: Les Halles

Hours: Open Mon., Wed.–Fri., 12 noon–10PM; Sat. and Sun., 10AM–10PM. Admission fee.

Parisians have called this vast structure the Pompidoleum, the refinery, the distillery, the supermarket, and the self-service or culture-mill. But about fifty thousand people visit it daily. The exterior consists of a melange of structural supports, heating and plumbing pipes, cooling ducts, electricity conduits, elevators, and escalators. What is normally placed inside a building, hidden behind walls, is here exposed on the outside. Before it was built, President Pompidou said, "I would passionately love for Paris to have a cultural center that is both a museum and a center of creation, where the plastic arts would be side-by-side with music, cinema, books, and audiovisual research." The resulting complex, built on a five-acre lot called the Plateau Beaubourg, just north of the Seine, was also supposed to be France's claim to becoming the center of today's art world.

Outside, jugglers, fire-eaters, and other entertainers congregate in the plaza. Their presence goes well with the Nikki de Saint Phalle and Jean Tinguely joyful fountain made up of a number of brightly colored objects among patterns of rising and falling water. Inside is the Public Information Library (BPI) with a million French and foreign books, periodicals, films, records, slides, and micro-index cards covering every area of human knowledge. There is also the Center of Industrial Creation (CCI), an environmental study center involving architecture, urbanism, advertising, and everyday objects. Below ground level is the Institute for Research Coordination Acoustic/Music (IRCAM) headed by Pierre Boulez. Its aim is to solve, through teamwork and mechanical means, problems in music composition.

Most of the space at the Beaubourg has been given over to the **National Museum of Modern Art,** devoted to contemporary art from fauvism up to the present. About 1,000 paintings are permanently displayed on the third and fourth floors, with about 600 more arranged on suspended panels visitors may lower from the ceiling by pushing buttons.

At the writing of this book the museum was being remodeled and reinstalled. When completed it is expected to continue showing its collection in chronological order, from 1905 to the present, with intimate alleyways to allow for a change of both pace and scale, in which drawings, letters, books, photographs, and other memorabilia can be seen at leisure.

Here is an outline of the collection with the names of paintings the museum suggests you "not leave without going to see."

Third Floor
Salon Kandinsky
Fauvism (Derain, Dufy, Matisse, Valminck)
German expressionism
French School, 1910–14
Cubism (Picasso, Braque, Gris)
Italian futurism
Russian avant-garde
The start of abstraction
Kandinsky, Kupka
Robert and Sonia Delaunay

Dufy, *Flag Bedecked Street* (1905)
Chagall, *To Russia, to Donkeys, and to Others* (1911)
R. Delaunay, *The Town of Paris* (1911)
F. Léger, *The Wedding* (1910–11)
F. Picabia, *Udnie* (1931)
Picasso, *Lady Seated* (1901)

Fourth Floor
Works of Matisse, Léger, Mondrian, Malevitch, Klee
Dada and the 1920s
Chagall and Rouault
The Montparnasse painters (Modigliani, Soutine)
Surrealism (Dali, Ernst, Miro, Magritte)
The 1950s
Lyrical abstraction (Hartung, Mathieu, Soulages)
The Cobra Group
Abstraction in the United States
Geometric abstraction
Pop Art, happenings, environment
Art and technology, op art
Hyperrealism
New figuration
Group support—surface
Conceptual art

Ben, *Ben's Shop* (1958–73)
Calder, *Josephine Baker* (1926)
Dubuffet, *Traveller without Compass* (1952)
Gnoli, *Hair Part* (1968)
Mathieu, *The Capetiens* (1935)
Matisse, *Roumanian Blouse* (1940)
Mondrian, *Composition in Blue and Red* (1937)
Pollock, *The Deep* (1953)
Saint-Phalle, *The Bride* (1963)
Soutine, *The Groom* (1928)
Tanning, *Bedroom 20* (1970)
Zao Wou Ki, *Composition in Blue* (1960)

MUSÉE DE L'ORANGERIE

Place de la Concorde, 1ᵉ

Metro: Concorde

Hours: Open Wed.–Mon., 9:45AM–5:15PM. Admission fee.

Monet, Claude (1840–1926), French
Nympheas (Waterlilies) (1919–26): basement
This series of murals covering the walls of two oval rooms that were spe-

cially constructed for them in 1921 represent a subject on which Monet started as early as 1899 and worked at until his death in 1926. He had been obsessed with the movement of wind and water and how clouds affected light on the surface of pools and on plants growing in them. Based on his observations of these phenomena he conceived this series to capture a flowing display of nature.

While the *Waterlilies* has always been admired as a central work of impressionism, and even described as the "Sistine Chapel of impressionism," there remains a question as to how much of an impressionist work it really is. *Waterlilies* does show Monet becoming freer in his brushwork as he used abstract forms. Monet himself insisted he was an impressionist but his work here shows a movement out of impressionism toward abstract expressionism.

Monet's Garden at Giverny
Monet used his water garden at his home in Giverny for his water lilies paintings. Now, after restoration, both garden and house are open to the public.

Giverny is about one hour by car northwest of Paris along the Paris–Normandy highway, or about one hour by train to Vernon—taxis available to Giverny—from the Gare St. Lazare. Open daily, except Mon., Apr. 1–Oct. 31; the house 10AM–noon and 2–6PM; the gardens 10AM–6PM; admission fees to both.

The restoration came about when Michel Monet, the artist's son and heir to the house at Giverny, left it to the Institute of France (his collection of paintings and drawings were left to the Marmottan Museum). So careful has been the restoration, done largely through the generosity of Lila Acheson Wallace, co-founder of the *Reader's Digest,* that to see the house today is to see how Monet lived and worked. There is the huge studio where he painted his water lilies series, a commission of the government of France.

Permanent Home of the Jean Walter and Paul Guillaume Collection
The space in the Orangerie that does not contain Monet's *Water Lilies* is used for the collections of two noted French art dealers. The woman who was married to both of them bequeathed their collections to the Orangerie.

The paintings range from impressionism to the art of the 1930s, featuring the works of Cézanne, Derain, Matisse, Monet, Modigliani, Picasso, Renoir, Rousseau, Soutine, and Utrillo.

Cézanne, Paul* (1839–1906), French
The works of Cézanne depict the full range of his art from the early *Outdoor Lunch* and *Landscape with Red Roof,* which have the striking colors and technique of impressionism, to the late *The Red Rock* and *In the Grounds of the Black Château,* which are expressed through the use of planes and colors. The still lifes, *Apples and Cakes* and, especially, *Fruits, Napkin and*

Milk Jug, show Cézanne's great contribution to modernism. In these paintings Cézanne has invented his own light, which he expresses through the use of color. Shadow is eliminated and modeling is achieved by placing related colors side by side. He also creates a new sense of perspective by shifting the angle of vision—allowing us to see the object from various angles—as in *Fruits, Napkin and Milk Jug,* where the glass is seen both from the side and from above. Thus, Cézanne influences every modern artist by creating truly plastic creations existing within their own independent worlds, owing nothing to anything preceding them.

Derain, André (1880–1954), French
The twenty-eight works by Derain at the Orangerie largely date from after 1920, when Derain had left the modern movement. Along with Matisse and Vlaminck, Derain had been one of the brilliant fauvists of 1900–1910, but his paintings at the Orangerie are those that seek security in the art of the past. Gone are bright colors in favor of deeper tones, and experimental forms have been replaced by traditional light and shade. Still, what we see of Derain at the Orangerie are works of quality, which form an interesting chapter in the modern movement, when a brilliant artist, frightened at his own daring, felt the need to organize and curb his own freedom.

Matisse, Henri* (1869–1954), French
At the start of World War I Matisse, who was then forty-eight years old and had been rejected for military service, left Paris for the south of France, where he continued to live until his death thirty-seven years later. His paintings done in and around Nice from 1917–24, some of which are displayed at the Orangerie, show he was influenced by the warm pleasurable surroundings of the Midi. *La Jeune Fille et le Vase de Fleurs* (1920), *Femme au Violon* (1921–22), *Odalisque à la Culotte Rouge* (1924), and *Odalisque a la Culotte Grise* (1925–27) depict languishing females in interiors saturated with pale sensual colors, accented by strokes of bright color in wall patterns, intricate textiles, and southern flowers. These are masterpieces of delicate color and use of line and shape to create a soothing and charming atmosphere of visual delights. But Matisse tired of this trend around 1926 and thereafter his art changed. He paid less attention to making his paintings pretty and infused them with tension and boldness of color.

Picasso, Pablo* (1881–1973), Spanish, lived in France
The early works by Picasso at the Orangerie, dating from 1903–6, when Picasso had recently arrived in Paris, reflect his poverty and loneliness. The large monochromatic figure paintings, *The Embrace,* a rare pastel, and *The Adolescents,* painted in Spain when poverty had forced him to leave Paris for the last time, are melodramatic but moving works of tender feeling for the subject matter. The paintings done on Picasso's return to Paris, *Nude Against a Red Background* and *Woman with a Comb,* which have more variety of color, show the artist's change of mood and his interest in expressing

himself in geometric terms, which eventually led to the revolutionary *Les Demoiselles d'Avignon* of 1907 and the creation of cubism.

Of the paintings done after 1918, there are two great *Bathers* from Picasso's neoclassic period, where he was influenced by the Greco-Roman art he saw on a trip to Rome in 1917. These large, sculpturesque, fleshy figures occupied him in the early 1920s until his mood changed again and he began to manipulate the human figure, as shown in *Woman with a Tamborine*, whose flattened forms and stirring contrasts of color have the expressionism that came to dominate his art.

Renoir, Pierre-Auguste* (1841–1919), French
Renoir studied art in the early 1860s in Paris where he met Monet, Sisley, and Bazille. His early *Snowy Landscape,* painted outdoors in natural light to catch a momentary "impression" of the scene, shows him as a young artist closely linked to the theory of impressionism. But the outdoor subjects of the impressionists were not Renoir's main interest. He is best known for scenes of people relaxing and enjoying themselves and, above all, the female figure and portraiture, where he shows a concern for form and volume as well as light and color.

Young Girls at the Piano (ca. 1892) is one of his scenes of young feminine beauty in an atmosphere that radiates a sense of contentment and well-being. It was so successful that it was purchased by the Louvre and Renoir repainted it several times. His many nudes, such as *Nude Woman in a Landscape* and *Reclining Female Nude*, which are also portraits of Gabrielle, the governess of his children, may remind you of eighteenth-century paintings by Boucher and Fragonard, but their balance of color and line is an achievement of a nineteenth-century impressionist with respect for the art of the old masters.

Renoir's portraits of his sons, his second son Jean (who became a famous filmmaker) playing with Gabrielle, and Claude, his third son, also called Coco, wearing a bright orange costume that has become the trademark of the Orangerie, show he was sensitive to the charms of small children as he was to all of his subjects. They are also examples of Renoir's mature style that show him combining the light of the impressionists with the strong forms that were always a part of his art.

Rousseau, Henri "Le Douanier"* (1844–1910), French
The reputation of this engaging "primitive" rests on two paintings at the Musée du Jeu de Paume, *War* and *The Snake Charmer*, and two more, *The Dream* and *The Sleeping Gypsy* at the Museum of Modern Art in New York. What we see at the Orangerie are lesser works, but still wholly enjoyable.

Rousseau, whose occupation until 1885 was that of a minor customs inspector (hence his name "Douanier") painted without the disciplines of drawing, perspective, and art history. Yet, his homemade paintings cannot be dismissed as merely routine. There is a charm to the flat decorative style of *The Marriage*, which may have been composed in the shape of a St. Andrew's Cross (the shape of an **X**). We are captured by the surrealistic quality of *The Cart of Father Junier*, where the subjects sit as upright and as still as the two trees in the background, and the impossible little dog seems to be the only animated figure. There is also a period charm to much of this art. We see Wilbur Wright's biplane, factory chimneys, and even the Eiffel Tower, all the results of modern technology that few painters during Rousseau's time (Seurat is an exception) put into their art.

Soutine, Chaim (1894–1943), Lithuanian, lived in France
Chaim Soutine was born in Lithuanian Russia near Minsk, the tenth of eleven children of a poor Jewish tailor. It is extraordinary that this man from the lowest rung of shtetl society, who was beaten by his coreligionists for wanting to be an artist (his two older brothers constantly taunted him, saying, "a Jew must not paint") was able to attend an art school in Minsk and finally emigrate to Paris in 1912. Only ten years later he became famous when the American collector Dr. Albert C. Barnes of Merion, Pennsylvania, purchased some 100 of his works.

But enthusiastic patrons and money did not make Soutine happy. He suffered all his life from artistic doubt. Looking at his landscapes you can see the swirling anguish of van Gogh's cypresses and the same rage of color. Soutine, who sold everything he painted, felt as isolated as van Gogh, who sold nothing. Soutine, however, claimed he learned about color from Rembrandt, not van Gogh.

Soutine used ugliness to communicate life. He distorted the features of his sitters, exaggerating shapes and sizes of cheeks, eyes, and ears. For Soutine this was visual truth. It is unlikely that *The Little Pastry Cook, The Choirboy*, and *The Painter Lejeune* were unhappy or irrational personalities, but Soutine saw them that way. In the end one of Soutine's own torments got the better of him. He died at the age of 49 from a perforated ulcer, from which he suffered for many years.

Another Jewish émigré to Paris with whom Soutine was friendly was the Italian born **Amedeo Modigliani** (1884–1920). Though he thought of himself as a sculptor, and may have introduced African sculpture to Brancusi, whom he met in 1909, he abandoned sculpture for figure and portrait painting by about 1915, probably because he failed to sell his work and because the stone dust aggravated his tuberculosis. The almond-shaped eyes and oval shaped heads of his figures, delicately tilted on slender necks, show he was influenced by African masks, but he also took from Cézanne, whose broken planes, firm composition, and soft colors are seen in *The Young Apprentice*. Though his work is among the most mannered, he never sacrificed the individuality of his sitter. The *Portrait of Paul Guillaume*, his patron and art dealer, attests to that. He is seen as a dapper young Parisian, exuding the self-confidence and contentment of his position. In admiration of Guillaume, and to be certain we know he is a very important person, Modigliani has inscribed the picture with the titles "Novo Pilota" (New pilot) and "Stella Maris" (Star of the sea).

MUSÉE D'ORSAY

9, quai Anatole France, 7ᵉ

Metro: Solférino

At the time of writing, this museum was still under construction. When completed, possibly by November 1986, it promises to be the quintessential museum of nineteenth-century French art, which the museum defines as dating from 1815 to 1914.

There is no better place in Paris to display nineteenth-century art than in the former Orsay Railway Station, which itself is a nineteenth-century structure. Under its huge iron-and-glass barrel vault will be a main street lit by daylight. So vast is this space that the sculptures displayed there will seem as though they were in open air. The permanent collection will have a space of 20,000 square meters (72,000 square feet) and there will be rooms for temporary exhibitions. An interdisciplinary approach, promised by the museum, will join painting and sculpture to the graphic and decorative arts, and virtually every other means of artistic expression of the period: photography, music, literature, and even early cinema.

As for the collection, the small sampling of painting and sculpture from the Orsay exhibition at the Musée de l'Art et d'Essai (the right wing of the Palais de Tokyo at 13 avenue du Président Wilson) is very impressive. Seurat's *Circus* and the works of other neoimpressionists, such as Henri-Edmond Cross (1856–1910) and Paul Signac (1863–1935), who developed in the 1880s and 1890s under the leadership of Georges Seurat (1859–91), and exhibited with him at the first Salon des Indépendants (1884), are of immediate interest for their experimental approach to expressing light and color on canvas; Gauguin (1848–1903) and his symbolist followers, who called themselves Nabis (from the Hebrew word for prophet), in particular Pierre Bonnard (1867–1947) and Edouard Vuillard (1868–1940), who in 1890 shared a studio in Place Pigalle, are overwhelming for their color; and there are more than ten scenes of Parisian night life by Toulouse-Lautrec (1864–1901), which seem as though they were made for a museum of nineteenth-century French art.

To go with these works, and many more that will come from the Louvre and provincial museums in France, is the famous collection of impressionist art from the Jeu de Paume, which will free that overcrowded little museum for special exhibitions. With this lineup of art works waiting to take their place in the old Gare d'Orsay, the promise of this museum should be easily fulfilled.

MUSÉE DU PETIT-PALAIS

Avenue Winston Churchill, 8ᵉ

Metro: Champs-Elysées-Clémenceau

Hours: Open Tues.–Sun., 10AM–5:30PM. Admission fee.

The Petit-Palais, like its big cousin the Grand Palais located across the street, was constructed for the World's Fair of 1900. At that time it was opened to present a history of world art from Egyptian antiquity to French impressionism. Today it is one of the most pleasant museums in Paris, a place where special art exhibitions are held and the home of part of the collections of the city of Paris, which features a wide diversity in art from the Middle Ages to the nineteenth century. (Its art works of the twentieth century were sent to the Musée Municipal d'Art Moderne at the Palais de Tokyo.)

Of the paintings on permanent display, see in the **Galerie Zoublaloff** (the plan of the museum displayed on the walls makes it easy to find your way), **room 1,** *Portait of Théodore Duret,* by Manet (1832–83), a masterpiece in its harmonious shades of grey relieved by touches of yellow, pink, and blue; *Portrait of Ambroise Vollard,* by Cézanne (1839–1906), in which Vollard, the art dealer who sold Cézanne's works, was said to have posed over 100 times before Cézanne thought that at least the front of his shirt looked reasonably well; and portraits by Pissarro (his wife), Gauguin, and Toulouse-Lautrec. **Room 2** has some of the best works by **Courbet** (1819– 77): *Juliette Courbet,* a portrait of the artist's sister; *Young Ladies on the Shores of the Seine,* an original composition that influenced the impressionists; *Proud'hon and his Children,* a portrait of the socialist philosopher whom Courbet admired; and *Le Sommeil,* one of the most beautiful paintings of the many nudes Courbet painted, and the most sensational and erotic, showing two girls interlocked in sensual slumber. In **room 3** there is a nude called *Marietta* by Corot (1796–1875), which is possibly the first nude Corot ever painted, done when he visited Rome. In the **Galerie Dutoit,** devoted to seventeenth-century Dutch and Flemish art, see *Self-portrait with a Dog,* by **Rembrandt** (1606–69), showing the artist wearing an Oriental costume and posing, for the first and last time, with a dog.

Before leaving the museum, visit the **Inner Courtyard,** which has a statue of *Venus Victorieuse* (1914–16) by Renoir. It is a quiet place to sit and relax.

MUSÉE PICASSO

Hôtel Salé, 5 rue de Thorigny, 3ᵉ

Metro: St. Sébastien-Froissart

Hours: Open Wed.–Mon., 10AM–5:15PM. Admission fee.

This museum, the newest in Paris, has the largest and richest collection of Picasso's art in the world. Almost all of it was acquired from Picasso's own collection after his death in 1973—the art works Picasso saved for himself. At that time, no one had seen it all, or even realized the extent of it: Picasso had kept 1,876 paintings, 7,249 drawings, 1,335 sculptures, 2,880 ceramics, more than 3,000 prints, 149 sketchbooks, and a personal collection of African art and works by Cézanne, Degas, Matisse, the Douanier Rousseau, Derain, Balthus, and others. Now that the best of this treasure trove is housed in the Hôtel Salé, a great town house that once was a tax collector's mansion (Salé means salt, in reference to the seventeenth- and eighteenth-century *gabelle*, or salt tax), which is an appropriate place for a collection that came to France in lieu of estate taxes owed by Picasso's heirs, it gives us a fresh look at the work of the best known artist in the world.

The Achievement of Pablo Picasso (1881–1973)

Picasso's early academic works painted from 1894 to 1899, when he was thirteen to eighteen years old and living in Barcelona, are best seen at the Picasso Museum in Barcelona. The collection here begins with his first arrival in Paris and the first of his famous "periods."

1901–4: *Blue Period*

Coming from avant-garde Barcelona, Picasso was already aware of modernism and concerned with the problems of the world when he first came to Paris. *The Death of Casagemas* (1901), a deathbed portrait of his friend who committed suicide, led him into his Blue Period. During this time Picasso alternated between Spain and France living where he could. His paintings of the poor, the crippled, and the outcast, done in grayish-blue monochrome, omitting almost all background detail, are reflections of his own misery.

1905–6: *Rose Period*

Early in 1905 Picasso's mood changed, perhaps because he met the beautiful Fernande Olivier, who became his mistress for seven years. Pinks and ochers succeeded blues and he painted more cheerful, natural scenes, like *The Two Brothers*, whose tranquil figures are more solid and fleshy than the frail, elongated earlier ones. Life became brighter for Picasso; the expatriot American collectors Gertrude Stein and her brother Leo bought his canvasses, and a wealthy Russian merchant remained his patron until World War I.

1907–8: *Iberian and African Period*

After the sweetness and delicate balance of the Rose Period Picasso's paintings started to idealize a natural, primitive life, inspired, in part, by Gauguin. Sculpture, too, took on added meaning. If modern painting in the new industrial age was becoming inexorably flat, sculpture still had access to the third medium and could serve as Picasso's private escape into a lost paradise. It is at this time, when Picasso was painting the monumental *Les Demoiselles d'Avignon* (in the collection of the Museum of Modern Art in New York, but represented here with the numerous studies that preceded, accompanied, and followed it), that he studied archaic Iberian sculpture and African and Oceanic tribal masks and figures, costumes, and magical objects, at the Musée d'Ethnographie du Trocadéro (now the Musée de l'Homme) in Paris. The *Demoiselles* is a turning point in the history of art because, like tribal sculpture, Picasso took the liberty of rearranging the human anatomy, so that we see objects from all sides at once, as the mind, not the eye, perceives them. It set artists free to move beyond the boundaries of nineteenth-century visual realism and question realism itself.

That is not to say that tribal art in itself was directly responsible for changing Western art—from perceptual and representational toward conceptual and abstract. Picasso and other artists had already started painting figures from several points of perspective, rather than a single point, as was traditional since the Renaissance. Only after those revolutionary steps were taken did tribal art, which had been around for a long time in Paris and elsewhere, become relevant and full of interest to modern art. In conversations Picasso had with William Rubin, director of paintings and sculpture at the Museum of Modern Art in New York, we learn Picasso was more interested and influenced by what he considered the magical force in primitive art. Mr. Ruben has said, "He [Picasso] believed that Western art had gotten too far from what might be called the magical roots of image-making. He felt that with nineteenth-century traditions of salon painting, art had gotten washed out, lost all of its power and juice. He wanted to restore it by going back to its roots." This meant embarking upon the adventure of cubism.

1909–17: Analytic Cubism, Collage and Construction Sculpture, Synthetic Cubism

Picasso, with his new friend, Georges Braque, developed cubism. *The Man with Guitar* (1911–13) is an example of analytical cubism on canvas in which reality is taken apart, examined from all sides, and reassembled in a system of interlocking planes. The color is limited to browns and grays to stress that form is the essence of painting, not color. Eventually, the subject matter in cubist art became dissolved in space and unrecognizable: both space and objects in it were eliminated. Then, in a second phase, cubists reasoned that the object, which had been reduced to its elementary geometrical forms, could no longer be put together for identification by the eye, but could be reassembled by the mind. This meant that color, line, and texture did not have to represent anything but themselves. Art could be anything—any common object like the seat of a chair, a piece of plumbing, even machinery.

Until Picasso, sculpture had been based on either modeling or carving, of building up or whittling down a solid mass, almost always depicting a living form. Picasso not only chose inanimate subjects but, more important, he went beyond modeling and carving by combining shapes into a constructed sculpture, and assembling open, transparent, elements. Space, which had previously only surrounded sculpture, now came to be surrounded by it. This launched the movement that came to be known as constructivism.

Before 1914, Picasso and others made collages and *papiers collés* (pasted paperwork), which, unlike analytical fragmentation of objects, was a synthetic construction of objects from forms not originally derived from them. This led to synthetic or "decorative" cubism, which was more pleasurable to look at than analytic cubist works. Bright colors and mood returned to Picasso's canvasses. Less stress was put on the distortion, or tearing down, of forms. The objects painted began to be identifiable again and the use of materials hitherto foreign to painting—sand, paper, fabrics—was interesting and exciting. But Picasso had gone as far as he wished to go with cubism. Other influences entered his life, and his art took on new dimensions.

1918–24: *Classic Period*
Picasso accepted an invitation to create the costumes and sets for a new ballet by his friends, Jean Cocteau, the playwright, and Erik Satie, the composer, being produced by Diaghilev. This brought Picasso to Rome in February 1917, where Diaghilev's company was appearing, for rehearsals of the new production. The Greco-Roman antiquity that Picasso saw in Italy was to influence his art for a number of years. Back in Paris, now with fame and fortune, he was introduced to high society by Olga Koklova, a dancer from the ballet he met in Rome and married in 1918. The world was moving fast for Picasso, perhaps too fast. As if to slow it down he painted giantlike, fleshy figures drawn and modeled in the classical style. Faces show little emotion. Massive bodies, more like statues than people, are rooted to earth. Their overbearing sense of calm suggested a slow-motion world that did not exist for Picasso, now on top of the art world in Paris.

1925–1930s: *Grotesque and Double Image Period*
During his Classic Period, Picasso continued with richer, more colorful, simplified, cubist works. Suddenly, in 1925, his work took a turn toward using interweaving arabesques and linear designs to distort and displace human features and forms. By the end of the 1920s and into the 1930s the distortions became grotesque and violent, with few, if any, recognizable human elements. The masks his figures often wear at this time and his double-face portaits reflecting a mysterious otherness, suggest that Picasso was not painting a face but a state of mind, drawing out the inner forces buried deep within the soul. He may have been influenced by Freud's theories, which brought attention to the counter forces of attraction and repulsion, violence and tenderness, love and death, and the surrealists, admirers of Freud, who formed a popular movement at the time and claimed Picasso as one of their own. Of course, Picasso's art was always a journal of his personal life, and definitely reflected the breakup of his marriage in 1931 and the start of his love affair with a young woman, Marie-Thérèse Walter.

1937–46: *War Years*
In the 1930s the surrealists were using the half bull and half man minotaur, the creature from classical mythology who periodically devours seven maidens and seven youths sent to him in tribute, as a symbol of the human beastialities of the time; Fascists were already established in Italy and Germany, and conflict and insurrection beset Spain. Picasso used the minotaur, but altered its symbolism to express human society as a mindless brute of nature innocent of its destructions. Then, in 1937, the minotaur went on a rampage in Spain. The defenseless town of Guernica was savagely bombed by Hitler, on behalf of Franco, with great loss of life. Picasso, still very much a Span-

iard in spite of more than thirty years absence from Spain, let out his rage in his masterpiece, *Guernica*, the huge tapestrylike painting said to be the most famous painting of the twentieth century. Though *Guernica* is now permanently displayed in Madrid, the Musée Picasso has some of the concurrent work, in particular the tragic portraits of Dora Maar, the young woman Picasso met in 1936 and lived with in the 1930s and 1940s. These portraits, like *Guernica*, use many of the artistic techniques Picasso had created in earlier years: the flat fragmentation of cubism; the dislocations of facial features and limbs; the magical abstracted forms of primitive tribal art; and the symbols of his Minotauromachy.

During the war and the occupation of France, Picasso painted on in Paris, unmolested by the Germans who banned the showing of his art. His work at this time includes some realistic portraits, double-image faces, austere still lifes, and sculpture.

Postwar Years/Late Picasso

Picasso's long life encompassed almost the entire range of modern art. To the very end he was a compulsive, curious, tireless worker who produced an incredible output of art in almost every medium. There are drawings, prints, and paintings based on variations of old master pictures. Ceramics also occupied him for a time, and he made sculpture in many modes, putting every kind of material to expressive use.

In all this art, numbering in the thousands, there are many themes, but the dominant one is Picasso's own rage at nature for staging the comedy of human life. He expressed nature's hold on man by depicting human sexuality with all its uncontrollable appetites of the flesh and the spirit. Like other artists in the modern era—most notably Edvard Munch—Picasso screamed out with rage. He could not accept the grotesque distortion of death, which he considered a violence on human existence. He left us, at age ninety-three, not only having defined exactly what modern art is, but also with a terrifying message for us to contemplate.

MUSÉE RODIN

77 rue de Varenne, 7ᵉ

Metro: Varenne

Hours: Open Apr.–Sept., Mon.–Sun., 10AM–6PM; Oct.–Mar., Mon.–Sun., 10AM–5:15PM. Admission fee.

Rodin, Auguste (1840–1917), French
The Rodin Museum occupies the Hôtel Biron, an elegant eighteenth-century mansion with a lovely garden. Rodin lived and worked at the Hôtel Biron toward the end of his life and arranged to turn it into a museum of his works. Though art critics looked at him as a classicist, not since the Renaissance had anyone created works in stone and bronze with a greater creative

power. His statue of *Balzac* attests to that. Rodin took nineteenth-century sculpture from naturalism to a culminating point of expressionism.

Rodin's genius could be focused on his expressive modeling, where he shows control over his surfaces and sensitivity to form. But even without closely assaying his technique, his genius is still always there. His figures seem to have an inner soul with psychological tensions like those present in Michelangelo's sculpture. Rodin depicts man torn between spiritual aspirations and everyday existence. He dramatizes this human condition in a highly symbolic way.

A complete display of Rodin's work is seen in the mansion and gardens. **Room no. 1** (entered from the card shop) has *The Man with a Broken Nose* (1864), Rodin's earliest masterpiece. It reminds one of an antique sculpture. There is also *Young Woman with Flowers in her Hat* (1865–70), a bust of Rose Benet, who shared Rodin's life for fifty years and married him when she was sixty-eight, just before she died. **Room no. 2** has works from Rodin's early period in Brussels. **Room no. 3** is dominated by *The Age of Bronze* (1875–76), which caused a scandal when it was exhibited at the Salon in 1877, Rodin having been accused of making it from a cast of a live model. Also in this room are *The Call to Arms* (1879), a study for a monument symbolizing the defense of Paris during the Franco-Prussian War of 1870, and several busts, including *The Alsatian Woman* (1880–82) and *Madame Alfred Roll* (1884). **Room no. 4** has *The Head of God* or *Creation* (1898), one of Rodin's most daring and, for its time, unconventional works, and *The Eternal Idol* (1889), which illustrates the theme of the couple, best known in Rodin's *The Kiss* (1886), which can be seen in **room no. 5**. Also in **room no. 5** is *Saint John the Baptist* (1878), which has an incredible sense of movement, and *The Cathedral* (1908), which is a figure of only two hands joined loosely together as if in prayer. **Room no. 6** has *The Thought* (1886–89), *Le Sommeil* (1889), and *The Convalescent* (1892), all memorials to a woman and former student of Rodin's to whom he was close from 1882 to 1898, who eventually went mad and spent the last thirty years of her life in an institution. **Room no. 7** has *Eve* (1881), a sort of mother earth, vulnerable and giving, and other pieces devoted to Rodin's *Gates of Hell*. In **room no. 8** there are portraits of women.

On the **first floor**, starting again from your left, **room nos. 9 and 10** are devoted to more studies of the monumental *Gates of Hell*. **Room no. 11** has studies for *The Burghers of Calais*. Return to the first floor hall to enter the **five rooms at the rear of the building**. To the left, **room no. 13** has paintings by van Gogh, Renoir, and Monet, at one time owned by Rodin, and busts of famous people: *Gustav Mahler, Mozart, Clémenceau, Bernard Shaw*, and others. **Room no. 14** is devoted to the Balzac commission. **Room no. 15** has sculpture exploring movement and the expressiveness of hands. **Room no. 16** is given to the theme of the couple, as in *The Kiss*, already seen in **room no. 5**.

The Gates of Hell (1880–1917): garden

In 1880 Rodin received a government commission to design a monumental bronze door for a museum of decorative arts. The museum was never built and Rodin never finished his door, but the project occupied him over much of his career, and from it he extracted many figures and groups which were cast as separate sculptures. These include, out of a total of 186 figures, such masterpieces as *The Thinker* (also seen in the garden in large size), *Eve*, *The Kiss*, and *The Prodigal Son*.

The theme of *The Gates* comes from the *Divine Comedy*. *The Thinker*, its most celebrated sculpture, with his chin resting in his right hand, is supposed to be Dante surveying tides of human misery. He and the other figures represent the psychic torments to which the mind is subjected in modern life. Coming before World Wars I and II, which brought European man the hell *The Gates* allude to, they are prophetic. If the work lacks unified composition it may be due to the dynamic effect of the figures bursting from the frame with an energy impossible to contain. This shows a classical disorder symbolizing the pessimism of Rodin's time. The idea of life as something to suffer through rather than to enjoy was a symbol to Rodin of the world's decadence. To highlight this negativism Rodin shows us man suffering alone, without human or divine comfort of any kind. That is the theme of the *Gates of Hell*.

The Burghers of Calais (1884–88): garden

This arrangement of free-standing figures was made to commemorate an incident of 1347 from the history of Calais. Six civic leaders of the town offered themselves as human sacrifices to the English king, Edward III, who had laid siege to Calais in the Hundred Years War. Edward had demanded their deaths as a condition of clemency for the city. The six men did survive because of the intercession of Edward's wife, Queen Phillipa, but as Rodin shows them they are walking out of Calais to what they assume will be death. Their haggard faces, gaunt bodies, and torn robes show their mental state. They have swollen hands and feet. If the figures seem to lack composition, wandering as individuals, it is because Rodin is telling us once again that man must face his destiny alone.

Balzac (1892–97): garden

The greatness of Rodin's art is seen not only in the expressive poses he depicted but also in the inner soul sensed by the spectator that Rodin gave his figures. Rodin's statue of Balzac is an example.

Balzac was a commission that Rodin cared very much about because he felt he had much in common with the man of letters, and that Balzac's novels, which probed all levels of early nineteenth-century French society, paralleled his own lifelong work with the *Gates of Hell*. Admiring Balzac as a man of ideas, Rodin set out to capture the essentials of the artist in a statue that would express his character and his detachment from the tides of conventionalism. To express Balzac's inner strength of character and intelligence, he wrapped the figure in the dressing gown Balzac wore while writing his novels. The head, with deeply cut features, makes a powerful impression. The patrons who commissioned the Balzac rejected the statue. The bulk of the body offended them, leading to a controversy. With this single statue Rodin pushed realism aside in favor of an expressive and artistic truth that was to determine the course of sculpture in the twentieth century. One cannot imagine what Maillol, Picasso, Lipchitz, and Moore would have done without Rodin's example.

Buildings

Paris is often considered the most beautiful city in the world. Its wide streets sometimes provide uninterrupted vistas—such as that from the Tuileries Gardens, through the Arc du Carrousel, the Concorde, and the Champs Elysées to the Etoile. Many eighteenth-century buildings of tasteful design line these streets, and there is the river Seine flowing through the center of the city, and many trees along avenues and boulevards.

Paris started as a trading center in Roman days on the Île de la Cité, but almost nothing of this early part of the city remains. The Merovingian Frankish kings, who replaced the Romans, ruled the territory until the eighth century. They built a castle on the site of the Palais de Justice on the Île de la Cité, but that has also disappeared. It was not until after Viking attacks of the tenth century and the succeeding struggles between the kings and the French nobles that Paris began to be built. The **Cathedral of Notre Dame** (see below), begun during the time of Philippe Auguste (1180–1223), is from this period. This was followed by the building of the **Sainte Chapelle** (see below) in 1248 under Louis IX, St. Louis, who came to the throne in 1226. Paris was then neglected until after the Hundred Years War ended in 1453. By that time the Gothic Age had run its course. The building projects started when peace came had a new sense of permanence and a new style brought to France by Renaissance artists imported from Italy. In the early sixteenth century this building took place outside of Paris, in the Loire Valley and at Fontainebleau, but before the sixteenth century ended Paris also got its share of great buildings—the palaces of the Louvre, the Luxembourg, the Palais-Royale, the Bibliothèque nationale, the Hôtel Carnavalet, and many of the churches of Paris are all from this period.

The Renaissance style then gave way to the classical baroque, which made its appearance in the Paris area with the grandiose **Chateau de Versailles** (see below), Louis XIV's great palace. It was the greatest building project Paris had ever seen, the greatest in all of seventeenth-century Europe. What was built afterward in Paris—under Napoleon I, the Restoration, and Napoleon III, never quite measured up, in the minds of some architectural historians, to the achievement of the Sun King.

The construction of famous landmarks continued, however: the Arc de Triomphe, the Madeleine, Les Invalides. Napoleon III engaged Baron Georges-Eugène Haussmann to rebuild and modernize Paris during the Second Empire, creating the parks of Vincennes and Boulogne, and the "grands boulevards" that traverse the city.

The late nineteenth century saw the construction of other Paris landmarks such as the Sacre-Coeur in Montmartre, which is an expression of the late nineteenth-century rage for all that was Byzantinesque, and the Tour Eiffel, built to celebrate the hundredth anniversary of the Revolution. But these constructions generally are not considered great works of art. The Art Nouveau-inspired entrances to the stations of the Metro, which are inventively designed and even exotic in some cases, are the most impressive architectural achievements from this period. They may be the last of the best to be built in Paris. Much of what has been built in the twentieth century has detracted from the city rather than added to her beauty.

NOTRE DAME

Île de la Cité, 4ᵉ

Metro: Cité

Hours: Open daily 8AM–7PM.

The building of Notre Dame, which started in 1163 and was not completed until the fourteenth century, covers the complete range of Gothic cathedral architecture, from early Gothic to high Gothic. Its builders began by throwing off the bonds of the Romanesque, but remained cautious in their use of ribbed vaulting and flying buttresses. Notre Dame was one of the first cathedrals to use flying buttresses, introduced over the nave aisles in about 1180. Builders were unsure how high they could go. Notre Dame is also the last cathedral to be built with tribune galleries, which explains why the cathedral does not have the large windows and slender pillars that make Chartres so light and airy. The original plan of Notre Dame was a simple double-aisled cruciform basilica without chapels—basically a rectangle, like the cathedral at Bourges. Over the years high Gothic elements were added to enhance the cathedral's beauty. One of these changes occurred during 1240–90 when chapels were inserted between the buttress piers. This widened the interior and recessed the original transept fronts, which led to the need to add one bay to each transept arm, and to let in more light. That work was done between 1250 and 1267 in the high Gothic style called **Rayonnant** after the radiating tracery of the rose windows. Another example of the high Gothic is in the thirteenth century chapels in the choir, which resulted in the light **flying buttresses** ideally viewed from the bridge over the Seine from behind the cathedral.

Notre Dame's place in the history of cathedral building is pivotal. It was probably the first with flying buttresses, but not so daring in its early construction to permit the builders to do away with the old tribune galleries. With the passage of time and the need for new construction, Notre Dame employed the thinnest of high Gothic transept walls that are virtually reduced to glass. Finally, it made use of the most advanced flying buttresses, which, around its choir and east end, span almost fifty feet.

West Front Facade (1200–1250)
The front facade seems flat, but its well-proportioned geometrical form pro-

vides horizontal and vertical elements that enliven it and join the body of the cathedral to its massive twin towers. It is likely that the builders had planned to add steeples to the twin towers, but the front facade seems to lose nothing without them. The openwork, height, and proportions of the towers and the sculpture of the three portals make this facade a masterpiece of high Gothic architecture.

Sculpture of the West Front

The trumeaux, jambs, tympana, lintels, and voussoirs of the arches of the three portals are covered with sculpture. The **central portal** is devoted to Christ, represented as a Gothic figure on the trumeau dividing the doorway that opens into two parts. It is not the equal of *Le Beau Dieu* at Amiens. The tympanum (1225–30) is devoted to the *Last Judgment* with a judging Christ full of compassion. Below are scenes of the Resurrection and the separation of the blessed and the damned. Above the tympanum, in the lowest voussoirs on the right are Romanesque-like riders of the Apocalypse as grim reminders of the terror that will accompany the second coming of Christ. Twelve apostles occupy the door jambs, and below them, at eye level, are twelve virtues placed above the corresponding vices.

The earliest sculpture on the west front is to be found on the **right portal** of St. Anne, dating from 1165–70. The *Virgin* here, seated under a canopy, resembles the Virgin of majesty type from Romanesque sculpture. While her pose is stiff and the fluting of her drapery is in the old style, her elongated oval face and delicate proportions make her more of a Gothic than a Romanesque figure.

The **left portal** is also devoted to the Virgin. In the tympanum she is represented in scenes of her death and resurrection—the first we know of such a combination in sculpture. This work, dating from 1210–20 and an example of Gothic refinement, does not subordinate itself to the architecture, but adapts to it in a harmonious way. Its simplicity of composition, with figures modeled in the round, makes it a precursor of the classic style.

Portal of the North Transept

This mid-thirteenth-century portal is rich in sculpture with an original *Virgin Holding the Child* (1250–60) standing in front of the central post dividing the doorway. She is shown as the Gothic conception of the Mother of God, her weight slightly off center, in a pose both elegant and proud, presenting her Son (broken away) to the faithful. She stands alone, without the Romanesque supportive function of statues that were part of the structure of the building. With her beauty and natural gesture she is the embodiment of the ideals around which the cathedral was built. As the only free-standing piece of sculpture to survive Revolutionary attacks on the cathedral, she has been a silent observer of the events joyful and tragic that have taken place around her. Like the cathedral itself, she is a survivor of them.

Gargoyles

The gargoyles, small, usually repulsive creatures on the balustrades and at every corner of arch and buttress, are best seen by climbing the north tower (open daily 10AM–5:45PM; admission fee). From street level, binoculars or the telelens of a camera are needed to see them. Positioned sitting, crouching, or standing, while leering, grinning, or grimacing, they represent every kind of monster that medieval man could conceive of. At a time when belief in Hell was universal, these little creatures symbolized the evil creatures who could not enter the church. They also had the purpose of frightening people about the fate awaiting them if they fell into the damnation of Hell. Calvinist iconoclasts, and revolutionary zealots of 1793, who came after them, left these monsters in place while they demolished the statues of kings, bishops, and saints. The former thought they were purifying the church; the latter thought they were purifying society.

SAINTE-CHAPELLE

Courtyard of the Palais de Justice, west end of the Île de la Cité, 4e

Metro: Cité
Hours: Open Wed.–Mon., 10AM–12 noon and 1:30–5PM. Admission fee.

In 1241 Louis IX, who became St. Louis of France, obtained the crown of thorns, a fragment of the true cross, and other relics of Christ's martyrdom from bankers of Venice, who were holding them in pawn from the emperor of Constantinople. When these objects arrived in Paris, Louis, barefoot, accompanied them through the streets before placing them in a treasury in his palace in the Cité. The Sainte-Chapelle was then built, in about four years (consecrated 1248), as a home for Louis's precious relics. Visible today is a restoration carried out in the nineteenth century to repair it from the destruction of the Revolution, which caused the dispersal of those relics as well as the melting-down of the golden containers that held them.

As a royal chapel the Sainte-Chapelle was once connected to the palace by a two-level porch that served as a lower church and upper church. The lower church was reserved for servants and the upper church for the royal family and the holy relics. Even in the **lower church,** with its gilt, rich decoration, carved capitals, and stained glass, one could not have felt very inferior to those who worshipped in the upper church. The difference in height between lower and upper churches is striking. The lower church is too low to have had a single vaulted nave, which is the reason for its two aisles. In the **upper church** there is a high vaulted ceiling, more splendid than the one in the lower church. The walls are further articulated. Twelve statues of apostles stand on corbels and are crowned with elaborate canopies. The stained glass windows extend from above eye level to the eaves, making this building the purest example of a Rayonnant structure in France.

It appears that this little building was designed in the form of a reliquary to hold those relics placed in it. That shape reflects the small-scale reliquaries of the thirteenth century.

Paris Environs

CHÂTEAU DE CHANTILLY AND LE MUSÉE CONDÉ

Chantilly, twenty-five miles north of Paris

Hours for guided tour of the château and the Musée Condé: Open Apr.–Sept., Wed.–Mon., 10:30AM–6PM; Oct.–Mar., Wed.–Mon., 10:30AM–5PM. Admission fee.

Château

Chantilly is an elegant château—actually two châteaux connected—on a triangular island set in a beautiful park laid out by Le Nôtre (1613–1700), who was responsible for the park at Versailles. While the château was attacked during the Revolution and the main body of the house destroyed, the Petit Château, built in 1560, survived to display its Renaissance exterior. Its semi-dormer windows give movement to each facade. Especially lovely is the balcony running along the water's edge on the south side. Facing the courtyard the semidormers of the first floor alternate with the windows on the ground floor, giving a chessboard effect.

The main building is a nineteenth-century reconstruction by the Duc d'Aumale done between 1876 and 1882 over the ruins of the old château. It represents the classical Renaissance style of the smaller adjoining château and has drawn from the designs of many other French buildings and monuments.

The **chapel** and decorated **apartments,** which have a collection of furniture and porcelain, can be seen only on a guided tour. In **La Chambre de Monsieur le Prince** the walls are lined with sculptured paneling painted white with gilt enrichments, and large paintings of animals in landscapes—a typical eighteenth-century motif. Another example of rococo decoration is the **Salon des Singes,** where walls are decorated with large panels of paintings of frolicking monkeys.

Le Musée Condé

This part of the Château may be seen without a guided tour. It shows the collection of the Duc d'Aumale—some 600 paintings. There are two early works by **Raphael** (1483–1520), *The Virgin of Orleans* (1505) and *The Three Graces* (1504) in the Santuario, room 15. In *The Three Graces* the naked flesh is modeled with a youthful freshness not seen in Raphael's later works. In the Galerie de Peinture are five paintings by Poussin, and in the Tribune, *The Mystic Marriage of St. Francis,* by Sassetta (ca. 1392–1451) and a portrait of *Simonetta Vespucci,* by Piero di Cosimo (1462–1521). While the museum is also rich in works by French painters—François Clouet, Watteau, Ingres, Delacroix—and a number of European masters, the treasure of the museum is its collection of illuminated manuscripts. There are two masterpieces.

Fouquet, Jean (ca. 1425–1477/81), French

Book of Hours of Étienne Chevalier (1453–60): the Sanctuario, room 15
These forty miniatures, acquired by the Duc d'Aumale in Frankfurt in 1891, were originally part of a book with a greater number of pages, some of which have been rediscovered elsewhere. The book was cut in such a way that the miniatures look like framed pictures.

Fouquet did this work after he returned from Italy. There is the idea of the importance of man in his pictures, as well as a new conception of space—a blend of Flemish and early Renaissance elements. Receding lines converge on a vanishing point while the thickly draped figures are brought right out front. We do not know if Fouquet met Fra Angelico in Rome, but it seems clear he owes something to the Italian master.

Limbourg, Pol de, and his brothers (late fourteenth century–ca. 1416), Flemish miniaturist

The Book of Hours (early fifteenth century): Cabinet des Livres (copies of the originals on display)
This great illuminated Gothic manuscript comes down to us from medieval France. It was made for the Duc de Berry by the Limbourg Brothers, whom we know little about, except that they painted for the duke, an early French patron of the arts. He filled his castles with art treasures of every description and maintained a large library. *The Book of Hours* was probably the finest book he owned. Much of what the duke collected, and his castles, have vanished, but it is hard to imagine anything more exquisite than *The Book of Hours*. It has a place in art history as well as in art, marking the beginning of a development in illuminated manuscripts where decoration ceases to be a conventional pattern and instead depicts realistic objects and scenes. Scenes typical of each month of the year are illustrated with an interest in nature, and we see details of the country life of medieval France as well as the duke's court. The artists remove the side of a house (February) to show us a woman warming herself by the fire. Northern Flemish painting gets its start from such manuscripts, taking the form of small, detailed paintings.

PALACE OF FONTAINEBLEAU

Fontainebleau, 37 miles south of Paris

Hours: Open Wed.–Mon., 9:30AM–12:30PM and 2–5 PM (until 4PM in winter). Admission fee.

This huge palace complex originated in the twelfth century as a hunting lodge for the kings of France. One of them, Francis I (1515–47), on military campaigns in Italy, was brought into contact with the Italian Renaissance. Impressed with the magnificence of the style, he imported Italian artists, one of whom was Leonardo da Vinci, to introduce it into Gothic France. Two of Leonardo's countrymen, the Florentine Il Rosso (1494–1540) and the Bolognese Francesco Primaticcio (1505–70), settled at Fontainebleau and are responsible for changing it into a great sixteenth-century palace that was further enlarged up through the time of Napoleon.

The entrance through the **Cheval Blanc** (White Horse Courtyard) is named after an equestrian statue of Marcus Aurelius that once stood there; it is also known as the Cour des Adieux, for the time in 1814 when Napoleon said farewell to his troops and went off to exile in Elba. Surrounding this courtyard the palace was built in the time of Francis I, except for the baroque horseshoe staircase in the center, added in 1634. This part of the palace includes the masterpiece known as the **Gallery of Francis I**, a 210-foot room designed by Il Rosso, unsurpassed elsewhere in the palace for its wealth of invention. Thirteen compartments along its walls contain stuccoed, painted compositions resting on wainscotting of carved walnut. Scenes are from the world of mythology, far from the previous Gothic art of France. The Fontainebleau School grew up around the palace and is credited with converting Italian mannerism into a French style as it introduced the Renaissance. (See the School of Fontainebleau, the Louvre).

Primaticcio succeeded Il Rosso in 1541 and though his masterpiece, the great Gallery of Ulysses, has disappeared, an example of his work is seen in the **Apartments of the Duchess of Etampes**, the mistress of Francis I. Here frescoes relating the story of Alexander the Great are framed by slender female figures in stucco done in the elongated, elegant mannerist style of the Fontainebleau School.

CHÂTEAU OF VERSAILLES

Versailles, 12 miles southwest of Paris

Hours: Palace open Tues.–Sun., 9:45AM–5:30PM; Grand Trianon open Tues.–Sun., 9:45AM–5PM; Petit Trianon open Tues.–Sun., 2–5PM; closed May 1. Admission fees.

Louis XIV disliked Paris, and perhaps never forgot his experiences there during the "Fronde," a revolt against the monarchy. But he had known happy hours at Versailles when as a boy he played there at the small château his father, Louis XIII, had built to serve as a hunting lodge. When Louis ascended to the throne in 1661, at the age of twenty-three, he moved the seat of government out of Paris to Versailles, and to demonstrate his power and wealth he began turning it into the greatest palace Europe had ever seen. He wanted it also as a place where he could maintain surveillance over the scheming nobility. He demanded they spend much of the year at Versailles, which is why it was built large enough to house 1,000 nobles and 4,000 servants, plus Louis's 15,000 soldiers, quartered near the main gate.

Louis called upon the great artists of his time: Louis Le Vau (1612–70), the architect; Charles Le Brun (1619–90), the painter-decorator; and Andre Le Nôtre (1613–1700), the landscapist, all of whom had already collaborated on the building of the Château of Vaux-le-Vicomte. This group, in the 1660s, went to work on Versailles. It is mainly their creation, although construction went on well into the eighteenth century. It has served as the model for similar national palaces built elsewhere in Europe: Portugal's Queluz, Spain's Royal Palace in Madrid and Le Granja, Austria's Schönbrunn, and Russia's St. Petersburg Peterhof, among others. It has some superb interiors—the Hall of Mirrors and the Royal Chapel—and the Petit Trianon, a fine little building in the great park.

The **exterior of the palace** from the Cour d'Honneur (entrance) seems unimpressive. For a better view of the exterior one may walk in the **gardens** on the west side, the result of Le Nôtre's landscaping, a masterpiece of terraces, sculptured cascades, fountains, statues, and vistas that give an illusion of space that recalls the background landscape of a baroque painting.

The **western facades** are examples of classical baroque architecture. Columns and pilasters of gray stone blend with the warmer tones of the sandstone fabric of the building. The ground floor, somewhat plain, is enlivened by rustication marking each course of stone. Above this the main level is made prominent by massive free-standing columns with an application of the orders in pilaster form. This level is topped by an attic story; a low balustrade borders the roof. Various baroque accents such as urns and trophies enrich the roof level and overcome the horizontal line of its great, 1,900-foot length.

The **interior of the palace**, monumental in its proportions, is best expressed in its famous 240-foot-long **Hall of Mirrors** designed by **Jules Hardouin-Mansart** (1646–1708), who also built much of the rest of the palace. Walls are ornamented with marbles and gilded bronze, a barrel vault decorated by Le Brun with rich stucco, and paintings glorifying Louis XIV. A row of arched windows, opening on the garden, emits light reflected by the huge mirrors on the far wall that visually extend the space and create a sense of stately formality.

Hardouin-Mansart is also the architect of the **Royal Chapel** (1689–1710), which has more grandeur than piety. It is one of the supreme baroque structures built in France. Its height is divided into two levels: the lower floor for the courtiers and the public, and the upper floor for the royal family and guests. The oval design and the plain white of the walls and pillars set off decorative elements, especially the painting of the *Resurrection* by Coypel in the half-dome of the apse. The chapel takes its Italian-style beauty from subdued color and the few curves, unbroken entablatures, and pediments in its structure.

One may try to picture Versailles as it looked when Louis XIV and later kings held a glittering state ball. There would have been a thousand guests in silk, lace, and velvet, bedecked with powdered wigs and jewelry. A thousand servants would attend such a crowd, while an orchestra would play music to blend with the conversation of the guests. When it came time for Louis XIV to make his entrance there would be a sense of expectation. Finally he would appear—the "Sun King" himself—the most powerful ruler in the world, the person who held the destiny of every individual in the palm of his hand. That was the purpose of Versailles—not just as a residence for the king, but more importantly to impress the world.

Petit Trianon

Northwest of the palace, about a twenty minute walk across the park.

About one hundred years stand between the start of Versailles and the start of the Petit Trianon (1762–68), built by Louis XIV's son, Louis XV, as a retreat for himself and his mistress, Madame de Pompadour. Within that time the baroque of Versailles gave way to the asymmetry and playful lightness of the rococo, the main effect of which was felt mainly in building interiors. By the time Jacques-Ange Gabriel (1698–1782) designed this gem of a building, architectural style was turning in the direction of classicism. The Petit Trianon, splendid in its proportions and in its poise and sophistication, reflects the return of the classic style. Its two stories are divided discretely by the cornices of its lower windows, while also drawn together by Corinthian columns which had regained popularity. There was no attempt to regain the pomp of the preceding century; nothing is overemphasized. The exquisite delicacy of its detail makes this building a masterpiece.

Nearby is the **Grand Trianon,** a larger château built by Louis XIV in 1687, where he enjoyed a solitary hour or two away from the crowds at Versailles; and not far away is Marie-Antoinette's **Hamlet,** an idealized farm where she pretended she was a shepherdess. Such was her dreamworld; she was found there in 1789 when the mob of the Revolution broke into Versailles.

_____ _Reims_ _____

CATHEDRAL OF NOTRE DAME

Entered from place de Cardinal Luçon

Hours: Open daily 9AM–8PM.

Reims Cathedral is the coronation church of the kings of France, a tradition that dates back to Clovis, king of the Franks, who was baptized in the fifth-century church of St. Reim, which stood on the site. The cathedral was also the scene of the coronation of Charles VII. After having survived the Hundred Years War, he was crowned king of France at Reims on July 17, 1429, while Joan of Arc, who had made his victory possible, knelt behind him. The cathedral was still not complete, though it had been started in 1211.

The layout of the **interior,** 454 feet in length, with its long nave, is unique. The transepts, choir, and chapels of the east end combine to create one large space, so as to accommodate a large congregation during a coronation ceremony.

The view looking down the nave to the west end is striking. The **rose window** there, set within a pointed arch, is echoed by a similar rose over the central doorway. A **trellis of sculpture** on the inside wall of the west end contains figures relating to the story of St. John the Baptist and the coming of Christ. Pier capitals of the nave depict genre scenes from daily life and beasts that relate to a growing Gothic fascination with the world of nature.

West Front and Sculpture

Though it took over two hundred years to complete the great west front (started in 1241), it is uniform in design. It has been criticized for being overdone, dripping with sculpture, but nevertheless seems to give the dramatic effect that was intended. All of it is monumental, from the two elegant towers, not identical, to the three recessed portals. Just below the towers is a gallery of kings with fifty-six figures, each fourteen feet tall. These represent the kings of France, with Clovis, shown with his wife and St. Reim, in the center. Below in three portals are statues in a variety of styles, from archaic figures in the right portal to high Gothic figures in the center and left portals. These are the star attractions at Reims.

The Annunciation and the Visitation Groups (ca. 1220–43): center portal, right jamb

The two inner figures representing the *Visitation* includes the *Virgin* and *St. Elizabeth* and are derived from antique statuary, a sort of classical rebirth in Gothic sculpture. They are robed in the classic style, with their weight balanced on one leg, but their faces are realistically portrayed in the Gothic style. The beautiful young *Virgin* is quite freely treated.

To the right of the two figures of the *Visitation* are the two figures representing the *Annunciation*. The simple *Virgin* of this group, with smooth drapery clinging to a rigid body, is in the style of Chartres, Paris, and Amiens. However, the *Angel* standing next to her is an unrelated work that owes nothing to antique examples or twelfth-century traditions. Coming about 1240, it is peculiar to the late style of Reims.

Smiling Angel (ca. 1240): left portal

This statue is related to the *Angel* of the *Annunciation*. With her smile she shows the change coming over thirteenth-century French sculpture. The sacred and the profane are mixed as the expression turns from the symbolic character of the Gothic style to the more lifelike sculpture of the Renaissance. It signals that Gothic art at Reims had reached the height of its possibilities.

Next to the Cathedral, at 2 place du Cardinl Luçon, is the newly renovated Bishop's Palace, called **Palais du Tau** because of its T shape. Its museum (open daily 10AM–noon and 2–6PM; admission fee) houses original works of sculpture from the exterior of the cathedral. In 1927 the authorities began to replace the sculpture on the building with copies so that the originals could be protected from air pollution and natural elements. The splendid figures from the west front and the transepts are here.

Strasbourg

CATHEDRAL OF NOTRE DAME

Place de la Cathédrale

This red sandstone cathedral was started shortly after 1176 on the site of an old Romanesque church. Its apse, crossing, and north transept—the oldest parts of the cathedral, built by 1225 over the foundations of the older structure—are in the late Romanesque style. Later the Gothic style was introduced, and embraced with a determination seldom seen elsewhere. This is evidenced in the **west front**, where the emphasis is on height: in the four buttresses, in the pair of towers, in the mullions of the windows, in the pointed gables, and in the steeple that rises 480 feet above the ground (only the height of Ulm Cathedral is greater). Height is further emphasized by the vertical lines in the screen of arcading that covers the facade.

Though the west front was started in 1277 and finished only in 1439, it is uniform in design. This is true also in the Gothic **interior** where the nave (1240–75) reflects the latest in high Gothic French construction of clerestory and glazed triforium, with vaulting shafts rising from floor to vaults. The fourteenth-century stained glass windows add to the majesty of the place.

In the Romanesque apse, however, the feeling is different, because of the low vaulting and the abstract carvings on the capitals. In the south transept, also completed in the thirteenth century in the heavy Romanesque style, where the church's miracle plays were performed, a lighter note is struck by the ensemble of sculpture known as the *Angel* or *Judgment Pillar* (1230–50). Here the pier which supports the vault is decorated with three tiers of figures—the evangelists, angels playing trumpets, and Christ with three angels carrying the instruments of the Passion—in the late Gothic style. They are so festive they take on the appearance of folk art. The south transept has a clock dating back to the fourteenth century (reconstructed in 1842) that is a tourist attraction; it should be seen at 12:30PM when the whole works spring into action (admission fee).

Sculpture of the Exterior South Transept

The Death of the Virgin (ca. 1230–40): tympanum
The influence of high Gothic French sculpture is recognizable in the delicate modeling of the faces and in the clinging materials with their numerous small folds, but the whole work also is invested with the expressionistic feeling that comes out of Rheinish Gothic Germany. Such an excited, dramatic presentation of the scene is not French.

The Synagogue and **The Church** (ca. 1250)
These two statues, to the right and left, are part of the overall theme of the

sculpture on the south portal—a superseding of the old law by the new. The preoccupation with this theme is thought by some scholars to reflect a reaction against the large Jewish community at Strasbourg during the Middle Ages, expelled in 1539.

The allegory of the *Synagogue* shows a forward-stepping young woman with drooping head leaning on a broken staff. Like much of the other sculpture at Strasbourg, it is more dramatic and delicate in modeling than its French prototypes. The *Church* is shown triumphant, with a gaze directed at the *Synagogue* that is confident and perhaps indulgent.

Sculpture of the Exterior West Front

Sculpture and architecture accent each other here, figurative sculpture and architectural detail are barely indistinguishable from each other.

Parable of the Wise and Foolish Virgins (ca. 1280): right side porch
On the left are the three *Wise Virgins* and their *Temptor,* a handsome young man, stylishly dressed, tempting one of them with the age-old device of an apple. His back, however, is being gnawed by hideous reptiles that symbolize the death of the soul. His victim, the silly-looking one nearest him, glows with pleasure and prepares to open her gown. The other two foolish virgins, the pleasure of the moment now past, are distraught with grief at the error of their ways and their promised damnation. On the other side, holding lamps that symbolize the truth of the church, are the three *Wise Virgins* who stand ready to follow the bridegroom into the sanctuary and thus to Christ. The earthbound realism of these figures, which do not have the calm, mystic repose of the statues of Chartres and Reims, show the difference between the French and German influence in sculpture at this time.

Most of the best-known sculptures on the exterior of the cathedral are copies of the originals. The **Musée de l'Oeuvre Notre Dame** at 3 place du Château, facing the south front of the cathedral, has the originals, as well as paintings, rare stained glass, manuscripts, and drawings of the original plans of the cathedral. These show that medieval cathedrals were not built stone upon stone without thought to planning.

Next door the **Château des Rohan,** a palatial eighteenth-century riverside home of a family that produced French statesmen and churchmen, houses a complex of museums including the **Musée des Beaux Arts,** known for its collection of old master paintings from the fourteenth to the nineteenth century, French and foreign. The château also offers tours of the Rohan apartments as they were in the eighteenth century.

Strasbourg has a museum of modern art (**Musée d'Art Moderne,** 1 rue du Vieux Marché aux Poissons) located in a former customs house at the old part of Strasbourg. Its collection of paintings and sculpture includes the big names of the twentieth century: Picasso, Dufy, Klimt, Chagall, Arp, Klee, and many impressionists. Not all of the permanent collection can be seen when special exhibitions are on display, which is often the case in summer.

(All museums open daily Apr.–Sept. 10AM–noon and 2–6PM; Oct.–Mar., Mon., Wed.–Sat., 2–6PM, Sun. 10AM–noon; admission fee.)

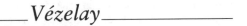

Vézelay

CHURCH OF THE MADELEINE

Though restored in the nineteenth century by Viollet Le Duc, this church remains one of the finest Romanesque churches in Burgundy. It had been a point of departure for pilgrims going to Santiago de Compostela in Spain, and was supposed to have its own precious relic, the remains of the body of St. Mary Magdalene, the existence of which was confirmed by the pope in 1050. In 1146 St. Bernard chose the church to preach the sermon that launched the Second Crusade. Among figures in attendance were King Louis VII and his queen, Eleanor of Aquitaine. Later, in 1190, before starting out on the Third Crusade, Philippe Augustus, king of France, and Richard Lion-Heart met at Vézelay and agreed to forget their differences in order to fight the infidel together.

Since Vézelay was dependent on Cluny, it is possible that the masons and sculptors who worked in that abbey (completely destroyed in the nineteenth century) also worked at Vézelay. The church they built was consecrated in 1104, burned in 1120, and rebuilt by 1132. We do not know how much of the old structure was destroyed and how much of the reconstruction followed its original lines. Later restorations and additions changed the luminous **choir**, 1215, into an early-Gothic style work, but its original Romanesque spirit remained in the thick wall holding the thrust of its ribbed vaults. The **nave**, built on a grand scale, is covered by groin vaults divided bay by bay with transverse arches, and is flooded with light because the architects opened the walls with large windows in the side aisles and clerestory. This explains the presence of large exterior buttresses, which had to be added to strengthen the walls. Unlike most Romanesque interiors, often so somber you can hardly see their sculptures, at Vézelay we can appreciate the pink stone, which has black accents on semicircular ribs supporting the vaults. Neo-Corinthian historiated capitals of the columns (ca. 1130–45), display a variety of animals, birds, and people in scenes out of everyday country life. There are also demons and fantastic monsters that seem to assault the guilty and the innocent alike. These are typically part of the iconography of Romanesque art, with anecdotal subjects taken mostly from the Old and New Testaments, although many of the scenes on the capitals still baffle interpretation.

Christ of the Pentecost Sculpture (ca. 1125–30): Tympanum of the center portal of the narthex
The covered portico (narthex) of the west front, which at seventy-two feet in length is like a little church on its own, opens into the nave, with the effect

of extending the length of the entire church. It is noted for the Romanesque sculpture of its tympanum over its central portal, which depicts the Pentecost—the descent of the Holy Ghost upon the Apostles. Christ, in the pointed oval, or *mandorla* shape, in the center, is shown in the expressive manner of the Burgundian Romanesque style. His fingertips give rise to rays that descend upon the head of each apostle, and His body, in a twisted, elongated form, recalls the influence of contemporary illuminated manuscripts on European sculpture. That the figure is flattened out, and that exaggerated movement prevails could not have concerned the sculptor, who portrays religious characters within the context of church dogma, in which the all-powerful Christ has the power to save mankind. Christ is shown here on the left side with clouds and open books, symbolic of wisdom and truth. On the right side, where the clouds are stormy and the books are closed, He condemns evil.

Riviera (Côte d'Azur)

_____Antibes_____

GRIMALDI MUSEUM (PICASSO MUSEUM)

Château d'Antibes, in the old town at the edge of the sea.

Hours: Open Mar.–June, Wed.–Mon., 10AM–12 noon and 3–6PM; July–Nov., Wed.–Mon., 10AM–12 noon and 3–7PM; Dec.–Feb., 10AM–12 noon and 3–5PM. Admission fee.

Picasso, Pablo* (1881–1973), Spanish, lived in France
If you are the director of a small museum that needs works of art, but you do not have the funds to purchase them, what do you do? Dor de la Souchère, curator of the Grimaldi Museum in Antibes, solved that problem by inviting an artist to make his studio in the museum, to paint and sculpt there, and to leave his work there.

Such an arrangment was made between Souchère and Picasso in 1946. Picasso, living in Antibes, needed studio space. Souchère had a museum in the Grimaldi Château in the old town of Antibes overlooking the Mediterranean, but no significant works of art. Picasso was given free reign of the museum's great hall. He worked there for six months and left behind twenty-three paintings, seventy-eight pieces of ceramics, thirty-three drawings, eleven oils on paper, one tapestry, two sculptures, and twenty-seven lithographs.

Among the works are the large *Joie de Vivre,* whose dancing, flowerlike woman may be taken from Françoise Gilot, who was living with Picasso, as well as *Still Life with Fish and Pitcher, Reclining Woman, Sleeping Atlantid, Squatting Woman, The Goat, Paloma and Her Doll, The Picador,* and others—all displayed on the white walls of this Mediterranean château where windows and terrace open to the sea. There was probably nowhere that Picasso enjoyed working more than he did at Antibes. He seems to have been inspired by the sea. His mural paintings are gay and full of life with fish, sea urchins, and fishermen, as well as leaping fauns, nymphs, and centaurs—important figures in Picasso's bestiary—in blues, grays, olive-greens, and browns.

The display of Picasso's **ceramics** has some of his best works; he had become interested in ceramics at the nearby village of Vallauris (see below). His enthusiasm for this art became so great that one year he produced more than 2,000 pieces.

_____Biot_____

FERNAND LÉGER MUSEUM

Four kilometers below the village

Hours: Open in summer, daily 10AM–12 noon and 2:30–6:30PM; in winter, daily 10AM–12 noon and 2–5PM. Admission fee.

Léger, Fernand (1881–1955), French
Fernand Léger, a native of rainy Normandy, once said, "I loath the Midi, I'll never go there—there's too much sun." His opinion of the Midi was not taken seriously, after his death in 1955, by those who built this little museum devoted exclusively to his art. It stands on a hill near the Nice-Cannes auto route with a gigantic ceramic wall in primary colors made up of 50,000 ceramic pieces set at angles to reflect the sun. The entrance hall has a window twenty-nine feet high by sixteen feet wide. There are two floors of galleries that display a complete collection of Léger's lifetime of work. The sun penetrates the galleries, lighting up Léger's paintings and bringing life to their colors.

An approach to understanding Léger's work is had in comparing him with Picasso. They were both born in 1881, arrived in Paris in 1900, and were subjected to the artistic currents of the city, but turned out differently. In Léger's cubism he refused to give up color for monochromy and insisted on the concrete rather than the fragmented, elusive cubism of Picasso and Braque. Léger was obsessed by a self-imposed mission to combine artistic reform with social reform, hoping to solve the problem of how the modern artist could get in touch with the people. Picasso, on the other hand, yielded to his moods and fancies. Apart from his *Guernica,* and *War,* and *Peace,* Picasso showed little concern for politics and social issues (even though he was a member of the Communist party). For Léger art was a constant, disciplined duty. He painted twentieth-century man and twentieth-century machinery as though modern society were his patron.

At the Léger Museum are solid, simple works with a plastic strength and cheerful openness to modern life. The evolution of Léger's art is traced from his cubist periods to the idealism of his late work.

Apart from the gigantic *Children's Garden,* a polychrome sculpture on the lawn outside, notable works inside include *The Woman in Blue* (1912), *The Big Barge* (1923), *Composition with Leaf* (1927), *Mona Lisa with Keys* (1930), *Four Girls on Bicycles* (1943–48), *The Constructors* (1950), and *Builder's Laborers with Aloe* (1951).

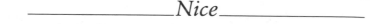

Nice

MARC CHAGALL BIBLICAL MESSAGE NATIONAL MUSEUM

Avenue du Docteur-Ménard (Bd. de Cimiez)

Hours: Open Oct.–June, Wed.–Mon., 10AM–12:30PM and 2–5:30PM; July–Sept., Wed.–Mon., 10AM–7PM. Admission fee.

Here is a museum built to display an art collection on a theme created by a single artist, Marc Chagall. The museum building, also a work of art, is built on a hill in Cimiez, the upper part of Nice, and is designed so that it hardly imposes itself upon the works it contains. Partially hidden by trees, with its large windows that take in the brilliant Mediterranean light, it appears to be without a facade. The pools that surround the building—the Chagall mosaic is reflected in one of them—add to a peaceful atmosphere.

Chagall, Marc (1887–1985) Russian, lived in France
Though Marc Chagall lived in France, the key to understanding his art is to remember he was born and raised in Russia of a poor Hasidic family. The themes and images of his art were already formed when he left Russia for Paris, in 1910, at age twenty-three. He returned to Russia in 1914, married Bella Rosenfeld, a wealthy, cultivated Jew of his hometown of Vitebsk, and became, in 1918, commissar of fine arts in Vitebsk. He settled again in Paris, in 1923, because the Revolution's enthusiasm for his art, and his Jewishness, declined. Many years later, he wrote to a friend that "the title 'a Russian painter' meant more to me than any international fame. . . . In my paintings there is not one centimeter that is free from nostalgia for my native land."

Many of Chagall's signature images are in the works of art shown in this museum, devoted to his interpretation of life as a religious experience. There are twelve large paintings based on the creation of man, the Garden of Eden, the stories of Noah, Abraham, Jacob, and Moses (Main room), and five large paintings illustrating the *Song of Songs* (Room of the *Song of Songs*). Also displayed are their 195 preparatory drawings, thirty-nine gouaches, and 105 engravings, lithographies, sculptures, stained glass windows, mosaics, and tapestries.

Chagall is best known and admired for combining naturalism with fantasy to convey the magic and power of love. His world of floating lovers and angels, set in acrobatic compositions, owes something to his life in Russia. From his provincial Jewish background, filled with stories of the mysterious world of the Cabala, comes his poetic idea of reality, which depends more on passionate impulses than rational causes and effects. In this enchanted world that gravity cannot hold down, people, animals, and objects are carried on the wings of love. From the pictorial world of Russian Orthodox icons, where the idea rather than the real is depicted in compartmental compositions that show scenes irrespective of a particular time and place, Chagall saw an art full of strange and unsettling vitality.

But there is another Marc Chagall whose sympathy for human suffering, not only as a Jew but as a universalist, is seen in many of his paintings. In *The Creation of Man*, Chagall has painted the crucified Christ as one of the figures in a celestial orbit around the sun. Christ on the cross expresses the theme of suffering inflicted by man upon man, but with the Jewish *tallis* (prayer shawl) around him he is not only a symbol belonging to Christians, he is also the inheritance of all descendants of the Jewish Jesus. This is further emphasized by the ladder, which always accompanies Chagall's crucifixion scenes. It stands for the bridge between man and God, a motif expectantly found in *Jacob's Dream*. Next to Christ on the cross it gives universal meaning to the crucifixion. Christ appears again in *Noah's Ark*, but there he is the infant Jesus, seen in the middle of a crowd with arms stretched out, symbolic, along with the Ark, of humanity's second birth.

Chagall's sympathy for human suffering is also seen in *Noah and the Rainbow*, where a mass of distressed people is fleeing what must be a Russian pogrom; in *Moses before the Burning Bush* a crowd of people in a tragic state of agitation represents the Exodus, reminder of human suffering in time of war.

Animals are everywhere in Chagall's art. He never forgot the animals slaughtered by the butcher near his home in Vitebsk. As part of his art they have a common destiny with man; like man they are born, live, and die, which explains animals with human faces and men with animal faces.

Finally, there are elements that have influenced Chagall's work outside his early life in Russia. His deeply saturated color—pure blues, greens, and reds—derives from his introduction to postimpressionism in Paris. Like the postimpressionists, Chagall believed he could make color say and mean anything. His color, which blankets his canvases, and his use of light, which infuses his art with an inner vitality and intimacy, expresses the mystery and poetry of the Bible. So too does music, which Chagall equated with painting. It is seen in the scenes of the *Song of Songs*, where David is playing the harp, and felt in the curves and circles of the compositions that suggest rhythms and vibrations.

MATISSE MUSEUM AND ARCHAEOLOGICAL MUSEUM

164 avenue des Arènes de Cimiez

Hours: Open May–Sept., Tues.–Sat., 10AM–12 noon and 2:30–6:30PM, Sun. 2:30–6:30PM; Oct., Dec.–Apr., Tues.–Sat., 10AM–12 noon and 2–5 PM, Sun. 2–5PM; closed Nov. Free admission.

This combination of two museums under one roof, the very old with the modern, is not such a good thing for the Matisse Museum, which suffers from cramped quarters. But both are indigenous to the area. The Archaeological Museum has a more valid claim to the site, since the structure, a seventeenth-century villa, rises from the remains of a Roman resort. Three Roman baths have been uncovered and new discoveries are adding to the collection of statues, pottery, jewelry, coins, sarcophagi, and other objects.

Matisse, Henri (1869–1954), French

The Matisse Museum is here largely because Henri Matisse lived in Cimiez at the old Hotel Regina from 1938 until his death. He left it only for a short time during the war to live in nearby Vence to escape the threat of Allied bombing.

The museum opened in 1963 with a collection of paintings, drawings, engravings, sculptures, pottery, and illustrated books, as well as Matisse's personal effects and private art collection that were donated by his family. The collection contains paintings of every period, so that aspects of Matisse's art may be traced from the somber style of his first painting, *Still Life with Books* (1890), to the 1947 work, *Still Life with Pomegranates*, which shows the artist as a master of color. There are also such works as *Still Life: A Harmonium, Young Woman with an Umbrella, Portrait of Laurette, The Square of the Moulin Ajaccio, Odalisque with Red Case, Nude in an Armchair, Reader at the Yellow Table, Rococo Armchair,* and the large decorative picture *Nymph in the Forest.*

An understanding of Matisse's art involves knowledge that his work went through a series of changes. He was first influenced by Cézanne. Later he became one of the original painters called Les Fauves (the Wild Beasts) and a prominent expressionist. Apart from any classification, Matisse said about his art: "There is an inherent truth that must be disengaged from the outward appearance of the object represented. This is the only truth that matters." To arrive at this truth Matisse simplified his paintings by subordinating what we think of as reality into an arrangement of form and color patterns. Today it is Matisse's color harmony that is most appreciated. The simplicity of his art during his late years was almost a form of sign language. In the Matisse chapel in Vence (see below), which he did from 1948 to 1951, the simplicity in Matisse's art is evident. The Matisse Museum has the complete drawings for the Chapel of Vence project, including the cut-out designs for the vestments Matisse planned for the priests.

St. Paul

THE MAEGHT FOUNDATION

Northwest of the Village of St.-Paul

Hours: Open July–Sept., daily, 10AM–7PM; Oct.–June, daily, 10AM–12:30PM and 2:30–6PM. Admission fee.

If you have ever wondered about art dealers who sold early works of Miró, Léger, Chagall, Braque, Giacometti, Calder, Bonnard, Matisse, and others to make fortunes for the artists and for themselves, you might visit a wooded hill above the medieval walled village of St.-Paul to see the result of a great art dealership, the Maeght Foundation (pronounced "Mahg"). It is a private museum and cultural center created by the Parisian art dealer Aimé Maeght. Since its opening in July, 1964, the works of contemporary masters, who were signed up by Maeght before they became famous, are displayed here indoors and outdoors. The museum was built by the architect José-Luis Sert of Harvard's Graduate School of Design.

This complex was meant to attract the public as well as provide a place where artists could meet, relax, and work if they wished. Thirty-nine thousand plants were brought in to create a Garden of Eden on what was once a parched hillside. This created environment has given rise to a harvest of outdoor sculpture. There are changing exhibitions drawn from Maeght's supply of art, shown in exhibition areas on different levels that follow the contour of the site. It is a kaleidoscope of twentieth-century art in a twentieth-century setting.

St. Tropez

MUSÉE DE L'ANNONCIADE

Place George-Grammont

Hours: Open Wed.–Mon., 10AM–12 noon and 3–7PM; closed Nov. Admission fee.

St. Tropez, one of Europe's most favored resorts, has a good art museum. Contemporary art is an indigenous part of the Riviera scene—the Matisse Chapel at Vence, the Maeght Foundation at St. Paul, museums devoted to Chagall and Matisse at Nice, to Picasso at Antibes, and to Léger at Biot. The museum at St. Tropez is in the former Annonciade Chapel (Chapel of the Annunciation), hence its name. There is a representation of the art of the twentieth century, including Georges Seurat's *Channel at Gravelines,* one of the few works by Seurat outside of Paris; two striking paintings by Vuillard,

Under the Lamp and *La Soupe;* Pierre Bonnard's lovely *Nude in Front of the Fireplace,* a painting of innocent sensuality, and his masterpiece *The Pink Road;* an early Matisse, *The Spanish Gypsy,* which foreshadows the expressionism of the Brücke movement in Munich; Rouault's *Biblical Landscape,* which has the evangelical feelings of his later expressionism; Derain's *Reflection on Water* and his two views of London, *Westminster* and *Bridge on the Thames;* Braque's vigorous *View of Estaque* in the style of the Fauves; and the simple *Port of Saint Tropez* by Albert Marquet.

Vallauris

Above Antibes off the road to Grasse

MUSÉE NATIONALE PABLO PICASSO

Chapelle du Chateau

Place de la Liberation

Hours: Open Apr.–Sept., Wed.–Mon., 10AM–12 noon and 3–7PM; Oct.–Mar., Wed.–Mon., 2–5PM. Admission fee.

Picasso, Pablo* (1881–1973), Spanish, lived in France
Picasso lived in Vallauris for ten years and revived its pottery and ceramics industry. His bronze statue, *Man with a Sheep,* is displayed in the central square in front of the church. In a small twelfth-century chapel in Vallauris Castle, now a national museum of modern art, are his famous paintings, *War* and *Peace,* on the crypt walls leading to the sanctuary.

These two large paintings come together at the top of the curving vault. They were completed in 1952 at the height of the cold war. One gets the impression that the horror of *War,* which shows a chariot of death with a horned and winged figure waving a bloody sword in one hand and a bowl of insects or germs (representing scientific warfare) in the other, will eventually overwhelm the noble figure protected by a shield emblazoned with the dove of peace and a spear bearing the scales of justice. On the opposite wall, depicting *Peace,* a white winged horse of life pulls a plow under a warm sun. A musician plays his pipes while a girl dances and a juggler balances birds and goldfish symbolizing the delicate balance of peace. Seen behind the horse are the benefits of peace: ripe fruit trees, bunches of grapes, a mother nursing her child. Between war and peace on the flat end wall, Picasso painted four figures: white, black, yellow, and red, representing the four races of Man. They are welcoming each other and holding doves of peace.

Vence

MATISSE CHAPEL (CHAPELLE DU ROSAIRE)

Foyer Lacordaire, Avenue Henri Matisse

Hours: Open July–Sept., Tues. and Thurs., 10–11:30AM and 2:30–5:30PM, Mon., Wed. and Fri., 3–5:30PM; Tues. and Thurs., 10–11:30AM and 3–5:30PM. Free admission.

Matisse, Henri* (1869–1954), French
Matisse came to Vence in 1943 to escape Allied bombing attacks he feared in nearby Nice, where he had lived since 1938. He installed himself in a box-like villa called Le Rêve (The dream) on the outskirts of Vence to wait out the war. Earlier Matisse had undergone surgery in Lyons and had recovered in Nice under the care of a young Dominican nun. The young woman had moved to Vence to a convent for invalid girls just across the street from Le Rêve. She was also an artist, and approached Matisse with a watercolor design she had made for the stained glass windows of a new chapel the nursing home was planning. Matisse became interested in the project and agreed to design the new building from the cross on top to the marble floor below, including its altar, its crucifix, its wall decorations, and its stained glass windows.

What Matisse did in Vence was unlike any of his other work. This "master of color," as he was known, finished the interior walls in plain white. He placed three large line drawings in black on white tiles on the walls, which emphasize the whiteness. On the rear wall are *The Stations of the Cross,* on the north wall of the nave the *Virgin and Child,* and in the sanctuary *St. Dominic.* His stained glass windows are the only source of color. Matisse evidently did not want his works of art to encroach on the building, a working chapel. In this sense they are acts of artistic humility. Matisse said, "What I have done is to create a religious space. I want those entering my chapel to feel themselves purified and lightened of their burdens."

Germany

The most important periods of German art were the fifteenth, sixteenth, and early twentieth centuries, times when German artists were at their most creative. Before the fifteenth century a great deal of art was produced in Germany, most notably Romanesque cathedrals. But it was not until the fifteenth and sixteenth centuries that a dynamic, original art came on the scene. In sculpture Tilman Riemenschneider (ca. 1460–1531), whose work reached a high point in late Gothic art, was the most gifted. In painting, the outstanding artists were Matthias Grünewald (ca. 1460–1528), Albrecht Dürer (1471–1528), Albrecht Altdorfer (ca. 1480–1538), and Hans Holbein the Younger (1497–1543), all of whom combined Gothic and Renaissance elements into a style that was recognizably German. The baroque and rococo styles, originally from Italy and France, found a welcome home in Germany; some of the finest works of architecture in Europe, especially pilgrimage churches, were designed in Germany in those styles. Germany also made its presence felt in the beginning of the twentieth century when a group of young artists broke with the old and struck out in their own direction, to expressionism and the abstract schools that derived from it. Similar work was being done elsewhere, and inspiration was drawn from van Gogh, Gauguin, Munch, and Ensor, but artists in Germany, such as those who belonged to Die Brücke and Der Blaue Reiter groups, plus the Bauhaus School and laboratory under the direction of Walter Gropius, made original contributions to art. They showed us a new way of looking at nature, even a new way of living, and their contributions have been as important as those achieved in the time of Dürer.

Today Germany has rebuilt its art museums destroyed in the last war and is increasing the quantity and the quality of its fine collections. It will continue to be a place where new ideas in art originate.

———————— *Bamberg* ————————

CATHEDRAL

Domplatz

This Romanesque cathedral is on a hill overlooking the lovely old town of Bamberg. It was built on the foundation of an earlier cathedral in the beginning of the thirteenth century and was largely completed by 1237. In spite of Gothic influences from France, the building remains essentially Romanesque with its four terminal towers, polygonal ends, lateral entrance, and round-headed windows and doorway openings. The steep ribbed vaults of the interior are in keeping with the transitional Gothic style, and the cathedral is best known for its Gothic statuary. Inspect the portals of the cathedral before entering: two on the north side and especially the *Adam portal* and the *Portal of Mercy* at the south and north sides of the east end respectively. They are richly molded and have statues (copies of originals now inside the cathedral) of late thirteenth-century Gothic design. The group in the tympanum of the Portal of Mercy, however, is purely Romanesque in character.

Gothic Sculpture of the Interior

Knight of Bamberg: At the north side of the steps leading up to the east apse
This realistic equestrian statue is one of the finest made in the Middle Ages, though the horse and the body of the knight are not memorable. The face, probably copied from the head of a king in Reims Cathedral, is a masterpiece of German Gothic art. Emphasis on bone structure accentuates its intensity in the forceful German style. This dry modeling succeeds in creating a medieval look of knightly courage.

Virgin from the Visitation Group: behind the *Knight of Bamberg* in the east choir
These sculptures show that if the artists working at Bamberg did not also work at Reims Cathedral, at least they saw it and adopted its style. However, at Bamberg their work is more dramatic. Notice the *Virgin*, whose right hand is missing, holding a book in her left hand. Her voluminous robe is decoratively arranged. Her head, framed by the mantle, is individualized, with the look of a mother who knows her destiny and has the courage to see it through. She is a different figure from the unreal Madonnas usually rendered in the Middle Ages, and from the sweet ones of the Renaissance.

See also, in the center of the nave, the tomb of Henry II, by Tilman Riemenschneider (ca. 1460–1531), the greatest of German sculptors; in the west, or St. Peter choir, the work of his contemporary, Viet Stoss (ca. 1438/47–1533), whose *Altarpiece of the Nativity*, a late work from 1523, completed when Stoss was very old, still has the spontaneity and mastery of execution that made him famous in his youth; and the early thirteenth-century sculptures of *Prophets* on the *St. George Choir Screen*, in the east choir, that display a Romanesque inspiration in the drapery, and indicate the forceful style the Gothic had to overcome when it first entered Bamberg.

On the north side of the Domplatz is the massive baroque **Neue Residenz** (1695–1704). Its luxurious apartments, each furnished with baroque furniture and Gobelin tapestries, reach a highpoint in the Emperor's Room

(Kaisersaal). There is also a **museum** with Cologne and Frankish late Gothic paintings. The museum is open daily, 9AM–noon and 1:30–5PM.

On the west side of the Domplatz is the sixteenth-century gabled **Alte Residenz**, a German Renaissance structure built as the bishop's palace. Next to it is the Alte Hofhaltung (Imperial Court) with a fine inner courtyard surrounded by half-timbered buildings and the remains of the old Diet Hall that dates to the eleventh century.

Berlin

PICTURE GALLERY (STATE MUSEUMS, PRUSSIAN CULTURAL FOUNDATION, IN BERLIN–DAHLEM)

Arnimallee 23/27, Dahlem

Hours: Open Tues., Thurs., Fri., Sun., 9AM–5PM; Wed., Sat., 9AM–8PM. Free admission.

The State Museums of Berlin, in the suburb of Dahlem, consist of many collections: Indian art, Islamic art, Far Eastern art, a number of ethnological museums, and a sculpture gallery (entrance on Lansstrasse, 8) that has examples of Italian Renaissance sculpture and Gothic sculpture from Germany and the Netherlands. Only the **picture gallery** will concern us here, a comprehensive collection of over 600 old master paintings from the thirteenth to the eighteenth century.

At the outbreak of World War II part of the collection was stored away for safekeeping in salt mines near Grasleben. These were found by American troops in 1945 and survived the war intact. However, paintings taken to the Flaktower at Friedrichschain in 1942 had a different fate. While they also survived the war, and were found on May 5, 1945, between then and May 10 they were mysteriously destroyed by fire. A total of 417 pictures, including works by Rubens, Van Dyck, Jordaens, Tintoretto, Titian, Veronese, Caravaggio, and others, were lost forever. It was one of the greatest destructions of art treasures in history, but the collection at Dahlem was so rich and well balanced that even after this loss it is still one of the finest collections of European paintings in the world.

Note: Owing to the frequent moving of paintings, room numbers are not given for the paintings in this museum.

Altdorfer, Albrecht (ca. 1480–1538), German

Nativity, no. 638 (1510)
Altdorfer is the sixteenth-century German painter who best expresses the Danube School's concept of landscape as the vehicle to express a sense of poetry and mystery. He anticipates the nineteenth-century romantics by three hundred years. He was also one of the first artists to introduce a feeling for

the magic of ruins. In this picture, the Holy Family is almost lost in the movement of light over the bricks of the ruined stable. It is the light from the moon in the upper left-hand corner which is the principal action in the scene. The religious drama is made to fit into the night landscape, rather than the landscape existing as a prop for the religious drama. The supernatural light from the Christ Child, who is supported by two angels, is no stronger than the luminous light filling most of the scene. Concentrating on landscape and light, Altdorfer goes far in taking the human element out of the picture and letting the landscape take over. Earlier, landscapes existed only as backdrops for religious, historical, or allegorical action.

Bruegel, Pieter, the Elder (ca. 1525–69), Flemish

Netherlandish Proverbs, no. 1720
This painting consists of a typical Bruegelian world of sinful, foolish people struggling vainly against the logic of society and the scheme of nature. Its composition, a kaleidoscopic wealth of detail where each scene is handled separately, consists of over one hundred scenes, each depicting a Flemish proverb to exemplify a type of folly.

Notice, in the center foreground, the blue hood being placed over an old man by his young wife dressed in red. This scene, which tells us that the old man is cuckold, is no larger than the others around it, but is meant to dominate the painting (at one time this painting was called *The Blue Hood*). The young woman's lying, cheating existence is symbolic of life in general, and the old man's impassiveness to it is meant to criticize society's acceptance of such behavior. Blue is used for the foolish and for victims of treachery. Red is the color for scoundrels who show contempt for society by cheating, which, to Bruegel, is defecating on the world. The fellow sitting half out of the window of the building on the left is doing just that on the blue globe below him. Even Christ, shown to the right of the old man in the blue hood, is being mocked by a treacherous monk, who has put a flaxen beard on Him and placed Him on a red chair.

Two Monkeys, no. 2077
This picture, showing two dejected monkeys sitting among hazelnut shells, chained in a dungeonlike enclosure, with the harbor of Antwerp visible behind them, has been interpreted in two ways. It may be Bruegel's statement of the plight of the Flemish provinces under Hapsburg domination, or simply a reference to a proverb "to go to court for the sake of a hazelnut," meaning that it is folly to sell one's liberty and happiness for a dubious gain. It was painted in 1562. By the following year, Bruegel, at his mother-in-law's insistence, had left his beloved Antwerp for Brussels. Perhaps Bruegel was agonizing over the decision to move when he painted this picture. It has been suggested that its small size means it may have been intended as a gift for a friend whom Bruegel had to leave behind.

Christus, Petrus (ca. 1415/20–ca.1473), Flemish

Portrait of a Young Lady, no. 532
After the death of Jan van Eyck in 1441, Petrus Christus became the dominant painter in Bruges until he gave way to Memling at the last quarter of the century. He represented the Bruges School between 1444 and 1473, and was influenced by Jan van Eyck, its founder. Christus is often considered merely a reflection of Jan van Eyck, but this is not entirely true. His *Portrait of a Young Lady* is original, and his most popular painting.

Notice its plain background, which does not distract one's attention from the head of the figure, gracefully framed by a black velvet hat. The almond eyes and silken luster of flesh are lovely and give life to the features. Christus's sensitivity to the solitude and elegance of the sitter makes this an exceptional work, equal to portraiture done by his predecessor.

Dürer, Albrecht* (1471–1528), German

Portrait of Hieronymus Holzschuher, no. 557E (1526)
This painting of the burgomaster of Nuremberg is one of the most admired pictures in Germany; reproductions of it are found in many German homes. It was done toward the end of Dürer's life, when he had assimilated the Italian Renaissance style into his work, so it shows the monumental form of Italian painting, with the careful detail and emotional agitation of his own northern tradition. He fits the sitter into a close-fitting aperture barely big enough to contain his chest and shoulders. The head is emphasized in such a composition, and its modeling, with penetrating eyes turned toward the viewer, is the mark of a strong personality—a strong-father type that has appealed to Germans from Dürer's time.

Another portrait by Dürer of a Nuremberg town councilor, *Jacob Muffel,* no. 557D, is an example of Dürer's energetic style, but this one is more reserved.

Eyck, Jan van* (ca. 1390–1441), Flemish

The Madonna in a Church, no. 525C (ca. 1420)
This early painting by Jan van Eyck is important in the history of European art because in it we can see the birth of modern painting. While it encompasses the medieval style (notice the impossible size of the Madonna, standing larger than life because she symbolizes the church), it shows in realistic detail the effect of light entering the window from the north. As the light plays upon the interior, Jan makes use of transitional half-tones, and distinguishes the brightly lighted portions from those lying in shadow. It is Jan's mastering of the oil technique that allows him to infuse his painting with these qualities, and it propels panel painting into the forefront, ahead of mural painting and book illumination, which are unable to match these spectacular effects.

Fouquet, Jean (ca. 1425–1477/81), French

Étienne Chevalier and St. Stephen, no. 1617 (ca. 1450)
This half of a diptych (the other half is in Antwerp's Royal Museum of Fine

Arts) is one of the few panel paintings that have come down to us by Jean Fouquet, the first French painter of importance. Fouquet is significant because he was an artist in the courts of Charles VII and Louis XI who broke with the Gothic tradition after he was introduced to the Renaissance style in Italy. In this panel he depicts Étienne Chevalier, the treasurer of France, and St. Stephen, Étienne's patron saint, who carries a stone, the instrument of his martyrdom. Both figures are rendered with a realism reminiscent of Jan van Eyck. We are observing Renaissance elements being introduced into France in the form of the architectural background and the accompanying perspective. No doubt most of this painting owes a debt to Flemish influence, but if you saw the other half of the diptych in Antwerp, you would also wonder if Fouquet had met Piero della Francesca in Italy.

Hals, Frans* (ca. 1580–1666), Dutch

Malle Babbe, no. 801C (ca. 1630)
Frans Hals's fame rests on pictures such as *Malle Babbe*. When we consider that this picture was painted about 1630, we see how far ahead of his own time Hals was.

For the characterization and spontaneous movement achieved in this painting the artist has abandoned the line and replaced it by brushwork. The tankard of beer, the woman, and the owl have been modeled by brush. Look at the painting close up; then stand back and take another look. The small patches of color blend with the dabs of white paint at a distance. The result is to depict people and objects as they really look, especially if the artist wishes to accord an instant of moving life. This is impressionism, but impressionism 150 years before it arrived on the art scene.

Who was Malle Babbe? The way Hals depicts her, she has been considered a madwoman, a gossip, and a "'merry toper" who went from tavern to tavern to get a drink. She is sometimes called the "witch of Haarlem" because of her wild look and the owl perched on her shoulder. The owl, as a symbol, can be a source of confusion. In medieval days the nocturnal bird was considered to be in league with the powers of darkness but it also typified foolishness, stupidity, and even drunkenness; there is a Dutch phrase, "He is as drunk as an owl." Judging from the size of the tankard Malle Babbe is holding, and the look on her face, the symbolism of the owl as drunkard seems apt.

Holbein, Hans, the Younger (1497–1543), German

Portrait of George Gisze, no. 586
Though Holbein painted what his wealthy clients wanted, he had an enormous talent which on occasion, such as in his *Portrait of George Gisze,* the Danzig merchant, was fully expressed. Unlike many of his portraits, this one has the strength of his sitter's personality. We are told about George Gisze not only by his shrewd dark gaze but also by the realistic Eyckian display of the materials of his trade: a box of coins open on the table, ink, receipted bills, and other objects, including a ball of string enclosed in a brass con-

tainer hanging from a shelf on the right. It is one of the most detailed paintings Holbein ever executed, probably done to advertise his virtuosity. Holbein had no lack of commissions for portraits, mostly from the English nobility. Unfortunately, few of them rise to the level of *George Gisze;* in some cases they are mere decorations.

Hooch, Pieter de (1629–ca. 1683), Dutch

Mother Beside a Cradle, no. 820B
De Hooch's reputation rests on pictures such as this one with its homey warmth and self-contained benevolence. It is what we expect of a seventeenth-century domestic Dutch interior. But De Hooch was also the artist of Holland's Golden Age that had the greatest command of spatial effects. In his pictures the manipulations of space are often more important than the depiction of human figures. One feels that De Hooch began his paintings with the architectural structure, and fitted in his figures afterward.

In *Mother Beside a Cradle,* the light enters through the open door to give an impression of deep space by binding the two rooms together, just as the small child in the kitchen is bound to her mother in the living room. A succession of parallel planes gives a refined spatial effect. Vertical lines are everywhere, but balanced by the strong horizontal lines of the stones in the living room floor. To help us enter the depth of the picture, an imaginary line runs through the mother's hands upward through the little girl's head to the open door. Such a geometrical construction in space allows De Hooch to achieve a harmonious tranquility. His warm colors are a part of this. It captivates us the way it does the little girl, who stands motionless, her foot reluctant to take the step into the outside world away from such a cozy environment.

Lippi, Fra Filippo (ca. 1406–69), Florentine

Madonna Adoring the Child, no. 69
A religious spirit prevails in this painting, unlike most other paintings by this pleasure-loving Carmelite monk. Yet as a Nativity scene it lacks what we expect: a cave, a shed, animals, and Joseph. Instead, there is young St. John the Baptist holding a cross, Romuald, the founder of the Camaldolite order (this painting was done for Lucrezia Tornabuoni, wife of Piero di' Medici, who had a penitential cell at the monastry of Camaldoli, in the Appennines), and the Godhead with the Dove of the Holy Spirit below him emitting a torrent of light. Since this painting was done in the 1450s, at the time of the Lucrezia Butti scandal, when Lippi fell in love with a young nun, it is likely a penitential picture. The ax in the tree trunk in the lower-left-hand corner is an image from John the Baptist's words (Matthew 3:10): "And now also the ax is laid to the root of the trees: therefore every tree which bringeth not forth good fruit is hewn down, and cast into fire." Lippi's signature on the ax handle records his penance. Of all Lippi's paintings, this one and the *St. Ambrogio Coronation* in the Uffizi are the only ones he ever signed.

Mantegna, Andrea (1431–1506), Italian

Mother and Child, no. S.5 (ca. 1455)

Here is Mantegna at his most spiritual. This painter of tantalizing, spectacular perspective moves us in this painting with a display of simple human feeling. The Madonna, holding the Child in her mantle of burnished gold, as if longing to return Him to the safety of her womb, shelters His frail head between her hand and her cheek with loving affection. Her sorrowful, pensive mood is perfect to convey the religiosity of the subject.

Note the Donatellesque relieflike conception of the Madonna's elongated neck and head. Donatello, a sculptor who worked on reliefs for the high altar of the Church of San Antonio in Padua from 1443 to 1453, had the strongest influence on the Padua school of painting, of which Mantegna was its greatest master.

Rembrandt?* (1606–69), Dutch

Man with the Golden Helmet no. 811 A (ca. 1648–50)

Until recently this painting, one of the most admired works of art in the Berlin gallery, was thought to be a Rembrandt, and the model of the portrait Rembrandt's brother, Adriaen van Rijn. The golden helmet did not tell us anything about Rembrandt's brother, who, like Rembrandt's father, was a miller. But it was known that Rembrandt liked exotic costumes for the painterly effects that he could draw from them. He often painted himself in similar attire. More important, Rembrandt was mainly interested in the spiritual depth of his sitters. The very Rembrandt-like golden helmet acts as a contrast to the withdrawn contemplative face of the man and thus makes his meditative mood a richer pictoral effect.

It is a beautiful painting and for generations the art viewing public has loved it, but it is not a Rembrandt. In November, 1985, the *Man with the Golden Helmet* was declared by Rembrandt scholars to be the work of an unknown seventeenth-century Dutch artist, "an independent original in its own right."

How can this happen? For over 100 years this painting was considered a Rembrandt by the highest authorities. Was it a fraud? Was the painting part of a swindle by art dealers, curators, and critics?

We must consider that in the nineteenth century, when the Berlin gallery bought the painting, art history, as we now know it, was in its infancy. There were few genuine experts. To make matters more difficult, anyone with a Dutch seventeenth-century painting to sell would call it a Rembrandt if he possibly could, and there was an eager audience of art connoisseurs who believed that the more Rembrandt's there were in the world the richer we would all be. As we learn more and new evidence emerges it becomes necessary to remove, or change, the authorship of some great paintings. But this does not make a painting like the *Man with the Golden Helmet* a lesser work of art than originally thought. It is still as wonderful an achievement as ever. It just is not by Rembrandt.

Vermeer, Jan* (1632–75), Dutch

Woman with a Pearl Necklace, no. 912B (ca. 1665)
This painting contains a recurring theme in Vermeer's art, the representation of a single figure: a young woman, usually shown in a domestic setting. Pearls, worn in the ear or on a necklace or both, appear often in Vermeer's art. One could speculate endlessly on the meaning: pearls have symbolized immortality, but also profane love or vanity. It is likely that Vermeer simply enjoyed painting certain objects. Pearls just fascinated him.

Vermeer has employed one of his basic compositions in this painting: a table to form a horizontal that balances the well-lit vertical of a woman standing. Horizontals and verticals are carried over into the accessories of the room—the seat, backs of chairs, and the curtain. Only the crumpled fabric on the table, the round jar, and decorative nails of the chair relieve these lines. Vermeer's trademark is also present—his ability to catch a moment of silence, when the figure is immobile, such as the woman here pausing to study herself in a mirror, trying to decide whether to tie the ribbon of her necklace.

Weyden, Rogier van der* (ca. 1399–1464), Flemish

Bladelin Altarpiece, The Nativity (central panel), no. 535
This altarpiece, dated after 1456, is from Rogier's latest period (the two wings are studio work; the *Nativity* in the center is from Rogier's own hand) and as such is more charming and serene than his emotional earlier work. Rogier has now found a way to control the dramatic tension of his earlier phase with a simplicity that retains the fervent mysticism. The donor, Peter Bladelin, the wealthy maître d'hôtel of Charles the Bold, is the perfect expression of this style. He has a priestlike yet courtly air about him. We have only to look at his face to believe in his simple, fervent devotion to the Virgin and Child.

The street scene in the background represents Middelburg, a small town northeast of Bruges in the Dutch province of Zeeland. Bladelin founded the town, and the imposing building on the left side of the street is probably his castle. The two holes in the ground, directly in front of Joseph, the Virgin, and Bladelin, suggest the cave of Bethlehem where Christ was born. The prominent column in the left foreground is, according to the *Meditations,* the column the Virgin leaned upon when about to give birth. The Romanesque architectural elements in the rest of the ruined building indicate that the New Law, the law resulting from the birth of Christ, is about to replace the Old Law. The candle that St. Joseph is holding, rather than meaning that the Nativity is taking place at night, probably has its origins in the writing known as the *Visions of St. Bridget,* in which the saint tells us that as soon as Christ was born, celestial radiance overpowered the light of the candle.

Among other works by Van der Weyden at the Berlin Gallery is the *Portrait of a Woman,* no. 545D, which may represent the artist's wife. This is based on little evidence, in that it is the only portrait by Van der Weyden in which the sitter looks at the viewer; Van Eyck's famous portrait of this wife in the Groeninge Museum in Bruges also shows the subject's eyes directed at the spectator. In any case, this portrait is an early work.

MUSEUMS IN BERLIN OF NINETEENTH AND TWENTIETH-CENTURY ART

Two museums in West Berlin specialize in German and European painting where Dahlem leaves off, around 1800 to the present.

The **New National Gallery** is located in the Tiergarten (Potsdamer Strasse 50, near Potsdamer Platz) in a rectilinear black steel and glass building designed by Ludwig Mies van der Rohe. Its German collection consists of the work of Caspar David Friedrich, Karl Friedrich Schinkel, Carl Spitzweg, Karl Blechen, Lovis Corinth, Max Lieberman, and Max Beckmann, among others. The museum is open Mon., Tues., Thurs., Sun., 9AM–5PM; Wed., Sat., 9AM–8PM; closed Fri.; free admission.

The **Brücke Museum**, at Bussardstieg 6, at the edge of the Grunewald, specializes in one school of twentieth-century art—German expressionism. Die Brücke (The Bridge) was an association of young artists who joined forces in Dresden in 1905–6 (moved to Berlin in 1911) to use art as an instrument of social rebellion and spiritual redemption. In artistic terms it was Germany's counterpart to the fauvist and cubist revolutions in Paris. The art of its members—Heckel, Schmidt-Rottluff (who gave the group its name), E. L. Kirchner, Max Pechstein, Otto Mueller, and others—are shown in this museum. (For a discussion of Die Brücke see Munich, Municipal Gallery in the Lenbachhaus.) The museum is open daily, 11AM–5PM; closed Tues.; free admission.

CHARLOTTENBURG PALACE

Luisenplatz

Hours: Open Tues., Thurs., Fri., Sun., 9AM–5PM; Wed., Sat., 9AM–6PM. Free admission.

This baroque Versailles-like palace has been restored after wartime bombing almost destroyed it completely. Its history goes back to 1695, when it was a small country house called Lutzenburg. The original part of the complex, the central portion with the pedimental portico facing the main front and an oval bay construction facing the garden side, is visible. Like so many other royal buildings, it was continually increased in size, especially after the death in 1705 of Sophie Charlotte, the wife of Friedrich III. The name of the palace was changed to Charlottenburg in her memory, and the baroque cupola, with the gilt statue of the goddess Fortuna on its summit, was built.

While the gardens of the palace are a delight, and its equestrian statue of *The Great Elector, Fredrick Wilhelm I*, by Andreas Schlüter (ca. 1662–

1760), in the forecourt, is done in the vigorous Roman baroque manner by one of Germany's great sculptors, the exterior of the palace is not its strong point. Apart from its cupola, its design is simple for a great Prussian building in the baroque style. However, inside is a riot of rich decoration, consisting of beautiful wooden paneling and fine furniture, paintings, sculpture, and handicrafts. Of note are the French paintings by Watteau, Chardin, and Boucher located in the Knobelsdorff wing in the Friedrich the Great Room. Of these the *Pilgrimage to Cythera* by **Watteau** (1684–1721) is outstanding, a second version of Watteau's masterpiece (the other on the subject is in the Louvre in Paris). You will also see Watteau's *Gersaint's Signboard,* which depicts the shop of the art dealer Gersaint, Watteau's friend. It was briefly used as a sign above the dealer's premises on a Paris bridge. Though it looks like a genre scene, it is an elegy for Louis XIV, whose portrait, in the far left, is being lowered into a box. This also refers to the name of Gersaint's shop, Au Grand Monarque. Notice that three figures have their backs turned away from us; a lady in pink on the left and a lady and gentleman looking at a painting on the right. Watteau was a master of the draped human back. In his hands the human back became as expressive as a face—reflecting and absorbing light, a myriad of folds and crevices, a silent personality of its own.

Cologne

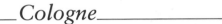

WALLRAF–RICHARTZ MUSEUM AND LUDWIG MUSEUM

Bishoff Garten Strasse

Hours: Open Wed., Fri., Sat., Sun., 10:30AM–5PM; Tues., Thurs., 10:30AM–8PM; closed during carnival, Dec. 25 and Jan. 1. Admission fee.

This arts complex—two museums under one roof and a 2,000-seat concert hall—housed in modern buildings between the cathedral and the Rhine, contains every period of German art from the Middle Ages to the twentieth century.

The **Wallraf-Richartz Museum,** formed in 1861, is known for its collection of fourteenth- and fifteenth-century paintings of the Cologne school, whose best-known painter, **Stephan Lochner** (ca. 1400–51), is represented by the *Virgin in the Rose Bower.* Painted around 1438, it has the medieval gold background, the idealized posture of the Virgin, and conventional flowers, leaves, and grass, but the new trends of the fifteenth century are beginning to come through in the draping of the Virgin's mantle, which suggests weight and volume. It also has the sweet and happy atmosphere that was the style of the early fifteenth-century Rhenish school, whose aim was to depict a world of hope and happiness through religion.

Also see the foreign paintings, in particular: *The Hunt Breakfast* by the French realist Gustave Courbet (1819–77), and *Four Girls on a Bridge* by the Norwegian preexpressionist Edvard Munch (1863–1944).

The **Ludwig Museum,** specializing in art of the twentieth century, is Cologne's newest museum, having opened to the public in 1986. It was mostly formed by Dr. Peter Ludwig and his wife, Irene, heir to a fortune in chocolate. For many years they have been among the world's premier art collectors and, as donors and lenders of a great stock of art to Europe's museums, their influence has been widespread. Here their collection touches most of the movements of twentieth-century art. High points are reached with American Pop Art—the Ludwigs seemed to have found the early works of Claes Oldenburg, Jasper Johns, James Rosenquist, Roy Lichtenstein, Robert Rauschenberg, and Andy Warhol before they became best-sellers—and the Russian avant-garde of 1917, when Kasimir Malevich (1878–1935) and his contemporaries tried to redesign life down to the smallest detail. The Ludwigs have contributed the works of a great many German artists of our own day, but it is the pre-1914 collection of German expressionist painting (once part of the Wallraf-Richartz Museum) that should get most of your attention. As the avant-garde of German art before World War One, which attempted to create a new way of looking at nature, their intensity of thought and feeling, expressed in striking color and bold new forms and compositions, equaled (and, in some cases, surpassed) the French Fauvists.

COLOGNE CATHEDRAL

Hours: Open Tues., Fri., Sat., Sun., 10AM–5PM; Wed., Thurs., 10AM–8PM; closed some holidays. Admission fee.

This cathedral, modeled after the cathedral at Amiens in France, is the largest church in northern Europe. Its construction took over 600 years, starting in 1248 and not ending until 1880; lack of funds to continue building was a problem for long periods of time. It does not have the perfect proportions of most French Gothic Cathedrals—it is too wide for its length, and its towers are too large for the size of the building—but it is still one of the chief monuments of Gothic architecture in Europe. Its towered facade, a nineteenth-century construction, is spectacular at 525 feet high, the highest cathedral twin towers in the world. The rest of the cathedral is immense: 468 feet long and 275 feet wide; the nave vault rises 150 feet.

Inside two works of art are of importance:

The Gero Crucifix (tenth century): in the first northern chapel of the ambulatory (left of the choir)
This is the earliest surviving piece of large-scale Ottonian sculpture and the oldest monumental crucifix in Europe. Its date had been disputed, but it seems probable that it was made for Gero, archbishop of Cologne (969–76), which would make it of tenth-century origin, instead of eleventh or even twelfth century as previously thought. Some Byzantine elements can be seen

in its stylization, but the swaying body, firmly modeled with a knowledge of anatomy, and the overall realism, are characteristics of Ottonian art.

Lochner, Stephan (ca. 1400–51), German

Adoration of the Magi Altarpieces (ca. 1440): south chapel off the ambulatory
This altarpiece was identified as Lochner's work by Albrecht Dürer, who paid two pfennigs to have it shown to him in 1520. The central panel depicts an enthroned, sweet looking Madonna, similar to the Virgin in Lochner's *Madonna in the Rose Bower* (Wallraf-Richartz Museum, Cologne), being adored by the Magi and their entourage. The left panel shows St. Ursula, the saint who, with 11,000 maidens as companions, was said to have died in a massacre in Cologne early in the Christian era. In the right panel St. Gereon, the other patron saint of Cologne, is depicted. The gold background and Gothic decoration make this a fine example of the international style. The artist augments the plasticity of form by deepening the shadow and colors, which are striking greens, browns, pinks, bluish whites, and brownish purples. As one of the first to master the oil technique, Lochner creates a rich tonal atmosphere that clings to the surface with a velvety sumptuousness. At the same time he keeps the lyrical, dreamy style he is known for.

Before leaving the cathedral square look at the *Dionysus Mosaic,* the great treasure of the new **Roman-Germanic Museum** at the southeast side of the cathedral. It was discovered by workmen digging an air raid shelter in 1941, and it dates back to about 22 A.D. Covering an area of twenty-three by thirty-four feet, and composed of about one million separate fragments, it shows the Greek god of wine, Dionysus, drunk, surrounded by dancing Bacchae, satyrs, Pan with a goat on a lead, and various evocations of food and drink. It is thought that it started out as the dining room of a Roman house, which would make its motif perfect. The museum is open daily, 10AM–5PM; Wed., Thurs., to 8PM; closed Mon. and some holidays; admission fee.

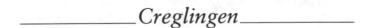

Creglingen

HERRGOTTSKIRCHE (CHURCH OF OUR LORD)

Near Creglingen, on the road to Blaufelden

Hours: Open Apr.–Oct., daily 8AM–6PM; Nov.–Mar., Tues.–Sun., 10AM–12 noon and 1–4PM. Admission fee.

Riemenschneider, Tilman (ca. 1460–1531), German

Altar of the Virgin (1505–10)
This limewood Flamboyant Gothic altarpiece is done by Germany's greatest

sculptor of altarpieces, also one of the last great Gothic illustrators. His work is so late in this regard that the character of his expression is sometimes thought to be between late Gothic and the Renaissance. Thus his figures have no Gothic harshness about them. The Virgin has a Renaissance charm about her previously unknown in Germany. That is not to say that Riemenschneider's figures are cut from real life or that they express Renaissance values. Their natural poses are more in the spirit of a pious approach to life, a search for truth through religion in the spirit of northern European man during the early sixteenth century.

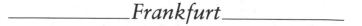

————————— Frankfurt —————————

STÄDEL ART MUSEUM

Schaumain Kai, 63

Hours: Open Tues., Thurs.–Sun., 10AM–5PM; Wed., 10AM–8PM; closed holidays. Admission fee.

This museum has German paintings by old masters such as Cranach, Dürer, Holbein, Elsheimer, Grünewald, and Hans Baldung Grien, and nineteenth- and twentieth-century artists, including Corinth, Kirschner, Beckmann, Marc, and others. Other European schools are also represented: Flemish paintings by van der Weyden, Bosch, Memling, Peter Brueghel the Elder, Jordaens, and Rubens; Italian paintings by Fra Angelico, Botticelli, Tintoretto, and Veronese; French paintings by Poussin, Claude Lorraine, Watteau, Chardin, Cézanne, Renoir, Manet, Picasso, Matisse, and others. The museum is best known for a Flemish masterpiece by van Eyck.

Eyck, Jan van* (ca. 1390–1441), Flemish

The Lucca Madonna: first floor, room A
Completed about 1437, this paintings shows a change from Jan's earlier Madonna paintings. His earlier Madonnas had a fragile charm, but this Madonna is a more massive type in a simplified setting. If it were not for the richly decorated throne, the interior could be that of a wealthy fifteenth-century burgher in the town of Bruges. Jan has also simplified the symbolic objects in the room, which signify what the future holds for the innocent Child who is feeding at His mother's breast: the fruit on the windowsill (man's fall in the Garden of Eden), the bowl of water (the Baptism), the flask of wine (the Last Supper), the empty candlestick (the apostles' desertion of Christ at the crucifixion), and the lions on the throne (the Resurrection).

Freiburg

FREIBURG MINSTER

Münsterplatz

This Minster of Our Lady started out as a Romanesque parish church (it was raised to the rank of cathedral only in 1827). The transepts and most of the two little eastern towers date from this thirteenth-century late Romanesque period. When the Gothic style had penetrated into the Upper Rhine area, the church was Gothicized with attention to work being done by builders at Strasbourg. The result was a fine Gothic structure that has a single **west tower front** (finished 1275), one of the best in Europe. Its proportions are harmonious; despite its height of 377 feet it does not appear top-heavy. Its ground floor is open to the interior and has a richly decorated hall. Above it is a chapel that has a narrow window with some tracery. There is also a clock story and above that a bell tower with an openwork octagon around it that dissolves into the spire with its filigree of tracery. The richly decorated interior offers a good idea of how German cathedrals looked before fires, wars, and the excesses of the Reformation emptied them of their treasures. Among the many art works are, in the chancel, paintings by Hans Baldung Grien and Hans Holbein the Younger; a silver Romanesque crucifix; the _Locher Altarpiece_ by Sixt Gumpp; and stained-glass windows. The museum is open July–Sept., 10AM–noon and 2:30–5PM; closed Sat.–Sun. and holidays; Admission fee in chancel.

Mainz

CATHEDRAL

You can see the red sandstone bulk of Mainz Cathedral and its Romanesque silhouette best from across the river. A close look at its structure reveals Gothic as well as baroque elements; its highest tower is baroque on top, Gothic in the center, and Romanesque at the bottom. While its main structure was built during the eleventh, twelfth, and thirteenth centuries and shows the German medieval preference for multiple towers, double apses (one on the west side as well as one on the east), and double transepts, other influences derive from additions and alterations made up through the eighteenth century. The **eastern end** best illustrates its original German design, with its projecting round apse surmounted by a gable and flanked by twin towers.

The **interior** in a toned-down design is overwhelming in scale. It is covered by rib vaulting in double bays above a generous clerestory, and has an enormous aqueductlike arcade on each side of the nave, with vaulted aisles beyond. Note that this conception of arcading shows a relation to the Lombard style of northern Italy, developed during the Holy Roman Empire's Hohenstaufen dynasty in the twelfth and thirteenth centuries. There is also a good collection of funerary monuments, outstanding rococo choir stalls, and some fine sculptures in the cloisters by the thirteenth-century Naumburger Master.

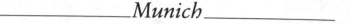

Munich

Museums

ALTE PINAKOTHEK (BAVARIAN STATE ART GALLERY)

Barerstrasse, 27

Hours: Open Wed., Fri., Sat., Sun., 9AM–4:30PM; Tues., Thurs., 9AM–4:30PM and 7–9PM. Admission fee.

As heir to the best royal collections in Germany, this gallery is one of the richest museums in Europe. Its fame is not only based on its collection of German paintings, which, with works by Altdorfer, Dürer, Grünewald, Cranach, and others, is unsurpassed. It also has an extensive collection of old master paintings of the European schools: Flemish, Dutch, French, Spanish, and Italian. All of it was saved during World War II, but its fine neoclassic building, dating from 1826–36, was severely damaged and not opened again until 1964. Today it is a model of modern museum planning.

Index to the Rooms of the Alte Pinakothek

Artists mentioned below have works referred to in the text that follows. You will find these works listed under the names of the artists, arranged alphabetically.

Ground floor, room 2a	Cranach
Ground floor, room 13	Cranach
Ground floor, cabinet 23	Bruegel
Upper floor, room 1	Gossaert (Mabuse), Memling, van der Weyden
Upper floor, room 2	Dürer
Upper floor, room 2b	Dürer
Upper floor, room 3	Altdorfer
Upper floor, room 4	Raphael
Upper floor, room 5	Titian
Upper floor, room 7	Rubens
Upper floor, room 8	Rubens
Upper floor, room 12a	Boucher

Upper floor, cabinet 9   van Dyck, Rubens
Upper floor, cabinet 16   Rembrandt
Upper floor, cabinet 21   Steen

Altdorfer, Albrecht (ca. 1480–1538), German

The Battle of Alexander (ca. 1529): upper floor, room 3
Among historical battle scenes in Europe, this is supreme. Napoleon said it was the best battle picture he had ever seen, and had it hung in his bathroom at St.-Cloud. After his defeat it was returned to Munich.

In the center of the swirling mass of miniature figures are the two protagonists and the story of the outcome. To the right in golden armor, with his visor up, riding on his horse, is Alexander the Great. He is pursuing the Persian King Darius, also dressed in gold, fleeing on his chariot. The Europeans of Altdorfer's time thought of the pagan Greeks as Christian kin. They are dressed in the uniforms of German soldiers, while the Persians wear Oriental turbans.

The drama on land is carried to the surrounding landscape and the sky, which seems engaged in a cosmic struggle between sun, wind, and clouds. One can look at this as suggesting that worldly events are but a small part of the greater universe. However, Altdorfer was a principal representative of the Danube School of painting, which emphasized the landscape over figures and objects. It was his style to paint this way no matter what the subject. Later, the nineteenth-century romantics were attracted to the sixteenth-century Altdorfer and his school, and used landscapes similarly to express meaning and mood.

Boucher, François (1703–70), French

Nude on a Sofa (1752): upper floor, room 12a
No visit to the Munich Gallery would be complete without seeing this rococo masterpiece of a reclining young nude, one of the most popular paintings in the museum. As a painting from court life of the middle of the eighteenth century in France, it depicts the sensuality of a time when a fifteen-year-old nude was treated as a treasured possession. In this case, she is Louise O'Murphy, who indeed is fifteen and the mistress of Louis XV. She was the first occupant of a house in the deer park near Versailles that Louis had built for "lovely little things" like Louise O'Murphy, and she was a favorite model for Boucher, the official court painter and director of the Academy. Her pose, an unnatural one, is an alluring invitation to join her on the disordered bed. Naturally this kind of painting was meant for intimate rooms such as Louise herself occupied. There is also a refined attitude about the picture. Notice the colors of prints and the touch of blue in the silk ribbon entwined around the girl's head and hand; blue and pink were favorite colors of the rococo. This is a sensual world whose lack of restraint is tempered with sophistication.

Bruegel, Pieter, the Elder (ca. 1525–69), Flemish

Land of the Cockayne (1567): ground floor, cabinet 23
This painting describes a Fools' Paradise where gluttony reigns supreme and, according to a Netherlandish text of 1546, "men have cast away every scrap of decency and virtue." In order to enter it one has to eat through a maze of cornmeal cake, but this discourages no one. Most of society is represented. We see a soldier, a peasant, and a clerk, each less like people than like geometrical forms (cone, sphere, cylinder). They are immobilized as spokes in the wheel of laziness, where they have only to open their mouths and all sorts of good things to eat will fall in.

The story is an old one, found in the folklore of every European nation ("the greatest fool is an idle glutton"), but Bruegel may have intended it to depict the kind of abstract utopia everyone in the Low Countries was dreaming about during a time of political and religious upheaval brought about by the Spanish Hapsburg domination. Rather than retreat into the Land of Cockayne, which is a Fools' Paradise, Bruegel is reminding his countrymen they must face the Spanish terror.

Cranach, Lucas, the Elder (1472–1553), German

Crucifixion (1503): ground floor, room 2a
Lucas Cranach was a painter whose work often epitomized the Danube School. His dramatic landscape is fundamental to his picture. He also employs new compositions such as this one where the viewer comes upon the scene at Golgotha from the side, so that one of the crucified thieves is partially hidden. Cranach's exciting colors and plasticity of form add to the drama, as does the movement in the approaching storm seen in billowing clouds and a gust of wind that has taken up Christ's loincloth.

Cranach painted a number of these dramatic crucifixions which were popular, but he was also a painter of innumerable young female nudes for the wealthy burghers and electors of Germany, a seemingly strange labor for a region so devoutly Protestant. The painting of *Lucretia,* ground floor, room 13, is such a picture. Her artificial pose and bland expression make its intentions obvious. She is there not to kill herself but to show off her nudity to an admiring male audience.

Dürer, Albrecht (1471–1528), German
During the sixteenth century, when the most important development in painting outside Italy took place in Germany, Dürer was the most highly regarded painter north of the Alps. His fame and talent were so great that even today, more than 450 years later, he is still commonly known as Germany's finest artist. His paintings, in the Northern oil medium derived from the medieval Flemish School, are treasured in the world's leading museums, along with his engravings and woodcuts, of which he was the great master in Europe. To look at his work without considering his drawings does not enable you to appreciate his talent and influence.

Dürer is also important, because he stands as a transitional figure—medieval but affected by the Renaissance. His love of microscopic detail is Northern, but his concern with perspective, with the weight of his figures, and with composition imply that he was familiar with the Italian Renaissance and learned from its masters. We know of two trips he made to Italy, but even without firsthand knowledge, communications between Germany and Italy were such that an artist of Dürer's imagination and talent would have been aware of the new style. He carried the Renaissance style into the Netherlands, where he made a trip in 1520. His fame was so great he was received like a prince. His celebrity was further spread by his writings, which tell of his affection for his parents, especially his father, a goldsmith from Nuremberg, whom he painted twice. He also expressed his belief in God, which his works of art make clear, going as far as representing Christ in his self-portrait. Yet in a survey of the achievement of Dürer, the religious themes are secondary to the Renaissance sophistication of his work and its influence in Germany. He was his own publisher of drawings and spread his art farther than other masters of his time. Not only a great painter of pictures, he remains one of the most influential popularizers of art in the history of Europe.

Self-portrait in a Fur Coat (1500?): upper floor, room 2b
The dating of this picture at 1500 derives from the date on the picture, which has Dürer's signature. However, many scholars regard this as the nonsense of some restorer. Dürer may actually be about six years older. His likeness shows more dignity, reserve, and monumentality than his self-portrait of 1498 (at the Prado, Madrid). His rich costume may be the one he mentions in his letters from Venice in 1506.

Dürer does convey a forceful idea in his character, which we know from his writings and the writings of contemporaries. Notice the Gothic expressiveness of the half-length frontal composition and the well-modeled right hand fingering the fur of the coat. This contrasts with the Renaissance softness of the face, framed by a wreath of curls, standing out against a dark background. There is no self-portrait in Europe in which the painter appears to be presenting himself more in the image of Christ. That is not to say this is a form of self-worship, as it has been thought to be. Dürer wrote that he humbly accepted his genius as a gift from God and believed in "living according to the Lord." Therefore, this painting would reflect Dürer's humility and a mystical feeling of serving as God's instrument. Believing the most important theme of art was to illuminate the Passion of Christ, Dürer naturally identified closely with Christ.

This religiosity is not depicted in the 1499 *Portrait of Oswald Krell* (upper floor, room 2b), a rich merchant from Lindau. Like all of Dürer's portraits, including his self-portraits, it is a powerful rendering of the sitter's character, emphasized by the ardent gaze of the fiery eyes. This device of the intent look or fiery glance of the sitter distinguishes Dürer's work from those of most of his contemporaries. It appears on the face of the saint on the right in his *Four Apostles*.

The Four Apostles (1526): upper floor, room 2
These pictures, which Dürer donated to the town of Nuremberg, are his last and perhaps his greatest paintings. They consist of two panels in the shape of large altar wings. It is possible that a planned central panel depicting the Madonna and Child had to be dropped after the Reformation in 1525.

The greater than life-sized figures represent, on the left, St. John and St. Peter and, on the right, St. Mark and St. Paul (since Mark was not one of the apostles the title is not correct). At the bottom of each panel are biblical texts written in German that warn against accepting false prophets and of mistaking human temptations for the Word of God. Thus Dürer intended to incite his native city against the radical Protestant sects of his day as well as against the Catholics. His own position was one with Luther's reforms. The four figures represent an expression of faith based on that thought.

Of importance to the history of art is that these four are Renaissance figures that have the humanistic spirit of the new age. Their classical drapery is worthy of the art of Giovanni Bellini, whom Dürer knew in Venice. Their powerful colors and form, though within the Germanic character, remind one of the most accomplished Italian sources, as do the compositions that set the figures against dark backgrounds to emphasize their powerful plasticity. These four figures may have had religious meaning in the sixteenth century, but today their power derives from their painterly presence, powerful because they exist as a superior work of art.

Dyck, Anthony van* (1599–1641), Flemish

Self-portrait (ca. 1622): upper floor, cabinet 9
During his short life Anthony van Dyck became famous throughout Europe as the greatest portrait painter of his time. He became the favorite of the Italian nobility of Genoa and the official court painter to Charles I of England, who knighted him and made it possible for him to live in England for five years in princely splendor. One of the greatest portraits painted by this temperamental dreamer, so concerned with worldly acclaim, is a self-portrait. This one, in which he proudly but discreetly shows the gold chain presented to him by Duke Ferdinand Gonzaga, was done when he was about twenty-three years old and traveling in Italy. He had already made a name for himself in his native Antwerp, where he was at one time Rubens's favorite assistant. His slightly girlish face belies his love of beautiful women, and his enigmatic smile gives his portrait a sensual quality that tells us that physical beauty was important to him. That is why he was highly regarded as a portrait painter: he showed what was most beautiful and elegant in his sitters. That applies to his own image in this self-portrait.

Gossaert, Jan, also called Mabuse (ca. 1478–ca. 1536), Flemish

Danae (1527): upper floor, room 1
After Jan Gossaert journeyed to Italy as part of the Burgundian court's visit to the pope in 1508–10, the experience seems to have dominated his whole life, with the result that he became the artist who introduced the Italian School into Flanders in the early sixteenth century. With the Italian School

came pagan figures of antiquity the North was unfamiliar with, though they were a part of Italian Renaissance literature. *Danae* represents Gossaert's finest painting in this manner; it was executed before Titian, Correggio, Rembrandt, and others portrayed the same story in painting.

According to Greek mythology, the Delphic Oracle told King Acrisios that he would be killed by one of the sons of his daughter Danae. To prevent such a fate he shut Danae in a bronze tower to keep her suitors away. But Jupiter fell in love with her and gained entrance to the tower in the form of golden rain. A son was born from this union who eventually killed his grandfather accidentally with a discus.

Gossaert has painted Danae at the moment when Jupiter, in the form of a shower of gold, is entering her chamber. He shows Danae as a soft-looking pretty girl holding out her blue cloak (a color usually used for the Virgin) to catch the golden rain—the golden semen of the god. Her garments fall aside enticingly to reveal her breast which, with the position of her legs, give the painting an erotic character. The classical columns that surround Danae, which Gossaert always included in one form or another in his paintings, are phallic symbols. To avoid too much sensuality that might have impaired the work, colors are toned to gray-blue and dull red.

Danae was not only an erotic story that people loved seeing in paintings and reading about, but also an example of the conception of a virgin through divine intervention—thus a prefiguration of the Annunciation.

Memling, Hans (ca. 1433–94), Flemish

The Seven Joys of the Virgin (1480): upper floor, room 1
The title of this painting is inaccurate. What is shown are scenes depicting the life of Christ and the Virgin set in a single large landscape. The actions are the following: the Annunciation, the Nativity (two donors, dressed in black, are introduced here by the ingenious idea of placing them outside the window watching the Nativity inside the ruined building, seen on the extreme lower-left-hand corner of the panel), the Annunciation to the Shepherds, the Appearance of the Star to the Three Kings, their visit to Herod, their Journey, the Adoration, the Massacre of the Innocents, the Flight into Egypt, the Temptation of Christ, the Resurrection, the Noli me Tangere, Christ at Emmaus, Peter on the Water, the Appearance of Christ to His Mother, the Ascension, Pentecost, the Death of the Virgin, and the Assumption.

A brown landscape is employed to bring out the little figures of reds and blues, with bright white applied throughout, and a conventional seascape in the background to relieve the density of the composition. The effect is somewhat confusing. You have to go from scene to scene before the work becomes a narrative delight, the only horror being the Massacre of the Innocents.

Raphael* (1483–1520), Florentine, born in Umbria

The Canigiani Holy Family (1506): upper floor, room 4
This painting was done when Raphael was living in Florence (1504–8) and

is one of a number from the period that have compositional arrangements in the Leonardoesque pyramidal form. Raphael employed it often to depict his popular Madonna and Child with St. John scenes, but this one has been expanded to include the Madonna's cousin, St. Elizabeth, and her aged husband, St. Joseph, which is something that Michelangelo also employed. In spite of drawing from two older Florentine masters, the result is Raphael's original work. This is evident in the color tones and the Raphaelesque sense of humanity. Original also is the northernlike landscape in the background, which includes a city similar to those in France and Flanders.

In the *Tempi Madonna* (upper floor, room 4), dated about 1508 and the last of Raphael's Florentine Madonnas, he is still borrowing from other artists, in this case Fra Bartolomeo. But Raphael's eclecticism has a purpose and an ultimate originality. We can see in his liberated colors how he is achieving new heights in his quest to create a harmony between form and feeling. It anticipates his Roman period when he develops a sense of expressiveness, a foremost example of high Renaissance painting.

Rembrandt* (1606–69), Dutch

Self-portrait as a Young Man (1629): upper floor, cabinet 16
One reason Rembrandt is considered such a great artist is that he could express character on canvas. This included his own character as well as that of his sitters, and no other artist has left so many portraits of himself. This early self-portrait, made when he was twenty-three, shows he was not a good-looking man (he was short of stature, as other self-portraits show), but one with a presence possessing the self-confidence of youth. The bold aspect of his character is brought out by the hair, nearly the main subject of the portrait. Notice how the accents of his locks seem to be scratched into the surface with the butt end of a wooden brush, leading us to feel this is the portrait of an angry young man preparing to challenge a society that had not yet given him acclaim.

Passion of Christ (five paintings): upper floor, cabinet 16
This series of paintings represents the first major commission given to Rembrandt (1632). They were done for Prince Frederick Henry of Orange, head of the official Calvinist party in Holland, yet they are like any Catholic painting. That they could have been executed in a country that had espoused Protestantism and banned visual church art is due to a toleration for non-Protestant belief. Therefore, the illustrating of the Bible by a Protestant for a Protestant prince in a Protestant country was acceptable; we know of no instance in which Rembrandt's religious paintings were denounced as heretical.

Of the five paintings *The Raising of the Cross* and *The Descent from the Cross* are the best, the other three being *The Entombment, The Resurrection,* and *The Adoration of the Shepherds.*

The Descent from the Cross might seem to have been inspired by Rubens, whose famous painting on the same subject in the Cathedral of Notre Dame in Antwerp Rembrandt was familiar with from engravings. But Rembrandt's *Descent from the Cross* is the antithesis of the work of Rubens. It is closer to Caravaggio than Rubens in its treatment of mysterious light and dark shadows to produce an emotional realism that seems true to life. A greater difference is in the arrangement of the figures in space and in the figures themselves. They are pushed back to the middle-ground. Christ is a pitiful dead mass falling in a heap into the arms of a supporter, instead of a heroic body with beautiful outlines. There are no ecstatic faces with blond hair against a luminous white sheet, as in the Rubens painting. The figures at the base of the pyramid-shaped composition are just discernible in the indeterminate sepia monochrome. Rembrandt included himself in the scene. He is the man dressed in blue who clutches Christ's lifeless right arm. In *The Raising of the Cross* Rembrandt is also there, as the man wearing the blue cap at the right of Christ's nailed and bloody feet. If you ever had doubts about Rembrandt's religious convictions, think of his painting his portrait into these two pictures symbolizing the crime and the anguish of the Crucifixion.

Rubens, Peter Paul* (1577–1640), Flemish

The Rape of the Daughters of Leucippus: upper floor, room 7
Rubens is best known for his mythological scenes done in a baroque style. This one, painted in 1618, shows the twin brothers, Castor and Pollux, sons of Zeus, carrying off the daughters of King Leucippus who were betrothed to another set of twins. There is tumultuous movement within its compositional structure of strong verticals and diagonals. The women's nude bodies are Venetian in color with transparent skin tones that add to their sensuality. The strength and sexual prowess of the men are echoed in the muscular movements of the horses, and the presence of the two cupids leaves no doubt about the outcome of the scene. One's imagination is stimulated by the background of land and sky.

Rubens and His Wife Isabella Brant: upper floor, room 7
When Rubens returned to Antwerp from Italy in 1608 his name had already been made. He had been the court painter to the duke of Mantua and had traveled widely, including a trip to Spain in 1603. He now assumed the position of court painter to the Hapsburgs in the Netherlands, and in 1609 he married Isabella Brant, the daughter of a humanist of Antwerp, Jan Brant, whose portrait is in the Pinakothek.

This double portrait was probably painted the year Rubens and Isabella married, as a record of the event. Isabella was eighteen and Rubens thirty-two. They are sitting before a honeysuckle bower, which forms a dark background. Isabella's hand on Rubens's shows her trust and devotion, and her eyes, with their mischievous expression, reflect pride in having gotten such a successful husband. Rubens's face is full of self-content and confidence. Formed together in the shape of an oval that fills the canvas, they are an image of the ideal couple, which they remained during seventeen years of marriage.

Helena Fourment with Her Son: upper floor, room 8
Four years after the death of his first wife, Rubens married Helena Fourment

when she was not yet seventeen. This portrait of her, about five years later with her son Frans, whose feathered beret enlivens the painting and gives it a delightful sense of pomp, indicates Rubens's contentment with Helena and the children she bore him (there were five, one born after Rubens death).

Rubens painted Helena's portrait at least nineteen times. See, in the Pinakothek, *Helena Fourment in Her Wedding Dress* (room 7) and *Helena Fourment with Gloves* (cabinet 9), and the charming *Rubens and Helena Fourment in their Garden* (room 8), painted only a few months after their marriage in 1630, showing them strolling in their garden in Antwerp on a summer day accompanied by Rubens's thirteen-year-old son, Nicholas, from his previous marriage with Isabella Brant.

Steen, Jan* (1626–79), Dutch

The Lovesick Maiden: upper floor, cabinet 21

Steen is Holland's great seventeenth-century painter of genre scenes, and is ranked after Rembrandt and Hals. He moralized a great deal, and many of his paintings (there are about 800 of them, of uneven quality, but a few dozen great enough to prove that he was a master) depict young ladies limply reposing on a chair. In some they are visited by a doctor, perhaps depicted as a quack, as our man in this painting must represent. The slip of paper in the girl's hand carries the message of the picture, "Medicine is of no avail for these are the pains of love." The statue of cupid above the alcove leading to the door makes clear the significance of the scene. So does the dog, a symbol of animal nature. The small stove on the floor may refer to the fires of love; the cord lying limp near it is symbolic of tying the knot of marriage the young woman pines for. More sensual, the ripe fruit at the edge of the table, opened and partly eaten, is an obvious reference to a recent love affair which the withering peel suggests is now over. The hope of the maiden is also reflected in the open wicker basket, which to Dutchmen of the seventeenth century symbolized the maiden's eagerness for carnal love.

Titian* (ca. 1487–1576), Venetian

The Emperor Charles V: upper floor, room 5

This is one of the court portraits that Titian executed for Charles V at the Congress of Augsburg in 1548. Charles had recently defeated the Protestant League at the Battle of Mühlberg, and invited Titian, the painter he most admired, to join his official party in Germany. From his position close to the emperor, Titian was able to see the struggle Charles was going through. He recorded Charles's inner turmoil on canvas. We are shown Charles seated but not relaxed. His deep-set eyes beneath arched eyebrows are reflections of his disbelief facing the determination of the Protestant princes. The vertical furrow in his brow and his firmly set mouth show his equally determined position. Dressed in black, he seems to be a tragic figure who may already have been thinking of abdicating (he abdicated in 1554 and retired to a monastery in 1556, two years before his death and one year after the conclusion of the Peace of Augsburg, which resulted in a compromise with the Protestant German princes). Charles looks older than his forty-eight years. There is a certain fragility about him that the space and grandeur Titian has given the picture—by leaving a large area empty above the emperor's head—cannot overcome. Titian has definitely given us an exact likeness of his sitter as well as a penetrating look at the inner thoughts of a man who has the troubles of Europe on his mind.

Crowning with Thorns (ca. 1570): upper floor, room 5
Only few masters complete their life's work with masterpieces that surpass what they did earlier, but in Titian we have an example. This *Crowning with Thorns*, as well as his *Pietà* in Venice (see Titian's *Pietà* in the Academy Gallery, Venice) is an expression of an intellectual style developed by Titian to give vent to his emotions. Painted at a late date and found in Titian's studio after his death, it is one of those religious paintings, showing the pain and death of Christ, that Titian did for himself and which, at his advanced age, he identified with. It uses a composition from his 1542 painting of the same subject (see Titian's *Crowning with Thorns* in the Louvre, Paris), but the mannerist tension built up in the earlier Louvre painting, where Titian has the dynamics of the *Laocoön* in mind, are absent from his painting. In comparison, this scene is quiet, almost devotional. Christ endures His pain exhausted and submissive, with His head at an angle to bear the blows of the sticks. The empty space of the archway reveals the original position of Christ's head before it was brutally knocked to one side. The triangles, diagonals, and counterdiagonals, often a part of Titian's compositions, are brilliantly arranged to represent the storm of violence and pain that surround Christ. Notice that color and brushwork supersede form. Reds, blues, and yellows are applied to the canvas freely with the brush almost as Rembrandt would do in the next century. The hazy blur and indefinite mass bring out the feeling of the scene as line and form could never accomplish. Such an advanced style of painterly expression was not widely understood by Titian's contemporaries. This painting was called unfinished for a long time, and probably was never fully appreciated until the late nineteenth century.

Weyden, Rogier van der* (ca. 1399–1464), Flemish

Adoration of the Magi (St. Colomba) Altarpiece: upper floor, room 1
This painting, often called the *St. Colomba Altarpiece* because it is believed to have been made for the Church of St. Colomba in Cologne, is from the end of Rogier's career, dated about 1462. The donor in the central panel at the extreme left, shown in a kneeling position with a rosary in his hands, is probably the mayor of the free Hanseatic city of Cologne. All three panels are executed with typical Flemish precision and excellence of color. Notice the striking yellow sleeve of the kneeling king in the central panel. Its brightness draws our attention to the Virgin and Child, as well as to the king kissing the Child's hand. The traditional blue of the Virgin's robe is carried over into the panel on the left, showing the *Annunciation,* and the panel on the right, showing the *Presentation in the Temple.* Similarly, the reds in the central panel, worn by Joseph, to the left of the Virgin, and by the kings, to the right (notice the rich brocade of the king who is raising his right hand), is

also carried over into the left and right wings. The hole in the ground, directly in front of the Virgin, has been interpreted as the cave of Bethlehem, the place where Jesus was born. More interesting is the Gothic church to the right in the central panel, and the Romanesque interior in the panel showing the *Presentation in the Temple*. By such an iconography Rogier is telling us that the Presentation in the Temple is a ceremony of the Old Law, but here taking place for Christ, Founder of the New Law. The Gothic exterior of the temple symbolizes the New Law (New Testament), but the Romanesque interior is also present to symbolize that the New Law has been built upon the Old Law (Old Testament).

MUNICIPAL GALLERY IN THE LENBACHHAUS

Luisenstrasse, 33

Hours: Open Tues.–Sun., 10AM–6PM. Admission fee.

The Lenbach Gallery, as it is popularly called, specializes in modern German paintings and French paintings that were influenced by them. The gallery has a highly regarded collection of this art because Munich was a center of modernism in the early part of this century, the city where an artist's society called **Die Brücke** (The Bridge) became the first group of German expressionists to discover and represent the spiritual meaning of nature. With five artists at its core (Kirchner, Heckel, Schmidt-Rottluff, Nolde, and Pechstein), all influenced by the expressionism of the Fauves in Paris, Die Brücke grew in numbers and influence. Before it fell apart at the start of World War I, it carried on a revolt against German classic painting and the romantic-realistic school. Their use of bold, unnatural colors and exaggeration of form to evoke an emotion rather than an impression was similar to what the Fauves had done in France, but done with a brooding emotionalism that made the pictures particularly German.

A more radical step, beyond fauvism and the work of Die Brücke, was taken in 1911 by the Russian **Wassily Kandinsky** (1866–1944). He and a number of German painters, whose aim it was to unleash forces they could sense behind the appearances of the physical world, founded a new group called **Der Blaue Reiter** (The Blue Horseman), a name taken from a painting by Kandinsky. They held exhibitions in Munich showing anyone's work that broke traditional molds. In his own work Kandinsky pursued abstract expressionism, abandoning representation altogether. His pictures became pure emotion, practically breaking down the barrier between music and painting.

Of Kandinsky there are about one thousand paintings at the Lenbach Gallery, and also works by Alexej von Jawlensky (1864–1941), Paul Klee (1879–1940), Franz Marc (1880–1916), August Macke (1887–1914), Lovis Corinth (1858–1925), and others from this period, who helped redefine the art of our century.

NEUE PINAKOTHEK

Barerstrasse, 29 (across from the Alte Pinakothek)

Hours: Open Wed., Fri., Sat., Sun., 9AM–4:30PM; Tues., Thurs., 9AM–4:30PM and 7–9PM. Admission fee.

The collection in the Alte Pinakothek is continued chronologically in this brand new forty-four million dollar building on the site of the original Neue Pinakothek, destroyed during World War II. There are paintings and sculptures here from the nineteenth century to the art of our time, including works by the best of the French impressionists and German expressionists. It is also a marvelous place to compare the works of the German schools with those of foreign painters of the same period. The German paintings are more emotional, violent, and distorted.

STATE ANTIQUES COLLECTION (STAATLICHE ANTIKENSAMMLUNGEN UND GLYPTOTHEK)

Königsplatz, 3

Hours: Open Tues., Wed., Fri., Sat., Sun., 10AM–4:30PM; Thurs., 12 noon–8PM; closed holidays. Admission fee.

This complex of antique art is located in two buildings. The **Staatliche Antikensammlungen** has a large collection of Greek vase painting, including some of the finest anywhere. There is a rich collection of Etruscan and Greek jewelry, and a collection of Greek figurines in bronze and terra cotta.

The **Glyptothek** holds a collection of Greek and Roman sculpture in a building considered one of the first museum constructions in Europe, erected in 1816–30 to house the collection of King Ludwig I of Bavaria. In this museum there are a number of high points.

Room 1

Two well preserved marble **Kouroi.** These are somewhat oversimplified statues of standing nude youths that date back to the sixth century B.C. Their features express an intelligence and enjoyment of life characteristic of Greek sculpture.

Rooms 7–9

In these rooms are the treasures of the museum, the fifth-century B.C. *Aegina Marbles* representing the battles for Troy, in two pediments. Though executed about fifty years before the Parthenon sculptures, they have an archaic quality, with figures that seem frozen with conventional grins even though they are in the heat of battle. They were discovered as fragments in 1811 and, about fifty years later were purchased by Ludwig I who asked a sculptor named Thorwaldsen to repair the work and refinish the stones. One wonders to what extent he changed their original appearance. While they do not compare with the *Elgin Marbles* in London, or with the collection in the Louvre in Paris, they are one of the important groups of Greek sculptures outside Greece.

Room 13

Here are Roman copies of some important Hellenistic works. A tiny relief, *Peasant Taking a Bull to Market,* and the lovely sculpture group, *Little Boy Struggling with a Goose,* are excellent.

STATE GALLERY OF MODERN ART (HAUS DER KUNST)

Prinzregenten Strasse, 1

Hours: Open Tues.–Sun., 9AM–4:30PM. Admission fee.

This building, the home of Bavaria's collection of contemporary art, was built by the Nazis and used to mock expressionist and abstract painting by staging the 1937 exhibition of "degenerate art." The paintings displayed here now are those of Munch, Picasso, Magritte, Matisse, Beckmann, Motherwell, and other leading artists of the twentieth century.

Continuing down Prinzregenten (toward the river), at number 9 you will find the **Schack Gallery** filled with nineteenth-century German paintings. The gallery is open Tues.–Sun., 9AM–4:30PM; closed Mon.; admission fee.

Buildings

ASAMKIRCHE (CHURCH OF ST. JOHN NEPOMUK)

Sendlingerstrasse

The work of the **brothers Asam—Cosmas Damian** (1686–1739), a painter and decorator, and **Egid Quirin** (1692–1750), a sculptor—was well appreciated in southern Germany. They built and rebuilt a number of ecclesiastical buildings with an aim of achieving an interior as close to real life as the scenery on a stage, with decoration in all the splendor the age could devise. They succeeded nowhere better than in this little church they built for themselves with their own money (1733–46). It was the project of Egid Quirin, a bachelor, whose house is adjacent to the church. He built another house for the priest next to the other side of the church. The work of his brother is also in the church and together they created probably the finest example of a baroque exterior and a rococo interior in southern Germany. Its whimsical Borrominesque **facade** rises from two boulders like a Bernini fountain (the Asam brothers studied in Rome) and is decorated with sculptured flowers and ribbons up to its mighty pediment. Inside, free to indulge their every fancy, they outdid themselves. All around the narrow room—there are no aisles or transepts—are curves in planes and masses. This makes the room look narrow, but emphasizes the height, a technique close to the heart of every baroque artist. The **ceiling** is painted in one large panel, which, like the rest of the room, is a picture of movement, emphasized by the darker colors of the church below it. The main feature, as in all Asam churches, is the centerpiece over the altar, a marvel of black and gold and marble. It seems to bulge, vibrate, and float away upward.

FRAUENKIRCHE (CHURCH OF OUR LADY)

Frauenplatz

The cathedral church of Munich was begun in 1470. The strange **onion-domed towers** of its facade, a curious feature on a church whose lower portions are Gothic, were completed in 1512, and are a distinctive landmark of Munich.

The cathedral, a typical brick-hall church, is 358 feet long and a nave over 100 feet in height. The interior underwent restoration in the eighteenth, nineteenth, and twentieth centuries, which spoiled some of it, but it is still striking, with rows of octagonal piers rising directly to the ceiling, and nave and aisles of equal height. When viewed from the entrance, the piers look as though they are hiding the windows of the chapels. This feature, and its simple white appearance, give the church a modern look.

NYMPHENBURG

Northwest of the city about 5 miles

Hours: Open Apr.–Sept., Tues.–Sun., 9AM–12:30PM and 1:30–5PM; Oct.–Mar., 10AM–12:30PM and 1:30–4PM. Admission fee.

This great park on the outskirts of Munich contains **Nymphenburg Palace,** an extravagant baroque royal residence; **Amalienburg,** a so-called hunting lodge; **Badenburg,** an elegant bathing pavillion; and **Pagodenburg,** a tea pavilion with Chinese motifs. It was all started in the seventeenth century as a summer residence for the Bavarian kings and completed in the eighteenth century. The buildings are of a German baroque design with French influences, and the park is laid out like Versailles. Its finest part is Amalienburg (1734–39), the French rococo masterpiece of the Flemish-born architect François de Cuvillies (1695–1768), who was a dwarf. Its centerpiece is a circular room, the **Hall of Mirrors,** where the room lights up on a sunny day from reflections from the windows. Its colors are a harmony of blues and yellows with silver decorations. Adjoining the central circular saloon are two smaller rooms on either side, completing this compact jewel of rococo design. It was one of the first examples of the elegant rococo in Germany.

———————*Speyer*———————

CATHEDRAL

Hours: Open Apr.–Sept., daily, guided tours 9AM–6PM (Sat. to 4PM); Oct.–Mar., daily, guided tours 9AM–12 noon and 1:30–5PM; Sun. and holidays, 1:30–4:30PM. Admission fee.

The foundation stone for this, the largest of German Romanesque cathedrals, was laid by Conrad II in 1030; it was completed in the twelfth century. The remarkable **crypt**, with its stout columns and cubiform (or block) capitals supporting a heavy groined vault, is from the early eleventh-century and an example of pure German Romanesque. Above, the **nave**, with spacious groin vaulted aisles on either side, and immense piers supporting its own high groin vault, which at the crossing is the tallest Romanesque example in Europe, is forty-five feet wide and 235 feet long.

Like so many other German churches, this one was devastated by wars, especially in 1689, when the French army of Louis XIV gutted the building. What you see today is an eighteenth- and nineteenth-century reconstruction that happily retains its Romanesque origins to a great degree. The style derives from Lombardy in Italy, part of the Holy Roman Empire when the cathedral was being built. The eaves gallery, upper clerestory, and decorative arcading, are all of this style, innovations that spread rapidly to other churches being built in Germany at the time. Today you can see elements of this Lombard style almost everywhere in the Rhineland.

_____ Ulm _____

ULM MINSTER

Hours: Open May–Aug., daily 7A.M.–6:45P.M.; Sept.–Apr., daily 9A.M.–4:45P.M. Admission fee.

Like the cathedral at Freiburg, Ulm is famous for its single towered **west facade**—the highest spire in the world at 528 feet. The structure was begun in 1377 and, except for its lofty tower, was completed in the fifteenth century. In the sixteenth century the tower was built, but the spire was not added until the nineteenth century. Unlike Freiburg, where the great front tower harmonizes well with the building, at Ulm the neo-Gothic tower overwhelms the rest. It is noted for its impressive size and Gothic appearance, but can be considered an excess of nineteenth-century romanticists who destroyed what was once a quaint Upper Swabian parish church. There is a lovely **triple porch**, which has fourteenth-century sculptures, and, in the interior of the church, carved **Gothic choir stalls** with strongly modeled lifelike figures.

_____ Vierzehnheiligen _____

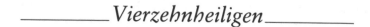

Near Bamberg

CHURCH OF VIERZEHNHEILIGEN (1744–72)

After the wars of religion ran their course in the seventeenth century, the artistic life of Germany came to a standstill and afterward became subservient to the Italian baroque. But at the end of the century it was showing signs of producing a German baroque style in the Catholic areas, in new church building. By the middle of the eighteenth century, when architects such as Balthasar Neumann were active, the baroque burst upon the German scene with spatial effects never before seen. Away went the mathematically logical plans of the Italians and in came unique spatial creations that had a greater sense of spiritual animation. The pilgrimage church of Vierzehnheiligen, one of many built to accommodate pilgrims who believed that a miraculous event had taken place on the site—in the case of Vierzehnheiligen it was a local herdsman who claimed he had visions of Christ and the Fourteen Saints of the Intercession—is such a church, one of the finest designs, by **Balthasar Neumann** (1687–1753).

From the outside, where the church commands a magnificent site on the crown of a hill, it is impossible to tell what splendor lies within. It has a tall twin-tower facade enriched by a variety of windows and a convex central section. It looks like a traditional basilican Latin cross plan with side aisles, transepts, and apse, but inside nothing corresponds to these expectations. There you will find spatial relationships that take their cue from ovals, ellipses, and semicircles that are deliberately intertwined. Whatever there is of transepts and crossing is encroached upon by the adjoining spatial units. Color is not a major focus, the scheme being largely white. The dynamic form created from stucco, iron, and sculptural decoration is enough to carry the effect to its convincing theatrical end. All this sounds like an irrational plan, but it delivers an emotional effect that is exhilarating.

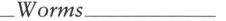

Worms

CATHEDRAL

Hours: Open Mar.–Oct., Mon.–Sat., 8A.M.–6P.M.; Nov.–Feb., Mon.–Sat., 9A.M.– 5P.M.; closed holidays. Admission fee to chancel.

Of the three great twelfth- and thirteenth-century Romanesque cathedrals in the Rhineland—Worms, Speyer, and Mainz—Worms is the most purely Romanesque and displays best the Lombard influence in its German design. That influence, represented in the quadripartite ribbed vaults, in the membered piers, and in the exterior Italianate arcaded balconies, is to be expected because the Rhineland and Lombardy were both in the Holy Roman Empire. When these features are combined with the German style of apses at both east and west ends, flanked by paired towers, and the variety of fantastic beasts upon window ledges and on plinths of piers and shafts, the building takes on a monumental German character.

Owing to the seventeenth-century war with the French, much of the interior of the cathedral was destroyed and had to be rebuilt. Today its outstanding decoration is a baroque **high altar** by **Balthasar Neumann** (1687–1753), a gilded, festive design somewhat out of place in the austere interior of massive stone walls.

——————— *Würzburg* ———————

RESIDENZ (1719–44)

Hours: Open Apr.–Sept., Tues.–Sun., 9AM–4:40PM; Oct.–Mar., 10AM–3:30PM; closed some holidays. Admission fee.

This great palace of the prince-bishops of Würzburg has some of the most magnificient baroque interiors in Europe. It was almost completely lost on the night of March 16, 1945, when in twenty minutes of bombing 5,000 buildings in the city were damaged or destroyed. But most of the Residenz was spared and the damaged portions have now been restored.

The Würzburg Residenz demonstrates the development of the baroque style in Germany during the first half of the eighteenth century and shows the extent the work of the German architect **Balthasar Neumann** (1687–1753) played in this late German Renaissance. While other architects worked on the palace, his is the greatest contribution, accounting for the design of the **Hofkirche**, the court chapel; the elegant **Kaisersaal**; and the famous **Staircase Hall**, whose ceiling was decorated by the Venetian Tiepolo.

Tiepolo, Giovanni Battista (1696–1770), Venetian

Ceiling (1750–53): front staircase hall
There are few easel paintings by Tiepolo, his expressive outlet was ceiling and wall paintings, and this is his finest. Perhaps his artistic spirit and his technique required gigantic surfaces. Whatever the case, he built up a reputation for that kind of work, and in the last decade of his life, in Madrid, he had more commissions to paint ceilings than he could fulfill.

Over the triple staircase, called the most beautiful in the world, Tiepolo painted a fresco showing Apollo as patron of the arts, with the personified seasons and the continents of the world, each symbolized by a dominant female. The unsupported vaulted ceiling is about one hundred by sixty feet. When the architect of the ceiling, Neumann's collaborator Hidebrandt, finished it, he feared for its survival, but it has not only passed the test of time, it also withstood the bombing of 1945.

As one ascends the first flight in the center and proceeds on one of the flights doubling back, one feels the boundaries of the room expand, because the spatial shell is larger than the width of the three flights of stairs. Tiepolo planned his fresco to develop this idea by massing colorful figures, set before a rapid recession of trees and buildings, along the rim of the painted zone. This creates the illusion that the staircase extends sideways as well as upward, a special baroque technique. Tiepolo has paid his debt to Balthasar Neumann, whose staircase inspired him to paint the masterpiece of his career; the architect appears in the fresco as the grey-haired man lying in the center beside the dog. As the final flowering of Venetian art, Tiepolo's work also pays a debt to Venice, whose two hundred years of painting, inaugurated by Veronese, he has celebrated with his light colors, his originality of composition, his realism, his movement, and the warmth and spirit of the entire work.

After ascending the staircase, one enters the **Kaisersaal** on the first floor. After the extraordinary Staircase Hall, it is no anticlimax. Its large rectangular apartment has its lower walls articulated with Corinthian columns, and there is a coved ceiling decorated with stuccowork and Tiepolo paintings that glorify the Emperor Barbarossa. In the large central oval panel is depicted *the Arrival of the Emperor Barbarossa's Bride Beatrix in the Sun Chariot of Apollo.*

In the **Hofkirche,** the court chapel of the palace, badly damaged in 1945, is a small, perfect baroque interior richly decorated but not overdone.

The **exterior of the palace,** especially its garden facade, is enriched by pilasters, cornices, engaged columns, and imaginatively curved gables. The eye is never diverted to one architectural element; instead, the whole baroque structure prevails.

Würzburg is also the city where the German Late Gothic sculptor Tilman Riemenschneider (ca. 1460–1531) settled in 1483. His work, in stone and wood, is a forerunner of Renaissance art; individualistic and highly refined, especially in the treatment of the female body, it is rare at that time in Germany. His life-size sandstone statue of *Eve* (1491–93), in the **Franconian Museum** (entrance on the right in the first courtyard on Marienberg Castle, open 10AM–5PM) is an example of this delicacy. Other sulptures by Riemenschneider are in the **cathedral.** These are the tombs of his patrons, Prince Bishop Rudolf von Scherenberg and Bishop Lorenz von Bibra (right side of the transept). A few steps away from the cathedral, the **Neumünster Church** has a *Virgin and Child* attributed to Riemenschneider (beneath the cupola).

Ireland

As early as the first century, the Irish produced exquisite art objects made of gold and carved from stone. During the seventh and eighth centuries, when Europe was lost in chaos and barbarism, the Irish created masterpieces of illuminated manuscripts that recorded and held Christianity together. The mastery of these precious books has never been surpassed. The *Book of Kells* can be seen today in Dublin's Trinity College Library with other illuminated books of almost equal importance.

In the centuries that succeeded the age of illuminated manuscripts, Ireland's history did not bring a development of painting and architecture. They did not fully emerge until the relatively late period of the eighteenth century.

The best place to see the range of Irish art, from the prehistoric to the modern, is Dublin. The National Museum displays ancient objects of art such as the *Tara Brooch* and *Ardagh Chalice*. Trinity College Library is the great repository of illuminated manuscripts. The National Gallery and the Hugh Lane Municipal Gallery are museums that display Irish painting, and the most important architecture is found also in Dublin.

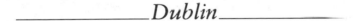

Dublin

Museums

HUGH LANE MUNICIPAL GALLERY OF MODERN ART

Parnell Square

Hours: Open Tues.–Sat., 9:30AM–6PM; Sun., 11AM–5PM. Free admission.

This museum is housed in Charlemont House, an eighteenth-century (1763) neoclassical town house built by Sir William Chambers (1723–96), the English architect, for the earl of Charlemont. In its day it was one of Dublin's finest houses. The Municipal Gallery, founded in 1908, made Charlemont House its permanent home in 1933.

The collection consists of nineteenth- and twentieth-century art built around paintings bequeathed to the museum by Sir Hugh Lane, but the Irish found the inheritance a cause for still another row with the British.

The dispute came about because Sir Hugh, a wealthy Anglo-Irish collector and curator of Dublin's National Gallery, who died on the *Lusitania* in 1915, had left his collection to the National Gallery in London where his paintings were on loan. His will provided the bequest go to Britain. But before sailing on the *Lusitania* Sir Hugh had a change of heart and made a codicil leaving his paintings to Dublin's new Municipal Gallery. When the Irish asked London for the paintings, the British stated that the codicil was invalid because it had not been witnessed by two people. Although the argument was logical and legal, it continued for fifty years. An agreement was at last reached in 1959, dividing the thirty-nine pictures in question into two groups to be exchanged every five years between Dublin and London. At the end of October, 1979, a new arrangement was made, to exhibit thirty paintings in Dublin and eight in London, during the following fourteen years. *Les Parapluies* by Renoir, the jewel of the collection, is to stay in Dublin for seven years and then transfer to London for a similar period.

Of the thirty paintings currently at Dublin, see, in **room 4** the portrait of *Eva Gonzales* (1870) by Manet (1832–83) and works by Monet, P. E. Theodore Rousseau, and Morisot. In **room 5** paintings of interest are *In the Forest*, by Gustave Courbet (1819–77), a portrait of *Honoré Daumier*, by Charles Daubigny (1817–78) and *Christ and the Soldier*, by George Rouault (1871–1958).

Renoir, Pierre-Auguste* (1841–1919), French

Les Parapluies (Umbrellas): room 4
Painted in 1883, *The Umbrellas* is a transitional work in which Renoir drew away from impressionist emphasis on atmospheric effects. Gone is the brightness of Renoir's earlier colors. The umbrellas' somber gray is repeated in the dresses of the women and the coat of the child restraining the little girl in the foreground. Renoir accents line and emphasizes design and structure. He seems fascinated with geometrical patterns. The curving shapes of the umbrellas are repeated in the brim of the man's hat, in the folds of the woman's dress, and in her basket. Even the child's hoop is part of the pattern of curves formed by the umbrellas, while the stick she holds relates to the handles. These geometrical patterns give rise to a sense of movement.

The Umbrellas is unlike what Renoir painted earlier or was to paint later in his career. It emphasizes formal design in contrast to his casually planned work. Forms are more sculptural and the intense reds and yellows of his earlier period are gone. But the cold manner in which Renoir treated his concern for sculptural form during his "harsh period" of the 1880s did not last. After 1890, while continuing with strong forms, he once again emphasized atmospheric effects and color.

Yeats, Jack B. (1871–1957), Irish: rooms 8–9

Jack B. Yeats was a member of the famous Yeats family. His father, John

Butler Yeats (1839–1922) was one of Ireland's finest portrait painters. His brother, William Butler Yeats (1856–1939), the great Irish dramatist, poet, and essayist, won the Nobel Prize in 1923. While Jack B. Yeats has not yet received international recognition, his work is appreciated in Ireland.

Yeat's work can be divided into three parts. The earliest phase (**room 8**) consists of his black and white illustrations done for English journals. Around 1905 Yeats began painting in oils. From this second period come many paintings that express Irish life: sporting figures, circus performers, peddlers, and figures from political and social life of the time. These works become more atmospheric until in his mature phase (**room 9**) he emerges as an expressionist, using thick impasto and rapid brush strokes to express a mystical quality his early works hinted at.

There are some common distinctions observed in all of Yeats's pictures. First, there is action, or something is about to happen; second, figures exist in isolation, experiencing their encounters alone.

About to Write a Letter (1935) gives us a simple statement of objects in a room, but accents a table in red, with its pen and paper waiting for the solitary figure of a man. In *Many Ferries* (1948) Yeats depicts an isolated figure looking down at the sea near Sligo. Although not much is happening, we realize that the figure and perhaps others seen below are having encounters with the world—moments of truth in their lives. In *Grief* (1951) Yeats makes an antiwar statement in a straightforward style. In the right foreground a young woman has her arm on the shoulder of a boy; an old man to the left of them with white beard holds his hands out in an attitude of prayer. Behind him is the figure of death. On the left side are soldiers with fixed bayonets led by a commander on a white horse. A city of Georgian houses is ablaze in the background.

Yeats might have been thinking of the recent world war, but his painting can stand as a statement against all wars. The young mother and child are symbols of those who always fall heir to the devastation caused by their elders.

NATIONAL GALLERY OF IRELAND

Merrion Square

Hours: Open Mon., Tues., Wed., Fri., Sat., 10AM–6PM; Thurs., 10AM–9PM; Sun., 2–5PM. Free admission.

The National Gallery of Ireland was named by people in the nineteenth century who hoped to make it a rival of the National Gallery of London. Like the London gallery it has old master paintings from all schools, with few chronological gaps. The Dublin gallery is unique for its collection of Irish painting. These are in rooms 7 through 3, reached via the small bookshop at the entrance on the ground floor. First, however, turn right off room 8 into room 29 to see an outstanding *Entombment* by Nicolas Poussin (1594–1665), which conveys an extraordinary sense of tragedy. Return to the Irish paintings in rooms 6 and 7 where there are eighteenth-century paintings by **Nathaniel Hone** (1718–81) and **George Barret** (ca. 1732–84). Nathaniel Hone, a portrait painter, is at his best in his affectionate portrayal of *The Piping Boy* (room 7), a portrait of his youngest son. Barrett's *Powerscourt Waterfall* (room 6), an example of his more original work, rich with trees and a massive waterfall, show him to be a good landscapist.

In **room 5** are works of **James Barry** (1741–1806) who, like George Barrett, was patronized by Edmund Burke (born Dublin 1729–97), the British statesman and member of Dr. Johnson's circle. Barry's *Adam and Eve,* or *Temptation in Paradise,* painted in Italy on a trip financed for him by Burke, shows a love of contour and outline associated with neoclassicism.

Rooms 2 and 3 display Irish painting of the nineteenth and the early twentieth centuries. Of interest is **Walter Osborne** (1859–1903), who studied in Belgium. His *St. Patrick's Close, Dublin* (room 2), where he captures the hopelessness of a Dublin slum street made palpable, and ironical, by a little boy with a whistle is one of his best. The paintings of **W. J. Leech** (1881–1968), a Dublin born artist who studied in Paris, show a French influence. See Leech's *The Goose Girl* and *Convent Garden, Brittany,* in the pointillist manner, using thick dabs of paint to emphasize light. (Both paintings are in room 2).

Before leaving room 2 look at the paintings by **Jack B. Yeats** (1871–1957). In *The Liffy Swim* (1923), where Yeats depicts the annual swimming race in Dublin's River Liffey—seen from the north bank, looking toward O'Connell Bridge—there is a wonderful sense of movement that tells us a race is in progress. Even the stationary mass of humanity, spectators at the event, contributes to the feeling of a race and thus becomes part of the action. Also, see two of Yeats's later works in a more expressionist style: *In Memory of Boucicault and Biancini* and *For the Road.* A major collection of paintings by Yeats is to be found at the Hugh Lane Municipal Gallery.

Yeats's father, **John Butler Yeats** (1839–1922), was an outstanding Irish portraitist who had a gift for capturing the personality of a sitter. Two portraits of his famous sons, *Jack B. Yeats as a Boy,* the painter, and *William Butler Yeats,* the poet, are seen on the ground floor staircase.

From room 2 go to **room 1,** the so-called Icon Room made to look like a church. Here is *The Attempted Martyrdom of Saints Cosmas and Damian* (third alcove on the right when you face the apse) by **Fra Angelico** (ca. 1400–55). In this painting the master of the early Italian Renaissance seems to delight in the triumph of good over evil.

Continue seeing the old masters on the second floor. The best of these are *The Village School* (room 37) by **Jan Steen** (1626–79), a superb seventeenth-century genre scene showing a masterful display of the emotions of young children; and two paintings (room 36) by **Rembrandt** (1606–69): *Rest on the Flight into Egypt,* a nocturnal landscape done in 1647 whose interweaving of light and dark brings out the elements of fear and loneliness, which Rembrandt, who was already in financial decline, probably identified with very closely; and *Portrait of a Young Woman,* which is typical of Rembrandt's early career in Amsterdam when he was in great demand as a portrait painter and confident about his future.

Additional paintings in the museum cover the Spanish, Flemish, and Italian schools, with some interesting works from Venice.

A large part of the collection of the **National Portrait Gallery** is housed in **Malahide Castle** (a few miles north of Dublin, bus no. 42), one of Ireland's oldest castles dating back to the fourteenth century. Apart from its portraits of men and women from Irish history, the castle with its collection of furniture and 250 acres of parkland is also an attraction. The great hall is one of the few medieval halls still in use in Ireland. The Oak Room has many examples of seventeenth-century Flemish carving. The castle is open Jan.–Dec., Mon.–Fri. 10AM–5PM; Apr.–Oct., Sat. 11AM–6PM; Sun. and bank holidays 2–6PM; Nov.–Mar., Sat., Sun., and bank holidays 2–5PM.

A great private art collection is seen at **Russborough,** a notable Palladian house (1740–50) in Blessington, County Wicklow (twenty-five miles south of Dublin). The house and collection are owned by Sir Alfred and Lady Beit. Among its many treasures are a series of six paintings by Murillo telling the parable of the Prodigal Son (dining room); the earliest known Velázquez, *The Servant Girl* (tapestry room); Gainsborough's *Cottage Girl with Dog and a Pitcher*, and five Venetian scenes by Guardi (music room); Vermeer's *Lady Writing a Letter with Her Maid,* one of only three Vermeers in private ownership, *The Letter Writer* and *The Letter Reader,* by Metsu, *The Lute Player,* by Hals, and a landscape masterpiece, *Castle at Bentheim,* by Jacob Ruisdael. The house is open Apr.–Oct., Sun. 2:30–6:30PM; June–Sept., Wed. 2:30–6:30PM; July–Aug., Sat. 2:30–6:30PM. Closed Apr.–May, Mon.–Sat.; June–Sept., Mon., Tues., Thurs.; Nov.–Mar.

NATIONAL MUSEUM

Kildare Street

Hours: Open Tues.–Sat., 10AM–5PM; Sun., 2–5PM. Free admission.

With this museum I shall divert from my plan to discuss only the greatest masterpieces of European painting, sculpture, and architecture. Rare items of beauty—the Tara Brooch, the Ardagh Chalice, the Shrine of St. Patrick's Bell, and the Cross of Cong, to mention a few—are displayed at Dublin's National Museum. As great pieces from European antiquity, they are the kind of decorative art that is often associated with Ireland.

The **Tara Brooch,** probably made to fasten the woolen cloak of a noble, and the **Ardagh Chalice,** a silver cup that must have brightened the altar of an early church, both date from the early eighth century and are miracles of delicate workmanship. The style of the two items is similar, and they may have come from the same workshop. Both have filigree work and glass studding of the greatest refinement. There is no Christian significance in their decoration of abstract patterns and animal ornament. Their artistic origins are Celtic and relate them to gold objects dating back to the pre-Christian era (before 432) on display in the main exhibit hall. Early Celtic artists followed the shapes and patterns they found in nature—circles, zigzags, and triangles—and saw things as three-dimensional.

Four hundred years after the Tara Brooch and Ardagh Chalice were made, Celtic design is still prevalent in Irish metalwork, such as in the **Shrine of St. Patrick's Bell,** made between 1094 and 1105 to enshrine the relic of St. Patrick known as the Bell of Will, and in the famous **Cross of Cong,** made ca. 1123 to enshrine a relic of the true cross. Neither compares in detail to the earlier Tara Brooch and Ardagh Chalice, but both are in the Irish Celtic tradition of complex ornamentation and animal motifs. A two-sided serpentlike head at the bottom of the shaft of the cross holds the cross in its teeth, allowing it to stand independently from its socket. It is a Celtic monster in a design already hundreds of years old when the cross was made.

A visit to this museum and its glorious treasures gives a quite different perspective to the Dark Ages as a savage time without the refinements and civilizing pleasures of art.

TRINITY COLLEGE LIBRARY

College Green

Hours: Open Mon.–Fri., 10AM–4:45PM; Sat., 10AM–1PM. Free admission.

The history of Trinity College dates back to Queen Elizabeth I, who established it in 1592 on the site of a former Augustinian monastery. Elizabeth thought an English place of higher learning in Dublin would keep her subjects home, away from the influences of Catholic universities on the Continent. Trinity remained the academic home of the Anglo-Irish until 1793, when Catholics were finally admitted. Today Trinity College is nondenominational.

An entrance passageway on College Green across from the Bank of Ireland leads into a cobbled courtyard called Parliament Square. Facing each other are identical templelike buildings, each with four Corinthian pillars, built by Sir William Chambers (1723–96), who, with Robert Adam, was one of the most influential English architects during the second half of the eighteenth century. Ahead is the campanile, and behind that is a row of red buildings known as the Rubrics, the oldest buildings remaining at Trinity (early eighteenth century).

At the right corner of Parliament Square is the somewhat French-looking three-story **Old Library** (1712–32) designed by Thomas Burgh (d. 1730). In its **long room** (at 209 feet in length this room deserves its name) are displayed extraordinary illuminated manuscripts: *The Book of Durrow, The Book of Dimma, The Book of Armagh,* and *The Book of Kells.*

The earliest of the manuscripts, ***The Book of Durrow*** (ca. 670), a copy of the Gospels in the Latin Vulgate, is smaller in page size than other illuminated manuscripts, and its range of colors—dark green, yellow, red, and black (which has now become dark brown)—is more limited. It shows the early custom of the left-hand page, called "carpet" page, being given over to ornamentation in the Celtic spiral style. It also has animal decoration and interlaced bands of Coptic or Mediterranean origin. The use of dots gives color without allowing it to appear too solid.

Why was an abstract, pagan style used in the *Book of Durrow* and in the illuminated manuscripts that succeeded it into the ninth century? Was the style mere decoration or did it say something to medieval readers?

The creators of the *Book of Durrow* were drawing on what they knew and on the objects in their possession. What they knew was from prehistoric and pre-Christian traditions, similar to Germanic and Oriental curvilinear and animal patterns. The objects in their possession were Celtic metalwork, a craft that went as far back as 2000 B.C. (See National Museum, Dublin).

The ancient artists expressed their awareness of the world around them in curving forms, because almost nothing in nature is a straight line. As time went on there was a merging of diverse elements of expression from as far away as Mongolia. Finally, Roman, Greek, Byzantine, Scandinavian, and North African arts played their parts.

While early Christian art was based on pagan motifs—spirals, intertwined animals, interlacing—it was adapted to Christian ideas. Among all the abstractions there is the Christian cross. Early Christian artists seemed to welcome the Celtic practice of merging subject with background. That way they could express the cross intangibly, like the mystical presence of God. The interlacing may represent running water, symbolic of fertility or purification. Interlacing may also serve to imprison biting animals and supernatural beasts—symbols of evil—and thus express the divine orderliness and predictability of Christianity in a disordered and unpredictable world.

The Book of Durrow served as a source for illuminated manuscripts that came after it, both in Ireland and England, such as *The Book of Dimma* (eighth century). This small book, meant to be carried by Irish missionaries who were preaching in Scotland and England, has interlacing and the use of dots that recall the earlier *Book of Durrow*. *The Book of Armagh* (ca. 807) contains the entire New Testament, and is also from this later period. Its black and white drawings of the Evangelistic symbols make it a more simple example.

The monastic artists were the great civilizers of the time. Many came from southern climates to spread the Gospel in northern Europe. They may have believed that their civilizing, Christianizing work would die with them unless they recorded what they knew. Every monk had to devote time to the monastery scriptorium. Monks with talent for illuminated writing were singled out to work in the larger monasteries. During the Viking invasions of the mid-ninth century the portable, concealable books kept Christianity alive until it could come out of hiding and flower.

The Book of Kells (late eighth century)

The *Book of Kells* represents the most sublime achievement of Irish Celtic art and probably the most well known. Originally a single large volume, in 1953 it was rebound into four volumes. There are always two volumes on display—one opened at an illuminated page and the other showing pages of text. The openings are changed regularly.

The *Book of Kells* and other books like it played such an important role in keeping the faith, by serving as a record of the religion when Christianity was threatened with extinction, that they grew to be revered as holy and were thought to have magical healing powers.

The twelve-hundred-year history of the *Book of Kells* is one of precarious survival. It was written and painted in about 800 in a monastery scriptorium still not identified. Some scholars believe its place of origin was Iona off the coast of Scotland. When the monastery there came under seige by Viking invaders in 806, the book was brought to Kells in County Meath for safety. In 1006 it was stolen from the church treasury of Kells and stripped of its gold cover. Two months later it was found wet and discolored, buried under a stone. It turned up in 1621 in the possession of the famous Irish historian, the Protestant bishop elect of Meath, James Ussher. Sometime after 1661 it was brought to Dublin and presented to Trinity College by Henry Jones, a one time scoutmaster in Cromwell's invading forces, later Protestant bishop of Meath.

Various artists worked on the *Book of Kells,* each embellishing it with his own style, but keeping within motifs used in earlier illuminated manuscripts—spirals, interlacing, dots, animals and vegetal decorations—to create an eclectic work. The range of color, the clear and rounded script, and the sense of balance and space on many pages leave no doubt that *The Book of Kells* was meant to be a work of art.

Giraldus Cambrensis, a twelfth-century Welsh scholar, in his *The Topography of Ireland,* had an appropriate statement to make about Irish illuminated manuscripts. Commenting on the *Gospel Book of Kildare,* now lost, Cambrensis wrote:

> If you observe these pages superficially, and in the usual careless manner, you could imagine them to be daubs, rather than careful compositions—expecting to find nothing exquisite, where, in truth, there is nothing which is not exquisite. But if you apply yourself to a more close examination, and are able to penetrate the secrets of the art displayed in these pictures, you will find them so delicate and exquisite, so finely drawn, and the work of interlacing so elaborate (while the colors are so well blended, and still so fresh), that you will be ready to assert that all this is the work of angelic, and not human, skill. The more often and closely I scrutinize them, the more I am inspired, and always find them new, discovering fresh causes for increased admiration.

Outside the Old Library is New Square, site of the **Museum** (1854–57), now the engineering school. It is next to the plaza of the New Library (1961–67).

The museum was designed by two Irishmen, Sir Thomas Deane (1828–99) and Benjamin Woodward (1815–61), but the inspiration for this Victorian masterpiece came from John Ruskin's *The Stones of Venice,* published in 1851. It is a Venetian Renaissance palazzo in a sea of green grass in the center of Dublin. The exterior has round arched windows, a roof with a heavy corbeled cornice, and polycrome marble discs on the facade. Inside the eclecticism of the nineteenth century runs wild in an asymmetrical profusion of columns, arches, and balustrades of varicolored marbles, with twin domes patterned in pinks and blues. Carvings of foliage and animals were executed by the O'Shea brothers of County Cork and an Englishman, a Mr. Roe of Lambeth. Following Ruskinian architectural philosophy, they were given a free hand to create as they wished.

Buildings

Along the north bank of the river Liffey (O'Connell Street side) are two late eighteenth-century neoclassical structures built by **James Gandon** (born London, 1743–1823). The **Custom House** (east of O'Connell Street), with its long south facade facing the river, accented by slightly projecting central and end bays and free-standing and recessed columns, and topped off with a baroque dome supported by a columned drum, is considered Gandon's masterpiece. Further up the river (west of O'Connell Street), Gandon's **Four Courts** building, which serves as the judicial seat of Ireland, also has a dome on top of a columned drum, but here the drum is larger, adding bulk to the central block and the wings on either side. The result is a composition of harmonious scale. Christopher Wren may have been the inspiration for these buildings.

On the south side of the river is the **Bank of Ireland** (built 1728–39), across the street from Trinity College on College Green. Formerly the old Parliament House, it was possibly designed in part by Lord Burlington (1694–1753), a proponent of Palladianism in the British Isles. The Bank of Ireland is the earliest large-scale Palladian public building in all of Britain and Ireland. With its dramatic sweep of Ionic columns surrounding a courtyard it is the grandest building in Dublin.

Within walking distance of the Bank of Ireland, at Merrion Square and Fitzwilliam Street, are examples of Dublin's famous **Georgian red brick row houses.** Though built by private developers in the second half of the eighteenth and the early nineteenth centuries, they are the result of town planning. Their severe wall-like facades are relieved sometimes by wrought-iron balconies and always by brightly colored classic doorways with fan-shaped transoms. The real beauty of these buildings, however, lies in their interiors where rich plasterwork is a feature.

The two ecclestiastical buildings in Dublin of note, and best examples in Ireland of early Gothic architecture, have been Protestant since the Reformation. **Christchurch Cathedral** at the top of Lord Edward Street (near the river Liffey, south side) was begun in 1172; its nave was completed in 1235. Late nineteenth-century restoration saved the structure, but reduced its original parts to the north and south transepts and the interior of the nave. An exterior feature is the Chapterhouse Arch, a covered bridge spanning the street between the cathedral and the Synod Hall. An idea of how the cathedral looked in the twelfth and thirteenth centuries is seen inside in the vaulting of the transepts and the arches of the nave. Of transitional style, between Norman and early English styles, they show the Gothic style of the Normans, with decorations in arches and capitals, but lack the refinement of the early English style. The crypt has impressive vaulting and extends beneath the entire church. For a time in the eighteenth century it served as a meat market. The cathedral is open Tues.–Fri. 9:30AM–12:45PM and 2:15–5PM; Sat. 9:30AM–12:45PM.

Contemporary with Christchurch is St. Patrick's Cathedral (begun in 1190), in the same neighborhood a few blocks to the south. Competing with Christchurch, started about twenty years earlier, the builders of St. Patrick's built their church larger. At 300 feet it is the longest Irish church, the only one that compares in size with churches in England and on the Continent. Like Christchurch, St. Patrick's underwent extensive restoration in the nineteenth century when it was almost completely rebuilt. It is amazing that the spirit of the original work still exists. The interior has a choir in early English style and a lady chapel in decorated Gothic. These parts are like the early construction.

Jonathan Swift (born Dublin 1667, died 1745), the author of *Gulliver's Travels*, was dean of St. Patrick's from 1713 to 1745. His tomb is in the south aisle to the right of the entrance porch. "Stella" (Esther Johnson) is buried nearby. We do not know if they married, but there is no doubt there was a love between them that lasted a lifetime. A reading of Swift's *Journal to Stella*, with its tender passages, tells us this.

St. Patrick's Cathedral is open Mar.–Oct., Mon.–Fri. 9AM–6PM, SAT. 9AM–4:30PM; Nov.–Feb., Mon.–Fri. 9AM–12:30PM and 1:30–6PM, Sat. 9AM–12:30PM and 1:30–4:30PM; admission fee. Choral services weekdays at 9:45AM and 5:45PM, Sun. 11:15AM.

Italy

No other country in the world has as much to offer the spectator of art as does Italy. That should be apparent from the size of this section on Italy relative to the space devoted to other countries. Italy presents the traveler with the greatest achievement in Western art. If it has any drawbacks, it is that almost all of it is Italian, with few great works from other countries. It covers four periods—classical, Christian, Renaissance, and baroque—each of which set a style that the rest of Europe followed. They dominated the artistic sense of the Western world down through the seventeenth century.

It started with ancient Romans, who immortalized in stone their great moments in history and their everyday life. Realizing the great works of Greek sculpture were superior to anything they could produce on their own, Romans copied Greek art faithfully or plundered it. Later, Christianity provided the impetus to the development of Italian art, first based on the Byzantine style, and later on the Romanesque, which the Italians never relinquished, even in the face of the Gothic. Then things began to change. The first great age of Western art, the Renaissance, started in Italy and ushered in modern art. Italian artists became world celebrities sought after by both king and church. At first their art was primarily religious in theme, but this slowly changed as the new spirit encouraged the glorification of man. When the baroque period arrived and artistic expression changed again, the Renaissance spirit proved to be lasting. By the seventeenth century, when Italy seemed no longer to lead the way, it passed on its cultural heritage to others. By that time Italy had made such an achievement in art that we cannot imagine what the world would be like today without some of the earliest developments of art there, and the works of Leonardo, Michelangelo, Brunelleschi, and others who created some of the most enduring masterpieces of all time. No place in the world more fully celebrated—and continues to celebrate—the artistic genius of man.

Arezzo

CHURCH OF SAN FRANCESCO

Piazza San Francesco

Hours: Open daily 12 noon–2:30PM and 7–9:30PM. Free admission.

Piero della Francesca (ca. 1416–92), Umbrian, under Florentine influence

As recently as the beginning of the twentieth century Piero della Francesca was not placed among the immortals of Italian artists, but today his works rank in importance with those painted by Masaccio and Michelangelo.

Piero was born in Sansepolcro, a small town near Arezzo, but in 1439 he visited Florence for a long stay and his technique and style evolved there. He learned from Domenico Veneziano, whom he worked for, and from the paintings he saw done by Masaccio. Thus Piero's paintings have the human grandeur of Masaccio's art and the poetic quality of light that comes from Veneziano. In later life his eyesight failed and he turned to mathematics, which had become his main interest. He wrote a treatise on the practical application of perspective in painting which he dedicated to his protector and patron, Federico da Montefeltro, duke of Urbino, whose portrait he painted in 1465 (Uffizi, Florence). The geometric form and logically constructed space of Piero's paintings are based on his mathematical theories. Piero was one of those who showed the way to the high Renaissance by experimenting with the placement of objects in space to create convincing images of the real world. Piero's pupil was Perugino, who in turn taught Raphael and Luca Signorelli, who influenced Michelangelo.

Scenes from the Legend of the True Cross: choir
After five hundred years some of the frescoes in this cycle are in bad condition, but remain to show Piero's achievement. They were executed between 1452 and 1464 and tell a popular story that was treated often in the figurative arts of the Middle Ages and even of the Renaissance.

The tale starts in the lunette on the right-hand wall. Here Adam, an old man, is dying and asks his son, Seth, to get the oil of mercy promised him by the Angel of Earthly Paradise. The Angel gives Seth instead a branch from the tree that Adam ate fruit of, and instructs him to plant it on Adam's grave, telling him that when it bears fruit his father will be in Heaven. The tree flourishes and is credited with working many miracles. But King Solomon cuts it down and uses it to build a bridge over the river Siloam. On the fresco below the lunette on the right-hand wall, we see the Queen of Sheba journeying to Jerusalem to see King Solomon. Gifted with prophecy, she recognizes the sacred wood, worships it, and tells King Solomon that it is destined to become the Cross of Calvary on which the Son of Man will be crucified. The prophecy holds true, and after the Crucifixion, not shown, the wood is buried, where it remains for two hundred years. The story then continues with the Emperor Constantine, who we see sleeping in the fresco on the window wall. He is faced with an imminent invasion by Maxentius, whose armed hoards are at the gates of Rome. An angel appears in Constantine's sleep, showing him a cross in the sky and telling him that if he will take up this sign he will be victorious. In the lower fresco on the right-hand wall we see Constantine on his white horse holding the cross and Maxentius fleeing from it. Constantine now becomes a Christian and sends his mother, St. Helena, to Jerusalem to recover the True Cross. She finds that a man by the name of Judas is the only one in Jerusalem who knows its hiding place. To make him reveal it, she has Judas placed in a dry well for six days without food until, on the seventh day, he asks to be brought up. We see that scene depicted on the window wall. He leads Helena to the Mount of Calvary where three crosses are dug up: Christ's Cross and the crosses of the two thieves executed with Him. On the left-hand wall, in the middle, below the lunette, we see the crosses unearthed. To distinguish the True Cross from the others we are shown, in the same fresco, the crosses being applied to a youth who had recently died at Jerusalem. As the third cross touches him he rises to life. Then, on the lower fresco on the left-hand wall, we see the continuation of the story where the king of Persians, after conquering Jerusalem, carries off the Cross to his palace, where it decorates his throne. But the Roman emperor Heraclius meets the Persians in battle and defeats them, beheading the king in front of his throne. In the lunette on the left-hand wall the Emperor Heraclius, barefoot and in humble dress, is seen returning the True Cross to Jerusalem by the gate through which Christ carried it out on His shoulders.

This cycle of frescoes shows a concern with basic forms. What Piero sees in everyday life he carefully records on these walls in a logical, clear manner. He has no time to concentrate on the elegance of line and the richness of surface decoration that characterized the works of earlier artists. With his depth of space and volume alone he achieves a representation of the real world—undemonstrative, indifferent to emotion, where even the women are plain looking. This somewhat abstract approach is, however, never devoid of a feeling for man. Piero is in step with Renaissance ideals in his confidence of human capacities. His figures are monumental, with a humanizing influence on the surrounding world. They are calm, confident, and rooted to the earth. No matter how otherworldly the narrative of his scenes may be, Piero combines that unreality with the real.

COMMUNAL PICTURE GALLERY AT SANSEPOLCRO

Via Aggiunti, 65

Hours: Open summer, daily 9:30AM–1PM and 3–6PM; winter, daily 10AM–1PM and 2–5PM. Admission fee.

Piero della Francesca (ca. 1416–92), Umbrian, under Florentine influence
About twenty-three miles from Arezzo is Sansepolcro, the little town where Piero was born and spent most of his life. In 1442 he was elected to the position of town councilor and he held it until his death.

In the Palazzo Communale you can see two of Piero's paintings. The **Polyptych of the Misericordia (The Virgin of Pity)**, room 5, the first work to have been commissioned from Piero, has a gold background in the medieval tradition that lingered on and was imposed on him by the churchmen (it was ordered in 1445 but delivered many years later). It has the glaring contrast of Piero's strongly modeled forms. Also here is *The Resurrection,* which Aldous Huxley called "the greatest painting in the world." There is also a moving *Crucifixion* by Luca Signorelli (ca. 1441–1523).

The Resurrection (late 1450s): room 5
True to his style, Piero has painted Christ, who has risen from His tomb, as a monumental sculptured figure. The only indication we have that movement has taken place is His upraised left foot. It may be surprising that an artist who almost ignores movement would want to paint a Resurrection, but Piero has done so successfully without sacrificing his style. He is so good at giving a static design vital meaning that Christ takes on a superhuman quality, outside time and space; His fixed, wide-open eyes reveal His eternal spiritual power. The soldiers asleep in the foreground form a compact sculptured group (Vasari said that the soldier into whose face we look is a self-portrait of the artist) and their color tones combine with the background's dark earth colors, symbolic of men struggling in earthly darkness while Christ stands out liminous and full of Heavenly light. The trees on the left are barren, while the trees on the right are green, recalling that on His way to Calvary Christ had said, "If they do this in the green tree what will they do in the dry?" meaning, "If they do this to me while I am still alive, what will they do when I am dead?" Thus the trees symbolize the world before and after the Crucifixion and the Resurrection.

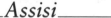

Assisi

CHURCH OF SAN FRANCESCO

Piazza Inferiore di San Francesco

Hours: Open all day in summer; closed 12 noon–2PM in winter. Free admission.

Assisi is the little medieval city of St. Francis (1182–1226), and this great Church dedicated to him is one of the most popular shrines in Italy. It is also one of the richest art galleries in Italy, with thirteenth- and fourteenth-century frescoes covering its walls, making it possible to see, probably better than anywhere else, the transition of Italian art from traditional Byzantine to the pre-Renaissance style.

The church was begun in 1228, the year of St. Francis's canonization and two years after his death. It was probably completed by 1239, although it was not consecrated until 1253. There are actually two churches, one above the other, and an enlarged crypt below the high altar of the lower church. Here the saint's tomb is located, having been uncovered in 1818 after lying hidden for five centuries.

Lower Church
This solemn cruciform church is spanned by huge Roman arches and is dark, low and mysterious. Its cavernous nave is lined with chapels that contain great works of àrt. The first chapel on the left has frescoes with *Scenes from the Life of St. Martin,* by **Simone Martini** (ca. 1284–1344), the Sienese painter. You will find Simone's work here, which dates from about 1328,

less Byzantinesque than most of his other work seen at Siena and in museums.

Many frescoes in the lower church are credited to Giotto, but they are most likely the work of his assistants (Giotto was at one time the director of the art work here). The work of Giotto's teacher, **Cimabue** (ca. 1240–1302), who first took Giotto to Assisi when he was still a young painter in training, is to be found in the right transept. Here is Cimabue's *Madonna Enthroned with Angels and St. Francis*. Though not painted during the saint's lifetime, it is considered a true portrait of St. Francis.

Upper Church

It is difficult to believe that the plan for the upper church was drawn at the same time as the plan for the lower church. The upper church is wholly different, Gothic rather than Romanesque, and is well lit with natural light. Its plan is simple, with a single large nave with no aisles at the sides. It is typical of the great mendicant churches, which needed large open spaces for religious programs that attracted great crowds. Similar to most other Italian versions of the Gothic, it differs from French buildings in its emphasis of the horizontal rather than the vertical. The tall windows of French Gothic cathedrals would be out of place in the hotter climate of Italy, so that the smaller windows at Assisi have large open spaces of empty wall between each of the short load-bearing columns. This space is available for decoration with frescoes, which adds to the impression of horizonality—an un-Gothic characteristic. Thus the nave, choir, and both transepts are covered with frescoes, some of the oldest of which were painted by Cimabue between 1279 and 1296, though the most celebrated frescoes are by Giotto, painted after the turn of the fourteenth century. Unknown painters of the late thirteenth-century Roman School painted the roof. It is believed that some of the work attributed to Cimabue is no doubt from these artists, whose school died early.

Cimabue (ca. 1240–1302), Florentine

Crucifixion (after 1279): on the left wall of the left transept
The finest of Cimabue's frescoes, in such bad condition it is difficult to appreciate, is this *Crucifixion*. The whites have oxidized and turned black with age, but the drawing and the composition of the work is still largely clear. It shows that while Cimabue is the last great Italo-Byzantine painter, he has refined the style with expressive elements that lead to the pre-Renaissance work of his pupil Giotto. Thus in this painting we can see Christ suffering on the Cross with the physical pain of a real person. A great wind seems to have enveloped the scene, no doubt a reference to the earthquake recorded in the Gospels. It sweeps the folds of Christ's loincloth to one side. While the outstretched hands of the figures below emphasize the crucifixion, what we see on the Cross is so expressive and intense that little else is needed.

Giotto di Bondone* (ca. 1267–1337), Florentine

Scenes from the Life of St. Francis (ca. 1302): starting at the wall at the right of the altar, along the nave, and finishing on the left wall

These twenty-eight frescoes below the windows have given rise to one of the most difficult unanswered questions in the history of art. There are no documents that refer to them as being done by Giotto's own hand or by anyone else's. Ghilberti, writing in the fifteenth century, said that Giotto "painted almost all of the lower part," and Vasari, in the sixteenth century, claimed the same thing. However, Vasari makes many erroneous claims of authorship in his writings, and Ghilberti's reference to the "lower part" may simply mean the lower church. That would be incorrect, because these were executed by Giotto's assistants. Even considering the frescoes to be examples of Giotto's early work, done before his superb accomplishment in the Arena Chapel in Padua, they differ from Giotto's style. Some of the compositions of the various scenes seem trivial for Giotto. There is a marked lack of facial expressions, and many faces are in the Byzantine three-quarter view. These and other elements of style and quality that differ from Giotto's known work elsewhere have given rise to doubts regarding the authorship of the work. Today it is dogmatically held by Italian scholars that all but four of the frescoes are by Giotto, with seven by assistants under his influence or in part by his own hand. Foreign scholars reject all of them as being by Giotto, considering them to have been done only under his influence. Whether by Giotto or not, the frescoes of the Poverello are among the most charming and best-loved works of art in Italy.

Here is a listing of the series with reference to those paintings that are considered in Italy to be by Giotto, partially by him, or under his direct influence.

Right wall

No. 1   *St. Francis Honored by a Man in the Market-place:* done in part by Giotto, the two figures at the extreme right were probably done by one of his pupils

The next eighteen pictures, which follow on the right wall and are carried over to the left wall, are by Giotto

No. 2   *St. Francis Gives His Cloak to a Poor Nobleman*
No. 3   *The Vision of the Palace*
No. 4   *The Crucifix Speaks to St. Francis at San Damiano*
No. 5   *St. Francis Renounces His Father*
No. 6   *The Dream of Innocent III*
No. 7   *The Pope Confirms the Franciscan Rule*
No. 8   *Vision of St. Francis Being Taken to Heaven in a Fiery Chariot*
No. 9   *Vision of the Empty Thrones*
No. 10 *Brother Sylvester Drives out the Demons of Arrezo*
No. 11 *Trial by Fire*
No. 12 *The Ecstasy of St. Francis*

No. 13   The Miracle of Greccio

Left wall

No. 14   The Miraculous Spring
No. 15   The Sermon to the Birds
No. 16   The Death of the Knight of Celano
No. 17   St. Francis Preaching before Honorius III
No. 18   St. Francis Appears to St. Anthony
No. 19   St. Francis Receives the Stigmata

Frescoes nos. 20 to 25 are attributed to Giotto's assistants under his direction

No. 20   The Death of St. Francis
No. 21   The Apparition of St. Francis to Brother Augustine and the Bishop of Assisi
No. 22   Hieronymus Convinced of St. Francis' Stigmata
No. 23   The Lamentation of the Poor Clares
No. 24   The Canonization of St. Francis
No. 25   The Apparition of St. Francis to Pope Gregory IX

The eighth group of pictures, nos. 26 to 28, are attributed to the unknown Master of St. Cecilia without Giotto's participation

No. 26   A Wounded Man Cured by the Invocation of St. Francis
No. 27   St. Francis Reviving a Woman
No. 28   Peter of Assisi Liberated by St. Francis

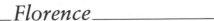

_____ Florence _____

Museums

ACADEMY GALLERY

Via Ricasoli 60

Hours: Open Tues.–Sat., 9AM–2PM; Sun. and holidays, 9AM–1PM. Admission fee.

The collection in this small museum was originally assembled in the eighteenth century for the study of the pupils of the Accademia di Belle Arti. It became considerably enriched from works taken from the suppressed monasteries and confraternites and today contains Florentine paintings of the thirteenth to the eighteenth century including, in Room no. 1, *Madonna Enthroned with Saints and Angels,* by Fra Bartolomeo (1475–1517); in Room no. 2, a *Madonna and Child with St. John,* by Botticelli (1445–1510), and an interesting fifteenth-century frontal painting from a marriage chest *(cassone)* representing a marriage between two Florentines that shows an excellent display of the fashions and customs of the time; and in the Main Hall, sculptures by **Michelangelo,** including his unfinished *Slaves* (ca. 1518), intended for the tomb of Julius II in Rome, his unfinished *St. Matthew* (ca. 1504), designed for the Duomo in Florence, his unfinished *Pieta di Palestrina* (1515–20), from Santa Rosalina, Palestrina, and, literally towering above all, his *David,* the most spectacular statue in Florence and the most famous work of art in the city.

Michelangelo (1475–1564), Florentine

Michelangelo was born in the isolated village of Caprese, a Florentine outpost above the Tiber Valley, where his father was the mayor, but the family moved back to Florence before Michelangelo was one year old. At the age of ten his talent at drawing attracted the attention of Domenico Ghirlandaio, the Florentine artist, but Michelangelo's father resisted the idea of his son becoming an artist. It took Lorenzo de' Medici to convince Michelangelo's father that art was a respectable profession. Thus at the age of thirteen Michelangelo entered the studio of Ghirlandaio, not only to learn to paint but as a wage-earning assistant.

Michelangelo's talents matured quickly and it was not long before he was invited to live in the Medici Palace, where Lorenzo the Magnificent treated him like a son. Surrounded by artists and scholars, Michelangelo learned the rudiments of sculpture from Bertoldo di Giovanni, who had been an assistant to Donatello. Michelangelo considered this the most important part of his training because he was always to consider himself a sculptor first, despite the fact that in the Sistine Chapel frescoes he created, completely by his own hand, some of the greatest works of painting in Europe.

Michelangelo's life with the Medici came to an end with the death of Lorenzo in 1492. His path led to Rome where, in 1498, at the age of twenty-three, he started his first famous *Pietà,* for St. Peter's. Thereafter he spent time in both Rome and Florence working for both the Vatican and the Medici, doing architecture as well as sculpture and painting.

Apart from Michelangelo's artistic skills, if one had to point to any single thing that made his art special it would be his use of the human figure in expressing ideas and emotions. No other artist, with the exception of Leonardo da Vinci, fulfilled that Renaissance ideal as well as Michelangelo.

David (1501–4)

This colossal *David* was created for one of the buttresses of the Duomo of Florence. The story of how Michelangelo chose an old block of marble abandoned by another sculptor is true. The marble had been lying outside the Duomo since the 1460s when, in 1501, Michelangelo decided to use it. Three years later, when Michelangelo completed the statue, the Florentines decided not to place it high above the ground as originally intended. Instead, it was placed in front of the entrance to the Palazzo Vecchio as a symbol of the Florentine Republic. It suffered from some rough treatment outdoors, by man as well as the elements, and in the nineteenth century was moved into the Academy Gallery where it stands today. (The *David* you see in the Piazza della Signoria is a copy).

The popularity of this statue is evident from the crowds that mill around it every day. Its triumphant nudity, its great muscularity and enormous size, glorify humanity in general and human beings in particular. It symbolizes human grandeur and beauty. The Renaissance idea is that man is the brightest, best, and most beautiful creature on earth; the heroic scale of *David* reassures us that this is true. Probably no other statue in Europe expresses that ideal as forcefully as this one.

The *David* was one of the most detailed statues Michelangelo ever did. In contrast to it his **Slaves,** lined up in the hall leading up to the *David,* are in an unfinished state, but no less powerful and expressive. Here the figures are still locked in the marble, but their twisting movements, as if trying to free themselves from their prison of stone, are powerful expressions of slavery. The statues were meant for the unfinished tomb of Pope Julius II in Rome, and one has to wonder if Michelangelo could have been displeased with the abandonment of the project. He must have seen, as we do, that to go further with these statues would not have improved their dramatic appeal. To call them unfinished is to mislabel them.

CONVENT OF SAN MARCO

Piazza San Marco

Hours: Open Tues.–Sat., 9AM–2PM; Sun. and holidays, 9AM–1PM; closed Jan. 1, Easter, May 1, June 2, Aug. 15, and Dec. 25. Free admission.

Angelico, Fra (ca. 1400–55), Florentine
The fifteenth-century Dominican Convent of San Marco is a museum because its most/celebrated tenant, Fra Angelico, and his assistants, painted exquisite frescoes on the walls of the monk's cells and in the public areas.

Fra Angelico was born Guido di Pietro and was trained as a painter before he entered the Dominican order. He eventually became priorate of San Marco in Florence, but his fame during his lifetime was as a painter. A Dominican writer referred to him as "the angelic painter," which is how he got his name.

In 1436 Cosimo de' Medici gave the Convent of San Marco, a former Silvestrine monastery, to the Dominicans, and financed its renovation. Michelozzo (1396–1472) directed the building project, and Fra Angelico was entrusted with decorating the interior. We have at San Marco a situation where an artist lived and worshiped in the building he worked on, so there are few places where you can feel closer to an artist—even one who painted five hundred years ago.

As you go through the chapter house, corridors, and monks' cells, all covered with frescoes done between 1438 and 1445, you will find that Fra Angelico was an artist of the Renaissance. However, because of the time in which he painted, and his own deep religious convictions, he applied the new methods of the Renaissance only to express the traditional religious stories. For example, you will see that he could use perspective without difficulty, but he did not dote on it. It was in the depiction of Christ, the Madonna, the saints, and other Christian figures that he lavished his artistic talents.

Annunciation

This large *Annunciation* is located at the head of the staircase in the upper corridor. It is true to the rules of perspective, but the figures, standing out in full light, seem reluctant to fit into it. There is a contemplative mood. Mary is seen sitting on a rough-hewn stool, in contrast to the classical elegance of the columns and capitals, which consist of four in Corinthian style and four in Ionic style, all in the same portico. Her bare chamber is seen in the background with a small barred window, probably symbolic of St. Antonino's advice to sweep clean the room of one's mind and to distrust the eye, the window of the soul ("evil comes in at the eye"). Fra Angelico's Virgin is worthy of such an ideal. While earthbound, she has a transparent quality about her reflecting the painter's personal mysticism. Beneath this painting is a legend inviting all passersby to say "Hail Mary."

NATIONAL MUSEUM (THE BARGELLO)

Via del Proconsolo 4

Hours: Open Tues.–Sat., 9AM–2PM; Sun. and holidays, 9AM–1PM; closed Jan. 1, Easter, May 1, June 2, Aug. 15, and Dec. 25. Admission fee.

It is ironic that the Bargello is a place where all that is best in mankind is displayed, for at one time it was a place of suffering and death. Its history goes back to the thirteenth century, when it was the residence of the town's magistrate and later of the *podestà*, or head of government (the Bargello is still known as the Palazzo del Podestà). When it became the residence of the *bargello* (police chief) and a jail, its courtyard served as a place for executions announced from its 185-foot bell tower. After the position of bargello was abolished in the nineteenth century, the building was turned into a museum, and the entire structure refurbished. Today, the Bargello is the greatest repository of Florentine sculpture.

Among the Bargello's treasures are the two demonstration **reliefs of the Sacrifice of Isaac** (Salone del Consiglio Generale) by **Brunelleschi** and **Ghiberti**. (For the story of the competition that led to these works see the Baptistery, Florence.) Other works include *Bacchus* (ca. 1497) by **Michelangelo** (1475–1564), a youthful work in which the artist shows his interest in depicting the male nude with a sensuality not seen since antique times (ground floor, room 1); and the small bronze *Hercules and Antaeus* (ca. 1475) by **Antonio Pollaiuolo** (1431–98), a subject this artist depicts at the height of violent struggle with its conflicting tensions and movement (second floor, Sala di Verrocchio).

In addition to the sculpture the Bargello has collections of ceramics, coins, arms and armor, ivories, enamels, and paintings.

Donatello (1386–1466), Florentine

Donatello, a genius of Italian sculpture, came from a branch of the Bardi family (one of the great banking families of Italy), but had a plain upbringing. We first know of him as a student of Ghiberti, but he became independent at an early age, setting up his own studio in 1406. He proceeded to make a name for himself by working for the cathedral of Florence, where some of his early statues have static, Gothic-like qualities he learned from Ghiberti. His work progressed to more dramatic sculptures that emphasized individual character. He created a new imagery in art, universal in its emotional appeal and expressiveness.

David (ca. 1430): first floor, Salone del Consiglio Generale
This *David*, probably the first nude free-standing statue since antiquity, revived, on a large scale, the antique concept of the beauty of the male nude. Yet there is no ancient statue it can be compared with. It is an original work, though we have seen other figures standing in relaxed poses. It has a sensuous surface texture that almost convinces us it is living flesh. The sharply chiseled details of the hair framing the face, and the feathers of Goliath's helmet caressing the right leg, add a touch of contrast that enlivens the figure. As a *David*, symbolic of Christ's heroic triumph over sin and death, one wonders how convincing it was to the Florentines. Its effeminate qualities, such as the richly ornamented leather boots and the pointed hat with laurel, make it more like Eros or Narcissus than David. It is a unique work for Donatello, devoid of the psychological expressionism of his earlier work or the religious fanaticism of his late work.

Verrocchio, Andre del (1435–88), Florentine

David (ca. 1475): second floor, Sala di Verrocchio
This statue of David, somewhat flat because it was meant to be viewed frontally, seems to react to Donatello's *David*. It is less prettified but lacks the strength of Michelangelo's statue of David in the Academy Gallery, whose powerful body convinces us that he is capable of heroic action. It has been suggested that the model for this statue was young Leonardo da Vinci, who as a boy assisted in Verrocchio's workshop in Florence. Leonardo was handsome in his youth and was a homosexual. If this is indeed Leonardo—and there is no proof that it is—it is fitting that he has the same ambiguous smile on his face that he himself would later depict in his greatest paintings.

PITTI PALACE, PALATINE GALLERY

Piazza Pitti

Hours: Open Tues.–Sat., 9AM–2PM; Sun. and holidays, 9AM–1PM; closed Jan. 1, Easter, May 1, June 2, Aug. 15, and Dec. 25. Admission fee.

Though this great palace carries the name of the Pitti family, it was a former residence of the Medicis, whose decendants occupied it until 1919, when it was acquired by the state. The Pitti family were the original builders of it, in the middle of the fifteenth century. The Pittis had competed with the Medicis for power and wealth, but in 1465 financial reversals forced them to reduce their building plans, and in 1549 the Medici Grand Duke Cosimo I acquired the property. In the succeeding centuries the palace was enlarged a number of times and decorated with part of the fabulous Medici art collection; many of the paintings presently on its walls were commissioned by the Medicis directly from the artists in the sixteenth and seventeenth centuries. They are still hung as they were when the Pitti was a private ducal collection seen only by invited guests, without any regard to period, school, or artist, within rooms sumptuously decorated with the grand duke's furniture. That is the charm of the place, and there are few collections in Europe that have such a grand setting. In the Pitti Palace you feel more like a guest of the grand duke than a spectator in a museum.

Lippi, Fra Filippo (ca. 1406–69), Florentine

Madonna and Child (The Pitti Tondo): Sala di Promoteo, room 18
This famous tondo (circular painting) was painted about 1452 for a merchant in Florence. Apart from being one of Lippi's finest panel paintings—it has the sense of space and clarity of composition learned from Masaccio without Masaccio's overwhelming sense of gravity—it is also one of the most important paintings in the history of Quattrocento art, one of the first to eliminate every vestige of the conventional, forbidding Madonna paintings of old, which displayed unreal Madonnas surrounded by equally unreal angels and saints. In Lippi's painting everything is fresh and new and exciting, depicting human joys and fears in heavenly themes. Renaissance painters, such as Botticelli and Domenico Ghirlandaio, were quick to grasp the idea, which had already been accomplished in sculpture by Donatello, Luca della Robbia, and Desiderio da Settignano.

The model for the Madonna is Lippi's mistress, the beautiful nun Lucrezia Buti, whom Lippi also painted in his Uffizi *Madonna and Child* (for the story of Lucrezia Buti and Lippi see Lippi in the Uffizi). She holds a cut pomegranate which has religious meaning; its red color represents the blood of Christ and its seeds the individual souls within the all-encompassing church. In the background are scenes from the life of St. Anne, Mary's mother. On the left, in a fashionable Florentine bedroom, Anne has given birth to Mary; on the right is Joachim descending the steps to tell Anne of the birth of Christ.

Perugino (ca. 1445–1523), Umbrian

Mary Magdalene: Sala di Saturno, room 5
The fame of Perugino is partly attributed to his having been the teacher of Raphael, but he was a master in his own right, as his *Mary Magdalene* shows. His work, and that of other Umbrian painters, such as Pintoricchio (ca. 1454–1513), often display charming Madonnas with peaceful landscapes as backgrounds. But in this painting, probably executed between 1496 and 1500, he has eliminated the sentimentality often associated with his art. In its grace and spiritual nobility the *Mary Magdalene* appears to be more Florentine than Umbrian; at one time it was attributed to Leonardo. You will see in Perugino's *Mary Magdalene* the artistic style that helped develop some of the genius of Raphael.

Raphael* (1483–1520), Florentine (born in Umbria)

The Madonna of the Chair (1515–16): Sala di Saturno, room 5
This Madonna painting is from Raphael's later Roman period. Unlike his earlier paintings on the theme, done in Florence, it does not have a pyramidal composition and an idylic landscape background. It is considered one of the deepest representations of the maternal instinct and the most celebrated of Raphael's Madonnas. It is also one of the finest tondi (circular paintings) created; the figures are so perfectly arranged within the circle that the viewer's eye is immediately drawn to them. The framework of the tondo offers a challenge to Raphael that he seems to enjoy. He positions Mary and the Christ Child in profile in order to make the composition less cluttered. He also brings the circular shape into his composition, suggested by the curvature of the Madonna's right arm and the Child's left arm. This turning of circular planes helps to produce a warm atmosphere enhanced by the lovely Venetian color, perhaps influenced by Titian.

An earlier Madonna and Child painting in the same room, dated about 1504–5, the start of Raphael's Florentine period, called the *Madonna of the Grand Duke (Madonna del Granduca),* because it was a favorite of the Grand Duke Ferdinand III of Lorraine, who purchased it in 1799, was painted when Raphael was beginning to be influenced by Leonardo. While Leonardo's famous pyramidal structure is not yet present, the shading is Leonardesque, even though Raphael makes it lighter. One can see Raphael's genius with geometric forms. Notice how the oval face of the Child is echoed in the oval face of the mother, and how both figures are modeled in rounded forms which, in their muted colors, bring out their gentleness.

The Lady with a Veil (La Velata) (1514–15): Sala di Giove, room 4
As the greatest eclectic of his age, Raphael painted this portrait in the Venetian style, for its superior color technique. So convincing are the color tones in this painting that it would appear Raphael was born into the Venetian School, even though there is no evidence of his ever visiting Venice (no doubt Raphael saw Venetian paintings in Rome brought there in 1511 by Sebastiano del Piombo). The Venetian richness of the painting is evident in the white and gold drapery of the dress, the deep dark eyes and chestnut hair, and the luminous flesh tones that set off the soft glow of the necklace. The painting is extraordinary as a study in white, a most narrow and elusive range of tones.

The sitter may be the famous Fornarina (baker's daughter or wife) recorded by Vasari as one of Raphael's mistresses whom he "loved until death." Raphael used her as a model for many paintings, and this one may have been conceived as a devotional painting of St. Catherine with the original religious references painted out.

In the Pitti's Sala di Saturno, room 5, two earlier portraits, *Agnolo Doni* and his wife *Maddalena Doni,* painted in Florence about 1506, also show Raphael as a great portraitist. They both have traces of the artist's recent Umbrian manner, especially in the floating hair of Agnolo Doni, which reminds one of something Perugino would have done. However, the Florentine style, just mastered by Raphael, is more in evidence and once again there is a debt to Leonardo; *Maddalena Doni* has certainly been inspired by the Mona Lisa. Both sitters look directly at the viewer in a straightforward way. They have a sense of proportion; the *Maddalena Doni's* round face accords perfectly with her whole figure.

Titian* (ca. 1487–1576), Venetian

The Concert: Sala di Venere, room 1
Titian, who had been an assistant to Giorgione, remained under the spell of the master of Castelfranco long after his death in 1510. This painting, dating to 1513–15, had for many years been attributed to Giorgione. The dreamy spirituality of the face of the Augustinian friar playing the harpsichord does look like the work of Giorgione, though the sensuousness of the face and the overall vigorous quality of the painting, expressed in the emphasis on structural forms, as in the tense, bony fingers of the friar, and in his taut neck and well defined jaw, are more like Titian's work than Giorgione's. Whether from the hand of Titian or Giorgione, these three figures, who make up a group portrait of musicians, emit strong psychological vibrations difficult for us to pin down but nevertheless fascinating.

Portrait of a Woman ("La Bella"): Sala di Venere, room 1
Here, in one of the finest examples of Titian's portraiture, is a clear explanation why the princes of Europe competed for his work. This one was in the collection of the duke of Urbino. It has been suggested that the woman in it is the Duchess Eleonora of Urbino, the duke's wife, whose features can also clearly be recognized in Titian's famous nude, *Venus of Urbino,* now in the Uffizi. It is more likely that the sitter is an unknown courtesan of the duke of Urbino who served as Titian's model several times. Whoever she may be in this painting, she has been traditionally known as "La Bella" for the beauty of her face. More beautiful than her face is the richness of detail, color, and texture typical of the style Titian used for court portraiture. In the magnificent gown Titian exhibits the whole range of his art, combining color, form, and light into an indissoluble whole. Paintings like this set a standard by which other portraits were judged, and its depiction of a three-quarter-length figure became popular within a short time after it was painted, about 1536–37.

Portrait of a Man ("Portrait of an Englishman"): Sala di Apollo, room 2
This painting, done between 1540 and 1545, came to be known as a *"Portrait of an Englishman"* because it was listed in the old inventories as a portrait of the duke of Norfolk. However, it is probably Ippolito Riminaldi, secretary to the duke of Ferrara, if we are to believe a portrait of that gentleman, in the Academy of St. Luke in Rome, not by Titian. In any case, our uncertainty of the sitter's identity takes nothing from the enjoyment of the work. It is one of Titian's best portraits out of a total of about two hundred. It has his knack of capturing a face at its most sensitive moment, when nature is revealed, here with a touch of nobility that made Titian popular

with the courts of Europe. The light vibration in the sitter's face and hands, as the rest of the body emerges from the dim background and the eyes, which communicate directly with the viewer, give this portrait a sense of drama and a vital character that are captivating.

Back in room 1 is a portrait of *Pietro Aretino* (ca. 1546), the slanderer, who, oddly enough, was a good friend of Titian's. His pamphleteering services could be bought by anyone. It is said that he died in 1566 after an uncontrollable fit of laughter.

Mary Magdalene: Sala di Apollo, room 2
This painting, like many others by Titian at the Pitti, came to the Medici collection from Urbino in the seventeenth century as part of a great number of paintings inherited by Ferdinand II's wife, Vittoria, the granddaughter of the last duke of Urbino. It is one of the paintings Titian did for the duke of Urbino between 1530–40 when he and the duke were close friends. As an example of Titian's mature work, it is bold and spontaneous with a rich warmth that is striking. No one has ever given Mary Magdalene more luxurious hair; as a nude this figure is as voluptous as Titian's famous Venus paintings.

UFFIZI GALLERY

Piazzale degli Uffizi, 6

Hours: Open Tues.–Sat., 9AM–2PM; Sun. and holidays, 9AM–1PM; closed Jan. 1, Easter, May 1, June 2, Aug., 15, and Dec. 25. Admission fee.

The Uffizi contains the greatest collection of paintings in Italy and the largest and best collection of Renaissance paintings in the world. These include many familiar masterpieces.

Its building, next to the Palazzo Vecchio, was commissioned in the late 16th century by Grand Duke Cosimo I de' Medici and built by Giorgio Vasari. Its original use was to accommodate the offices *(uffizi)* of the Medici government of Florence, which is why it is connected to the Palazzo Vecchio on one side and, by way of the Ponte Vecchio, to the Pitti Palace on the other side. Its conversion into a public museum started as early as the eighteenth century and it was a fully functioning museum by 1795.

Index to the Rooms of the Uffizi Gallery

Artists mentioned below have works referred to in the text that follows. You will find these works listed under the names of the artists, arranged alphabetically.

Room 2	Giotto
Room 3	Martini
Rooms 5–6	Gentile da Fabriano
Room 7	Piero della Francesca, Uccello
Room 8	Lippi

Rooms 10–14	Botticelli, van der Goes, van der Weyden
Room 15	Leonardo da Vinci
Room 20	Dürer
Room 21	Bellini
Room 25	Michelangelo
Room 26	Raphael, Sarto
Room 28	Titian
Room 41	Rubens
Room 43	Caravaggio
Room 44	Rembrandt

Bellini, Giovanni* (ca. 1430–1516), Venetian

Sacred Allegory (ca. 1490): room 21
You can appreciate this small panel for its color alone. Color unites the detached objects and figures with the surrounding space and creates a whole with a dreamlike beauty. The fascination of this painting lies in what it means, a problem never fully explained. Its mysterious feeling evokes the mood of Giorgione, a student at Bellini's studio, to whom this painting had been attributed until the late nineteenth century.

One explanation calls the painting an allegory of the church with the Madonna enthroned on the left and St. Catherine of Alexandria and St. Catherine of Sienna at each side of her. Behind the railing, as though guarding the enclosure, are St. Paul with a sword and St. Peter near the open gate (St. Paul's attribute is a sword, with which he was executed, and he is often paired with St. Peter, who has the keys to the gates of Heaven). In the center is the Tree of Life from which the children, representing human souls, pick fruit. To the right stand St. Job and St. Sebastian, the two plague saints. Beyond the railing stretches the most fantastic landscape to be found in Bellini's work probably symbolic of the world and its problems. The centaur on the right represents vicious inclination, while the hermit in his cell indicates a refuge from the temptations of an evil world.

If this is a religious picture, whether or not the explanation above is a valid one, it is unique for its unorthodox composition, completely out of the realm of accepted fifteenth-century religious painting.

Botticelli, Sandro (1445–1510), Florentine
Botticelli was forgotten for centuries and only rediscovered by English artists in the nineteenth century. He had been trained by Fra Filippo Lippi and had mastered his teacher's soft style so that when Lorenzo de' Medici encouraged the painting of nonreligious themes based on ancient history, mythology, and philosophy, Botticelli's training—with his own style, which added a lean vigor to Lippi's art—was a perfect background for painting the pictures the Medici most admired. That style was best expressed in Botticelli's *Primavera (Spring)* and *Birth of Venus,* today the most popular paintings in the Uffizi.

Primavera (ca. 1478): rooms 10–14
What could be more enchanting than an allegory of Spring drawn from the ancient Latin authors. Horace tells how the three Graces, dressed in trans-

parent garments, danced before Mercury (the man with the upraised arm on the extreme left, who has been identified as Giuliano de' Medici), as Spring's arrival, shown in the center as a pregnant Venus symbolizing nature's fruitfulness, is preceeded by Flora, the goddess of flowers blown forward by the West Wind as she metamorphoses into the flower-clad goddess on the left. To go with such a refined, unreal world, into which the Medicis probably enjoyed escaping to forget their daily troubles, there is a virtuosity of line that adds to the movement of the composition, from the West Wind on the right to the vibrancy of Flora, then to the quiet Venus who continues it with her outstretched hand, then to the curves of the three Graces, only to be stopped by the masculine Mercury.

Birth of Venus (ca. 1482): rooms 10–14
The *Primavera* was done for Lorenzo di Pierfrancesco de' Medici, second cousin to Lorenzo the Magnificent. It hung in his villa at Castello along with the *Birth of Venus*. Vasari saw them there together in the sixteenth century. That is why the movement in the *Birth of Venus* is reversed, since the pictures were probably intended to hang on opposite walls of the same room.

As in the *Primavera* the subject of the *Birth of Venus* is inspired by mythology, but contemporized during Botticelli's time by a poem written by one of the humanists in Lorenzo's circle. According to the poem, Venus was born of the sea. Botticelli shows her being carried across the water in a shell propelled by the winds on the left. A maiden on the right awaits her arrival with a garment to cover her nudity. This was revolutionary, personal painting for its time, because nudity had only been tolerated when applied to Adam and Eve or a crucified Christ. Botticelli's nude goddess, who gracefully covers her nakedness with her hands and her golden hair, has no religious purpose and is meant only to re-create the impression of an ideal classical statue of an early Greek or Roman model. Like the *Primavera,* it is a masterpiece of line and movement. Botticelli has disregarded the Florentine interest in mass to emphasize his subtle linear pattern. We surrender to it emotionally, without intellectual concern.

Caravaggio* (1573–1610), Italian

Youthful Bacchus: room 43
This painting is among the first done by Caravaggio in Rome after he arrived there in 1589. Some scholars consider it to be a self-portrait. With the bedsheet draped over one shoulder of the figure, it also seems imitative of ancient Roman statues of pagan deities. Though Caravaggio was young when he painted this picture (about sixteen), and had not yet developed the dramatic style that was to follow, the work shows he was already a naturalist and an accomplished painter of the still life. Without the basket of fruit this painting would not be the masterpiece it is.

The *Sacrifice of Isaac,* in the same room, has a landscape in its background unusual in Caravaggio's work. However, this painting may not be authentic.

Dürer, Albrecht* (1471–1528), German

Adoration of the Magi (1504): room 20

If ever there was a painting by Dürer that reveals how well he combined his Northern style with the Italian Renaissance, it is this central panel from an altarpiece, the wings of which are dispersed in German museums. It has the detail and emotional intensity of the North, which befits Dürer's main occupation of engraver. Dark outlines drawn with the brush are filled in with brilliant colors of red, blue, and green, which give it the gemlike quality we are accustomed to seeing in Flemish painting. While these elements make it more alive and flowing than most Italian works, it becomes a masterpiece in its use of the Renaissance idea of large-scale geometrical arrangement—in this case a diagonal, like the composition in Leonardo's famous painting on the same theme in the Uffizi. The largeness of the conception and grandeur of the figures suggest a new spirit in the Northern schools. Dürer's art and influence carry it as far as the Netherlands.

Gentile da Fabriano (ca. 1370–1428), Italian

Adoration of the Magi (Strozzi Altarpiece): Rooms 5–6

This altarpiece, done for Palla Strozzi, one of the most powerful men in Florence, was completed in 1423 and is signed by the artist. It was placed in the sacristy of the church of Santa Trinità in Florence where it remained until the early nineteenth century.

Gentile was one of the leading painters of the international style, which in this work bursts forth in all of its unreal splendor, courtly pomp, and fairy-tale elegance. The altarpiece teams with so much life and color that the story it is supposed to tell is almost lost. Yet this picture is not merely a masterpiece of decorative painting; there is concern with modeling and perspective. Look at the rounded head of the figure to the right of the third king, and the foreshortened figure who is taking off the king's golden spurs. When we remember that Masaccio was to paint his famous frescoes in the church of the Carmine in 1424, one year after Gentile completed this Adoration, they are remarkable figures for these times. In the predella scenes at the bottom, for the first time in Italian painting there is a real sky in the background. It has its own source of light within the picture, casting shadows and acting on objects in a natural way. Gentile is also the first Italian painter, as far as we know, to paint night scenes, and to adopt the atmospheric discoveries that Donatello made in sculpture, a medium far ahead of painting at this time. This is not to say that Gentile da Fabriano made a contribution to Renaissance art like those of Masaccio and Piero della Francesca. Gentile remained one of the last and best of the international Gothic painters.

Giotto di Bondone* (ca. 1267–1337), Florentine

Madonna Enthroned (ca. 1310): room 2

It is convenient to compare this altarpiece by Giotto with a similar altarpiece in the same room, depicting the *Virgin and Child,* by his teacher, Cimabue (ca. 1240–1302). Giotto has been called the founder of Renaissance painting even by his contemporaries. Boccaccio (1313–75), the poet, referred to him as one who resuscitated painting after it had been "in the grave" for centuries.

Boccaccio was criticizing the Italo-Byzantine style dominant during Giotto's time, reflected in the altarpiece by Cimabue. This style derives from the early mosaicists and is a carryover from the Eastern or Greek culture. That is a hieratic, formal, decorative, linear, two–dimensional style with gold-leaf backgrounds.

Giotto's work, while retaining elements of the *maniera byzantina*, departs from it with innovations that lead to the Renaissance. The Virgin has become a more real, stately figure with a face painted from a living model. She sits on a real throne and is holding a real baby. The gold background is still there, but the figures in front of it are three-dimensional forms powerfully modeled by contrasting light and shade. Compare the garments worn by Giotto's *Madonna and Child* with those worn by the same figures in Cimabue's work. Giotto is aware that there is a body beneath the garments and uses the folds of the drapery to reveal bodily forms, whereas Cimabue ignores this realistic approach. Greater differences are found in the kneeling angels in the foreground of Giotto's painting. They clearly occupy the space between the throne and the spectator, in contrast to the stylized, oddly placed prophets in Cimabue's painting. Finally, while the old symmetrical arrangement of the side figure is still maintained in Giotto's work, and the saints are smaller than the Madonna, the composition is enhanced by an illusion of depth achieved by the way these figures overlap each other. The new vision that Giotto achieves in this altarpiece and in his frescoes elsewhere not only narrates but represents, and sets the pace for painting in the West for the coming five hundred years.

Goes, Hugo van der* (ca. 1440–82), Flemish

Portinari Altarpiece: rooms 10–14

When this altarpiece was painted in 1476–78 and put on display in Florence (it was installed in the church of the hospital of Santa Maria Nuova in about 1483, and transferred to the Uffizi in 1897), it immediately became famous. Tommaso Portinari, who commissioned it, was a wealthy banker and an agent of the Medici living in Bruges.

Executed with precision, superior draftsmanship, and use of the oil technique, the van der Goes triptych had all the characteristics of the Flemish School that impressed the Italians, plus one other—it was the largest Flemish painting ever seen in Italy. It proved that northern minuteness of detail—a kind not seen in Italian painting—could coexist with Italian monumental scale. Notice the still life of flowers in the foreground, symbols of Mary and her future sorrows. The sheaf of wheat signifies Bethlehem, and the harp in the tympanum of the Romanesque church in the background indicates that Mary and the Child stem from the house of David.

Of significance also is the realistic detail of the three shepherds and the position Hugo gives to these lowly rustic types. Prior to the *Portinari Altar-*

piece these characters were generally placed discreetly in the background, but here, in keeping with the Flemish style of treating a sacred scene in the context of everyday reality, they have been made a major part of the picture. To the Florentines this seemed to dramatize the event.

Notice also that Hugo makes use of spatial distortion in the scale between the figures. Their relative sizes are based not on the laws of perspective but on their importance in the composition. Mary, Joseph, and the shepherds in the central panel are placed in the middle ground and are larger than the angels around them. In the left panel Tommaso Portinari and his sons are smaller than St. Anthony the Hermit, on the left, and St. Thomas, standing behind Portinari holding a lance. Similarly, in the right panel, St. Margaret, in red, and St. Mary Magdalene, with her jar of ointment, loom larger than Portinari's wife and daughter. This technique, Gothic in origin, is handled by Hugo with a sense of imagination.

Leonardo da Vinci* (1452–1519), Florentine

Adoration of the Magi (1481–83): room 15
This unfinished picture is Leonardo's first Florentine masterpiece. It was commissioned by the monks of a now-vanished monastery near Florence who had to order another from Filippino Lippi when Leonardo put the painting aside to join the glittering court of Ludovico Sforza in Milan. Even if it had been finished it is possible that the monks would not have appreciated its lack of concern with traditional religious symbols that a work intended for public devotion was expected to have. It is more of a study in group psychology and physical action than a religious picture, different from the customary joyful, calm, static Adoration paintings of the fifteenth century. It anticipates all that Leonardo was to accomplish in composition, light, movement, and the human type.

What appears at first as chaos is actually a careful composition of light and shade. In the center are the brightly lit Virgin and Child. Around them figures sway in adoration as though drawn by an electrical force. Their phantomlike forms emerge out of the deep shadow, some with dark cavities where eyes and mouths should be, reminding us of Leonardo's unfinished *St. Jerome* at the Vatican Picture Gallery in Rome. Hands reach heavenward and some faces bear that blind look of wonderment common to religious ecstasy. This agitation is countered by the calm of Virgin and Child and the two contemplative figures on either side of the picture. One, a young man, represents the beauty of youth, and the other, an older man, represents aged wisdom. The agitation is carried into the background where we see prancing horses and active humans, but they too are countered by solid architectural forms and the surrounding landscape. Though an unfinished picture, the chiaroscuro and the psychological relationships between the figures, arranged in a pyramidal composition, are again indications of what is to come from Leonardo.

The Uffizi also displays a charming *Annunciation* (room 15), an earlier work (1472) painted partly by Leonardo when he was a member of Verrocchio's workshop in Florence. Leonardo's touch can be discerned in the kneeling angel and in some of the elements of the landscape.

Lippi, Fra Filippo (ca. 1406–69), Florentine

Madonna and Child with Two Angels (ca. 1455–60): room 8
Fra Filippo Lippi started in life as an orphan, having lost both of his parents before he was three years old. A poor aunt tried in vain to care for him. Failing in this, she persuaded the fathers of the Carmelite monastery in the neighborhood to take him in when he was only eight years old. Here he grew up, robbed of a normal childhood and, as it turned out, far from suited temperamentally to lead the life of a monk. On the contrary, he was destined to become an artist. When he came in contact with Masaccio, who was at work on the Brancacci Chapel in Santa Maria del Carmine (see Santa Maria del Carmine, Florence), he decided to become a painter, and was probably trained by the master himself.

As an artist Lippi was eminently successful and obtained the patronage of the Medici. His career as a monk came to an end when, while serving as a chaplain in a Carmelite convent in Prato, he ran away with Lucrezia Buti, a beautiful young nun. In 1457, Lucrezia gave birth to his child, Filippino, who became the famous painter Filippino Lippi (1457–1504). Filippo married Lucrezia in 1461, and it is her portrait that you see in this painting (she is also the Madonna in the Pitti Tondo)

Lucrezia is one of the most beautiful Madonnas ever painted. Fashionably coifed, her hair in artful disarray, with a linen veil and pearls, she is shown as a young Medici beauty. Her sense of solemnity is in her modestly downcast eyes and her hands clasped in prayer. Religiosity is also suggested in the landscape seen through the windows in the background—the seashore may be symbolic of Mary as the "Star of the Sea and Port of Our Salvation," and the rocks refer to the Virgin birth from the vision of Daniel, who saw a stone fall from a mountain, smash an idol, and then grow to become a mountain that filled the entire earth. All this is countered by the fat, healthy baby held by an angel who looks at us with a far-from-angelic grin. The pleasant realism of the painting is in keeping with the humanizing ideas of the time, and with the character of Filippo Lippi himself, who was more attuned to the present life than to the pursuit of the next.

Coronation of the Virgin: room 8
This richly detailed panel, executed for the high altar of St. Ambrogio between 1441 and 1447, is filled with more figures than any other painting by Filippo Lippi. He may have considered it his masterpiece, since he painted his portrait into it—he is the monk on the left resting his chin on his hand (in the past Lippi was considered erroneously to be the older man dressed in blue—actually a portrait of the donor—kneeling in prayer on the right). Lippi's casual, almost vulgar looks bespeak a pleasure-loving temperament. Apart from the center of the picture, where God is crowning the Virgin— both represented larger than the other figures—the painting has numerous

figures whose looks have no spiritual significance. The female figure on the right, in front of two little children, is one of them. She is supposed to be a saint, but is shown as a Florentine lady dressed in her best clothing and, typical of Lippi, with a stylish hairdo. She takes her place with other saints in the foreground, but this center group reminds one more of luxury, sensual love, and profane beauty than of religious spirituality, reflecting Lippi's need to combine heavenly happiness with earthly happiness, and his disinclination to reject materiality from his paintings. Even the numerous figures of angels, holding white lilies, symbolizing the purity of the Virgin, have nothing angelic about them. They wear pagan-looking wreaths of roses in their hair instead of conventional aureolas around their heads. The only figures that evoke fifteenth-century religious sentiment are St. Ambrose, standing on the extreme left, and St. John, on the extreme right, who is dressed in camel's hair fabrics and holds the Cross in one hand. This painting turned out to be a very popular work, bringing Lippi more commissions and increasing his reputation as one of the best painters in Florence.

Martini, Simone (ca. 1284–1344), Sienese

Annunciation (1333): room 3
It is ironical that one of the finest works of Sienese art should be a treasure of the Uffizi in Florence. The two cities, Siena and Florence, were competitors in all things, including art, which differed greatly; Sienese painting was conservative and highly religious, holding to the medievalism of the Italo-Byzantine tradition into the fifteenth century, while Florentine art tended toward the rational and critical attitudes that led to the Renaissance.

This painting by Martini (the two saints on the sides are attributed to his brother-in-law, Lippo Memmi) is one of the most sophisticated examples of Siena's mystical art. It is typical of the style that the entire panel is painted in gold leaf, which adds to its brilliance. It is unique for its expression of movement, not ordinarily found in the two-dimensional patterns of the Sienese School. Notice the arrival of the angel Gabriel, one of the most refined figures ever painted in Sienese art, whose plaid cloak floats in the breeze of his previous movement. He has come to announce to Mary, whose purity is symbolized by the vase of white lilies in the center, that she will bear the Son of God: "Greetings most favored one! The Lord is with you" (Luke 1:28). Movement is also expressed in the Virgin's Oriental-like undulation of line as she tremulously shrinks at hearing the news.

Martini deliberately painted this altarpiece, the first we know of completely devoted to the Annunciation, with a northern Gothic design and feeling, a style popular during his time, although it had not penetrated his native Siena to any great degree. He has abandoned the clean-cut shape of Sienese paintings and has emphasized the Gothic in an elaborate construction of pointed arches. True to his conservative training, he does not go over completely to the Gothic style, but he blends the Sienese-Byzantine tradition with the French flamboyant international Gothic to create a new sense of refinement.

Michelangelo* (1475–1564), Florentine

The Doni Madonna (ca. 1503): room 25
This painting was done for Angelo Doni, a Florentine weaver, to celebrate his marriage to Maddalena Strozzi of the banking family. These two are immortalized in portraits painted of them later by Raphael that now hang in the Pitti Palace. According to Vasari, Doni, who was tight with his money, at first tried to pay Michelangelo less than the agreed sum. But where Doni may have been successful in pressuring other artists to accept less, Michelangelo was of a different temperament, and Doni ended up paying double.

As for the tondo (round painting) itself, it is not the most admired of Michelangelo's paintings—the inharmonious colors of pink and orange have disturbed viewers and so has the cold, strained sculpturesque quality of the central figures—but anything from Michelangelo is of importance, especially when it is his only preserved panel painting. Look at Michelangelo's brilliant, original, tightly coiled composition, whose round shapes in the holy figures in the front, and the perimeter of the panel itself, are ingeniously stabilized by the horizontal line of figures in the background, foreshadowing the nude figures of the ceiling of the Sistine Chapel. A symbolism gives meaning to the picture, something viewers have struggled with for a long time.

The nude youths in the background, despite their reminder of classical antiquity, probably represent humanity before God gave the Law to Moses, as the holy family, Christ, Mary, and Joseph, represent humanity under the Law. The dry font, in which the youths are posed, where an infant John the Baptist looks out toward Christ, reminds us of the coming baptism in which the nude figures will be united with the Christ Child who wears a headband, the ancient symbol of victory. The white cloth the youths seem to be spreading resembles the bands in the entombment that wrapped the dead body of Christ. Additional Christian symbolism abounds in the holy figures in the front: Mary and Joseph appear to be giving the Child as a gift to humanity (this is a play on the name "Doni," which means "gifts" in Italian), and the position of the Christ Child above His mother may suggest the descent from the Cross, or the prophecy of the Virgin birth in Lamentations, "The Lord hath trodden the virgin, the daughter of Judah, as in a winepress." The distant mountains on the right symbolize the mountain of Daniel's vision in which a stone fell and filled all the earth—a prophecy of the Virgin birth. The water on the left suggests the Virgin's titles as the Star of the Sea and the Port of Salvation.

The most interesting symbol in the painting is probably the most delicate—the flower rising alone in the middle ground, silhouetted against the stone enclosing the dry font. It recalls Isaiah's prophecy of the Virgin birth, "For he shall grow up before him as a tender plant, and as a root out of a dry ground."

Piero della Francesca* (ca. 1416–92), Umbrian, under Florentine influence

Federico da Montefeltro, Duke of Urbino, and His Wife, Battista Sforza
(ca. 1465): room 7

The duke of Urbino was a scholarly man who surrounded himself with artists, philosphers, and poets. Piero della Francesca dedicated his own treatise on mathematical perspective to him. He was a military leader whose deformed profile resulted from the blow of a sword in a tournament that cost him the bridge of his nose and his right eye. Piero painted the duke and his wife in profile not only because it was stylish, and a convenient way to hide the Duke's blind right eye, but also to create an official portrait in the tradition of medal design, to call attention to the commemorative nature of the picture. The profile portrait does not hamper Piero's solid style. He is still able to render his figures in a realistic, rounded mass with an idealized landscape in the background.

On the back of the diptych are delightful scenes of the duke and his wife each riding on a triumphal car symbolizing their fame and virtues. With the duke is a Winged Victory and the four Cardinal Virtues: Justice, Prudence, Fortitude, and Temperance. Battista Sforza's car, pulled by unicorns symbolizing chastity, is attended by the Theological Virtues: Faith, Hope, and Charity. The total effect is so clear and sparkling that one wonders if Piero had come in contact with Jan van Eyck or Rogier van der Weyden of Flanders.

Raphael (1483–1520), Florentine (born in Umbria)
In many ways the life and career of Raphael, though short (he died at the age of thirty-seven), is the quintessence of the Renaissance. Of all the great artists of that period he is the most self-confident and his art, an assimilation of the best of the new, the most sublime. Like the Renaissance itself, he was a phenomenal success and lived more like a prince than an artist. Once he left his provincial Umbrian home of Urbino, where he was trained by his father, a local painter, and by Perugino, the Umbrian master, and went to Florence, he digested the work of Leonardo and Fra Bartolomeo. There he had a meteoric rise that led to Rome and the ultimate status of favorite of the Renaissance popes. After the death of Bramante he was given the position of architect of St. Peter's even though his experience with architecture was meager in comparison to that of other men.

His first success in Florence came with a series of Madonna paintings executed between 1504 and 1508. They are probably what he is best known for today, and they made him famous because they were the kind of paintings the patrons of his time wanted to see: a compromise between the classical past and the Christian present. Their pyramidal compositions, borrowed from Leonardo, created a Renaissance monumentality without Leonardo's elaborate, problem-creating designs. They have always been admired for their completeness and serenity, perhaps a reflection of the artist's personality.

While Raphael set a standard with his Madonna paintings, he was also a superb portraitist with an uncanny power to portray the characters of his subjects. This was especially so when he painted someone he felt close to, such as Baldassare Castiglione, the author of the *Book of the Courtier* (portrait in the Louvre, Paris). Basically all of Raphael's portraits display an extraordinary sympathy and affection for his sitters.

At the Vatican in Rome, where Raphael did a series of frescoes for Pope Julius II, he executed his greatest and most intellectual work. Nowhere is there a greater harmony of content through a balance of real and idealized elements. The frescoes at the Vatican show that Raphael understood what Renaissance artists were striving to realize throughout the fifteenth century.

Madonna of the Goldfinch (ca. 1506): room 26

This is one of Raphael's most admired Madonna paintings, and is also typical of Raphael's famous pyramidal compositions. The three figures are enclosed within a triangle (derived from Leonardo), the basis for the classical monumentality of the scene. Trace the outline of the triangle starting at the right foot of the curly headed St. John, proceeding upward to the Virgin's head and down again along her left side. Notice how the figures within the triangle are related to its sides in a succession of lines running almost parallel to those of the Virgin. For example, the infant Christ's left side is parallel to the Virgin's left arm and leg, and St. John's left leg is parallel to her right leg; his right back and lower right leg are parallel to her right arm. All this helps to create a stable composition. But the Virgin's pose is even more telling, for while the upper part of her body faces her pointed left foot, strengthening the left side of the triangle, the turn of her head and the direction of her gaze downward toward St. John (the patron saint of Florence) consolidates the right side of the triangle. The Madonna is a noble idealization of womanhood, with a shapely figure, a beautiful face, and children who are real, healthy babies any mother would be proud of. With its subdued color and setting within a peaceful Umbrian landscape is a quiet scene considered one of the most sublime representations of the Madonna and Child in the history of art.

Portrait of Leo X with Two Cardinals (ca. 1518): room 26

This triple portrait is from Raphael's mature period in Rome, and is a masterpiece in coloring, texture, and detail. The pope is shown holding a gold-framed magnifying glass similar to one Raphael must have used to paint the tiny detail of the illuminated manuscript on the table and the classical vine scrolls on the bell. All three men are Medicis, the most powerful family in Italy at the time. To the left of the pope is his cousin, Giulio de' Medici, son of the murdered Giuliano and subsequently Pope Clement VII; to the right of Leo is his cousin Cardinal Luigi de' Rossi. All of their faces are illuminated by the cross-light that is part of the X-shape composition. One source of the light is seen in the reflection of the window in the polished brass sphere on the chair back, which shows a distorted reflection of the room and a hint of the figure of Raphael painting the scene. It reminds one of the *Arnolfini Marriage* by Jan van Eyck with its famous convex mirror in the background, and urges us to remember that Raphel came in contact with Flemish painting during his early training at the court of Urbino. Yet Flemish detail and striking color do not overwhelm Raphael's monumental structure and his reliance on form. Even the obscured architecture in the background adds to the permanent aspect of the figures, especially Leo, whose hulking presence dominates the picture. His fleshy cheeks imply that he loves good food and drink as much as he loves his manuscripts.

Rembrandt* (1606–69), Dutch

Portrait of the Artist as a Young Man and Portrait of the Artist as an Old Man (two paintings): room 44

No famous painter has ever left more portraits of himself than Rembrandt. They number over one hundred and encompass his entire life—a virtual autobiography in art. They all differ from one another in pose and psychological content. In the Portrait of the Artist as a Young Man (Rembrandt is about twenty-eight years old), where he has dressed himself up in a metal collar and gold chain, we see his taste for the masquerade. Notice the extraordinary glow of light shining on the hard collar to emphasize the softness of flesh above it. In the Portrait of the Artist as an Old Man (dated about 1664), painted when he is about fifty-nine years old, after his brief period of prosperity has come and gone and his life now is one of disappointment, and bankruptcy, his appearance is that of a mournful, antiheroic character who is not giving an inch—even though he has been rejected as an artist by the burghers of Holland. He has the look of a man who has seen the worst, survived it, and will continue to struggle, certain that posterity will vindicate him.

Rubens, Peter Paul* (1577–1640), Flemish

Portrait of Isabella Brant: room 41

This portrait of Rubens's first wife, whom he married in 1609, was painted not long before she died in 1626 at the age of thirty-five. Her keen, almond-shaped eyes and kindly, intelligent face, with fine lips that extend upward into charming dimples, point to a vivacious personality we know Rubens adored. His eulogies of her make it clear that she was a perfect companion. Her death interrupted his work for four years.

Sarto, Andrea del (1486–1530), Florentine

Madonna of the Harpies (1517): room 26

Andrea del Sarto is one of the best of the painters who came into maturity after the high Renaissance style of Leonardo, Michelangelo, and Raphael had already been established. He was not affected by the mannerist crisis of the 1520s, but continued the tradition of the older masters. His Madonna of the Harpies, named for the harpies that adorn the pedestal on which the Madonna and Child are placed (their role is to lead souls to Heaven), has the monumentality of Fra Bartolomeo, the sculptural qualities of Michelangelo, and some figures borrowed from Raphael. This does not mean that Andrea del Sarto's work is devoid of originality. We have not seen such a charming infant Christ before, full of childish grace and playfulness as he climbs his mother's neck. There is also the Venetian color whose harmonious fusion of tones shows not only skill but also a sense of beauty and originality. Working within the confines of established principals, Andrea del Sarto unifies the various elements of the Roman high Renaissance grand style and establishes himself as its foremost master in Florence, the city that made it possible in the first place.

Titian* (ca. 1487–1576), Venetian

The Venus of Urbino (1538): room 28
This nude, embodying the sixteenth-century idea of feminine beauty, is one of Titian's best-known works. The model may have been the paramour of the duke of Urbino, who met Titian in 1532 when he was commander of the Venetian army. A close relationship developed between the two men, and Titian executed many works for the court of Urbino, including the Pitti's *"La Bella,"* a portrait of the same woman depicted here as Venus. But is this Venus? There is nothing mythological about the scene; one must admit that she looks quite like a duke's mistress. She gazes directly at us like a woman of worldly experience, at peace with herself as she reclines in luxurious nudity waiting for a maidservant to find her a garment worthy of her position and beauty. Her golden flesh tones are carried into the depth of the picture to the tapestry and rising sun, seen through the window, illuminating a phallic pillar.

Uccello, Paolo (ca. 1397–1475), Florentine

The Battle of San Romano (ca. 1450): room 7
The technique of perspective had already made itself felt in Florence, where Brunelleschi (its inventor), Donatello, and Masaccio used it to advantage. Uccello, whose origins as an artist were Gothic, embraced it wholeheartedly, and it led him into the realm of the Renaissance. No artist was so caught up in it as Uccello, although his perspective was different from Masaccio's. Masaccio used it to form a new conception of man and his place in the world, whereas Uccello used it to escape into a world of fantasy. His *Battle of San Romano*, one of three paintings intended to be placed side-by-side in the Medici palace in Florence (the other two are in the Louvre in Paris and the National Gallery in London), is based on a battle that took place in 1432 between Florentines and Sienese. Uccello's conception is unrealistic. Nowhere is there an accurate depiction of the horror and violence of war. The men look like toy soldiers and the horses look like those on a merry-go-round. The flatness of the figures comes of a lack of light and shade. As compared with a balanced work of Masaccio, this is a wholly geometric, decorative creation. Its harmony of color and changing line make the basis of Uccello's fantastic stylization. It has the effect of fusing reality with fantasy, somewhat akin to modern art. Reality is transferred by Uccello's imagination into something new—not something rational but something that still reveals truth. It is probable that Uccello knew how to deal with perspective more accurately than he shows. He certainly knew how to use light and shade. He seems to have subordinated these elements to his artistic expression.

Weyden, Rogier van der* (ca. 1399–1464), Flemish

The Entombment: rooms 10–14

Rogier visited Italy in 1449–50, traveling to Rome, and it is likely that this painting was commissioned by the Ferrarese court and executed in Italy. He must have stopped in Florence, because the compositional scheme of *The Entombment* is similar to one painted by Fra Angelico that, in Rogier's time, was the predella of the high altarpiece of San Marco in Florence (now at the Bavarian State Art Gallery, Munich). Otherwise there is little of the Italian influence in Rogier's painting, except for the broad landscape in the background, probably requested by the Italians who commissioned the work; Rogier, unlike van Eyck, thought the inclusion of nature a disturbing influence. All the rest is purely Rogierian, with nothing narrative about the picture. Rogier simply presents the torn body of Christ as an object of piety and adoration. Christ's feet and hands are still in the position of the Cross, and in keeping with this image all of the figures are thin and wavering rather than large and monumental. There is an uncompromising gravity to it all, anchored in the Gothic tradition and, of course, in Rogier's personal style.

Buildings

CATHEDRAL GROUP

Piazza del Duomo

The cathedral group consists of three buildings: the Cathedral (Santa Maria del Fiore); the Campanile (bell tower) next to it; and the Baptistery (San Giovanni), across from the front of the cathedral.

The Cathedral (Duomo)

Hours: Open daily 7:30AM–12 noon and 2:30–7PM. Free admission.

The Cathedral of Santa Maria del Fiore (St. Mary of the Flower, an allusion to the lily in the coat of arms of the city, pertaining to the tradition that Florence was founded in a field of flowers) was begun in 1296 using plans drawn up by **Arnolfo di Cambio** (ca. 1245–1301), but taken over after his death by a number of other artists including Giotto. The cathedral took so long to build (1296 to 1461) that it encompasses the Gothic style, which the main body of its building represents, as well as the Renaissance, the style of its massive dome.

The proud, competitive Florentines, anxious to outdo the Pisans and the Sienese, asked Arnolfo to create a design for a cathedral more splendid than any other devised by human invention. His original design was mostly carried out, and the Duomo of Florence is, with the exception of St. Peter's in Rome, the greatest of all Italian churches. Its size, 555 feet in length and 340 feet in breadth, was so large that it created a problem in the construction of its dome. No one knew how to build one large enough until, in 1434, Brunelleschi accomplished the feat.

The Latin cross plan consists of four large bays with aisles half the width of the nave bays. Massive angular piers support its stone vault and a heavy cornice running all round the building. The length of the nave is twice as high as it is wide, giving a unity to the interior space. The east end expands into an octagon on three sides which contain polygonal chapels as well as a drum spanning a width of 140 feet. Above it is Brunelleschi's great dome.

Brunelleschi, Flippo (1377–1446), Florentine
The father of Renaissance architecture, one of the most important architects in history, came to architecture on the rebound. Trained as a goldsmith and a sculptor, he lost a competition, in 1401, to Ghiberti, for a commission to decorate a bronze door of the Baptistery in Florence, so he turned to architecture. He built the first structures in Florence to ignore the Gothic style as though it had never existed, using architectural innovations of his own based on classical Roman buildings he had studied as a young man. His simplified yet grand designs, supported by mathematical formulas, became dominant in his time. He was the first artist to translate the Renaissance feeling into bricks and mortar; in that respect he can be considered the world's earliest modern architect. Some of his outstanding buildings in Florence are San Lorenzo and the Old Sacristy (begun 1419); the Foundling Hospital (1419–24); the dome of the cathedral (1420–36); the Pazzi Chapel (1429); the design for Santa Maria degli Angeli; and Santo Spirito (begun in 1436).

Cathedral Dome
More than one hundred years after Brunelleschi's dome was built, Michelangelo, when working on his own dome for St. Peter's in Rome, said he now had an opportunity of surpassing the dome of Florence. "I will make a sister dome. Larger yes, but not more beautiful." Michelangelo was confident of being able to construct a larger dome because he had Brunelleschi's dome to study. When Brunelleschi started his dome he had only the dome of the Roman Pantheon to learn from, a dome not feasible for Florence. Therefore, what Brunelleschi accomplished stands out as an original work with few architectural elements borrowed from classical structures.

Brunelleschi was limited by the construction that had already taken place. The building already had an octagonal base for the crowning dome. Most every other part of the church had also been completed. It only lacked a dome to span the 140 feet across the opening, about 180 feet above the ground. Flying buttresses could not be used, since there would have been no place to put them. He could not build a hemispherical dome, like the dome of the Roman Pantheon, because the weight of its concrete would have crushed the existing drum. The only solution was to build a dome pointed in sections and supported on ribs with the lightest possible weight between them. This he did by buttressing the octagonal substructure of the crossing with a series of half-domed apse chapels and using eight major ribs, which you can see from the outside, springing from the angles of the octagon, and a minor series of ribs between them. The skeleton was completed by horizontal arches tying the major and minor ribs together and absorbing the side thrusts. It also had the first known set of two shells, an outer and an inner one, which reduced the weight. The large lantern at the top was placed there to weigh down the ribs, preventing them from breaking open. As part of the building project Brunelleschi had to create new mechanical devices for handling the stones. He even built a canteen above ground to save the men wasting time going down to ground level for their meals.

No other Renaissance work of art in Italy better demonstrates the spirit of the Renaissance than Brunelleschi's great dome. It tells us in a tangible way that man can solve any problem and achieve any result—in an aesthetically pleasing way that expresses his artistic feeling—if he only puts his intelligence and talent to it.

After the glittering exterior of the cathedral its **interior** seems almost plain. But it has a splendid marble pavement, fifteenth-century stained glass by Ghiberti in the nave, frescoes by Vasari and Zuccaro in the cupola (crossing), and many other works of art by major Renaissance artists. During restoration, parts of the Duomo may be closed and art works covered or removed. The greatest art treasure of the church, Michelangelo's *Descent from the Cross,* has been moved to the **Museo dell'Opera del Duomo** across from the cathedral's east end.

The Campanile (1334–87)

Giotto (ca. 1267–1337) is given credit for the design of the bell tower (to the right of the cathedral), but changes were made after his death (he is buried in the cathedral at the corner nearest to the Campanile). For one thing the Campanile never received the 150-foot spire that Giotto wanted to add to the 276-foot-high structure. It did, however, receive the same rich marble decoration that adorns the cathedral, and statues by **Donatello** in its second-story niches. What you see there today are copies; the originals, including the famous *La Zuccone* (a realistic portrait of a bald, ugly man), are in the **Museo dell'Opera del Duomo** located across from the cathedral's east end. This museum is highly worthwhile visiting and contains a number of other Donatello pieces, including his polychrome wood statue of *St. Mary Magdalene* which, until recently, stood in the Baptistery.

The Baptistery (San Giovanni)

Hours: Open Mon.–Fri., 12 noon–5:30PM; Sat., Sun., 9AM–5:30PM. Free admission.

No one seems certain of the age of the Baptistery. It may have had pagan origins. We know from fourteenth-century sources that people of Florence believed it was a temple of Mars converted for Christian usage. In any case it was the first Christian church in Florence and to ths day one of the most important sites to the Florentines.

Though it has a fifth-century Roman foundation, what you see today is a proto-Renaissance structure of the eleventh or twelfth century. A pitched roof covers a vast dome decorated with thirteenth-century Byzantine mosaics. Extensive use of green and white marble in geometrical patterning is used throughout the interior, including a floor that shows signs of the Zodiac. It also contains works of sculpture by Donatello and Michelozzo, but its most celebrated piece, *St. Mary Magdalene,* by Donatello, has been removed to the Museo dell'Opera del Duomo across from the back of the Duomo.

Ghiberti, Lorenzo (1378–1455), Florentine

East door of the Baptistery ("Gates of Paradise"): door facing the front of the Duomo
The first decade of the quattrocento saw the start of many projects to glorify the city of Florence. One of these was a competition to decide which sculptor should decorate the north doors of the Baptistery. What is today the south doors, by Andrea Pisano (ca. 1270–1348), had already been completed in 1336 and was in place as the east doors, across from the entrance to the Duomo; later moved to its present position on the south side (the side closest to the Campanile) to make room for Ghiberti's *Gates of Paradise.* Seven sculptors showed their designs, but it came down to deciding between panels by Brunelleschi and Ghiberti. Ghiberti won and it turned Brunelleschi away from sculpture to architecture. The two competing panels, which show the *Sacrifice of Isaac,* are today on display at the Bargello. When you see them you may decide that the wrong man won. Brunelleschi's design may be a bit dramatic, but it is pictorally realistic with concern for the filling of architectural space. Ghiberti's panel is sentimental and confused, even lumpy.

Ghiberti went on to execute what is today the **north doors** (1403–24) in twenty-eight panels, showing the principal events in the life of Christ, the evangelists, and the fathers of the church. He then did the **east doors** (1425–52), which Michelangelo termed *Gates of Paradise,* showing stories of the Old Testament in ten panels. Starting from the top, from left to right, they represent (1) *Creation of Adam and Eve, the Temptation and Expulsion;* (2) *Adam Tilling the Soil, the Story of Cain and Abel;* (3) *The Flood, Noah's Sacrifice and Drunkenness;* (4) *Abraham and the Angels, and the Sacrifice of Isaac;* (5) *The Story of Esau and Jacob;* (6) *Joseph Sold into Slavery;* (7) *Moses Receives the Law;* (8) *The Fall of Jericho;* (9) *Battle against the Philistines and David Kills Goliath;* and (10) *Solomon and the Queen of Sheba.*

These panels also show that Ghiberti outgrew the deficiencies of his demonstration panel. The "Paradise" series is his most mature work, with a Renaissance feeling for harmony of composition that counteracts the limits of bas-relief. Their sense of depth borders on the pictorial, and their greatest attribute is that they are works of sculpture that communicate like paintings. There is also a wealth of landscape detail that further adds to a pictorial impression, as does the architecture, shown in correct perspective. They are three-dimensional pictures, like paintings in bronze, as they have been described.

MUSEO DELL'OPERA DEL DUOMO

Piazza del Duomo 9

Hours: Open Mon.–Sat., 9:30AM–1PM and 3–5:30PM; Sun., 10AM–1PM. Admission fee.

This small museum contains works of art removed from the Duomo, the Baptistery, and the Campanile. Its most important works are Michelangelo's *Descent from the Cross;* the two *Cantorie (Singing Galleries)* by Donatello and Lucca della Robbia; Donatello's *St. Mary Magdalene;* and bas-reliefs from the Campanile executed by Donatello, Andrea Pisano, Lucca della Robbia, and Alberto Arnoldi.

Michelangelo* (1475–1564), Florentine

Descent from the Cross (ca. 1550–55): mezzanine
This statue, with its Gothic-like expressionism, is the result of Michelangelo's religious impulse of his later years, brought on by the Counter-Reformation and his friendship with certain religious reformers. No longer does Michelangelo seek to glorify man. Instead, he surrenders to man's final fate, depicted by the figures of the statue who are powerless to prevent Christ's descent into the tomb. When Michelangelo did this statue he was at least seventy-five. He carved his own likeness in the head of the hooded figure of Joseph of Arimathea, the rich man who gave Christ his own newly cut tomb. This was Michelangelo's way of merging his own identity with that of Christ.

This is another statue that Michelangelo did not finish. In this case he claimed the stone was faulty and he could not work with it. He started to destroy it and he succeeded in smashing the left arm and left leg of Christ before his pupils stopped him; they were able to mend the arm, but the leg has disappeared. His pupils finished the figure of Mary Magdalene on the left, which has come out looking timid and stiff, unworthy of the other figures. When faced with the reality of his own death, perhaps this most dynamic man of the Renaissance could not, after all, accept it. The unfinished state of this statue has for many symbolized man's inability to accept his tragic fate.

Michelangelo intended that this statue be placed on his own tomb in a chapel he owned in Santa Maria Maggiore in Rome. If you have seen what turned out to be his tomb in Santa Croce in Florence, which includes uninspired sculpture, you may think it a pity that this magnificent statue has not been removed from the Duomo to adorn the master's tomb.

Donatello* (1386–1466), Florentine, and **Luca della Robbia** (1400–82), Florentine

Cantorie (two): first floor, room 1
These two marble Cantorie, gallery parapets, used to support the console of the cathedral organ. In the *Cantoria* by Donatello (1433–39), the master de-

picts classical cupidlike children, no doubt suggested by Roman reliefs. They dance and sing along the gallery with a sense of unrestrained abandon found only in children. Their dynamic action is in contrast to *Luca della Robbia's Cantoria* (1431–38) illustrating Psalm 150 (inscribed on the frieze and the two stylobates immediately beneath the columns) in which the reader is asked to praise God "in the sound of the trumpet," "lute and harp," "cymbals and dances," "strings and pipe," and to "let everything that hath breath praise the Lord!" The young Florentine boys and girls do indeed praise the Lord dancing, playing musical instruments, and singing. They are carefully arranged on each panel in the classical tradition of an Augustan frieze. Not a detail has been left out. Their clothing falls in natural rhythms over their young bodies, reminiscent of Roman togas, and their faces are right off the streets of Florence, where Lucca watched children playing a discus-throwing game. The two most celebrated panels of the series are the two end pieces; the one in which the singing children are seen full-face, and the group in which the children are in profile. One can almost hear their music and see their drapery swing in time to the beat. They are justly famous as some of the loveliest presentations of children in the history of sculpture.

Also in room 1 is Donatello's shocking *St. Mary Magdalene* in wood (under the Cantoria), moved here from the Baptistery, and Donatello's sixteen statues from the niches on the Campanile, including the famous *Habbakuk*, popularly known as "Lo Zuccone" (Baldhead). In the next room are relief panels from the Campanile. The panels by Andrea Pisano (ca. 1270–1348/9) illustrating (1) *Conquest of the Sea*, (2) *Conquest of the Earth*, (3) *Agriculture*, (4) *Trade*, (5) *Christianity*, and (6) *Architecture*, are thought to have been designed by Giotto.

ORSANMICHELE

Via dei Calzaiuoli

Hours: Open daily 8AM–12 noon and 2–7PM. Free admission.

This building was once a grain market and its upper part a granary. A painted figure of the Virgin on one of its pilasters became an object of devotion that attracted such large crowds that it was decided to turn the building into a church in the late fourteenth century. The various guilds of Florence commissioned statues to be placed in niches on the exterior of the building the city granted to them as their own. This led to competition between guilds and sculptors for the best statue, with the result that Orsanmichele displays some of the best sculpture of the Florentine Renaissance. Its interior has a Gothic **Tabernacle** (1339–59) by **Andrea Orcagna** (active 1344–68) rising in stately beauty to the roof of the church. It is of marble, inlaid with mosaic and gold, with reliefs at its base. The old miraculous image, destroyed by fire, was replaced by the *Madonna and Child* by Bernardo Daddi (active ca. 1312–48), Giotto's pupil.

Sculptures on the Exterior of the Building

Beginning at the corner of Via dei Calzaiuoli and Via dei Lamberti, and progressing to the right down Via dei Calzaiuoli:

St. John the Baptist (1414–16) by Ghiberti (1378–1455)

Special permission had to be granted to use this bronze statue, instead of the customary marble. Ghiberti worked only in bronze, but since he was the sculptor of the bronze doors of the Baptistery of Florence, permission was granted. The statue reflects Ghiberti's international Gothic style, fashionable at the time, but mannered when compared to the work of Nanni and Donatello at Orsanmichele.

Doubting Thomas (1466–83) by Verrocchio (1435–88)

This statue replaced one of St. Louis by Donatello (now in the Museum of Santa Croce) and Verrocchio felt the pressure of having to outdo the older statue. The task was difficult because into a niche designed for one figure he had to fit two figures. He did this by reducing the scale of the figures and by placing only Christ in the main part of the niche. The arrangement of the thick robes of both figures accentuates the upward movement and brings both figures into the central part of the niche.

St. Luke (1601) by Giovanni Bologna (1529–1608)

This is the last statue to be placed in Orsanmichele. It is by a Flemish artist who had great success in Italy and made Florence his home.

St. Peter (1408–13) attributed to Donatello (1386–1466) but possibly by Cinffagni (1385–1450)

St. Philip (1412–16) by Nanni di Banco (died 1421)

Four Crowned Saints (ca. 1412) by Nanni di Banco (died 1421)

These four Christian sculptors were martyred for refusing to make a pagan statue for Emperor Diocletian. With their neat appearance they stand like Roman senators displaying the moral dignity of exalted figures. Nanni avoids Gothic tendencies in his work by drawing inspiration from the antique world.

St. George (ca. 1417, original in the Bargello) by Donatello (1386–1466)

This statue marks the point when Donatello begins to assert his individuality. It shows the realism, pent-up energy, and psychological depth of many of his statues to follow. The marble relief below (also a copy; original in the Bargello), showing St. George killing the dragon is an attempt at exploring the problem of spatial suggestion and is a forerunner of the sculptor's revolutionary bronze, Feat of Herod (1423), in the Baptistery at Siena.

St. Matthew (1419–22) by Ghiberti (1378–1455)

St. Stephen (1428) by Ghiberti (1378–1455)

St. Eligius (ca. 1410–11) by Nanni di Banco (died 1421)

St. Mark (1411–13) by Donatello (1386–1466)

St. James (early 15th century) attributed to **Niccolo di Pietro Lamberti** (ca. 1370–1451)

Madonna (1399) attributed to **Niccolò di Pietro Lamberti** (ca. 1370–1451)

St. John the Evangelist (1515) by **Baccio da Montelupo** (1469–1535)

PIAZZA DELLA SIGNORIA

This great piazza has been the heart and soul of Florence since medieval times. Its architecture and sculpture is almost a review of the city's history and art—a microcosm of Florence itself. An equestrian bronze statue of *Duke Cosimo I de' Medici* by **Giovanni Bologna**(1529–1608), the first of the Medici family to rule Florence, stands on the north side of the piazza. On the southeast corner and dominating the piazza is the fortresslike **Palazzo Vecchio** with its lofty tower. To the left of it is the *Fountain of Neptune* (1565–75) by **Bartolomeo Ammanati** (1511–92). A plaque in the pavement in front of the fountain marks the spot where the Dominican preacher-reformer, Savonarola, was hanged and burned on May 23, 1498. To the right of the fountain, on the steps, are two small bronzes by **Donatello** (1386–1466): a copy of *Marzocco* (1418–20) (the original is in the Bargello), the heraldic lion of Florence whose rear end captured enemies of Florence were often made to kiss; and *Judith and Holofernes* (1456–60), which the Florentines regarded as a symbol of liberty and a warning to tyrants. To the right is the copy of **Michelangelo's** *David* and the crude *Hercules and Cacus* (1534) by the Mannerist sculptor **Baccio Bandinelli** (1493–1560). It indicates the decline of artistic sensibility and an uncertain taste at the Medici court. Two small statues (hermae) flank the entrance to the Palazzo Vecchio. They once served as posts securing a chain across the entrance.

Loggia Dei Lanzi (1376–81)

The Loggia, on the south side of the piazza, was built to provide shelter for the politicians and merchants who often discussed business here. It got its name, *Lanzi (Lancers)*, from Duke Cosimo I's Swiss lancers who were housed nearby. Its wide, lofty Romanesque arches, supported by strong compound piers, are a welcome relief to the austere massiveness of the Palazzo Vecchio, just across the corner from it. Of the many statues in the Loggia, the best, one of the finest statues in Florence, is the one by Cellini under the first arch.

Cellini, Benvenuto (1500–71), Florentine

Perseus with the Head of Medusa (1553)
Cellini is the Italian goldsmith and sculptor (also a writer) who created the famous gold saltcellar for Francis I now in the Kunsthistorisches in Vienna. Here he tells the story of Perseus, the son of Danae, who beheaded Medusa, one of the three snake-haired Gorgons of Greek mythology. Cellini shows him standing in heroic naked splendor with the sword Mercury gave him in

one hand (like Mercury he wears a hat with wings) and the monster's head in the other. He is splendidly modeled but static, as if to reduce the brutality of the scene. Cellini was aware of Donatello's *Judith and Holofernes* on the piazza and of the parallel between that statue and his own. He uses a cushion for the base of his statue—appropriate for *Judith*, but out of place for *Perseus*.

Cellini has placed his signature on the strap crossing Perseus's chest, as Michelangelo did on his *Pietà* in St. Peter's. This is a tribute to Michelangelo. As a nude of the post-Renaissance period, *Perseus* owes its existence to Michelangelo's marble nudes of the early Cinquecento.

PALAZZO VECCHIO (begun 1298)

Piazza della Signoria

Hours: Open Mon.–Fri., 9AM–7PM; Sun., 8AM–1PM. Admission fee.

The exterior of this superb Gothic palace owes its design to **Arnolfo di Cambio** (ca. 1245–1301) and was built largely in the early fourteenth century. The interior is of much later origin. It was the residence of the ruling Medici in the sixteenth century and up to the present the seat of the municipal government of Florence. Its main feature is its overhanging upper story supported by machicolations, with dark openings and crenellation. This overhang is repeated in the slender soaring tower, 300 feet above the piazza, with an elegant arch at its top that relieves the impression of military architecture. The *interior* has monumental halls and apartments decorated by some of Italy's greatest artists, and though only about one third of the palace is open to public inspection, it includes the rooms with the finest works of art.

Verrocchio, Andre del (1435–88), Florentine

Putto with Dolphin (ca. 1470s): the Cortile
This lovely little statue of a boy holding a dolphin in the center of a fountain (the original is in the palazzo) was originally in Lorenzo de' Medici's country villa at Careggi. It has a lifelike, mischievous appearance, with a large head and chubby legs, reminding one of Luca della Robbia's terra cottas in Florence in which the Christ Child usually shows these characteristics. It is the first statue of the Renaissance with multiple, merging viewpoints that encourage the viewer to walk around it to appreciate its composition. What appears an insignificant statue is actually a forerunner of the work of Michelangelo, who carried the effect further in marble, and of Pollaiuolo, who mastered it in bronze.

SAN LORENZO AND THE MEDICI CHAPEL

Piazza San Lorenzo

Hours: Open Tues.–Sat., 9AM–7PM; Sun., 9AM–1PM. Admission fee.

San Lorenzo, the parish church of the Medici family, is the first large basilica that **Brunelleschi** (1377–1446) built in Florence (begun in 1419). Though it incorporates many architectural elements established one hundred years earlier in Santa Croce, it improves on the older church in a more harmonious architectural plan. Its shape is a Latin cross with small chapels at either side and around the transepts. Everything is done to precision, with the basic module a square; the plan is a geometrical repetition of this unit. The interior walls were designed by Michelangelo. He had a plan for the exterior unfinished walls, but it was never carried out. The outstanding works of art inside the church are two **Bronze Pulpits** by **Donatello** (1386–1466) opposite each other in the nave. They are examples of Donatello's latest work and were finished by his pupils after his death. They are of great historical interest; from them Savonarola delivered some of his most stirring sermons, even denouncing the Medici.

The Old Sacristy of the church was begun in 1419 by Brunelleschi and completed in 1428. It is one of the first centrally planned buildings of the Renaissance and in its exact proportions (the walls are equal to the sides of the square plan) forms a perfect cube; simple arithmetical proportions were the essence of Brunelleschi's art. The plastic decorative details are largely by Donatello, which include on the walls stucco medallions of the Four Evangelists, circular stucco reliefs with scenes from the life of St. John the Baptist in the spandrels, and on the sideboard a bust of young *St. Laurence* to whom the church is dedicated.

To the left of the church is the **Laurentian Library** where rare illuminated manuscripts are exhibited. It can be reached from the piazza, or from the church going through the lovely cloisters and climbing the **staircase** designed by Michelangelo and Vasari.

Michelangelo* (1475–1564), Florentine

Medici Chapels (New Sacristy)
Enter from the Piazza Madonna degli Aldobrandini, on the right side of the church (open Tues.–Sat., 9AM–7PM; Sun., 9AM–1PM; admission fee). On ascending the stairway you will be in the **Chapel of the Princes**, a somber, richly decorated baroque burial place for the Medici grand duke Ferdinand and his descendants. It contains larger-than-life-sized statues of them, walls lined with rare marbles, and a dome frescoed in 1328, by Pietro Benvenuti (1769–1844), with scenes of the Old and New Testaments.

On the left is a passage leading into the **New Sacristy** built by Michelangelo between 1520 and 1534. It contains the famous **Medici Tombs** with Michelangelo's allegorical figures and two of the Medici princes depicted alive. To the left of the entrance is the **Tomb of Lorenzo d' Medici** completed in 1519. Lorenzo is shown in contemplation, and below two recumbent figures represent *Dawn,* to the right, and *Twilight,* to the left. Opposite is the **Tomb of Giuliano de' Medici** completed in 1516. The figure of Giuliano, dressed in classical armor, typifies energy and leadership and below him are *Day,* to the right, and *Night,* to the left. The male figures of *Day* and *Twilight* are unfinished.

Dawn, a beautiful female nude, tries to raise herself to face a new day in an image of despair. *Twilight,* beside her, an old man, is a picture of weariness. Only the muscular tension in their bodies seems to prevent them from sliding off the curved sarcophagus, which, scroll-like, became a standard form of baroque art. On the opposite tomb, *Day* is a colossus in a twisted pose with an energy that seems about to burst forth, and *Night,* a female figure with the body of a man, is a picture of despondency and exhaustion—a sleep of unfulfilled desires symbolized by the supportive figures of an owl (restlessness) and a mask (false dreams). Spiritual victory of the soul comes, as *Dawn* and *Twilight,* representing the passage of time that corrupts the body in the sarcophagus, are overcome by Lorenzo. *Day* and *Night,* the corrupting influences of nature, are also overcome by the commanding, virtuous Medici figure above.

Though Michelangelo essentially belongs to the high Renaissance, and is one of its founders, these figures are not of this style. Their restless horizontals and verticals contrast with the conventional Madonnas and monumental classical figures that lack the emotional tension and imaginative modeling found here. It is likely that mannerism was born in the Medici Chapel.

SAN MINIATO AL MONTE

Located above the Piazzale Michelangelo on Viale Galileo

Hours: Open daily 8AM–12 noon and 2–7PM. Free admission.

Not every work of art in Florence is from the Renaissance. This basilica was completed in 1062 and is of Tuscan-Romanesque design. Its **facade,** based on mathematical forms (square, triangle, semicircle), with a thirteenth-century Byzantine mosaic above the window of its upper floor, dates from the twelfth century and could be considered a proto-Renaissance piece. It was copied widely during the Renaissance not only in Florence but elsewhere. **Inside** is a patterned stone floor dating to 1207, with abstract Romanesque designs of heraldic beasts and the signs of the Zodiac, and a beautiful marble screen and pulpit with carved figures, rosettes, and lace work ornament. The nave is divided into three aisles with some columns originating from early Romanesque buildings in Florence. Marble veneering and the bright painted ceiling and trusses, lit up by strong light entering through clerestory windows, make the interior colorful. There are also works of art by Italian masters.

SANTA CROCE AND THE PAZZI CHAPEL

Piazza Santa Croce

Hours for cloisters, museum, and Pazzi Chapel: Open summer, Mon., Tues., Thurs.–Sun., 9AM–12:30PM and 3–6:30PM (to 5PM in winter). Admission fee.

The great religious movements of the thirteenth century required preaching churches in Italy that could accommodate large crowds. Two of the finest

Florentine Gothic churches of this period, Santa Maria Novella (Dominican) and Santa Croce (Franciscan), owe their existence to the preaching orders that still occupy them today.

Of the two, Santa Croce is the larger and was built in rivalry with its crosstown Dominican competitor. It was probably planned between 1294 and 1301 by **Arnolfo di Cambio** (ca. 1245–1301), the architect who created the plan for the Duomo. After Arnolfo's death his design seems to have been faithfully carried out, and was completed in 1442 (but its colorful facade is entirely nineteenth century).

Though there are similarities between Santa Croce and Santa Maria Novella, a basic difference between the two churches is the richly treated open-trussed wooden roof of Santa Croce, as opposed to Santa Maria Novella's stone vaulting. Therefore, at Santa Croce there is no need for heavy piers, only octagonal light columns. The effect is of loftiness and openness. It makes a pleasing sight to view the length and breadth of Santa Croce (460 feet long by 134 feet wide) from the entrance looking back to the tall triumphal arch with its light-filled apse.

Santa Croce serves as the Pantheon of Florence, where some of the greatest figures in Italian history have been buried. You can see Michelangelo's disappointing tomb, designed by Vasari (1570), in the south aisle, first altar. Most of the other tombs are also devoid of artistic value, but the church makes up for this with many works of art, such as a fine relief of the *Annunciation* (1428–33) by **Donatello** (1386–1466) in the south aisle, fifth column, and his wooden *Crucifix* in the north transept, Bardi Chapel, not to be confused with the Bardi Chapel containing Giotto's frescoes (see Santa Maria Novella, for the story of how Donatello's *Crucifix* inspired Brunelleschi's famous *Crucifix*); and early frescoes (ca. 1330–66) illustrating the *Life of the Virgin*, by Taddeo Gaddi (1300–66) in the Giugni Chapel (formerly Baroncelli Chapel) located at the end of the south transept.

Frescoes have always been a high point of Santa Croce. At a time when the French were dissolving the wall in church architecture to make way for great areas of colored glass, the Italians were mastering the use of the wall. In so doing they turned to their great painters to decorate their churches with frescoes. Santa Croce was the recipient of the work of the great Giotto.

Giotto di Bondone* (ca. 1267–1337), Florentine

Frescoes in the Bardi and Peruzzi Chapels: fourth and fifth chapels immediately to the right of the chancel

These two chapels were decorated by Giotto and his assistants in the 1320s during the height of Giotto's career. Both chapels were whitewashed in the eighteenth century, made visible again in the nineteenth century, when they were badly restored with tempera (1853), then freed of their overpaint in 1958. As a result, the frescoes in the Peruzzi Chapel are almost totally ruined. However, those in the Bardi Chapel, representing scenes from the *Life of St. Francis*, are largely in good condition and show a mature, accomplished style with an integration of figures in space and a realization of architectural form. In the fresco showing *St. Francis Undergoing the Test by Fire before the Sultan,* with its inlaid marble architecture, there is a more restrained emotion than in Giotto's earlier work, combined with a soft light that reminds one of sixteenth-century Venetian painting. On the left we see the Moslem priest lifting his mantle in a gesture of defense when he hears that St. Francis will walk into the fire to prove that his God is greater than Mohammed. The two black slaves, one pointing to St. Francis, are the earliest known representations of black people in Western art, and are depicted with a sensitivity to their features and color. All of the figures are more imposing than those Giotto painted twenty years earlier in the Arena Chapel in Padua. The sense of space is also deeper.

Brunelleschi, Filippo* (1377–1446), Florentine

Pazzi Chapel (1429–30)
To the right of the church, in the first cloister (fourteenth century), is one of the most beautiful buildings in the world, the Pazzi Chapel, built by Brunelleschi as a chapter house and a family burial chapel. It probably comes closer to the Renaissance ideal of perfection than any other building in Florence.

It has a small portico with a vaulted ceiling adorned with glazed terra cotta rosettes by Luca della Robbia (1400–82) and a frieze of cherubim by Desiderio da Settignano (1428–64). Behind this rises a small dome. Its simple white interior is relieved by terra cotta roundels of the Twelve Apostles by Lucca della Robbia, and by other decorations.

As in other buildings by Brunelleschi, there is an abandonment of the complicated Gothic style and a search for a restrained, quiet effect, here expressed through a reliance on the square and circle. The result is a little jewel of a building whose strongest points are proportion, scale, and composition reflecting architectural harmony and order.

Museo dell'Opera di Santa Croce
To the right of the entrance to the first cloister is the church museum which begins in the former refectory. It contains a great number of art works salvaged from the restoration of the church and cloisters, including frescoes by Taddeo Gaddi and Orcagna, a bronze statue, *St. Louis of Toulouse* (1423) by **Donatello,** and the important *Crucifix* by **Cimabue** (ca. 1240–1302), now restored after the 1966 flood when it was almost completely destroyed.

SANTA MARIA DEL CARMINE
Piazza del Carmine

Hours: Open daily 9AM–12 noon and 3:30–6PM. Free admission.

If the Brancacci Chapel, with frescoes by Masaccio, had perished in the fire that destroyed the original church in 1771 (rebuilt by 1782), Santa Maria del Carmine would have no importance in the history of art. But the chapel survived (along with the sacristy and another chapel) to be the guardian of one of the greatest treasures in Western painting, an artistic achievement that brought painting out of the Middle Ages into modern times.

Masaccio (1401–28), Florentine

Masaccio's Frescoes in the Brancacci Chapel (1425–26): end of right transept
Not all of the frescoes on the walls of the chapel are by Masaccio. Starting from the upper left is the small *Expulsion of Adam and Eve,* and to the right of it the large *Tribute Money,* both by Masaccio. So are *St. Peter Baptizing,* on the upper level to the right of the altar, and immediately below it, *St. Peter and St. John Distributing Alms,* as well as the painting of *St. Peter Healing the Sick with His Shadow,* on the lower level to the left of the altar. The others are by Masolino (1383–1447), Masaccio's teacher, and by Filippino Lippi (1457–1504).

The *Tribute Money,* the greatest of the works here, is divided into three parts. In the center the tax collector demands payment from a calm, majestic Christ who turns to Peter and tells him how to get money from the mouth of a fish. In the left background Peter is seen catching the fish. On the right, Peter, with an air of indignation, is shown paying the tax collector. This kind of composition is called "continuous narrative" since it represents consecutive events of a single story in a unified space. The landscape in the background is varied slightly so that each event stands alone.

It is difficult to believe that this fresco is exactly contemporary with Gentile da Fabriano's *Adoration of the Magi* in the Uffizi. Masaccio ignored the international Gothic style as he eliminated all surface decoration and details and got down to the real significance of the subject. He uses the newly discovered laws of perspective, learned from Brunelleschi, to give the illusion of three dimensionality to his figures and objects. There is one source of light with modulating shade to render the forms realistically, and he has introduced aerial perspective into the backgrounds. Objects in the distance become smaller and their outlines less distinct as they recede from the eye. He paints the apostles around Christ as individual characters, determined men of action who look like real Roman citizens of old. The tax collector is dressed in the style of Masaccio's own time; the calf of his leg is so real you can reach out and touch it. In the painting of Christ we have a real hero in the down to earth sense. The movement of the composition starts with Him and is convincing; He is an expressive power who operates in the real world, instead of the static medieval world. All these figures have a classical calm, balance, and dignity that make up what Masaccio was aiming for: correct proportions between man and nature, where man comes out looking very good. The sense of moral responsibility in Masaccio's figures is a far cry from the flights of medieval fancy in Gentile da Fabriano's work.

In the fresco depicting *Adam and Eve* Masaccio continues to reestablish the ideal of mass and to sacrifice detailed articulation to give a quick comprehension of subject matter. The powerful bodies are modeled with planes of stark shadow and in full frontal light. They look like real people with real emotions: Adam holds his bent head with his hands, and Eve seems to cry out. It is clear that they are moved by the force of their emotions. The archangel, foreshortened to create an illusion of depth, only hovers above without touching them. The impact of the scene is immediate and more powerful than any detailed depiction of the event.

These frescoes by Masaccio were a great leap forward, but that is not to say they were less religious than the old art. They were, instead, a new conception that added vitality to an old story and placed it in step with the times. Only an artist of imagination and genius could have conceived them. They showed the way to other artists into the Renaissance and the modern age. Leonardo, Raphael, and Michelangelo came to the Brancacci Chapel to study them. The achievement of Masaccio makes him heir to Giotto and Brunelleschi and the true ancestor of Michelangelo.

SANTA MARIA NOVELLA

Piazza Santa Maria Novella

Hours for cloisters: Open Mon.–Thurs., Sat., 9AM–2PM; Sun., 8AM–1PM.

Santa Maria Novella, built for the Dominican Order, was the first monumental church built in Florence. It has Gothic attributes of pointed arches and windows, and ribbed stone vaults instead of an open timbered roof, but no flying buttresses, because the walls are solid. Typical of the Gothic in Italy, Santa Maria Novella is modified by classical proportions and reaches for a sense of human scale, for breadth rather than height. This is due not only to the Italian rejection of the French Gothic striving for towering height and the complicated engineering system that goes with it, but also to the need for the accommodation of a large group of people in a space who can see and hear a preacher. The main element of the design is a large square nave with aisles on either side that are much longer than they are wide.

A great deal of time was taken to build this church (begun in 1279, completed in 1470). For the **front facade, Alberti** (1404–72), the architect who planned it, came up with a Renaissance design mixed with Gothic forms. Multicolored marble is used for geometrical pattern. A classical gable crowns the center portion marking the nave, while scrolls at the sides indicate the aisles. The space is divided so that the height of the building is equal to its width, thereby forming a single large square. This gives it a harmony of proportion that is pleasing to the eye and typical of Alberti's work. The large piazza in front of the church affords views of the entire facade and has been used for church festivals and for chariot races.

The **interior** of the church is museumlike, displaying objects of art from the artists of Florence. The most outstanding of these are a series of frescoes by Domenico Ghirlandaio (1449–94) completed about 1490, a wooden crucifix by Brunelleschi (1377–1446), and the *Holy Trinity* fresco by Masaccio (1401–28).

The **fresco cycle by Ghirlandaio** is located in the sanctuary, or Tornabuoni Chapel, and depicts scenes from the *Life of the Virgin* and *St. John the Baptist*. Assistants helped Ghirlandaio with this monumental work and among them was the young Michelangelo, thirteen years old. The most striking feature of these frescoes is the modernizing of sacred history by the introduction of contemporary portraits of well-known Florentines, both men and women. This work remains one of the best representations of the customs, clothes, and furnishings of fifteenth-century Florence.

The wooden *Crucifix* by **Brunelleschi** is found above the altar in the Gondi Chapel, the first chapel on the left of the choir (north transept). It is said that Brunelleschi created it after he saw Donatello's *Crucifix* for Santa Croce and told Donatello that his Christ looked like an ordinary peasant. Donatello challenged him to make a better one. When Donatello saw this *Crucifix* he agreed it was superior to his own. It is the only surviving sculpture in wood by Brunelleschi.

Masaccio's *Holy Trinity* fresco may have been painted just before the completion of his masterpieces in the Brancacci Chapel of Santa Maria del Carmine in about 1426. It became hidden by an altar when the church was reconstructed in the sixteenth century, and it was not rediscovered until the nineteenth century. Restored to its original place today, in the north aisle beyond the third altar, it demonstrates Masaccio's spatial technique to allow the viewer to see everything from a single viewpoint. In this case it is from below the crucified Christ. Masaccio obviously consulted with Brunelleschi, the founder of Renaissance perspective and the greatest architect of his day. Brunelleschi's influence is particularly noticeable in the architectural frame, a great barrel-vaulted ceiling. With it architectural illusionism entered the scene of Renaissance painting.

To the left of the church is the entrance to the **cloisters,** decorated in calm green tones, and off the cloister is the **Spanish Chapel** (Cappelone degli Spagnoli), formerly the chapter house of the Dominican monastery. It was erected in about 1340 to celebrate the Festival of Corpus Christi. Its present name is due to its serving as the chapel of the Spanish residents of Florence since 1506. It has a completely frescoed Giottesque interior; the fourteenth-century artists who worked on it have not been completely identified, but it is believed that much of the work is by Andrea da Firenze or Bonaiuto (ca. 1343–77). The pictures glorify the Dominican order.

Mantua

DUCAL PALACE GALLERY AND MUSEUM

Piazza Sordello

Hours: Open (guided tours) Tues.–Sat., 9AM–2PM; Sun., 9AM–1PM. Admission fee.

This rambling, fortresslike palace was the seat of the powerful Gonzaga family who ruled Mantua from 1329 until 1708, when the duchy came to an end with the annexation of Mantua by Austria. During the fifteenth and sixteenth centuries, under Gonzaga rule, the court at Mantua was one of the most splendid and enlightened in all of Italy. Gonzaga Renaissance princes, such as Lodovico III (1444–78) and Giovanni Francesco II (1484–1519), and his wife, Isabella d'Este (1474–1539), were patrons of poets and painters and built the family collection into one of the most outstanding in Italy.

Each building of the complex (it was built from the fourteenth to the eighteenth centuries) consists of an isolated, symmetrical block enclosing rectangular courtyards. At one time many of the more than 450 rooms were lavishly decorated, but from the seventeenth century they fell into decay. Extensive restorations in the twentieth century, still going on, have restored some of the apartments to their original splendor. You can see the **Paradiso of Isabella d'Este**—four jewel-box rooms, connected one to the other—which Isabella used for her private retreat. When she occupied them they contained paintings, books, musical instruments, and other precious things. She was an art critic and collector and dealt with the most talented artists and craftsmen of her day. Though her treasures have been scattered all over the world, the splendor of the Paradiso, with its intricately carved ceilings and marble reliefs, is a treat.

Mantegna, Andrea (1431–1506), Italian

Frescoes in the Camera degli Sposi (1474)

The celebrated frescoes in the Camara degli Sposi (marriage chamber) by Andrea Mantegna were executed for Lodovico Gonzaga. Ludovico had lured Mantegna with a high salary to be official court painter when the artist was a rising young artist. Mantegna put him off for four years, but in 1460 moved to Mantua to work for the Gonzagas exclusively. Mantegna held the position for the rest of his life, forty-six years, leaving Mantua only for brief visits to Florence and Bologna, and to spend two years in Rome.

Before coming to Mantua, Mantegna was already a master of perspective, so when Lodovico asked him to decorate this corner room in one of the palace towers, and to make it seem larger than it was, Mantegna was up to the task. The result is one of the most distinguished rooms in Italy, with every inch of walls and ceiling covered with frescoes, showing Lodovico and his family in ceremonial activity. Mantegna achieved an illusion of extended space by painting views of open countryside on the walls, and arranging his monumental life-sized figures above or around real doors and fireplaces, thus changing our normal angle of vision and making us see what he wanted us to see. Though the characters displayed have heroic qualities, with a sculptured presence of strength, each face, costume, and movement is individually characterized. As real people they are as convincing as Mantegna's space is deceptive.

The ceiling is the most extraordinary exercise in illusive painting. Here the flat surface is painted to resemble sculpture in marble and mosaic in gold. In the center is the optical illusion of a round window out of which women, animals, and *putti* are leaning over a parapet apparently looking down into the room. To add to the realistic effect, Mantegna has painted a basket of fruit placed precariously on the edge of the parapet. It is the greatest example of illusionist painting in the early Renaissance.

PALAZZO DEL TÈ

Viale Tè

Hours: Open Apr.–Sept., Mon.–Sat., 9:30AM–12:30PM and 3–6:30PM, Sun., 9AM–1PM; Oct.–Mar., Mon.–Sat., 9:30AM–12:30PM and 2:30–5PM, Sun., 9AM–1PM. Admission fee.

In 1524 the marquis of Mantua commissioned **Giulio Romano** (ca. 1492–1546) to create a small palace for his mistress outside the city gates on land adjacent to his stud farm (Gonzaga horses were prized throughout Europe and many princes had received them as gifts from the Mantua court). The building, named either for the T-shape of the avenues that led up to it, or from the many *tigli*—linden trees—that grew there, was completed by 1535. It consists of four main buildings enclosing a square courtyard with exterior facades compressed by a deliberate rustication. The **courtyard facade** is the most fantastic with great columns, between which are windows capped by massive pediments, where one triglyph suddenly drops out of place, leaving a blank hole above it. No one had ever seen such construction before.

The **interior**, even more a riot of mannerist decoration, was also executed by Romano who, as Raphael's favorite pupil, had worked on the Villa Farnesina in Rome. The frescoes of the **Sala di Psiche** are devoted to the story of Psyche and Cupid in great detail. The wedding feast, covering two entire walls, has a variety of gods, nymphs, animals, and some indelicate scenes. The **Sala dei Cavalli** has frescoes showing six Gonzaga horses life-sized in a *trompe-l'oeil* decoration. The famous **Sala dei Giganti** (Room of the Giants) is almost frightening in its brilliant illusionism. It is a mannerist scene of total chaos, the room painted in a continuous vision of the destruction of the rebellious giants who attempt to storm Mount Olympus with thunderbolts from the hand of Jupiter. The palaces of the giants seem to collapse upon them and upon the spectator too. It is the epitome of mannerist illusionist painting where you see nothing of the room's real walls and ceiling. It enjoyed great success in Italy throughout the sixteenth and seventeenth centuries.

Milan

BRERA PICTURE GALLERY

Via Brera, 28

Hours: Open Tues.–Sat., 9AM–2PM, Sun., 9AM–1PM. Admission fee.

The Brera looks solid with age, almost impregnable, but during World War II a good part of it was almost destroyed. The works of art had been removed for safekeeping, but if Napoleon had been alive he might have wished that the nude neoclassic statue of him by Canova (1757–1822) in the court-yard, had not survived. The marble version he saw displeased him. The bronze seen here, dating from 1809–11, is reduced in size from the original fourteen-foot-high model. Canova thought that nudity best expressed the he-roic qualities of Napoleon, whom he idealized. He had made a plaster bust of the subject in Paris in 1802. He simply added a nude figure derived from antiquity, a long pike in one hand, and a globe with the figure of Victory in the other. It is appropriate that Napoleon should stand here, since it was his ideas of liberalizing cultural activities that gave museums the impetus to form themselves.

Once past this statue (there is also a dusty array of others representing literary figures and scientists placed between the columns and on the walls of the porticoes), a spectacular double-ramped staircase leads to the collec-tion of paintings gathered from convents, churches, and palaces of Italy. It represents every major school of Italian art as well as some paintings by other European artists.

Bellini, Gentile (ca. 1429–1507), Venetian

St. Mark Preaching in St. Euphemia's Square in Alexandria: room 5

Gentile Bellini was a member of a famous family of Venetian painters. He specialized in large ceremonial paintings and knew something about the Ori-ent, even though he had never visited Alexandria. In 1479 he had been sent to Constantinople by the Republic of Venice at the request of Sultan Mo-hammed II, who wanted his portrait painted by the "best artist in Venice." Gentile painted the sultan's portrait (now in the National Gallery, London), but cut his visit short when, it is said, the sultan, wishing to prove that a painting Gentile showed him of the severed head of John the Baptist was anatomically incorrect, had a slave decapitated in front of him. Gentile knew what Orientals looked like, and painted them into his view of Alexandria's main square, with a great Byzantine church in the background. Notice the seated Arab women. They enrich the picture with their mysterious presence. He also knew how to draw Moslem minarets and the flat-roofed eastern houses along the square. We have Gentile to thank for the painting of town-scapes and landscapes that became popular in Venice during the eighteenth century.

Gentile started this painting in 1505 for one of the Scuole in Venice (fra-ternal organization), but illness prevented him from finishing it. His brother, Giovanni, completed the work in 1507 and probably softened it, because it is not done in the severe linear style Gentile often used.

Bellini, Giovanni* (ca. 1430–1516), Venetian

Pietà: room 19

This early Pietà, dating from 1465, is the finest production of the many Pie-tàs that Giovanni Bellini executed. He was always searching for ways to ex-press the emotion of the tragedy. Great thought has gone into this Pietà to create a religious statement as well as one that has human and psychological meaning.

Mastering color, even without the more expressive oil medium he was to adopt later in his career, Giovanni Bellini uses color as part of the expressive language. Notice how the cold purple and steely blues lock the figures into the chilly early morning landscape, creating a mood of desolation. Yet the triumph of Christ's sacrifice does not go unnoticed. His body is bathed in light and His fist is tightly closed in the attitude of a fallen but unvanquished hero. Bellini's ability to explore human emotions with a depth of humanity never before seen in his time, except in the sculpture of Donatello, is what makes him the leading painter in Venice of the quatrocento, one of those who built the basis for the high Renaissance of the cinquecento.

Mantegna, Andreas (1431–1506), Italian

The Dead Christ (ca. 1466): room 18

Mantegna's name is almost synonomous with the technique of foreshortening, a basis of Renaissance realism. *The Dead Christ* is the epitome of an exaggerated version of it done for shock effect. No matter what angle you view it from, the three dimensionality of the heavy corpse is convincing and weighs upon your emotions. It is impossible to escape the feet with their glaring wounds, creases, and lines, carried over into the folds of the sheet and the granulations of the marble slab. As you keep looking you come to focus on the head raised on a pillow; it shows the fact of death, and absorbs the emotional tension of the picture.

Notice the two masklike faces of the mourners to the left. They are not needed, and if you place your hand in front of you to block out their presence the picture actually improves.

Piero della Francesca* (ca. 1416–92), Umbrian, under Florentine influence

The Brera Altarpiece: room 25

This altarpiece was done by Piero for the great humanist prince, the duke of Urbino, Federico da Montefeltro, Piero's patron as he was to many painters, poets, and philosophers during his life (1422–82); the duke is shown, with his characteristic profile, kneeling in prayer on the right side of the foreground. It is thought that the painting was begun in 1472 (though probably not completed until the early 1480s), the year the duke's son and heir, Guidobaldo, was born and the year his wife, Battista Sforza, died at the age of twenty-six (she had already given birth to four daughters). It has been suggested that the Madonna represents a portrait of Battista; there is a resemblance to the portrait Piero did of her earlier (now in the Uffizi in Florence). More meaningful is the explanation that Battista, which means "Baptist" in Italian, is represented by the empty space in front of St. John the Baptist (the figure on the extreme left side) opposite her husband, the duke. The egg, hanging in the center over the Madonna, is that of an ostrich. Apart from the ostrich egg often being hung over altars dedicated to the Virgin (it was a symbol of Virgin birth), the ostrich itself was considered a symbol of absent friends and thus a reminder of Battista now dead. There is further emphasis of this theme in the sleeping child, who foretells the death of the adult Christ. His awakening is His Resurrection, which the duke and the Madonna are praying for and the saints waiting for. This Resurrection will also assure Battista eternal life with Christ.

Apart from its symbolism, this altarpiece has been criticized as an inferior work by Piero della Francesca. Piero's eyesight was failing, and his shortsightedness may have led him to entrust the painting of certain parts to others; the Flemish-looking hands of the duke were not painted by Piero, and the saints seem to lack the weight and vigor of his earlier work. Still, the Albertian architecture and the soft light penetrating it and reflecting from it, plus Piero's quiet monumentality, make this a great work if not a perfect achievement.

Raphael* (1483–1520), Florentine (born in Umbria)

Marriage of the Virgin: room 26

This is an early work by Raphael, signed and dated in 1504 (above the colums of the temple) when Raphael was still under the influence of his teacher, Perugino. The polygonal temple in the background, the piazza with geometric tiles painted in sharp perspective, and the figures in the foreground converging from either side, are directly from Perugino.

Raphael's Marriage of the Virgin tells the story of Mary's marriage to Joseph. We see the suitors on the right presenting their rods to the high priest with the understanding that the one whose rod blooms is to have the hand of Mary. Joseph's rod is shown with a flower at the end of it, while a man at his left side is breaking his rod in disgust. The women to the left of Mary are other virgins of the temple. Although only a few of the faces are turned toward the ceremony at the center, they are all related to one another and make up a pictorial design by their similar proportions and coloring. Raphael cleverly fits his composition into the arched shape of the frame of the picture, stressing the half-circular form of the Bramante-like domed temple. Even the heads of the two central figures, Mary and Joseph, are curved in a manner to harmonize with the shape of the picture.

Signorelli, Luca (ca. 1450–1523), Umbrian

The Flagellation (ca. 1475): room 27

Italian artists were the first to present the human body in action, Signorelli's principal subject. His male nudes, in the form of executioners, archers, mercenaries, and other athletic types, prefigure Michelangelo's gigantismo of the high Renaissance. To Signorelli man was the center of the universe and his body and movement a never-ending source of interest. Notice the strong lines that define these male nudes, their variety of movement, bulging muscles, and marked sinews. Each one is modeled in strong light. The column to which Christ, the most magnificent physical specimen of them all, is tied serves as a classicizing element in the composition, as do the nude figures.

Signorelli was probably the pupil of Pero della Francesca, but one can only point to the reflected light as of Piero's influence. Otherwise there is more of the physical vigor of Pollaiuolo in this work.

Tintoretto* (1518–94), Venetian

Discovery of the Body of St. Mark (1562–66): room 4
This canvas is one from the series Tintoretto painted for the Scuola Grande di San Marco (others in the series are in the Academy Gallery, Venice). It shows a scene in the crypt of the old Christian church in Alexandria, now ruled by pagan Saracens, in which a group of Venetians is rummaging through sarcophagi to find the body of their patron saint, which they intend to bring back to Christian Venice. St. Mark himself appears on the left to put a stop to the well-intentioned despoiling of the tombs. On the right, to balance the action of his raised left hand, is a group representing a man and woman possessed by the devil, and a victim of the plague asking for St. Mark's help. The powerful composition creates tension with its succession of arches, painted in perspective, moving rapidly inward. So rapidly do they move away from us that if it was not for the saint's outstretched hand, placed over the vanishing point of the perspective, the motion would continue and the painting would lose its cohesiveness and disturb its main focus of attention. As with all of Tintoretto's paintings, the chiaroscuro and Venetian color is paramount in adding mystery and excitement to the scene.

CATHEDRAL

Piazza del Duomo

Milan Cathedral is the only true northern Gothic building on a large scale in Italy. As one of the largest and most elaborate churches in the world, it is 490 feet long, 298 feet wide, and 268 feet high in its interior; it could hold about 40,000 people. It is adorned by 2,245 Gothic gargoyles and other statuary.

All of this started in 1386 when Gian Galeazzo Visconti, the ruler of Milan, ordered that it be built. The project extended over centuries and included the work of many foreign architects and craftsmen. It was completed under Napoleon in 1805.

The exterior of shining white marble (even the roof is marble) is the most ornate example of the Gothic anywhere. With its flying buttresses and intricate lacework in stone surrounding the tall tracery windows of the aisles, and the three large ones of the apse, it has been called an "Italian wedding cake" and a "transparent marble mountain." Yet Milan Cathedral does succeed. It is impressive inside where it has a cruciform shape, four aisles, a double transept, polygonal choir, ambulatory, and domelike vault. Its vast space and the beauty of its proportions, with its forest of clustered pillars that support its roof, produce a solemn, mystical sensation.

SANTA MARIA DELLE GRAZIE

Piazza Santa Maria delle Grazie

Hours: Open Tues.–Sat., 9AM–1:30PM and 2–6:30PM, Sun., 9AM–3PM. Admission fee.

This church, known throughout the world because its refectory contains Leonardo's *Last Supper,* is otherwise worth seeing. It was built between 1465 and 1490, and in 1492 partly rebuilt by Bramante (1444–1514), who is responsible for the striking tribune and cupola. One wonders if he was not inspired or helped by Leonardo (himself an architect) who was at work on the *Last Supper* next door. The cubes, hemispheres, and half cylinders of the exterior are right out of Leonardo's own drawings. This complex geometric design is carried inside where it provides a lovely spaciousness.

Leonardo da Vinci (1452–1519), Florentine
Leonardo da Vinci was endowed with a combination of intellectual and artistic qualities such as few men have possessed. With his personal charm and strength of character he was the most dynamic personality of the high Renaissance in Italy, around whom a school of painting grew.

Leonardo's genius made itself present at an early age, and it was not long before he became architect, sculptor, painter, musician, engineer, and scientist—the ideal Renaissance man, imbued with the spirit of inquiry and search for excellence. (At the Ambrosiana Library and Picture Gallery in Milan, Piazza Pio XI, 2, are over one thousand of his sketches and notes covering scientific and artistic subjects.) His paintings are unique in combining Masaccio's and Piero della Francesca's analytical approach with Botticelli's decorative, poetic, and linear art to achieve his own Leonardesque style. That style, with its poetic sentiment, searching analysis, pyramidal composition, and blending of light and atmosphere into a mysterious *sfumato,* was copied by painters during and after his time.

A brief chronology of Leonardo's life starts with his birth in the village of Vinci, the son of a notary and a peasant girl his father did not marry. He was brought up in his father's house with the affection of a childless stepmother, and probably remained in Vinci until the age of fourteen. Afterward, he went to Florence with his father—his stepmother having died young—and in about 1469 entered the studio of Verrocchio. From 1480 he began to receive his own commissions and in 1482 got what he considered to be his great opportunity, an invitation to enter the service of the duke of Milan, Ludovico il Moro. He prospered in Milan and took part in its Golden Age when it was one of the most lavish, enlightened courts of Europe. This came to an end, however, when the duke of Milan was taken off to France as a prisoner by Louis XII. Thereafter Leonardo moved on to Mantua and Venice, and finally arrived back in Florence, where he stayed until 1506. Then he returned to Milan, having obtained the patronage of Charles d'Amboise, but when the French were driven out of Milan in 1512, he joined Giuliano de Medici in Rome. He stayed there until 1515 when at the death of Giuliano he accepted an invitation from the French king, Francis I, to settle in Amboise and act as his official engineer. He died at Le Clos-Lucé on May 2, 1519, and was buried in the cloister of the church of St. Florentin in Amboise (his supposed remains are now at the Chapelle St. Hubert at the Château d'Amboise).

The Last Supper (1495–98): refectory
Throughout its history Leonardo's painting has led a charmed but fragile life, and it is amazing that any of it has survived. Leonardo painted it on a dry wall in oils, rather than on a wet wall as in fresco painting, and it started to deteriorate only about twenty years after it was completed. Over the centuries it was continually touched-up and little of the original was probably visible when, in August, 1943, during an air raid on Milan, the roof and one wall of the refectory were demolished. The painting was not harmed; you can see a picture of the destruction on the refectory wall. In 1947 the restoration of the painting was begun and all the touching up of former centuries removed. As a result, though most of Leonardo's masterpiece is gone, today it is probably more like the original than it had been for hundreds of years.

Prior to Leonardo's *Last Supper* the scene had been depicted by other artists using static compositions, where the apostles were isolated, with Judas set apart from the rest. These earlier paintings concentrated on events after Christ had disclosed that one of the twelve would betray Him, and therefore were concerned with the Eucharist (the first communion of the apostles). For the first time Leonardo chose to depict only the earlier moment in the drama when Christ says, "Verily I say unto you, one of you which eateth with me shall betray me." This sets off a shock wave that moves from Christ to either side, where the apostles are arranged in four sets of threes. Instead of isolating the betrayer, Leonardo shows the dramatic effect the announcement has on all the guests at the table.

In Leonardo's mingling of the mathematical with the poetical, he reaches for the underlying meaning of all life. Leonardo was aware of the symbolic meaning Christian tradition gives to various numbers, and he set up his composition to play upon them so as to add to the mystery of the scene.

Starting with **three** (each group consists of three apostles) we have the number of the Trinity, the most sacred. **Four** (there are four groups of apostles in Leonardo's composition) is the number of the Gospels in the New Testament (Matthew, Mark, Luke, and John), of the Cardinal Virtues (justice, prudence, fortitude, and temperance—the benefits to be derived by man from the Eucharist), the Rivers of Paradise, which stand for the symbols of the Gospels, and the seasons of the year. Three plus four makes **seven,** the number of the Gifts of the Holy Spirit (wisdom, intellect, consolation, strength, knowledge, piety, and fear of God), and the Seven Sacraments (Baptism, Confirmation, Confession, Communion, Holy Orders, Matrimony, and Extreme Unction). Three times four is **twelve,** the number of the apostles and of the gates of the New Jerusalem, the months in the year, the hours of the day, and the hours of the night. These arithmetical arrangements, with their symbolic meanings, make order out of the dramatic confusion of the scene.

But there is no confusion as to where Christ is sitting. His presence is distinct from the others by virtue of His calm manner, His position at the center of the table, at the vanishing point of the perspective. The second window behind Him is a symbol of revelation and a reference to His being the second figure of the Trinity. We have to look for Judas, even though he is next in importance in the scene, because a wrongdoer is likely to hide and has to be discovered. He is the only figure in dark shadow, leaning on the table in the first group to Christ's right. His face is in contrast to the inquiring expression of St. Peter and the youthful innocence of St. John, with Judas in his group of three. He is also the only apostle who does not protest, since he knows it is he whom Christ is referring to, and he is also the only one who reaches for food, indicating he has received the sacrament unworthily.

The other apostles are depicted in varying intensity of action, balanced with movements inclining toward or away from the center. The contrasts in their behavior are a credit to Leonardo's study of human character. Starting from the right hand of Christ is the group including John, Peter, and Judas, already mentioned. In the next group, St. Andrew, grey bearded, lifts his hands in astonishment; St. James Minor, who resembles Christ, reaches out for St. Peter's shoulder; St. Bartholomew, at the end of the table, has risen from his seat and leans forward as if not certain he heard Christ correctly. On the left side of Christ St. James Major, with extended arms, shrinks in horror; St. Thomas behind him raises his probing forefinger; St. Philip, with his hands on his breast, expresses love for Christ and his own innocence. In the second group on Christ's left, St. Matthew turns to his two companions and points to Christ; St. Thaddeus speaks to Simon expressing his consternation; and Simon, the oldest of the apostles, is thoughtful and distressed.

Can you imagine how *The Last Supper* must have looked when it was in new, luminous and richly decorated condition? It is a credit to Leonardo's genius that this painting, even though a ghost of its former self, is enough to establish him as one of the greatest painters who ever lived.

————————Naples————————

NATIONAL MUSEUM OF CAPODIMONTE

Parco di Capodimonte

Hours: Open Tues.–Sat., 9AM–2PM, Sun., 9AM–1PM. Admission fee.

This museum, located at "The Top of the Hill," or Capodimonte, is one of the most pleasant museums in Italy. It is set within a huge Bourbon palace built by Charles III, king of Naples, and surrounded by gardens. Its picture gallery, on the second floor, contains a collection from every Italian school. There is also a display of furniture, glassware, Flemish tapestries, porcelain, and enamels.

Bellini, Giovanni* (ca. 1430–1516), Venetian

Transfiguration: room 8
During Bellini's long career he was constantly improving his style and technique. In this painting, from the late 1480s, he places the figures in the landscape instead of relegating the landscape to a background with figures in front of it, a decisive point in his development. Bellini has also changed the established depiction of the Transfiguration itself. Prior to this picture the Transfiguration was shown as a supernatural event with Mount Tabor represented as a lofty peak. But here a familiar landscape that could be anywhere replaces it to give a natural, balanced rendering of the scene. Bellini sticks close to the text from Mark which says that Christ appeared in "raiment white and glistening." He uses Christ's white robe, shaded with tones of gray and green, to translate Christ's presence to the colors of the hills and the white clouds in the background. The makeshift fence running diagonally across the foreground may represent the fragility of life, and the chasm behind it the grave, each suggesting barriers that must be crossed to fully understand the Transfiguration.

Bruegel, Pieter, the Elder (ca. 1525–69), Flemish

The Parable of the Blind (1568): room 20
This painting, which depicts the Gospel story where Christ likens the Pharisees to blind men ("Let them alone, they be blind leaders of the blind, and if the blind lead the blind, both shall fall into the ditch"), has a composition that is a high point of European art. Bruegel has concentrated upon the critical moment when the leader of the blind men has fallen into the ditch and the others, one by one, are about to follow. The movement is on a plane of a descending diagonal reinforced by the staffs the figures are holding, and by the sloping ground. It is a hopeless, pathetic scene, contrasted by the verticals in the background, the most prominent being the church. Perhaps the church also had symbolic meaning to Bruegel as a force unable to stop the catastrophe we are witnessing, or other catastrophies in the world. The low-toned cold grays, olive greens, and off-reds add further to the austere atmosphere of the scene and imbue it with a sharp intensity.

In painting this picture Bruegel may have been thinking of wandering preachers of various sects who, in his day, attracted large crowds of followers. It is significant that this painting was one of Bruegel's last (it was completed one year before he died), and may reflect his tragic sense of life. Considering the accuracy with which he painted each blind man (specialists have pointed out that each figure is suffering from a definite form of blindness, such as the central figure whose white patch on his cornea shows him to have leucoma) it may indicate his fear that he too would become blind. During Bruegel's time people thought blindness was caused by diseased vapors rising from the stomach to the brain, and we know that Bruegel was suffering from a stomach ailment at the end of his life.

In the same room is also Breugel's last work, *The Misanthrope* (1568), whose unfinished condition (it has suffered with age) adds to its pathetic statement of renunciation. T'.e colors here are also quiet—mauve, gray, dull green, grayish brown—to depict a gloomy outlook on the world. No wonder the strange old man is a misanthrope. As he is seeking solitude in the countryside, which to him appears deserted, and oafish scoundrel, representing the world, is stealing his money. When the old man discovers the theft it will not surprise him because he already feels that mankind is a faithless lot who have polluted the beauty of nature.

Titian* (ca. 1487–1576), Venetian

Danae: room 19
Titian painted the erotic mythological story of Danae several times. His *Danae* at the Prado in Madrid is similar to this one, showing the recumbent maiden on a bed receiving Jupiter is the form of a shower of gold. But at Madrid an ugly maidservant, interested only in material gain, selfishly stretches out her apron to collect the gold; Danae waits only for love. In this *Danae*, painted for the powerful Farnese family during Titian's visit with them in Rome in 1545, only cupid occupies the picture with Danae. As in the Prado picture she is daringly depicted as a beautiful maiden lying in a position to receive the love of Jupiter. Her warm, glowing body makes her one of Titian's most sensual women, in a career that included the most beautiful reclining nude Venuses ever painted in Europe. (For the story of Danae see Gosaert's *Danae* at the Bavarian State Art Gallery, Munich).

Pope Paul III and His Grandsons: room 19
Titian's sojourn in Rome in 1545 was a great success. He was welcomed by everyone, including the Farnese pope, Paul III, and in a splendid ceremony was made a citizen of Rome. This portrait of the pope and his two grandsons was done at that time and is one of Titian's finest works, making use of his mastery of light and color to cover a vast range of gradations. It was listed in the Farnese inventory as a "sketch," rather than a completed painting, which shows a lack of understanding of Titian's free brush work.

Titian's painting shows the pope as an old man with an inner energy and vitality of spirit visible in the eyes. He was used to corruption, having been made a cardinal because his sister, Julia Farnese, known throughout Rome as "La Bella," had been the mistress of Alexander Borgia. He was no fool and thoroughly disliked his grandsons, especially the untrustworthy one on his left, the son of the cruel Pierluigi Farnese, the Pope's son who was murdered a few years after this painting was completed. He was the last of the Renaissance popes, and while he was an unwilling supporter of the Counter-Reformation, he created the basis for its success: the Jesuit order and the Council of Trent.

NATIONAL ARCHAEOLOGICAL MUSEUM

Piazza Museo

Hours: Open Tues.–Sat., 9AM–2PM, Sun., 9AM–1PM. Admission fee.

Note: Some rooms in the museum may be temporarily closed due to recon-

struction necessitated by damage done in the earthquake of November 23, 1980.

This museum has one of the finest collections of antique statues, frescoes, and mosaics in Italy, plus an interesting display of everyday household goods—kitchen utensils, drawing instruments, tables, coins, crystals—that were buried in the ash and mud after the eruption of Vesuvius in 79 A.D. Its sculptures include pieces that came to the museum from the famous Farnese collection in Rome and Parma. Of these *The Farnese Hercules* (room 12), a larger-than-life piece, is a second-century B.C. Greek marble copied from a fourth-century B.C. Lysippian bronze showing a massive male figure leaning on a club draped with the skin of a lion. It not only shows the conquering hero with his exaggerated muscles—the superhuman brute strength he is famous for—but also depicts him in a moment of contemplation or weariness, which adds a human dimension to his character. Another large piece, the largest of all known ancient statues intended to be seen from all sides, is *The Farnese Bull* (room 16), which is a marble Roman copy of a Hellenistic work of the second century B.C. It is the basis of a group composition in pyramidal form involving two sons of Antiope avenging wrongs done to their mother by tying the cruel Dirce to the horns of a wild bull to be dragged to her death. Other statues are *Harmodius and Aristogeiton* (room 1), *Orestes and Electra* (room 7), *The Dead Amazon* (room 9), *Venus Callipygus* (room 9), *Venus of Capua* (room 14), *Youth and a Dolphin* (room 25), *The Dancing Faun* (room 61), and *Drunken Silenus* (room 116).

The Roman wall paintings and mosaics in the museum have no equal anywhere as examples of the way wealthy Romans decorated their homes in ancient times. You will see an almost infinite variety of themes and subjects, usually showing dark backgrounds with figures standing out in relief. Many of the subjects of these paintings were drawn from Hellenistic works, including landscapes that have a surprising freedom of expression.

Alexander Mosaic (second century B.C.): mezzanine, room 61
This mosaic, one of the most celebrated works of ancient art, was found in 1831 in the House of the Faun in Pompeii. Over one million tiny stones make up its surface, which includes many different colors to achieve its four primary tones—white, black, red, and yellow (no blues). It is probably a faithful copy of a lost fourth-century B.C. Greek painting and may have been made in Alexandria, where complex work of this kind was a specialty.

We are looking at the moment when Alexander the Great, the beardless figure at the left, is routing the Persians under King Darius at the Battle of Issus in 333 B.C. The king, reaching out to help his fallen general, who has been transfixed with a spear, is being led away on his chariot by the retreating army. The landscape is only barely indicated by means of a shattered tree trunk, but the long lances rising above the scene, and the overlapping figures which artfully compress the volume, combine to suggest three-dimensional space. Notice the face of Alexander with his exaggeratedly large eyes. He is shown as a man who realizes his destiny, which his victory at Issus brought to reality. It is the historical start of the Hellenistic Age.

Orvieto

CATHEDRAL

This cathedral was begun in 1290 (not completed until about the late six-teenth century) to commemorate the Miracle of Bolsena (1263; see Raphael Stanza, Vatican), the reliquary of which is kept in a tabernacle over its altar. It was built in competition with the Cathedral of Siena, which it resembles, and like that building is one of the architectural masterpieces in Italy of the period of transition from late Romanesque to Gothic. Notice the pointed Gothic pinnacles and cusped gables of its front facade, and the round Romanesque arches and horizontal zebra banding of its interior. Only at Siena and Orvieto can you see such a mixture of these two dominant styles.

The lower part of the Gothic front facade is the work of Lorenzo Maitani (ca. 1275–1330), a Sienese who also worked on the facade of his native city's cathedral. The upper part of the facade is by Andrea Orcagna (active 1344–68) and Andrea Pisano (ca. 1270–1348), the authors of the various sculptures and bas-reliefs. The colorful mosaics are modern and so are the bronze doors (1963–65).

The interior is of basilican shape, round-arched, timber-roofed, with a square sanctuary, projecting transepts, and heavy cylindrical columns. Its great art treasure is a series of frescoes by Signorelli.

Signorelli, Luca (ca. 1450–1523), Italian

Frescoes in the San Brizio Chapel (1499–1504): end of right transept
Fra Angelico started a fresco cycle of the *Last Judgment* on the walls of this large chapel in 1447, but had finished only two of the vaulting compart-ments before he was called to Rome by the pope. Signorelli was originally employed to finish Fra Angelico's work on the ceiling, but in 1500 he got the commission to continue with the walls.

Signorelli does not have the artistic gifts of Michelangelo, but has the same interest in the movement of the human body, and a Michelangesque imagination to go with it. His work here represents the first colossal painting of the cinquecento.

On the left wall is the ***Sermon of the Antichrist,*** a subject that fascinated the medieval mind. The drama begins with the fall of the evil spirit driven out of Heaven by the angel. We see the Antichrist preaching in the fore-ground with a demon on his back telling him what to say. At the foot of the pedestal on which he stands are vases with coins and other enticements to tempt souls. The crowd around him consists of all sorts of people, one of whom is Dante to the right. In the background, a Renaissance temple is be-ing looted of its treasure. Soldiers are beheading people. Victims are being stripped. In the foreground, at the extreme left edge, are portraits of both Signorelli (the older man with clasped hands) and Fra Angelico (the younger man painting). Their black dress enhances their presence in the painting which has many pale blue, rose, and brown tones. They seem to observe the evil in the world with a detached assurance of knowing that only the true Christ is the way to salvation.

Other easily identifiable paintings are the **Resurrection of the Dead,** significant for being the most ambitious nude composition of its day; and the most grotesque and crowded scene, the **Damned Consigned to Hell,** which depicts people tortured by demons dressed in the colors of contemporary German soldiers.

Padua

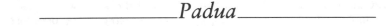

CAPPELLA DEGLI SCROVEGNI (ARENA CHAPEL)

Corso Garibaldi

Hours: Open Apr. –Sept., daily 9AM–12:30PM and 2:30–5:30PM; Oct.–Mar., Mon.–Sat., 9:30AM–12:30PM and 1:30–4:30PM. Admission fee.

Giotto di Bondone (ca. 1267–1337), Florentine

If you look at Giotto's work outside the chronological flow of the history of art in Western Europe, you may think that it is somewhat primitive. But if you view it with the understanding that until Giotto came onto the scene Western painting was medieval in outlook and appearance, then the frescoes in this little chapel in Padua will take on more meaning. Giotto helped to change painting in Italy to a style based on human reality and the illusion of depth. This style was taken up in the major centers of Italy, with only Venice, strongly tied to Byzantium, resisting.

Giotto was born in the little town of Vespignano, north of Florence, into a peasant family. He showed talent for drawing at an early age and was sent to Florence to be trained by the painter Cimabue, whose few surviving works, while Byzantinesque, show some transitory elements. With Cimabue Giotto went to Assisi where frescoes were being painted on the walls of the Church of St. Francis. Here, at the center of the growing Franciscan movement and also a center of art activity, Giotto learned painting in the old two-dimensional style. He also formed his own ideas based on depicting the rounded forms of ancient sculptures and the real emotions of people. He became director of the works at Assisi and was later called to Rome to help celebrate the jubilee of 1300. He completed a mosaic of *Christ Saving St. Peter* there and perfected his three-dimensional style, drawing from observations of Rome's ancient sculpture. In about 1304 he was called to Padua, where the family of moneylenders, Scrovegni, built this small, plain building that stands today in a garden next to fragments of a Roman amphitheater—hence the name Arena Chapel. If ever usury served a noble purpose it was here. In order to help the repose of his father's soul (Reginaldo Scrovegni is so notorious for the sin of usury that he appears in the seventh circle of Dante's Hell), Enrico Scrovegni commissioned young Giotto to cover his chapel with frescoes depicting the *Lives of the Virgin and Christ.*

The Scrovegni Chapel

The narrative starts with the top row of six frescoes on the window side showing scenes from *The Life of the Virgin.* Fresco no. 1, *The Expulsion of Joachim from the Temple,* shows the priest, who must perform his duty, turning Joachim out of the temple because he has given Israel no children. Joachim, clinging to a lamb he has offered but that has been rejected, is standing at the edge of a step like the edge of an abyss leading into the blue void at his right. In the background, on the left, is a young father being blessed. Such an emotional, realistic impression of this story was unprecedented in Giotto's time. In fresco no. 2, *Joachim Returns to His Sheepfold,* we see the future father of the Virgin taking refuge with shepherds in the wilderness. Here, too, Giotto injects a dramatic sense into his painting. Joachim, humiliated, looks downward, with his hands wrapped in his mantle. Even his dog, a symbol of fidelity, senses there is something wrong. From the look of the shepherd facing us we see that he accepts Joachim reluctantly. The natural rock in the background accentuates the psychological moment and frames the figures. Fresco no. 3 shows *The Vision of Anna,* who is visited in her home in Jerusalem by an angel who tells her she will conceive and bear a child. A servant on the back porch is oblivious to the miracle of the angel appearing. The charming little building has a classical pediment with a Roman-like medallion containing a bust portrait uplifted by angels. The front wall has been removed, and as in Giotto's other frescoes, the background and objects in the scene symbolize a complex reality in the way they would be used in a stage setting. The depth of the space is brought out by the foreshortening of the angel, seen from above, and by the more brightly lit architectural frame against the darker recesses of the interior, a principle Giotto always followed. Fresco no. 4 shows *The Sacrifice of Joachim* and fresco no. 5 *The Vision of Joachim,* where an angel comes down to tell him that a child will be born to Anna. It is the first painting in Italy that so forcefully depicts sleep as part of drama. Two diagonals divide this picture: one by the downward movement of the angel continuing along Joachim's back, the other from the top of the pyramidal rock down through the crevice. While one diagonal isolates Joachim, the other connects him with the hovering angel and the approaching shepherds. The last fresco in this row is the *Meeting at the Golden Gate.* Joachim and Anna, having both received the good news, greet each other with great warmth. Their feelings are mirrored in the faces of the women standing to the right. As they embrace, Joachim's cloak tightens about his back, giving form and weight to his figure. The depiction of such tender love between a man and a woman was unknown in painting before Giotto.

The story continues with six pictures on the opposite wall, starting with the frescoes in the front: *The Birth of the Virgin, The Presentation of the Virgin in the Temple, The Presentation of the Rods, The Watching of the Rods, The Betrothal of the Virgin,* and *The Virgin's Return Home.*

On the Triumphal Entry Arch there is, at the top, a scene of *God the Father Dispatching the Angel Gabriel;* below it on the left, *The Angel Ga-*

briel; on the opposite side, *The Annunciaton,* and directly below it *The Visitation.* The story continues on the window wall with scenes from *The Life of Christ* in the middle row of frescoes. These consist of five pictures between the windows starting with *The Nativity,* the one nearest the back wall. Until this Nativity was painted, medieval Byzantine tradition required that the scene take place in a cave. But Giotto has adopted a shed, probably derived from the Gothic art he had seen on a visit to France. One shepherd has his back turned to us, showing that Giotto was mastering space by placing his figures in it any way he chose. In fresco no. 2 we see *The Adoration of the Magi,* somewhat idealized and abstract, with light, limpid tones. Fresco no. 3 is *The Presentation in the Temple* and fresco no. 4 is a *Flight into Egypt,* where the Virgin sits upright on her horse, framed by a great pyramidal rock. The combination of stillness and movement conveys a sense of danger and mystery. This series ends with the last fresco showing *The Massacre of the Innocents.*

Six pictures continue the story in the middle level on the opposite wall: *Christ Disputing with the Elders, The Baptism of Christ, The Marriage at Cana, The Raising of Lazarus, The Entry into Jerusalem,* and *The Expulsion of the Merchants from the Temple. The Pact of Judas* is on the Triumphal Entry Arch beneath *The Angel of Gabriel.* Then the story shifts to the lower level on the window wall with five more frescoes. The first shows *The Last Supper,* the second *The Washing of the Feet,* and the third is Giotto's famous *The Kiss of Judas,* where the vicious animallike features of Judas are contrasted with the noble countenance of Christ. Notice how Judas's yellow cloak and bulky figure engulfs Christ but does not bend or move Him. It is a classic example of the confrontation between good and evil. To the left Peter, with a halo around his head, is about to cut off the ear of Malchus, the high priest's servant. A dark-hooded imp of a soldier with his back to us tries to restrain Peter. On the right the high priest is shown in a vacillating attitude as his out-stretched finger begins to contract and his massive cloak bunches up into little folds, in contrast to Judas's stretched and rounded garment. These three figures—the grotesque soldier, Judas, and the high priest—are significant for their time because they have breadth and mass. They stand with real weight in a real world and express real emotion, as opposed to the decorative, abstract figures of traditional painting during Giotto's time. The wall is completed with fresco no. 4, *Christ before Caiaphas,* and the last fresco, *The Mocking of Christ.*

On the opposite wall, lower level, the story continues with six more pictures. Starting from the back we first see *The Road to Calvary* and then a *Crucifixion* which is the first modern depiction of this scene in Italian art. Instead of the unrealistic, triumphant Christ of the medieval mosaics, we see a real dead body, with solid weight, hanging from the Cross. Two blocks of figures on either side of the Cross accent the tragedy. To the left Mary is seen collapsing. To the right Roman soldiers are disputing Christ's robe. Mary Magdalene is at the foot of the Cross, where she will always be in Western art from now on. A famous *Pietà* comes next, where the action is directed toward the dead Christ being held by His mother. Two of Giotto's famous figures, who show only their solid backs, hold His head and hand; Mary Magdalene looks down at Christ's feet, which she is supporting with her hands; St. John stands over Christ with his hands outstretched, in form similar to the sweeping rock in the background; and angels turn overhead. These figures, solidly placed on the earth, depict signs of grief unprecedented in Giotto's art, but their display of emotion is calm in comparison to later versions of the scene done by Giotto's successors. The wall is completed with depictions of *The Angel at the Tomb and the Noli Me Tangere* (both in one picture), *The Ascension,* and *The Pentecost.*

As you leave the chapel you will see on the entrance wall the largest scene of all, *The Last Judgment.* Here Giotto does not emphasize the torments of Hell, as other painters were to do later. He does show Judas, Christ's betrayer (to the left of the blue devil), hanging for his crime. On the other side he paints his own portrait among the blessed (fifth from the left in the bottom row) and that of Enrico Scrovegni, the donor of the chapel, shown presenting a model of the building. High above the masses of figures are two angels, on either side of the windows, rolling back the heavens to reveal the gates of Paradise.

Significance of Giotto's Achievement

Before the Arena Chapel Italian art had neglected the importance of the expression of mass. With Giotto, however, figures take on realistic weight, volume, and consequently depth. Giotto's technique is that of an accurate rendering of what we actually see in the real world. This is not to say that Giotto is a realist. He simplifies his figures to eliminate whatever might hinder his emphasis on weight and volume, and to reduce figure and design to fundamentals. Similarly, his settings, both architectural and landscape, are simple statements of the locale, not an attempt at realistic representation. His primary concern is with figures and their reactions; everything else is secondary.

Giotto's art is noted for the warm human sympathy he injects into his characters, often depicted with a dignity and restraint that balances the dramatic tension of the stories. This departure from the art of the Middle Ages leaves the characters under the artist's control, an essential of Renaissance art. It is Renaissance art that Giotto inspires. The heirs to his artistic legacy become Brunelleschi, Donatello, and Masaccio. With them the genius of Giotto is continued and passed on up through the nineteenth century.

CHURCH OF SANT' ANTONIO

Piazza del Santo

Hours: Open daily 9AM–12 noon and 2:30–6:30PM. Free admission.

The pilgrimage church of Sant' Antonio owes a great deal to its proximity to Venice, evidenced by its seven Byzantine domes on high cylindrical drums over its nave, transepts, and choir. To go with them are two minaretlike bell towers. This Byzantine quality is mixed with Romanesque and Gothic ele-

ments—notice its Romanesque round arches and Gothic pointed windows—
to make for an interesting edifice. Its dim, vast interior, with rough bare
walls, disappoints, and if it were not for **Donatello's High Altar bronze reliefs** showing the *Miracles of St. Anthony* (1446–50), and his equestrian
statue on the piazza outside, the church would be just a curiosity. The
bronze reliefs in Sant' Antonio show Donatello's work at its most mature,
full of dramatic religious intensity and an intellectual concern for solving
problems of form and perspective. Lively foreshortened figures and vast architectural settings project movement in relief sculpture as never before, with
attention directed toward the center of each scene, where the saint is performing a miracle.

Donatello* (1386–1466), Florentine

Equestrian Statue of Gattamelata (ca. 1450): Piazza del Santo
In 1443 Donatello left Florence and went to Padua for ten years where, away
from the competitive climate of Florence, he was free to explore his own
style. His presence in Padua gave rise to a school of painting that formed
around him and helped spread the Florentine Renaissance to the Veneto,
where it had lagged behind. This equestrian statue was probably ordered by
the Venetian senate as a memorial to Erasmo da Narni, called Gattamelata,
captain-general of the Republic of Venice, who died in Padua in 1443. It was
the commission to do this statue that brought Donatello to Padua.

The *Gattamelata* is not the first equestrian monument of the Renaissance or even of the late Middle Ages. There were others, but the artistic
accomplishment of this one made it the forerunner of all those that stand
today throughout Europe and even America.

Donatello seems to have been inspired by the antique statue of *Marcus
Aurelius* on Rome's Campidoglio, and by the ancient bronze horses of San
Marco in Venice. Even the head of Gattamelata, which is not a real portrait,
seems based on busts of Julius Caesar. But this is not a mere copy of other
works of art. Donatello infused it with an intellectual energy and a mood of
philosophical humanism that was unkown earlier. His figure represents the
Renaissance ideal of a commanding, intelligent personality capable of greatness in battle. To the fifteenth-century mind the ideal could be expressed as
reason overcoming the brute force of the animal.

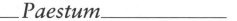

Paestum

CITTÀ ANTICA

Hours: Open Tues.–Sun., 9AM–one hour before sunset. Admission fee.

Temple of Neptune
As early as five hundred years before Christ this was the wealthy Greek colony of Poseidonia (city of Neptune). The Sybarites, from Sybaris, founded it
to facilitate the movement of goods by caravan from the east coast of Italy

to Cumae on the west coast. They were an energetic, intelligent people, as the ruins of the three temples indicate. In 273 b.c. the Romans occupied the city and changed its name to Paestum. These enormous and majestic ruins were unknown to the Middle Ages and even to the Renaissance, and were rediscovered only in 1740.

Of the three Doric temples the so-called Temple of Neptune, which may have been dedicated to Hera, wife of Zeus, is the best preserved; in fact, it is the best preserved of all Greek temples anywhere. It is not as fine as the Parthenon in Athens, built a hundred years later, but it has all the qualities of Greek temples elsewhere—fine fluting on its columns, which reduces their robust dimensions; a slight vertical bulge of the shaft (entasis) in each column to avoid the illusion of sagging inwards; and unity of design within a compact form. Originally it was covered with stucco made to look like marble, and details of its entablature were colored in reds and blues. In their present ruined condition these temples are still quite beautiful.

Your ticket of admission entitles you to visit the worthwhile small museum, which contains many objects from the site, some recently discovered.

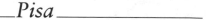

Pisa

CATHEDRAL GROUP

Piazza del Duomo

The cathedral group at Pisa, displayed on a broad expanse of green grass, is one of the most famous architectural complexes in the world and the best example of the Tuscan Romanesque style in Italy. It was begun in 1063, and of the four structures within the group—the Cathedral, the Leaning Tower, the Baptistery and the Camposanto—the first two and part of the third were completed in the eleventh and twelfth centuries. Their uniformity comes in all being built of the same white marble from quarries near Pisa.

Cathedral (Duomo)

Hours: Open daily 7:45AM–1PM and 3PM–sunset. Free admission.

This building was planned on a grand scale, by a Greek architect, as a five-aisle Latin-cross basilica with three transepts, a flat roof, and no dome. The present dome is probably a Gothic addition. Its construction, with round arches over pillars, became famous as Pisan Romanesque design and was copied throughout Tuscany and beyond. In no other church of this size is there such lavish use of loggias and blind arcading. Their richness is in a fusion of the characters of the Orient and the Mediterranean. Inside the effect is one of monumentality, in changing views seen through rows of columns and bridgelike galleries over arcades that separate the transepts from the nave. There is black and white horizontal banding of marble throughout, a standard feature in Romanesque buildings in Italy.

Pisano, Giovanni (ca. 1245/50–after 1314), Pisan

Pulpit (1302–11): nave, beneath cupola.
This pulpit was partly destroyed by the burning of the cathedral in 1595 and by the dispersal of its panels afterward. It was finally reassembled and restored in 1926.

Giovanni Pisano is the son of Nicola Pisano, sculptor of the pulpit in the Baptistery. While the older man's work shows little of the Gothic spirit, Giovanni's has more Gothic feeling and less of the classical elements of his father's sculpture. The reliefs on the panels show the new religious feeling of the Gothic Age. In the *Crucifixion* panel everything is pushed to the extreme. Mary is fainting, the figures on the crosses are twisted in agony, and the group around the scene seems transfixed. The other panels represent *The Birth of the Baptist and the Visitation, The Birth of Christ, The Announcement by an Angel to the Shepherds, The Adoration of the Magi, The Presentation in the Temple and Flight into Egypt, The Massacre of the Innocents, The Betrayal and the Passion of Christ,* and *The Last Judgment.*

Baptistery

Hours: Open Mon.–Fri., 9AM–1PM and 3PM–sunset. Free admission.

This building, a rotunda with a huge hemispheral dome, was begun in 1152 and developed over a few hundred years into a mixture of Romanesque and Gothic styles. The ground floor is Romanesque. The building continues above with Gothic finials and pointed arches—not a unified result. But the interior happily maintains its original Romanesque design. It is distinguished by a large octagonal font (1246) in the center by Guido da Como and, its treasure, the pulpit by Nicola Pisano.

Pisano, Nicola (ca. 1220/25 or earlier–ca. 1284), Pisan

Pulpit (1260)
This hexagonal pulpit is the masterpiece of the elder Pisano. Three of its seven columns are supported upon the backs of fierce lions; the central column rests on a group of men and animals. Above, trilobe arches rest on the outer pillars supporting the platform which is surrounded by the five panels of reliefs representing *The Nativity, The Adoration of the Magi, The Presentation, The Crucifixion,* and *The Last Judgment.*

Nicola's chief talent lay in depicting the human form in the classical style. Notice the monumental Virgin in the *Adoration of the Magi* panel. Light and shade define her body and her classical Roman head is framed by wavy strands of hair. In the *Presentation in the Temple* panel, where the protagonists are in Roman robes, classical design persists. On the left-hand corner below the *Adoration* panel, the most striking of the figures is shown representing the Christian virtue of *Fortitude.* His nakedness places him in the classical spirit of art rather than in the medieval.

Leaning Tower (Campanile)

Hours: Open daily 7:45AM–1PM and 3PM–sunset. Free admission.

In this famous building, begun in 1174 (completed 1350), the Pisan passion for blind arcading and loggias is pronounced; there are six stories of concentric rings of them embellished with lozenge ornaments in the upper sections of the arches. It blends with the cathedral near it and in spite of its dramatic tilt comes off as an elegant structure. Details of construction indicate that the tower settled into the ground at an angle even while being built. The builder made the angle of inclination slightly greater near the bottom than further up, to mitigate the settling as the tower rose.

Camposanto

Hours: Open daily 9AM–sunset. Free admission.

This large cloister, which blends Romanesque solidity with Gothic weightlessness in a symmetrical design, was built in 1278 around a rectangular green filled with earth taken from the Holy Land (*camposanto* means cemetery). It was badly damaged in 1944, but there are still enough Etruscan, Roman, and medieval sculptures left to make a visit worthwhile, plus medieval frescoes interesting for their content if not for their artistic quality. Of these, see the ***Triumph of Death,*** possibly painted about 1350 by either Orcagna or Francesco Traini (Cappella Ammannati).

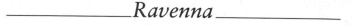

Ravenna

There is no other place where you can more convincingly enter the Christian world of the fifth and sixth centuries than at Ravenna. A great number of early mosaic masterpieces have been preserved in this city, which at various times during its Golden Age was the seat of the emperors of the West, and the administrative capital of the region controlled by the emperor of Constantinople.

Here, color and light are supreme. The materials that make up the mosaics—small cubes of enamel, glass, marble, and even mother-of-pearl—absorb and reflect light, giving off a brilliance no other medium can equal. They are not subordinate to the architecture that contains them, but assume a dominant role.

TOMB OF GALLA PLACIDIA

Via San Vitale, 17

Hours: Open daily 8:30AM–6:30PM. Free admission.

Who was Galla Placidia? She was the daughter of Emperor Theodosius the Great, who was captured by Alaric when he and his Goths sacked Rome in

410. She witnessed Alaric's secret burial in the Busento River and married his successor, Ataulf, only returning to her people when Ataulf was slain. Later, her son, by a Roman general, became Valentinian III, emperor of the West.

This building is supposed to be her tomb but historians believe she was buried in Rome where St. Peter's now stands. Rough-looking from the outside, the tomb contains some of the finest mosaics in Ravenna (ca. 450). The small windows of the building are original, so the coloristic effect of light falling on the sparkling surfaces of the mosaics is the same as it was in the fifth century.

Look up at the deep blue **dome** of the building, studded with eight hundred gold stars, and around it with symbols of the four evangelists (Matthew, Mark, Luke, and John). The Latin cross in the center symbolizes Christianity as the embodiment of order and harmony in a mysterious world. This is emphasized in the circles of stars which grow smaller, creating the illusion that the sky is receding as the eye moves toward the apex, and also seeming to give additional height to the dome.

Within the **wall surface** of the arches, directly beneath the dome, are figures representing the apostles. They point to the cross in the dome with their right hands, while at their feet are white doves at vessels and fountains that sprinkle water, symbolizing the good Christians who move toward the holy water that will give them everlasting life.

Notice the scenes in the **lunettes** of the cross-arms. There are two stags among acanthus tendrils. The stags symbolize the souls of the world crying out to God. In the lunette opposite the entrance, St. Lawrence, the Roman martyr venerated in the antique world, is about to be condemned to the flaming gridiron. He is hurrying toward it because he is anxious to give up his life for his faith. The four books in the gold cabinet, representing the four Gospels, symbolize that faith.

Above the doorway is a scene depicting the Good Shepherd (Christ) in a pastoral landscape. He is a human figure, young, beardless, and with a softness and heavenly sense achieved by the arrangement of the colors in the mosaic pattern. This theme recurs in the catacombs and is a part of the early Roman Christian tradition.

The mosaics in this little building, done in the Hellenistic-Roman realistic style, give us a mystical feeling of unlimited space. The effect is unlike any other work of art.

BASILICA OF SAN VITALE

Via San Vitale, 17

Hours: Open daily 8:30AM–6:30PM. Free admission.

This church was begun in 527, less than one year after the death of Theodoric and the accession of Justinian as emperor in Constantinople. It was undertaken by Justinian in absentia to assert his Italian claims, but it was not until his armies physically took Ravenna in 540 that construction was pursued in earnest, to come to completion about 547.

The architectural plan is of a centralized church as opposed to an oblong basilica. Therefore the axis is vertical, leading the eye upward from the central floor space to the dome, instead of running horizontally through the center of the building, dividing it lengthwise. This type of plan was derived from the ancient circular tombs of Greece and Rome.

The plain red brick exterior contrasts with the interior, where two large rectangular panels of mosaics, high points of Ravenna's masterpieces, face each other in the **sanctuary.** The one depicting *Justinian and his Courtiers* has all the pomp and luxury of the Byzantine court as the emperor offers the liturgical vessels as imperial gifts (the *oblatio Augusti et Augustae*—an offering made by Byzantine emperors at Easter to the most important churches in the city). It shows the figures in frontal view, characteristic of Byzantine art, with Justinian in his purple mantle standing out in the center. His face is probably a portrait of the way he really looked, being a juridical substitute for his actual presence—Justinian lived in Constantinople and never visited Ravenna. His face could have been copied from imperial medals distributed in the Byzantine provinces, but most likely it points to the presence here of mosaicists from Constantinople. A prominent place is also given to Bishop Maximian, who carries a jeweled cross symbolizing his authority and has his name inscribed above his head. Tall and lean, he appears to be of strong character, aware of his own importance even in the presence of the emperor.

On the opposite side in the sanctuary is the panel depicting *The Empress Theodora and her Servants.* Here the color is more vibrant and again we see tall slender figures with an air of dignity and luxury. The empress stands aloof and wears a jeweled necklace around her shoulders and a splendid crown. The five women in the right corner have stereotyped faces resembling each other, but the two ladies near the empress are set apart and may represent Antonina, the wife of General Belisarus who captured Ravenna in 540, and her daughter, Giovannina, said to be a close friend of Theodora. Notice the small fountain and the open door. They may allude to the death of Theodora, who died in 548; if this is so the date assigned to these mosaics (547) would have to be moved forward a few years.

The **half-dome of the apse** is distinguished by its *Christ Enthroned* in which Christ appears as a clean shaven young Roman instead of the bearded sorrowful figure of later times. Notice the figure of the Archbishop Ecclesius on the right side, the man who started the construction of the church—see the model he is holding.

When one stands in San Vitale, surrounded by the magnificence of its mosaics, the realization of how different the Oriental Christian church can be is felt. Such color and decoration exist nowhere else.

ORTHODOX BAPTISTERY

Via Battistero

Hours: Open daily 9AM–12 noon and 2:30–6:30PM. Free admission.

The Baptistery of the Orthodox is a converted Roman bath house dating back at least to 450, perhaps from 396. It is octagonal in plan with three projecting apses, covered with a central dome. The **mosaics in its dome** are its main attraction and are some of the finest in Ravenna. Focus on the central medallion first. It shows the baptism of Christ and is the focal point on which all of the ornament converges. Its gold background, partly restored, projects the rocks and flowers outward and emphasizes the transparency of the water in which Christ is immersed. Notice that a river god emerging from the water is carrying a swamp reed in his left hand, symbolizing aquatic divinity, and in his right hand a green cloth, with which to dry Christ's body after the baptism. Later representations of the baptism replace this figure with angels who hold the cloth. Also look at the twelve apostles holding crowns and separated from one another by slender floreate candelabras that extend up to the central medallion. Each apostle is seen in a portrait depicting facial structure and individual character—something that did not occur again until the Renaissance. Below them, the decoration is symbolic of the omnipotence of Christ.

ARCHIEPISCOPAL MUSEUM

Piazza Arcivescovado, 1

Hours: Open Mon., Wed.–Sat., 9AM–12 noon and 2:30–6PM, Sun., 9AM–1PM. Admission fee.

This museum is the archbishop's residence, located near the Baptistery, where among works of art from the original cathedral and from San Vitale is the beautifully carved ivory covered **Bishop's Throne of Maximian** dating from the sixth century. It is the most impressive example of sculpture of this period, with figures representing the story of Joseph, the life of Christ, St. John, and the Evangelists. Notice that the design is not yet fully Byzantine, but it has also ceased to be Roman. You can see a vague angularity and stylization that will become more pronounced in later times as pure Byzantinesque.

The **Archiepiscopal Chapel,** on the third floor, was the bishop's private chapel, also used to administer the sacrament of penance. It was constructed at the end of the fifth century during the reign of Theodoric the Great, and is rich in mosaics, but not the kind where many colors are used or sharply contrasted. It employs an extensive gold background instead of the traditional blue. Of special interest, in the **lunette above the vestibule door,** is the figure of **Christ** as a warrior. It shows Him in the act of trampling on the heads of a serpent and a lion (derived from the psalm: "Rise above the viper and crush the lion and the dragon"). His pose is frontal, as in other mosaics of the period, and He holds a long cross against His right shoulder and, in His left hand, an open book inscribed with the words, "I am the Way, the Truth, and the Life."

BAPTISTERY OF THE ARIANS

Piazzetta degli Ariani

Hours: Open daily 8:30AM–12:30PM and 2–6:30PM. Free admission.

This is a small octagonal building with four apses. The date of its construction is unknown, but it was built during Theodoric's reign (493–526). It is of interest for its **dome,** decorated with mosaics similar to those in the Orthodox Baptistery (see above).

Like the Orthodox Baptistery, there is a central medallion showing the baptism of Christ, but here the composition is better balanced. St. John the Baptist is standing on Christ's left, while a figure representing the River Jordan, with two red crayfish claws ornamenting his head, is on Christ's right. Below the medallion are the twelve apostles separated by palm trees and, as a variant to the same procession in the Orthodox Baptistery, a throne bearing a cross studded with gems is introduced into the circle. The position of the throne behind the baptism, creating the point where the apostles meet, unfortunately disturbs the perspective of the scene in the central medallion and the figured frieze around it.

Other differences between this work and the mosaics at the Orthodox Baptistery are the more subdued color here and the lack of individuality in the faces of the apostles. They all look alike, while at the Orthodox Baptistery each is an individual portrait.

SANT' APOLLINARE NUOVO

Via di Roma

Hours: Open daily 8AM–12 noon and 2–6:30PM. Free admission.

Theodoric the Great built this church in 500 as an Arian cathedral. Sixty years later, after the Goths had been already driven out of Ravenna, it was consecrated as a Catholic church and dedicated to St. Martin, the former bishop of Tours (370), a famous destroyer of pagan shrines. Its round belfry, to the right of the front of the building, was erected in 1000 and is derived from the turrets of Roman walls, a typical construction around Ravenna.

The mosaics along both walls of the long nave are unique, one of the high points of the mosaic masterpieces in Ravenna. Each wall is divided into three horizontal sections of mosaics starting above the arches: the first runs along the wall between the top of the arches and the moulding at the base of the windows, the second covers the area between each window, and the third is at the very top between the windows and the ceiling.

Of the **upper level mosaics,** the ones on the left wall have scenes referring to the life and miracles of Christ, while those on the right wall show the Passion of Christ. Ornamental squares, designed with large shells shaped like the open wings of an eagle, above which two doors face each other, separate each panel. On the left wall the drama starts with Christ's first miracle—the

Water turned into Wine at the Marriage in Cana—and proceeds to the *Healing of the Paralytic.* Christ is depicted as a beardless young man in these scenes, but on the right wall, showing the Passion of Christ, he is older, with a beard. This difference does not mean that the left and right walls were executed at different times. Their overall style is the same. No adequate explanation has ever been given for this difference.

Notice the panel depicting *The Last Supper* on the right wall. It is one of the earliest representations of this scene. Christ and His disciples are seen reclining Roman fashion around a table. Christ, robed in imperial purple, is seated at the left and is larger than the other figures. At the other end of the table, Judas is seen in profile looking horrified as Christ prophesizes his treachery.

On the **level below the upper mosaics** are solemn figures robed in white. They are probably prophets or saints, and like the upper panels they belong to Theodoric's time and are executed in the Hellenistic-Roman style. However, the large **lower strip of mosaics** are of a later date and are well within the Byzantinesque tradition.

At the right side on the lower level, the wall is occupied by the male figures. There are twenty-six saints all clad in white garments, except Saint Martin at the front of the line, dressed in an amethyst robe. All bear crowns sparkling with gems, and at their feet are white and red flowers. They are approaching Christ enthroned between angels. Similarly, on the opposite wall is a solemn procession of twenty-two virgin saints headed by the Three Magi bearing gifts as they advance toward the Madonna enthroned between angels. Two cities are shown. On the left wall is the town of Classis, with its Roman buildings, the sea, and ships. On the right wall is Ravenna, with its churches and the palace of Theodoric. Both the men and the women are all in the same attitude, more Eastern than Western. They seem to repeat the rhythm of the Greek marble columns below, and create a mood of mystic devotion.

SANT' APOLLINARE IN CLASSE

Via di Roma (three miles from Ravenna)

Hours: Open daily 8AM–12 noon and 2–6:30PM. Free admission.

This church, the largest of all the basilicas in Ravenna, was begun in 534 on the spot where St. Apollinaris, the first bishop of Ravenna, was buried. It consists of a nave and aisles with an apse and a fine round tower off to the side of the building, not unlike the tower at Sant' Apollinare Nuovo. Though the rich marble that once covered its walls was carried away by Sigismondo Malatesta in 1449 to embellish the church of St. Francis in Rimini, the apse vault and the rood-arch still retain their rich mosiacs, mostly dating from the sixth and seventh centuries.

At the center of the highest part of the **rood-arch** is a bust of Christ in a round medallion. The four symbols of the Evangelists are to the left and right of him. The one represented as a calf (St. Luke) has a head drawn in profile, but both nostrils appear as if seen from the front. (Was Picasso, one thousand years later, inspired by this?) Beneath these figures are twelve white sheep, representing the apostles, which have come out of the sparkling towns of Jerusalem and Bethlehem, symbolizing the church of the Hebrews and the church of the Gentiles. Lower on the arch, beneath two golden green palms, are the Archangels Michael and Gabriel depicted as identical. Their banners carry the Greek words "Atioc, Atioc, Atioc" (Holy, Holy, Holy).

The great **vault** has the Hand of God at the top with two half-figures of Elijah and Moses emerging from reddish clouds. A central medallion, studded with gems and containing a great cross with the face of Christ in the center, dominates the area. Below it, on a green meadow, stand three lambs that, because this composition represents the Transfiguration, symbolize the three apostles, Peter, James, and John. At the center of the green meadow is St. Apollinaris with white sheep, symbolizing those faithful to Christ.

The mosaics here do not have the brilliance of those at San Vitale, but the freedom and simplicity of their compositions are more pronounced. They mark the end of the series of mosaics preserved in Ravenna in the Hellenistic-Roman and Byzantinesque styles.

Reggio di Calabria

NATIONAL MUSEUM OF MAGNA GRAECIA

Piazza de Nava on Corso Garibaldi

Hours: Open May–Sept., Tues.–Sat., 9AM–1:30PM and 4–7PM, Sun., 9AM–12:30PM; Oct.–Apr., Tues.–Sat., 9AM–4PM, Sun., 9AM–12:30PM. Free admission.

As its name indicates, this museum is devoted to displaying exhibits that document the history of the colonial cities of Greece in southern Italy. These antiquities (coins, jewelry, gold, silver, glass, terracottas, marbles, and bronzes) are shown on the first two floors. The _Riace Bronzes_ have a room to themselves in the marine archaeology section in the basement.

Riace Bronzes (fifth century B.C.)

These statues were found in August, 1972, in the Ionian Sea a few hundred yards off the little town of Riace. An amateur archaeologist, on the last day of his vacation in Calabria, was deep-sea fishing in about twenty feet of water when he saw a hand and arm sticking up out of the sandbed beneath him. Some days later a crew of divers hoisted to the surface two life-size bronze statues of Greek warriors.

After an initial cleaning in Reggio, the statues underwent complete restoration and study in Florence, which since the flood of the Arno in 1966 has been a center of sophisticated restoration techniques. Two thousand years of encrusted sand deposits were carefully removed from the statues. Sand and lime were sucked out of their interiors through holes cut in the feet, and steel rods were inserted as supports and as protection against seismic tremors. (Both statues now stand on earthquake-resistant pedestals.)

The cleaning and study revealed that the statues were in near-perfect condition. All that was missing were their shields and spears and, in the case of statue B, the smaller of the two, one of his eyes.

The statues, excellent examples of rare bronze sculpture from the golden age of Greece, were preserved by the sand that covered them. Statue A, standing nearly seven feet high, has a terrifying look. His eyes, a composition of ivory, amber, and limestone, his lips of copper with a reddish tint, and teeth and eyelashes of silver intensify his proud and majestic expression. His veins and musculature are beautifully delineated as though made of marble. He appears to be resting after a victory in battle. Statue B, somewhat smaller in size, is equally as fine. He strikes the same pose as statue A, but his attitude is one of philosophical meditation, giving him a less terrifying appearance.

There has been considerable speculation as to who the two figures represent, how they came to be in the Ionian Sea, and who made them. Some scholars suggest the two sculptures were made to commemorate the Athenian victory over the Persians at Marathon. Others suggest that statue A represents Achilles, who has avenged the death of Patrocles, while statue B is Hector in melancholy contemplation over the last battle he must fight and will not survive.

It is suspected that they were on their way by ship from Athens to Rome, or they may have been intended to adorn the ends of a pediment on one of the four Greek temples in Agrigento or Siracusa in Sicily, when the ship sank.

Who made them? No one knows. But if they are the work of Phidias, as has been suggested by a leading authority on Greek art, they are among the rarest antique bronze statues in the world.

_____ *Rome* _____

Museums and the Vatican

BORGHESE MUSEUM AND GALLERY

Via Pinciana

Hours: Open Tues.–Sat., 9AM–2–pm, Sun., 9AM–1PM. Admission fee.

This lovely seventeenth-century palace, situated in Rome's finest park, was built by Cardinal Scipione Borghese, nephew of Pope Paul V, in 1613–16. It served as a suburban villa and summer retreat and a place to hold lavish banquets and enjoy the Borghese art collection, assembled largely between 1605 and 1633. In 1902 it was purchased by the state and turned over to the city of Rome, but not before the original layout and the park had been much altered, and a large part of the sculpture collection removed in an enforced sale to Napoleon (some of it is exhibited in the Louvre in Paris). This museum presently comprises, on its upper floor, one of the finest collections in Europe of seventeenth-century Italian paintings and, on its ground floor, an incomparable collection of Bernini sculptures, among other works.

Sculpture—Ground Floor

Canova, Antonio (1757–1822), Italian

Pauline Borghese (1804–8): room 1
This statue has thrilled observers for over a century because Pauline Borghese was Pauline Bonaparte, the favorite sister of Napoleon, and her statue shows her as Venus reclining "topless" on an Empire couch.

Even in an age when nudity was fashionable, this statue was thought to be daring. Pauline Borghese was a notorious woman known for her fantastic clothes and jewels and a procession of lovers. She did not have any love for her wealthy husband, Prince Borghese, and she left him, establishing herself in the Villa Bonaparte, which stands near the Porta Pia.

Considering the modest place that today's art critics have given to Canova's neoclassical sculpture, this piece, with its formal purity and lack of sensitivity, is merely a sculptural curiosity.

Bernini, Gian Lorenzo (1598–1680), Italian
The precocious genius of Bernini was noticed by Cardinal Scipione Borghese, who introduced Bernini to the pope when he was only a young boy. The pope, given a demonstration of Bernini's spontaneous drawing, declared, "This child will be the Michelangelo of his age." Bernini's name came to epitomize the artistic activity of the papacy in the seventeenth century.

The scupltures discussed below were executed by Bernini for his first patron, Cardinal Scipione Borghese (his 1632 bust by Bernini is in the gallery upstairs in room 14). They are youthful works conceived in the mannerist spirit, when Bernini was only in his twenties, but all are works of accomplishment from the hand of a gifted sculptor. Later, when Bernini did monumental sculptures designed for an architectural setting, his work became purely baroque.

David (1623–24): room 2
When you compare Bernini's *David* with the statues of David done a century earlier, such as Donatello's or Michelangelo's, you realize how different the style became. The previous *Davids* stood in self-contained regal splendor with a determination that seemed to be within the statue itself. Bernini's *David,* on the other hand, shown in the act of delivering the blow from his sling that will kill the giant Goliath, is a figure engaged in action who affects the observer with a display of physical movement. Its aggressive pose is designed along a diagonal not only to allow for maximum movement of the figure but also to take full possession of its space.

Apollo and Daphne (1624): room 3
This lovely group represents the popular story, from Ovid's *Metamorphoses,* of how Cupid, in a spiteful mood, shot Apollo with a golden arrow (the kind that encourages love), but shot the nymph Daphne, the daughter of the river god Peneus, with a leaden one (the kind that puts love in flight). Thus she ran from Apollo as she was pursued by him. When she could run no more she prayed to her father to save her, whereupon she metamorphosed into a tree.

Bernini gives the scene a diagonal arrangement that moves the eye out of the group rather than into it, in contrast to Renaissance sculpture where figures are capable of movement only within the block. The movement here is spectacular, with Apollo, an effeminate figure reminiscent of the *Apollo of the Belvedere* at the Vatican, just catching up to the nymph while both are still in flight. His left arm is around her lithe body, but she is already turning into a laurel tree, sprouting roots from her toes and leaves from her hair and fingers. Nothing previous to this statue extends the limits of marble carving as dexterously and with such convincing texture of flesh; it functions as though the original limitations of the block of stone never existed.

The Rape of Proserpine (1621–22): room 4
The subject matter of this statue is also taken from Ovid's *Metamorphoses.* Proserpine, the daughter of the corn goddess Ceres, was picking flowers when Pluto, the king of the underworld became overwhelmed by her beauty. We see him, a virile figure wearing a crown on his head, carrying Proserpine down to his kingdom below. The myth tells of Proserpine's return to earth each spring for a third of the year, becoming part of the Greek rites to promote the fertility of crops.

This statue is not as successful as the two mentioned above. It retains mannerist characteristics and the problem of space is not completely solved. It could be considered a study that made possible the achievement of the artist's *David* and *Apollo and Daphne.*

Paintings—Upper Floor

Caravaggio (1573–1610), Italian
After the deaths of Raphael and Leonardo, and before those of Michelangelo, Titian, and Tintoretto, the high Renaissance had ended and was replaced in part by a new creative movement of young artists called mannerism. Within the changing conditions of the time, brought on by the Protestant reformation in the north which undermined the assurance of the high Renaissance, the old values could no longer be maintained. In painting, mannerism opposed the classicism of the Roman high Renaissance by imbalance, distortion of scale, and conscious exaggeration of color and line to give meaning to the restlessness of people and their world. But this elusively complex art was only partially popular and did not perpetuate itself much into the seventeenth century. Most painters were in fact opposed to mannerism and maintained an eclectic art borrowed from high Renaissance masters.

The artist whose protest against both the Italian mannerists and eclectics had the most influence on the art of the early seventeenth century, whose art lay the seeds of the baroque style, was Caravaggio. He came from the small town of his name in Lombardy near Bergamo. When he first arrived in Rome in 1589 or 1590 he was not well trained. In an academic sense he was diffi-cient in drawing, in creating a composition that included more than one fig-ure, and in the art of fresco painting (he never painted one). He may have started out as a specialist of still life; two paintings in the Borghese men-tioned below, and others elsewhere by Caravaggio, have baskets of fruit with a single figure. As his technique and style grew, he moved toward the cre-ation of a new art taken from everyday experience. This included, to the shock of some of his patrons, the depiction of the lower classes of society: Gypsies, strolling musicians, card players, and criminals. Thus he became a leader of a new school known as realists, or naturalists, which had enough of an impact to influence such painters as Ribera of Spain and even Rem-brandt. His lighting effects—not the light of nature but of art—aimed for intensity by the use of chiaroscuro, and became a means of piercing the veil of appearances to the essence of everyday things. The new style was his way of revolting against the formalism of his time and that of the age that had preceded his. He lived his short life with the intensity of his art, in riotous living and bouts of physical violence. He had to leave Rome in 1606 because he killed a man, and he died, at the age of thirty-seven, of sunstroke in the Italian summer, attempting to return from Naples to Rome on foot.

In **room 14** are several paintings by Caravaggio that date from his ar-rival in Rome (1590) to the end of his Roman period (1606). The *Boy with Fruit,* also known as *Young Bacchus Ill,* and *Boy with a Basket of Fruit* both date from 1590 when Caravaggio was seventeen. They show his skill as a painter of still lifes, as well as his more modern style. The *Boy with Fruit* is thought to be a self-portrait of Caravaggio convalescing from malaria. We know he stayed at the Hospital of the Consolation in Rome to recover from it; the yellowish complexion of the figure is an obvious reference to the dis-ease.

The *David with Goliath's Head, St. Jerome Writing,* and the *Madonna of the Palafrenieri,* also known as the *Madonna of the Serpent,* are from about 1606. The latter was painted for the Confraternity of the Palafrenieri, of Grooms of the Vatican Palaces, but was removed by the authorities from St. Peters because of its excessive realism. It was given to Cardinal Scipione Borghese, whose bust by Bernini is also in this room. All three paintings are works of drama and tension, using common folk as models. The magic of Caravaggio's light, which reveals and hides at the same time, has a dark background that serves to heighten the contrast between dark and light.

Raphael* (1483–1520), Florentine (born in Umbria)

Deposition: room 9
This painting was done in 1507, near the end of Raphael's Florentine period. He had observed the works of Michelangelo in Florence, and that is reflected here in the powerful figures engaged in a carefully thought-out theatrical

scene (there are sixteen preparatory sketches, and possibly more that have been lost). In spite of the preparation, he has overdone his painting. He usually was able to strike a vibrant emotional chord, but here the composition is strained. Missing is the unifying force so often found in his later work. This work is valued, however, as a basis for Raphael's huge Roman frescoes. After this painting was completed, Raphael arrived in Rome, in 1509, and was employed in the Vatican to decorate the apartments of Pope Julius II.

Titian* (ca. 1487–1576), Venetian

Sacred and Profane Love (ca. 1515): room 20
This is one of Titian's most enigmatic works as well as one of his finest early paintings. It has had many titles and many romantic interpretations. Its current title, *Sacred and Profane Love,* is widely accepted. The painting is superbly executed in color tones from white and silver-grays to earth colors. We are shown two beautiful women who have the same face. One is dressed in a rich Venetian costume belted under the bodice. She wears gloves and holds a closed jar in one hand and roses in the other. Behind her is a landscape of a town with a fortified medieval tower, a huntsman on the road, and, in the countryside, two rabbits (symbols of love). The other woman is nude except for a white scarf across her lap and rose-red cloak around her left arm. She holds a small urn from which a flame rises, and behind her is a meadow where huntsmen have caught up to a rabbit and a shepherd is tending his flock. There is a lake and a town with a church steeple rising above it. Both women sit at the edge of a fountain with Cupid looking at his reflection. A golden bowl filled with water sits at the fountain's edge. The sculptured scenes on the side of the fountain show a powerful horse being led by one groom while others flee, a man being beaten, and a woman being led by her hair. It is obvious that the nude woman is speaking to the clothed woman, her sister, and the clothed woman is listening to her.

While part of the charm of the work is that its meaning is obscure, the nude figure is thought to represent Heavenly Love exhorting her clothed sister to take her advice. The image of the horse refers to the lower senses, which may run away with abandon, and the figures being abused derive from ancient initiations into the rites of love, which can be painful and disruptive. There is a reference to Christian baptism in the presence of the water in the well and in the golden bowl: that is, to enter into the realm of Heavenly Love one must leave the old life behind and be born again. The fortress of false chastity must be abandoned, symbolized by the ancient tower. The clothing of the dressed figure, the locked belt, and the roses must be dropped, and the jar opened. The rabbit must be subdued. The church, symbolized by the steeple, must sanctify the love, and it must be as eternal as the flame in the lamp held up to Heaven.

Perhaps the clothed woman has been unlucky in love. The roses she holds have thorns, symbolic of the wounds of love. In spite of these wounds and the possibility that the lower senses may disrupt the ideal union, the painting seems to say that the clothed woman must trust in love in order to achieve its eternal, heavenly side.

CAPITOLINE MUSEUMS AND GALLERY

Piazza del Campidoglio

Hours: Open Tues., Thurs., 9AM–2PM and 5–8PM; Wed., Fri., 9AM–2PM; Sat., 9AM–2PM and 9–11:30PM; Sun., 9AM–1PM. Admission fee.

This complex of museums and a picture gallery is located in buildings facing each other on the Piazza del Campidoglio. On the left side of the piazza is the **Capitoline Museum (Palazzo Nuovo)**; facing it, on the right side of the piazza, is the **Palazzo dei Conservatori**, which has behind it the **Palazzo Caffarelli** or **Museo Nuovo.**

At the back of the piazza is the **Palazzo Senatori** (the town hall of Rome) erected over the ancient Tabularium (78 B.C.), where Roman books of law had been kept.

To the east of the Capitoline Museum is the church of **Santa Maria di Aracoeli** (sixth century), which occupies the site of the citadel of ancient Rome. Do not allow the plain exterior to mislead you. The nave is richly decorated with twenty-two ancient columns brought from the Forum and the Palatine, and a rich ceiling commemorating the victory of the papal fleet over the Turks in 1571. In the south aisle (first chapel) are frescoes depicting the life of St. Bernadino by Pinturicchio (ca. 1454–1573). Outside, the flight of 124 marble steps leading up to the entrance of the church was built in 1348 as a votive offering from those who survived the plague in Rome.

Campidoglio

The Campidoglio is largely the result of Michelangelo's plan for the reconstruction of Rome in 1536, during the reign of Pope Paul III. His design called for new facades for the existing Palazzo Senatori and Palazzo dei Conservatori, and for a new building, now the Capitoline Museum, or Palazzo Nuovo, on the left side of the piazza. During Michelangelo's lifetime work was begun, but the project was not completed until the seventeenth century, well after Michelangelo's death, with modifications to his original design.

What Michelangelo was striving for—to create an architectural effect worthy of the Roman past—was essentially achieved. The flanking palaces, with their open porticoes and giant order of pilasters, converge toward the triangular ramp of the Palazzo Senatori, creating a grand effect. Verticals and horizontals are evenly distributed all around the piazza, so that it has been described as "an outdoor room with three walls."

The *Equestrian Statue of Marcus Aurelius,* in the center of the piazza, is part of Michelangelo's plan. It was he who removed it from its original home on the Lateran and placed it in its present position. Its base, with emblems of the reigning popes and the city of Rome, is also his work. The statue itself, of guilded bronze weighing two tons, is the only equestrian statue of a Roman emperor to come down to us from the second century. It survived being melted down only because medieval Rome erroneously thought it was a statue of Constantine, the first Christian emperor.

Capitoline Museum (Palazzo Nuovo)

This museum, in spite of its name, is only a part of the Capitoline Museums and Gallery. With the Palazzo dei Conservatori and the Palazzo Cafferelli, it consists of a large collection of Greek and Roman sculpture that got its start as early as 1471, when Pope Sixtus IV gave a number of valuable bronze sculptures to Rome and placed them in the Palazzo dei Conservatori. Later, various acquisitions expanded the collection. In 1734, after obtaining the Cardinal Albani collection, it was opened to the public.

Dying Gaul (second century B.C.): first floor, room 1
This marble copy of a bronze original from the Pergamum Acropolis represents a late Greek style that flourished in Pergamum. It was influenced somewhat by the surrounding cultures of Asia Minor, but by the time it was cast Hellenistic sculpture had slipped into exaggerated forms, which its style reflects. That is not to say that the statue's lack of refinement, compared to what had come before it, makes it an inferior work of art. It is dignified, with a lifelike aspect restrained and in good taste, and is a tribute to the humanism of the artist who made it. The figure represents one of the invading Gauls, a people who penetrated into Greece and Italy in the last half of the third century B.C. and were reviled in Greece as barbarians. There is no doubt about the Celtic origin of the figure, as evidenced by his matted hair and mustache and the twisted gold ornament around his neck. In spite of this, the figure is shown as a human being dying with a dignity worthy of a Greek hero. His head is not especially noteworthy, but the vigorous modeling of his body, in an attitude of tragic realism, has always been admired.

Satyr Resting (fourth century B.C.): first floor, room 1
This is one of the best copies of the *Anapouonemo Satyr* of Praxiteles, one of the most popular statues of ancient times (there are over seventy copies of it extant), and an example of Praxiteles' finest style, with the figure in the supple S-curve for which the artist was famous. Leaning on a tree trunk in careless abandon, with a leopard skin thrown over his shoulder, the figure shows Praxiteles' preference for the cheerful side of existence. This description of it was made by Hawthorne, for whom it was the *Marble Faun* of his romantic novel of 1858: "The whole statue unlike anything else that ever was wrought in the severe material of marble, conveys the idea of an amiable and sensual creature, easy, mirthful, apt for jollity, yet not incapable of being touched by pathos."

Wounded Amazon (ca. 440 B.C.): first floor, room 3
Pliny tells in his *Natural History* of a competition between the greatest Greek artists of the time (Polykleitos, Phidias, Kresilas, and Phradmon) for a bronze statue of an Amazon (the legendary race of warrior-women who came from the Caucasus and invaded Athens, but were repulsed by Theseus, king of Athens) to be set up in the Artemision of Ephesus. Three of these Amazons are known to us, of which this Roman copy is one, but art historians have been unable to assign definite authorship to any of them. While this woman warrior, displaying her wound on her right side as the weight of her body is

supported by her left side, has often been attributed to Polykleitos, its less refined composition and realistic attitude probably make it a work of Kresilas.

Capitoline Venus (second century B.C.): first floor, room 7
This Roman copy is famous for everything about her from the neck down. From there she is a picture of feminine softness and grace as she steps into her bath. Her modesty in covering her breasts with her hand only serves to emphasize them, while her head turns shyly to the side. However, the beauty of her body is impaired by the too-large head weighed down by the hair, and the common facial features.

Palazzo dei Conservatori

This palace, across the piazza from the Capitoline Museum, was begun by Nicholas V about 1450 and, as noted, was remodeled from designs by Michelangelo. It continues the great sculpture collection in the rooms of the Conservatori, the Museum of the Palace, and the Palazzo Caffarelli (Museo Nuovo), the former German embassy. A picture gallery on the second floor at the southwest end of the Palazzo dei Conservatori has a largely undistinguished collection of Italian and foreign paintings.

Spinarius (Thorn Picker) (first century B.C.): Sale dei Conservatori, room 3
This Roman bronze of a boy picking a thorn from his foot is one of the statues donated by Pope Sixtus IV in 1471 that started the museum. The body of the figure, with its commanding use of space and plastic modeling, shows the artist has learned from the Greek statues that were in Rome during the Augustan age. Only the severe head indicates its Roman origin.

Bronze Bust (Brutus?) (second century B.C.): Sale dei Conservatori, room 3
There is considerable confusion over this bust, of which only the head is antique. It may be an Italic-Etruscan work, and if so the Etruscan sculptor has been skillful in imitating Hellenistic portraiture. However, there is a possibility the bust is indeed Greek. There is a concern for detail that is missing in Etruscan sculpture, and it was not unknown for Greek artists to do portraits of famous Romans.

We cannot be certain whom the bust represents. It is thought to be Lucius Junius Brutus, not the Brutus who was Caesar's assassin, though, judging from coins of 509 B.C. with the profile of Marcus Brutus, there is a resemblance. Lucius Junius Brutus led a revolt in 509 B.C. against the last of Rome's kings, abolishing the monarchy and bringing the Republic to Rome, in which he served as first consul. The bust, with its strong features and stern, determined eyes, looks like a man who could accomplish such a feat.

DORIA PAMPHILI GALLERY

Palazzo Doria Pamphili, Piazza del Collegio Romano 1A

Hours: Open Tues., Fri.–Sun., 10AM–1PM. Admission fee.

This collection is housed in one of the finest palaces in Rome and is still in the possession of the heirs of the family that founded it. The building dates to the sixteenth century, but much of what is visible today was constructed in the eighteenth century by the architect Gabrielle Valvassori (1683–1761). His work included closing the upper loggia of the inner courtyard to create the three wings that make up the picture gallery, and the fourth wing that has the **Gallery of Mirrors**. His facade facing the Corso has been criticized, especially the windows on the first story, which have overbearing baroque pediments in which the bases of an attic story are inserted. While these architectural elements enliven the long, flat surface on the Corso, there could have been a better way to do it. The Gallery of Mirrors is behind the facade, one of the most splendid rooms in Rome. Its vault is decorated with trompe-l'oeil architectural motifs and allegorical paintings by Milani.

The collection of paintings dates back to the period of the infamous Donna Olimpia Pamphili, sister-in-law of Pope Innocent X, and consists of many works by old masters, including *Rest on the Flight into Egypt*, by Caravaggio (1573–1610), plus some of his other early paintings; another *Flight into Egypt*, by Annibale Carracci (1560–1609), a classical landscape of early seventeenth-century Roman painting; *The Daughter of Herodias with the Head of John the Baptist*, by Titian (ca. 1487–1576), a work of Titian's youthful period, full of brilliant color; and *The Mill*, by Claude Lorraine (1600–82), and other paintings by this seventeenth-century French master.

Velázquez* (1599–1660), Spanish

Portrait of Innocent X: gallery 3, second cabinet
This painting of Innocent X has been called one of the greatest portraits in Europe. It was painted in 1650 by Velázquez when he was in Rome buying antique art for Philip IV of Spain, at a time when Innocent X, the former Giambattista Pamphili, was seventy-three. Its intensity of characterization makes it famous and Velázquez a master of portraiture. But there is a controversy: Velázquez shows us a shrewd, implacable man, not the kind to be manipulated by a woman. Yet there are stories of how Donna Olimpia, Innocent's sister-in-law (her bust by Alessandro Algardi, ca. 1602–54, is seen in Gallery I), bullied him, stealing his money as he lay dying in bed, that make it difficult to believe in the portrait Velázquez painted. In the same room is a *Bust of Innocent X* by Bernini (1598–1680), who knew the pope well. Also done in 1650, it shows the pope as a kind, gentle dreamer. Is the Velázquez portrait an inaccurate portrayal, a portrait to flatter him, or does it picture the true character of the pope? It is a question that will probably never be answered.

NATIONAL GALLERY OF ROME

The collection of the National Gallery of Rome is divided into two sections: one is located at the **Palazzo Barberini**, near the piazza of the same name, and the other at the **Palazzo Corsini**, across from the Villa Farnesina near the Tiber. Of the two, the Palazzo Barberini holds the major part of the collection. For entrance to the Palazzo Corsini, Via della Lungara, 10, telephone (06) 65422323, apply to the director a day or two in advance.

Palazzo Barberini

Via della Quattro Fontane 13

Hours: Open Tues.–Sat., 9AM–2PM, Sun., 9AM–1PM. Admission fee.

The Palazzo Barberini, one of the best examples of Baroque architecture in Rome, was constructed in the seventeenth century for the family of Pope Urban VIII on the site of the old Sforza Palace. Its first architect, Carlo Maderno (1556–1629), died before the work was completed, and Bernini (1598–1680) completed the construction. Its three-story facade, which has three orders that follow the classical sequence of Doric, Ionic, and Corinthian styles, are attributed to him. Notice the illusionist arches feigning a perspective recession in space in the upper windows. They are a typical painterly device of the baroque.

On entering the palace, you will see a staircase that leads from the ground floor loggia to the **piano nobile.** The oval one to the right was designed by Borromini (1599–1667), Moderno's nephew, who helped in the original design of the palace. The staircase on the left is the work of Bernini. The landing at the top of the staircase leads to the **Great Hall,** famous for a huge illusionist frescoed ceiling, *The Triumph of Divine Providence* (1639) by Pietro da Cortona (1596–1669), his masterpiece. The name might well have been "The Triumph of the Barberini Family," because it shows the antecedents of the family, indicated by three huge Barberini bees being carried to Heaven by the Virtues (Faith, Hope, and Charity).

The collection of paintings covers the period from the thirteenth to the eighteenth century and includes works by Italian and foreign old masters. Among the best are a triptych of the *Last Judgment, Ascension and Pentecost* by **Fra Angelico** (ca. 1400–55), which shows in its central panel Christ decreeing the end of the world. Below, the condemned, of which many are monks, are being sent to Hell; *Portrait of Stefano Colona,* by **Bronzino** (1503–72), showing the captain of Charles V in armor; the famous *La Fornarina* attributed to **Raphael,** but in spite of the master's name on the band around the subjects arm, it is mostly the work of Raphael's assistant Giulio Romano (ca. 1492–1546). The sitter may be Raphael's mistress; paintings by **Caravaggio** (1573–1610): *Narcissus,* a study in self-love; *Judith and Holofernes,* a realistic rendering of decapitation; and *Young St. John the Baptist,* a somewhat romantic picture where the real subject is the light that evokes by contrasts in shadowing the lifelike expression of the face, to which our eye is led by the red draperies forming the base of a triangle below; a *Nativity* and a *Baptism of Christ* by El Greco (1541–1614), probably sketches for pictures on the subjects now scattered throughout Europe, showing El Greco's dramatic lighting and heavy brush strokes; *Christ and the Adul-*

tress by **Tintoretto** (1518–94), an early work with a clear, illuminating light and a harmony of colors that mark it as Venetian; a *Portrait of Erasmus* by **Quentin Massys** (1466–1530), typical of this Flemish artist's presentation of the sitter through his work, and a *Portrait of Henry VIII* by **Hans Holbein the Younger** (1497–1543), painted in 1540, showing the king on the day of his marriage to Anne of Cleves (though there is some dispute whether it is entirely from the hand of Holbein).

NATIONAL MUSEUM OF THE VILLA GIULIA

Viale delle Belle Arti

Hours: Open Tues., Thurs.–Sat., 9AM–2PM, Wed., 9AM–2PM and 3–7:30PM (in winter, Wed., 9AM–6:30PM), Sun., 9AM–1PM. Admission fee.

You can enter the ancient world of the Etruscans in this museum, which offers a complete panorama of the artistic production of the Etruscan people. There are sarcophagi, ceramics, goldsmith's work, and sculptures, all displayed in a splendid sixteenth-century palace, built as a suburban villa by Pope Julius III, that has been called "the jewel box containing the jewels."

These pre-Roman works of art are indeed "jewels." We have only recently learned to appreciate them as something far more than crude sculpture attempting to imitate the Greek style. Depicting slender figures of priests and gods, sometimes with distorted anatomies, and sometimes with archaic smiles on lifelike faces, they are original, expressive works that seem modern today. The vigor and animation of this art achieved a perfection of expressiveness that is highly accomplished.

Apollo of Veii (ca. 500 B.C.): room 7
This terra cotta work, with a clinging robe that seems to flutter in the wind, probably adorned the roof of the Temple of Apollo at Veii when that city was at the height of its splendor. It has Hellenic characteristics in the treatment of the hair, the eyes, even the lips, but it also has an expressive, individual face that can only be described as Etruscan—a sharp profile, slanting eyes, and an enigmatic smile.

Sarcophagus of a Married Couple (sixth century B.C.): room 9
This beautifully balanced terra cotta group of a deceased couple, reclining in the Etruscan fashion on a banqueting couch, reveals the emancipated state that women enjoyed in Etruscan society, which shocked the Greeks and the Romans. Even though the Ionian inspiration in the work can be seen, as in others of Etruscan origin it does not detract from its originality. The fashionable pointed shoes and dome-shaped cap of the lady are typically Etruscan, and despite the likeness in the two faces, with their archaic smiles, the intent of personal identification is clear. There are few poses of a male and a female in the history of Western sculpture as intimate as in this 2,500-year-old couple.

NATIONAL ROMAN MUSEUM (MUSEO DELLE TERME)

Piazza dei Cinquecento 69

Hours: Tues.–Sat., 9AM–1:45PM, Sun., 9AM–12:45PM. Admission fee. (Free admission on first and third Sat., and second and fourth Sun. of each month.)

This museum, with antique sculptures that have been copied over and over again by Renaissance artists, occupies halls of the Baths of Diocletian (you will visit the bath before the museum) and parts of a Carthusian monastery. There is also a fine collection of paintings, mosaics, glass, and jewelry, which, with the statuary, comprises one of the most important archaeological museums in the world.

Note: Restoration of the building has made it necessary to move portions of the collection to other locations in Rome. Check with the museum. Tel. (06) 460530. What follows is a description of works of art as they would normally be displayed in the museum.

Apollo of the Tiber (460 B.C.): room 2
This nude god with flowing locks of hair was found in the Tiber River in fragments in 1891. It is a Roman copy of a Greek bronze original once thought to be by Phidias but now considered to be by Hegias or Kalamis. In any case, it is a work of genius which, with its head slightly inclined, communicates an impression of isolation and spirituality, an example of Greek art at its cultural peak.

Discobolus (Discus Thrower) (460–450 B.C.): room 3
The *Discus Thrower* is a splendid example from the classical period when Greek sculptors achieved mastery over their art. It is also a dynamic example of the introduction of motion into sculpture, a departure from the earlier static poses in Greek art. It made the sculptor, Myron, famous, as ancient sources record. As a display of the moment pent-up energy is about to be released like a coiling spring in the male body, his work has never been surpassed. Notice how the musculature is boldly depicted in broad planes with just enough detail to be convincing—the balanced compositional effect, rather than anatomical accuracy, is the aim. The original bronze, which did not need the supporting tree trunk behind the figure, may have been even better. (Of the copies in existence, two are in this room; the Terme's Lancellotti copy is reputed to be the finest.)

Boxer (first century B.C.): room 3
This bronze statue is signed by Apollonius, son of Nestor, an Athenian sculptor who also signed his name to the *Belvedere Torso* at the Vatican. Both pieces show the figure in the same sitting attitude with bulging muscles. The artist probably took the model from an earlier Hellenistic statue, perhaps of the realistic Pergamene School, and reworked it to be more brutally realistic

to satisfy the tastes of his own time, far removed from the high classical fifth- and fourth-century B.C. period. Every detail of exhaustion, physical disfigurement and punishment past and present is depicted in this boxer who has just finished a fight. His hands are bound with straps of leather with bands of lead at the knuckles known as *caestus* (killers). Yet mixed with this brutal realism are classical stylistic elements such as the treatment of the beard and the hair.

Wounded Niobid (ca. 440 B.C.): room 3

This Roman copy from a Greek original may have been part of a group of wounded Niobids from the pediment of a temple. It shows one of the daughters of Niobe (wife of the king of Thebes and granddaughter of Jupiter) dying from an arrow shot into her back by Apollo. Niobe's seven sons and seven daughters were all killed by Apollo this way to punish her for trying to dissuade the Theban women from worshipping Leto, Apollo's mother, and instead to worship Niobe. The loss of her children caused Niobe such grief that she turned into stone, which, however, continued to cry.

This Niobid is shown falling, her left knee nearly touching the ground. She tries to pull the arrow from her back and in so doing her robe falls down, leaving her beautiful body uncovered. The firm modeling of the figure, rendered with a sense of human sympathy, make it one of the most sublime examples of how the Greek figure could become an instrument for communicating suffering and death. It is almost as exceptional a work as those found among the Parthenon marbles, which are contemporary with it.

Venus of Cyrene (fourth century B.C.): room 3

This Greek original, one of the most sensual female figures to come down to us from the Greek world, was found in the Baths of Cyrene in 1913. It shows a goddess rising from the sea, probably lifting her arms to squeeze out her wet hair. Beside her is a dolphin with a fish in its mouth. One can imagine the study and care that went into the carving of this Venus. The patina of the marble and the soft modeling give it a warmth that makes it almost come alive.

Hellenistic Prince (ca. 160 B.C.): room 3

The heroic pose and proportions of this bronze statue, and the rendering of the hair, the deep-set eyes, and disdainful mouth, indicate it may be a figure inspired by Lysippos's lost statue of Alexander the Great holding a spear. He has also been compared to the faces of Sulla and Lucullus from their likeness on Republican coins, but cannot be identified with certainty.

Maiden of Anzio (fourth–third century B.C.): room 3

This statue was found at Anzio in 1878 and is considered an original masterpiece of Greek art, though some scholars insist it is a copy. It shows a young woman carrying a tray with a roll of cloth, a laurel twig and a box on it, probably offerings for an act of adoration she is performing. Judging from the modeling of the disordered robe, the sculptor was highly accomplished, possibly belonging to the School of Lysippus.

Head of a Roman Girl (second century): room 3
This portrait of a Roman girl was probably done for a wealthy Roman family by a Greek artist living in Rome. The exquisite hairdo frames her perfect face with curves over her forehead and around her ears. The innocence of childhood is captured in her sweet face, just dignified enough for her future high position in society. The accuracy of detail combined with a slight idealism place it firmly in the Greek tradition of portraiture.

The Ludovisi Throne (ca. 470 B.C.): room 2 (between the Grand Cloister and the garden)
This three-sided relief, making up what appear to be the sides and the back of a throne, is an original Greek work from the archaic period, one of the treasures of the museum. Its name derives from being found in the Ludovisi Villa in Rome, but nothing else about its origin is known.

On the back is seen Aphrodite being born from the sea, as the legend goes. She seems to smile with newfound life as she is helped out of the waves by two maidens standing on a pebbly shore holding out a cloth to cover her below the waist, the upper part of her body being revealed by her wet, clinging garment. The design and sculptural technique achieve a greater degree of feminine charm than previously found in Greek sculpture. The artist's sense of design avoids rigidity in the composition, centered on Aphrodite's soft profile and curvy body, by making the horizontal folds of the cloth flow effortlessly into the vertical pleats of the garments of the two maidens.

On one side of the throne is a naked young girl playing a love song on a flute; on the other side a young bride in a closely draped garment is dropping incense into a brazier in honor of Venus.

VATICAN MUSEUMS AND GALLERIES

Vatican City, entrance in Viale Vaticano

Hours: Open July–Sept., Easter, Mon.–Sat., 9AM–5PM (no admission after 4PM); Oct.–June, 9AM–2PM (no admission after 1PM); closed Sun. (except last Sun. of the month when admission is free), Jan. 1, Feb. 11, Mar. 19, Easter Sun. and Mon., May 1, Ascension Thurs., Corpus Christi, June 29, Aug. 14 and 15, Nov. 1, Dec. 8, 25, and 26. Admission fee.

Everyone knows the Sistine Chapel and Raphael's Stanze contain great works of art, sightseeing events on their own that have the effect of overwhelming the rest of the Vatican. But the Vatican has a great deal more on display than these two attractions—over one thousand rooms and chapels— and you cannot see them all in a single visit. You should visit the Vatican Museums more than once and break your visits into sections.

Note: You can choose from four color-coded itineraries of varying lengths of time. The shortest, directly to the Sistine Chapel and back, takes an hour and a half. The longest, the highlights of which are described below, takes at least five hours if done at one time.

The long route will take you first to the **Gregorian-Egyptian Museum.** Beyond it lies the **Courtyard of the Pigna,** named for its giant pinecone fountain (first century A.D.), a pleasant but puzzling Roman antiquity. A door in the courtyard opens to the **Chiaramonti Gallery.** Founded by Pope Pius VII (Chiaramonti) in the early nineteenth century, little of its huge collection of sculpture, arranged by Canova in a section of Bramante's east corridor, is of great significance. Beyond the Chiaramonti Gallery lies the Pio-Clementine Museum, named for Pius VI and Clement XIV, the popes responsible for its reorganization in the mid-eighteenth century.

Pio-Clementine Museum

Many pieces on display in this museum, which holds the pontificate collection of ancient sculpture, are outstanding, in spite of the unfortunate fact that all the male sculpture has been disfigured by plaster additions to the genitals. What follows is a room-by-room review as one would normally proceed through the museum.

Hall of the Greek Cross (Sala a Croce Greca)
This room, designed in the shape of a Greek cross, is guarded at its entrance by two large **sphinxes** of red and gray Egyptian granite found during the construction of St. Peter's. On the pavement is a large **mosaic** with the bust of Minerva. The left and the right walls of the room contain two giant **sarcophagi** in porphyry from the time of Constantine the Great (306–37). The one on the left is for his mother, St. Helena; the one on the right for his daughter.

Circular Hall (Sala Rotonda)
In the floor of the center of this room, fashioned after the Pantheon to contain statues and busts of ancient gods and emperors, is the great polycrome *Mosaic of Otricoli.* In the center is a magnificent basin in porphyry found in the Baths of Titus.

The sculpture includes *Bust of Jupiter,* a colossal head of serene beauty; the *Barbarini Juno,* a noble female statue; *Hercules* in gilded bronze, found near the Theatre of Pompeii; the *Emperor Claudius* represented as Jupiter; and the statue of *Antinoüs,* the favorite of Hadrian (the drapery is modern, restored from the original bronze by Thorvaldsen).

Hall of the Muses (Sala delle Muse)
This lovely room, with a vestibule at either end and a ceiling decorated by Conca (1680–1764), owes its name to its statues of the nine Muses, which were found, along with the statue of Apollo, in a villa near Tivoli. Of greater interest, however, is the superb bust of *Pericles,* probably a copy of a famous work by Cresilas (first vestibule), and the famous *Belvedere Torso* (center of main room), which is supposed to be a seated Hercules. When this first-century B.C. torso was discovered, at the time of Julius II, buried in the Campo dei Fiori, it caused a sensation. Michelangelo, among others, was impressed by its portrayal of muscles in action. It is signed by the same Apol-

lonius, son of Nestor of Athens, who carved his name to the *Seated Boxer* in the Terme Museum in Rome.

Animal Room (Sala degli Animali)

Here, as the name implies, you will find a collection of animal statues, some from antique fragments, but most by the eighteenth-century sculptor F. A. Franzoni (1734–1818). Part of the floor is paved with antique mosaics, and built into the walls are reliefs and two mosaics from Hadrian's villa at Tivoli. Of special interest is the marble statue of *Meleager,* found about 1500 in a vineyard on the slopes of Janiculum. The mythological hero is seen resting on his lance between his dog and the head of a boar.

Gallery of the Statues (Galleria delle Statue)

This gallery was originally a summer house of Innocent VIII and included a chapel with frescoes by Mantegna and Pintoricchio. It was converted into a museum by Clement XIV and later extended by Pius VI. In the conversion the frescoes were destroyed. Only some remains of the paintings by Pintoricchio can be seen.

In its present form the hall contains a series of antique statues, most copies. The most notable are the *Apollo Sauroctonos,* a copy of a famous bronze by Praxiteles; and the treasure of the room, *Sleeping Ariadne,* a Roman copy of a master artist's work of the mature Hellenic School of the third century B.C. The story from Greek mythology of how Ariadne, the daughter of King Minos of Crete, helped Theseus to kill the Minotaur but was then abandoned by him on the island of Naxos while she lay asleep, to be awakened by Dionysus who took her as his wife, has been used by many European painters and sculptors. The gentle inclination of the head and the turn of the beautiful arms of this statue did not escape Michelangelo. In his *Night* and *Dawn* at the Medici tombs in Florence he adopted it in part. The pedestal of the *Ariadne* is formed by a sarcophagus on which struggling giants are being turned into hydras. On either side of the entrance are the two *Barberini Candelabra,* the most beautiful candelabra that have come down to us from the Roman era.

Gallery of Busts (Sala dei Busti)

This series of small rooms contains busts of the likenesses of famous people from the Roman Empire. There are *Marcus Aurelius, Hadrian,* the head of *Caracalla, Julius Caesar,* and others that make up a display of historical as well as artistic interest.

The Mask Room (Gabinetto della Maschere)

The small mosaics of theatrical masks from Hadrian's villa that are set into the floor give this room its name. Its chief attraction is the *Cnidian Venus,* second-century Roman copy of an original fourth-century B.C. Greek statue by Praxiteles. While its head is that of another copy of the same statue and its limbs are restorations, it is still an excellent copy of one of the antique world's most famous statues, whose face was put on Cnidian coins. This was the Cnidian way of paying homage to their beautiful *Aphrodite* or *Venus.* Pliny tells that poets wrote about it and people from all over the Greek world traveled great distances to see it. She is the goddess of love, a nude with a pensive expression and a soft, vibrant sensuality.

Cabinet of Laocoön (Gabinetto de Laoccente)
You will have to return to the animal room and enter the **Courtyard of the Belvedere** to get to this room. The courtyard is the place where Pope Julius placed the first classical sculptures of the Vatican and around which the entire collection was formed. It is a welcome place for the visitor to rest before entering the Cabinet of Laocoön to see the most famous piece of sculpture in the Vatican museums.

Laocoön and His Sons (second–first century B.C.)
The discovery of this statue in 1506 by a wine grower who unearthed it near the Baths of Titus created a sensation because it was the first Greek original discovered in Italy for which there was reliable written information concerning the name of the artist. The Roman writer Pliny saw it in the palace of the Emperor Titus and wrote that it came from the island of Rhodes and was the work of three sculptors—Agesandros, Athenodoros, and Polydoros, a father and his two sons. Pliny also left a description of the Rhodian School of sculpture, which developed in the third century B.C. and was one of the most productive in the ancient world. It was known for its colossal bronze sun-god *Helios* rising to a height of 105-feet near the city harbor. Pliny described this statue and wrote that an earthquake destroyed it fifty-six years after it was erected. He also said that the island had over one hundred colossal statues, any one of which would have made a city famous. The *Laocoön* is part of the tradition of this school of sculpture. It is also part of a famous ancient story, that of the *Wooden Horse of Troy*.

Laocoön, a principal character in the story, was a Trojan priest wise enough to see the treachery of the Greeks who left a huge wooden horse outside the city when they retreated from Troy. (The horse was filled with soldiers who attacked once the Trojans pulled it inside the city.) Virgil says that Laocoön urged the Trojans not to accept it—"Beware of Greeks bearing gifts." For his wisdom Athena, who favored the Greeks, sent serpents to kill him. We see the snakes attacking Laocoön and his two sons, vainly trying to free themselves. On the left one son has already been bitten and is dying. His father, in the center, is trying to keep the serpent's head away from his thigh. The older son is trying to escape by pulling away to the right.

Renaissance artists were impressed by the Laocoön, none more than Michelangelo, who urged Pope Julius II to acquire it for the Belvedere courtyard. He must have felt close to the ancient sculptors who executed the *Laocoön*, because he copied various parts of it in his own masterpieces: the positions of the legs of *Moses* in San Pietro in Vincoli, and of *Jonah* on the ceiling of the Sistine Chapel, are almost identical to the *Laocoön*. One could say that all of Michelangelo's powerful figures on the ceiling and in the *Last Judgment* of the Sistine Chapel were done in the spirit of the Laocoön.

What evoked Michelangelo's admiration still impresses us today; the mastery of design and technique and the exaggerated, violent action of figures shown in conflicting tensions, but still part of a tightly knit triangular composition. Our own generation is better able than our ancestors to view the *Laocoön*. A final restoration of a piece found in 1906 took place as recently as 1960, restoring a lost arm to the central figure.

Cabinet of Apollo (Gabinetto dell'Apollo)

At one time the statue in this room, *Apollo Belvedere,* considered to be a Roman copy of a late fourth-century B.C. Greek bronze original attributed to the Athenian sculptor Leochares, was one of the most famous works of art in the world. Connoisseurs of neoclassical art in the eighteenth and nineteenth centuries considered it the most pure representation of the Apollonian character from classical antiquity. Like the *Laocoön*, it was brought to the Vatican by Pope Julius II after being discovered in the last years of the fifteenth century on one of the Della Rovere properties near Anzio. But, unlike the *Laocoön*, it is not admired today as it was in the past. It is considered dull, with an affected pose that misses the mark of great Hellenistic sculpture.

Cabinet of Canova (Gabinetto del Canova)

Here you will find three works by the nineteenth-century Italian sculptor Antonio Canova (1757–1822): *Perseus, Creugas,* and *Demoxenes*. The last two, boxers, are overdramatized. The *Perseus* was ordered by the Vatican to replace the *Apollo Belvedere,* which had been stolen, and transported to Paris by Napoleon, and is no better than the statue that inspired it.

Cabinet of Hermes (Gabinetto dell'Hermes)

The statue of *Hermes* in this room is a marble Roman copy of the fourth-century B.C. Greek original by Praxiteles. It probably shows Hermes in the form of Psychopompos, the conductor of souls to Hades, the realm of the dead. Found in the ruins of a building erected by Hadrian, it was formerly called the *Antinoüs of the Belvedere.*

Cabinet of Apoxyomenos (Gabinetto dell'Apoxyomenos)

The remaining rooms on this floor are of minor importance with the exception of this room off the round vestibule. In it, as its name suggests, you will find *Apoxyomenos ("The Scraper"),* a Roman copy of a Greek bronze by Lysippos from about 330 B.C. It depicts an athlete after his gymnastic exercise scraping the dusty oil from his right arm with a strigil. He is a magnificent figure: relaxed, well-proportioned, with most of his weight resting on his left leg and his right leg slightly outstretched. His raised arms occupy the upper space with a rhythm that is a masterpiece of three-dimensional movement.

In order to visit the rest of the museum you have to return to the Hall of the Greek Cross to go upstairs to the next floor. The most notable item there is the *Discobolus,* a marble copy of Myron's famous fifth-century B.C. bronze, but it is inferior to another marble copy in Rome's Capitoline Museum.

Next, on the second floor, is the Gregorian-Etruscan Museum, a collection of Etruscan art and Greek vases formed in the nineteenth century housed in sixteenth-century rooms. It makes up one of the most important collections of its kind in the world.

The Gregorian Etruscan Museum

Room 1 has sarcophagi from Tuscania. Room 2 has objects from the royal tomb of Regolini Galassi, unearthed in 1836. There are weapons and household effects, including gold jewelry which is barbaric by classic Greek standards but shows a high degree of artistic skill. Small rooms numbered 12a and b have Greek originals, including a fragment of a *Horse's Head,* probably from the west pediment of the Parthenon.

The vase rooms, 14–17, with an excellent collection from the vicinity of Rome, will allow you to follow the development of Greek vase painting from its rise through its high point to its decline, that is, from the black-figured vases to the red-figured vases. They show Greek life in all its forms, including some freely expressed erotica typical of this art.

A long gallery joins the Etruscan collection to the Raphael rooms and the Sistine Chapel. Along the way, you will have views of the Vatican gardens; sarcophagi and vases in the **Candelabra Gallery;** tapestries designed by Raphael; sixteenth-century frescoed maps; the **Apartment of Pius V** with rare Flemish tapestries; and the **Sobieski Room,** which gets its name from its huge painting of the *Victory of Vienna* won by John II Sobieski, king of Poland, over the Turks.

The Raphael Stanze

Raphael* (1483–1520), Florentine, born in Umbria
Raphael arrived in Rome from Florence in the summer of 1509, when Pope Julius II was having his apartments on the second floor of the unfinished Vatican palace decorated with frescoes. Julius was so taken by young Raphael (he was twenty-six) that he ordered paintings of other artists already at work on the rooms to be removed, and entrusted the entire project to Raphael.

Stanza della Segnatura: room 2

This second room is the first room decorated by Raphael. He left Sodoma's completed ceiling intact, but covered up the already decorated walls with bricks to start anew. First he undertook the *Disputà* (1509–11), the most complete portrayal of the doctrine of the Eucharist in Christian art, and the only great sacred poem in Renaissance painting. It is a masterpiece of balance and form, tracing the Sacrament from its origin in Heaven, where we see God the Father, Christ, the Madonna, and St. John the Baptist, with apostles, patriarchs, and saints enthroned around them in a wide circle. Beneath, on earth, the great figures of the church are engaged in meditation and in discussions on the nature of the Sacrament. With such large groups set on two levels, Raphael's skill lies in the variety of poses set within a symmetry that creates a balance and that is spirited and dignified. Various figures represent St. Jerome (at the left of the altar with his head bowed, contemplating his translation of the Bible), St. Gregory (sitting to the right of St.

Jerome, and probably a portrait of Julius II before he grew his beard), Sixtus IV (standing to the right of the altar next to Dante at his side), Bramante (the bald man leaning on a parapet at the lower left side of the picture), and others who make this work not only a glorification of the Sacrament but also a vast historical scene. The realities of Raphael's time are depicted and merged with the theme that within the church—the protector and supporter of the arts and sciences—lies truth.

The same idea is carried over into the second fresco in the room, facing the *Disputà*, the so-called *School of Athens* (1509–11). Here the illustrious men of philosophy are shown together without the intervals of time and space that separated them, just as in the *Disputà* the great figures of religion are depicted. In the center, framed by a distant arch beyond which is an infinite blue sky, stand Plato and Aristotle. Plato, carrying the *Timaeus* in his left hand, points to Heaven with his right, indicative that Heaven is the realm of ideas that through superior intellect could be brought down to earthly forms; and Aristotle, holding his *Ethics*, points downward to earth, implying that all philosophy must be derived from experience. On each side of these two characters is a group of listeners. To the left of them is Socrates making a point while counting on his fingers. A bearded man in this group beckons to another to come hear what Socrates has to say. Above them in a niche is a nude Apollo which suggests that Raphael had seen a drawing of Michelangelo's *Dying Slave*. In the niche on the opposite side is Athene, and directly below is an old man wrapped in a dark red mantle with the white beard and piercing eyes of Pope Julius II. This man is looking across to a group surrounding Pythagoras, who is writing in a book. The elegant youth dressed in white above him, gazing out with the worldly confidence typical of Raphaelian youths, is a portrait of Francesco Maria, duke of Urbino, a nephew of the pope. Further to the left, the well-rounded man with a laurel wreath on his head is Democritus (the Greek philosopher who thought that the world was made up of tiny particles—atoms), and behind him the small boy with a beautiful head of hair is Federico Gonzaga, who lived at the Vatican at that time and was a favorite of Julius II. In the group to the right is a bald Archimedes (a portrait of Bramante) bending over his slate. Beyond him and his youthful admirers are the natural philosophers: the geographer Ptolemy holding a terrestial globe, and Zoroaster (a portrait of Castiglione) holding a celestial globe. These two turn toward two figures at the edge of the picture, portraits of Sodoma dressed in white and of Raphael himself. One wonders how much Sodoma appreciated this compliment, since it was his paintings that were covered up to make space for Raphael's frescoes. Perhaps he felt like Diogenes, the cynic, sprawled out on the steps oblivious to the crowd around him.

With this painting Raphael reached the height of his artistic achievement and created, along with Michelangelo's Sistine ceiling, one of the greatest murals of the sixteenth century. The arrangements of figures have ideal formal and spatial harmony, and nowhere has the humanism of the Renaissance been expressed more deeply; the patriarchial characters, clad in massive drapery, achieve monumentality of form as well as spirit; their arrangement in a half circle creates a perspective that is exciting and believable; and the noble architectural background is taken out of Bramante's designs for the new St. Peter's itself.

Raphael, as one of the greatest eclectics in art, had no doubt borrowed from Michelangelo's frescoes in the Sistine Chapel. That project was nearly completed when Raphael started to paint in the Stanza della Segnatura. While Raphael has retained his own style, he has also changed its appearance into that of Michelangelo's high Renaissance Roman grand manner. His figures, strongly modeled, have new possibilities of action as form and line sweep with ease between them. They and their overall composition are the epitome of the clarity, completeness, and assurance of the high Renaissance in Rome.

When the Sistine Chapel was reopened in August, 1511, and Raphael saw Michelangelo's astonishing new art on the ceiling, he seems to have rushed back to his own painting to record the presence of Michelangelo as the inspirational force of high Renaissance art. Thus Raphael has painted Michelangelo into the scene as Heraclitus (the Greek philosopher who held that reality is change and permanence an illusion), a solitary figure in deep thought scribbling on this marble block in the middle foreground. His powerful form recalls Michelangelo's own figures on the ceiling of the Sistine Chapel, and he wears the rough garb of a sixteenth-century stonecutter instead of the flowing robes of the other philosophers and their attendants, in keeping with Michelangelo's character and the reality of his everyday appearance.

Stanza di Eliodoro: room 3

Following the Stanza della Segnatura, Raphael worked on the Stanza di Eliodoro from 1512 until 1514. Julius II died before Raphael completed it, but the new pope, Leo X, extended Raphael's contract. The theme of the room is the aid given by God to his chosen people, represented by Julius II, in their hour of need. Around the window facing the Cortile dei Pappigalli is the famous *Mass of Bolsena.* Here the story is told of the Eucharistic miracle of 1263 still celebrated on the feast day of Corpus Christi. A Bohemian priest who doubted the mystery of the presence of Christ in the Eucharist was celebrating Mass at the little town of Bolsena when, in elevating the host, blood began to flow from five gashes in the wafer, resembling the five wounds of Christ. The consecrated Host shed drops of red blood in the form of a cross on the Corporal (cloth) on which it was resting. When Julius II was marching northward in 1506 to engage rebellious cardinals backed by the French, he stopped at the Cathedral of Orvieto, which still preserves the blood-stained Corporal as a sacred relic, to pray before entering battle near Bologna. His victories there were attributed to the intervention of the relic. Thus this painting illustrates the infallibility of the church of Rome and the suppression of the schism by Julius. It also shows that Raphael's style, like that of Michelangelo's, never stood still. Only two or three years after the painting of the frescoes in the Stanza della Segnatura, there are already signs of the new baroque manner. The great arch that encircles the whole composition is part of the more solid architecture. Great balanced masses fill the spaces on either side of the altar, with Pope Julius II in prayer at the right, and the priest holding the miraculous wafer at the left. Below, on the right, are the Swiss soldiers who Julius had used in his battles. They are some of the most handsome youths Raphael ever painted, with uniforms in rich Venetian color, in the strong modeling of Michelangelo.

On the opposite side of the room is the *Deliverance of St. Peter from Prison* showing the story, in triptychlike form (according to the Acts of the Apostles 12:3–11) of Peter being freed from Herod's prison by an angel of the Lord, being led out, on the right, in a trance, and, on the left, the soldiers waking up to look for their escaped prisoner. This story had special meaning for Pope Julius II who had been praying in the church of St. Peter in Chains (San Pietro in Vincoli) in Rome, where he had been cardinal, when news reached him of his unexpected victory over the French in 1512. Thus the fresco represents the deliverance of the papacy from the French invader. Since Julius died while Raphael was executing the work, it also stood for the liberation of Julius from the earthly prison into the eternal light of Heaven.

As a rare night scene in Renaissance art it reminds us of Piero della Francesca's *Dream of Constantine* (Church of San Francesco, Arezzo). But Raphael's work, painted about fifty years later, is more ambitious and is rendered with greater imagination in illumination; light emanating from four different sources is the artistic theme. First, and most dramatic, is the halo-like light of the angel in the center, behind the black bars, producing an almost blinding aura by the device of contrasting light and dark. It also adds to the horror of the prison and the sight of the old man in chains. Second, on the right, the angel again lights up the darkness, illuminating the soldiers sleeping on the stairs as she leads St. Peter away to safety. Third, on the left, the light from the torch, held by the soldier rousing his comrades to get up and search for the escaped prisoner, is reflected by the figures, adding tumult to the scene. Fourth, the light of the moon shining through the clouds adds to the grimness of the scene. It is the boldest night scene executed in the Renaissance.

The other two walls in the room show the *Expulsion of Attila from Rome by Pope Leo I* and the *Expulsion of Heliodorus from the Temple.* They are depicted with heroic action that owes a great deal to Michelangelo, and if any of Raphael's works can be labeled baroque these two are the ones. Their baroque action reminds one of Rubens, and their classical manner reminds one of Poussin, both artists of the next century.

Stanza dell'Incendio and Sala di Costantino: rooms 1 and 4

In these rooms, where the basic themes are the activity of the popes throughout history (in the Stanza dell'Incendio, 1517) and the triumph of Christianity over paganism (in the Sala di Costantino, 1520–24), most of the work is by Raphael's assistants and is below the artistic heights reached by the master.

The Loggia of Raphael

From the Sala di Costantino one enters the Loggia of Raphael, a long arcade gallery that at one time was open and afforded a view of all of Rome.

The vaulting of each of its thirteen bays contains four biblical scenes, collectively known as Raphael's Bible, designed but not painted by Raphael (1517). The design for each pair of wall columns is different and depicts Roman decorations discovered in the buried vaults of Nero's Golden House. These were designed and executed by Giulio Romano and others (1519).

Next, pass through the richly decorated *Chiaroscuri* room to get to the exquisite little chapel of Nicholas V.

Chapel of Nicholas V (Niccolina Chapel)

If you ever thought that **Fra Angelico** (ca. 1400–55) was the last painter of the Gothic period rather than one of the first Renaissance painters, a visit to this exquisite little chapel will change your mind. Fra Angelico was at the end of his career when, with the help of his pupil, **Benozzo Gozzoli** (1420–97), he covered these walls with frescoes depicting scenes from the lives of St. Stephen and St. Lawrence. They were executed between 1447 and 1449 and are clearly works of the Renaissance, with a sincerity and clarity of vision remarkable for that early date.

St. Lawrence Distributing Alms: lower part of wall

St. Lawrence is shown standing before the poor and the infirm distributing wealth from the church treasury. He is solidly drawn, wearing a dalmatic decorated with golden flames, referring to his martyrdom on a grill. The figures around him are not submissive, but seem proud and even noble, worthy of the saint's generosity. At the extreme left a woman, depicted madonna-like, fondles her baby as she momentarily forgets her poverty. Two children to the right of Lawrence are delighted with what he has given them. In the background is the open Renaissance portal of a church and a view of its interior, which has majestic columns that give a convincing illusion of space. The painting is a Renaissance scene of the first magnitude, with fine figures and rich architecture directed toward the impulses of charity and respect for the individual.

The route now doubles back through the Raphael rooms and descends to the Borgia apartments, the Gallery of Modern Religious Art, and the Sistine Chapel.

The Borgia Apartments

These apartments, whose rooms, leading one into another, are richly decorated with wall frescoes and gilded ceiling vaults, are named after the Borgia Pope, Alexander VI, who had three of the rooms decorated by **Pinturicchio** (ca. 1454–1513). Take special note of Pinturicchio's fresco, *Disputation of St. Catherine of Alexandria,* in room 4, the Hall of Saints. Catherine is the patron saint of bastards which, in view of the Pope's numerous progeny, justifies her presence here.

Continuing from the Borgia apartments is the *Gallery of Modern Reli-*

gious Art, which displays a collection of works from some of the world's modern artists: Francis Bacon, Marc Chagall, Salvador Dali, Giorgio de Chirico, Max Ernst, Paul Gauguin, Wassily Kandinsky, Paul Klee, Oskar Kokoschka, Fernand Léger, Marino Marini, Henri Matisse, Henry Moore, Edvard Munch, Pablo Picasso, Auguste Rodin, Maurice Utrillo, and many others.

Sistine Chapel

This chapel (as large as a church, 133 feet long by forty-three feet wide) was built in 1473–81 by Pope Sixtus IV della Rovere (1471–84), hence its name "Sistine." Many Renaissance masters—Boticelli, Perugino, Signorelli, Rossellini, Pinturicchio, and Ghirlandaio—decorated its lateral walls in 1482 with scenes from the Old and New Testaments, but these frescoes are overwhelmed by Michelangelo's ceiling and his giant fresco of the *Last Judgment* on the west wall. They are one of the greatest achievements in the history of painting, though executed by a man who was really not a painter. Michelangelo has signed his name to this work as "Michelangelo, Sculptor."

Michelangelo* (1475–1564), Florentine

Sistine Ceiling (1508–12)

This immense ceiling, of almost an acre in area, forty feet above the ground, was not a favorite project of Michelangelo. He did not consider himself a painter and had, in fact, done little painting, though recent findings show he knew the fresco technique well. Bramante and his other rivals, who wished to see him distracted from sculpture, in which no one could compete with him, urged Pope Julius II to insist that Michelangelo take the commission. After trying to extricate himself from the project, even suggesting that it be given to Raphael, the pope's favorite, Michelangelo reluctantly had to accept. He began the work on May 10, 1508, with plans to divide the ceiling into three zones: the central zone has nine main panels framed in painted architecture—four large ones alternately with five smaller scenes telling the story of the Creation of Man to the Flood and the Drunkenness of Noah. On either side of them, in the second zone, are immense figures of sibyls and prophets; in the remaining zone, directly above the windows, and in the triangular spandrels, or spaces between the arches, are biblical ancestors of Christ. The arrangement is unified with a series of decorative nudes perched on the painted architecture to soften its lines and to afford transitions.

Perhaps the most moving painting from the central series, done in lighter colors to draw attention to them as the principal panels of the ceiling, is the *Creation of Adam* (fifth ceiling fresco from the altar end). It is the epitome of Michelangelo's scultpurelike painting where he relies on the form of the human figure to the elimination of almost everything else. The landscape is reduced to a minimum, though color is of more importance than scholars first thought (restoration of the ceiling, begun in 1981, will take twelve years to complete at a cost of three million dollars, and has revealed more color in Michelangelo's frescoes than could previously be seen through the dirt and layers of varnish and overpainting—early restorers, unable to remove the dirt, had applied deeper shadow to maintain contrast). But color and detail are not of first importance. Adam lies on the bluish-green earth, there only as a background. The figure of God, supported by His angels, floats through the air with grace and ease. As His index finger almost touches Adam's—the focal point of the painting—one can sense the electriclike charge that will infuse life into man. Yet Adam regards his Maker reluctantly as though he realizes that the gift of life will bring sorrow. His massive nude figure is Michelangelo's ideal of the body drawn with the familiarity of anatomy of a great sculptor, done out of his mind without the aid of a model. Further demonstration of Michelangelo's mystery of drawing of the male nude is in the four figures that frame the composition and in sixteen others on the ceiling. They resemble athletes of classical Greek art and, with Adam, have that sense of figural vitality that Michelangelo infused into his paintings.

After seeing the nude figure of Adam, examine the fully clothed figure of *Jeremiah* (first prophet on the left side of the ceiling from the altar end). In deep contemplation, he is one of the most expressive of the group of prophets and sibyls depicted on the ceiling and illustrates Michelangelo's love of sheer power. Yet in spite of his bulk, it still seems that he could rise to move around in the illusion of three-dimensional space in which he is sitting. This characteristic of Michelangelo's art, where his figures assume a living monumentality that is highly convincing, is what makes Michelangelo such a communicator of profound thoughts, even in our own age, when visual imagery takes second place to the written word. It is difficult to imagine words expressing more meaningfully the universal message of the unity of man's body, mind, and spirit. Michelangelo's art compels us to think of human relationships and of our own destiny.

The Last Judgment (1536–41): west wall

Michelangelo was more than twenty years older when he was called back to the Sistine Chapel to decorate its west wall. In the intervening years he had become embittered at his and Italy's misfortunes (Rome had been sacked in 1527 by mercenaries of Emperor Charles V's army) and, being older, was concerned about his own destiny. The youthful hope of redemption that he expressed in his ceiling frescoes is not present in *The Last Judgment*. Instead there is a hopeless, sinister, vengeful depiction of mankind, making it less of a Christian work than you might expect to find in the Vatican. But it is also what you would expect from Michelangelo, and represents a new style not seen on the ceiling and that goes beyond the art of the Renaissance.

Covering an area of about 200 square yards and containing 391 major figures, it has an extraordinary energy of movement and form that seems to start with the trumpeting angels in the lower center and then moves to the left where the dead, in various stages of decomposition, are being rescued by angels (Michelangelo's angels have no wings) and carried up to Heaven. In the center is a beardless, muscular Christ surrounded by the blessed who seem to be filled with fear at his presence, because Michelangelo's Christ has come as a judge rather than a saviour. As He raises His arm in condemnation the damned souls, on the lower right side, are seen falling straight into Hell.

Two figures are of special interest. One is St. Bartholomew holding his flayed skin (a symbol of his martyrdom) directly below Christ to the right. The face on it is that of Michelangelo, his grotesque testimonial to his own presence on earth. However, the face of St. Bartholomew, holding the skin, is a portrait of the satirist Pietro Aretino, who attacked Michelangelo in his writings because he could not convince the master to paint his own version of the Last Judgment. The other figure on the wall that represents the vengeance of Michelangelo is Minos, king of Hell, actually a portrait of Biagio da Cesena, the papal chamberlain. He is depicted in the extreme lower right corner of the door with ass's ears, a nasty expression on his face, and a tail in the shape of a serpent wound around him. His place there derives from his remark to the pope, when they were inspecting Michelangelo's unfinished work, that it was improper for a chapel to have such a display of nudity and genitals (later, one of Michelangelo's followers, Daniele da Volterra, was engaged to cover the figures with painted drapery). Not only has Michelangelo put Biagio da Cesena where he belongs, but has aimed Minos's gnawing serpent at his genitals.

Michelangelo's *Last Judgment* became the most famous and notorious painting in Italy. The young painters who came to view it saw Michelangelo's angry shapes as a revolt against the standards of high Renaissance art and were quick to react. Michelangelo's *terribilità* had already been an inspiration to a growing group of painters called mannerists whose work showed human figures in strange new ways rather than in classical poses. *The Last Judgment* gave them more confidence and ultimately led to the baroque style that came to dominate European art for at least one hundred and fifty years.

Continue to follow the itinerary, which includes a gem of a little room of Roman frescoes named after its treasure, *The Aldobrandini Marriage,* the Vatican Library, and the New Wing (Broccio Nuovo).

New Wing (Braccio Nuovo)

The splendid New Wing (Braccio Nuovo) contains several sculptures of first rank, among them *Prudicitia,* no. 23, a copy of a third–second-century B.C. Greek original showing the goddess of maidenly modesty; *Demosthenes,* no. 64, a copy of a popular third-century B.C. Athenian statue of the orator who was born about 385 B.C. who had to overcome physical impediments to become one of the greatest speakers of ancient Greece; *The Nile,* no. 106, a colossal group statue copied in the second century in Rome from a Hellenistic prototype showing the river god with sixteen children clambering over him, symbolic of the number of yards by which the Nile rises to irrigate the land; and the *Giustiniani Athena,* no. 111, a Roman copy from a popular fifth-century B.C. Greek bronze original—with her helmet pushed back, her breastplate decorated with the Gorgon Medusa, her spear, and the Acropolis snake coiled at her feet, she is surely Athena born of Zeus.

Augustus of the Prima Porta (after 20 B.C.), no. 14
This great Roman marble statue in armor was discovered almost intact in 1863 in Livia's villa (the second wife of Augustus) near the Prima Porta on the Via Flaminia. It is a magnificent Roman statue of an emperor, with a splendid head and the armored dress of a general. He holds a scepter in his left hand and his right hand is raised in an oratorical gesture. His feet are bare in keeping with heroic style, and the dolphin ridden by a cupid is a reference to the Julian clan that claimed descent from Venus.

At the Quattro Cancelli you can descend to the restaurant for a well-deserved lunch, and then complete your itinerary with a visit to the Picture Gallery.

Picture Gallery (Pinacoteca)

This splendid gallery, started by Pope Pius VI in the eighteenth century, is housed today in a Renaissance-style building built during this century and completed in 1932. Though not all of the schools of Italian painting are to be found here, there is a display of about 500 religious paintings from the eleventh century onward. This includes an altarpiece, *St. Peter in the Chair and Saints* (ca. 1469) by Giotto and assistants (room 2); works by Raphael (room 8): *Coronation of the Virgin* (1503); *The Madonna of Foligno* (1512) and *The Transfiguration* (1520), mentioned below, plus ten famous *Tapestries* woven in Brussels from Raphael's cartoons drawn in 1515–16 (see Gallery of the Raphael Cartoons, Victoria and Albert Museum, London); and paintings by Titian, Veronese, Ribera, van Dyck, and other old masters.

Caravaggio* (1573–1610), Italian

The Desposition (1602–4): room 12
Here is one of the best religious works by an artist who introduced realism into European painting. Figures depicted are humble people drawn from everyday life, for its time an original concept in a religious painting. The light, somewhat subdued for Caravaggio, is nevertheless filled with a dramatic intensity, while the composition reaches out to invite us into the picture; notice that it starts with the pointed corner of the slab, which is repeated in the pointy elbow of Nicodemus holding Christ's legs, while Christ's right hand and white sheet touch the slab, leading our eye upward to His lifeless body and then to the figures holding Him, the point of greatest tension. The sculptured quality of the figures reminds one of Michelangelo; only the young woman with her hands raised in the background seems out of place and may have been added later by a baroque artist.

Leonardo da Vinci* (1452–1519), Florentine

St. Jerome (ca. 1482): room 9
This unfinished drawing has always been considered a genuine Leonardo. It was found damaged in Rome in the nineteenth century. There is a story that it had been cut in two, and that one piece was found in a junk shop and the

other was found by a Cardinal Fesch in the shop of a shoemaker. Later Pope Pius IX bought it from the cardinal's heirs.

Only Leonardo could have painted the human body depicted in this picture. He had begun to study anatomy by dissecting corpses, and the emphasis he gives to the skeletonlike form of the old man and the muscles beneath his skin shows Leonardo as a scientist as well as an artist. The head of St. Jerome comes directly out of Leonardo's collection of drawings. He liked to collect what he considered grotesque heads, and when he saw one on the street he would follow the person around all day, then go back to his studio and draw his features from memory.

What may make this picture so impressive is its unfinished state. The drab olive background emphasizes the penitent saint who had only wild beasts and scorpions for company in the desert. What better way to reveal the ascetism of the saint than in this naked old man, the only human figure in a bleak background?

Raphael* (1483–1520), Florentine, born in Umbria

Transfiguration: room 8

This is Raphael's last painting. He began it in 1519 and died the following year before he could finish it. There is a dispute as to how much of it was by the master's own hand, but it is generally agreed that the upper half is by Raphael and the lower half by Giulio Romano and Francesco Penni from Raphael's sketches.

The work is heroic in scale and conception to convey the forceful gestures of exalted persons engaged in a great event. It communicates not only by form and structure, but also by a complicated lighting that with the movements of the figures connects upper and lower parts. Still, each part is treated separately, as seen from eye level, instead of from one point of view at ground level, which would have required foreshortenings and the distortion of noble forms. Since form is one of the main means of expression in this painting, as in all of Raphael's art, nothing is done to disturb that element. Reality is sacrificed for it. Even the light, important in communicating the dramatic quality of the scene, is made to fall along forms to emphasize their volumes.

This statement of form and light was put on display at Raphael's funeral in the Pantheon, and was a testimonial to his genius and style at the end of his brief career.

Ancient Roman Remains

ARA PACIS (ALTAR OF PEACE)

Between the Via di Ripetta and the Lungotovere at the Tiber

Hours: Open June–Sept., Tues.–Sat., 9AM–1PM and 3–6PM, Sun., 9AM–1PM; Oct.–May, Tues.–Sat., 10AM–4PM, Sun., 10AM–1PM. Admission fee.

This modern building, constructed in 1937 across from the remains of the mausoleum of Augustus, contains reconstructed fragments, found over a period of four centuries, of a monumental pagan altar executed in 13 B.C. in honor of Augustus. Marble friezes (north wall) show a rather formal procession of people, some of whom may represent portraits of the family of Augustus. They show how official Augustan art relied on the classicism of Greek reliefs. On either side of the doors of the monument are reliefs of legendary characters. The best preserved (east entrance) depicts a shapely young mother idealized as the Earth goddess Tellis flanked with personifications of Air and Water. This theme of the Earth pacified and made fertile is adapted from Hellenistic compositions and here is a return to tradition in the Augustan Age.

CASTEL SANT' ANGELO

Lungotevere Castello, on the Tiber

Hours. Open Tues.–Sat., 9AM–1PM, Sun., 9AM–12 noon. Admission fee.

The Castel Sant' Angelo was once the mausoleum of Hadrian. Constructed in 136, it had white marble walls surmounted by statues and a bronze two-wheeled chariot drawn by four horses on its summit. Like the Colosseum, it is an example of the massive proportions of Roman buildings.

The bronze angel that now rises above it recalls how the structure got its present name. According to legend, in 590 Pope Gregory the Great was leading a procession to pray for the end of the plague when he saw above the castle the Archangel Michael sheathing his sword, thus predicting an end to the plague and giving the castle its name.

In the fifth century the structure was converted into a fortress. In the fifteenth century it was connected by a covered corridor to the Vatican, which enabled popes to use it as a place of refuge. It was successfully used as such in 1494 during the invasion of Charles VIII and in 1527 during the sack of Rome. The castle contains sumptuously furnished papal apartments started by Alexander VI and completed by Paul III. However, much of the structure today is a military museum.

COLOSSEUM

Piazza del Colosseo, end of Via dei Fori Imperiali

Hours: Open daily 9AM to one hour before sunset. Admission fee for upper levels.

This huge arena, dating to the first century, is the most impressive of the ancient structures in Rome and the one that best gives an idea of the great scale in which the Romans worked. Vespasian (69–79), the conqueror of Jerusalem, undertook its construction, using thousands of Jewish slaves he had taken prisoner. Its inauguration in 80 A.D. by Titus (79–81) lasted for one hundred days, at which time 5,000 animals were killed and mock naval battles held (the floor of the Colosseum could be flooded for such events). During the next three hundred years it was used for gladiatorial combats and was also the scene of barbarities during the Christian persecutions. The blood sports were terminated by Honorius (395–423) in 404. In the centuries that followed it was damaged by an earthquake, used as a fortress during the Middle Ages, an arena for bullfights, and in the fifteenth, sixteenth, and seventeenth centuries as a stone quarry by builders of Rome's Renaissance palaces, churches, and monasteries. What you see today is only about one third of its original structure. Only the intercession of Pope Benedict XIV (1740–58) in the eighteenth century prevented it from being completely leveled. He declared it to be sacred ground in memory of the Christian martyrs who perished in it. Thereafter, some restoration was carried out, but we will never be able to realize the total effect when it was completely intact. It held about 50,000 spectators, who could be protected from sun and rain by canvas awnings strung from poles. The dimensions of its oval are approximately 660 by 512 feet, and originally it was 200 feet high (it is now 160 feet high). Its floor has been removed to show a network of ramps and corridors beneath it.

Its exterior walls reveal the Roman combination of arch and column, known as the Roman arch order. The structure rests on the arches, but those are enframed by an engaged column on each pier, which supports an entablature; the columns and entablature create a rectangle around the arch. The sturdiest order is placed at the bottom, the lightest at the top; thus the capitals on the lower columns of the first level are Doric; on the second, Ionic; on the third, Corinthian. Renaissance architects frequently copied this design.

The Colosseum should be seen not only in daylight but also illuminated at night. Like many ruins, when seen at night its damage is more hidden and the structure takes on an extra dimension provided by the spectator's own imagination.

ARCH OF CONSTANTINE

Piazza del Colosseo, next to the Colosseum

This construction exemplifies the combination of arch and column even though the columns in this case are free standing, supporting only the statues. It dates to the fourth century when it was built to celebrate Constantine's victory over the tyrant Maxentius at the Milvan Bridge in 312. Unlike earlier similar constructions, which have only one opening, it has three: a large opening in the center flanked by smaller ones.

Most of its decoration is made up of reliefs taken from earlier monuments (second century) in Rome. Contemporary art in Constantine's time had declined and local artists were not capable of doing the earlier fine work. The rude fourth-century statues on the bases of the columns and the long narrow reliefs beneath the medallions forming a frieze over the side arches contrast with the admirable reliefs on the inner side of the central archway and the two reliefs on top on either side of the arch. This is not to say that it fails as a monument whose aim is to convey the military greatness of imperial Rome. It succeeds by virtue of size, scale, bold proportions, and decorative richness.

THE ROMAN FORUM

Via dei Fori Imperiali

Hours: Open Oct.–May, Wed.–Mon., 9AM–5PM; June–Sept., Wed.–Mon., 9AM–7PM. Admission fee.

First view the Forum from the terrace of the Via del Campidoglio. (Steps lead down to the ruins below.) From this vantage point you can get a view of what was the political and religious center of ancient Rome long before the Christian era. The ruins mostly date from the second and third centuries and remained intact until the sixth century. Then followed a period of vandalism when the Forum was used as a stone quarry. It was then abandoned for centuries and became a rubbish dump and cow pasture. Restoration, starting in the nineteenth century, brought it to its present state. Whatever could be salvaged is being preserved.

Below you are the three columns of the **Temple of Vespasian,** erected in 79–96 A.D. in honor of Emperor Vespasian and his son Titus. The columns and entablature are of the best Roman period. It contains the remains of a frieze that depicts sacrificial implements. Behind it, to the right, are the eight columns of the **Temple of Saturn** built in 497 B.C., which make it one of the oldest structures in the Forum. At one time it served as the state treasury. To the left is the well-preserved **Arch of Septimius Severus** dating from 203. It was erected in honor of the emperor and his two sons, Caracalla and Gela, and originally had a bronze chariot containing these three figures mounted on its top. Further into the Forum, to the right, are three columns of the **Temple of Castor and Pollux.** These are the most ancient ruins here, dating to 484 B.C. The temple itself was erected to honor Rome's first military victory in the early days of the republic. In the distance, almost immediately behind the three columns of Castor and Pollux, is the **Arch of Titus** erected to commemorate the victories of Titus and Vespasian in the Judaean war in which the Romans destroyed the city and temple of Jerusalem in 70 A.D.

A walk among the ruins gives a different perspective, as though you were walking down the Broadway of ancient Rome. A close look at the **Arch of Septimus Severus** shows, in a sculpture panel of the north face, the emperor addressing his troops; another depicts the siege of Babylon. Other battles are shown in the panels of its south facade. In the frieze are shown conquered Africans paying tribute to Rome. The **Arch of Titus** has sculptured reliefs. The coffered interior of the arch has carved squares depicting the Romans carrying off spoils from their victory over the Jews. While the scenes are realistically executed they are not strong on design or artistic maturity.

Accessible from the Roman Forum is the **Palatine Hill,** once the best residential section of ancient Rome. The ruins here will give you an idea of the splendor of the palaces that once stood on the site, especially the **House of Livia,** probably occupied by the wife of Augustus (27 B.C.–A.D. 14). In three of its rooms there remain frescoes and friezes of interest.

PANTHEON

Piazza della Rotonda

Hours: Open Tues.–Sat., 9AM–1PM, Sun., 9AM–12 noon. Free admission.

The pantheon is the only ancient Roman building that has come down to us intact, rescued from decay and plunder by being declared a Christian church in 609. As such it can be considered a tangible link between the ancient and the modern city of Rome.

It was originally built in 27 B.C., probably in rectangular form, under Marcus Agrippa, the son-in-law of Augustus, to commemorate the victory of Actium over Antony and Cleopatra. It was then rebuilt by Hadrian in 110–125 A.D. in the large circular form seen today, dedicated to seven pagan gods of the solar system, the bronze statues of whom once stood in the seven niches that surround the single room of its interior. At one time it was covered with marble but that and the original gilt bronze tiles of its roof have disappeared.

Today we marvel at the Pantheon for its concrete **dome,** rising 140 feet above the ground. Its placement within massive walls (over twenty feet thick) allows the cylindrical outer mass utmost visibility. The dome itself is almost hidden from the outside, one of the first buildings in which the builders were more interested in the interior space than in exterior form. But the exterior is impressive in size and in its simplicity of shape. It is such an imposing mass that it hardly needs the colonnaded portico in front of it.

Within, the building is more impressive. Its circular shape contains perfect proportions—the diameter of the rotunda (143 feet) is exactly equal to the height from floor to summit, and the height from floor to cornice is equal to that from cornice to apex. The chapels of the ancient gods, now occupied by saints, are niches built into the wall at intervals, part of the main spatial area rather than separate volumes. The undersurface of the dome is marked off in trapezoids by horizontal rings crossed at regular intervals by bands radiating from a single opening in the center of the dome, which lights the whole building. Below the beautiful marble pavement runs a drain to carry off rain, which enters from the opening in the dome (twenty-eight feet in diameter).

From the time of the Renaissance the Pantheon became a burial place for the famous in Italy. This is no better expressed than in the tomb of Raphael, whose fame and accomplishments outshine those of the other deceased occupants of the Pantheon.

Churches, Squares, and Buildings of Christian Rome

CAMPIDOGLIO

(See Capitoline Museum and Gallery)

PALAZZO FARNESE

Piazza Farnese (the French Embassy), behind Campo dei Fiori

Hours: Open Sun., 11AM–12 noon. Free admission.

Do not be put off by the fact that the Farnese Palace is the home of the French embassy and that it is open to the public only on Sundays for one hour. It is the finest Renaissance palace in Rome and if you cannot see the interior a look at its **front facade** is still worthwhile. This was built by **Antonio da Sangallo, the Younger** (1483–1546) between 1534 and 1546 but completed after his death by **Michelangelo,** who added the widely projecting cornice and the balcony. Notice that there are no vertical divisions of the facade by columns or pilasters. Its main feature is the three long rows of windows cleverly varied by the shape of their pediments. Their structural members stand out from the smooth wall creating a refined decoration that relieves what could have been a monotonous block.

The **entrance vestibule** by Sangallo, itself a masterpiece, has a barred vaulted central aisle supported by a powerful Roman Doric order of polished granite columns. This leads into the splendid **inner courtyard,** the palace's masterpiece. Sangallo must have been inspired by the buildings of ancient Rome, for this is no longer quattrocento work but an arcaded quadrangle with Roman arches supported by columns attached to piers, as in the Colosseum. Michelangelo's contribution here was the upper story where he designed superimposed pilasters crowned by carved Corinthian capitals. While they are mannerist features whose function is purely ornamental, they were necessary to relieve the Roman severity of Sangallo's design.

The outstanding feature of the interior is the **Galleria** with its beautiful **frescoed ceiling** (1597–1603) by **Annibale Carraci** (1560–1609). Its subject is the loves of the gods as related by Ovid and Virgil. In the center of the vault is *The Triumph of Bacchus and Ariadne,* while other panels show *Mercury Handing the Golden Apple to Paris,* various episodes of *The Legend of Galatea,* and, in the background, *Andromeda Freed by Perseus.* While this fresco creation had often been considered a revival of Raphael's mythological scenes, such as his *Galatea* in the Villa Farnesina, just across the Tiber from the Farnese palace, it is really a work done at a higher pitch, and is more imaginative. With the interrelationships of its paintings, its simulated stone herms and atlantes that carry into the vault the lines of the pilasters below, its bright colors and robust forms with their surging movements, Carracci's work is one of the finest examples of early baroque ceiling painting in Europe.

PIAZZA NAVONA

This beautiful piazza, decorated with three baroque fountains, preserves the shape of the ancient stadium of Dormitian that once stood on this site. The buildings that today surround it are constructed on the foundations of the stadium's terraced seating.

The most outstanding building on the piazza is *Sant' Agnese in Agone* built on the west side on the spot where the saint was supposed to have been martyred. Its lucid facade and elegant dome, flanked by perforated twin towers, was built by **Borromini** (1599–1667) in 1653–57. With the neighboring buildings, all baroque, and those wonderful fountains, it contributes to forming one of Rome's most beautiful piazzas.

Starting from the south end, the fountains are as follows: *The Moro Fountain* (begun in 1575) by Jacopo della Porta, but altered by Bernini; *The Fountain of the Four Rivers* (begun in 1648) by Bernini; and *The Neptune Fountain* (1878) by Antonio della Bitta and Zappalà.

Bernini, Gian Lorenzo* (1598–1680), Italian

The Four Rivers Fountain: center of piazza
The four figures surrounding this fountain represent the four great rivers of the world: the Danube, the Nile, the Ganges, and the Plata. Notice that the Nile is covering his eyes as though not wanting to look at the facade of Sant' Agnese in Agone built by Barromini, Bernini's rival in architecture. Their religious meaning derives from the Christian idea of the Rivers of paradise at the foot of the mountain on which the Cross stands. The Roman obelisk, which tops the fountain in the center, is crowned by a dove, the traditional symbol of divine light and eternity, alluding to the all-embracing power of the church. These objects, the sprawling river giants and the gushing water, combined with the huge rock formation, make this the most dynamic baroque fountain in Rome. It also blends well with the surrounding architecture, especially the church.

ST. PETER'S BASILICA

Piazza San Pietro

Hours: Open Oct.–Mar., daily 7AM–6PM; Apr.–Sept., daily 7AM–7PM. Free admission.

In 1506 Pope Julius II decided to tear down old St. Peter's and build a new one larger and more magnificent than any other church in Europe, a basilica to glorify the church of Rome in the face of northern Protestantism. Today you approach St. Peter's by walking down the Via della Conciliazione, that broad street built to commemorate the signing of the Lateran Treaty in 1929, which leads into the Piazza San Pietro and has, from its beginning, the famous view of the great basilica. You will see that what Julius II started in 1506 is indeed the most glorious church in Christendom.

Of course, what Pope Julius II began in 1506 he never lived to see completed. It took 106 years to build St. Peter's. Many artists, including Bramante, Raphael, and Michelangelo, had a hand in it, along with a multitude of popes directing them. It therefore has a complicated building history, with many changes being made along the way. What we see today, on a site once occupied by the Circus of Nero, where early Christians were martyred and where old St. Peter's had stood since the early fourth century, is a huge, essentially baroque building that owes much of its design to **Michelangelo** (1475–1564). He devoted the last thirty years of his life to it, and refused any salary.

While Michelangelo liked Bramante's original plan, modifying it only for practical reasons, most of the present exterior (apart from the east front facade) is Michelangelo's construction and, when he died in 1564, at the age of eighty-nine, a considerable part of the basilica was built, right up to the top of the drum. In the seventeenth century **Carlo Maderno** (1556–1629) built the long nave to achieve the present Latin cross shape (not part of Michelangelo's Greek cross design), making the length of the church 611 feet long, and a facade made necessary by that addition (which obscures some of the dome). Some controversy exists as to how much of Michelangelo's design went into the **great dome,** the most striking feature of the church. When it was built between 1585 and 1590 by Giacomo della Porta (1539–1602) and Domenico Fontana (1543–1607), modifications were made to Michelangelo's slightly pointed dome. However, the original conception, spanning 157 feet and rising to a height of 452 feet above the ground, in a fluid baroque style, is largely Michelangelo's.

Most of the sides of St. Peter's are difficult to see, but the east **front facade,** facing the great piazza, is as impressive from a distance as it is close up. The work of Maderno, as noted, is palacelike, with eight huge columns and four pilasters, all with decorative Corinthian capitals. These support a huge entablature in the center of which there is a triangular pediment. A baroque attic extends across the facade, and above this level is a balustrade surmounted by statues of Christ, St. John, and eleven of the twelve apostles (St. Peter is not represented). Clocks adorn each end of the facade, and at either end, at street level at the beginning of the front steps, is a statue of *Emperor Charlemagne,* to the left, a work of Cornecchini (1685–1740); and *Emperor Constantine,* to the right, by Bernini (1598–1680).

The **piazza** itself is also the work of **Bernini,** a square of majestic beauty (1,100 by 785 feet). It is surrounded by a curving colonnade of four rows of columns atop whose classic balustrade are sculptured figures of saints (162 of them). The obelisk in the center was brought from Egypt to ancient Rome and at one time stood in Nero's circus. On either side are fountains; the one to the right by Maderno and the other by Fontana.

The great **interior** of the basilica, measuring a total area of over 163,000 square feet, is occupied by many works of art by the great artists of Italy, including Bernini, who did the huge bronze *Baldacchino* (canopy) above the supposed tomb of St. Peter under the dome. Its twisted columns make up a dramatic baroque form and, while many people find it overdone, it animates the void under the dome with a sense of movement.

With such an array of artists contributing to the interior of a church, it would ordinarily be difficult to single out one work as being far above the others, but at St. Peter's this is easy. It is Michelangelo's incomparable *Pietà*, conveniently located in the first chapel on the right aisle.

Michelangelo* (1475–1564), Florentine

Pietà (1498–99/1500):
The *Pietà* represents Michelangelo's first religious commission, given when he was twenty-three by a French cardinal in Rome. Perhaps the Northern-style depiction of the dead Christ lying on His mother's lap came from the cardinal, because there is no reference to it in Italian art. Before Michelangelo's *Pietà* Christ was shown in Italy as a child asleep on His mother's lap, not as a grown man, as he appears here. However, the overall style of the *Pietà* was not unique. It has a Leonardesque pyramidal composition and, though loosely arranged with freely flowing lines and contours, is full of quattrocento detail and classical purity of figures—something Michelangelo would soon abandon. It is the only work Michelangelo ever signed; his name is carved into the strap that crosses Mary's bosom. Vasari tells us that when the *Pietà* was first exhibited in St. Peter's Michelangelo overheard another artist claiming the work belonged to him. Michelangelo said nothing, but that night stole into St. Peter's and carved his signature on the statue.

The *Pietà* is placed too high to be viewed properly. It was intended to be low enough to enable the viewer to look directly into Mary's face (to compensate it is tilted forward). It is that beautiful, serene face, the face of a girl of no more than eighteen—even though the son she is holding is far older—that not only counteracts the expression of death of the figure of Christ but is also the greatness of the work. By giving Mary a beauty spared by the laws of age, Michelangelo has placed the story of Christ outside time and space, giving it a universal significance that has lasted to this day.

SAN LUIGI DEI FRANCESI

Piazza San Luigi dei Francesi, off Via Giustiniani

This church, completed in 1589 and noted today for its richly decorated chapels, is the national church of France in Rome. The second chapel on the right has frescoes showing incidents from the life of St. Cecilia by Domenichino (1581–1641) and an altarpiece by Guido Reni (1577–1642), a copy of Raphael's *Bologna St. Cecilia*. However, the great treasures of the church are paintings by Caravaggio.

Caravaggio* (1573–1610), Italian

The Calling of St. Matthew (ca. 1601–3): north aisle, fifth chapel

This painting, one of three in the St. Matthew cycle here, is located to the left of the altar which has *St. Matthew and the Angel;* to the right is the *Martyrdom of St. Matthew.* The *Calling of St. Matthew* was a perfect theme for Caravaggio because it lent itself to the low-life genre that Caravaggio was wont to paint: gamblers, cardsharps, mercenaries, and other unsavory characters. We see St. Matthew at his desk in the custom house counting money, which Caravaggio depicts like one of the small taverns he himself often frequented in the side-streets of Rome. On the right Jesus approaches: "And He saith unto him, follow me. And he arose and followed Him" (Matthew 9:9, Mark 2:14, Luke 5:27). The three Gospels go on to say that Matthew (or the publican Levi) then gave a banquet in honor of Jesus who sat in the company of other publicans and sinners. Thus the people in this painting are the same types who attended the feast in the House of Levi. Even Jesus is depicted as a poor peasant instead of an idealized religious character, and St. Matthew, pointing to himself as if to say, "Who, me?" is shown as a common card player.

What is equally original, however, is the genius of Caravaggio's dramatic sense of light. Practically all of the figures are steeped in darkness, but a great beam of light, striking down from the right and passing along the wall behind them, illuminates the face of the dandyish youth at the table and comes to rest upon the face of Matthew, while at the same time it illuminates only the hand and the lower part of the face of Christ, who is accompanied by St. Peter. This spirituallike light, which illuminates only some things from a source not explained, dramatizes the religious event and brings it down to earth.

No less original is the composition, with its large area above the figures exploiting the psychological effect. It promotes the physical presence of the figures, and places them in the emptiness and darkness of the world juxtaposed with the figure of Christ emerging from the darkness, saying, "Follow me."

SAN PIETRO IN VINCOLI

Piazza San Pietro in Vincoli, near Via delle Satte Sale

This old church, founded in the fifth century (restored in 1475 and 1503) as a shrine for the chains with which St. Peter was bound, is noted for its tomb of Pope Julius II, the most unhappy project in Michelangelo's career. The original conception of the tomb was more extensive than what you see today. It was to have thirty-eight statues and as many bronze reliefs, and was to stand under the dome in St. Peter's Basilica. Because of arguments between the artist and the pope and other problems, the present structure has only the famous *Moses* in the center and the flanking figures of *Rachel* and *Leah,* executed by Michelangelo.

Michelangelo* (1475–1564), Florentine

Moses (ca. 1515–16)
This statue was made to be viewed from below, not from eye level, which is why its torso is unusually long. You get the best view of it from a crouching position. Much has been written about the statue representing Moses having just come down from Mt. Sinai, angry at the sight of his people worshipping the golden calf. In this interpretation Moses is about to rise up and smash the tablets (God's law). It is more likely, however, that Michelangelo has depicted Moses not in anger, but with a prophetic inspiration from receiving God's law directly from the Almighty. The figure can only resemble the massive philosophers and sibyls on Michelangelo's Sistine Ceiling. From his knitted brow to his powerful legs, Moses has that same powerful *terribilità*, with muscles and veins bulging to create an image of moral and physical grandeur. His voluminous beard, like a tumbling cataract, adds to the fierceness like nothing seen in marble in classical times, a model that served the baroque style for over one hundred years.

The curious horns on the head of Moses are those conventionally shown in Christian art. They stem from a deliberate mistranslation of the Hebrew words "rays of light" or "shining" used in the Bible to describe the face of Moses when he returned from Mt. Sinai. To avoid endowing an Old Testament figure with a halo, even one who is the precursor of Christ, the Vulgate translates the word as "horns."

SANTA MARIA DELLA VITTORIA

Via Venti Settembre

Bernini, Gian Lorenzo* (1598–1680), Italian

Vision of St. Teresa (1644–47): north side, fourth chapel, the Cornaro chapel
Bernini called this statue his greatest work. Others have called it his worst, criticizing it for its melodramatic treatment of a religious subject that should be shown in a more dignified way. Keep in mind that it was executed at the height of the Counter-Reformation in Italy, when the prevailing style leaned toward the emotional and the theatrical in order to appeal to the faithful to stand firm in the face of Protestantism. In this Bernini's statue is eminently successful.

The attitude of the centerpiece, showing St. Teresa of Avila in an ecstatic vision, described by some as orgastic, is described by the saint herself in her autobiography: "I did see an angel not far from me toward my left hand, in corporal form. . . . I did see in his hand a long dart of gold, and at the end of the iron head it seemed to have a little fire, this he seemed to pass through my heart sometimes, and that it pierced to my entrails, which me thought he drew from me, when he pulled it out again, and he left me wholly enflamed in great love of God. . . ."

The execution of the scene by Bernini is masterful. He has arranged the chapel as a theater, placing his central group so that sunlight from the window above (best seen in the afternoon), reinforced by the rays behind (which remind one of the golden rain in which Jupiter chose to visit Danae—see Gossaert, *Danae,* Bavarian State Art Gallery, Munich), suggest every texture of flesh, cloth, and metal. It is one of the most imaginative fusions of the pictorial, sculptural, and architectural aspects of art.

SANTA MARIA IN ARACOELI

(See Capitoline Museums and Gallery)

SANTI COSMA E DAMIANO

Off the Via dei Fori Imperiali

This early Christian church dates back to 527 and occupies a large rectangular hall of the Forum of Vespasian, up against the north side of the Roman Forum. You pass through a seventeenth-century cloister in order to enter the church. Inside, you see splendid sixth-century mosaics in the apse (restored in the seventeenth century). Their early date and flat appearance has not yet placed them firmly in the medieval style; the faces, attitudes, and clothing of the figures still show individuality and do not form a mere pattern, as they would later in the Italo-Byzantine style.

In the center stands Christ, sustained by clouds, carrying a rolled book in one hand, symbolic of the Old Law which He has inherited; His other hand is open, symbolizing peace. At His feet flows the river Jordan, the symbol of His baptism. His commanding appearance on the wall is unlike any other mosaic in Rome.

On Christ's left side are St. Felix (Pope Felix IV, who reigned 526–30 and built the church) presenting a model of the church; St. Cosma and St. Paul; on Christ's right are St. Peter, St. Damian, and St. Theodore. The crowns these figures carry are symbolic of their martyrdom. The sheep underneath represent the apostles issuing from the cities of Bethlehem and Jerusalem. On the face of the triumphal arch is the lamb on a gemmed throne surrounded by seven candlesticks (the Seven Lambs of Revelation), angels and symbols of the Evangelists.

SPANISH STEPS

Piazza d'Espagna

These splendid steps, built in 1723–25 by Francesco de Sanctis (1693–1740), leading in elegant curves from the Piazza d'Espagna, where there is a fountain in the form of a boat by Bernini, up to the Church of Trinità dei Monti, belong to the late stages of the baroque and the early rococo. They were designed for near as well as distant views, making it impossible to see them all from one vantage point without moving up and down the stairs. Once you do that (the ascent is gentle) you will find that they are equally effective from short as well as long views. This built-in movement contains a dynamic baroque effect tempered with the grace of the eighteenth century.

TREVI FOUNTAIN

Via della Stamperia off Via del Tritone

In the fifteenth century there was only a simple basin here used by washerwomen. It was and still is the terminus of an aqueduct built by the Romans to bring water to the city. Bernini was asked to design a grand fountain for the site and made a sketch for the present structure, built by two architects in the eighteenth century. It shows a baroque figure of Neptune in the central niche of the triumphal arch, with more refined rococo elements. The facade of the Palazzo Poli forms a backdrop for the fountain, giving stability to its design.

Rome has other fountains considered works of art, such as Bernini's *Fountain of the Triton* in the Piazza Barberini, and his spectacular *Fountain of the Four Rivers* in the Piazza Navona.

VILLA FARNESINA

Directly opposite the Corsini Palace on Via della Lungara 230, at Via Corsini

Hours: Open Mon.–Sat., 8:30AM–1:30PM. Free admission.

This little pleasure palace was built by a Sienese associate of Raphael, **Baldassare Peruzzi** (1481–1536), perhaps best remembered as Bernini's principal assistant. This building is his masterpiece; he also carried out an entire fresco series in two of its major rooms and part of a third. He built it between 1509 and 1511 for Agostino Chigi, a papal banker, who had become so wealthy that he underwrote the ambitious projects of Julius II and Leo X. Chigi often entertained Leo with lavish banquets in the luxurious rooms decorated with pagan scenes.

The building is in the shape of a central block with projecting front wings. Having no balustrades or balconies, the exterior looks severe, but one should remember that the exterior walls were once covered with frescoes long since withered away. That explains the discrepancy between the bareness of the walls and the richness of the frieze below the eaves. The interior of the palace has rooms decorated with frescoes by Raphael and his assistants, Sodoma, Sebastiano del Piombo, and, of course, by Peruzzi himself.

Raphael* (1483–1520), Florentine, born in Umbria

The Triumph of Galatea (ca. 1513): Loggia of Galatea
Raphael has left out most of Ovid's text and instead concentrates on the

Venus-like Galatea, seen in the middle riding the waves in a shell. Her shape, in the form of a figure eight, is an idea that Raphael was to develop further. Notice the sense of movement and color within a classical composition. The figures are pointed inward or outward, with perfect balance and control, around the riding Galatea. The broad sea-light acts on the figures to bring out their skin tones and muscular forms, which adds to the exciting pagan abandon of the scene. This composition and color will later, in the seventeenth century, impress and inspire such classicists as the Frenchman Nicolas Poussin. As for Raphael, *The Triumph of Galatea* remains his most light-hearted work based on an antique theme and was probably to him what the *Birth of Venus* was to Botticelli or the *Bacchanal* to Titian.

Rome Environs

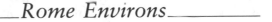

Tivoli, nineteen miles east of Rome

VILLA D'ESTE

Piazza Trento 1

Hours: Open Tues.–Sun., 9AM to one hour before sunset; Apr.–Sept., gardens illuminated and open until 11:30PM. Admission fee.

If the movement of water from hundreds of fountains creates its own architecture, the Villa d'Este at Tivoli is a great work of art. A Renaissance palace once part of a Benedictine abbey, it was started in 1550 by Cardinal Ippolito d'Este, son of Lucrezia Borgia and Alfonso d'Este. It is modest and even severe in some places, though it does have an admirable central hall frescoed with arabesques and classical figures and some lovely rooms on the garden side of its courtyard. It is the wonderful gardens, with scores of fountains and rows of cypress trees, that are the main attraction here—one of the most successful creations of its kind in Europe. They are on the side of a hill to benefit from a stream diverted to supply the fountains with a flow of water. Paths lead the visitor from level to level, and there are balustrades, urns, stairs, and fountains, which, while not refined Renaissance architectural pieces, are appropriate for their setting of moss, lichens, and overhanging trees. One never escapes the sound of splashing water, some of it falling in a cascade. The sounds must have been music to the ears of Franz Liszt (1811–86), who lived at the villa from 1865 to the end of his life. The fountains are splendid at night, when the gardens are illuminated.

Near Tivoli are the ruins of *Hadrian's Villa* (135 A.D.), the emperor's favorite residence. It was originally made up of exact replicas in miniature of the monuments and buildings he admired most in his travels throughout the world. (It has the same hours as the Villa d'Este.)

Siena

CATHEDRAL (DUOMO)

Piazza del Duomo

Hours: Open Apr.–Oct., daily, 9AM–7PM; Nov.–Mar., daily, 9AM–5PM (Piccolomini Library until 2PM in winter). Admission fee for library.

The cathedral at Siena, built during a span of about 150 years (1250–1400) when great Gothic cathedrals were being raised in France and elsewhere, is the finest achievement of Gothic architecture in Italy. This does not mean that the Gothic style as it is known north of the Alps is reflected at Siena. Gothic architecture was alien to Italy and never acquired prominence there. Even when it did have some influence, as it does in this cathedral, it was held down by Romanesque elements, such as the maze of massive piers in the interior, its broad fanlike ribs, and zebra patterning that stresses the horizontal instead of the vertical. This Italian version of the Gothic, which avoids soaring heights, dissolution of walls, and flying buttresses, could hardly be called Gothic if it were not for its magnificent front facade (a decorative screen rather than a structural part). Its upper part is Gothic, though its lower part, with its deeply recessed portals, is Romanesque.

Exterior facade

We owe the lower half of the exterior facade to **Giovanni Pisano** (ca. 1245/50–after 1314) who worked on it as chief architect from 1290 to 1297. As the greatest sculptor of his day he has adorned the portals at the level of the architraves, and the exterior buttresses with a collection of beasts and biblical figures, many in lively animation, endowing the facade with a vigorous life (most of the original statues are in the Museo dell'Opera del Duomo). The Gothic upper part of the facade is more flamboyant, with turrets, gables, finials, and slim dark openings. Polychrome marbles are used throughout. The Venetian mosaics are modern, having been installed in 1877.

Interior

The outstanding feature of the interior design is the hexagonal crossing where the cupola spans the width of the nave and aisles. It is the only architectural element that can compete with the array of rich decoration, including the ornate **floor,** which has an inlaid marble pavement consisting of fifty-six historical and other designs.

Pisano, Nicola (ca. 1220/25 or earlier–ca. 1284), Pisan

Pulpit (1265–68): nave
Of all the works of art in the cathedral, the pulpit, with its sculpture by Nicola Pisano, creator of the pulpit in the baptistery at Pisa, is the most valued. Its shape is octagonal and it is supported by pillars of marble resting upon

the backs of lions and a central column, the base of which is adorned with allegorical figures representing the arts and sciences. The Renaissance staircase was added in 1543.

Notice the panels of reliefs representing *The Visitation* and *The Nativity*, *The Adoration of the Magi*, *The Presentation in the Temple* and *Flight into Egypt*, *The Massacre of the Innocents*, *The Crucifixion*, and *The Last Judgment*. They are the first creations of modern Italian art, as distinguished from the art of the earlier Middle Ages. Nicola collaborated with his son Giovanni, the architect and sculptor of the lower half of the cathedral's front facade, and other students in his workshop, in order to execute them in such a short time. Perhaps the influence of the younger men made itself felt in the more modern feeling of the compositions and in the figures, especially the vivid depiction of the muscular figures of *The Last Judgment* panels, and the portrayals of the Madonna, shown as a winsome young woman with none of the massive dignity of earlier Italo-Byzantinesque forms. One wonders if Nicola had come in contact with the Gothic sculpture of the North. While there is nothing to prove that he did, master masons traveled considerably around Europe in the thirteenth and fourteenth centuries and Nicola may have had some understanding from them of the new Gothic forms being done in France. Nicola had just finished the Pisa baptistery when he was called to Siena; after his experience at Pisa he may have better understood how to blend old forms with the emerging classical forms. In any case, this work was a step forward, providing artistic elements that eventually led to the Renaissance. It must have had a strong influence on other sculptors and even painters.

Pinturicchio, Bernardino (ca. 1454–1513), Italian

Piccolomini Library: entered from the north aisle
It is a delight to find a magnificent Renaissance library built into part of the north aisle of this Sienese cathedral, but here it is, one of the finest, best preserved creations of the Renaissance, covered with frescoes by the last important painter of the Perugian School.

Pinturicchio had assisted Perugino in the Sistine Chapel frescoes in Rome and returned to paint an apartment at the Vatican for Pope Alexander VI. But these frescoes, done for Francesco Piccolomini, who became Pope Pius III, as a monument to his family and especially to his uncle, Pope Pius II, whose books and manuscripts the library was intended to receive, are Pinturicchio's masterpiece.

The frescoes, started in 1502 and completed in 1508, glorify the life of Pope Pius II (Aeneas Silvius Piccolomini) whose career is shown to be connected with the great events of the period. Ten compartments have scenes painted in clear, brilliant colors that are well preserved. In the first one, showing Aeneas Silvius as secretary to Cardinal Capranica, setting out from the port of Genoa for the Council of Basel (at which Aeneas was so disloyal to the papacy that he had to do penance before Pope Eugenius IV—an incident the frescoes do not show) we see a violent storm at sea, the earliest naturalistic storm scene in Western art. Though far from what Turner was to do three hundred years later in England, it is delightfully convincing in the way the dark sheets of rain, bent by the wind, are shown battering the cardinal's galleys. Raphael, a student of Perugino, may have assisted Pinturicchio in these frescoes; it is sometimes suggested that the youth on the horse to the left is Raphael's portrait.

A wall of carved marble forms the entrance, executed around 1500 by Lorenzo Marrina (1476–1534) of Siena. Above the altar to the right of the entrance is a wall panel of Pinturicchio's representation of the enthronement of Pope Pius III in 1503.

MUSEO DELL'OPERA DEL DUOMO (CATHEDRAL MUSEUM)

To the right of the cathedral

Hours: Open Arp.–Oct., daily, 9AM–7PM; Nov.–Mar., daily, 9AM–2PM. Admission fee.

In the early fourteenth century the builders of the Cathedral of Siena, in competition with the cathedrals being built in Florence and Orvieto, determined to make their cathedral the largest and grandest in Italy. Their plan was so grandiose that it called for the present cathedral to serve merely as a transept to a new cathedral. Work commenced on this project but the plague of 1348 so depopulated the town that the scheme had to be abandoned and was never renewed. The museum is located in an unfinished part of the new cathedral in what was supposed to be the nave. Apart from containing Giovanni Pisano's original statues and sculpture fragments from the facade of the cathedral (mentioned above), it has a number of fine Sienese paintings from the thirteenth century.

Duccio di Buoninsegna (ca. 1255–ca. 1318), Sienese

Maestà: first floor
This multipaneled altarpiece, a masterpiece of Sienese painting, is one of the finest works of art in Italy. Its early history is well documented. The town of Siena wished to reaffirm its devotion to the Madonna, protectress of the republic, and commissioned Duccio to undertake the painting on October 9, 1308. When it was completed on June 9, 1311, a procession of clergymen and citizens carried it from Duccio's workshop to the cathedral, where it was put on the high altar, to remain there until 1506. It originally consisted of panels painted on both sides, each with a predella. The large panel of the Madonna surrounded by angels faced the congregation, and the other side was made up of smaller panels with scenes from the life of Christ. In 1771 the front and back were separated. Later, a few panels were lost. Today, others are in the National Gallery of London, the National Gallery of Washington, D.C., and the Frick Collection in New York.

The Sienese School of painting was more conservative than the Florentine school, holding to the conventional Byzantine-medieval style derived from the fifth-century mosaicists. This was characterized by an oriental-style depiction of the Madonna with an oval face and long slender figure, a profuse use of gold background and halos, a lack of individuality in the faces of the adoring angels and saints, and a flat, two-dimensional pattern. Duccio's *Maestà* remains faithful to this tradition, but for the first time there is an attempt to break free from the rigidity of medieval symmetry and repetition and enter the realm of poetic form. This is not to say that Duccio's work goes as far as Giotto's frescoes in the Arena Chapel in Padua, which Giotto was executing at the time the *Maestà* was completed. Giotto's work almost completely breaks with the medieval tradition. Duccio, on the other hand, achieves a new refinement of line and an elegance of expression within the Italo-Byzantine style.

Compare Duccio's enthroned Madonna with others of the period in the museum. She appears just as regal but more gently maternal. Her monumental proportions seem more refined and humanized. The little Christ Child looks more like a real baby than a medieval prop. And in the draped head of St. Agnes, the last standing figure to the right, is a sensitivity to realistic beauty that lesser painters of Duccio's time never attempted.

In the smaller panels Duccio goes further to express himself in realistic terms, employing spatial techniques that compare with Giotto's. He keeps to the traditions when depicting Christ and the Virgin, but pushes his realistic style to new heights in treating the minor figures in the narrative. There is a feeling of space in many of his scenes, a three-dimensionality unknown in Siena.

Of course, Sienese art was to remain within the Christian mystery of the church. It was in Florence that art emerged from the original source of inspiration and entered the brilliance of the Renaissance. But Duccio's *Maestà* is a gem within the confines of old traditions, and an indication of the changes that were about to take place elsewhere.

BAPTISTERY OF ST. JOHN

Piazza San Giovanni (beneath part of the cathedral)

Hours: Open daily, 9AM–1PM and 3–7PM. Free admission.

The Baptistery, which forms the crypt of the cathedral, contains a fifteenth-century hexagonal **font** designed by the Sienese Renaissance sculptor **Jacopo della Quercia** (1374/75–1438). It is decorated with bronze reliefs, one of which, *Zaccharias in the Temple,* is by Quercia himself. Others are *The Birth of John the Baptist,* by Giovanni di Turino; *The Baptism of Christ* and *St. John in Prison,* by Ghiberti; and *Herod's Feast,* by Donatello. Between the panels are figures representing *Fortitude,* by Goro di Neroccio; *Justice, Charity* and *Prudence,* by Giovanni di Turino; and *Faith* and *Hope,* by Donatello. The marble upper part of the font, with small prophets in niches and the crowning figure of *St. John the Baptist,* are also by Quercia. The angels are by Donatello and Giovanni di Turino.

Donatello* (1386–1466) Florentine

Herod's Feast (1423–27)

This panel of Donatello's set new standards for sculpture in early Renaissance Italy. As one of the first sculptures done with elaborate perspective, many sculptors learned from it. The architectural background is merely a tour de force bearing no relation to the surrounding reality, done only to demonstrate the artist's mastery over the newly discovered laws of perspective. There is also the dramatic tension and emotional approach to narrative he is famous for. Donatello chooses the moment when the executioner brings in St. John's head on a tray to the king, who reels back, raising his hands in horror. The children around him cry out and scramble away. Salome's mother, Herodias, seated at the table, who urged her daughter to ask for St. John's head in return for her exotic, naked dance, is trying to explain this to the king. One of the guests at the table covers his eyes with his hands, and at the far right Salome has stopped her dance.

NATIONAL PICTURE GALLERY

Via San Pietro, 29

Hours: Open Tues.–Sat., 8:30AM–1:45PM, Sun., 8:30AM–12:45PM. Admission fee.

This museum, in the fourteenth-century Buonsignori Palace (restored in the nineteenth century), has the greatest collection of Sienese paintings in the world. All the masters native to the city of Siena are represented: Duccio, the Lorensetti brothers, Monaco, Martini, and others. Theirs is a beautiful medieval world without much care for perspective, movement, or anatomy. The spiritual beauty of it all is peaceful, golden in color, and insulated from artistic trends elsewhere.

TOWN HALL (PALAZZO PUBBLICO)

Piazza del Campo

Hours: Open Apr.–Sept., Mon.–Sat., 9AM–6:30PM, Sun., 9AM–1:30PM; Oct.–Mar., Mon.–Sat., 9AM–2PM, Sun., 9AM–1PM. Admission fee.

The growing importance of independent towns in medieval Italy gave rise to the building of town halls to house the government and the family of the *podestà*. The Palazzo Pubblico, begun in 1294 and completed in the middle of the fourteenth century (the third story was added in the fifteenth century), with its tall, slender tower, castellated roofline, and Gothic fenestration, is an example of one of the finest. It was part of a plan to create a new city center, of which the **Piazza del Campo** was the focal point. Since the thirteenth century people have gathered on this piazza when the Palio horse races are held in August. In 1425 crowds formed in front of the **Cappella di Piazza** (the loggia at the foot of the tower, built in 1348–52 to fulfill a vow made during the plague of 1348) to hear Fra Bernardino, the great preacher, exhort them to end their wicked behavior, especially that of the ladies who, like their Florentine contemporaries showed off their charms by cutting their dresses low and making extravagant use of cosmetics. A pyre was erected on the Campo to burn cards, dice, false hair, and obscene books and pictures.

Near the center of the piazza is the beautiful *Fonte Gaia* (Joyous Fountain) erected in 1419 by **Jacopo della Quercia** (1374/75–1438). Its large rectangular basin is enclosed on three sides by a low wall covered on its interior face with sculptures of the Madonna, the Virtues, and various biblical scenes, all placed in niches. The present sculptures are copies installed in 1868. The original panels are in the Palazzo Pubblico.

The **interior** of the Palazzo Pubblico is well preserved, with a series of rooms that housed the offices and the living quarters of government officials. It is noted for rooms that contain original frescoes by some of Siena's leading painters.

Martini, Simone (ca. 1284–1344), Sienese

Maestà (1315): first floor, Sala del Mappamonde
Simone Martini was a pupil of Duccio and probably assisted the master with his painting of the *Maestà* in the Cathedral of Siena. This forty-foot-wide *Maestà* in the Palazzo Pubblico, completed four years after Duccio's masterpiece, seems to be the first known work by Martini. While Martini continues to exploit the decorative qualities of Duccio's brilliant color and elegant line, he is sensitive to the contemporary French Gothic style and to the innovations of Giotto, whose work he must have seen in the church of San Francesco in Assisi, where he later painted his own frescoes in the lower church.

Although the arrangement of the kneeling saints in the foreground remind one of Duccio's work, the two kneeling angels are shown in profile in the manner of Giotto. Duccio's Byzantine throne has been replaced with a slender Gothic one with lofty wings, reminiscent of those in French cathedrals. The use of a huge canopy, arranged in depth to create a unified space, is ingenious, and the worshipping saints, standing around the throne, are more graceful than in Duccio's painting.

On the opposite wall of the room is a later work (1328) possibly by Martini, the equestrian portrait of *Guidoriccio da Fogliano,* the condottiere who served Siena as captain of war in 1326 and won a victory for the city. He is shown on horseback clothed in a sumptuous blanket while visiting his troops, seen within a sweep of landscape. The dark blue background is an abstract medieval entity with the rider placed before it rather than in it. A hoof of the horse seems to touch the frame, while another one is on the ground; the two hooves on the horse's right side are impossibly lifted at once. In spite of its inaccuracies and medievalism, this is a charming, fairy-tale-like painting uniting in the same rhythm rider, horse, and landscape.

Lorenzetti, Ambrogio (ca. 1290–1348), Sienese

Allegory of Good and Bad Government (series of frescoes): first floor, Sala della Pace
This room was named after the Council of Nine who ruled Siena after 1270.

The frescoes on its walls were placed there in 1337–43 as a reminder to the government of the effects their decisions and policies might have on the city. As important secular paintings of the Middle Ages, they charm us with a picture of life and society in Italy in the fourteenth century, in spite of deterioration.

On one wall, showing the *Effects of Good Government in the City and Country,* we see the town of Siena with her towered palaces and cathedrals; her streets and scenes of prosperity and gaiety. Everyone has something to do, whether it is building, manufacturing, or trading. Young girls are dancing and children are playing in the square. In the country, people are equally prosperous and happy, bringing their bountiful harvest to the town. It is a scene of peace and prosperity with an intelligent, energetic population.

On the adjacent wall is a complicated *Allegory of Good Government* with symbolic figures modeled with sculpturesque opulence, such as the reclining figure (third from the left of the king) representing Peace. She wears a finely pleated white tunic inspired by antique sculpture.

On the opposite wall is the *Allegories and Effects of Bad Government,* in very bad condition.

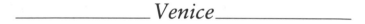

Venice

Museums

ACADEMY GALLERY (ACCADEMIA)

Campo della Carita

Hours: Open Tues.–Sat., 9AM–2PM., Sun., 9AM–1PM. Admission fee.

At the Academy Gallery you can see the full range of Venetian painting from its inception to Tiepolo. About eight hundred paintings are displayed, many brought to the gallery from churches, monasteries, and scuole (fraternal orders). The Academy itself occupies the site of an old church, a monastery, and the Scuola Grande della Carita. Some of its rooms retain splendid ceilings.

Venetian painting is different from that of Florence and Rome. Having turned itself toward the Orient, Venice was little influenced by the classic antiquity and Christian medievalism of the other Italian city states. Open to new ideas, Venice introduced into Italy the technique of oil painting with its remarkable power to extend the range of visual awareness. Venetian painters began to draw with a brush stroke instead of a pencil line, which led them to concentrate on color. Their style spread throughout Europe and is with us today. There is no better place to see this world of exquisite color and light than at the Academy Gallery.

Index to the Rooms of the Accademia

Artists mentioned below have works referred to in the text that follows. You will find these works listed under the names of the artists, arranged alphabetically.

Bellini, Gentile (ca. 1429–1507), Venetian

Procession in Piazza San Marco (1496): room 20
Gentile Bellini is the older brother of Giovanni Bellini (ca. 1430–1516). Both were sons of Jacopo Bellini (ca. 1400–70), patriarch of the Bellini family of painters, himself a painter and father-in-law of Andrea Mantegna (1431–1506). Although most of the work of the elder Bellini is lost, he is given credit for inspiring his two sons and for establishing a studio in Venice that determined the course of Venetian painting in the fifteenth and sixteenth centuries.

    Gentile Bellini established himself as a portraitist and painter of ceremonial scenes, which he produced for charitable and religious foundations in Venice. This painting, part of a cycle relating to the Miracle of the True Cross, was done for the Scuola di San Giovanni, a confraternity in Venice. The scuola had a relic, a fragment of the True Cross, which was proudly carried in a golden reliquary under a canopy through the Piazza San Marco. Bellini was commissioned to record such a procession with the members of the scuola dressed in monastic habits. It is a work, like Gentile's other ceremonial pictures, with a linear style and an overabundance of detail. It is a painting done with a great deal of affection, whose interest is in its description of contemporary Venetian life and buildings. We have Bellini to thank for showing us what the lost Byzantine mosaics on the front of St. Mark's Cathedral looked like. The mosaics on the facade today are mostly modern.

Miracle of the Cross at Ponte di Lorenzo (1500): room 20
In this painting, part of the series made for the Scuola di San Giovanni, Bellini records an incident that occurred when the holy relic fell into the canal. According to Gentile, the relic floats and is rescued by a friar who is buoyed up by it. Notice the black man to the right preparing to swim in the canal, the gondolas, and the richly dressed buxom ladies, lining the banks of the canal. There is little sophistication in the presentation of these figures, but they make Gentile's paintings as charming and interesting today as they were when he painted them.

Bellini, Giovanni (ca. 1430–1516), Venetian
This youngest of the Bellini family of painters was its greatest artist. He became the dominant painter of Venice; at one time his students included both
Giorgione and Titian. He was the most innovative of painters, reacting
against Crivelli's expressive function of line and Mantegna's definition of
sculptural planes and contours. Bellini's method was to master tonal gradations and light, and fuse his figures into the space around them by means of
color modified by light. When the oil medium came along he mastered that
as well, with the result that his expression burst forth on a new plane of
perfection, creating visual harmonies never seen before in Venice. Giovanni
Bellini brought the Venetian School up to the door of the high Renaissance,
clearing the way for Giorgione, Titian and Veronese.

Enthroned Madonna and Child (San Giobbe Altarpiece): room 2
This altarpiece, one of the most imposing Giovanni ever executed, was done
for the chapel in the Venetian hospital of San Giobbe (St. Job) and probably
dates from the middle 1480s. Notice that the Renaissance architecture is
conceived so as to look like a continuation of the chapel that once contained
the painting. Figures are seen in proportion with their surroundings, a
rounded apse of a church with marble cornices and pilasters and a gilded
vault. The Madonna is seated upon a Renaissance throne in hieratic solemnity, holding the Child with one hand and raising her other hand in an act
of blessing. To the left is St. Francis drawing viewers into the act of worship.
Job, the old man with the white beard, is the patron saint of the hospital.
On the right of the Madonna is St. Sebastian, patron saint of the sick. These
nude figures of Job and Sebastian are painted with supple realism by means
of integrating planes of light into the shaded parts of the body.

Madonna of the Small Trees: room 5
Of the many Madonna pictures that Bellini painted, this one, painted and
signed in 1487, is among his finest; it was probably done a little after the
San Giobbe Altarpiece. Bellini was constantly searching to vary his Madonna
paintings, to express his devotion for the Mother and Child. Here, in addition to the customary monumentality of his composition, he adds the novelty
of a landscape seen on either side. Light that penetrates the green silk curtain
imparts a softened outline to the figures, which helps to present them as symbols of harmony and gentleness.

Carpaccio, Vittore (ca. 1465–ca. 1525), Venetian

Departure of the Prince from Britain, His Arrival in Brittany, and
Departure of the Betrothed Couple for Rome (1495): room 21
This talented late quattrocento painter did a number of large-scale narrative
paintings for the Venetian scuole, those charitable societies of laymen that
were the focus of social life for citizens beneath the patrician class. His series
depicting the Life of St. Ursula (1495), which he did for the Scuola di Ursula
(the scuola was destroyed but the series of paintings were reassembled in the

Academy), takes an imaginative approach to depicting Venice—the color is bright and rich, the architecture bizarre, and the populace more splendidly attired than they really were—yet there is a feeling of what the city was like. Carpaccio was an excellent painter-chronicler of Venice.

This is the case in the *Departure of the Prince from Britain, His Arrival in Brittany, and Departure of the Betrothed Couple for Rome,* the richest of the scenes in the series. On the left is Britain, separated by a flagpole from Brittany, on the right. But both are united by a sky with large floating clouds, and since Carpaccio's idea of the perfect harbor is Venice, he takes occasion to celebrate his own city. We see the dazzling effect of Venetian light on buildings, high-masted merchant vessels in the harbor, and the rich dress of people in a ceremonial. An orderly crowd of spectators views the event from various vantage points. It is a genre scene in which an episode from history and legend is based not on the exploration of the subject but on the pictorial qualities of a scene.

Giorgione (ca. 1477–1510), Venetian

Giorgione is one of the geniuses in sixteenth-century Venice who made Venetian painting supreme in Europe, challenged only by Michelangelo in Rome. He lived only a short time (he died at the age of thirty-three), but his influence, referred to as "Giorgionism," was enormous—carrying composition and color from Bellini (after Giorgione arrived in Venice, at an early age, from Castelfranco, the small town of his birth, he entered Bellini's studio) to Titian (later, on his own, Giorgione used the young Titian as his assistant: thus the difficulty of telling Giorgione's work from Titian's early paintings) and finding a new way to express man and nature in which form, space, and mood are unified into a mysterious, poetic whole.

The Tempest (ca. 1505–10): room 5

This small painting known as *The Tempest,* but also as *The Soldier and the Gypsy* or as *Giorgione's Family,* is thought to be an enigma never to be solved, an example of how Giorgione never gave exact meaning to his paintings. The painting may have some meaning involved in Giorgione's humanist ideas or in ancient philosophy. If it were not for the fact that an X ray examination of the painting has revealed that in place of the soldier there was once another nude woman, greater credence would be given to the idea that the broken columns represent the virtues of fortitude and moral strength, and that the allegorical figures—a soldier, representing valor, and a gypsy, representing feminine abandon—have uncertain lives, and are therefore unmoved by the approaching storm. They are one with nature, a part of the uncertain world Giorgione has painted, in a Renaissance idea that valor and feminine abandon should be brought together. Even with the contradiction brought on by the X-ray examination, this seems to be the best explanation.

This small painting is the first of a new genre in which the poetic mood is most important, especially if it conveys man's life as it relates to the world of nature. On this level, without the consideration of narrative content, *The Tempest* is considered one of the masterpieces in European painting.

Tintoretto (1518–94), Venetian

Along with Veronese, Tintoretto, who was born in Venice and spent his life there, is the last great painter of Venice's sixteenth-century Golden Age of painting. His actual name was Jacopo Robusti: "il Tintoretto" (the little dyer) is a nickname he acquired after his father's profession. He drew a great deal of his inspiration from the *terribilità* of Michelangelo, and in his mature style his mannerism anticipates the baroque. Thus he is a painter of the dramatic and unexpected; figures are posed obliquely or in diagonals, with foreshortenings that accent the scene. His de-materializing light resulted in paintings unique for their energy and movement. His teacher may have been Titian, and it is said that when Titian saw one of his drawings he dismissed him for fear of future competition. But Tintoretto remained a lifelong admirer of Titian, and on his studio wall he displayed the inscription: "the color of Titian and the drawing of Michelangelo."

St. Mark Freeing a Christian Slave: room 10

This painting tells the story of a slave from Provence who left his master without permission to go to Alexandria to venerate the relics of St. Mark. On his return he was sentenced to be punished by having his eyes gouged out and his legs broken with hammers. At the moment of his torture, St. Mark comes down from Heaven to save him, as we see in Tintoretto's painting. The slave's master is falling off his throne in astonishment and servants, henchmen, and bystanders are reeling with surprise. There is brilliance of color and movement in the composition, especially in the swooping St. Mark suspended in mid-air.

    St. Mark Freeing a Christian Slave, done for the Scuola Grande di San Marco in 1548, was Tintoretto's first success. It eventually brought him major commissions and established him as the creator of a new style never before seen in Venice. It was a combination of Michelangelo's figure movement with Titian's color, a synthesis that did not care much about reality, in favor of achieving a mannerist expressionism that broke with the classical tradition of clear, ordered forms. As Tintoretto's personal style, it was maintained throughout his entire career.

    Another painting in the series that Tintoretto did for the scuola, *The Transport of the Body of St. Mark* (room 10), shows St. Mark's followers reclaiming his body from pagans who were about to burn it after dragging him alive through the streets of Alexandria for two days until he died. A storm, visible in the picture, intercedes and allows the Christians to triumph. The pagans are seen rushing off in all directions.

Titian (ca. 1487–1576), Venetian

Titian is the grand old man of Venetian painting, who did more to popularize the school throughout Europe than anyone else. Like many other Venetian painters he was not born in Venice. He came from Cadore in the nearby Dolomite Mountains. At the age of about nine, he and his older brother entered Bellini's workshop in Venice. Later he became Giorgione's assistant. By 1510, at the age of twenty-three, he seems to have become independent, yet his early paintings were still under the influence of Giovanni Bellini. It took a long time for him to free himself from the spell of Giorgione, whose unfinished works he completed after Giorgione's death at the age of thirty-three. But the influences of Bellini and Giorgione were only early phases Titian went through in a long career as a painter (sixty-five years or more). He developed his own style that allowed him to free the brush from the task of recording details and, therefore, from the restrictions of draftsmanship. His method was to build up layers of oil paint as many as thirty or forty, which absorbed or reflected light as he chose. When the light was allowed to penetrate a thin outer paint to the dark underpaint, the effect was a dark area or a shadow; when the light was not allowed to penetrate a thicker surface layer, it shone back into the viewer's eye and caused a light area. Painting this way, using the brush with broad short strokes that de-emphasized detail, Titian was able to achieve a convincing impression of volume and form, but not to concentrate on it at the expense of color and light. This technique also permitted a freedom of expression adaptable to portraiture. Titian became known as the greatest portrait painter in Europe, an accomplishment helped along by his ability to bring out the character of a sitter. He was also able to create masterful compositions for his paintings, which often relied on the diagonal to break up the previously accepted symmetry of high Renaissance pictures. Titian's style was based on an original technique and structure. With the intellectual content and emotion of his paintings he achieved popularity and was copied widely in Venice and elsewhere. He became painter to kings and princes of Europe, and wealthy in his own right. By 1531 he was able to purchase a palatial residence in Venice, overlooking the lagoons and Murano. It was here, it is said, that Charles V, while visiting Titian in his studio, showed his respect for the master by picking up a brush the painter had chanced to drop; not a small gesture from the emperor of most of the known world.

Presentation of the Virgin in the Temple (1534–38); room 24

This painting is located in the place for which it was painted; it was a mural for the Scuola della Carita, which has been incorporated into the maze of buildings that make up the Accademia. It is in Titian's so-called Flemish style: crisp brush strokes give a jewellike finish with a wealth of detail. Also jewellike is the Virgin herself, seen climbing steps, her blue skirt in hand, toward the high priest, Zacharias, who awaits her at the top. Her mother, Anne, stands below with an assortment of people (many of whom are probably portraits), and there is an old woman, reminiscent of a Carpaccio figure, sitting in the foreground with a basket of eggs (it has been suggested that she is a portrait of Titian's mother). The ruined classical statue at the lower right-hand corner represents the coming change from a pagan world to a Christian world, while Jewish law is represented in the Virgin's consecration as the "chosen vessel" of Christ's Incarnation. In every case the figures are small in relation to the architecture, Renaissance in style, with the pink-and-white-diamond pattern of bricks on the back wall, obviously inspired by the Doge's palace. In the background is a landscape from Titian's mountain village of Cadore, and Titian's idea of the pyramid of Gaius Cestius in Rome.

position, in great scale, shows St. Catherine as a princess sumptuously dressed and crowned with jewels. Typical of Veronese, the two angels seated

Pietà (1676): room 10

This painting, considered Titian's last work, is a jewel of a painting, with brushwork exposed without a care for line or form. His color is moving and his composition dynamic, with triangles that cross or converge upon Christ. Titian intended this painting to be for his own tomb in Santa Maria Gloriosa dei Frari. However, it was left unfinished at his death and completed by others, and unfortunately later disfigured by poor restoration. In the figure of Joseph of Arimathea, the old man looking directly into the face of the dead Christ, Titian has made a likeness of himself, just as Michelangelo did with a piece of sculpture—*The Descent from the Cross* in Santa Maria del Fiore, Florence—intended for his own tomb. The Magdalene, dressed in green, has rich masses of light brown hair; with her right arm outstretched she is crying out to the world expressing man's struggle against injustice, suffering, and death.

Veronese, Paolo (1528–88), Venetian

Veronese is one of the artists responsible for Venetian domination of painting in Europe in the sixteenth century. He originally came from Verona, as his name suggests, but it did not take him long to become thoroughly Venetian. In fact, he is the most typical of Venetian artists, known for painting a world of pageantry with monumental decorations. His religious paintings have little spiritual depth, only noble gestures, quiet reserve, and ceremonial opulence. The fullness of color is an important part of his depiction of the fullness of life. There was no Venetian artist as much a colorist as Veronese. He never subdued his color as Titian did, or resorted to the intricate chiaroscuro of Tintoretto. Color remained the source of his inspiration—the essence of his visual imagination. His paintings were popular with the public, although their worldly spirit prompted the church to censure him. He was questioned before the Inquisition about his practice of inserting worldly detail into sacred pictures. His answer was, "If in a picture there remains unfilled space, I adorn it with figures according to my invention." That probably explains Veronese's painting—he raised decoration to the level of art.

Feast in the House of Levi (1573): room 10

This is the painting that got Veronese into trouble with the Inquisition. It was supposed to be a picture of *The Last Supper* for a convent, but the commissioners looked askance at the presence of "buffoons, drunkards, dwarfs, Germans, and similar vulgarities," and Veronese was excused only when he agreed to make minor changes at his own expense and change its title from *The Last Supper* to *Feast in the House of Levi*.

Christ sits at the center of the table conversing with the guests, who are busy eating and drinking. The rich classical architecture adds to the opulence. Even the sky above Christ is elegant, as is part of the fabric of colors below. It is certainly not a religious scene, but a Venetian feast.

A similar picture in the Academy Gallery is Veronese's *Mystical Marriage of St. Catherine* (room 11) dating from the 1570s. Its Titianesque com-

All this detail has been subordinated to the glowing Virgin pausing as she nears the high priest. She has been placed as the focus of the composition. at the lower left, dressed in white and gold brocade, green silk, and orange taffeta, are arguing over a piece of music and not paying attention to the holy ceremony.

CORRER MUSEUM

Piazza San Marco

Hours: Open Mon., Wed.–Sat., 10AM–4PM, Sun., 9AM–12:30PM. Admission fee.

The palatial Correr Museum faces St. Mark's across the piazza. Originally formed by Teodoro Correr, a rich Venetian who donated it to the city in 1830, its Picture Gallery (Quadria), which shares the building with a large historical collection, includes paintings by the Bellinis, Antonello da Messina, the Flemish masters Dieric Bouts and Hugo van der Goes, and works by Carpaccio, one of Venice's favorite sons.

Carpaccio, Vittore (ca. 1465–ca. 1525), Venetian

Two Courtesans (ca. 1520): room 15
Carpaccio loved to depict the colorful life of his native Venice. Although the two ladies have long been considered women of loose virtue, they are probably just women of the nobility all dressed up with no place to go. They look bored, seated on a balcony trying to amuse themselves with a collection of birds and dogs. Notice the red shoes near the boy standing on the left. They are those precarious *choppines,* sometimes eighteen inches high, worn by Venetian ladies for hundreds of years until they were abolished in the seventeenth century. Wives and daughters tottered on them as if walking on stilts.

GUGGENHEIM COLLECTION

Palazzo Venier dei Leoni (on Grand Canal) San Gregorio 701

Hours: Open Mar.–Dec., Sun.–Fri., 12 noon–6PM, Sat., 6–9PM. Admission fee (free admission Sat.).

This is the famous collection of modern and contemporary art owned by Peggy Guggenheim. Until her death in 1979, she pursued the art of the twentieth century with a passion that began in 1937, when she opened a London gallery. She started a second gallery in New York during World War II, called *Art of this Century,* which became the most important of its day and introduced the New York School, what came to be called abstract expressionism.

Despite her success in New York, Peggy Guggenheim returned to Europe after the war and took up residence in Venice in the Palazzo Venier dei Leoni, an unfinished eighteenth-century palace. It was here that she continued to collect and to build her own museum, opened to the public in 1951. Administered today by her uncle's museum, the Solomon R. Guggenheim Museum of New York, it is still set within Peggy Guggenheim's Venetian palace and sculpture garden, where the statue of the nude rider, *The Angel of the Citadel,* by Marino Marini, serves as a modern-day counterpart to Venice's famous equestrian statue of the condottieri Bartolommeo Colleoni by Verrocchio. The collection of works by some of the best artists of the century (Braque, Picasso, Duchamp, Mondrian, Picabia, Kandinsky, Brancusi, Ernst—Peggy Guggenheim was once married to Max Ernst—de Chirico, Pollock, and Gorky) is representative of cubism, abstraction, futurism, surrealism, and abstract expressionism.

Buildings and Monuments: Churches, Scuole, Palaces

CA' D'ORO (GIORGIO FRANCHETTI GALLERY)

Palazzo Ca' d'Oro, located on the Grand Canal, enter from Via 28 Aprile

Hours: Open Tues.–Sat., 9AM–2PM, Sun., 9AM–1PM. Admission fee.

This little palace, whose name, "Golden House," derives from its once gilded facade, was built in 1422–40 and is usually referred to as a Gothic building. However, its only Gothic style is in the pointed arch. With its qualities of color, light, opulence, and exotic fantasy, one can describe it as "pure Venetian."

Like other Venetian palaces, it has lovely arched portals at the level of the water and open loggias in the upper stories which, with decorative features applied lavishly, screen the living rooms that run across the front of the building and provide comfortable vantage points where the pageant of canal life could be watched. It gives us a look at how wealthy noblemen lived in Venice during the Golden Age of the republic.

As for the interior, it is almost as rich as its facade and contains an excellent collection of paintings given to Venice, along with the building, by Baron Giorgio Franchetti in 1915. Within this collection are works by Vivarini, Carpaccio, Bordone, Titian's famous *Venus before the Mirror,* and the unfinished *St. Sebastian* by Mantegna (both on the first floor).

MONUMENT TO COLLEONI
Campo San Zanipolo, at Santi Giovanni e Paolo

Verrocchio, Andre del (1435–88), Florentine

Equestrian Statue of Colleoni (1481–88)
Bartolomeo Colleoni (1400–75), the soldier of fortune from Bergamo, successfully led the armies of Venice in 1445 and willed his fortune to Venice on condition that an equestrian statue be erected to his memory. The result is by Verrocchio (completed after his death by Leopardi), the pupil of Donatello and teacher of Michelangelo.

No doubt Donatello's equestrian statue of *Gattamelata* in nearby Padua inspired Verrocchio, but the *Colleoni* is more technically advanced in the raised foot of the horse, which involved a difficult calculation of balance. It is also more dramatically presented. The figure is seen thrusting his shoulder forward and riding into battle with the determined attitude of a man who expects to be victorious and is ready to use brutal force. One can almost feel the tension in his body, which is transmitted to his lively horse—a display of dynamic energy and a fierce, commanding presence. Verrocchio's *Colleoni* freed equestrian statues from the constraints of Donatello's *Gattamelata* and set a standard of sculptural force that has lasted to our own time.

The unfinished **Santi Giovanni e Paolo** (Gothic, begun in 1234), to the left of the *Colleoni,* is the church where many of the doges of Venice and other dignitaries are buried. Adjacent to it, the **Scuola di San Marco** has a rich early Renaissance (1485) facade with a relief of St. Mark over its front portal.

DOGES' PALACE

Piazzetta San Marco

Hours: Open Apr.–Oct. 15, Mon.–Sat., 8:30AM–6PM, Sun., 9AM–1PM; Oct. 16–Mar., Mon.–Sat., 9AM–4PM, Sun., 9AM–1PM. Admission fee.

The Doges' Palace dates from the fourteenth century, but parts were built in the fifteenth century and later. It is a magnificent example of Gothic civic architecture, but owes little to the medieval fortified palaces and town halls of central and northern Italy. The Gothic style here is transformed into a flamboyant Byzantine luxuriance so original that it ignores structural principals to express the character of Venice. Its facades facing the Piazzetta and the Grand Canal use fragile interlacing arches instead of heavy piers to carry the wall masses above them. It is amazing that it has not fallen down. Apart from sinking into the soft ground somewhat, it has survived for over five hundred years. The structure is a success from an aesthetic point of view because one is so dazzled by the color and design of the wall (a diagonal diamond pattern of rose and white) that one forgets the lack of balance and architectural logic.

The **courtyard** is typical of Venetian Renaissance design rich decoration. Foremost here is the **Stairway of the Giants** (1485–89) by A. Rizzo (active ca. 1465–1500) with its two colossal statues of *Mars* and *Neptune* (1554) standing above (representing the military and naval power of Venice) by Sansovino (1486–1570), the architect who designed the library facing the Doges' Palace on the Piazzetta. The doges were sworn into office at the top of these stairs.

Inside is a reflection of the richness of Venice in her days of glory. To view the principal rooms, ascend the **Scala d'Oro,** a golden staircase (1538–59) designed by Sansovino (1486–1570), decorated with gilded stuccoes, to the **Atrio Quadrato** on the third floor, or *secundo piano nobile.* This anteroom has a sixteenth-century gilded wooden ceiling with Tintoretto's painting of *Justice Presenting the Sword and the Scales to Doge Girolamo Priuli.*

Enter the **Sala delle Quattro Porte** (Hall of the Four Doors). To the right of the entrance is a painting by Titian, *Doge Grimani Kneeling before Faith,* probably finished by the artist's nephew, and on an easel between the windows G. B. Tiepolo's *Neptune Offering Venice the Riches of the Sea.*

Next, enter the **Sala dell'Anticollegio** in which ambassadors used to wait for an audience with the doge. Its finest paintings are Tintoretto's *Bacchus and Ariadne* (on the door walls between Tintoretto's *Mercury and the Graces and Minerva Dismissing Mars*) in that artist's lyric style, and the sensuous *Rape of Europa* by Veronese (opposite the window wall), remarkable for its use of color.

The magnificent **Sala del Collegio** is the room where the doge sat in state. Its ceiling, decorated with Veronese's paintings, is the most beautiful in the palace. Notice, especially, the centerpiece at the far end showing *Justice and Peace Paying Homage to Venice.* Above the doge's throne is another masterpiece by Veronese, *Doge Venier Offering Prayers of Thanksgiving to Christ for the Victory of Lepanto.* There are also paintings by Tintoretto on the wall opposite the fireplace.

Now enter the **Sala del Senato** where meetings of as many as 120 senators were held. There are two paintings in this room by Tintoretto, *Descent from the Cross* on the wall over the tribune and, on the ceiling, *Venice, Queen of the Seas.* The door to the right of the tribune leads to the antichiesetta and the adjoining **doge's private chapel.** If open enter it to see a marble *Madonna and Child* over the altar by Sansovino.

Returning to the Sala delle Quatro Porte, pass through the Sala d'Oro into the **Sala del Consiglio dei Dieci,** the seat of the Council of Ten (judiciary), to see Veronese's famous *Youth and Age* (far right-hand corner of ceiling) depicting an old man in an Oriental costume accompanied by a graceful young woman. The room next door, the **Sala della Bussola,** has the infamous Bocca di Leone (Lion's Mouth) into which anonymous denunciations were placed.

The Saletta dei Tre Inquisitori, a room used for interrogating suspected enemies of the state, leads down to the State Armory collection dating back to the fourteenth century. The Scala dei Censori redescends to the primo piano mobile (second floor), where you will find the **Sala del Maggior Consiglio,** the assembly hall of the Great Council and the most splendid room in the palace. In this room the Great Council of over one thousand noblemen made the laws and elected the magistrates. At the far end of the wall, above the doge's dais, is the largest oil painting in the world, **Tintoretto's** *Paradise* (about seventy by twenty feet). Tintoretto followed the canto 13 of Dante's *Divine Comedy* in portraying the scene. Christ and Mary are shown silhouetted against a glaring light that provides the source of illumination for the picture. In this way Christ and Mary remain the dominant characters in a picture that contains hundreds of swarming figures. Also in this room is a magnificent ceiling divided into fifteen main sections. Note particularly the large oval central panel, *The Triumph of Venice,* by Veronese, in which the artist expresses his love for Venice. A doorway to the left of the dais leads to a loggia and stairs down to the Bridge of Sighs.

SAN GIORGIO MAGGIORE

Isle of San Giorgio Maggiore

Hours: Open daily 9AM–12:30PM and 2–7PM. Free admission.

This church, in the harbor on an island of its own across from the Doges' Palace is striking at night when its elegant facade is illuminated. It was built by **Palladio** (1518–80), who did not live to see it completed in 1610 by Scamozzi. Palladio had turned to church architecture during the 1560s, and at San Giorgio we see how his genius solved the problem of how to put a classical front on a church with a high central nave and lower side aisles. The answer was to build two temple fronts, one tall and narrow and the other, as if placed behind the first, wide and low. Typical of Palladio's refined design are Corinthian columns across the facade done with a restraint and beauty that made him famous.

The interior of the church, in the shape of a Latin cross, is empty at the crossing under the dome, as if it were the spacious hall of some elegant villa. It contains a number of paintings and other works of art, but those of Tintoretto are the main attraction.

Tintoretto* (1518–94), Venetian

Last Supper (1592–94): chancel, right wall
This great painting is one of Tintoretto's last and the summation of his original style. It has his characteristic deep perspective, where the action takes place in depth rather than across the breadth of the canvas; it is a *Last Supper* removed from the classical symmetry of Leonardo's in Milan. On its right side it has powerfully modeled people and realistic elements; even a cat is trying to get at the food. It also has Tintoretto's dramatic light-on-dark technique, here pushed to the limit to de-materialize the color yet retain the basic forms. We can easily see Christ giving the Host to a disciple, but otherwise there is no individualization of the apostles, who remain nameless abstractions whose substance is light and shadow—perfect symbolism for the Christian mystery.

See also, in the chancel, left wall, Tintoretto's *The Gathering of Manna,* a scene set in a spacious, detailed landscape.

SAN MARCO (BASILICA OF ST. MARK)

Piazza San Marco

Hours: Open Mon.–Sat., 9:30AM–5:30PM, Sun., 2–5:30PM. Admission fee to Pala d'Oro and Treasury.

If you have ever wondered how close Byzantium and Venice were, San Marco will put the question to rest. While San Marco is a conglomeration of many styles and architectural techniques, its basic elements are purely Byzantine.

The present basilica replaced a Romanesque church that had been built on the site in 829, but was burned by the Venetian populace in 976 to show their displeasure with a dictatorial doge. The present church was started in 1063 (a large part of the facade dates from the early fifteenth century and other parts were built into the sixteenth century), copied from the Church of the Apostles in Constantinople (destroyed in 1463). Its plan is in the form of a Greek cross with arms of equal length, roofed with domes at the end of each arm and at the crossing, where a large central dome dominates. The exterior portions of the domes are timber and metal-sheathed structures that stand clear of shallower inner stone domes and make a weatherproof shield for them.

The **front facade** from the west end of the piazza is one of the great sights in Europe. The recesses above the Romanesque arches that dominate the front contain Byzantine mosaics dating as far back as the thirteenth century (the large central mosaic showing the *Last Judgment* is from 1836). The fanciful second story has blind arcades and a central window with balusters, mosaics, turrets, and an eclectic array of other Byzantine, Romanesque, and Gothic elements that blend well. This decoration includes the famous **Hellenistic bronze Horses** that have been there for over 700 years and are as much a symbol of Venice as the Venetian lion. No one has traced their exact origin, but it is thought that they started out in ancient Greece or Rome, and they may have once graced Trajan's Arch. They arrived in Venice in 1204 after the sack of Constantinople. In 1795 Napoleon took them to Paris and put them on the gates of the Tuileries. They were returned to Venice in 1815 after the fall of Napoleon. Today the originals have been removed from San Marco because atmospheric pollution threatens to damage them irreparably. The originals are on display in the Basilica's museum.

The **interior** of the basilica is an intersection of two gigantic halls with the crossing lit from windows cut into the stone. It has glittering mosaics, rare marbles, and richly colored stones. The vaulting niches and walls are adorned with mosaics (about one acre in total surface, representing the work of six centuries). Notice Old and New Testament scenes with elongated figures in gold color reflecting Byzantinesque mystery and opulence. At the altar and apse, which are raised and screened, is the famous *Pala d'Oro,* a gold altarpiece at the back of the main altar. It is the great art treasure of San Marco, made up of gold and silver plaques, enamels, and precious stones— hundreds of rubies, topazes, emeralds, garnets, amethysts, and pearls. There is also a **Treasury** filled with a profusion of reliquaries, enamels, and Byzantine works of art taken from Constantinople in 1204.

A doorway to the right of the main entrance of the basilica leads up a staircase to the **museum** located in the galleries above the church. Here are the original four gilded bronze horses, fragments of early mosaics, Oriental carpets, tapestries, and painted covers made for the Pala d'Oro. From the loggia on the facade there is a fine view of the piazza and of the Gothic sculpture, and the galleries give the best view of the mosaics on the walls and floor. (There is an admission fee.)

SANTA MARIA GLORIOSA DEI FRARI

Campo dei Frari (Rio Terra San Stin)

Hours: Open Mon.–Sat., 9:30AM–12 noon and 2:30–6PM, Sun., 2:30–6PM. Admission fee.

This Gothic church was started in the 1330s by Franciscan friars, but was not completed until the 1440s. Its beautiful campanile was completed earlier, in 1396, and is second in height only to that of St. Mark's. While its plain brick exterior is not particularly attractive, inside it has a striking architectural feature in its **transepts,** onto which opens the chancel with its six terminal chapels on either side of the main apse. Their stained glass windows give a welcome feeling of space. The church also serves as the Pantheon of Venice and has tombs of all periods. Compare the early, plain looking tombs with the elaborate later ones. They reflect the history of Venice, which went from an early simplicity to increasing splendor and to extravagance made possible by great wealth.

Titian* (ca. 1487–1576), Venetian
Among the artists buried in the Frari is Titian. The master lies beneath a nineteenth-century work of little merit, but this defect is made up for by two of his paintings, treasures of the church.

Assumption of the Virgin (1516–18): chancel
Located on the high altar and designed to be seen from a distance, this monumental painting is like a powerful force pulling the viewer toward it. It glows with a golden haze and excites with the red of Mary's tunic and the red robes worn by two of the figures. Its heroic figures are the epitome of the high Renaissance style in Venice, with a difference that sets it apart from the paintings of Raphael in Rome. In Raphael's work form, not light, is most important; light is applied to form already existing. In Titian's work light, with its varying degrees of shade, is an expression of form, and color the substance from which it is made. Thus color, light, and space give the *Assumption* its appeal, along with its dramatic sense of movement. The Virgin seems to soar heavenward with a vitality that needs no assistance from the angels. As her body is miraculously united with her soul, nothing can stop her from overcoming the gravitational pull below. The figures on the bottom form a compact base for the composition, most of which is floating in the air, and their thrusting movements add to the soaring effect of the scene.

When the *Assumption* was installed in the church in 1518, it established Titian's reputation as a master. Venice had never before seen a painting so exciting, with such energy. It created a new pictorial style that anticipated the baroque. One wonders what Bernini would have done without its influence.

The Madonna of the Pesaro Family (1519–26)

The fame Titian achieved with the Assumption brought him many commissions, such as this votive painting located on the second altar in the left aisle. It was done for the Pesaro family whose illustrious member, Jacopo Pesaro, bishop of Paphos and commander of the papal galleys, defeated the Turks at the battle of Santa Maura in 1502. It has the same kind of color as the *Assumption,* but its dynamic element is its revolutionary composition. The figures are arranged in diagonal depth like a human pyramid. Titian breaks with tradition and places the Madonna and Child enthroned on the steps of a heavenly palace in full daylight before a portico of monumental columns, instead of placing them in the center of the picture. St. Peter sits on the Virgin's right with his open book and the keys to the Kingdom of Heaven. A soldier holding an olive-crowned flag with the arms of the Pesaro family presents a captured Turk, and Jacopo Pesaro himself kneels at the left. At the right kneel five members of his family, the youngest, clad in white silk, looking out with a frank, inquiring gaze. Above them St. Francis is seen recommending the family to the Virgin. The asymmetrical composition of diagonals and triangles, with depth conveyed by the contrast of lighted and shaded zones of color, breaks with the classical tradition.

Among the many other works of art in the Frari is the famous *Enthroned Madonna and Child,* known as the *Frari Madonna,* by **Giovanni Bellini** (ca. 1430–1516). It is located in the **sacristy** in the position for which it was painted in 1488, and is still in its original frame. In fact, this altarpiece was made for its frame. The capitals inside the picture are identical with those of the frame, increasing the illusion that painting and frame are one. However, Bellini's use of oil paint plays an even greater part in creating the illusion of reality; it allows him to create a realistic atmosphere of light and shadow that seems to come from the frame.

See also, in the **first chapel in the choir,** to the right of the chancel, the wooden statue of *St. John the Baptist* (1438; recently restored) by **Donatello** (1386–1466). It must have astonished Venice when it arrived at the church from nearby Padua in 1451.

SANTA MARIA DELLA SALUTE (CHURCH OF ST. MARY OF SALVATION)

Rio della Salute

Hours: Open daily 8AM–12 noon and 3–6PM. Free admission.

No church in Venice, including St. Mark's, is more photogenic than Santa Maria della Salute. The masterpiece of **Baldassare Longhena** (1598–1682), an architect of prominence in Venice in the seventeenth century, it occupied him for more than twenty-five years (1631–56).

The idea to build the church came from the Venetian senate. It was to serve as an offering of thanks for the end of the plague of 1630, which had taken nearly 50,000 lives. Its name, Santa Maria della Salute, signifies both health and salvation. The Venetians wanted a church that would impose itself on the small scale of the city and could be seen from everywhere, especially from St. Mark's and the Doges' Palace. Thus the fantastic baroque mass dominating the entrance to the Grand Canal is a perfect example of architecture used for religious and emotional effect. Even its color, basically white, has its theatrical appeal by reflecting an enormous amount of light.

Its central plan, recalling the buildings of ancient Rome, is that of a regular octagon surrounded by an ambulatory. Its interior is dominated by its large **dome** which has an inner and an outer vault, the outer one consisting of lead over wood. There is also a dome over its **sacristy** (admission fee), which forms an almost independent unit and is distinguished for its ceiling paintings by **Titian** (ca. 1487–1576): *Cain Killing Abel, Sacrifice of Isaac,* and *David and Goliath.* These were done in 1542 for another church, but were removed to the Salute. Notice that Titian's figures are like the clouds he has painted around them: twisting, weaving, and interpenetrated by light and color. They are Titian's first paintings in the style of the Roman baroque—heroic, powerful, and masculine—and are in contrast with his early altarpiece (located in the sacristy to the left of the high altar) done about thirty years earlier: *St. Mark Enthroned between Saints Cosmas, Damian, Roch, and Sebastian.* They also show that Titian knew the baroque works of Michelangelo.

Also in the same room in the sacristy is *The Marriage at Cana,* by Tintoretto (1518–94). It is a typically immense painting and one of the few Tintoretto signed.

SCUOLA DI SAN ROCCO

Campo San Rocco, at the east end of the Frari Church

Hours: Open Mon.–Fri., 9AM–1PM and 3:30–6:30PM, Sat., Sun., 10AM–1PM and 3–6PM. Admission fee.

This building, begun in 1515 for the religious confraternity of St. Roch, has a pretentious Renaissance facade with basket-handle arches and fluted Corinthian columns, but its main claim to fame is its interior, decorated with paintings by Tintoretto, fifty-six in all, that took him twenty years to complete.

Tintoretto* (1518–94), Venetian
In the **lower hall** are scenes from the early life of Christ and the Virgin (on the wall opposite the staircase). See *The Flight into Egypt,* almost an impressionistic painting, and *The Adoration of the Magi,* a painting that also has modern rapid brush strokes that seem far ahead of Tintoretto's time.

In the **upper hall** is *The Nativity* (on the wall opposite the staircase), remarkable for its original composition, and the celebrated *Crucifixion,* which Tintoretto regarded as his masterpiece.

Crucifixion (1565): upper hall, Sala dell'Albergio
This is the largest painting in the scuola, and at approximately forty feet in length rivals in size and dramatic power Michelangelo's famous *Last Judgment* in the Sistine Chapel in Rome.

There are eighty moving figures in its composition, but somehow all of them revolve around the Cross, which is so tall it almost reaches the frame. With Christ at the top of it, He is positioned as if looking down from Heaven. The two crosses of the thieves have not yet been hoisted into place, so nothing disturbs the dominance of Christ's central Cross. The main thrust of the eye upward toward Christ starts at the pyramid of figures below the Cross, and is supported over the vast area of the canvas by a series of diagonals that appear in a multitude of forms.

The language of form, strong as it may be, is not the dominant conveyor of feeling in this picture. As in practically all of Tintoretto's work, dramatic color is what speaks to us. Tintoretto's light-and-dark technique takes over, communicating excitement, mystery, and even the supernatural. Tintoretto transforms the scene into a luministic network where forms emerge out of the shadows to take their place in a surrealistic nocturn, where the self-generating light is within Christ himself, drawing those to him who will listen.

Sicily

Agrigento

This is the greatest concentration of Doric Greek temples anywhere in the world (Zona Archaeologica open daily 9AM to one hour before sunset). Five in all, they were part of ancient Acragas of the Greeks, who founded the city as early as 582 B.C., and of Agrigentum of the Romans. According to Pindar, the Greek poet who saw the temples when they were new, Acragas was "the most beautiful city of mortals" and the "friend of pomp." No city ever built so many temples, one alongside the other, as this city dedicated to war and art. With their ally, Syracuse, it won battles over the Carthaginians and enslaved tens of thousands of them for agricultural work and great construction projects. Its military fortunes changed to defeat, and in 406 B.C. it was emptied after a siege and a sacking by the Carthaginians under Hannibal. It then made a comeback, but was taken by the Romans in 261 B.C. It never regained the wealth and power it had during its golden age in the fifth century B.C. and eventually was reduced to a mere village, with only the ruins of its temples to testify to its past glory.

View the Valley of the Temples (open 9AM to one hour before sunset) first from the town high above the site. Then follow the panoramic road, Strada Panoramica, to visit the various temples: **Temple of Juno** (Tempio di Giunone Lacinia), middle of the fifth century B.C.; **Temple of Concord** (Tempio della Concordia), probably built between 450 and 440 B.C.; **Temple of Hercules** (Tempio di Ercole), sixth century B.C.; **Temple of Olympian Jupiter** (Tempio di Giove), fifth century B.C.; and the **Temple of the Dioscures** (Castor and Pollux), fifth century B.C.

TEMPLE OF CONCORD

This is the best preserved of the temples of Agrigento because it was converted into a Christian church in the sixth century. It still has its cella (the enclosed inner sanctuary that once contained the statue of the divinity) whose wall openings were made by the Christians. Its fine state of preservation reminds one of the Temple of Neptune at Paestum, but this temple, built about a quarter of a century later, is more elegant. It has thirty-four columns with the architrave and pediments still standing. In the corner are staircases leading to the top of the temple.

One does not have to know anything about architecture or archaeology to appreciate the intelligence and civilizing refinement that went into this Greek temple. The builders were masters who knew how to express the pride and youthful vigor of their city in architecture, and in so doing created a monument to the harmony of proportion, of forms that dissolve into rhythms, and of surfaces that absorb and reflect light and change color, and apparent shapes.

The new **Archaeological Museum** (open Tues.–Sat., 9AM–2PM, Sun. 9AM–1PM; admission fee) next to the church of San Nicola, north of the temples, has a wealth of objects from the site, the most notable of which is a colossal **Telamon** in Room VI (the figure of a man used like a supporting column) from the Temple of Jupiter. There is one at the temple site lying among the fallen rocks, but this reconstructed one, erect and twenty five feet tall, better shows its powerful structural and decorative effect among the columns of the temple. (The museum is open Tues.–Sun., 9AM–2PM closed Mondays). Admission fee.

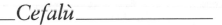

_____*Cefalù*_____

CATHEDRAL

Piazza del Duomo

Hours: Open daily 9AM–12 noon and 3:30–7PM. Free admission.

The Cathedral of Cefalù, started by the Norman King Roger II in 1131 (the nave was completed in 1160 and the facade in 1240), reflects various styles brought to Sicily by its several conquerors. Its double entrance is in the style of churches in Normandy and England; its two handsome towers are like North African minarets; and inside its Romanesque basilica plan has a short nave whose columns have Byzantine and Romanesque capitals. The church also has wooden-trussed roofing that dates back to 1263, when it was restored; an east end with a sanctuary covered by groin vaulting and a pointed semidome flanked by two deep tunnel-vaulted chapels; and a transept covered partly by tunnel-vaulting and partly by wooden roofing.

To go along with this Sicilian Romanesque architecture are **Byzantine mosaics** in its semidome (1145), the treasure of the church. It shows an almost menacing hieratic half-length figure of Christ whose stern appearance the medieval mind thought to be good for man. Its chromatic richness makes it the masterpiece of Sicilian mosaics and indicates that it was probably executed by a great craftsman of Constantinople.

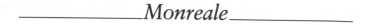

Monreale

Five miles from Palermo

CATHEDRAL (SANTA MARIA LA NUOVA)

Piazza Vittorio Emanuele

Hours: Open Tues.–Sat., 9AM–12:30PM and 4–7PM, Sun., 9AM–12:30PM. Admission fee.

This festive Christian basilica was built by Norman kings who, in Sicily, admired the Byzantine-Arab style. Thus there is a blend of the Norman-Romanesque, Byzantine mosaic decoration with Moslem pointed, interlacing arches. The building dates to 1174 when it was started (completed in a short time, by 1189) and even though a fire in 1811 caused great damage, which resulted in additions that do not harmonize with the original twelfth century parts, it is still an architectural masterpiece of the Middle Ages.

The plan is that of an early Christian basilica consisting of a wide, well-lit nave, narrow aisles, and antique Corinthian columns supporting pointed Moslem arches. Its open timber roof is brightly painted, and its eastern apse and choir is decorated with Byzantine mosaics, as is almost every available wall elsewhere. The half-figure of Christ in the apse reminds one of a similar figure at Cefalù Cathedral, but that one is more accomplished. The mosaics in the nave illustrate scenes from the Old Testament; those in the aisles and transept show the history of Christ.

The exterior of the church is not as fine as the cathedral at Cefalù, apart from its magnificent bronze doors, unequaled in Sicily. The interlacing pointed arches on the three apses, which rise up steep and solid in three stories, seem overdone. The two thick blocklike tower bases of its front facade have disparate, unattractive terminations, and the heavy portico of 1770 between the towers appears out of place. The **cloisters** (1172–89) are the best example of twelfth-century architecture here. They have twenty-five arches of the Moslem pointed form on each side of the court, supported by 216 columns in pairs, with a group of four columns at each corner. The decorations on these columns are delightful, showing scroll-work, chevrons, fluting, spiral bands, and mosaics. Notice the square fountain house, the monks' lavatory, at the south corner. It is so lovely it reminds one of the Alhambra.

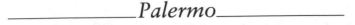

Palermo

CATHEDRAL (CHURCH OF THE ASSUNTA)

Corso Vittorio Emanuele

This cathedral is exotic as a conglomeration of many diverging styles. Much of it was built in 1172–85, but its south facade is from the fifteenth century and its interior, unhappily spoiled, was rebuilt between 1781 and 1801, including its inharmonious baroque dome. In spite of architectural faults it is a pleasing sight from the outside, especially its beautiful south facade with rich arcading and cresting and a fine Gothic portico with a carved gable and three pointed arches.

NATIONAL ARCHAEOLOGICAL MUSEUM

Piazza Olivella 4

Hours: Open Tues.–Sat., 9AM–1:30PM, Sun., 9AM–12:30PM. Admission fee.

This museum has Greek and Roman antiquities found at archaeological sites in Sicily, and its lovely setting, among the seventeenth-century cloisters of the Philipines, a suppressed monastery, enhances the attraction of its collection.

Its greatest treasures are the *Metopes of Selinus* (metopes are the square slabs in a Doric frieze that sometimes contain sculpture) in the Salone di Selinunte on the ground floor. These relief carvings from the ancient temple of the Greek colony of Selinus show freedom of composition and an understanding of the human form, though they are among the oldest known sculptured Greek metopes in existence (second quarter of the sixth century B.C.). They point to the future development of Hellenic sculpture, which will later have the classic grace and fine proportions that this early work lacks.

NATIONAL GALLERY OF SICILY

Palazzo Abbatellis, Via Alloro 4

Hours: Open Wed., Fri., Sat., 9AM–2PM, Tues., Thurs., 9AM–2PM and 4–7PM, Sun. and holidays, 9AM–1PM. Admission fee.

This Renaissance palace was restored after World War II damage by bombs, to contain the most complete collection of Sicilian art from the Middle Ages through the eighteenth century. Its ground floor is devoted mostly to sculpture and includes the works of Antonello Gagini (1478–1536), the best Sicilian sculptor of the sixteenth century, and a masterpiece by Laurana.

Laurana, Francesco (ca. 1430–ca. 1502), Italian

Bust of Eleonora of Aragon (ca. 1467): ground floor, room 4
This was done for Eleonora's tomb in the cloister she had founded. Laurana was a master of portraits of women in sculpture and somewhat modern in our sense of art. His purity of line, which transcends surface appearance, tends toward the abstract. He shows us a frozen likeness of his sitter that ignores detail in favor of a cool schematized beauty, almost masklike in appearance, and mysterious.

The first floor contains paintings of which the most important are by **Antonello da Massina** (ca. 1430–79), the Sicilian painter who learned the oil medium from Flemish artists traveling in Italy and helped introduce it to Venetian painters during the fifteenth century. There are also some fifteenth and sixteenth century Flemish paintings that go well with his work.

PALACE OF THE NORMANS (PALAZZO DEI NORMANNI)

At the Piazza del Parlamento

Hours: Open Mon., Fri., Sat., 9AM–12:30PM. Free admission.

Cappella Palatina (Palatine Chapel)

Hours: Open Mon., Tues., Thurs.–Sat., 9AM–1PM and 3–5:30PM, Wed., 9AM–1PM, Sun., 9–10:20AM and 12:15–1PM. Free admission.

This architectural masterpiece is within what remains of the royal palace, the former seat of the kings of Sicily. It was built by Roger II between 1132 and 1143 as a miniature church that probably served as a model for the Cathedral of Monreale. However, it is more lavish than that structure. Its basilican interior, with slender columns of marble dividing the nave from the aisles, has twelfth-century **mosaics** that are purely Byzantine in style and are enhanced by the chapel's tall pointed arches of Moslem form, and by an elaborate oriental stalactite ceiling. The **floor,** as well as some of the wall space, is inlaid with rare marbles, and there is an ornate **pulpit** and a carved marble Norman **candelabrum.** Though a Christian church dedicated to St. Peter, filled with scenes from the Old Testament and the lives of Christ, St. Peter, and St. Paul, it may remind you of the Moorish Alhambra in Spain.

Above all this splendor are the apartments of King Roger where the mosaic decoration continues in examples of Byzantine art used for secular decoration—a series of hunting scenes.

Segesta

DORIC TEMPLE (424–416 B.C.)

Hours: Open daily 9AM to one hour before sunset. Free admission.

This mysterious Greek temple was part of the ancient city of Egesta, which was not totally Greek. It was founded by Elymeans, probably descendants of Trojan emigrants going as far back as the twelfth century B.C. But Hellenic art exerted great influence. Their temple, which remains as it was when work on it was interrupted by war, looks rough from close up, but from a distance, silhouetted against the surrounding hills, it is magnificent. Its unfinished state shows columns that are smooth and unfluted, indicating that this work was done last, so it could be made perfectly rectilinear. This meant difficulties for the builders, but perfection in their work. The construction of such a temple showed that the people had confidence in the permanence of their city. The city, however, was sacked in 309 B.C. by Agathocles, the Syracusan warrior who ruled much of Sicily, and its ten thousand inhabitants were slaughtered.

About one kilometer away is the site of the unexcavated Hellenistic town where you can see a Greek theater (fifth century B.C.) hollowed out of the rock. The views of the surrounding countryside are excellent.

Netherlands

While the art of the Low Countries during the fifteenth and sixteenth centuries is largely the art of what is today Belgium, the art of the seventeenth century is that of the Netherlands. During this period of religious, political, and economic transition, encompassing the crystallization of changing forces in the preceding century, Holland emerged as an independent Protestant republic, increasingly proud and rich. Amsterdam became Europe's leading port, after the ruin of Catholic Antwerp, and with it a new art emerged that was not created for and about the church. Iconoclasm had destroyed much art in the churches, and the new spirit that evolved was a product of the period and the place and all that had gone into its making. It portrayed the new country and the people that created it in every aspect of everyday life. It did this on a prodigious scale. Enormous numbers of paintings were produced for the new middle class that, free from the restraints of Catholicism and foreign domination, and prospering under an early capitalist society, grew rapidly. Not only were a great number of works of art produced, but there were also a great number of works of genius. One has only to look at the roster of names: Hals, Steen, Hobbema, de Hooch, Ruisdael, Vermeer, and, the greatest of all, Rembrandt, to know that this was a special time equal to the early Renaissance in Florence, the Age of Elizabeth in England, and the era of Louis XIV in France. The great art of Holland's Golden Age is still there for us to enjoy, displayed in the country's leading museums.

Amsterdam

Museums

REMBRANDT'S HOUSE

Jodenbreestraat, 4–6

Hours: Open Mon.–Sat., 10AM–5PM, Sun. and public holidays, 1–5PM; closed Jan. 1. Admission fee.

This is the house that Rembrandt bought in 1639 and moved into with his young wife Saskia. Twenty of the most productive years of his life were spent here. His son Titus was born here and it was here that his wife died. Finally, he went bankrupt here and had to give the house he loved to his creditors. It was purchased in the early part of this century by the city of Amsterdam and restored to the way it looked when Rembrandt lived in it. The restorers knew exactly the way it looked then because Rembrandt's bankruptcy brought the city's Insolvency Office down on him and an assessor made a record of everything in the house. The inventory describes the furniture and even tells us where everything was placed. It is worth visiting because Rembrandt was the greatest Dutch artist and one of the greatest artists in the history of European painting. The magnificent collection of his etchings is also on view here.

RIJKSMUSEUM

42, Stadhouderskade

Hours: Open Mon.–Sat., 10AM–5PM; Sun. and public holidays, 1–5PM; closed Jan. 1. Admission fee.

No one would visit the Rijksmuseum with anything in mind but to see Dutch paintings. The museum has works by Spanish and Italian masters, but the overwhelming intention is to display the glory of Dutch painting, and most particularly Dutch painting of the seventeenth century.

The museum dates back to the time of Louis Napoleon, whom Napoleon Bonaparte put on the throne of the new kingdom of Holland. The day after Louis moved into the Town Hall on the Dam, on April 21, 1808, he issued a decree establishing what he called a Great Royal Museum and stocked it with works from the House of Orange. The period following the French Revolution, when the Louvre in Paris got its start, was a time of the creation of national museums, among them the Prado in Madrid and the Berlin Galleries. The Rijksmuseum came out of that mold.

During the nineteenth century there were short periods of expansion as a result of purchase, gifts, and legacies, and always in the direction of Dutch art. In 1885 the Rijksmuseum moved into its present building and the municipality of Amsterdam transferred to it some of its greatest masterpieces: Rembrandt's *Bridal Couple,* Vermeer's *Woman in Blue Reading a Letter,* and Ruisdael's *Mill at Wijk by Duurstede.* By the turn of the century the Rijksmuseum already had its great collection of seventeenth-century Dutch art intact.

The collection of paintings, while the high point of the museum, are not the only works of art. There are collections of drawings and prints, sculpture, silver, jewelry, glass, ceramics, textiles, and furniture. It is one of Europe's greatest presentations of a nation's art.

Index to the Rooms of the Rijksmuseum

Artists mentioned below have works referred to in the text that follows. You will find these works listed under the names of the artists, arranged alphabetically.

Room 210   Avercamp
Room 211   Hals
Room 214   Hobbema, Ruisdael
Room 216   Kalf, Steen
Room 218   Steen
Room 221   Maes, Rembrandt
Room 221a   Maes
Room 222   Hooch, Vermeer, Witte
Room 222a   Terborch
Room 224   Rembrandt

Avercamp, Hendrik (1585–1634), Dutch

Large Winter Scene (early seventeenth century): room 210
The winter landscape is almost exclusively Dutch. It owes a great deal to Flemish sixteenth-century landscapes, of which Pieter Bruegel's work has a direct bearing, but there is little else in Europe, before or after the seventeenth century, that one can refer to.

Hendrik Avercamp, a deaf mute who lived in the remote village of Kampen, was a master of the winter landscape. His *Large Winter Scene*, with its high sky and cool silvery atmosphere, is typically Dutch. The high viewpoint provides a depth of field for us to see a crowd of happy people on a frozen canal. They are skating, riding in sleds, making conversation, even falling on their faces, and playing *kolf* in the center foreground of the picture—the forerunner of our modern ice hockey and golf. The buildings add color and warmth to the scene, especially the large honey-colored brewery on the left. In spite of the cold winter scene, this picture has a charm that many summer landscapes cannot offer.

Hals, Frans* (ca. 1580–1666), Dutch

The Jolly Toper (The Merry Drinker) (ca. 1630): room 211
In the seventeenth century beer was already a national drink of Holland, and as today Dutch breweries made some of the best beer in Europe. In Haarlem, the town in which Frans Hals lived and worked, there were over seventy breweries. It is not surprising to find drinkers depicted in many Dutch paintings of the period. *The Jolly Toper* is only one of many paintings by Hals in which he shows drinkers.

We do not know the identity of the man drinking in *The Jolly Toper*. It may be a portrait, or it may be a genre scene, or an allegory representing the pleasures of drinking. In any case, it is Hals at his best using his impressionistic technique—two hundred and fifty years ahead of its time—to capture the flux of life and the living presence of the figure.

Was Hals one of the first impressionists? Look at the head of *The Jolly Toper* close up. It appears to be a wild and loose complex of irregular brush strokes, patches of color, and dabs of white paint. Now step back and take another look, and it resolves itself into a coherent impression that suggests form and texture. Hals recognizes this method of painting, not understood or used again until the nineteenth century, as the best way to depict spontaneous character and the actual look of things. It is one of the great discoveries in the history of painting. When you think of Frans Hals, this aspect of his genius should come to mind.

Hobbema, Meindert (1638–1709), Dutch

Watermill: room 214

Next to Jacob van Ruisdael, his teacher, Hobbema is Holland's greatest landscape painter. Hobbema did not enjoy that reputation during his lifetime. He seemed unable to earn a living from painting, and probably painted very little after the age of thirty; it was not until the eighteenth and nineteenth centuries in England that his paintings came to be appreciated.

Hobbema often painted one scene many times. There are many *Watermills* by him. This one is famous for its treatment of diffused sunlight and subtle nuances of color. Notice, on the right side of the painting, that just enough of the landscape opens up to allow the eye, carried by alternating shades of light and dark, to explore the depth of the picture. It is a lovely scene, uncomplicated, with rich coloring of reds, greens, and browns.

Hooch, Pieter de (1629–ca. 1683), Dutch

Interior with Mother and Child or Maternal Duty (ca. 1660): room 222

Pieter de Hooch and Jan Vermeer had much in common: they were contemporaries (de Hooch was born only three years earlier than Vermeer); both painted typical Dutch interiors, where a mother, or lady of the house, is engaged in a domestic occupation; both probably learned perspective from Carel Fabritius; and both men were friends—at least during the time that de Hooch lived in Delft (from 1655 to about 1665), Vermeer's native city. However, of the two, Vermeer is the greater artist. De Hooch produced masterpieces only during the period of time he spent in Delft with Vermeer. When he moved to Amsterdam, to become a society painter, he lost his "magic" and became a second-rate artist.

Maternal Duty is one of those paintings from de Hooch's Delft period that clearly explains why his reputation is unshakable. One cannot imagine a more tender scene. We see a mother arranging her child's hair. A little dog, perhaps the child's pet, seems to be patiently waiting. There is a rich palette of deep golden yellow, red, and brown-reds, that adds warmth, as does the play of light entering from the garden in the rear, which merges the two rooms. It is an ideal Dutch seventeenth-century domestic scene.

There is more to this painting than its obvious charm. De Hooch has mastered the depiction of spatial and architectural elements. He concentrates on them so intensely that his human figures become subordinated to his architectural structure. Notice that he does not seem to need the people that inhabit the house, nor does he seem confident in depicting their faces. He relies on his sense of space and composition to make his painting convincing.

Also in the Rijksmuseum (room 222) see de Hooch's **The Pantry** (ca. 1658) and **The Small Country House** (ca. 1665), done in Amsterdam, but early enough so that de Hooch still had the skills he mastered in Delft. These paintings have different forms and objects, but are a demonstration of his spatial genius and his ability to depict light falling on bricks and stones, enriching his colors with a warm glow typical of the Dutch spirit of the time.

Kalf, Willem (1619–93), Dutch

Still Life, No. 1320: room 216

The greatest master of the still life was Willem Kalf, who was born into a wealthy family in Rotterdam and spent some time as an artist in Paris before settling down in Amsterdam. His mature still lifes, of which this is a noted example, break with the tradition of symbolic meaning in still lifes in which flowers, rotting fruit, hourglasses, and even skulls stood for the transience of life. That tradition was born out of the still life elements in early fifteenth-century religious paintings, where various objects symbolized meaning related to the religious content of the composition. With Kalf, the objects themselves and their possibilities for composition, rather than their symbolic meaning, are most important. His best still lifes have visually rich objects, such as this Dutch silver jug, blue china dish (a rare Oriental porcelain he used in other stills), and fragile wine glass, theatrically arranged with a mysterious quality about them. Their warm colors, set against a dark background, show that Kalf understood Rembrandt. Notice how he has combined Rembrandt's chiaroscuro technique with a little of Vermeer's color sense relating to the blue-yellow harmony seen in the fruit and the dish.

Maes, Nicolaes (1634–93), Dutch

An Old Woman Saying Grace or Prayer without End (1655): room 221A

Here is a painting by one of Rembrandt's most prominent pupils in the late 1640s. The influence of Rembrandt is obvious. At times Maes can be so much like the great master that some paintings attributed to Rembrandt have now been credited to Maes. Notice Rembrandt's warm harmonies of red and touches of yellow, and that wonderful black and white within a golden chiaroscuro.

However, many of Maes's paintings have their own unmistakable characteristic of a quiet melancholy, such as seen in *An Old Woman Saying Grace*. It is interesting because it seems to be critical of the woman, who feels that her time on earth is running out—symbolized by the hourglass on the windowsill, encased in a red frame. She is praying too much and is thus out of touch with reality. With her eyes closed, she will not be able to prevent the cat from climbing onto the table and stealing her dinner of salmon. The keys hanging on the wall refer to the keys to paradise, the open book is the Bible, and the inverted funnel is a reference to folly. This is an appropriate criticism of human character during a time when a prosperous, talented Dutch people believed in living life to the hilt, far from thoughts of the hereafter.

In room 221 see *Dreaming* by Maes, which has another melancholy character: in this case a young woman leaning on a cushion in an open-arched window.

Rembrandt (1606–69), Dutch

To be "truly gifted" is a term that is sometimes loosely used, but in the case of Rembrandt it is an apt description of his talent. Rembrandt's ability to communicate the deepest human experiences on canvas was something that could not be totally learned. It must have come from within, a genius he was born with. Rembrandt's innate talent exhibited itself at an early age. We know that from the many sketches and portraits that he made of his family in his youth. Rembrandt himself was certain of his own genius. He left his native Leyden to seek fame and fortune in Amsterdam.

In Amsterdam, almost immediately the rich burghers gave Rembrandt more commissions for portraits than he could handle. He earned a good deal of money, married a well-to-do Frisian beauty, Saskia van Uylenborch, who appears in many of his paintings, and, in the manner of Rubens, bought a mansion in the Breesstraat. However, while his creative genius continued to grow, his popularity declined and with it his finances. His group portrait, *The Night Watch*, was poorly received by the company of Captain Banning Cocq, commissioners of the painting, who did not realize that they were destined for immortality in one of the most famous pictures ever painted. His wife died while still young, and finally bankruptcy caused him to move out of his beloved mansion. But he never ceased to paint—with a genius rarely seen from the very beginning of painting in Western Europe. His gift for capturing human emotions and intellect on canvas is noticeable in many of the paintings he undertook—religious scenes, landscapes, and, above all, portraits. Whatever powers Rembrandt had, to paint as he did, they made him one of the most universally admired artists in the world.

The Night Watch (1642): room 224

From the size of this painting you can see that *The Night Watch* represented an important commission. It was given to him by a company of musketeers who had a meeting house on the street where Rembrandt lived. It had been the custom of companies, or civic guards (really social clubs), in seventeenth-century Holland to have group portraits painted in the form of a gathering of the members in a somewhat static composition, with good representations made of each member's face. But Rembrandt had a different idea. He created more of an historical painting than a group portrait, and depicted the members of the company at a time of action, when they are about to "fall in" under the command of Captain Cocq, their leader shown in the center with a red sash across his chest, and move out into the sunshine. The title "Night Watch" was erroneously given to the painting in the early nineteenth century when the picture, covered with the dirt of more than a century, appeared to look like a night scene. The company will have a day of shooting at the popinjay (either the live green woodpecker of Europe, or merely at the figure of a parrot used as a target), symbolized by the dead bird hanging from the little girl's belt. It is a lighthearted and festive occasion, so that the dwarf on the left with a fool's cap, the company fool wearing oakleaves on his helmet and shooting off his musket, and the man in an old fashioned top hat, fit right into the scene.

Of Rembrandt's painterly technique, the picture has baroque action vigorously united by a dramatic chiaroscuro with intense color accents. The colors yellow and red (Rembrandt's favorites) are on either side of the captain, set against the noncolor, black, in the center of the composition. The yellows and reds, especially the red sash worn by the captain across his black costume, have the effect of pushing forward the black of the picture, giving it a dramatic impact. This gives a sense of movement welling up from the dark background and bursting forth into the sunlight of the day.

There has been a controversy concerning the part *The Night Watch* played in the decline of Rembrandt's popularity. Even though Captain Cocq loved the painting and had a watercolor copy made of it for his private collection, it is said that it was not looked on favorably by the other members of the company who had paid an equal share (one hundred guilders each) and found that only parts of their faces were shown. They felt a group portrait should not draw the spectator's attention to the main action instead of the individual portraits. To be sure, after painting *The Night Watch,* Rembrandt's commissions for portraits declined, and he experienced financial ruin. Others say this is nonsense. People who saw the painting in the company's house admired it and remarked how superior it was to other paintings in the room done by popular artists of the day. In any case, in 1715 *The Night Watch* was transferred to the War Council Chambers of the Town Hall (at this time some of it was cut away to make it smaller). But in 1715 Rembrandt was not alive to see his largest painting hung in the most important public building in Amsterdam.

The Syndics of the Cloth Guild (1662): room 221

As fine a painting as *The Night Watch, The Syndics of the Cloth Guild,* done twenty years later, is the masterpiece of the group portrait. In this painting Rembrandt gives equal prominence to each sitter, but it is a credit to his genius that his picture is not monotonous and static. The six men, each looking out at some point, wear wide brimmed black hats (except the individual in the rear who is possibly a servant), black coats, and plain white collars. This mode of dress and harmony of color in a composition held together by the rich warmth of the tablecloth, presents the sitters to us as a group. At the same time, they are individuals; Rembrandt has caught their attention at a moment when they are acting with a sense of individual responsibility.

The Jewish Bride (ca. 1665): room 221

No one knows for certain that this is actually a Jewish couple. There is an argument that it represents the wedding portrait of Rembrandt's son Titus (the man does resemble Titus), who died only a few months after his marriage. But Rembrandt's close ties with the Jewish community of Amsterdam are well known, and if Rembrandt was able to find patrons to allow him the liberty that a great artist desires, such as painting his subjects in costumes not contemporary with the time, it was in the Jewish community.

Apart from whom the painting represents, it has been admired for its magical coloring. It is painted with a pageant of colors intensified by the red of the bride's dress and the greenish undertones of the garment of the man, heightened by the brightness of the yellow on his arm. An evocation of tender love is transmitted to us in the touch and gentle embrace of the couple, in spite of the fact that they do not look at one another. The left arm of the man drawn around the bride's shoulder, his right hand lying gently on her breast, the light touch of their hands, represents a quiet act of physical communion that Rembrandt felt strongly about at the end of his life. Rembrandt showed the act of touching in many of his other pictures that depict tender moments, or express spiritual or intellectual contemplation, but this painting stands as his greatest achievement in depicting love between a man and a woman.

Ruisdael, Jacob van (1628/29–1682), Dutch

The Mill at Wijk by Duurstede (1670): room 214

Landscapes, as subjects in their own right and not merely as backgrounds, were an important part of the vast production of seventeenth-century Dutch painting. These were realistic landscapes, not imaginary ones like those painted in Flanders and in Italy. The Dutch people, who loved their land and were realists at heart, preferred them that way. This is not to say that Dutch landscape painters painted out-of-doors, as would the French impressionists of the nineteenth century. They made trips into the countryside to sketch what they saw, but did the actual painting in their studios. Memory and the love of the land must have played a great part.

Of the many hundreds of Dutch landscape painters during the seventeenth century, the most talented was Jacob van Ruisdael. He came from a family of painters—his uncle was Salomon van Ruysdael, one of the founders of the school of landscape painting at Haarlem—and he was already an independent master painter at the age of eighteen. He was a sick man all of his life—he never married—and that, with his ability to see behind the countryside he painted, may be the reason for the thoughtful melancholy in his canvases. His masterpiece, *The Mill at Wijk*, has a peace and calm about it evocative of the searching, moody personality of the artist, in spite of the dramatic tension created by the triangles formed by land and water pressing up against each other, and in the ominous, turbulent sky against which the vertical mill stands out thrusting its arms against the approaching storm— symbolic of heroic Dutch resistance to the elements of nature. It is a carefully worked composition of strong tension built around water, land, and sky, in which the zigzag pattern of the painting directs our eyes to every corner, as do the alternating tones of light and dark.

Steen, Jan (1626–79), Dutch

Paintings of common people engaged in everyday activities were an important part of the new realism of seventeenth-century Dutch art, and no genre painter of that time is more prominent than Jan Steen. He was an educated man and an accomplished artist, but also a man of the people, operating a brewery in Delft and later a tavern in Leyden, his native city. Having produced about 800 paintings during his lifetime (at his death 500 remained unsold), his work is uneven, but enough of his paintings are of a quality to rank him as a great master.

Steen's zest for painting is reflective of his own zest for life his paintings depict. He seems to have lived out his own paintings, because we often see his rotund figure, with drink in hand, smiling and part of the scene everywhere (in the Rijksmuseum's *The Prince's Birthday,* room 218, he is the high-spirited man in the center, answering a toast). One might say that he overdid it, but what made Dutch seventeenth-century genre painting so special, especially Jan Steen's paintings, was that the artist derived his scenes from direct visual experience. Steen seemed to love the people in his pictures, and even when he took a moralizing position concerning their behavior, which he often did, one feels that he was only trying to be entertaining and did not expect to be taken too seriously.

The Feast of St. Nicholas (1660–64): room 216

This picture is typical of Steen's domestic scenes in which we see a setting within a house or a tavern, always peopled by the lower middle class. In this picture there are three generations of a family, ten figures, on the occasion of the visit of St. Nicholas before Christmas (December 5) when children receive toys and good things to eat. The father of the children is holding the smallest in front of the chimney to show where St. Nicholas came from. Steen loves to paint children and is a master at it. He captures their actions and emotions at every age, such as the roguish little girl in the center, refusing to show her mother her gifts, one of which is a doll in the form of a saint (which this little girl is anything but), and the older boy behind her, crying because he has received a birch-rod in his shoe, being held up by his sister in a mocking way, showing he has been bad and will be punished. Steen is careful to let us know that the grandmother, in the far background, has a gift for him behind the curtain, and soon he will be smiling.

The composition is carefully worked out. The figures, which lean in one direction, are balanced by those leaning in the other; right and left are held together by movement, gestures, glances, and expressions. The convivial merrymaking has resulted in a clutter of various objects which spill onto the floor, but no one seems to mind. This is a solid, happy family enjoying life as they knew it.

The Toilet: room 218

Steen is known for being the most daring of the seventeenth-century Dutch painters. This painting, and similar versions of it elsewhere, is partly responsible for that reputation. We see a pretty young lady sitting on a bed taking off her red stockings. There is a dog, her slippers on the floor, and a chamberpot. Nothing is very suggestive, even though her legs are crossed so that her thighs show. But Steen's contemporaries would have seen more. To them this woman was a prostitute. The dog refers to animal desires; the slippers, thrown off on the floor, to a moral looseness, or an "anything goes" attitude; and the chamberpot to a bad reputation. The stockings, the elements of action and most conspicuous objects, are most telling. The Dutch word for stocking is *kous,* also a seventeenth-century Dutch gutter word for vagina.

Other paintings by Steen are *The Sick Lady* (room 216), where a woman is suffering from lovesickness that the visiting doctor cannot cure, and a typical tavern scene, one of Steen's best, *The Prince's Birthday* (room 216).

Terborch, Gerard (1617–81), Dutch

Brothel Scene or *Gallant Conversation* (1653–55): room 222A

Gerard Terborch was one of the better genre painters of seventeenth-century Holland. He came from a grade of Dutch society above that of Steen and his paintings reflect his cultured sense of taste. He always seemed to have commissions to paint portraits, not only the result of his knowing the "right people" but more likely due to his talent for recording the fine clothing and furniture of the Dutch bourgeois. Notice his rendering of the girl's silver-gray satin dress. It is an example of his ability to achieve illusionist imitation of textures. So delicate and refined is his touch that though this painting depicts a brothel, with a cavalier speaking to a procuress in the presence of a prostitute, who is seen only from behind, thus discreetly hiding her face, it looks like a proper scene. A prudish owner of the painting erased the coin the man is holding in his right hand, and for most of its history it was called *Parental Admonition, Fatherly Advice,* and, more simply, *A Company in an Interior.* Even Goethe fell for this deception. He saw the procuress, with a glass of wine in her hand, as the girl's mother lowering her eyes so as not to be too attentive to the father's admonition. But the man is too young to be the girl's father, and the partly erased coin he is holding removes any false interpretation.

Terborch seems to have repeated himself in many of his paintings. In his genre scenes we see the same figures, the same furniture, and other details. He even repeated this entire painting. Another version of it is in the Dahlem Museum in Berlin. It is almost entirely the same except for the dog (a symbol of animal desire), which is omitted.

Portrait of Helena van der Schalke (ca. 1644): room 222A

Terborch excelled in the execution of the full-length portrait. This one, of a little girl who looks old beyond her years, represents the highest level of his art. The triangular form of the little girl is completely self-sufficient compositionally. No furniture, accessories, or background of any kind is needed. Terborch is able to give her the look of a little idol, lighting her up with a white light reflected from the pavement with a gaze made intense, and a bit macabre, by the neutral ground surrounding her.

There may be a direct influence of Velásquez in Terborch's technique. Terborch traveled widely and visited Spain, where he painted a portrait of Philip IV. He must have become familiar with Velázquez's work at that time. This portrait seems to have the psychological penetration often achieved by the Spanish master.

Vermeer, Jan (1632–75), Dutch

There was probably no artist who chose to be so withdrawn from the public as Jan Vermeer. He lived his entire life in Delft and supported his wife and nine children as an art dealer selling other artists' paintings. His own paintings were rarely for sale, and when a French connoisseur, Balthasar de Monconys, visited him in 1663 to see his work, he reported in his diary that Vermeer had "none of his works to show me." The artist remained almost totally unknown until about one hundred years ago when he was rediscovered and put on the level of Holland's greatest seventeenth-century artists. His thirty-nine paintings, a small amount for an artist with such a reputation, are considered treasures of art. The Rijksmuseum has four of the best of them. They show that Vermeer's art was different from the art of his contemporaries. The stillness of his figures, his absolute clarity combined with positive colors (especially yellows and blues), are in the realm of still lifes, though no still lifes by Vermeer survive. Vermeer was concerned with showing the visable, the known, the "here and now"—milk pitchers, the texture of fabrics, chairs and tables, even pictures and maps on the wall. Of course, human figures play a part in his art, but they are treated with the same passion and tenderness that are devoted to objects, leading one to say that Vermeer was not very interested in the human soul, as Rembrandt was, but in the soul of things.

The Kitchenmaid (ca. 1658): room 222

This scene is considered to be one of Vermeer's finest paintings. Some critics feel he never surpassed it. It has always been popular with the Dutch, since the Rijksmuseum acquired it in 1908. The woman in the painting pouring milk has been referred to as the "Mother of Holland" the provider of food, especially milk.

While Vermeer treats the woman with sympathetic interest, he lavishes the same attention on every other object in the painting. Even the imperfections of the wall, with its holes and occasional nail, are important to him. His use of the pointillé technique (the little points of light that he spreads over the surface of things to bring out their highlights) on the bread enables us almost to feel its texture. The scene is lit up by the light from the window on the left, and the plain kitchen wall forms a background to bring out the heavy figure and objects that Vermeer seems to love to paint.

Woman in Blue Reading a Letter or **Young Woman** (ca. 1665): room 222

This painting also depicts a pregnant woman engaged in a simple activity— reading a letter—but here she is not a maid but the lady of the house. It seems a simple painting, but it is actually a masterful balance between the figure and space. The light from the left of the picture allows for a clear view of the figure and the objects around her. The cool blue of the woman's blouse, contrasted with the fine yellows, is important in rendering this effect. Everything you see is planned. The rectangular and round forms, the diagonals and verticals, are all there to make you look at every object. They provide a happy equilibrium of essential formal elements. That is what makes this painting, and many others by Vermeer, masterpieces.

The Love Letter (ca. 1666): room 222
This is another of Vermeer's domestic scenes. Now we are shown both the lady of the house and the maid. The maid has just brought the lady a letter, and the lady has interrupted her music to receive it. The interpretation that the lady has received a love letter is had from the seascape on the wall, behind the figures, which in seventeenth-century Holland was a metaphor for love. A book of 1634, *Images of Love,* refers to a seascape with the lines "Love is like a sea, the lover like a ship, your favor, my love, is the harbor; your rejection a reef." The lute the lady has set aside is also significant, because music making in seventeenth-century Holland was a sign of love, even of lovemaking, for it symbolized harmony between lovers.

An illusion of depth is seen in the shadowed, crowded foreground, on either side of the open door. We look directly into the room on the second plane of the picture and, though the figures we see are caught in a moment of suspended animation—typical of Vermeer's art—everything is so brilliantly painted, including the objects on the floor and the shining pearl in the lady's ear (Vermeer loved to paint pearls), that we become caught up in the scene.

There is some disagreement as to how we are seeing the scene and where it is actually taking place. Some students of Vermeer's art consider the open doorway, leading into the room with the woman, to be not a doorway at all but a mirror reflecting the figures in another part of the room in which Vermeer was working, sitting in a position with his back to the curtain, chair, and mirror.

The Little Street (ca. 1658): room 222
Vermeer observed this street scene from the back window of his own house in Delft. The two old houses represent the old men's home on the far left and the old women's home on the right. Vermeer probably painted them because he knew they would be torn down to make way for a new building to house the Guild of St. Luke, of which he was a member. It was not an uncommon practice in seventeenth-century Holland for artists to paint buildings they knew would be demolished and disappear forever.

This is one of the two landscapes, or cityscapes, we have by Vermeer, but it does not really depart from the principles of his interior scenes. There is the same concern for patterning of geometric forms, the same open doorway we can look into, and the same attention to the texture of things. One could almost say it is an interior scene turned out-of-doors, or even a still life. Vermeer's ability to combine the everyday world with the eternal is the genius of this painting. Max Liebermann, the major exponent of German impressionism, called it the most beautiful easel painting in the world.

Witte, Emanuel de (ca. 1616–ca. 1691), Dutch

Interior of a Gothic Church (1680–82): room 222
With the exception of several paintings of a diversified subject matter (see *The Fishmarket,* room 226, in the Rijksmuseum), de Witte specialized in church interiors. All of them show a church in daily use, both for religious

services and other activities. In this painting the figures include a sexton and a gentleman speaking together beside an open grave. This humanizing aspect of de Witte's interiors makes his churches look convincing, yet all of them are imaginary, though this one contains motifs from both the Nieuwe Kerk and the Oude Kerk in Amsterdam. But the Dutch burgher did not want pictures of church interiors that did not exist, so de Witte's paintings brought him little success. We admire them today because of their flexible architectural elements. Being imaginary, the works rearrange the architecture to increase spatial effect, and his light gives the architecture a scenic quality with horizontal and vertical effects that attract the eye into the depth of the space. It may be all purely imaginary, but it seems very real.

STEDELIJK MUSEUM (MUNICIPAL MUSEUM)

13, Paulis Potterstraat

Hours: Open Mon.–Sat., 9:30AM–5PM; Sun. and public holidays, 1–5PM. Admission fee.

The Stedelijk Museum is everything that a major museum of modern art should be. Its collection, which covers the period 1850 to the present, is made up of many new and revolutionary trends in visual art, and its exhibition and acquisition policy follows art being produced in both the United States and Europe. The result is that the museum displays practically every current development in the art of the 1960s and 1970s.

It is also refreshing to find a museum operated with the same dynamic spirit that is reflective of its own collection. It is continuously reaching out to the public with innovative events in the form of special exhibitions and retrospectives. There is something different going on every month, as well as a building program that is improving its facilities.

Some of the highlights of the museum's permanent collection are works by French artists, or artists associated with France. These include Manet's *Sketch for "A Bar at the Folies Bergère";* Monet's *La Corniche de Monaco* and *The Garden at Giverny;* a still life and *La Montagne Sainte-Victoire,* by Cézanne; van Gogh's *Montmartre* and *La Berceuse;* Picasso's *Still Life with Guitar* and *Seated Woman with Fish-hat;* Léger's *Three Comrades;* and Chagall's *The Fiddler* and *Portrait of the Artist with Seven Fingers.*

German expressionism is presented by Kandinsky's *Landscape with Houses* and *Improvisation 33;* Kirchner's *Three Nudes in the Forest* and *Nude behind a Curtain: Franzi;* Kokoschka's *Portrait of William Wauer;* and Beckmann's *The Painter and his Wife.*

Of great importance is a collection of works by the artists who formed a group around the publication called *De Stijl* (The Style) in 1917. They formulated the concept of a new world not dominated by private interests in which individualism would become irrelevant. One might think this a strange manifesto for artists to espouse, but they were searching for a general universal style, which finally led to pure geometrical abstraction. **Piet Mondrian** (1872–1944) called it neoplasticism and reduced his paintings to horizontal and vertical lines and rectangular planes. He restricted his use of color to the three primary colors—red, yellow, and blue—and the noncolors—black, white, and gray. **Theo van Doesburg** (1883–1931), the central figure in the movement, had the idea to issue the publication. At first he painted much like Mondrian, but later added diagonal lines to make his compositions more dynamic. There was also an attempt to put the basic concept of *De Stijl* into architecture, typography, and advertising. Of this movement the museum shows paintings by Mondrian and van Doesburg in room 207.

The museum also has the largest collection outside of Russia of the works by **Kasimir Malevitch** (1878–1935) in rooms 202–6. This Russian painter created a new form of abstract painting he called **suprematism**, meaning the supremacy of the senses. Like Mondrian's work, Malevitch's paintings ignored physical reality and played an impor.ant part in bringing about a revolutionary change in art.

Not limited to painting, the museum also displays its collections of prints, posters, photographs, films, and industrial design. There are concerts of modern music every Saturday afternoon from October to April. These start at 3PM and are free to museum visitors.

VINCENT VAN GOGH MUSEUM

7, Paulus Potterstraat

Hours: Open Mon.–Sat., 10AM–5PM; Sun. and public holidays, 1–5PM; closed Jan. 1. Admission fee.

Along with works in the Kröller-Müller Museum in Otterlo, the finest colection of Vincent van Gogh's work is to be seen in the Vincent van Gogh Museum in Amsterdam (opened in 1972). This museum is the next door neighbor of the Stedelijk Museum, where the van Gogh collection used to be housed and displayed.

About 200 paintings by van Gogh and his contemporaries are on display in chronological order. Additionally, there is a periodically changing selection of the museum's vast collection of drawings.

Gogh, Vincent van (1853–90), Dutch

Vincent van Gogh was the first great Dutch painter since the seventeenth century. During a ten-year career as an artist, he gave a new form to impressionism, injecting it with the freedom needed for emotional personal expressionism. In this respect he is sometimes called an expressionist. Along with his postimpressionist contemporaries, Paul Cézanne (1830–1906) (the forerunner of twentieth-century cubism and the abstract forms derived from it), and Paul Gauguin (1848–1903), who used simplified, solid, well-defined forms, encompassing flat colors and lighting without shadows (Gauguin referred to it as synthetism; today we call it symbolist art), Vincent van Gogh is one of the founders of modern art and a legendary figure in the history of Western painting.

While somewhat close to the colorful expressionist painting of Gauguin, Vincent's art was different from that of both Cézanne and Gauguin. His use of expressive distortions, achieved with his frenzied brush strokes that made form and color one, were the most personal and emotionally charged paintings ever seen. He freed artists to be completely themselves, without the restraints even of impressionism, and he made it possible for them to paint what they felt about everything and everyone that came within their range of vision.

What a pity it was that Vincent was tormented by loneliness and largely ignored by the very humanity he so loved and wished to communicate with. We see it most directly in his early work in which, more than that of any other artist of the nineteenth century, including Gustave Courbet (1819–77) and Jean François Millet (1814–75), he expressed feelings of shame at the state of society and showed sympathy for the oppressed and poor. He was a religious man who, after failing to make a career as a salesman in the family art gallery in Paris and London (his uncle was the manager of The Hague branch of the Goupil Art Gallery of Paris), turned to the ministry. As a preacher he lived among the poor coal miners of the Borinage district, near Mons, of Belgium, and administered Christianity to them with such fervor that his superiors in Brussels, who considered such literal Christianity shocking and Vincent eccentric, dismissed him. But it was in the Borinage that Vincent began to draw sketches, and with this developing interest in painting he went to Brussels and then to The Hague to study art. Returning to his parent's home in Brabant he observed the poor peasants of the region and painted his first masterpiece, *The Potato Eaters,* which shows a moving intensity of feeling for poor, hard-working people. In the meantime, Vincent's brother Theo was establishing himself in Paris with the Goupil Art Gallery and was friendly with such impressionist painters as Camille Pissarro, Henri de Toulouse-Lautrec, Edgar Degas, and, most important, Paul Gauguin. He invited Vincent to Paris in February, 1886, to meet these men. Through the impressionists Vincent discovered the expressive powers of pure color and became interested in the perspective effects of Japanese prints. In less than two years he transformed his art from the dark tones of *The Potato Eaters* to the more dynamic colors of impressionism. Yet Vincent was never an impressionist. He entered the periphery of the world of impressionism only to transform it and, feeling that he was not succeeding as an artist in Paris, left for Arles, where he produced a new art.

Vincent's new art took form under the bright sunlight of Provence. His colors intensified enormously and came to express personal emotions. In his voluminous letters to his brother he tells us what they mean. The yellow is pure light and also love, the blue an infinity like the night sky, red and green "the terrible passions of humanity." His varicolored brush strokes, which he learned from the impressionists, became larger, freer, and stronger, and with them came an emphasis on sinuous curving movements, which in his last year came to mirror his tormenting emotional tension.

While Arles was a revelation to Vincent, he became lonely and made the mistake of inviting Gauguin to stay with him. Both men could not have been more different in personality and their constant arguments were too much for Vincent's nerves. Shortly before Christmas, 1888, van Gogh and Gauguin had one of their violent arguments over Vincent's idea for a brotherhood of artists—a house for art in Arles—which may have precipitated Vincent's first attack of madness (probably epilepsy). He cut off part of his left ear and was committed to a mental institution at Saint-Rémy, twelve miles from Arles. He spent a year there, where he produced some of his best canvases, all indicative of the recurring epileptic attacks: twisting movements with exciting, intensely blazing colors.

Toward the end of van Gogh's stay at Saint-Rémy, Theo sold one of his paintings for four hundred francs—the first and only one ever sold, apart from one commissioned portrait for twenty francs—and suggested he spend the money at Dr. Gachet's private sanatorium at Auvers, near Paris. Vincent put himself under Dr. Gachet's care, but the attacks became more frequent. On July 27, 1890, van Gogh went into a nearby field and shot himself. He died two days later with his brother Theo at his bedside. Theo died six months later and the two were reunited, side by side, in the little cemetery at Auvers.

Van Gogh's life may have been filled with hardship and loneliness, but he was never without a creative conviction based upon his genius. He often wrote of himself as preparing the way for future painters.

A recommended list of paintings follows below. It should be combined with the larger collection of the artist's work at the Kröller-Müller Museum at Otterlo.

The Potato Eaters (Nuenen, 1885): first floor
A Pair of Shoes (Paris, 1886): first floor
Harvest at La Crau (Arles, 1888): second floor
Boats on the Beach at Saintes-Maries (Arles, 1888): second floor
Still Life: Vase with Fourteen Sunflowers (Arles, 1888): second floor
Vincent's House on the Place Lamartine (The Yellow House) (Arles, 1888): second floor
Vincent's Bedroom in Arles (Arles, 1888): second floor
Wheatfield with a Reaper (Saint-Rémy, 1889): second floor
Still Life: Vase with Irises (Saint-Rémy, 1889): second floor
Wheatfield with Crows (Auvers, 1890): second floor

Buildings

The **Royal Palace** located on the Dam Square, which started out as a town hall, is the largest architectural masterpiece in Amsterdam. Designed by Jacob van Campen (1595–1657), it was begun in 1648, when the war with the Spanish ended and Holland was recognized as an independent republic. It was completed in 1665 and assumed the function of a royal palace in 1808. It is an immense rectangular block containing two courtyards separated by a massive central hall. Its style is usually referred to as Dutch Palladianism, but many of its features are unlike the Mediterranean tradition: the two courtyards are not accessible from the main floor, in contrast to those in Italian buildings; and the exterior, with its four projecting pavillions at the angles and the large cupola that rises above the pediment of the front, is un-Italian. The interior, with its royal apartments, can be visited during summer months, Mon.–Fri., 10AM–12 noon and 1–4PM; admission fee.

The **Nieuwe Kerk** is also located on the Dam and serves as the national church of the Netherlands. Originally a Catholic church, it dates to the last decade of the fifteenth century. It is largely of Gothic design with an interior wooden roof supported by massive grouped pillars.

Of greater interest in church architecture is the **Oude Kerk** at Oudekerksplein, which was begun in the fourteenth century and combines Gothic and Renaissance styles unique in Amsterdam. Its sixteenth-century tower is typical of a fine lofty Dutch steeple. Another church with an excellent bell tower is the fourteenth-century baroque **Westerkerk** at Prinsengracht, corner of Westermarkt, built by **Hendrik de Keyser** (1565–1621). Rembrandt is buried there.

De Keyser is credited with creating a Dutch Renaissance style out of a medieval one. He worked in Amsterdam during the prosperous, high-spirited early seventeenth century, when the city was being enlarged and when the famous canals—Herengracht, Prinsengracht, Keizergracht, and others—were being planned. The lovely tall houses along these canals owe their vaired gables to him. Prior to De Keyzer, gables had been stepped, but he worked out systems for scrolled sides, strapwork decoration, finials, and a pediment at the apex. These decorations, best seen during a cruise on the canals, are an important reason why Amsterdam is still such a charming city.

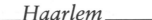

Haarlem

FRANS HALS MUSEUM

Grote Heiligland, 62

Hours: Open Mon.–Sat., 10AM–5PM; Sun. and public holidays 1–5PM; also last week in Mar.–first two weeks in May, and last two weeks in July–Sept. 1, Sat. and Mon. evenings, 8:30–10:30PM, and Easter Sun. and Whitsun, 8:30–10:30PM. During spring and summer the museum has evening concerts; several rooms are lit by candlelight and period music is performed in the inner court and in the Renaissance hall. Admission fee.

Haarlem, a small town, observed the development of museums in Amsterdam, The Hague, and Rotterdam. When citizens realized that they too had a fine collection of paintings, mostly works of their native son Frans Hals which hung in municipal institutions, they decided to form a museum of their own. The original collection has never been surpassed by later purchases.

In 1862, after a number of rooms were set aside in the Town Hall, the museum was opened to the public. Because of lack of space, in 1906 the town bought the seventeenth-century old men's home and converted it into the museum you see today. It specializes in the Haarlem School of painting and possesses some of the best works of sixteenth- and seventeenth-century masters: Jan van Scorel, Johannes Verspronck, Jan de Bray, and, of course, Frans Hals. But there is also an excellent collection of modern Dutch paintings after 1945. A recent extension of the museum has made possible a permanent exhibition of works by such twentieth-century Dutch painters as Karel Appel, Corneille, Lucebert, and other members of the so-called Cobra Group.

Hals, Frans (ca. 1580–1660), Dutch
Frans Hals is one of the brilliant masters of seventeenth-century Dutch painting and an innovator of a new style. He was almost exclusively a portraitist, and the Haarlem museum is outstanding for its collection of many of his group portraits.

There was a long history in Holland of local militia groups organized as guilds to protect their towns against attack. These groups gradually became social organizations as well as civic bodies, and by Hals's time it was common practice to decorate their buildings with group portraits of their members. Traditionally, these portraits took the form of the members being placed in two rows, in order to allow an even exposure for each individual. But in 1616 Hals broke with that tradition in his first great group portrait, the *Banquet of the Officers of the Haarlem Militia Company of St. George,* a landmark in the history of Dutch art. In this painting Hals abandoned the boring rows of portraits and instead divided the group into figures standing, sitting, and bending toward one another. He used sweeping diagonals and, by subtly arranging the heads of most of his subjects on the same level, achieved a new kind of unity. Notice how the flag forms a diagonal, repeated in the groups of men standing on the right and seated on the left. It enlivens the composition and enchances the illusion of space.

In later group portraits Hals's compositions became even more lively and his brushwork achieved a new kind of freedom. In the group portraits of the *Officers of the Haarlem Company of St. Hadrian* (ca. 1627) and of the *Officers of the Militia Company of St. George* (ca. 1627), both have animated compositions where two groups are linked by long diagonals, and each group shows a central seated figure around which other men are arranged, some seated and some standing. Of greater significance is the elimination of the line, replaced by brush strokes that model forms by strong contrasts of color in small patches. This allows for the depiction of people and objects as they really look, infusing movement and the spontaneity of live action into a scene. The color patches and dabs of white paint blend only at a distance and are more effective than drawing and graduated modeling in light and shade. It anticipates nineteenth-century impressionism, and only Velázquez and the late Rembrandt were familiar with such a technique during Hals's time. Later painters of the seventeenth and eighteenth centuries overlooked it completely.

In the 1630s the same vivacity of style is still seen in Hals's *Officers of the Militia Company of St. Hadrian* (ca. 1633) and in the *Officers of the Militia Company of St. George* (ca. 1639), but with a tendency toward restraint in compositional setting and in color, especially in the 1639 painting.

By the 1640s a melancholic strain enters Hals's work, which the dignified character of the group representing the *Regents of the St. Elizabeth Hospital* (ca. 1641) clearly shows, and sets the tone of his painting in the last decades. By the time Hals paints his last group portraits, the *Regents of the Old Men's Home* and the *Regentesses of the Old Women's Home,* painted about 1664 when the artist was over eighty, almost all of the color disappears, the paint is applied more thinly, and the composition has become simple and subdued.

Despite constant patronage—at times Hals had more portraits than he could handle—he appears to have been poor and in debt to local merchants. Stories of his being an alcoholic are probably exaggerated, and a popular story of his being a wife-beater is clearly incorrect; actually, Hals seems to have held a respectable place in his community. He belonged to a number of prestigious societies in Haarlem and surely would never have received commissions to paint portraits for the various associations and individuals that patronized him all his life if he had a bad personal reputation. His production of paintings, about 250 (about 200 of them commissioned portraits), is not large for a painter who found painting easy and lived to a very old age. Possibly many of his pictures were stored away in attics and basements and through the years lost. His work began to be highly treasured only in the middle of the nineteenth century.

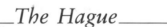

The Hague

MAURITSHUIS

29, Plein (8, Korte Vijverberg)

Hours: Open Mon.–Sat., 10AM–5PM; Sun. and public holidays, 11AM–5PM; closed Jan. 1. Admission fee.

The Mauritshuis has been closed for restoration for a number of years (completion scheduled for end of 1986 or 1987). An important part of the Mauritshuis collection of paintings has been moved to the Johan de Withuis, 6, Kneuterdijk, not far from the Mauritshuis, where it will be on display until its permanent home at the Mauritshuis is fully restored.

The Mauritshuis itself is a work of art, having been designed by Jacob van Campen (1595–1657) in 1633 for Prince Johan Maurits Van Nassau, a general and later governor of the Dutch colony in Brazil. It is a lovely little

Renaissance palace with a simple plan set in a rectangular block that has a front of five bays composed of large sandstone orders with brick in the side parts and sandstone alone in the middle bays. The decorative doorway is approached by entrance steps and above a central pediment rides a Dutch-style hipped roof.

Fabritius, Carel (1622–54), Dutch

The Goldfinch

Carel Fabritius is important to us today as a link between Rembrandt and Vermeer, the two greatest artists of the Golden Age of Dutch painting. He was Rembrandt's most talented pupil, but was not content to copy the master's style. He developed his own in which he put dark figures against light backgrounds, in contrast to Rembrandt's dark backgrounds, and used cool silvery colors instead of Rembrandt's warm browns, reds, and golds. After leaving Rembrandt in Amsterdam, Fabritius moved to Delft in the early 1650s where the young Vermeer became his pupil. It is certain that Vermeer developed his own cool harmony of colors from Fabritius, even though Vermeer came to use more tonal contrasts, especially yellow and blue. On October 12, 1654, at the age of thirty-two, Fabritius died in an explosion of a powder magazine that destroyed a good part of Delft. No doubt many of his pictures also perished, so that only about twelve of them survive today, too few to perpetuate his reputation.

The Goldfinch is considered his masterpiece. It was meant to be a panel decorated in trompe l'oeil (realistic representations so that the objects look real rather than painted), perhaps for a door designed to cover a fireplace when it was not in use. The recording of the play of light on the wall and the bird's plumage is outstanding.

Holbein, Hans, the Younger (1497–1543), German

Portrait of a Man with a Falcon (1542)

Looking at this portrait, painted at the end of the artist's life, we can understand why Holbein was the supreme court painter of portraits in England during the first half of the sixteenth century. We do not know the name of the sitter, who is only twenty-eight, but he is certainly a nobleman, since he is carrying a falcon. Everything about him is aristocratic. He looks slightly beyond us with a haughty gaze; he appears self-contained and confident; and he is dressed in the finest wools and silk of the time. It is surely Holbein's gift to be able to present his subjects at their best, or, at least, the way they wanted to look, while maintaining their exact likeness.

The Mauritshuis has three other portraits by Holbein. The Portrait of the Falconer Robert Cheseman was painted nine years earlier than the Portrait of a Man with a Falcon, and although the pose is different, the essence of the picture is very much the same. The Portrait of Jane Seymour is one of several, very similar portraits Holbein did of Henry VIII's third wife (see Holbein's Jane Seymour in the Kunsthistorisches Museum, Vienna). However, in the Portrait of a Young Woman the sitter is not from the aristocracy and may represent the artist's wife. These paintings and the *Portrait of a Man with a Falcon* were transferred by Prince Willem III from England to The Hague after he became king of England. After his death the British asked for their return, but without success.

Mieris, Frans van (1635–81), Dutch

The Soldier and the Girl (1659)

Frans van Mieris, like Jan Steen, came from Leyden and also was a painter of genre scenes. But, unlike Steen, he had no trouble finding customers. He was famous not only in Holland but also abroad—his patrons included archdukes Cosimo of Tuscany and Leopold Wilhelm of Austria. As a result, his paintings are mostly of aristocratic society, with resplendent interiors, and portraits of the wealthy. He was also not adverse to doing the kind of genre painting we see here, euphemistically called *The Soldier and the Girl*. It is actually a picture of a brothel. Erotic subjects depicted in paintings were by no means rare in Calvinist Holland, and this is one of the best of them.

We see a man wearing a steel cuirass (a piece of defensive armor consisting of a heartplate and a piece for the back) and therefore identifiable as a soldier (in seventeenth-century Holland soldiers were considered a lower element of society, associated with licentiousness). A young lady is pouring him a glass of wine, and in the background two dogs are copulating (a reference to the Italian proverb, "As is the lady, so is her dog"). Other signs in the picture tell us that this is a house of ill-repute: the mattress and bedding hanging from the second floor, the drunken patron slumped over the table, and the couple at the door. Mieris's technique has colors stronger than those used by other contemporary artists, and is particularly effective in the rendering of glittering fabrics. Notice the silver luster of the lady's skirt and the red tunic of the soldier. Focusing on these refinements alone, it is understandable why Mieris was such an important figure in Dutch painting.

Rembrandt* (1606–69), Dutch

The Anatomy Lesson of Dr. Tulp

This painting, completed in 1626 when he was twenty-six, launched Rembrandt's career in Amsterdam. The group portrait of Dr. Tulp and his onlookers was different from anything that had ever been seen. Dr. Tulp was a well-known figure of the time—the foremost surgeon of Holland and the treasurer and burgomaster of Amsterdam. With such establishment backing Rembrandt was never without a commission to do a portrait for almost ten years, up to the time he painted *The Night Watch*.

We see Dr. Tulp demonstrating the muscles of the forearm of a cadaver, which was that of a criminal from Leyden called Aris. A textbook by Vesalius stands open at the feet of the corpse and as an aid for the doctor. A sheet of paper one of the onlookers holds contains a drawing of the forearm and the names of the onlookers, or subscribers. Only three of the men seem to be absorbed in Dr. Tulp's demonstration. The other four, of which one in the background and one on the far left may have been late subscribers and added at a later date, seem only to be interested in having their portraits painted.

The work is not without faults. Dr. Tulp is shown in a self-conscious pose, the composition is unbalanced, and the lighting concentrates too much on the cadaver, which, without the rigidity of death, is unconvincing. Against these imperfections we should note the skillful portraits of the three attentive men and the unification of all by means of light. That light throughout the composition creates a feeling of excitement, as though the lesson is a dramatic production—which, in seventeenth-century Holland, it probably was.

The Mauritshuis has additional masterpieces by Rembrandt: *Susanna Bathing* is Rembrandt's treatment of the popular story, *Susanna and the Elders* (see Tintoretto's *Susanna and the Elders* in the Kunsthistorisches Museum, Vienna), in which he uses his wife, Saskia, as the model for Susanna; *Two Young Negroes,* a painting where the subjects are treated with naturalistic accuracy; *Homer,* a sensitive portrayal of old age; and *Saul Listening to David,* possibly done by Rembrandt's students, which shows the somber figure of the sick king wiping tears from his eyes, while David appears lost in his music.

Steen, Jan* (1626–79), Dutch

The Inn

This painting is typical of Steen's genre scenes in which everything seems to be going on at one time. But this is not as casual a scene as it may appear to be. Steen is making a statement, and the gray silk curtain, which seems to have been raised to reveal a theatrical production, calls our attention to what is happening.

We see people, young and old, male and female, even children, drinking, socializing, and eating oysters. Since oysters are a legendary aphrodisiac, one could read only sexual meaning into the picture. Actually, sexual pleasure is only one of the many pleasures Steen is referring to, though it may be the strongest. We focus on the little boy hiding in the attic blowing bubbles, with a skull next to him. That another name for the picture is *The Life of Man* gives us the real meaning of the picture. In the bubble Steen is referring to the classic adage *homo bulla*—"man is a bubble," or life is fragile. This is not to suggest that the bubble is used in the medieval sense, to depict the fragility of life and thus the renunciation of worldly pleasures in favor of a higher ideal. On the contrary, this is seventeenth-century Holland, and Steen is likely saying, "If life is short, enjoy it to the fullest while you can," which is exactly what these people are doing.

Another painting by Steen in the Mauritshuis, where oysters as an aphrodisiac play a part, is *Girl Salting Oysters*. The pretty girl with the flirtatious look suggests that it is for you, the spectator, that she is salting oysters.

Additional masterpieces by Steen are *The Poultry Yard, Merry Company,* and *The Lute Player,* a portrait of the artist's wife, Grietje, the daughter of the landscape painter Jan van Goyen.

Vermeer, Jan* (1632–75), Dutch

View of Delft (ca. 1660)

This glittering view of the old city of Delft, where Vermeer spent his entire life, is presented like a still life, with a quiet, penetrating beauty typical of most of Vermeer's paintings. In the background, on the right, with sunlight shining on it, is the tower of the Nieuwe Kerk, where Vermeer was baptized. On the left, above the roofs of the city, the spire of the Oude Kerk, in which he is buried, is also visible. The painting's fascinating beauty was observed by the French art critic Etienne-Joseph Théophile Thoré, who fell in love with it in the mid-nineteenth century, and thus started a new interest in Vermeer that resulted in the late recognition he deserved as a master.

Notice the sensitivity to color and the play of light, further enhanced by the use of pointillé. By lighting up the salmon-colored sand in the foreground, Vermeer makes us enter the picture from the bottom, where our eye moves across the silky pale-blue water to the city, with light shining on roof tops, and then to the sky where the sun, breaking through clouds, provides the light that illuminates and harmonizes the blues, reds, and yellows of the buildings.

The *View of Delft* is likely the greatest landscape painting in seventeenth-century Holland, a time when there were many artists specializing in landscape painting. Apart from the extraordinary technique, it has a freshness of vision helped along in that it was painted from nature, instead of from a sketch or from memory.

Girl in a Turban (ca. 1662)

This painting was also praised by Etienne-Joseph Théophile Thoré, who called it "La Gioconda du Nord." She does have a mysterious charm with an almost Leonardoesque tenderness. As she casts a glance at us over her left shoulder, there is a mild harmony of colors that seems to glow with an inner radiance, like that of the pearl in her ear. Vermeer does not do much drawing of her face. With his gift for simplicity and his genius at expressing himself with color and light, he produces a portrait with much character and charm. Whoever she is (there has been speculation that she is the artist's daughter), she has, like the *Mona Lisa,* a look that is eternal.

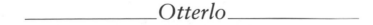

Otterlo

KRÖLLER-MÜLLER MUSEUM

Hoge Veluwe National Park

Hours: Open Mon.–Sat., 10AM–5PM; Sun. and public holidays, 11AM–5PM (Nov.–Mar., Sun. and public holidays, 1–5PM); sculpture garden, Apr.–Oct., 10AM–4:30PM. Admission fee.

You can reach the museum by train to Ede, Arnhem, or Apeldoorn, from where there are connections by V.A.D. bus to Otterlo or Hoenderloo. From June to September there is a direct bus line between Arnhem station and St. Hubertus via the museum.

Few women in Europe, other than Peggy Guggenheim (see the Guggenheim Collection, Venice), collected as extensively and brilliantly as Hélène Kröller, the former Hélène Müller. In 1934 she gave her collection to the state. The museum, located in the largest national park in Holland, at one time was owned by the Kröllers and was built to house Mrs. Kröller's art collection.

While the fame of Mrs. Kröller's museum has always rested on its collection of the works of **Vincent van Gogh**—276 pieces in all—there are also paintings from the sixteenth and seventeenth centuries by such masters as Baldung and Cranach, antique Chinese and Greek ceramics and jade figures, and paintings, sculptures, and drawings from the nineteenth and twentieth centuries. More than sixty sculptures are displayed outdoors, on either side of the path leading to the main entrance and in the largest sculpture park in Europe.

For a discussion on the life and work of Vincent van Gogh see Vincent van Gogh Museum, Amsterdam. Some of the most important paintings by van Gogh are listed chronologically as follows, and are to be found in the exhibition area surrounding the patio:

The Loom (Nuenen, 1884)
Self-portrait (Paris, 1887)
Interior of a Restaurant (Paris, 1887)
Orchard in Blossom surrounded by Cypresses (Arles, 1888)
Haystacks in Provence (Arles, 1888)
The Sower (Arles, 1888)
Café Terrace at Night (Arles, 1888)
Portrait of Lieutenant Milliet (Arles, 1888)
La Berceuse (Arles, 1889)
The Postman (Arles, 1889)
The Garden of the Asylum at Saint-Rémy (Saint-Rémy, 1889)
Two Women and Cypresses (Saint-Rémy, 1889)
Field of Olive Trees (Saint-Rémy, 1889)
Road with Cypresses (Saint-Rémy, 1890)

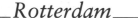

_____ *Rotterdam* _____

BOYMANS-VAN BEUNINGEN MUSEUM

18–20 Mathenesserlaan

Hours: Open Mon.–Sat., 10AM–5PM, Sun. and public holidays, 1–5PM; closed Jan. 1 and Apr. 30. Admission fee.

Rotterdam became in the twentieth century one of the wealthiest and most important commercial centers in Europe and determined to have a great museum of art to compare with those in The Hague and Amsterdam. Rotterdam acquired, through donations and purchases, an excellent collection of paintings, and built, in 1935, one of the finest museum buildings in Europe. In 1958, with the acquisition of the Van Beuningen collection, which included such treasures as van Eyck's *Three Maries at the Sepulchre* and Pieter Bruegel the Elder's *The Great Tower of Babel*, it reached a level not only with great museums of Holland but also those elsewhere in Europe. It covers the range of painting and sculpture from the van Eycks to the present day. Its setting in the heart of the city (only a fifteen-minute walk from the Central Station), with a garden and park behind it, make it a convenient and lovely place to visit.

Bosch, Hieronymus* (ca. 1450–1516), Flemish

St. Christopher and the Christ Child: first floor, room 4
This is Bosch's interpretation of the story of St. Christopher as told in the Golden Legend (a collection of the lives of the saints written in the thirteenth century by Jacobus de Voragine). It tells of a giant who wished to serve the most powerful person in the world. At first he worked for a king, but left him when he learned the king was frightened of Satan. He then served the Devil, whom he also deserted when he saw him trembling before the crucifix. Then a hermit induced him to carry people across a river by telling him that through this service he would find the mightiest of masters. Doing this, he came one day to carry a small child who grew heavier and heavier with each step he took. When this puzzled the giant, the child told him He was Christ and that he was therefore carrying the weight of the world on his shoulders. Thus, the giant became known as Christopher (bearer of Christ) and, in the Roman Catholic church, the patron saint of travelers. (In spite of the charm of this story, the Council of Trent in the sixteenth century tried unsuccessfully to abolish it because of its doubtful historicity and in 1969 St. Christopher was removed from the Catholic church calendar.)

In Bosch's *St. Christopher* the stooping giant carrying the child across the stream is dominant, but there are also some of the enigmatic objects that Bosch is known for. At the left-middle ground is a man hanging a bear (a symbol of gluttony), a dragon (a symbol of the Devil) rearing up from behind a wall and frightening a bather in the river, and in the background a city burning (symbolizing sin). There are also fish, probably symbolizing Lent, and the figure at the water's edge may be the monk who introduced the giant to Christ. Yet if the monk's dwelling is meant to be the cracked pitcher a (symbol of idle vanity) in the dead tree behind him, which also has a beehive being raided by a climber, it is puzzling. To add to the confusion is one of Bosch's curious irregular shaped barks struck through the branch of the tree so as to shield the pitcher, which may be symbolic of worthlessness, or a useless protection from the all-seeing eye of God. These are references to the corrupt world that Bosch uses in his art, and are unique to his imagination.

The Vagabond (ca. 1510): first floor, room 4
This painting used to be called the *Prodigal Son,* but there is little reason to believe that it represents an episode from that famous parable. The main figure in the picture, drawn on a larger scale than its surroundings, may represent the greater part of humanity reduced to poverty because of its sinfulness. We see the vagabond at the moment when he is tempted to turn toward the tavern, a symbol of the world and the Devil. The dilapidated condition of the tavern and the unsavory characters in it show us that it leads to a life of ruin. There is no doubt that it is also a house of ill repute. The swan on its sign is a symbol of lust, there is a man in the doorway with his hand on a woman's breast, a woman at a window is looking for a new customer, and a man is urinating in the yard. Yet the vagabond has only to enter through the gate at his left to escape the lure of the tavern and acquire a life of peace and prosperity. His weakness makes him hesitate, not knowing which way to go.

In room 4 the museum also has the **Marriage Feast at Cana** (ca. 1475–80), probably a copy of an early work by Bosch and not in good condition. Most of it has been repainted and parts cut away. It too employs the tavern as a symbol of evil.

Bruegel, Pieter, the Elder (ca. 1525–69), Flemish

The Tower of Babel (ca. 1564): first floor, room 5
This version of the story of the *Tower of Babel* was probably done by Bruegel after his much larger painting of the same subject, now in the Kunsthistorisches Museum in Vienna. Unlike the larger painting, this one has little detail at the base of the tower and in the surrounding countryside, so that nothing detracts from the main point of the story. Even King Nimrod himself has been left out. Its dark colors and threatening clouds indicate that the stupid idea to build a tower to heaven, based on incorrigible human vanity and the sin of pride, is doomed to failure and that the end is already near.

Eyck, Hubert van (ca. 1370–1426), Flemish

The Three Maries at the Sepulchre (ca. 1420): first floor, room 3
This early Flemish painting, which once may have been part of a diptych, or even a polyptych (a cleaning has revealed evidence of rays of light on the right edge of the picture which may have come from an adjacent panel), has been attributed to Hubert van Eyck. There is also a possibility it is by both van Eyck brothers, Jan and Hubert, if Hubert existed at all. It shows the discovery of the Resurrection with the three Maries approaching from the left, a characteristic of early Italian primitives. Each Marie is dressed in a different colored costume, but they are united by their white headdresses. The three sleeping soldiers are also colorfully attired, but in their inaction they are depicted in contrast to the figures on the left. Above Christ's empty grave the angel, with yellow and blue wings, is clearly separate from the earth-

ly figures by its small size. The carefully drawn plants that can be identified with botanical accuracy and the imaginary skyline of Jerusalem showing the Mosque of Omar have qualities that are characteristic of the Flemish School.

Magritte, René (1898–1967), Belgian

On the Threshold of Liberty (1929): first floor, room 33

This painting is one of the most difficult of Magritte's to decipher. We are looking into a room with a cannon pointed toward a rear wall, though some say it is pointed at the woman's torso. For some, too, there is a sense of eroticism in the nude and in the woods, and even in the bare wood with its grain. The closed facade of the house next to the open sky suggests an interchangeability of indoors and outdoors, emphasized by the cannon in the room. Harness bells on a sheet of corrugated metal indicate the sound of trotting horses, and the paper-cutout pattern below the fire combines incongruous mixtures. All these elements suggest a world in disorder and full of contradictions. As its title suggests, the work is meant to stimulate thoughts into unbounded areas of the imagination.

Rembrandt* (1606–69), Dutch

Titus at his Desk (1655): first floor, room 9

Rembrandt was very attached to his son Titus, born of his marriage to Saskia van Uylenborch. The portrait of Titus at his Desk, when the sitter was about fourteen, is one of those personal paintings Rembrandt did in his mature period when he felt free to do as he liked. The boy is shown in a pensive mood, daydreaming. His hand and thumb, pressed against his chin, heighten the play of light on his face, giving him a contemplative mood. The reddish, brownish tonalities of the work and that marvelous old desk hold the picture together, establishing forms and textures so important to Rembrandt.

Portugal

Portugal, a small country comprising less than one-fifth of the Iberian peninsula, has its own artistic history separate from that of Spain. It may have less of a story to tell, and it sometimes suffers from a lack of definition and originality, but in comparison to Spanish art, with which it is too often confused, Portuguese art is brighter, without the brooding dark mysticism of Spain. It is also an art that is not well known beyond its borders, because its greatest genius has been expressed in architecture and the sculpture and decorative elements used with architecture. You have to travel to Portugal to see and appreciate it.

There are two great periods of architecture, both coming after Portugal's success in worldwide exploration and empire building. The sixteenth-century Manueline style, essentially Gothic, dominated Portugal into the Renaissance. It came at a time when the discovery of Brazil and sea routes to India and the Orient provided great wealth, which King Dom Manuel, for whom the style was named, spent lavishly on palaces and churches. The style features rich surface decorations, the equal of Spanish Plateresque, applied to Gothic forms derived from various parts of Europe.

The eighteenth-century Joanine style, named after King Dom João (John V), features splendid decoration and rich embellishment, like the earlier Manueline, but applied to baroque architecture in massive scale. It was financed from the royal fifth the king received on all the gold and diamonds of Brazil, whose mines the Portuguese had developed.

During these periods of fabulous prosperity, foreign artists worked in Portugal, which explains the eclectic nature of Portuguese architecture and sculpture; but no artist, foreign or Portuguese, emerged with the unmistakable originality to be considered a genius. Theirs was a combined effort of three centuries drawing on Moorish, Spanish, and northern influences, to create the fantastic compositions and ornamentation that are the most original forms of Portuguese art.

Portuguese painting was also affected by influences from outside the country. The important figures in its history, Nuno Gonçalves and Domingos António Sequeira, are little known outside Portugal, but nevertheless rank as European old masters. Of the two, the fifteenth-century Gonçalves is considered Portugal's greatest painter. His *St. Vincent Altarpiece,* showing Flemish influence in style and technique, is the major treasure of the Museum of Ancient Art in Lisbon.

Domingos António Squeira, the early nineteenth-century painter, whose work can also be seen at the Lisbon museum, was a fine portraitist who used light to express dramatic and romantic effects, as Goya did in Spain, though there is no evidence Sequeira ever visited Spain or saw Goya's paintings. But that is where the similarity between the Portuguese Sequeira and the Spanish Goya ends. Goya was a pessimist who saw the dark side of life; Sequeira was an optimist who painted with a strong sense of faith in the future and a warm approach to life that is typically Portuguese.

Alcobaça

MONASTERY

Hours: Open daily 9:30AM–5:30PM. Admission fee.

The royal monastery at Alcobaça, built between 1158 and 1223, is one of the finest Cistercian buildings in Europe. The Cistercians, called white monks because of their white habit, were a reformed Benedictine order that originated in France in the eleventh century. They were known as great builders of monasteries and churches. Although they first favored the Romanesque style, which reflected their spirit of poverty, they later became the principal disseminators of Gothic architecture, of which this monastery is an example. In fact, Gothic architecture entered Portugal by way of the Cistercians at Alcobaça.

Notice the typical Cistercian clean, simple interior, which uses cross-ribbed vaulting so that the aisle vaults are only a little narrower and lower than the nave vaults, to give the effect of an open-hall church. It contrasts with the seventeenth- and eighteenth-century baroque front facade which, while restrained in design, is ornate by comparison.

The history of the church dates back to a vow made in the early twelfth century by King Alfonso Henriques. He swore that he would build an abbey dedicated to St. Bernard of Clairvaux, the preacher of the Crusades, if he captured a Moorish stronghold. After he achieved his goal, he invited Cistercian monks to settle in Alcobaça and financed the construction of the church and monastery.

The most interesting history of the church relates to two **royal tombs** in the transepts. These ornately carved flamboyant Gothic tombs, positioned opposite each other, belong to Inês de Castro (in the north transept) and King Pedro I (in the south transept). The king arranged the tombs so that when he and his beloved Inês woke on the day of judgment they could see one another at first glance. Their story is one of the great love affairs and includes an extraordinary coronation, one that took place after death.

Inês de Castro was a Spanish lady-in-waiting to Constanza of Castile, who for reasons of state married Dom Pedro, the son of the king of Portugal, in 1340. The king, seeing that his son was madly in love with Inês, exiled her from the court. In 1345, when Dom Pedro's wife died, Inês returned and she and Dom Pedro resumed their love affair. This went on for ten years until the old king, suspicious of Castilian pretensions to the throne of Portugal, consented to Inês de Castro's assassination, which took place on January 7, 1355. Two years later, when Dom Pedro ascended the throne, he revealed that he had been secretly married to Inês, who had been the future queen of Portugal. He had her body exhumed, dressed it in a purple robe, and crowned her in a ceremony in which he forced the courtiers who had rejected her to kiss her lifeless hand. He then placed her in her tomb in Alcobaça and planned his own tomb across from it, in the south transept.

Batalha

MONASTERY

Hours: Open summer, daily 9AM–7PM; winter, daily 9AM–5PM. Admission fee.

This Gothic monastery, begun in 1387 but built mainly in the fifteenth century, like the monastery at Alcobaça, owes its construction to a vow. King John I promised to build a monastery when the Portuguese defeated the Spanish, which they did at the Battle of Aljubarrota (1385). This battle resulted in the expulsion of the Spanish army and assured Portuguese independence from Spain.

Its richly decorated **facade** is a delight to behold from a distance as well as close up. It has flying buttresses supporting the nave and choir, and, on the left, one of the finest cloisters in the Manueline style in Portugal. Here you will find some of the richest surface decoration on any piece of architecture in Europe, depicting sea shells and twisted ropes intermingled with exotic Oriental forms.

The **interior** of the church has soaring multiclustered piers that rise to a quadripartite English-type vault. There is a clerestory but no triforium. To the right of the entrance is the square **Founder's Chapel** (1434) which has a lantern tower supported by columns. The tomb of King John I and those of his wife and children are here, including that of his famous son Prince Henry the Navigator, all under Gothic canopies.

In the eastern end of the church, John's successor, Edward, started to build a great **funeral rotunda**. Though it was continued by Manuel the Great, who gave his name to the Manueline style, it was never completed. One enters it through a porch containing a sixteenth-century doorway decorated in the most elaborate Manueline design, which is carried over into the unfinished, octagonally shaped roofless chapel.

The elevations of the structure at Batalha follow the French Gothic style; the vaults, with longitudinal and lateral ridge-ribs, follow English examples; the facade is like the English Perpendicular style; the spire on the tower is German in appearance; the fussy tracery on the facade is of French flamboyant·pattern; and the flat roofs, which could be called Portuguese, are also common to the Mediterranean. Batalha is thus an excellent example of Portuguese eclecticism. While the architects may not have succeeded in creating a distinct national style, they did succeed in creating a beautiful Gothic building.

_____Lisbon_____

Museums

THE GULBENKIAN CENTER FOR ARTS AND CULTURE

Ave de Berna, 45

Hours: Open Tues., Thurs., Fri., Sun., 10AM–5PM; Wed., Sat., 2–8PM; Admission fee weekdays; free admission weekends.

This museum, opened in 1969, houses part of the collection of the late Armenian oil magnate Calouste Gulbenkian. The variety of the collection is staggering. During his lifetime Gulbenkian collected over 3,000 items that range from 4,000-year-old Egyptian sculpture to modern art. In addition to Persian, Mesopotamian, and oriental treasures, the museum contains one of the world's great collections of Islamic art.

The European collection is distinguished by its excellent paintings from the Hermitage Museum in Leningrad. These Gulbenkian purchased from the Soviet government in 1929 and include two paintings by Rembrandt (1606–69), *Portrait of an Old Man* and *Pallas Athene;* an adoring portrait by Rubens (1577–1640) of his young wife Helena Fourment; a landscape, *Fête à Rambouillet,* by Fragonard (1732–1806); and *Cupid and the Three Graces* by Boucher (1703–70). The Hermitage purchase also includes the statue of *Diana* by Houdon (1741–1828) and a collection of silver made for Catherine the Great.

A modern wing is devoted primarily to Portuguese art, where the paintings of Almada Negreiros (1893–1970), Portugal's best-known modern artist, can be seen. Though technically skillful, his art, like that of so many other Portuguese artists represented here, is not original, being derived from leading European and American schools.

All this is displayed with taste and care in a modern structure of concrete, bronze, and glass, with each room designed to fit the objects it displays. The building itself is designed around the collection, and its location in a seventeen-acre park in the center of Lisbon makes it appealing.

MUSEUM OF ANCIENT ART

Rua das Janelas Verdes, 95

Hours: Open Tues., Wed., Fri., Sat., 10AM–5PM; Thurs., Sun., 10AM–7PM. Admission fee.

Established in 1883 in the former palace of the counts of Alvor, this is Portugal's national art museum and the best place to see Portuguese painting, which largely begins in the fifteenth century. It is an art that has always been affected by influences from outside the country, never establishing itself as a great school of national painting. That is why Portuguese painting has never won fame outside the country.

Yet Portugal did produce two noteworthy painters, Nuno Gonçalves and Domingos António Sequeira. Of the two, the fifteenth-century Gonçalves is the greater, but Sequeira (1768–1834) is also a painter who can be considered an old master. The museum has a collection of his neoclassical allegorical scenes. The originality of his portraits shows that he was not bound by neoclassicist conventions and may be considered a romantic. See Sequeira's work, with other Portuguese paintings, one flight up on the first floor.

Gonçalves, Nuno (active 1450–71), Portuguese

St. Vincent Altarpiece (ca. 1467–70): first floor
This large polyptych, of which two central panels and four lateral ones survive, marks the beginning of the Portuguese school of painting. It was found in 1882 in the monastery of São Vicente de Fora in Lisbon, and attributed to Nuno Gonçalves. Each oil painting has figures paying homage to the youthful martyr St. Vincent, seen in the two large panels. The others in this vast gallery of figures consist of the king and courtiers, knights, the clergy, fishermen (a reminder of the importance of the sea to Portugal), and a member of the Jewish community (he is the man in the far right-hand panel holding an open book referring to the Old Law). This array is a cross-section of Portuguese society in the fifteenth century.

Note that the style of the painting, though inflexibly ironed flat, is somewhat like that of the van Eycks of Flanders. Perhaps Gonçalves was influenced by Jan van Eyck when he came to Portugal in 1428 to paint the portrait of the daughter of King John I, who married van Eyck's patron, Philip the Good, duke of Burgundy. Gonçalves's work makes use of the same Flemish lustrous oil technique, the realistic observation of faces and other details, and the mannerism of Flemish portraiture. A difference is in the absence of a precise indoor or outdoor setting—rooms filled with objects or landscapes that depict every flower. Gonçalves's composition disregards space and concentrates on rows of figures, one after the other, like people in a tapestry. He captures the mood of these people, subordinating the religious theme and de-emphasizing the background.

The museum's collection of foreign paintings on the ground floor reaches its heights with the *Temptation of St. Anthony*, by Bosch (ca. 1450–1516) (see below), *Salome*, by Cranach (1472–1553), *St. Jerome*, by Dürer (1471–1528), a *Virgin and Child*, by Memling (1435–94), *Virgin and Child with Saints*, by Holbein the Elder (ca. 1460–1524), and a fine painting, *The Twelve Apostles*, by Zurbarán (1598–1664). There is also a collection of gold and silver objects formerly in the possession of Portugal's royal family.

Bosch, Hieronymus* (ca. 1450–1516), Flemish

The Temptation of St. Anthony: ground floor, room 4
This painting marks the pinnacle of Bosch's achievement. He may have been inspired to paint it by a cult of St. Anthony in the town where he lived, but most likely the story of the saint's ascetic life in the desert, where he experienced hallucinations, provided the occasion for Bosch to employ his inventive imagery. The St. Anthony story best expresses themes that dominated Bosch's art: man's pursuit of the flesh at the expense of his spiritual welfare, and the monastic ideal of a life secure from the world in anticipation of God. Bosch's monsters and devils in *The Temptation of St. Anthony* are the most original of his demonic inventions; this painting represents the creation of a new iconography in Western art.

The hallucinations that beset the saint assume two forms: the demonic and the erotic. In the left panel we see the saint borne aloft on the backs of demons and, in the center portion, worn out by his attackers, he is helped back to his hut by fellow hermits. Under the bridge, demons plan their next attack while a demon messenger skates toward the saint with a letter (possibly a letter of indulgence). At the lower left a bird gulps down its newly hatched young and, on the road ahead of the saint, a group of demons is approaching the saint's hut, which has become a brothel. A kneeling man is shown in an obscene posture, his head pierced by an arrow (indicating that lust leads to folly and self-destruction). In the right panel, the devil queen appears nude under a rotting tree surrounded by her cohorts. St. Anthony turns the other way only to be beckoned to a grotesque outdoor feast given by agents of the devil. In the background the devil-queen's castle is shown, complete with a dragon swimming in the moat.

The culmination of this havoc, unleashed by the devil, takes place in the center panel whose composition, like the other two panels, is a large landscape with many small figures. Even the main figure of St. Anthony, and the master demon orchestrating the chaos and horror—the man dressed in red with a black top hat sitting against the parapet with his back to us—are set in the middle ground. The composition indicates that the painting is more than an episode out of the life of a saint—it is a depiction of the human condition. St. Anthony and his temptations represent the situation of the human soul in a world of sin, ravaged by the fires of hell and dominated by the devil. We can see that a black mass, or "witches' sabbath," is being conducted. Almost overwhelmed by the crowd of demonic figures coming from all directions, St. Anthony is positioned between Christ, in the ruined tower, and satan, leaning against the parapet. He faces the viewer with his right hand raised in blessing, a gesture echoed by Christ within the tower. Thus St. Anthony has overcome the power of the devil and emerges triumphant through the strength of his faith in Jesus Christ. His steady gaze is one of assurance.

Buildings

JERÓNIMOS MONASTERY

Praça do Império (near the Tower of Belem facing the river.)

Hours: Open daily 8AM–9PM. Free admission.

This celebrated Hieronymite monastery (dedicated to the followers of St. Jerome) is the largest in Portugal and one of the largest in Europe. It was built between 1502 and 1519 to honor Vasco da Gama, who in 1497 sailed from near the site to India, thus opening up the east to Portugal and bringing great wealth to the country. Da Gama's tomb is in the church.

As a sixteenth-century work that fuses flamboyant Gothic with early Renaissance designs, the monastery is an example of the Manueline style, derived from a mixture of the dominant styles of other countries—often the flamboyant northern style and the plateresque style of Spain—to create something like an original Portuguese design. It takes its name from Dom Manuel I who reigned from 1495 to 1521, and is characterized by fantastic forms used as surface decoration: twisting ropelike shapes intermixed with sea-shell and Oriental designs.

The convent church in this complex, **Santa Maria de Belem**, which has three naves of the same height covered by a single vault, is well endowed with Manueline decoration, inside and out, and has ornate carvings, especially in its **south door**. It also has an octagonal cloister with a double gallery vaulted throughout and sumptuously decorated with sculpture.

TOWER OF BELEM

Avenida Marginal, on the Tagus River

Hours: Open Tues.–Sun., 10AM–5PM; closed holidays. Admission fee.

This piece of military architecture, located close to the Jerónimos Monastery, was built between 1515 and 1520 and is also an example of the Manueline style. It has a mixture of Gothic and Venetian elements with a blocklike tower rising from a fortified terrace that dominates the river. True to its style, it is embellished with designs of rope and knot moldings, cupolas, cornucopia spires, flowerlike surface forms, and other imaginative twisting and turning decorative features.

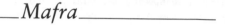

Mafra

MONASTERY

Hours: Open Wed.–Mon., 10AM–5PM; closed Dec. 25. Admission fee.

The childless King John V of Portugal made a vow to build a monastery if God granted him and his wife a child. The couple had a daughter, so the building project began at Mafra in 1717. At first John intended to build a small facility, but the plan grew in proportion to the growth of his wealth, derived from a royal tax of a fifth of all gold and diamonds mined in the Portuguese colony of Brazil. A German goldsmith, J. F. Ludovice (1670–1752), was put in charge of the building. He employed Italian architects and some 30,000 craftsmen from all over Europe. The work proceeded rapidly and the basilica was consecrated in 1730.

The **basilica** is the focus of the front facade that is one side of a gridiron of 850 square feet, which includes a palace surrounded by courtyards. Thus the church and convent are a part of the palace, an arrangement similar to that found in German baroque monasteries. However, Italian architectural elements prevail, such as in the facade wings connecting the end pavilions to the church, the nave of the basilica, the bulbous spires, the Roman Doric arcade of the courtyard, and the concavely curved drum and dome, the first great baroque dome erected in Portugal.

Notice the many marble Italianate statues and altarpieces in the basilica. So much sculpture was shipped to Mafra from Italy, or was made at the workshops at Mafra, that a school of sculpture grew up around the monastery which spread the art throughout Portugal.

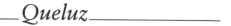

Queluz

ROYAL PALACE

Hours: Open Fri.–Wed., 10AM–5PM. Admission fee.

If you have seen the baroque palace-convent at Mafra, you will find that the palace at Queluz, a good part of which was built between 1747 and 1752, represents a reaction against that earlier monumentality. It was intended to be a summer palace, not a religious complex, and is designed in the eighteenth-century rococo style, with a pastel-colored exterior. Some of its decorations inside and out are as dainty as its pink and white colors, but there is also a rustic quality about the place that makes it somewhat heavier than French taste would have permitted.

The central part of the palace is the two-storied block at the north end of the garden court, surrounded on three sides by low buildings faced with garlanded windows. The park facade is grander, with Doric columns and a theatrical cascade of stairs. The palace as a whole has changing facades and is always both lovely and interesting to look at from any viewpoint. The interior is what you would expect of a great rococo palace: a light design embellished with huge chandeliers and blue-and-white tiles covering the lower half of the walls. It has an elegant touch throughout.

Sintra
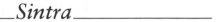

In this lush elevated section of Portugal the country houses of the nobility of Europe and Portugal are in a tradition started by the kings of Portugal. Kings have inhabited the Moorish-style **Sintra Palace** (open daily, 10AM–5PM; closed Tues.; admission fee), erected over the remains of an eighth-century Arab structure, since the time of King John 1 in the fourteenth century. The most striking feature of the exterior is the pair of conical chimneys, resembling inverted funnels, that go well with the Manueline decorative elements. Notice, also, the painted ceilings of the interior. None are more lovely than the ceiling of the **Hall of Swans,** whose painting of swans with crown-shaped collars of gold was ordered by the king in 1432 to remind him of his daughter, who had been delighted by two pet swans sent her by her fiancé Philip the Good, duke of Burgundy, before she left Sintra to live with him in Flanders.

A short distance away is **Pena Palace** (open daily, 10AM–5PM; closed Tues.; admission fee), a nineteenth-century construction located on one of the highest peaks in the area. It was built around an old monastery in a conglomeration of several styles, and includes Arab minarets and Gothic turrets. Actually, the palace's surroundings are more interesting and enjoyable than the buildings, and are worth more of your attention.

Tomar
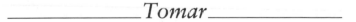

THE CONVENT OF CHRIST

Hours: Open daily 9AM–12:30PM and 2–6PM (to 5PM Sept. 23–Mar. 21). Admission fee.

This great monastery of the Knights of Christ was built from the twelfth to the seventeenth century around the preceeding Knights Templar sanctuary, or **rotunda,** and contains seven cloisters. It is richly designed and decorated to express Christianity triumphant in the world of exploration and conquest, the time when Portuguese explorers in ships bearing the red cross of the Knights of Christ on their sails opened up the East for commerce and imperialistic adventure.

The twelfth-century rotunda leads into a late Gothic building that includes a chapter house containing a remarkable **window,** the finest example of Manueline decoration in Portugal, covered with an array of spiraling coils reminiscent of Indian temples and Moorish mosques as well as with northern Gothic forms. The exotic shapes contain references to the sea, since the window was intended as a monument to Vasco da Gama. It took imagination to arrange the ropes, seaweed, coral, fishing nets, and other decorations into a single architectural framework.

Of the seven cloisters, the outstanding one is the **main cloister,** constructed between 1557 and 1560 in the Renaissance style. The cloister's skillful manipulation of Doric and Ionic columns is reminiscent of Roman architecture, and as a Renaissance structure it is almost unmatched in sixteenth-century Portuguese architecture. Another example of the classic Renaissance mix is found part way up the hill that leads from the town of Tomar to the Convent. It is the small Chapel of the Conception (Consepção), built about 1550, with a pure classical design outside and a Renaissance style in the manner of Brunelleschi inside.

Spain

Napoleon said that "Europe ends at the Pyrenees." While it is true that Spain is somewhat isolated geographically, she shares Europe's political, cultural, and religious heritage to an extent that makes the emperor's statement mere French chauvinism. Still, a look at Spanish art does lend credence to the concept of Spain as non-European, for it is strikingly different from the art of France, Italy, Germany, and the Low Countries.

Spain's uniqueness in this area arises from dual aspects of a single historical fact—the domination of the Moors from the eighth to the eleventh centuries. The elaborate surface decoration of many of Spain's finest buildings is of Moorish origin, and the Islamic emphasis on nonrepresentational design continued to exert a strong influence on Spanish art even after the Christian conquest. The intensity and long duration of the Christian struggle against the Moors left a fanatical strain of religiosity in Spanish art, making it morbid and mystical compared to medieval art in the other countries of Europe. This combination of styles—the Moorish and the Christian—gives Spanish art a quality not found elsewhere.

Spain has fostered the development of some of the most original artists in Europe. The country's fervent Catholicism has not inhibited the individuality essential to creative genius. In the case of El Greco (1541–1614), a Greek by birth but a Spaniard by choice, religion was an inspiration. Though El Greco worked within the religious context that had given rise to so much mediocrity in late sixteenth-century Spanish painting, his artistic expression is so individual that he belongs to no school. Those who came after him learned from his example, and his influence extends as far as twentieth-century expressionism.

Velázquez (1599–1660), generally considered to be Spain's greatest artist, painted for the Spanish royal court instead of the church. Even against this background of conservatism, Velázquez anticipated impressionism by his use of light and color, 200 years before the movement emerged in France.

With Goya (1746–1828), the individuality that had become a hallmark of Spanish painters began to border on the radical. Goya was so far ahead of his time that some of his paintings resemble the best modern art.

Spanish architecture, characterized by a highly developed sense of individuality, also falls into familiar European categories: Romanesque, Gothic, Renaissance, and baroque. At best, the Moorish influence gave Spanish interpretations of these styles a character of their own; at times an ornate surface decoration called plateresque dominates the design. Plateresque decoration is still popular in Spain today.

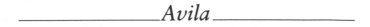

Avila

Avila is known for the **town walls** that enclose the medieval city. With their eighty-eight twelfth-century towers and nine city gates, they are one of the most fascinating sights in Spain, best seen from the road to Salamanca. The walls are such an important part of the town that the **cathedral's apse** is built right into the eastern angle of the wall. The apse is also the most interesting part of the cathedral, otherwise a cold, dark structure, grim in contrast to the rest of Avila. Its slim shafts, enclosing the apse, owe a debt to French design, and it was probably a Frenchman who started building it in 1160.

Avila's Gothic **Church of San Vicente** (just outside the city walls on the east side, the same side as the cathedral [open 11:30AM–2PM]) also has the French to thank for the twelfth-century sculptures on its south portal, which resemble those on the tympanum of Vézelay in Burgundy. The Avila artist used a sense of unimpeded movement to relate the figures to each other. The freely flowing draperies of the column figures have been beautifully rendered and, inside the Romanesque interior, the cenotaph reliefs tell of the martyrdom of St. Vincent and his two sisters, St. Sabina and St. Cristeta, with refined and delicate touches (ca. 1180).

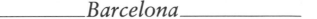

Barcelona

Museums

MUSEUM OF CATALAN ART

National Palace, Montjuich Park

Hours: Open Tues.–Sun., 9:30AM–1:30PM. Admission fee.

This museum has an important collection of Romanesque and Spanish Gothic frescoes and altarpieces assembled from provincial Catalonian churches.

The superb twelfth-century wall paintings are of greatest interest, especially those from San Clemente at Tahull. Of these, *Christ in Majesty* (room 14), by an artist known to us today only as the **Master of Tahull**, is the finest example. In this work you will find the traditional Byzantine linear rendering of Christ, but with a strength of characterization usually missing from Italian-Byzantine work of the period. It is one of the finest examples of the Romanesque style in painting anywhere in Europe.

Take notice of the Gothic altarpiece by **Luis Dalmau** (active 1428–60), *The Madonna of the Aldermen of Barcelona* (no. 1 in room 60). This outstanding work of Gothic painting was executed in 1445 by an artist who had been sent to Flanders by his patron, Alfonso V. If you have seen the great van Eyck masterpiece in Ghent, *The Adoration of the Lamb,* which Luis Dalmau also saw, you will notice the extent to which the Barcelona altarpiece was inspired by van Eyck's work (the singing angels are almost exact copies).

Rather than single out any of the fine works in this museum, you should look at the collection as a whole, letting yourself sink into the medieval world of Catalonia where religion was the all-encompassing totality of life. The **museum's building,** a huge palace built for the 1929 Exposition, covers nearly eight acres of ground on Montjuich Hill, which affords views in one direction over the port of Barcelona, and in the other over the entire city. The museum's Great Hall covers more than one acre, with a ceiling at a height of over sixty feet. It is a splendid setting for a collection of ecclesiastical art that represents the triumph of the church over the Dark Ages and the great awakening of European civilization.

MIRÓ CENTER FOR CONTEMPORARY ART

Montjuich Park

Hours: Open Tues.–Sun., 11AM–8PM. Admission fee.

Close to the Museum of Catalan Art is the Miró Foundation. Joan Miró (1893–1985), a Catalan by birth, established it to display avant-garde works. José Louis Sert, his friend and fellow Catalan, who was dean of Harvard's School of Architecture, designed the building. It offers a constant variety of shows and exhibitions, and is a wonderful setting for Miró's art. His great tapestry and oil paintings, and his sculpture placed in and around the building and on an outdoor terrace overlooking Barcelona, show Miró as a surrealist who writes in a language of his own as much as he paints images that invade every part of his canvases. These images, familiar, unexpected, and fanciful, are statements of the unconscious; a spontaneous and natural flow for which Miró said, "I have no responsibility." His objects are short statements of what for Miró is their most characteristic trait—most often the ones we least expect. That is what makes his simple-looking pictures complex. We expect to see a representation of Miró's ideas on canvas; instead, Miró packages them in hieroglyphic archetypical figurations.

PICASSO MUSEUM

Calle de Montcada, 15

Hours: Open Mon., 4–8:30PM; Tues.–Sun., 9:30AM–1:30PM and 4–8:30PM. Admission fee.

Picasso lived in France for sixty-nine years, but Spain and Barcelona were stamped on his personality. Barcelona was the city where Picasso came to live at the age of fourteen, where he became an artist and first began to study modern art. He was always friendly to the idea of a Picasso museum in Barcelona, and when one developed there he supported it generously.

The museum was founded when Jaime Sabartés, a native of Barcelona and friend and secretary of Picasso, presented his collection of Picasso's work to the city. The Berenguer d'Aguilar Palace, dating to the fifteenth century, was chosen as the site to display it, and the Picasso museum opened in 1963. Later the museum received an impetus from the artist himself, who donated fifty-eight paintings, including his *Maids of Honor* series (forty-four paintings based on the theme of Velázquez's famous painting, *The Maids of Honor*). In 1970 Picasso donated more than 800 of his early works.

Picasso, Pablo * (1881–1973), Spanish, lived in France

Maids of Honor Series (1957)
This series of paintings, based on Velázquez's *Maids of Honor (Las Meninas)* in the Prado Museum, Madrid, was not the only time Picasso did variations based on the work of an old master. Prior to the *Maids of Honor* series, which was done after Picasso moved to the villa La Californie at Cannes in 1954, he did a series after Delacroix's *Women of Algiers,* and had worked on a Poussin, Cranach, Courbet, El Greco, Manet, and Giorgione. Studying the work of others was Picasso's way to reexamine the problems of art.

In Velázquez's painting he studies the relationship between the painter, his model, and the viewer. Velázquez shows himself painting the Spanish royal couple, whom we see in a mirror on the back wall. The Spanish princess and her ladies-in-waiting are viewing the scene. Though they give the painting its title they are not the main subject. Finally, viewers of the painting are able to stand at a position outside the painting that is level with the king and queen.

This interaction between artist, model, and viewer fascinated Picasso. He produced forty-four variations of it, reaching out in various directions within the cubist technique. Sometimes he paints the figures separately, sometimes in groups. He achieves Velázquez's effect of distance by overlapping dark and light planes. He feels so much at home with Velázquez's painting that he paints his own paintings into the picture. Thus he brings Velázquez into the twentieth century through his own personal artistic language and forges a link between modern art and great art of the past: each artist's exploration of form and space.

MODERN MUSEUM OF ART

Cindadela Park

Hours: Open daily 9AM–7PM. Admission fee.

This museum is mainly devoted to the works of Barcelona artists from the end of the eighteenth century to the early twentieth century. Its one hall of contemporary art adjoins an **inner courtyard** that has an exciting display of sculpture by Josep Guinovart I. Bertran, a Barcelona artist born in 1927. Carved tree trunks in various sizes and shapes—some painted, some with metal canopies, some decorated with cord—clutter the space, bending and seemingly reaching to their sides and thrusting upward to make contact with hanging mobiles. Mirrors surrounding them add to a forestlike feeling.

Buildings

No two ecclesiastical structures in one city are more unalike than the **Cathedral of Barcelona** (Plaza de la Cathedral) and the **Church of the Sagrada Familia** (between the plaza Sagrada Familia and the plaza Gaudí). More than 500 years separates the construction of the traditional Gothic cathedral and the modern church, a fantastic structure without historical precedent.

The **cathedral** (open daily 7:30AM–1:30PM and 4–7:30PM) was founded in 1298 but completed in the fifteenth century. It has a three-aisled nave, a transept that does not project beyond the outer walls, an ambulatory, and chapels in the recesses between the buttresses. The height of its nave and aisles give a French Gothic feeling and its spatial design is reminiscent of the German hall-church. A huge collection of art treasures has remained intact through the centuries. In the Barcelona Cathedral you can get a better idea of what a great church looked like in the Middle Ages than in almost any other place. Among its many altarpieces and other works of art, see, in the third chapel in the ambulatory (on the side of the cloisters), the fifteenth-century altarpiece by **Barnardo Martorell** (d. ca. 1452), *Altarpiece of the Transfiguration* (1449). No other Gothic painter in Spain seems to have reached Martorell's degree of refinement. His drawing is meticulous; though done in the Gothic international style, with an overabundance of rich elements, nothing detracts from the main theme. It is a perfect blend between the essential and the accessory.

The Romanesque door leading from the church to the cloister (viewed from the cloister) has white marble carvings that may date back as far as the eleventh century. The **cloister** itself is a fifteenth-century garden with palm and orange trees and a small pond with geese. Its fountain has a delicate little sculpture (fifteenth century) of St. George slaying the dragon. At the far corner of the cloister is the **Chapel of Santa Lucia,** a survivor of the old Romanesque cathedral that stood on the site. Its exterior facade has Romanesque carvings. Another chapel in the cloister serves as the **cathedral museum** (open 11AM–1PM; small admission fee). Here is *La Piedad* (Piety), an intensely moving painting on wood by Bartolomé Bermejo (active 1474–95) showing the dead Christ on Mary's lap with blood pouring from his side.

The door leaving the cloister (Door of Piety), opposite the fountain, has fifteenth century carvings possibly done by the German sculptor Michael Lochner. A second door leaving the cloister exits onto the Calle Obispo Irurita. Walking toward Plaza San Jaime, the **wall of the Flamboyant Gothic chapel,** part of the Provincial Council building (Generalitat), is ornamented with gargoyles, lattice work, and a medallion of the Catalan patron, St. George, slaying the dragon. Crossing the plaza, the City Hall (Ayuntamiento) has a facade on the small street of the Ciudad that dates back to the Gothic period. Inside the City Hall (open Mon.–Fri., 10AM–1PM and 5–7PM) the **Salon of the One Hundred** is named for the occasion, in 1374, when the city's 100 guildes met to form a city council. The Gothic arches and delicate rosette window of this room contrast sharply with the Chronicle Room next door with its ornate Victorian decoration.

The **Church of Santa Maria del Mar,** close to the Picasso Museum, is one of the best examples of early Catalonian Gothic style. A seamen's church built in the 1300s, it has a simple truncated facade flanked by two towers. Inside, the nave has an immense vault with an unusually wide distance— about fourteen yards—between the supporting arches. Beautiful stained glass windows, illuminating the entire church, lessen the severity of the austere functional architecture.

The **Church of the Sagrada Familia** was begun in 1883 and remains unfinished today. Its architect, the Catalan **Antonio Gaudí** (1852–1926), worked on it intermittently until his death in 1926. The church was begun by another architect as a neo-Gothic structure, but when Gaudí took it over he superimposed so many of his own imaginative designs and made such ingenious use of materials that it became a completely original structure. While reminiscent of Moorish, African, and Gothic designs, it is completely original. Its abstract decorative details are a delight, particularly the design of its wrought-iron, but its outstanding features are the four spires of one transept. Looking like corncobs that taper into sunbursts, the spires soar 350 feet high.

Elsewhere in Barcelona, Gaudí attempted to translate the sinuous lines and organic shapes of art nouveau into architectural terms. The **Casa Battló** (1905–7), at 43 Paseo de Gracia, looks like it was molded out of dough and garnished with whipped cream. The larger **Casa Mila** (1905–10), at 92 Paseo de Gracia, does not have the colorful mosaics of the smaller structure, but has twisting and turning stone forms and wrought-iron balcony railings that provide a burst of energy and excitement the smaller structure does not have. Gaudí enthusiasts should also see **Güell Palace,** just off the Ramblas on the Calle Nueva dela Rambla (open daily 11AM–2PM and 5–8PM, except holidays). Gaudí built it for his patron, Eusebio Güell, a rich nobleman. Its exterior is plain for a Gaudí building, but inside there are more than forty different types of columns made of a variety of materials, and imaginative designs for windows, doors, ornaments, and furniture. Gaudí's designs are also seen in **Güell Park,** a park the Güell family donated to the city. It has Gaudí's serpentine bench that encircles the playground, and imaginative gates and buildings.

Burgos

CATHEDRAL OF SANTA MARIA

Hours: Open daily 10AM–1:30PM and 4–6:30PM. Admission fee.

The Gothic cathedral at Burgos was begun in 1221 and took over 300 years to complete. From 1442 onward, three generations of the same family worked on it, which may account for the harmonious exterior, which consists of twenty-two pinnacles and spires rising high. When silhouetted against a blue sky or lit up at night, it is the main attraction at Burgos. A closer look at the building leaves much to be desired: restoration done in the eighteenth century to its west front replaced old portals with cold, uninviting classical doorways; there is a slight crudity to the filigree spires that betrays the German origin of their designer, Hans of Cologne (father of the family of architects mentioned above). The central lantern is overdone, with a mixture of Gothic and Renaissance plateresque details, and the tall-galleried screen walls of its three entrance fronts are out of place in a cathedral with low-pitched roofs.

Apart from these many defects, the **interior**, with its ornate chapels, will not fail to impress you. The huge octagonal chapel at the east end (**Capilla del Condestable,** 1482–94) has an attractive plateresque decoration, and the upward view into the vault, enriched with stained glass through the tracery, is magnificent.

The storied cloisters and old chapter house date to the first half of the fourteenth century. The cloisters have a diocesan museum containing a collection of tapestries and other works of art.

Cordova

LA MEZQUITA (CATHEDRAL)

Hours: Open Apr.–Sept., 10:30AM–1:30PM and 3:30–7PM; Oct.–Mar., 10:30AM–1:30PM and 3:30–6PM. Admission fee.

The site of the Mezquita (mosque) was once occupied by a Roman temple and later by a Visigothic church. After the Moslem conquest of Córdoba in 711, the church was used as a place of worship by both Moslems and Christians. In 785, the Christians sold it to Abdal-Rahman I who pulled it down and built this great mosque on its site. Later, the Mezquita became the largest Moslem house of worship after the mosque in Mecca, establishing Córdova as the western center of Islam and absolving the Moslems in Spain from having to make the long pilgrimage to Mecca. After the Christians reconquered Córdova in 1236, the Mezquita was converted into a Christian church by the insertion of a few chapels into its interior. Then, in 1523, Charles V authorized the construction of a cruciform church within the Mezquita. Although it took about 100 years to complete the church, Charles had second thoughts about the project as early as 1526. When he saw the construction he said, "You have built here what you or anyone might have built anywhere else, but you have destroyed what was unique in the world."

Still, the Mezquita is an exciting sight in its present condition. Its original dimensions are so great that it swallows up the cathedral within it. Most of the original 856 **columns** of porphyry, jasper, and multicolored marble, many with capitals taken from Roman and Visigothic buildings, are only about thirteen feet high, but the double rows of horseshoe arches increase the overall height of the roof. (These arches are not of Moorish origin but taken by the Moors from the Visigoths.) There is a mesmerizing effect in the many rows of these columns and the heavy vaults they support. See the small octagonal **Mihrab** (chapel) on the southeast side of the Mezquita. It is roofed over with a single piece of carved white marble and its outer walls inlaid with sumptuous mosaics from Byzantium.

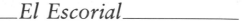

El Escorial

SAN LORENZO DEL ESCORIAL

Hours: Open Tues.–Sun., 10AM–1PM and 3–7PM (winter until 6PM); closed holidays. Admission fee.

This sixteenth-century monastery consists of a church, which also contains the mausoleum of the Spanish monarchs (Pantheon of the Kings), and a royal palace and museum. It is so large and its walls so austere that it may be better viewed from a distance. Close up, the walls, which lack projecting windows to create an interplay of light and shadow, can be monotonous. The building's history helps explain its somber appearance. It was built by Philip II to commemorate his army's victory over the French in the Battle of San Quentin in 1557. During the battle, the Spanish destroyed a church dedicated to St. Lawrence, on his feast day, August 10. In atonement, Philip dedicated his immense monastery-palace-tomb to St. Lawrence, whose gruesome martyrdom may have appealed to him. It is probably no coincidence that the ground plan of the Escorial recalls the gridiron on which St. Lawrence was roasted alive. A large quadrilateral was built between 1563 and 1584. It is 225 yards long by 175 yards wide and encloses a church. There are 2,700 windows, 1,200 doorways, and eighty-six staircases. The monastery occupies the left side of the complex with cloisters called the Patio de los Evangelistas adjoining the church.

Church

The church is approached from the Escorial's main entrance (tourists use the entrance on the opposite side of the building to enter the Escorial), which leads into the principal courtyard, the Patio de los Reyes. Six gigantic statues of Old Testament monarchs adorn the main facade, which has huge Doric columns at ground level. The great dome of the church, which is a beautiful Italian Renaissance structure, cannot be seen from the courtyard. View it from the car and bus park or even further away.

Inside the church, the plan is a Greek cross with four great piers faced with fluted pilasters that support the huge dome. It was built with the plan of St. Peter's in Rome in mind, but on a smaller scale. In keeping with the overall look at the Escorial, it has plain granite surfaces, but the presence of a number of works of art relieve the austerity—a great retable at the east wall, paintings, and sculpture by Leone and Pompeo Leoni.

Pantheon of the Kings
This octagonal crypt lies underneath the church. It is unique in having niches in its wall, one on top of the other, for the sarcophagi of thirty-six Spanish monarchs. Less important members of the Spanish royal family are accommodated in an adjoining room. While there are marble and gilt bronze decorations in this hall of death, nothing can relieve the feeling of gloom that is often associated with the Spanish Hapsburg kings.

Palace
The palace occupies about one fourth of the Escorial's total space and is located on the left side of the complex. The **apartments of Philip II** consists of a series of relatively small, bare rooms of which Philip's modest bedroom is the main attraction. A wooden partition opened beside his bed so that, bedridden during his last months, he could watch mass being celebrated in the church. A copy of Bosch's *Hay Wain* can be seen here (original in the Prado), together with some other Flemish and German pictures that Philip liked.

The presence of lovely rococo decoration and furnishings in much of the rest of the palace is due to the later occupancy of it by Bourbon kings in the eighteenth century, who used it as a summer residence. Thanks to them the walls are covered with tapestries which, in the Banquet Hall, include a number of genre scenes by Goya.

New Museum
This museum, located at the north end of the palace, was created in 1963 in several vaulted rooms restored for displaying the best paintings of the Escorial. The finest of these include, in room 1, four paintings by Bosch (ca. 1450–1516), including the *Mocking of Christ;* and a small triptych, *Descent from the Cross* by Gerard David (ca. 1460–1523); in room 3, paintings by Titian (ca. 1487–1576); in room 4, more paintings by Titian, including a large *Last Supper;* and paintings by Tintoretto (1518–94), including a very fine *Birth of Christ;* in room 5, paintings by Ribera (1591–1652) done in the Italian style; and in room 6 an interesting large religious painting, *The Tunic,* by Velázquez (1599–1660). Above these rooms are two large rooms containing *Christ on the Cross between the Virgin and St. John,* by Rogier van der Weyden (ca. 1399–1464), in which the fine modeling of the figures stand out against the dark background to make a powerful religious statement; and the *Martyrdom of St. Maurice,* by El Greco, arguably the best painting in the Escorial.

El Greco* (1541–1614), Spanish

Martyrdom of St. Maurice
This large painting was commissioned by Philip II in 1579 for the chapel of the saint in the church of the Escorial. It tells the story of the soldier saint and his Theban Legion (Roman troops from Thebes in Egypt) who served in

Gaul in the third century. Under the influence of Maurice (from Moorish), they refused to worship pagan gods and were executed by the Emperor Maximian Herculeus.

On the left side the executions have begun. Maurice is seen in two places, conversing with his staff in the foreground and mourning the dead soldiers at the side. The blues and yellows, which predominate, lessen the severity of the scene, and the serpentine composition of the doomed legionaries is unusual. The masses of naked human bodies recall Michelangelo, though Italian influence in this painting has almost vanished, being replaced by a new realism and relentlessness of detail that is entirely Spanish. El Greco's signature is on the paper held in the serpent's mouth, the symbol of evil or of earth (lower right hand corner).

Though this painting is considered a great work of art today, it did not satisfy the king, and El Greco received no further royal commissions. It was relegated to an unimportant corner of the palace and only properly reinstated by Velázquez, who admired El Greco. The king's rejection of the painting, putting an end to El Greco's brief association with the court, was El Greco's loss but posterity's gain. Henceforth, El Greco was able to paint as he pleased, a free man in Toledo.

Granada

ALHAMBRA

Hours: Open daily 9AM–7PM; closed Dec. 25, Jan. 1 and Good Friday. Admission fee.

The Alhambra was built by the Arab conquerors of Spain as a fortress (its name is a corruption of the Arabic "red castle"), a palace and harem, and a residence for court officials and their families. Construction was carried out mainly in the fourteenth century. Its two finest sections, the Court of Myrtles and the Court of the Lions, were built under different rulers: Yusuf I (1334–54) and Mohammed V (1392–1408). After the Spanish Catholic kings conquered it in 1492, the palace was left to decay. Charles V demolished part of it to build his adjoining Renaissance palace, which was left unfinished. Only in the second half of the nineteenth century was serious restoration begun. Although the Alhambra today is an incomparable sight, we will never fully obtain its original splendor when all of the wall decorations were intact, and luxurious furnishings, including a profusion of silk carpets, were everywhere.

The plan of the Alhambra reflects the history of its construction, during which new additions were frequently made. This partially explains why the two main open courts lie at right angles to each other, and other parts veer out, sometimes at sharp angles, from the central plan, or plans. In any case, the composition of each part is always based on the rectangle, with central courts the main focus around which rooms are arranged. If you ignore the elaborate Moorish decoration, you may conclude that the Alhambra is arranged according to the classical tradition of Greece and Rome.

Water is a vital presence in the Alhambra, whose architects valued its aesthetic qualities, though no doubt it had a practical value and some religious significance as well. Fountains play and pools shimmer in the open courts and within some of the buildings, enlivening the palace with light, sound, and movement.

Note the extraordinary surface decoration. Because Mohammed forbade representational art, associated with idol worship, Islamic artists poured their talent into elaborate design inspired by their knowledge of mathematics. Mosaic tiles cover the lower walls, with painted stucco decoration used above. Wood, also painted, is used in ceilings, beams, and eaves. The decoration was worked out according to a precise plan that took into account the height and location of doors and windows. Oddly enough, considering the planning that went into it, surface decoration was not intended to be permanent in the way such elements were considered a permanent part of Christian buildings in Europe. There was an expectation of future modification; in fact, the decorations in the Alhambra today do not all comprise the original motifs once used.

Court of Myrtles

This open court, with a long, narrow pool of water in the center, is graced by a six-columned portico at the south end. Its northern end is charming, consisting of an open portico with a small central cupola, a ceiling of wooden marquetry, and elaborately decorated niches at each end. In back of the portico is the **Sala de la Braca**, with a modern ceiling (restored in 1890) of astonishing beauty, and behind it is the **Hall of Ambassadors**, a square room built into the largest, highest tower of the Alhambra. Its wall and ceiling decorations of tiles and stucco are exquisite. The Islamic inscriptions on the walls, written in the form of poetry, say this throne room was used by Jusuf I for both business and pleasure. It is also the place where Ferdinand and Isabella signed the infamous decree expelling the Jews from Spain.

Court of the Lions

This part of the Alhambra, begun in 1377 by Mohammed V, is a favorite. The central court has a fountain resting on the backs of twelve little lions and a complete arcade running around its four sides supported by 120 white marble columns. On the western side is the **Sala de los Mozarables,** with a Renaissance ceiling. The eastern side, the Sala de los Reyes (Hall of the Kings), has three separate square units, rich vaulting, and stalactite arches. The north side leads into the Sala de las dos Hermanas (Hall of Two Sisters), whose name derives from the story that two sisters, members of the king's harem, perished from love sickness in viewing the amorous scenes in the garden below—scenes from which they were excluded. If there is any truth to the story, the sisters could not have succumbed in more beautiful surroundings. Overhead is a muquarnas cupola (a cupola with Islamic stucco work, frequently consisting of stalactite or honeycomb forms) set over an octagon. The room is surrounded on three sides by long rectangular halls, one of which leads to the elaborately decorated Mirador (lookout) de la Daraxa, overlooking the gardens of the same name. On the western side of the court is the Hall of Abencerrajes, which also has a muquarnas cupola, this one set over an eight-pointed star. The inscription on the walls of the Court of the Lions' complex indicate that it was built for pure pleasure.

PALACE OF CHARLES V

Adjoining the south side of the Alhambra

Brief mention is made here of the unfinished palace of Charles V (1516–56). Begun in 1525, it is an Italian Renaissance building with a facade in the form of a triumphal arch. Its circular center court is one of the few purely classic designs in Spain and affords a comparison between European and Arabic design. There could not be two structures of similar magnitude so unalike. The Alhambra, which is constructed in human terms, is certain to be your favorite.

GENERALIFE

Located above the Alhambra

This small complex served as the summer palace for the Islamic kings of Granada. Its Arabic name can be interpreted to mean "garden of the architect" or "noblest of gardens." While some of the buildings are earlier than those in the Alhambra, they have been altered and modernized and their surface decorations damaged. The pleasure garden with fountains and pools framed by orange trees, cypresses, and other vegetation is an illustration of the Arab genius for landscape architecture. Around its central garden court are two loggias and two complexes of buildings. There is also a view of the Alhambra below, whose plain exterior gives no hint of the richness within.

CATHEDRAL (SANTA MARÍA DE LA ENCARNACIÓN)

Off Gran Via de Colon

Hours: Open daily 10:30AM–1PM and 4–7PM. Admission fee.

This large cathedral was begun in 1523, consecrated in 1561, and completed in 1714. It is, unfortunately, a bad mixture of Renaissance and baroque elements based on a medieval plan. Even the novel idea of substituting a tall dome on stilts for a sanctuary, replacing the apse, is poorly executed. The dome rises to a majestic height of 148 feet, but its design is awkward and its baroque decoration uninspired.

Of real interest and artistic value here is the **Capilla Real (Chapel of the**

Kings [open 11AM–1PM and 4–7PM; admission fee]) attached to the south transept of the cathedral. This late Gothic building (1504–21), with finely detailed lacework vaulting, contains the **tombs of Ferdinand and Isabella,** the Catholic rulers who expelled the Moors from Spain. Their tombs have elaborately carved white marble effigies and sculptured decoration in the Renaissance style. In accordance with Isabella's will, a candle has been kept burning outside the tomb since 1521. Mementos belonging to Ferdinand and Isabella are kept in the sacristy, which also houses part of Queen Isabella's superb art collection, including works by Rogier van der Weyden, Memling, Dieric Bouts, and Botticelli.

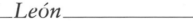

León

CATHEDRAL (SANTA MARÍA DE REGLA)

Hours for cloister: Open in summer, daily 9AM–1:30PM and 4–7PM; winter, daily 11AM–1:30PM and 5–7PM; closed Sun. afternoons. Admission fee.

The cathedral at León was begun in 1255 and, except for its towers, completed in 1303. It follows thirteenth-century northern French examples in plan, structure, and elevation, lacking only a high roof in the northern manner. Even the triple portals of its west front and south transept are arranged like those at Chartres, and many of the sculptured figures have the refined faces one sees at the cathedral at Reims.

The principles of northern Gothic architecture were applied at León on a reduced scale, which structurally weakened the building to the point that, centuries later, it was in danger of collapse. This necessitated restoration in the mid-nineteenth century, at which time many openings, including the triforium, had to be walled up. However, the magnificent **stained glass,** which is the chief glory of the cathedral, remained intact. Although unrest in the fourteenth century interrupted the decoration of the cathedral, the thirteenth- and fifteenth-century glass sections blend perfectly. Only at Chartres can comparable stained glass be seen today.

Though not typically Spanish, the rich brilliance of León's stained glass, together with the perfect vertical lines and graceful proportions of its interior, make this cathedral one of the most artistically important in Spain.

SAN ISIDRO

Plaza San Isidro

Hours: Open in summer, daily 9AM–2PM and 4–6PM; winter, daily 10AM–1:30PM and 3:30–8PM. Admission fee.

This church is one of the finest Romanesque structures in existence (1054–twelfth century). Its **Pantheon of the Kings** (1054–67) was a burial place for the early kings of León and Castile, and has superb Romanesque architectural elements, particularly the sculptural decoration of the capitals. The expertly designed system of domed-up groin vaults, just above the columns, have well-preserved frescoes painted in 1175.

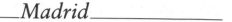

Madrid

Museums

CERRALBO MUSEUM

Ventura Rodriguez, 17

Hours: Open Tues.–Sat., 10AM–2PM and 4–7PM; Sun., 10AM–2PM; closed Aug. Admission fee.

The elegant decoration of this fine house has faded and is in need of restoration, but it will give you an excellent idea of the way a wealthy Spanish family lived and the art they collected. Its ground floor chapel has a painting of *St. Francis of Assisi,* by El Greco. In the Long Gallery there are two large late baroque religious scenes by Francisco Herrera "El Mozo" (1622–85), which cover the walls at each end. Painted in a brilliant, loose, and sketchy technique, stressing chiaroscuro, semitransparent tones of vermillion, orange, and ultramarine, which add to the airy soaring effect, they show the influence of Herrera's study of painting and architecture in Rome. Between them is a portrait of a woman by Titian done in the Italian Renaissance manner with a landscape seen through an open window; and Tintoretto's portrait of a man dressed in black with a theatrical light shining on his face.

Upstairs there is an armor collection that would do a castle proud, displayed against seventeenth-century Flemish tapestries. The main dining room is filled with paintings of still lifes, and the billiard room next to it is a portrait gallery with Dutch, Flemish, French, Italian, and Spanish works. Of these a portrait of *Louis XIV,* by Rigaud (1659–1743), the most distinguished portraitist during the Old Regime, is most notable.

LAZARO GALDIANO MUSEUM

Calle Serrano, 122

Hours: Open Tues.–Sun., 10AM–2PM. Admission fee.

This little museum came into existence in 1948 when Don José Lazaro gave the state his art collection and a large mansion in which to house it. It is one of the most charming small museums in Europe, with a collection of fine old master paintings, ivories, bronzes, jewelry, and sculpture tastefully displayed throughout its thirty rooms.

Start at the **top floor** and work your way down. In **room 20** there are Flemish paintings: a portrait by Joos van Cleve; a *Madonna* by Gerard David; a framed altarpiece of the three kings by Jan Gossaert, also known as Mabuse; and paintings by Bosch.

Bosch, Hieronymus* (ca. 1450–1516), Flemish

St. John the Baptist in the Wilderness
We are accustomed to seeing paintings by Bosch in which there are a great number of small creatures. This painting is one of those in which a single character occupies the foreground. St. John is seen not as an emaciated ascetic suffering in the desert, but as a solid figure larger than life; if he stood upright he would cover the entire picture. The saint, meditating on the lamb, the symbol of God, is distracted by the thought of sexual pleasures, as indicated by the open fantastic fruit in front of him, a symbol of nature. The landscape in the background, with forests, meadows, lakes, and mountains, is very Flemish in its portrayal of detail and variations of light.

Room 21 has seventeenth-century Dutch masters: *Firmado,* a portrait by Rembrandt; still life paintings by Metsu and de Heem; and a landscape by Hobbema. **Room 22** continues with Dutch and Flemish paintings: a work by Jan Brueghel; a portrait of a man by van Dyck; paintings by David Teniers; and a *Landscape with Cows,* by Albert Cuyp (1620–91), the noted painter of animals, particularly cows, set in placid landscapes lit by an Italianate golden sun. **Room 23** has Spanish paintings: three by Zurbarán, six by El Greco, and two small portraits by Velázquez. **Room 24** continues with Spanish paintings showing works by Ribera, Murillo, and others. **Room 25** has eighteenth-century English paintings: *Dedham Vale,* by Constable, and portraits by Lely, Romney, Gainsborough, and Reynolds. Notice the portrait of *Lady Sondes,* by Reynolds (1723–92). The subject has her face turned to the right with a marked look of displeasure. **Room 27** has eighteenth-century Italian paintings including Guardi and J. B. Tiepolo. **Room 30** is filled with portraits by Goya (1746–1828) and works from his renown "black period" in which he paints a nightmarish world filled with repulsive creatures that express the demonic forces that take over the world when reason loses control.

The rooms on the **first floor** are richly decorated with ceiling paintings from the school of Goya. Some of the children from royalty that appear in the ceiling paintings are shown as adults in portraits by Spanish artists hung on the walls. Before leaving, see, on the **ground floor, room 6,** a small portrait of a woman with a green shawl over her left shoulder. The museum attributes it to Leonardo da Vinci, but it is really by Ambrogio de Predis (ca. 1455–1517), with whom Leonardo lived during his first years in Milan. He rose to the position of court painter to the Sforza family in Milan and attained fame as a portrait painter.

EL PRADO

Paceo del Prado

Hours: Open Tues.–Sat., 10AM–6PM; Sun., 10AM–2PM. Admission fee.

The Prado is one of the world's great art galleries, a rival of the Louvre in Paris and the National Gallery in London. Most of the art works were formerly owned by Spanish royalty, whose collections were so rich that they have provided almost every room in the Prado with a masterpiece.

The concept of a Spanish national gallery dates back to the early eighteenth-century, when the Age of Enlightenment was inspiring a new interest in history and museums all over Europe. It took almost 100 years for plans to get underway, but they were halted by the Napoleonic Wars. Only after the restoration of Ferdinand VII did the museum come into being. Housed in the present building, planned fifty years earlier as an academy and museum of the sciences, the Prado opened its doors in 1819.

In the past the Prado was thought to be a stuffy place where nothing new ever happened. The museum's conservative directors seemed content to watch over the collection and open the doors on time. But change is now in the air as a result of the liberalism of post-Franco Spain. The building is undergoing improvement and public activities are being updated, but whatever modernization comes to the Prado, its priceless collection need no improvement.

Index to the Rooms of the Prado

Artists mentioned below have works referred to in the text that follows. You will find these works listed under the names of the artists, arranged alphabetically.

Bermejo, Bartolomé (active 1474–95), Spanish

Santo Domingo de Silos (1474–77): ground floor, room 49
By the late fifteenth century, Spanish painting had begun to emerge from medievalism to follow Franco-Flemish patterns. Bermejo, a widely traveled painter from Cordova, seems to have been influenced by the Flemish School. The sharpness of detail in the central panel of his altarpiece shows the Flemish influence, down to the seven little figures carved into the chair. These figures represent the Seven Virtues—Faith, Hope, and Charity (the theological virtues) at the top; Prudence, Fortitude, Temperance, and Justice (the four ancient cardinal virtues) at the sides. Yet the severe frontal pose, the angularity of line, and the robust, dramatic appearance of the saint leave no doubt of the artist's Spanish origin.

Bosch, Hieronymus (ca. 1450–1516), Flemish
Bosch's haunting paintings have been a source of mystery for centuries. His abstractions of natural form and his fantastic juxtaposition of the beautiful and the grotesque have led some to call Bosch the first surrealist. To be sure, many of his imaginary figures are stranger than anything done by twentieth-century painters of that school. Bosch's fantastic images are original; one would have to look to Romanesque sculpture for a source that might have nourished his imagination. His art is a revelation today, as it was in the late fifteenth century.

Most interpretations of Bosch focus on the hallucinatory world of the subconscious his paintings evoke. In the past some scholars interpreted his work as an expression of the heretical religious doctrines of the fourteenth century. Ingenious as these explanations may be, it is more likely that Bosch, a religious member of a pious layman's lodge (the Brotherhood of Notre Dame), was using unconventional means to express conventional ideas. His paintings suggest that God may be approached through hard work and an avoidance of sin, especially gluttony and lechery. He reveals a voyeuristic contempt for those whom he perceived to be adversaries of the Lord.

The Prado has the world's greatest collection of Bosch's paintings, most of which express these themes. In rooms 43 and 44, *The Garden of Delights*, *The Hay Wain*, and *The Temptation of St. Anthony* are works full of his extraordinary forms, freaks, and monsters; *The Adoration of the Magi*, sponsored by a donor whose portrait appears in the foreground, is more conventional, though Bosch was unable to resist sticking a few worldly evils in the background.

The Garden of Delights (ca. 1500): first floor, room 44
The left and right wings of this triptych probably represent heaven and hell. Does the central panel depict earthly bliss or a depraved orgy? The creative imagination of Bosch eludes analysis, so there are many interpretations of this painting.

Wilhelm Fraenger, the art historian, has pointed out that this triptych may represent a commission given to Bosch by an heretical nudist sect, such as the Brethren of the Free Spirit, or the Adamites. These cultist groups, which flourished during Bosch's day, worshipped God in a direct, unorthodox, and somewhat pantheistic way, seemingly at one with animals and plants. The sexuality they prescribed was one of innocent joy in a tranquil world where the earth yielded her fruit abundantly and without effort. According to Fraenger, the left wing represents the Garden of Eden at the time of the marriage of Adam and Eve; who walked the earth naked and unashamed. The right wing, representing hell, is reserved for those who do not follow the teachings of the sect. Notice the pig in the lower right hand corner. It is dressed in the habit of the Beguines, another liberal sect that was at odds with the Adamites, and is trying to seduce a victim.

Judging from Bosch's other works and what we know of his life, however, it is hard to believe that he would have undertaken the kind of commission that Fraenger has suggested. The central panel may indeed be humanity giving itself to various forms of sensuality, especially eroticism and gluttony, but not in innocent joy. Notice the circular pool in which female figures are bathing. Men are riding wildly around them on the backs of various animals. From their antics we can see that they are in a general state of excitement, no doubt brought about by the sight of the women, one of whom is already climbing out of the water. Thus, Bosch shows sexual attraction between men and women, which he considered sinful. According to medieval moralists, women, following the precedent of Eve, took the initiative in leading men into lechery and sin. The fantastic vegetablelike forms in the water may be erotic symbols inspired by popular songs and slang of Bosch's time. The fish may be phallic symbols from old Flemish proverbs. The bubble or glass bowl sheltering the lovers may stand for the fragility of life and the temporary pleasures to be derived from physical love. The strawberries (at one time this triptych was called "The Strawberry Tree") all over the landscape may refer to the vain glory of life, no sooner enjoyed than gone. Some scholars have seen the fruit, nibbled by the lovers in the garden, as metaphors for sexual organs. The result of sexual indulgence is depicted in the panel on the right, a vivid hell.

Bruegel, Pieter, the Elder (ca. 1525–69), Flemish

The Triumph of Death (ca. 1562): first floor, room 44
The medieval concern with death lingered on into the sixteenth century, and during Bruegel's time was intensified by the turbulence in the Flemish provinces. Philip II of Spain, in his campaign against the Calvinist heresy, later brutally repressed the Flemish. Executions became widespread in Flanders after Bruegel painted this political picture disguised as allegory. Death appears in many guises: wielding a scythe, a mysterious figure in a hooded cloak. Sometimes he mocks his victims by dressing in their clothing. Whatever the form death takes, man is helpless in the face of his powers.

In the lower-left-hand corner, death is holding an empty hourglass over a fallen king; a skeleton helps himself to the money that cannot buy life. To the right of the king a cardinal (dressed in blue to indicate dishonesty) is carried off, and above a skeleton plays a musical instrument as he drives a wagon loaded with skulls. At the lower-right-hand corner death interrupts a party: some of the guests attempt to defend themselves with their sword; a jester crawls under a table; and two oblivious lovers are mocked by a skeleton with a musical instrument. There is a marvelous figure of death, on a horse whose skin barely covers its bones, running roughshod over a multitude (humanity) and driving them with his scythe into an ovenlike enclosure (a precursor of the Nazi ovens of World War II?). The distant hills are ablaze with fires of destruction, underscoring the idea that death is omnipresent and overpowering.

Bruegel was careful not to arouse the Spanish authorities with paintings that could be considered critical of their rule in occupied Flanders. He kept hidden the paintings he felt too dangerous for public view. On his deathbed he asked his wife to burn a number of paintings so that they could not get her into trouble. *The Triumph of Death* was one of Bruegel's less controversial paintings, apparently just a rendering of a common medieval theme. Today we know that it was also a record of the thousands who were dying at the hands of the Spanish soldiers and in the Inquisition.

Dürer, Albrecht* (1471–1528), German

Self-portrait (1498): first floor, room 44
Prior to painting this portrait, Dürer had spent time in Italy, where he became interested in the Italian concept of the artist as a gentleman. His portrayal of himself in aristocratic dress, with a self-confident, reserved expression, is different from the way he would have portrayed himself in his native Germany, where the artist was regarded as a craftsman. While there is something of the Northern spirit about this painting, the landscape is Southern and reminiscent of Leonardo. So is the parapet on which the arm creates a horizontal defintion. It is a painting that expresses the new Renaissance style which Dürer brought north of the Alps.

See also (room 44) Dürer's life-sized paintings of **Adam** and **Eve** (1507). Here again we have the German painter who introduced the southern Renaissance to the north. His figures stand against a black background to emphasize the silhouette, their supple modeling more Italian than Gothic, and in Eve we have a new ideal of feminine beauty with long slender thighs, high breasts, and sloping shoulders, an erotic appeal unusual for Dürer.

El Greco* (1541–1614), Spanish

The Resurrection and **The Pentecost** (two paintings) first floor, room 9B
These two works belong to El Greco's mature phase, from 1603 to about 1608. By this time the master's art had undergone an evolution. His space exists so that figures can float freely in it, and, in the case of *The Resurrection*, so that Christ can flow out of it altogether. His colors are at their most intense: earth tones at their warmest and deepest. He is elongating his figures to dematerialize them, but he is using greater contrasts of light and shadow to propel them upward, emphasizing their mysticism and religious poi-

gnancy. In these paintings and others of this period. El Greco depicts a powerful spirituality. His themes are those of his time, but his artistic technique is so advanced it belongs to the late nineteenth and twentieth centuries.

Goya, Francisco (1746–1828), Spanish

Goya is one of the first great artists born in the eighteenth century whose art belongs to the nineteenth century. He is a forerunner of the romantic movement and of impressionism (a style he used fifty years before the movement surfaced in France). Even expressionists and surrealists of the twentieth century can trace their lineage to Goya.

Goya came from a modest background in the northern province of Aragon and was known in his youth for his short temper and dissolute ways. Scandals forced him to leave the town of his birth and later Madrid, where he worked with Tiepolo in the Royal Palace. He later returned to Madrid, settled down, married, and worked his way up to the position of court painter. His position did not subdue his temperament, which he expressed through art. It seems astonishing that Goya kept his post as court painter unchallenged, for he painted, with great realism, the court of Charles IV as stupid and corrupt. He also showed the horror of Napoleon's occupation of Spain; some of his great paintings on this subject are moving commentaries on injustice and cruelty. His macabre strain found full expression in the nightmarish fantasies that link him to some of the painting of our own time—with Ensor, Munch, and the surrealists.

The Family of Charles IV (1800): first floor, room 32

Shortly after Goya was appointed first painter to the king in 1799 he painted his official portrait showing, in the center, the king, Charles IV, wearing a white wig and looking older than his fifty-one years. At his side is his little son dressed in red, and the domineering queen with her arm around her daughter. To the king's left is an older daughter holding her baby; her husband, the prince of Parma, is at her side. The young man in blue on the left is the prince who became Ferdinand VII. The lady next to him, with her face turned away, is supposed to represent a future bride whose identity in 1800 was unknown. On the left, in shadow, Goya slyly depicted himself at work—an idea no doubt suggested by Velázquez's Maids of Honor.

The harmony of the figures and the warm colors accented by touches of white make The Family of Charles IV a brilliant work. But its primary fascination lies in its depiction of the royal family as an unattractive, dull-looking lot. But for their fine clothes, elaborate wigs, and precious jewelry, they might be an ignorant family of peasants. So different is this portrait from the usual flattering idealization that some people find it hard to believe the family of Charles IV resembled these unimpressive folk. Yet if the king had regarded the figures as unflattering caricatures, the painting would surely have been destroyed. Goya had gone deaf in 1792 and, cut off from the world of sound, he learned that appearances were not always the whole truth. He became interested in the character rather than outward appearance of his sitters. What he saw in the royal family were some unattractive, dull-witted people who let the destiny of Spain slip through their fingers.

Maja Nude and *Maja Clothed* (1796–98): first floor, room 38
These pictures are as famous as any Goya ever painted and as impressive as any. While there has been speculation as to the identity of the woman, the reference to her as a Maja indicates she was simply a pretty working-class girl fond of stylish clothes. Goya may have gotten the idea for the painting after seeing Giorgione's *Venus,* or more likely Velázquez's *Rokeby Venus,* a picture then in the possession of his friend the duchess of Alba (rumors that the model was the duchess herself appear unfounded; from pictures we have of the duchess she was never so attractive as this beautiful young woman). It is more reasonable to assume that Goya simply wanted to paint a nude without mythological justification or classical pretension. The realism of the nude is more sensational when placed beside the clothed version. Goya has done everything in drawing, color, and pose to make her alluring. The composition, which places the figure diagonally across the space, with arms folded behind the head to counter movement in that direction, is brilliant. Nudes may be rare in Spanish painting, but with his *Maja* Goya succeeded in painting the most naturalist nude in the annals of great painting.

The Third of May (1814–15): first floor, room 39
This painting records the mass executions by Napoleon's soldiers of Spanish citizens who were suspected of taking part in the insurrection against French rule on May 2, 1808. (The uprising itself is dramatized by Goya in his *The Second of May 1808* in the same room.) It is a painting whose subject is as meaningful for our own time as it was for Goya's. The victims are helpless in the face of brutal force. Those who have met their fate lie in a heap on the blood-soaked ground. Others marked for execution hide their faces in horror. The victim in the white shirt facing the firing squad raises his hands in a defiant gesture, but others are sinking to their knees. The background is made up of the diagonal of a hill running from the left, met and countered by the horizontal of the soldiers and the lifeless city on the right. Above this is a morbid dark sky, adding to the somber tone of the picture. Yet it is the depiction of the executioners that is most meaningful. They are huddled together in an unfeeling mass—faceless, anonymous: a vivid symbol in the art of repression and tyranny.

The Witches' Sabbath (1821–22): ground floor, room 67
After the executions of May 3, 1808, Goya seemed to become obsessed by all the tragedies that can befall ordinary people when reason loses control. He shares this feeling more with Goethe, Mozart, and Beethoven, his contemporaries, than with the painters of his day, who as classicists upheld the moralizing, humanistic values of the Age of Enlightenment and did not see the demonic forces underlying them. Goya dared to express the darker currents in human nature, especially in one of the "Black Murals" taken from his country home near Segovia. In this strange painting, demonic creatures

form a seething background for Satan, who appears as a goat dressed in a monk's cassock; a white shrouded figure being raised from the dead; and an innocent-looking girl sitting on a chair, properly clothed and hiding her hands in a muff. What is a nice girl doing in a place like this? Has she unknowingly strayed into this scene of evil, or is she a gullible victim of propaganda? Whoever she is, her innocent presence contrasts with the wickedness of the others, and heightens the horror of the scene.

Goya found that drawing and color are not necessarily the most important elements of painting. His blobs of black, brown, and white are painted with violent strokes, which sets the emotional tone of the painting and give the figures a random quality. Such plastic forms call to mind Munch and the expressionists who 150 years later were to take inspiration from Goya's precocious expressionism.

Master of Flémalle (ca. 1378–1444), Flemish

St. John the Baptist and Heinrich Werl and *St. Barbara:* first floor, room 40
These two panels, parts of a triptych (the center panel, probably a crucifixion, is lost), are considered among the best work of the Master of Flémalle (thought to be the Tournai painter Robert Campin). They were painted in 1438 for the donor, Heinrich Werl, a professor at the University of Cologne. An inscription at the base of the panel, near the figures of the donor and St. John, reads, "In the year 1438 I painted this likeness of Master Heinrich Werl of Cologne." This is the only dated painting of the Master of Flémalle, considered one of the originators of the Flemish school of painting, preceding Jan van Eyck. If you have seen *The Wedding Portrait of Giovanni Arnolfini,* by Jan van Eyck, at the National Gallery in London, you will recognize the convex mirror reflecting St. John's and the donor's backs.

Heinrich Werl was a Franciscan monk who was part of the Council of Basel (1431–39). He is shown here kneeling, with his hands in an attitude of prayer, facing the missing center panel. St. John the Baptist, his patron, is identified by his attribute the lamb (derived from the Fourth Gospel, 1:36: "John looked toward Jesus and said, 'There is the lamb of God' ").

The panel with St. Barbara shows the saint reading a prayer book (symbolizing the Word of God) in a typical Flemish room with a cozy fire. Her main attribute is the tower under construction seen through the open window (her pagan father had a tower built to hide her from suitors). The room contains objects symbolizing her purity: the iris, the pitcher and basin, and the white towel. The translucent carafe, half-filled with wine, symbolizes the Last Supper, because Barbara, like Christ, was betrayed and killed for her beliefs.

Memling, Hans (ca. 1433–94), Flemish

The Three Kings Altarpiece (1470): first floor, room 41
Hans Memling was the leading painter in Bruges during the last quarter of the fifteenth century, heir to the Flemish tradition of Jan van Eyck and Rogier van der Weyden. Clearly he drew from both of these masters. He also

added personal elements based on strict symmetry, balance of composition, and the moderation of color tones, to create an eclectic Flemish style. In the *Three Kings Altarpiece* we see an excellent example of this style. The dramatic tension of Rogier van der Weyden's art has been reduced to a somewhat static solemnity, and Jan van Eyck's luminous colors, muted to delicate tones, better suit Memling's calm emotional approach.

On the right wing is an austere depiction of the *Presentation in the Temple*. The infant Jesus has been brought by Mary and Joseph to the temple in Jerusalem to be "consecrated to the Lord." According to Mosaic law, the first-born of all living things was to be sacrificed to God; children were redeemed by the payment of five shekels to the priest. Joseph's purse, strapped to his belt, alludes to this custom. In his left hand he carries two doves in a small cage, to be used in the Mother's purification rite, which required the sacrifice of "a pair of turtle doves or two young pigeons" (Luke). Simeon, wearing a priest's vestments, had been told that he would not die until he had seen the Messiah. He takes the infant Jesus in his arms saying, "Lord, now lettest thou thy servant depart in peace, according to thy word: For mine eyes have seen thy salvation" (Nunc Dimittis, Domine). Anna, the older woman in a white coif, is seen with her hand raised in a gesture of prophecy. The small figures and the scene in the square face the open door of the temple, directing attention toward the presentation of the Child.

The central panel, *The Adoration of the Magi,* shows two of the kings kneeling in devotion to the Child as the richly attired black king enters on the right. The scene is executed with a perfection of design and was Memling's definitive statement on the subject. Ten years later, when he painted a smaller Adoration (see Memling Museum, Bruges, Belgium), it was similar down to the face of the man peering in at the window.

The *Nativity,* shown on the left wing, is a warm, tender scene in which Mary is depicted as a young Flemish girl. The severity of the architecture, carried from panel to panel, is absorbed by the assimilating calm and spirituality of Memling's art.

Murillo, Bartolomé Esteban (1618–82), Spanish

The Immaculate Conception (ca. 1660): no. 2809, first floor, room 16 B
Your attention is called to this religious work, typical of Murillo, because it was considered a masterpiece in the eighteenth century when Murillo was held in higher esteem than Titian, Rubens, and Velázquez. Today, however, Murillo is likely to arouse distaste because of his sentimentality. His scenes look more like pretentious clichés in religious calender art than great works of the baroque period. The pietistic sentiment of the Virgin's pose (hands clasped to her breast, eyes rolling upward) strikes the viewer as exaggerated. The drawing is weak and the saccharine pinks and blues add to the banality of the work. Yet if you have seen some of Murillo's low-life genre scenes, you know that he was a talented painter. Only when he allowed the theme of his religious painting to get in the way of his art did his work sink to the mediocre.

Raphael* (1483–1520), Florentine, born in Umbria

Portrait of a Cardinal: first floor, 2

Raphael must have welcomed the opportunity to paint a portrait in oil at a time when he was executing his great series of frescoes at the Vatican, about 1510–11. The less restrictive medium enabled him to paint in greater detail and to model the figure more accurately, aspects of painting he considered important. He captured the appearance of the sitter so well that we feel we have seen him before. As one of the great eclectics, Raphael is using what he learned from Leonardo during his Florentine period, 1504–8. The cardinal's left arm, resting on the base of the picture (which has obviously been cut down), and the oblique positioning of his body and head appear to be taken from the composition of the *Mona Lisa.* The color, though, is all Raphael's. The glowing red of the cardinal's vestments contrasts with the delicate pallor of his face with a rather grand effect. The cardinal was not a good-looking young man, but painted by Raphael he becomes part of a carefully balanced decorative beauty.

The Holy Family with the Lamb: first floor, room 2

This painting, from Raphael's Florentine period, also owes a debt to Leonardo, in this case his *St. Anne with the Virgin, Child, and Lamb* in the Louvre. Since *St. Anne* was completed in 1508 in Milan, and *The Holy Family* is dated 1505–7, Raphael must have come to know Leonardo's work through the cartoon, which was exhibited in Florence in 1501. (It has since disappeared.)

While Raphael borrowed from the greatest artists of his time (Michelangelo, Fra Bartolomeo, and others, in addition to Leonardo) he combined what he took from them with his own artistic vision. The touching expressions of the Virgin and Child and the refined choice of colors are his own.

See also in room 2 Raphael's *The Holy Family,* known as *La Perla* after Felipe IV referred to it as "the pearl of my pictures," and *The Holy Family of the Oak, The Virgin with the Fish,* and *The Virgin of the Rose.*

Ribera, José de (1501–1652), Spanish

The Martyrdom of St. Bartholomew (ca. 1639): first floor, room 25

Little is known of Ribera's life in Spain. At an early age he went to Italy and settled in Naples, where he was influenced by Caravaggio's style. He made an almost immediate success in Naples, under Spanish rule since the fifteenth century. Many of his paintings were sent to Spain, introducing Caravaggism, with its use of strong chiaroscuro and poor working people as models, to Spanish artists. So while Ribera spent his career in Naples, he nevertheless belongs to the history of Spanish art.

But Ribera was no mere follower of Caravaggio. He developed an independent version of Caravaggio's naturalism, which his great *Martyrdom of St. Bartholomew* shows; the wide Y-form composition is more grand and free than Caravaggio's, and the faces look distinctly Spanish, though Ribera had lived in Italy for almost thirty years when he painted this picture. Ribera's technique emphasizes his realistic modeling, creating an exciting surface texture that intensifies the naturalistic illusion. This technique is effective at producing an unpleasant grimness of tone, appropriate for a painting of a saint being hoisted into the air by three rough-looking henchmen to be skinned alive. Though Ribera has chosen to show us only the preparation of St. Bartholomew's horrible torture, his unprotected nakedness and stretched muscles are pathetic enough to arouse horror, compassion, and awe in the viewer. By forcing the viewer to anticipate the torture to come, Ribera creates dramatic tension that might have degenerated into revulsion if the skinning were shown in clinical detail.

Rubens, Peter Paul* (1577–1640), Flemish

Rubens was closely connected to the Spanish court. At one time he acted as a diplomat for Philip IV, traveling to England in 1629 on a mission to clarify the terms of an alliance between England and Spain. He was one of Philip's favorite artists and the recipient of many royal commissions. As a result of these commissions and Philip's purchase of Rubens's effects after the artist died in Antwerp, the Prado today has some of the most outstanding examples of the artist's work.

Portrait of Marie de' Medici (1622–25): ground floor, room 60

Philip IV was not the only enthusiastic supporter of Rubens. His greatest patron was the queen-mother of the French royal court, Marie de' Medici, who honored him with an enormous commission: twenty-two huge canvases for her residence in the Luxembourg Palace in Paris. Rubens was fond of her, which this portrait of her at the age of fifty shows. He hides her unattractiveness by using a soft light to minimize the contours of her cheek and hide her double chin. Thus he shows his patron in regal opulence with enough likeness so that she could recognize herself with satisfaction.

The Judgment of Paris: ground floor, room 61

Rubens had painted this popular mythological scene before (see his painting in the National Gallery, London) in which Paris, the shepherd, seen sitting on the left in contemplative thought, must choose the most beautiful goddess in the world. The goddess of his choice will be presented with the golden apple that Mercury, at Paris's side, is displaying in his left hand. This version of the scene was painted in 1638–39 when Rubens was suffering from gout and near the end of his life, but he is still capable of depicting a story with rich vitality, using color and movement to the greatest advantage. Unlike the London *Judgment of Paris,* where the figures are clearly detached from one another, the composition of Rubens's painting connects the figures in a graceful sweep across the canvas. Mercury's hand holding the apple is close enough to Minerva's flowing scarf almost to touch it; Venus's vermilion robe touches Minerva's thigh; and Juno's elbow pushes forward in front of Venus's arm.

The three goddesses are all nude portraits of Helena Fourment, Rubens's second wife, who was about twenty-five when she posed. The governor of the Spanish Netherlands, Archduke Ferdinand, was entrusted with sending the painting to Philip IV in Spain, and he did so with a letter announcing its departure from Antwerp in 1639: "It is without doubt, in the opinion of all painters, Rubens's best work. I have accused him of only one fault, on which point he gave me no satisfaction: the extreme nudity of the three goddesses. The artist responded that exactly in that consisted the merit of the picture. The Venus in the middle is a very good portrait of the painter's wife, the most beautiful of all the ladies in Antwerp."

The Three Graces: ground floor, room 61
Here are the handmaidens of Venus, the goddesses of joy and all social occasions. They are grouped in their usual pose so that the two outer figures face the spectator and the one in the middle faces away. They have been a subject of much allegorizing and were popular with collectors during the Renaissance and baroque periods. Rubens may have seen them, as the Florentine humanist philosophers of the fifteenth century did, as three phases of love (*beauty* arousing *desire* leading to *fulfillment*—notice the sexual implication of the three stags in the background), because he included a portrait of his second wife Helena Fourment on the left, and his first wife Isabella Brandt (whom Rubens deeply loved; she died in 1626) on the right. It is said that after Rubens's death Helena wanted to destroy the painting, but her confessor persuaded her not to burn it. It was acquired by Philip IV from Rubens's heirs and stands today as the finest female nudes Rubens ever painted.

The Garden of Love: ground floor, room 61
This painting, probably set in Rubens's own garden in Antwerp, depicts the elegant, pleasure-loving society the artist was a part of. Richly dressed women loll about while elegant cavaliers whisper sweet words of love into their ears. An idealized self-portrait of Rubens is seen on the left embracing his young wife, Helena Fourment. He is inducing her, with an assist from Cupid, to enter into the Garden of Love, a lavish baroque scene enriched with the primary colors of red, blues, and yellows. Its composition leads the eye from the lower left across the group of happy people, on a diagonal line, upward to the Renaissance fountain whose water flows from the ample breasts of a Venus mounted on a dolphin (Venus was born of the sea). Other symbols of love are the statue of the Three Graces under the portico, and the flock of winged putti with flowers, bows, and arrows, and a flaming torch symbolizing the "fire of love."

This lovely scene of graceful good manners, all dedicated to the pursuit of pleasure, was not just a fantasy of Rubens's but reflects the lives of the artist and his wealthy contemporaries. A priest of the time described the amorous revels of the upper classes: "They used to sit under a green arbour or go on the water to get an appetite, or again in the afternoon they would mount their carriages and make a pilgrimage to Venus, a fashionable walk; when evening came, they sang or danced the whole night and made love in a way that cannot be told." Such a description explains why Rubens's painting was so popular in its day. Its popularity continued through the eighteenth century, when it had an influence on French painting, especially the *fêtes galantes* and *fêtes champêtres* of Watteau. It appealed to Philip IV of

Spain, who has been described as a religious fanatic. The Spanish king hung it in his bedroom.

Titian* (ca. 1487–1576), Venetian

Charles V at Mühlberg: first floor, room 9
Titian had been introduced to Charles V at Bologna in 1530 and thereafter Charles favored him as his official painter, knighting him in 1533. Of the many portraits Titian executed for the emperor, this one, done in 1548 to commemorate Charles's victory over his Protestant rivals in Germany at the Battle of Mühlberg, was the most ambitious. Charles was in his full glory and asked Titian to attend the Congress of Augsburg as part of his official entourage. The event seemed to have inspired Titian, who shows us the emperor, wearing armor, astride a magnificent black horse. While this is not a battle scene, the dynamic landscape conveys the mood of triumph and shows how the dramatic relationship between figure and landscape, an important part of religious painting, could also be applied to portraiture. It is the first royal equestrian portrait, and it started a tradition carried on by Rubens, van Dyck, and Velázquez in the succeeding century.

In the same room is Titian's portrait of *The Empress Isabella* (ca. 1545). Titian painted it long after the death of the empress in 1539. He uses color to convey an essential mood. The orange of the sky is reflected in the highlights of Isabella's hair; the blue of the mountains is mirrored in her eyes. This link between figure and landscape suggests Isabella's remoteness, while her rose and purple dress recall the warmth of her presence. Titian's technique gives portraiture a new dimension and raises it from the production of a likeness to the level of great art. When the emperor retired to the monastery at Yuste this picture went along with him.

Bacchanal (1520): first floor, room 9
This painting and its companion, *The Worship of Venus* (1522), in the same room, are two of three paintings Titian did for Alfonso d'Este, the duke of Ferrara, who wanted sensual pictures to adorn a room in his palace. Titian, ready to please a wealthy patron, gave him what he wanted by painting the first orgy in Venetian art. We see a pagan scene from classical legend—the men and women of Andros, where Bacchus made a brook run red with wine, enjoying each other as they drink themselves into a stupor. On the music sheet in the foreground is the inscription, "He who drinks but once knows not what drinking is." The orgiasts seem eager to find out, and are shown ridding themselves of inhibitions, like the little boy who is unselfconsciously relieving himself. They dance, make love, and fall asleep. Even their old leader, on the hill in the upper right background, has succumbed. He lies spread out on the ground, aglow with wine and lit up by the rich light penetrating the clouds above. Below him, in the right-hand corner, is a beautiful female nude, her breasts uplifted, lying in expectant ecstasy. You have probably seen her before as Goya's *Naked Maja* (Prado, room 38) painted 280 years later. Her body gleaming in sunshine, this nameless beauty gives substance to the mood of rapture that Titian painted with obvious enjoyment.

In the same spirit and in the same room is Titian's *Danae* (1554), painted for Philip II. It is similar to an earlier version of the same scene (1545) now in the Capodimonte Museum in Naples. The only difference is the substitution of the maidservant for Cupid. Otherwise the figure of Danae waiting to receive the love of Jupiter is exactly the same. (See Titian's *Danae* in the Capodimonte Museum, Naples). For the story of Danae, see Gossaert's *Danae* in the Alte Pinakothek, Munich).

Velázquez, Diego (1599–1660), Spanish

Velázquez was the greatest painter in the history of Spanish art and a leading painter of seventeenth-century Europe. He came from a noble family in Seville, where he also received his training as an artist. He moved to Madrid in 1622 and remained there as court painter to Philip IV until his death thirty-seven years later. He built up a close relationship with the king, who made him a knight of Santiago. Philip also kept a key to Velázquez's studio so that he could watch the painter at work.

The genius of Velázquez was in his ability to paint what was clearly visible to the eye. The few Madonnas and mythological scenes he painted are far from his best work; in that respect he was similar to some of his seventeenth-century contemporaries, namely, Caravaggio, Vermeer, Hals, and Le Nain, and different from previous Renaissance masters who portrayed what they imagined. This is not to say, however, that Velázquez lacked an awareness of Italian Renaissance art. He saw it all around him at the Hapsburg court in Madrid, and visited Italy for two years to purchase Italian paintings for Philip IV (some of the Italian paintings in the Prado, such as the Tintorettos, were purchased by Velázquez). Most likely he remained faithful to his visual approach to painting because he lacked the ability to envision what he could not see. As court painter his job was to paint portraits that showed real people in actual settings. Some of his portraits in the Prado—those of Philip IV and his family, and others treasured by leading museums of the world—attest to Velázquez's excellence as a portrait painter.

Velázquez discovered from his portraiture the nineteenth-century idea that a rapid visual impression can be more revealing than a drawn-out interpretation. There is a somewhat flat appearance to his figures, and his colors and light are strikingly natural—the way we see things at a first glance. It is a style that links him with the future—to the late eighteenth-century Goya, to Manet in nineteenth-century France, and to the impressionist tradition.

The Surrender of Breda (The Lances) (1635): first floor, room 12

This picture was painted to commemorate the Spanish victory over the Dutch in 1625. Velázquez was not present at the scene, but had prints and descriptions of the event and may have taken the elements of the composition from a Bible print representing Abraham and Melchizedek.

We are shown Justin of Nassau, governor of Breda, delivering the keys of the city to Ambrogio Spinola, the Genoese general who commanded the Spanish forces. The latter became famous for his clemency at Breda, which Velázquez has emphasized. As the only figures isolated against the open landscape, the two men dominate the scene. Spinola puts his hand on Justin's shoulder in a superb example of seventeenth-century noble magnaminity. On the right, the victorious Spaniards press close to the two generals, restrained only by the magnificent chestnut stallion. Their tall lances, breaking into the sky in a bold rhythm, are symbolic of their victory and give this picture its popular name, *Las Lanzas*. On the left, the defeated Dutch are less lively; some show indifference to the proceedings.

The greatness of the picture lies in its skillful combination of baroque and classical elements. Its baroque character is revealed in the liquid spontaneity of the brushwork, the dramatic use of chiaroscuro, and in the general grandeur of the scene. Classic influence is reflected in the lack of diagonal lines and turbulent movements, which creates a mood of serenity in a painting about military conquest. Everything, especially the symmetrical composition and the counterbalancing of figure with figure and form with form, emphasizes the significance of the event.

The Spinners (The Fable of Arachne) (1657): first floor, room 11
The true subject of this picture has only recently been brought to light. It concerns the story of Arachne and Minerva from Ovid's *Metamorphoses*. Arachne, a girl from Lydia, was famous for her weaving. Her accomplishments came to the attention of the goddess Minerva, who challenged her to a contest. But Arachne made a picture in her tapestry mocking the follies of Jove, Minerva's father, showing him disguised as a bull. For her insult, Minerva changed Arachne into a spider (the ancients believed that the spider's web was woven). In the elevated room in the background we see the helmeted Minerva raising her arm to curse Arachne who is standing before her large tapestry, a picture of *The Rape of Europa* after a copy by Titian. The presence of the cello may be indicative of the belief that spiders were sensitive to music.

Velázquez painted this picture one year after his *Maids of Honor* masterpiece (see below), and may have wanted to prove that he could paint another just as original. The idea may have come to him from visiting the Santa Isabel tapestry repair shop, where he saw women spinning and winding yarn. In any case, he succeeded in painting a picture that equals *The Maids of Honor*.

The composition is highly complicated and beautifully balanced. If you look at the more strongly lighted upper room, your attention will be directed down to the lower room by the rays of light traveling in a diagonal line directly toward the young woman working on the right. The movement of the young woman's arm toward the left and the line of her left foot point to the older woman on the left who is spinning. A composition so complicated is filled with subtleties, such as the ladder on the right wall that catches the light; it is an indispensable element in the composition, and without it the central symmetry would be too obvious. If you look at the picture long enough you will probably see some of the other techniques Velázquez has used to hold it together.

Velázquez may have had his favorite artist, Tintoretto, in mind when he painted *The Spinners*. The color and light is Tintorettesque, and so are the sharp movements scattered about the canvas. But Velázquez's work is more true to life than any work by Tintoretto.

The Maids of Honor (Las Meninas) (1656): first floor, room 15A

This is one of those famous paintings whose quality is as great as its reputation. While it is a superb portrait of the Infanta Princess Margarita, the demure-looking little girl in the center, it is also a genre scene in which Velázquez (on the left) included himself in the process of painting a double portrait of the king and queen. A reflection of their portraits is visible on Velázquez's large canvas in the mirror on the back wall. Velázquez was always busy painting pictures of the king and queen, and it must have been a regular occurrence for the little infanta, surrounded by her ladies in waiting, to wander in to see what was happening. A courtier on the stairs is casually looking in through the open door. The *Maids of Honor,* unlike most formal portraits of royalty, is a natural scene that has no particular significance; therein lies its charm. The relaxed poses and optical realism draw the viewer into the world of the family. Also of note is the composition, a pattern of rectangles—in the pictures on the wall, the windows, a door, and the big canvas on which the artist is painting—countered by the undulating curve formed by the different heights of the people's heads. Like *The Spinners,* the painting exists in a vast, dimly lit space more expressive in its subtleties than a well-lit scene where every detail is clearly visible. In that sense Velázquez is giving us only a fleeting glance at what is happening; he knows how to use his paint and brush to create the textured variations of such an observation. In so doing he maintains a sufficient illusion to make things look real, even though they disintegrate as they get farther away.

The title of the picture seems not to make much sense. The two young ladies, or *meninas,* waiting on the little daughter of the king (one is offering her a little red vase on a tray and the other is attentively watching) are not the main subjects of the painting. Its previous title, *The Family,* would be more appropriate. In addition to the maids of honor there are the dwarfs in the employ of the royal household, the governess of the infanta, and the gentleman in attendance to the royal ladies behind her, the royal steward in the open door, Velázquez himself, a member of the royal Spanish court, and the king and queen in the mirror.

Veronese, Paolo* (1528–88), Venetian

Venus and Adonis (1530): first floor, room 8A

This is one of the Italian paintings that Velázquez brought back to Spain for Philip IV. He was obviously fascinated with Veronese's treatment of light: the picture looks as though it had been painted out-of-doors from direct observation. Notice the circles of light on the forehead, right elbow, and hip of Venus, which come from sunlight filtering through the trees. Such accurate observation of optical phenomena is rare in Renaissance painting, but not in the works of Veronese, a Venetian master colorist with few equals.

Typical of Veronese is his depiction of the story of *Venus and Adonis* in its most idylic aspect. Rather than show Venus trying to restrain Adonis from the hunt she knows will kill him, or showing her grieving over his dead body, Veronese depicts a moment of calm when Adonis is lying asleep. The dogs are alert as if anticipating excitement to come. They are kept from waking Adonis by Cupid and by Venus, who shields him with her fan and cradles his head on her lap.

Weyden, Rogier van der* (ca. 1399–1464), Flemish

Descent from the Cross: first floor, room 41

This is an early painting by Rogier van der Weyden, dating from about 1435, but it remains his best-known masterpiece, one of the most important works of the fifteenth-century Flemish school. It was originally painted for a church in Louvain, but later sold for a high price to Mary of Austria, queen of Hungary. She took it with her to Spain in 1556, and her brother, Charles V, sent it to the Escorial in 1574. Somewhere along the way the painting's two wings, showing *The Resurrection* and *The Four Evangelists*, were lost. It came to the Prado in 1939.

The ten large, exquisitely modeled figures look as though they have been carved from stone, though they are painted in the naturalistic Flemish style. They stand out against a depthless gold background, a Gothic decoration, but are presented with a psychological subtlety absent from most medieval art. Emphasis is on the figures; the artist has gone so far as to eliminate a background landscape, standard in a scene of this sort. The cross is only summarily indicated, to give a reference point to the picture and lessen the horizontal movement in the composition. The interrelationship between the figures gives a dramatic tension that is brought out by the overall swaying of the figures—a pulling and stretching in various directions. The position of Christ's body, hinged in three parts at hips and knees with one arm trailing, is echoed in the fainting body of the Virgin. The downward pull of these two figures expresses the profound grief of the scene.

Zurbarán, Francisco (1598–1664), Spanish

St. Luke Painting the Crucified Christ (ca. 1630s): first floor, room 29

There is a natural asceticism and rustic simplicity in the works of Zurbarán that we can justly think of as Spanish. In his case these qualities are further emphasized by his Extremaduran temperament, which made him a popular artist of religious themes, so popular that Philip IV called him a "painter to the king and king of painters."

In this painting, which shows Zurbarán as a master of simple themes, solitary figures, and strong forms in large spaces, he makes a powerful statement with dignity and feeling. It has been suggested that Zurbarán included a self-portrait in the guise of St. Luke, the patron saint of artists. This, however, cannot be substantiated.

Zurbarán's art was especially appealing to the ascetic taste of the monastic orders in Spain for which he did many paintings. You will find in his little *Still Life,* in the same room, in which objects are arranged in a row, a mystical quality that suggests a spiritual meaning.

CASÓN DEL BUEN RETIRO (ANNEX OF THE PRADO)

Plaza Filipe IV, 2

Hours: Same as hours for the Prado. Entrance is included in the Prado's general admission price.

This lovely little building was selected to house Picasso's *Guernica,* which, at the artist's behest, was to remain in New York's Museum of Modern Art until democracy returned to Spain. In September, 1981, the painting finally arrived in Madrid from New York and went on display at the Casón del Buen Retiro in October, marking the one hundredth anniversary of Picasso's birth. Placed behind bullet-proof glass because of its value ($40 million) and its controversial subject (the Spanish Civil War), the painting is the main attraction here, though part of a collection of other Picasso works that will be expanded in future years.

Picasso, Pablo* (1881–1973), Spanish, lived in France

Guernica (1937)
In 1936 Picasso accepted a commission from the government of the Spanish Republic, then engaged in a civil war with the Spanish Fascists, to create a mural for the Spanish Pavilion at the Paris World's Fair. For six months Picasso produced nothing; then, on the afternoon of April 26, 1937, German bombers, flying for General Franco, destroyed the defenseless Spanish town of Guernica. Moved by a newspaper description of the attack, Picasso immediately began work on the mural, which he finished in six weeks. He named it after the town of Guernica as a memorial to the innocent dead and as a manifesto decrying the brutality of modern warfare.

Though war has been commonplace in every century, Picasso's picture is a singular tragic statement about war. In the first half of the twentieth century, warfare was waged on a massive scale against entire civilian populations as a part of military strategy. *Guernica* forces us to confront the tragic consequences of anonymous random destruction by giving us a close view of home and farm after an aerial attack. Taking Goya's *The Third of May* a step farther, Picasso chooses to show us *only* the suffering of the victims; those who inflicted the suffering do not witness it.

Picasso's painting, done just before the outbreak of World War II, was a portent of things to come. Many of the great cities of Europe later came under even more brutal attack. But since Guernica and her population were among the first to suffer from this twentieth-century terror, Picasso's painting has become one of the most important works of contemporary art.

Guernica, done entirely in blacks, whites, and grays, recalls the way Picasso learned of the town's destruction in Parisian newspapers; the stippled hide of the horse suggests newsprint. The cubist technique Picasso once used to create serene still lifes now splits and fragments forms to convey the chaos of war. If you thought the cubist style incapable of conveying expressionist feeling, a glance at *Guernica* ought to dispel your doubts.

The bull, the horse, and the female heads are familiar from Picasso's earlier works. Although these shattered, distorted figures lack the physical reality of human beings and animals, they tell the story of inhuman warfare in realistic terms. Shocked and powerless, grieved and in pain, their mouths gape wide with almost audible cries in the terror and devastation that smashes down upon them. The effect is remarkable because there is almost no sign of bombing. Only the building in flames, the electric light above the horse's head which suggests an explosion, and the lance in the horse's flank, thrown from above, indicate an aerial attack.

In spite of the clear message this picture conveys, there is also a degree of ambiguity in the presence of the bull. All the figures seem to be turned toward the bull, crying out to him. The woman on the extreme right is an exception because she is being consumed by the flames of the burning building. The figure of a woman looking in from the window, surveying the scene with a lamp in her hand, is directed toward the bull; the woman below her is also leaning toward the bull (her back forms one side of a triangle, the other side of which Picasso makes clear by drawing a table into the scene, which also adds to the feeling that this is inside a house, perhaps a peasant's house, with Spanish block tiles on the floor). The wounded horse, which symbolizes labor and domesticity, is turned toward the bull, as well as the mother and her dead child below the bull, and the head of a smashed statue lying on the floor. The statue itself, with its severed limb holding a broken sword in hand, is among the telling elements of the scene. No doubt it comes from Picasso's earlier still-life paintings of academic plaster casts that are known to all artists. Here it suggests the traditional, ordered world now shattered by the disaster at Guernica. The broken sword suggests that conventional weapons are outdated, no match for the mechanized warfare that rains down upon the defenseless town. The transparent flower near the hand gives only a faint hope of resurrection and adds to the pathos of the painting.

Now we come to the bull. It is clearly not one of the victims in *Guernica*. It seems to have wandered in on the scene from outdoors. It stands upright with its smoking tail symbolizing power yet to be let loose. Is its latent energy one of good or one of evil? Is its cold stare, directed out of the picture, one of meditative thought or an expression of triumph? Picasso said the bull represents "brutality and darkness," so, if we are to believe Picasso, the bull is a symbol of energy gone evil. But Picasso also said, when asked again about the meaning of the bull by curators of the Museum of Modern Art in New York, that "The bull is a bull. . . . It's up to the public to see what it wants to see." The ambiguity is seen in the bull, which in the bullring is an evil figure that may wound the horse and the bullfighter, but in the end, after putting up a brave and hopeless battle, changes into a heroic figure. If you feel the bull is a symbol of evil, the victims' screams are screams of accusation. If, on the other hand, the bull is symbolic of the spirit of the Spanish people that sustains them through the worst of times, the bull is a hopeful sign that good will ultimately triumph.

Whatever interpretation you subscribe to, Picasso has made a powerful artistic statement about the victims of twentieth-century destruction.

SAN FERNANDO ACADEMY OF ART

Calle de Alcala, 13

When this book went to press this museum was still closed for restoration. Before attempting to visit it check with the tourist board. If it is open you should not miss the fine paintings by Goya (1746–1828) in this museum. The four small panels, probably from 1801—*The Procession of the Flagellants, The Bullfight, The Inquisition Tribunal,* and *The Madhouse*—and the often-reproduced *Burial of the Sardine* (1793) are especially important and clearly show how original an artist Goya was. His exaggerated colors, which have a black tonality, are vigorously applied, and his unusual forms, to be seen again in the "Black Murals" (see *The Witches' Sabbath* in the Prado), will remind you of twentieth-century expressionism.

There are a number of other fine paintings in the museum, namely, those by Zurbarán, Murillo, and Ribera.

Buildings

THE ROYAL PALACE

Plaza de Oriente (entrance in the Plaza de la Armería)

Hours: Open summer, Mon.–Sat., 10AM–1:30PM and 4–6:15PM; winter, Mon.–Sat., 10AM–12:45PM and 3:30–5:15PM; Sun. and holidays, 10AM–1:30PM. Admission fee.

This large eighteenth-century palace, constructed between 1738 and 1764, was designed by Italians, which explains its long Italianate facades. It is built around one great interior court with two extending wings, each about 600 feet in length, that form a second larger courtyard (the one you will walk through to enter the palace).

Before entering, notice the Italian horizontal emphasis on the balustrade and entabulature, and the building's two stories, spanned by a giant order of Doric pilasters interrupted by Ionic engaged columns on the pavilions. All this stands on a ground floor of rough stone.

Inside, a tour conducted in the language of your choice will take you to fifty-five splendid rooms, among which is the fine rococo **throne room,** which has a ceiling representing the glory of the Spanish monarchy painted by the Venetian **G. B. Tiepolo** (1696–1770). There is also the small **porcelain room** with its walls and ceiling covered in glazed ceramics; an elaborate marble and stucco **staircase** to ascend to reach the apartments on the first floor; an excellent collection of Flemish tapestries; some old master paintings, and more rooms painted by Tiepolo, who went to Madrid in 1762 at the invitation of the king. Tiepolo's paintings are in the throne room (*Apotheosis of Spain,* 1764), the guard room (*Aeneas Conducted to the Temple of Venus,* 1764–66), and the queen's anteroom (*Apotheosis of the Spanish Monarchy,* 1764–66).

SAN ANTONIO DE LA FLORIDA

Paseo de la Florida

Hours: Open July–Sept., Mon., Tues., Thurs.–Sat., 10AM–1PM and 4–7PM, Sun., 10AM–1PM; Oct.–June, Mon., Tues., Thurs.–Sat., 11AM–1:30PM and 3–6PM., Sun., 10AM–1:30PM. Admission fee.

Goya, Francisco* (1746–1828), Spanish

Frescoes Depicting the Miracle of St. Anthony (1798): dome
You will be fascinated with this little church, located between the Parque del Oeste and the Manzanares. The series of frescoes that Goya painted in its dome depict a scene from the life of St. Anthony in which the saint brings a murdered man back to life to testify to the innocence of the saint's father, who was accused of the murder. Many of the figures, arranged around the circular railing, appear more typical of a genre scene than a religious picture. They seem more concerned with themselves and everyday life than with the miracle taking place. One critic has described it as "more of a popular fiesta than a religious scene."

The religious figures are depicted the way Goya's independent mind saw them, not the way we may expect to see them. Nevertheless, the painting qualifies as a religious work of art. Goya's aim was first to delight the eye of the visitor, who would then notice the religious theme—an approach that seems to have been understood by the clergy and the king. They had the church raised by the pope to a privileged position under the direct control of the royal court.

The church contains Goya's grave. He died in exile in Bordeaux, but his remains were brought to Spain in 1888. When his tomb was opened it was found that his skull was missing. To compound the mystery there was a nineteenth-century painting in Spain called "Goya's Skull" by Dionisio Fierros, which has also vanished. To this day the mystery remains unsolved.

Salamanca

Salamanca is one of the most elegantly beautiful cities in Spain, with many buildings of artistic importance that give testimony to its rich past. The **Plaza Mayor** (1720–33), in the center of the city, is one of the great squares in Europe, an eighteenth-century descendant of the seventeenth-century Plaza Mayor in Madrid. Unlike that square, Salamanca's has retained much of its original character. Its architect was **Alberto de Churriguera** (1676–1750), a member of the Churriguera family of architects who gave their name to the flamboyant baroque in Spain, often referred to as Churrigueresque.

Close to the square, off the Rua Mayor, is the **Casa de las Conchas** (1483), a palace covered with sea-shell decoration containing some exquisite windows and grilles. The shells are not only decorative but also create interesting shadows by dispersing the rays of the sun.

Further down the Rua Mayor, to the right, is the **University of Salamanca,** which in the fourteenth century ranked second to the one at Paris. The religious fanaticism and corruption of the sixteenth century caused it to go into a decline. See it for its facade (1516–29), one of the best examples of the Renaissance plateresque. An early interpretation of the Renaissance style in Spain, Renaissance plateresque can be compared to a type of Flemish mannerism that also influenced English and German architects. In Spain the style is more ornate, with much carved or stucco decoration. That is not to say that the buildings themselves are Renaissance structures. They retain basic medieval characteristics, with Renaissance features in their decoration.

Continuing down the Rua Mayor, a short distance from the university, are the **Old and New cathedrals** (open 10AM–1:45PM and 4–7:45PM; admission fee), joined in one unit, the old flanking the new on the right. The New Cathedral is a sixteenth-century Gothic structure with Renaissance decoration. It was built to accommodate the growing population of university students and faculty. The difference in scale between it and the Old Cathedral will give you an idea of how large the university had grown by the time the new structure was built. Its west facade (1513–31) is decorated with plateresque ornament and is a sight of extraordinary splendor. Its interior, however, is solemn, in part because of the heavy bands of capitals encircling every pier, and an unusual square east end. The Old Cathedral, entered by way of the New Cathedral, is more interesting (built 1120–78). It has a fine dome with a high drum supported on pendentives, pierced with two rows of windows and topped off with a stone ribbed cupola. Its tall lantern on the exterior, the famous Torre del Gallo, floods the sanctuary with light and illuminates the fifteenth-century altarpiece that decorates the walls.

If, after seeing the cathedrals, you proceed down to the Tormes River, you will find the **Puente Romano,** a fine Roman bridge with twenty-six arches. The nearest fifteen are the original work of the ancient Romans, built under the emperors Trajan and Hadrian. The remainder of the bridge dates from 1499 and 1677.

_____Santiago de Compostela_____

CATHEDRAL

This cathedral, which holds the remains of St. James, the patron saint of Spain, was the terminus of the pilgrimage routes that started in northern Europe and Italy during the Middle Ages. While pilgrimage churches sprang up along the various routes, Santiago de Compostela is the greatest of them all, and the greatest Romanesque church in Spain—a fitting climax to the pilgrimage. It is an eleventh- and twelfth-century construction with a barrel-vaulted nave of great length (310 feet) and cross-vaulted single aisles. There are bold transepts (200 feet across) and a French-style chevet with ambulatory and radiating chapels in a cruciform plan. The cathedral's dimensions and interior layout were planned for rich ceremonial worship and processions.

While the exterior of the cathedral is baroque, having been rebuilt in the eighteenth century, its interior is Romanesque and its exterior south transept portico, called La Puerta de las Platerías, built in 1103, has some fine twelfth-century Romanesque sculpture. Most important, however, is the porch at the west entrance, called the **Portico de la Gloria.** Consisting of three doorways with column figures (the central portal having a tympanum and a trumeau), and figures on the walls of the narthex, the portico is an outstanding complex of Romanesque sculpture, depicting figures with religious fervor and a variety of terrifying monsters. These were sculptured (1168–88) by one **Master Mateo** (active second half of twelfth century), who is buried in the church. Mateo seems to have learned from the masters of Burgundy, but his art is first-rate Romanesque.

Segovia

Segovia has almost as much of a medieval atmosphere as Toledo, but with a more varied architecture dating back to the Romans. Segovia is probably best known for its impressive **Roman aqueduct.** On the eastern side of the city, it is formed by 118 arches in two tiers, constructed in granite blocks without mortar, and is 2,700 feet in length and 102 feet in height. Dating to the first and second centuries A.D., it is an engineering marvel as well as an architectural legacy. It still functions as an aqueduct.

On the western edge of the city is the **Alcázar** (open daily, 10AM–2PM and 4–6PM; Sat.–Sun., 10AM–6PM; admission fee), a fortified palace named for a Moorish castle that once stood on the site; many of its interior rooms have spectacular Mudéjar ceilings. While some parts of the building date back to the fourteenth century, most of what you see today was built in the nineteenth century. Isabella the Catholic was living in the Alcázar when she was called upon to become queen of Castile.

Segovia's **cathedral** (open 9AM–1PM. and 3–6PM; admission fee), built between 1520 and 1577 (located on the Plaza Mayor), is an example of the Gothic lingering in Spain after other countries had already turned to Renaissance designs. It is the last cathedral of first rank in Europe to be built in the Gothic style, beautifully expressed in the seven-chapel chevet with gently sloping flying buttresses and ornate crocheted pinnacles. Inside, slender clustered shafts, supporting the Gothic vaulting, create a soaring verticality, directing the eye heavenward. Segovia cathedral sums up what Gothic architects expressed hundreds of years earlier.

There is an important piece of Renaissance sculpture in Segovia, but you will have to cross the river to visit the Hieronymite monastery of **El Parral** (open daily, 9AM–1PM and 3–6:30PM; Sun. 9AM–12PM and 3–6:30PM) in order to see it. There, in the church of the monastery, making up the main altar is a great stone reredos with a triptych composition consisting of sculptured figures. Its execution in 1528 by two Spanish artists helped introduce Renaissance art into old Castile.

Seville

If any one city can be called the most Spanish of cities in Spain, Seville would qualify. It combines Moorish architectural elements in its Christian styles and has an almost completely Moorish **Alcázar** (southeast side of Plaza del Triunfo, across from the cathedral [open 9AM–12:45PM and 4:30–7PM; admission fee]), which dates back to the eleventh century (though most of the present structure dates from the fourteenth century). Somewhat similar to the Alhambra in Granada, the Alcázar has lovely gardens surrounded by a Hall of the Ambassadors that is decorated in the colorful, ornate Moorish style. Seville was also the home of the painter Murillo (1618–82), who lived at no. 2 Pl. de Alfaro in the charming Barrio de Santa Cruz section, and whose work can be seen in the chapel of the Hospital de la Santa Caridad (Calle de Santander) and in the Fine Arts Museum (Plaza del Museo), where other fine works from the Spanish school are shown. Seville also has parks that are masterpieces of landscape architecture, and the largest of all Spanish cathedrals, which combines the Moorish Giralda minaret into its structure.

CATHEDRAL

Hours: Open daily 10:30AM–1PM and 4–6PM (3:30–5:30PM in winter). Admission fee.

The Seville cathedral is the largest Gothic structure in the world, and the largest, highest church in Spain. Its site was once occupied by a mosque that was used as a church from 1248, the date the city was liberated from the Moors, to 1402, when the mosque had to be replaced because of age and damage from an earthquake. The new cathedral was completed by 1506.

Although the cathedral is in the Gothic style, it contains classical, Renaissance, and baroque elements. One of its outstanding features is the original Moorish twelfth-century **tower (the Giralda)**, the only part of the old mosque saved from demolition. In 1568 the Giralda was crowned with a Renaissance bell tower and a statue representing *Faith,* which rotates in the breeze. The statue and the Giralda have become symbols of the city of Seville. While the tower is the most distinctive feature of the cathedral's exterior, the apsidal end is also an accomplished piece of architecture. Much of the remainder of the exterior is restored or altered, and the almost flat roofs and horizontal buttresses do not make the best Gothic designs.

The cathedral is built on a Moorish grid square plan (430 by 237 feet). The wide nave has four massive aisles with surrounding chapels. Its height rises 130 feet; quadripartite vaults are supported on immense clustered piers with lovely little foliated capitals. A balcony takes the place of a triforium, extending along the base of clerestory windows with rich curvilinear tracery.

The interior shows remarkable unity and fine proportions for its great size. Numerous works of art by foreign masters as well as Spanish artists are worthy of attention, particularly the crucifixion sculpture called *The Merciful Christ* (1603) by **Juan Martínez Montañez** (1568–1649), located at the altar of the Sacristía de los Cálices, a sixteenth-century Gothic addition to the Sacristía Mayor on the south side of the cathedral. It is a work of piety showing Christ looking down from the cross at one of his followers, who kneels at his feet. Christ's face is serene, with tenderness and understanding; his eyes express profound sadness for the sins of man.

Toledo

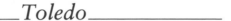

CATHEDRAL

Hours: Open daily 10:30AM–1PM and 3:30–7PM (to 6PM in winter). Admission fee.

Toledo Cathedral is based on the French Gothic model but retains a Spanish appearance. It was built over a long period of time from the early thirteenth century into the sixteenth. The **exterior** is dominated by a 301-foot three-storied tower, flanking the west front on the north side. It is easily seen from an irregularly shaped little plaza that also contains the archbishop's palace and a fine town hall. Houses of the town unfortunately interfere with the view on the other three sides of the cathedral.

The most important features of Toledo Cathedral are in its large **interior**, probably filled with more religious art treasures than any other church in Europe. The nave is simple and majestically Gothic, with multishafted piers and foliated capitals carrying pointed arches. Above are a quadripartite vault and clerestory windows that still have much of their original glass. There is also a magnificent rose window.

First, go to the **Capilla Mayor.** It has the finest altarpiece in Spain, which rises in sculptured piers of glittering richly colored scenes from the New Testament. A number of artists worked on it from 1498 to 1504, and though many of them were northern European, it still looks Spanish. There are other similar works in Spanish churches, but this one is larger and more beautiful than most.

Behind the high altar is the *Transparente,* the most famous work in the cathedral, but not the best. It is an eighteenth-century work by **Narciso Tomé** (active 1715–42) and nowhere has baroque theatricality and ostentation been carried to greater lengths. The marble carvings are a confusion of columns, carved cornices, and angels floating up to the Virgin perched near the top of the roof; Christ is seated in the clouds with his prophets and the heavenly host. The painting makes ingenious use of light from a hidden source that heightens the effect of shape and color.

Next, look at the **coro,** or choir. It has a superb set of **carved stalls** with many figures in the upper row on the south side carved by Spain's leading Renaissance sculptor, **Alonso Berruguette** (1480/90–1561). The figures, muscular and powerful without being too thick-set, will remind you of the best Italian sculpture of the period, perhaps even of Michelangelo.

The sacristy, to the left of the high altar, has been turned into a museum of paintings. The best of them are *The Taking of Christ* by Goya (1746–1828) and a number of works by El Greco.

SANTA MARIA LA BLANCA

Calle de Los Reyes Catolicos

Hours: Open daily 10AM–2PM and 3:30–6:45PM (to 5:45PM in winter). Admission fee.

This building is today a five-aisled church on a rectangular plan with multi-level roofs. It was originally a twelfth-century synagogue, converted to a church after the expulsion of the Jews from Spain in 1492. Notice the beautiful decoration of the capitals, the wall arcades, and the horseshoe arches. Their ornamental patterns show the influence of the Moors among whom the Jews lived undisturbed in Spain.

Close by, on the Calle de San Juan de Dios, is the Synagogue del Tránsito (open daily 10AM–2PM and 4–7PM; closed Sun.–Mon.; admission fee) founded in the fourteenth century. It too was seized by the Christians but has now been restored. Here you can see Hebrew lettering worked into the Moorish designs. It was built by Samuel Levi, treasurer to the crown, who was robbed and executed by Pedro the Cruel (1334–60).

CHURCH OF SANTO TOMÉ

Calle de Santo Tomé

Hours: Open daily 10AM–1:45PM and 3:30–6:45PM (to 5:45PM in winter). Admission fee.

El Greco (1541–1614), Spanish
El Greco's real name was Domenikos Theotokopoulos, hence his nickname El Greco or "The Greek." He was born on the island of Crete but received his artistic training in Venice. He seems never to have forgotten what he learned there, and throughout his career his art was influenced by the drama of Tintoretto's works and the late paintings of Titian. El Greco's style was intended to express the mystic emotionalism of the Catholic Counter-Reformation, which was even more sharply felt in Spain than in Italy. The fervid faith of the time needed a new, highly charged way of presenting the old Christian stories. El Greco achieved the effect by elongating his figures in an abstract way, rather like the figures he had seen distorted for emotional effect in the Byzantine art of his native land. To the elongation he added a whitish light that flickered over the forms, increasing their upward movement. The church was El Greco's best customer. His symbolic distortions communicated the religious intensity sought by church patrons. Because El

Greco broke many conventions of his day to convey emotion, we can look upon him as a modern expressionist who gave eloquent voice to the spirit of an age. This is the greatness of El Greco: though he painted 300 years ago for patrons as far removed from our own way of thinking as those behind the Spanish Inquisition, his manner of expressing himself was modern, and his insight into the human soul transcends history.

Close to the Church of Santo Tomé, in the Calle de Tránsito, east of the synagogue, is a reproduction of the kind of sixteenth-century house El Greco must have lived in, called for touristic purposes El Greco House. The art displayed is of little interest, but the house is worth visiting.

The Burial of Count Orgaz (1584–88)

This most admired of El Greco's paintings was based on a local fourteenth-century legend in which Gonzalo Ruiz, of the nearby town of Orgaz, was buried in 1323 with the miraculous intercession of Sts. Stephen and Augustine. The ascent to heaven was a favorite subject of El Greco; in this painting the heavens open up to receive the soul of the count, depicted as a cloudlike form borne aloft in the arms of an angel.

Notice that El Greco has painted the figures in heaven with his characteristic elongated proportions and his luminous white light. They float weightlessly in space. In the lower half, the figures are drawn naturally with their feet firmly on the ground. Contrasted as they are, the two parts are still visually coordinated, with each part subordinate to the whole.

El Greco depicted the mourners as members of the contemporary nobility and clergy, and is supposed to have included his own portrait in this picture. He has been identified as one of the mourners in the front row, a little left of center, his chin under the gesturing right hand of a nobleman whose left hand is waving toward the count.

Switzerland

Swiss art has always been determined by the artistic tendencies of its neighbors France, Germany, and Italy. In every artistic epoch, Romanesque, Gothic, baroque, and modern, the influence of these countries on Swiss artists predominates, with little of the Swiss simplicity and moderation making itself felt. In the nineteenth century Switzerland did make an original contribution with the work of Ferdinand Hodler (1853–1918), whose symbolist paintings became world famous and an influence on the expressionists of Germany. Similarly, the work of the Swiss painter Paul Klee (1879–1940), whose modernism took the form of a new picture-writing style, created one of the basic building blocks in the structure of twentieth-century modern art. One might even say that Switzerland found its true place in the art of our own time, and that this destiny has been reflected in its excellent museums. They have outstanding collections of French impressionist paintings and of artistic movements that followed. You can expect to find a display of modern art in Switzerland comparable to that in any European country. Swiss museums have intelligent, far-sighted purchasing programs and have been blessed with contributors numbered among the greatest collectors of art in the twentieth century.

Basel

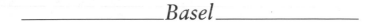

KUNSTMUSEUM (FINE ARTS MUSEUM)

St. Albangraben, 16

Hours: Open Oct.–May, Tues.–Sun., 10AM–12 noon and 2–5PM; June–Sept., Tues.–Sun., 10AM–5PM. Admission fee.

This art museum has the distinction of showing the first art collection that came into public ownership. In 1661 the city and the University of Basel purchased a collection of paintings, woodcuts, and engravings from the family of the fifteenth-century printer Johannes Amerbach. Some of the paintings in the Amerbach collection were once owned by Erasmus of Rotterdam, who bequeathed them to Amerbach's son. Before the seventeenth century ended the collection was on public display, and in succeeding centuries about 3,000 works of art were added.

While the collection started by specializing in fifteenth- and sixteenth-century Swiss and German Renaissance art—it has works by Konrad Witz, Hans Holbein the Younger, Mathias Grünewald, and Lucas Cranach the Elder—the museum also has nineteenth-century Swiss painting. Most notable, and most popular, among these works is *Isle of the Dead* (first floor, room 36) by **Arnold Böcklin** (1827–1901), painted in 1880. It is a mood painting in a symbolist sense, and makes a strong impression. It is the first version of five that Basel-born Böcklin was to paint.

The Kunstmuseum has a collection of twentieth-century art (second floor) that includes works by Corinth, Kokoschka, Chagall, Klee, and others purchased in the Nazi auction of Decadent Art in 1939. To this the museum has added cubist and constructivist art. The cubist collection is perhaps the best anywhere and includes masterpieces by Picasso, Braque, Gris, Léger, and Delaunay. There is also a large group of modern American paintings and sculptures and, of course, the works of Swiss artists.

Holbein, Hans, the Younger (1497–1543), German: first floor, rooms 9–11

The Kunstmuseum is best known for its portraits by Holbein, who was born in Germany but settled in Basel when a young man. Though he later left the city for England, he maintained his family in Basel. It was in Basel that Holbein met the famous author, Erasmus of Rotterdam, who was in residence there in 1523. You can see one of the profile portraits that Holbein did of *Erasmus* that year, and a number of other portraits, including *The Holbein Family,* done in 1528 when the artist returned to Basel after his first stay in England.

While Holbein's Basel paintings in the Kunstmuseum do not represent his best work (in England, free of the German tradition, Holbein's work is more accomplished) they do come from the hand of the greatest portraitist of the first half of the sixteenth century. Holbein could capture the personality of his sitters and at the same time present them at their best in a carefully designed picture. He set a standard in portraiture that lasted to the time of van Dyck.

Witz, Konrad (ca. 1400–ca. 1446), Swiss

Heilspiegelalter (Redemption Altarpiece panels): first floor, room 2
Konrad Witz, like Holbein, was another German-born artist who became a citizen of Basel. Not much is known about him except that he was the greatest Swiss artist before Holbein. The Kunstmuseum has nine of the twelve surviving panels from his major work, the *Heilspiegelalter,* probably done in 1435/36. These panels show an individuality, and do not follow the fanciful international style dominant during the early fifteenth century. Instead, Witz has provided strongly modeled figures that have the plasticity of sculptural forms, reminding one of Masaccio (1401–28) in Italy, and of the sculptor Claus Sluter (ca. 1350–1406) in Burgundy. Some attempt has been made to

provide a sense of perspective, though this is not worked out according to a precise formula. We know that Witz's influence on the artists of the first half of the fifteenth century in Switzerland and Germany was enormous. It gave way in the second half of the century to the Flemish style, which replaced Witz's forceful forms with more elegant models and concern for naturalistic detail.

Kokoschka, Oskar (1886–1980), Austrian

The Tempest or *The Bride of the Wind* (1914): second floor, room 9
This painting was created by Kokoschka to express the approaching end of his affair with Alma Mahler, widow of composer Gustav Mahler. Its greatness as a piece of expressionistic art is that its abstracted forms provide a statement of the turbulence of life, where serenity and peace can be found only in the miracle of human love. The two people sleeping are surrounded by a swirling, nightmarish mass, where color is of little importance; light and line are used to convey the mood. They have found refuge in this confusion, but their distorted forms reflect the toll life has taken physically and mentally.

Berne

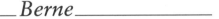

KUNSTMUSEUM (FINE ARTS MUSEUM)

Hodlerstrasse, 12

Hours: Open Wed.–Sun., 10AM–12 noon and 2–5PM, Tues., 10AM–12 noon, 2–5PM and 8–10PM. Admission fee.

Although this museum has some fine early Italian paintings—see *Virgin and Child* (ca. 1290) by Duccio (ca. 1255–ca. 1318) on the main floor, room 2— it specializes in works of the nineteenth and twentieth centuries: French impressionists and cubists (cubist paintings donated by the Rupf Foundation), including examples by Braque, Gris, Léger, and Picasso, among others, with an emphasis on Swiss artists, especially Paul Klee.

Hodler, Ferdinand (1853–1918), Swiss: main floor, room 15
It is gratifying to find a museum on a street named after an artist, especially one as good as the Swiss painter Ferdinand Hodler. The museum devotes a room to his works, where you can see his masterpiece, *Night,* another called *Day,* and his *Chosen One,* in which he has painted his son, then six years old. These are large oils and tempera on canvas, treated like frescoes.

Hodler and his symbolist paintings became famous in Europe in the 1890s. He is often grouped with the Art Nouveau painters because of the influence he had on the Berlin and Vienna Secession (the name given to avant-garde artistic movements in Germany and Austria at the end of the nineteenth and the beginning of the twentieth centuries, in which the Nabis, Fauves, Munch, Kandinsky and the Brücke artists, Klimt, and finally Kokoschka displayed their work). But Hodler's work is less decorated, with a spiritual dimension easily felt by the viewer. In *Night* (1889–90), the ghost of death is seen surprising one of the sleepers. It is symbolic of man's age-old fear of the night, of darkness, of what may happen while asleep. It is the fear of the unknown that death represents. The coloring, with the sleeping figures draped in black, adds to this symbolism. The female nude, seen from behind, sets up a brilliant tension between the realism of the scene and a spiritual feeling conveyed by a lack of spatial relations.

Klee, Paul (1879–1940), Swiss: ground floor, rooms 17–21
While the Berne museum is located on Hodler Street, it is best known today for the work of Paul Klee. Through the Klee Foundation the museum has the largest collection of Klees in the world, over 2,000 works.

Paul Klee developed a kind of picture-writing style that has been likened to Chinese calligraphy, to the art of primitive people, and even to drawings by children. It is abstract with a curious way of communicating dreamlike images, similar to those in modern music and poetry.

If you look at Klee's work as a mirror of processes of the organic world, you should find the key to Klee. Still, you need imagination to understand him.

Lugano

GALLERY VILLA FAVORITA

Castagnola–Lugano (east of Lugano–half hour walk from center of Lugano, or take steamer from main boat dock)

Hours: Open Tues.–Sun., 10AM–12 noon and 2–6PM. Admission fee.

The Villa Favorita, on the shores of Lake Lugano, holds one of the largest private art collections in the world, with a great number of old master paintings. It was formed in this century, with a large fortune behind it, the Thyssen steel holdings.

The collection got its start when Baron Hans Heinrich Thyssen bought some sculpture by Rodin. Later, the baron's father began to amass old master paintings. The depression years of the 1930s, when parts of private collections were sold to raise cash, helped the Thyssen collection grow. Many paintings were bought for sums that seem ridiculously low.

Earl Spenser, an English aristocrat, in 1934 sold the baron's father the only surviving oil portrait in England of **King Henry VIII** by **Holbein** for about $7,500. A **Ghirlandaio portrait**—the present baron's favorite painting—was acquired when many of Pierpont Morgan's paintings were sold. Bargains were also picked up from the Barberini collection in Rome, such as a **Caravaggio** acquired in 1935 for $16,000.

There are many Italian masterpieces to be seen: from the Bellinis of Venice there is an *Annunciation,* by **Gentile Bellini,** and from his younger brother, **Giovanni,** *Nunc Dimittis,* which tells the story of Simeon, a priest of the Temple who was told he would not die until he saw the Messiah; there is part of an altarpiece by **Duccio,** the leading painter of early fourteenth-century Siena; a portrait of a man with penetrating eyes by **Antonello da Messina,** the Italian painter of the early Renaissance who helped introduce Flemish detail into Italian painting; and many other old masters, including Bernardo Daddi, Fra Angelico, Piero della Francesca, Uccello, Raffael, Titian, Tintoretto, and Veronese.

From Germany there is the only authenticated portrait by **Altdorfer,** the painter of Danubian landscapes; **Dürer's** *Jesus Among the Scribes,* contrasting the youthful hands of Jesus with the crinkled hands of the old scribe, one of the most interesting depictions of hands in all of art; and from Dürer's most gifted pupil, **Hans Baldung,** a nearly life-size sensual *Adam and Eve.*

There is a rare **Petrus Christus** (there are only twenty extant in the world) representing the *Virgin in a Barren Tree* with fifteen letter A's hanging from its branches referring to the angel's greeting, "Ave Maria" or "Ave gratia plena Dominus tecum—Greetings most favored one! The Lord is with you." The apple held in the infant's hand is the fruit of the Tree of Knowledge and therefore alludes to him as the future Redeemer of mankind from Original Sin. The barren tree may refer to the power of God to bring the dried-out tree back to life through the Tree of Life, or it may symbolize the Tree of Jesse and the prophecy of Isaiah that a Messiah would spring from the family of Jesse, the father of David. Other works from fifteenth-century Flanders are a **Jan van Eyck diptych** painted to look like marble; a *Madonna Enthroned with Child,* by **Rogier van der Weyden;** a *Crucifixion,* by Gerard **David;** and portraits of men by the **Master of Flémalle** and **Memling.**

Spanish painting starts with five works by **El Greco** and ends with two by **Goya.** In between there are five examples of seventeenth-century Spanish painting by **Velázquez, Zurbarán,** and **Murillo.**

Seventeenth-century Holland is well represented with a *Self-portrait* of about 1643 by **Rembrandt;** landscapes by both Jacob **and Salomon van Ruisdael;** genre scenes by **Jan Steen,** and his *Self-portrait with a Lute;* interior scenes by **Pieter de Hooch;** a *Still life* by **Kalf;** society portraits by **Gerard Terborch;** a *View of Haarlem,* by **Vermeer;** and other Dutch paintings by Cuyp, Dou, Witte, Hals, Hobbema, Maes, and Wouwerman. Flemish art of the seventeenth century is shown with the works of Jacob Jordaens, Anthony van Dyck, and Rubens.

Finally, from France, there is an interesting work by **Clouet** with three figures representing a watchmaker and a man and woman in love; *La Toilette,* by **Boucher;** a *Still life,* by **Chardin;** a *Landscape with the Flight into Egypt,* by **Claude;** a delightful *Seesaw,* by **Fragonard;** and paintings by Lancret, Le Nain, Nattier, and Watteau.

The baron also collects modern art and does not specialize in any particular period. The result is a collection perhaps more comprehensive than any other in private hands.

It is a joy to view this collection in the surroundings provided for it by the baron's father, who in 1937 built the Villa Favorita. It is also gratifying that the paintings are kept in a better state of preservation than they would be in most public museums. Surrounded by a superb collection of furniture, they are a joy to see.

_____ Winterthur _____

KUNSTMUSEUM (FINE ARTS MUSEUM)

Museumstrasse, 52

Hours: Open Tues.–Sun., 10AM–12 noon and 2–5PM. Admission fee.

This museum was established in the mid-nineteenth century as a community museum specializing in works by Winterthur artists, but it soon expanded to become international in scope. When it moved into its present building in 1916, which it shares with the city's collection of natural sciences, it began to acquire the works in the areas it currently displays: the art of Winterthur from 1700 to the present; Swiss art since the beginning of the nineteenth century; and European art since impressionism.

Noteworthy are paintings by the eighteenth-century portraitist from Winterthur, Anton Graff; the Swiss painters Arnold Böcklin, Ferdinand Hodler, Felix Vallotton, and Paul Klee; French paintings by Claude Monet, Edouard Vuillard, Pierre Bonnard, Henri Rousseau, and Ferdinand Léger; works by Kandinsky, Oskar Kokoschka, Max Beckmann, Max Ernst, and Picasso; and sculptures by Rodin, Maillol, Brancusi, Jacques Lipchitz, Jean Arp, and others.

Graff, Anton (1736–1813), Swiss: No special room and shown only for a few months during the year
Anton Graff, born in Winterthur, rose to be a painter of considerable importance in Germany and Switzerland. An enormous number of his portraits exist in the museums of central Europe. (The twenty-eight in the Kunstmuseum are typical of his work.)

Though Graff's output of paintings and drawings number about two thousand, including eighty self-portraits, they are accomplished works that depict the ladies and gentlemen of the wealthy merchant class and the aristocracy with a sense of individuality that is admirable for a society portraitist. Graff did not reach the artistic heights in portraiture of some of his contemporaries, especially those in England (Gainsborough, Reynolds, Lawrence, Raeburn, and Romney), but in German portraiture Graff's accomplishment must be rated at the top.

THE OSKAR REINHART COLLECTIONS

Oskar Reinhart, a businessman of Winterthur, devoted his adult life to collecting and studying art. Over a period of sixty years (he died in 1965 at the age of eighty) he built up one of the finest private collections in Europe, and in 1951 set up the Oskar Reinhart Foundation to place part of his collection on public display as a gift to Winterthur. This collection is housed in an old school, and consists of about 600 works of eighteenth-, nineteenth- and twentieth-century German, Swiss, and Austrian artists. (*Stiftung Oskar Reinhart,* Stadthansstrasse, 6. [Hours: Open Mon., 2–5PM; Tues.–Sun., 10AM–12 noon and 2–5PM; first Thurs. of every month, also 8–10PM; admission fee.])

After Reinhart's death his private collection was given to Winterthur and since 1970 has been on display at Am Romerholz, his former home. The works of art there are the best part of his collection, consisting of French paintings from Poussin to Cézanne, and German, Flemish, Dutch, and Spanish old master paintings. (*Sammlung Oskar Reinhart "Am Roemerholz,"* Haldenstrasse, 95. Hours: open Tues.–Sun., 10AM–4PM; closed Mondays.) Admission fee.

Zurich

KUNSTHAUS (FINE ARTS MUSEUM)

Heimplatz, 1

Hours: Open Mon., 2–5PM; Tues.–Fri., 10AM–9PM; Sat., Sun., 10AM–5PM. Admission fee.

This museum of the city of Zurich is famous for its temporary exhibitions. It organized the first Hodler exhibition in 1917 and the first Picasso retrospective in 1932. It also has a large permanent collection that includes a sculpture garden with works by Rodin, Matisse, Lipchitz, and Burckhardt, among others.

On the **first floor** are European paintings dating back as far as the thirteenth century, including Dutch paintings from the sixteenth and seventeenth centuries (rooms 5–10). However, most of the space on this floor is given to the display of Swiss art. Room 11 is devoted to the works of **Arnold Böcklin** (1827–1901), an artist popular in Switzerland and Germany during the last quarter of the nineteenth century, who has been credited with influencing the art of the twentieth century. Such artists as Max Ernst, Salvador Dali, and Giorgio de Chirico were attracted to his imaginative themes, often revolving around an Arcadian landscape peopled by nymphs, shepherds, and all sorts of fantastic figures—fine stuff for surrealists and their world of secret desires that reflect the subconscious.

In room 12 is the work of a Swiss painter who preceded Böcklin, whose imagination was perhaps greater, **Johann Heinrich Füssli** (1741–1825), a native of Zurich. (Füssli lived most of his life in London where he became known as Henry Fuseli.) He grew up in the intellectual circle of Zurich where his father, Johann Caspar Füssli, was a portraitist, scholar, and historian. He became well schooled in works of literature, especially English. See the painting *J. J. Bodmer Speaking to the Artist* (1781). (Bodmer was a friend of Fuseli's father and the translator of Milton into German.) Fuseli painted scenes from Shakespeare, such as *Falstaff in the Washbasket* (1792). His paintings and drawings have a Michelangelesque quality in the modeling of his human figures, always the focus of his work. Fuseli was right for his time; his obsession with fear and sex expressed the incipient romantic movement in England, on which he had an influence. Paintings that depict dreams (nightmares) and erotica, in which the horse plays a role in Fuseli's iconography, are admired today and are the subjects of psychoanalyzing. See *Midsummer Night's Dream* (1793/94).

The works of another Swiss painter, **Ferdinand Hodler** (1853–1918), are shown in rooms 18–20. The discussion of Hodler's art in the museum at Berne refers to his influence on the avant-garde artistic movements in central Europe at the end of the nineteenth century, and to his pictures that seek to express intangible absolutes. Of pictures here see *The Truth* (1902), where Truth reigns supreme in the midst of dark ragged figures representing falsehood and deception who are unable to face the reality of Truth in the light of the day. But Hodler also painted excellent portraits (see *Portrait of Mlle. Duchosal* [1885], *The Student* [1874], and *Self-portrait* [1892], where he expresses the inward presence of his sitters as well as their physical appearance. He has also done roughly modeled landscapes with powerful brush strokes that evoke the grandeur of his native Switzerland (see *Evening at Genfersee* [1898] and *Silva-Planersee* [1907]). Coming at the end of the nineteenth century and at the early part of the twentieth, and basing his art on the expression of formal elements in painting, Hodler brought Swiss painting from impressionism to symbolism, and inspired others to experiment with abstract forms that came to dominate modern art.

The first floor also has the finest display of the Swiss sculptor **Alberto Giacometti** (1901–66). In Giacometti's *The Forest* and *The Chariot* (room 21), both from 1950, are the results of his lifelong experiments in expressing the isolation of the human figure in contemporary society. These elongated, emaciated figures, whose volumes are reduced to cracked masses anchored to the ground by baselike forms, powerfully evoke the mystery of life.

On the **second floor**, in rooms 1–2, are the works of expressionism. Here are two paintings by **Oskar Kokoschka** (1886–1980): *Lovers with Cats* (1917), which has the expressive qualities of Kokoschka's *Tempest* (Kunstmuseum, Basel); and one of Kokoschka's portraits, *Else Kupfer* (1910), which shows Kokoschka as a fine portraitist. Here is the finest collection outside Scandinavia of the work of the Norwegian painter **Edvard Munch** (1863–1944). Included are Munch's *Music on Carl Johan Street* (1889), *Winter Night* (1900), *Portrait of Albert Kollmann* (1901), and *Harbor at Lübeck* (1907).

The collection continues with a group of impressionist and postimpressionist paintings in rooms 3, 4, and 14, the art of Kandinsky, Miró, Léger, and Picasso in rooms 9 and 11, and an excellent collection of the work of **Marc Chagall** (1887–1985) in room 10. See here two examples of Chagall's mature work, *Above Vitebsk* (1922) and *The Lights of Marriage* (1945), where his images are expressed on several spatial planes and his people and objects float through the air immune from the laws of gravity. (see Marc Chagall Biblical Message National Museum, Nice, France.)

STIFTUNG SAMMLUNG E. G. BÜHRLE (BÜHRLE COLLECTION)

Zollikerstrasse, 172

Hours: Open Tues., Fri., 2–5PM. Admission fee.

This private museum houses the collection of E. G. Bührle, the Swiss industrialist, famous for its nineteenth- and twentieth-century paintings by the masters of impressionism, postimpressionism, and expressionism. A partial list will give you an idea of its quality: five paintings by Pierre Bonnard; a *Still Life* and three other paintings by George Braque; *Mother and Child* by Mary Cassatt; landscapes and portraits, including a self-portrait, by Paul Cézanne, seven paintings in all; *Russian Marriage,* by Marc Chagall; two readers and a landscape by Camille Corot; eight paintings by Edgar Degas, including portraits, domestic scenes, and dancers; four works by Paul Gauguin; seven paintings by Vincent van Gogh from 1884 to 1890; eight paintings by Edouard Manet; *Reader in Blue,* a Parisan scene and a still life by Henri Matisse; *Sleeping Nude,* by Modigliani; four paintings by Claude Monet, including landscapes and *Breakfast at Sisley's;* four paintings by Picasso; six paintings by Renoir; *In the Shade and the Sun* and *The Parade,* by George Seurat; and many more of the greatest names of nineteenth- and twentieth-century art. There are also French, Italian, Dutch, and Spanish old master paintings, and a collection of sculpture.

Glossary

Aisle: In cathedrals, lateral divisions that can be applied to nave, choir, and transepts. (See diagram, Latin-Cross Plan.)

Ambulatory: A processional aisle encircling an apse. (See diagram, Latin-Cross Plan.)

Apse: A semicircular or polygonal end to a church. (See diagram, Latin-Cross Plan.)

Arcade: A series of arches, purely decorative, open or closed (blind) with masonry, resting on piers or columns.

Arch: A construction spanning an opening designed to support its own weight and that of the structure above it. There are many different arches: the *Gothic,* or *ogee,* is pointed with a double curve; the *Romanesque* is semi-circular; and the *Moorish* is horse-shoe-shaped.

Architrave: The lowest member, or beam, of a classic entabulature. (See diagram, Greek Orders.)

Barbican: Outer defense of a castle or city wall. Usually a double tower over a gate or bridge.

Baroque Art (seventeenth century):   This style, a reaction against Renaissance classicism, originated in Italy as an outgrowth of the mannerism of the late sixteenth century and as an emphasis of the Catholic Counter-Reformation. Thus, it appeals to the emotions rather than the intellect. In architecture, it is most noted for its massiveness and theatricality, expressed with curved facades, textured variety, and illusions of depth and movement; in painting, it often presents bold and contrasting color, with dynamic compositions that imply great and sometimes violent movement, with backgrounds that open up as though there were greater areas beyond, instead of being contained and complete in themselves; in sculpture, dynamic and sometimes exaggerated compositions with emphasis on recessive modeling.

Basilica: A Roman hall-like rectangular structure flanked by aisles with its roof supported by rows of pillars. In Roman times, these were public places of business. In Christian times, they became churches; eventually, apses at the east end and narthexes at the west end were added, and then transepts were added to form the Latin cross plan.

Bay: The compartment between two columns and vaulting shafts.

Boss: In ribbed vaulting, a stone ornamental projection, usually carved with foliage or figures, used to conceal the intersection of the ribs.

Buttress: Masonry built out to strengthen a wall to resist thrust. (See also **Flying Buttress.**)

Byzantine Art (fourth–fifteenth century):   This style originated in the Byzantine Empire (Constantinople). It was the first art style developed to serve the Christian religion and, as such, it provided the dominant Christian iconography for over one thousand years. Its characteristics in paintings and mosaics are flat Oriental-looking two-dimensional figures that have little weight and depth. That is, physical reality and humanistic expression are omitted in favor of expressing an abstraction of the divine. Adopted by the West after the fall of the Roman Empire, we see it, especially, in the form of rich mosaics in Ravenna and Venice, but all art in Italy before the Renaissance is influenced by this style, which is often unsigned by the artist because he is making no claim to creating a personal work. Not until the arrival of the Renaissance does the West break away from Byzantine Art and begin to base its art on the emotions rather than just the mind.

Capital: The crowning member of a column or pier, giving support to superimposed arches or vaulting ribs. (See diagram, Greek Orders.)

Cella: The interior walled-in portion of a classic Greek or Roman temple that served as the sanctuary.

Chancel: The area of a Christian church around the high altar, reserved for the clergy; known also as the sanctuary or presbytery.

Chapter House: A room in a church set aside for administrative functions. It is often polygonal and vaulted in cathedrals.

Chevet: A French term for the grouping at the east end of an apsidal church, containing an ambulatory and radiating chapels.

Chiaroscuro: A technique in painting that uses strong contrasts between light and shade with emphasis on artificial light to achieve dramatic effects. Caravaggio in Italy and Rembrandt in Holland exemplify this technique.

Choir: As an architectural term, it refers to the eastern arm of a cathedral. (See diagram, Latin-Cross Plan.)

Cinquecento: The Italian term for the sixteenth-century High Renaissance period in Italy.

Clerestory: The upper part of the nave, choir, and transepts, containing windows above the aisle roofs. (See diagram, Gothic Cathedral.)

Column: An architectural support, often round and composed of a base, shaft, and capital. (See diagram, Greek Orders.)

Contrapposto: A torsion of the axis of the body as when the shoulders face in a different direction from the hips.

Corinthian: The most ornate of the three classic Greek orders; characterized by its bell-shaped capital covered with acanthus leaves. (See diagram, Greek Orders.)

Cornice: The highest portion of an entablature or a roof line; a moulding that projects the farthest outward from a building.

Crossing: The part of the church where the transepts cross the nave. (See diagram, Latin-Cross Plan.)

Cruciform: See **Latin-Cross plan.**

Crypt: A vault beneath a building, partly or usually below ground.

Cupola: A dome or spherical roof covering a circular or polygonal form.

Decorated Style (ca. 1300–75):   The evolution of the Gothic style in England into more elaborate forms. Window tracery is marked by more curves, and reverse curves and ribbing are more complex. This style anticipates the Flamboyant style that later spread through France in the fifteenth century.

Diptych: A painting composed of two hinged panels usually used as an altarpiece.

Doric: The simplest and most solid of the three classic Greek orders. (See diagram, Greek Orders.)

Drum: The circular base of a dome or cupola.

Early English Style (ca. 1200–1300):   The basic Gothic style in England, characterized by ribbed vaults with pointed arches, elaborate mouldings, a flat east end, a lantern tower covering the crossing, and west front towers.

Elizabethan Style: A continuation of the Tudor (Gothic) style, which flourished in England until the sixteenth century and afterwards.

Entablature: The top portion of a column, which consists of the three horizontal moldings (architrave, frieze, and cornice). (See diagram, Greek Orders.)

Expressionism: This is a term that refers to a main and permanent tradition in the art of the late nineteenth and twentieth centuries. It encompasses the work of artists who express their innermost emotions spontaneously, which often gives rise to distortion of forms and imaginative use of harsh color. As a movement in art, expressionism started in northern Europe in 1885 with such artists as van Gogh, Toulouse-Lautrec, James Ensor, Edvard Munch, and Ferdinand Hodler. In the twentieth century it has led to the development of abstract expressionism, which is so subjective an expression of art that it contains no reference to, or evocation of, reality.

Fan Vault: A vault of the English Perpendicular period (late Gothic, sixteenth century) in which the length and curvature of all of the ribs, fanning out in all directions from a single pillar, are similar and serve a decorative rather than a structural purpose.

Fauvism: From the French *Fauves* (wild beasts); used to describe a group of young unknown painters, led by Henri Matisse, who displayed their work at the autumn salon in 1904 in Paris. Fauvism in France came to be synonymous with expressionism.

Finials: An ornamental element above a gable, canopy, or pinnacle.

Flamboyant (fifteenth century): An architectural style, displaying ornate flame-shaped tracery, used mainly in France at the end of the Gothic period, but developed in England, where it is referred to as the Decorated style.

Fluting: Grooves, usually vertical, running up the shaft of a column or pilaster.

Flying Buttress: A buttress in the form of an open arch rising from the exterior of the aisle of a Gothic cathedral. While outwardly decorative, its function is structural, directing the thrust of a high vault across the roof of an aisle to the main buttress. (See also **Gothic Art.**)

Fresco: A technique of painting in which the artist applies the colored pigments directly onto a wet plaster wall so that the picture becomes part of the wall.

Frieze: The middle division of the horizontal mouldings that are placed above columns. The moulding below the frieze is the cornice. All three mouldings (architrave, frieze, and cornice) make up the entablature. (See diagram, Greek Orders.)

Gable: A vertical decorative triangular piece of wall above a door or window.

Galilee: A porch used as a chapel or an entrance vestibule in cathedrals. In France it is usually an entrance vestibule, or narthex; in England it is usually a large porch not necessarily at the western end.

Genre Painting: Pictures of scenes from everyday life.

Gothic Art (ca. 1150–1500): The dominant style of the late medieval period, often associated with architecture and specifically with northern European cathedrals. It is largely characterized by the pointed arch, which eventually replaced the heavy round Romanesque arch; soaring heights with walls that came to contain greater areas of window space made possible by the development of great vaults supported by piers, instead of resting on thick walls as in the Romanesque style; and the discovery that the outward thrust of the weight of the vault could be absorbed by masonry arches (flying buttresses), which were connected to heavy piers set into the outward walls of the aisle. With the constant development of these building techniques, the style became more and more graceful and even fragile as walls, built higher, became thinner, and windows, decorated with stained glass, become large and more glorious. (See diagram, Gothic Cathedral.)

Greek-Cross Plan: The layout of a church in the shape of a cross whose arms are of equal size; a form common in Baroque churches.

Hammerbeam Roof: A wooden roof in which projecting beams take the place of tie beams. The ends of these are usually decorated.

Hellenic Art (fifth–fourth century B.C.): The Classic Age of Greek art; the first humanistic art that, in sculpture, glorified man and portrayed him as a god, with particular emphasis on anatomical proportion and

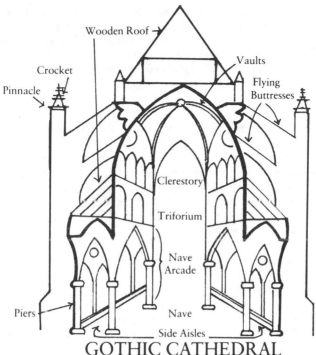

GOTHIC CATHEDRAL
Showing Major Interior and Exterior Elements.

detail, and realistic movement of the body; and, in architecture, used the column (not the arch) and emphasized perfect porportion, simplicity, and restraint.

Hellenistic Art (fourth–second century B.C.): Pertaining to the spread of Hellenic art throughout the Mediterranean area, largely by the conquests of Alexander the Great (d. 323 B.C.). It is different from Hellenic art in its greater realism, emotion, movement, and size.

Impressionism (last third of the nineteenth century): A movement credited with the start of modern art as we know it today, when strict rules of painting were discarded in favor of innovative techniques to reproduce, on canvas, what the eye really sees in nature and what is instantly assimilated by the mind without regard for meaning. Basic to its technique was the idea that varying sources of light could change the color of objects and therefore one's impression of what one sees. Using open brush strokes, with little or no drawing, painters placed bright colors directly on the canvas in immediate juxtaposition so that they would blend in the viewer's eye. Also, for the first time, painters often worked out of doors painting subjects previously considered unpaintable—rain, fog, snow, etc.

International Gothic Style (late fourteenth century): The elegant style of painting that developed in the courts of France and Burgundy before the Renaissance and spread throughout Europe, thus linking Italian painters with Northern painters. It is known for its detail and extravagant costumes, but no real concern with reality.

Ionic: The classical Greek order between Doric and Corinthian and characterized by the spiral volute of the capital. (See diagram, Greek Orders.)

Jacobean Style (early seventeenth century): An architectural style in England between the reign of Elizabeth I (1558–1603) and James I (1603–25). A continuation of the Elizabethan style with the addition of foreign influences, resulting in more ornamentation, or what can be considered a version of Italian mannerism. At its worst, it can be grotesque and vulgar; at its best, it is crisp and rhythmical.

Jamb: The side-piece of a doorway, window, or fireplace, usually spread out in Gothic buildings.

Keep: The innermost and strongest structure, or central tower, of a medieval castle.

Lady Chapel: A chapel dedicated to the Virgin Mary, usually situated, in England, beyond the east end of the sanctuary of a church.

Lancet Window: A narrow window terminating in a pointed untraceried head, common from about 1150 to 1250.

Latin-Cross Plan: The layout of a church in the shape of a cruciform, where one cross bar is longer than the other. This is the plan of most Christian churches in the West. (See diagram.)

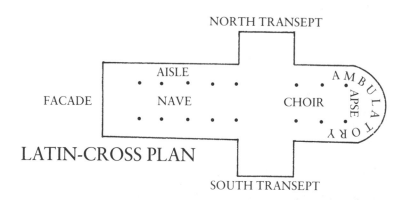

LATIN-CROSS PLAN

Lintel: A horizontal beam or slab of stone joining the two jambs of a doorway and usually forming and supporting the base of the tympanum or other architectural elements above it.

Lunette: A small arched opening in a wall.

Mannerism (sixteenth century): A term used to describe a part of the artistic tendency in the post-Renaissance era in which a new freedom of expression resulted in the exaggeration of established High Renaissance motifs. The classically posed became artificial and pretentious, color went from the balanced and harmonious to the purely decorative and chiaroscuro, composition went from the harmonious and often centralized to the conflicting and acentral. It was exported from Italy all over Europe and eventually gave way to the baroque in the late sixteenth century.

Manueline Style: The Portugese style, so called after Dom Manuel I, who reigned 1495–1521; the equivalent of the Spanish Plateresque. It features rich surface decorations in the form of seashells and twisted ropes intermingled with exotic Oriental forms.

Medieval: A term that means "of the Middle Ages," referring to a period of about ten centuries (fifth to fifteenth) from the collapse of the Western Roman Empire to the rise of the modern world.

Metope: A square, or almost square, slab in a classic frieze between two triglyphs, usually enriched with relief carving. (See diagram, Greek Orders.)

Mosaic: A design of colored glass, stone, or tile cut into small pieces and set in the mortar or plaster of walls, floors, or ceilings. The design may represent figures or it may be floral or abstract.

Mullion: A slender vertical stone bar that divides a Gothic window into separate segments.

Narthex: A covered porch stretching across the western end of many large churches on the continent.

Nave: The western arm of a church, often separated from the choir by a screen for assembly of the congregation. From the Latin word *navis* (ship), because the church was thought of as a ship that carried the faithful safely through the stormy seas of life. (See diagram, Latin-Cross Plan.)

Neo-Classicism (late eighteenth–nineteenth century): The period of classic revival stimulated, in part, by new archaeological discoveries of Greek and Roman works of art and writings, giving expression to the new political and social realities of the time (the American and French Revolutions and the Napoleonic period). It swept away the ornamental rococo style and substituted strict rules of composition and design. In painting, color was deemphasized in favor of sharp outlines; in sculpture, works were based on Hellenistic styles and became static in comparison to the more plastic and pictorial post-Renaissance sculpture; in architecture, Greek and Roman forms dominated, sometimes reproducing antique models in their entirety.

Ogive: A pointed arch.

Orders: A formal system of base, column, and entablature in classic architecture. (See diagram, Greek Orders; Doric, Ionic, and Corinthian.)

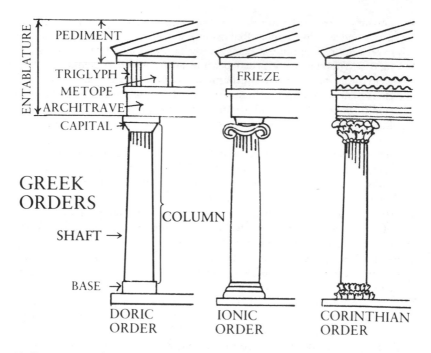

Pediment: The triangular structure supported on the entablature over porticoes, doors, and windows. (See diagram, Greek Orders.)

Perpendicular Style (ca. 1375–1500): The last phase of Gothic in England. It is characterized by a slenderness of design, particularly seen in the flattened stone vaults supported by ribs that fan out (fan vaulting), but with windows that are more austere, divided by long vertical mullions set very close together and intersecting with horizontal mullions. The window tracery gives the style its name.

Perspective: The apparent decrease of objects in size as they recede into the distance.

Piano Nobile: The main story of a building; generally placed immediately above the ground story.

Pier: A supporting mass of masonry from which arches or vaulting spring. It is usually composed of a collection of shafts and therefore may be of various shapes.

Pilaster: A columnar form flattened against or imbedded in a wall.

Plateresque: A particularly ornate form of Flamboyant architecture, popular in Spain in the sixteenth century.

Pointillé: A technique in painting in which thick bright paints are distributed as highlights over a dark area to give the illusion of glittering light without changing the basic value of the form.

Polyptych: A painting executed in more than three hinged panels.

Portico: A porch whose roof is supported by columns or piers.

Post-Impressionism (late nineteenth century): This was the reaction against Impressionism by such artists as Cézanne, van Gogh, and Gauguin, who brought the ideas of the impressionists further along by exploring new meanings of color and structure, thus rejecting the naturalistic aims of the impressionists leading to the first conscious use of expressive distortion, or what we call abstraction.

Pre-Raphaelite Art (mid-nineteenth century): A romantic movement in painting started in 1848 by a small group of English painters to protest against the mediocre painting of their time. They emphasized the Gothic and what they considered the pure forms of art that existed in the early fifteenth century before the time of Raphael. Pre-Raphaelite art is characterized by minuteness of precision and detail and a devotion to figure subjects with a narrative content often depicting a dreamlike world anchored by religion and legend.

Predella: A small strip of paintings along the base of an altarpiece.

Quattrocento: The Italian term for the fifteenth-century Renaissance period in Italy.

Renaissance art (fourteenth–early sixteenth century): A period of transition from the medieval to the modern, based on a revival of rediscovered classical art, which led to a new interest in man and a greater appreciation of life in the present world. In painting, a new approach to reality led to the development of perspective and a modeling in light and shadow; in sculpture, a revival of classical qualities led to refined surfaces, detailed realism, a sense of movement and characterization in portraits: in architecture, classical facades and interiors were emphasized and secular buildings became prominent for the first time in Italy.

Retable: A painted or carved altarpiece standing behind the altar in a church.

Rococo Art (eighteenth century): A continuation of the seventeenth-century baroque style, but lighter with greater delicacy giving an impression of heightened elegance and refinement. In painting, a playful, fluid, and decorative style, associated mostly with France, in which the main subject matter was the worldly pleasures of aristocratic society, but also some genre motifs that emphasized domestic virtues; in sculpture, a continuation of the richness of the baroque, but with increased pictorial qualities; in architecture, a change from the magnificent grandeur of baroque exteriors to a concentration on elegant and intimate interiors that displayed the greatest and most elaborate ornamentation and skilled workmanship in European history.

Roman Art (second century B.C.–fifth century A.D.): Most important accomplishments are in architecture where the true arch, the vault and the dome were used—for both engineering and aesthetic purposes—in monumental works that structurally were more progressive and utilitarian than the conservative Greek buildings. Greek orders were retained for decorative use, however, and a major Roman contribution to art was the preservation of Greek forms through adaptation and direct copying in sculpture and the pictorial arts, as well as in architecture.

Romanesque Art (eleventh–twelfth century):   A style that varied widely in different locations and developed over a long period of time prior to the eleventh century. Its basic elements are found in classic early Christian, Byzantine, and barbarian styles, which were fused into the Christian iconography of the Middle Ages. It is best known in architecture, which gives it its name from the use of the round Roman arch, but Byzantine domes were also used and a great variety of purely decorative elements, such as sculptures that were conceived as an integral part of architecture. In the pictorial arts the illuminated manuscript dominated and, because of its small size, helped to disseminate the different artistic styles throughout Europe.

Romanticism (nineteenth century):   A reaction against nineteenth century neo-Classic art. In architecture, it revived the Gothic; in painting, it opposed the linear and the sculpturesque style of the Classic Revival in favor of dynamic designs, bright colors, and emotional subject matter; in sculpture, it added greater movement and power to overly static designs. Romanticism rejected tradition, was emotional, subjective, individualistic, experimental, and interested in nature, especially in its wild and primitive state; neoclassicism accepted tradition, appealed to reason, was objective, typical, based on clear, measurable, ordered forms, and emphasized universal thoughts and ideas.

Rose Window: A circular stained glass window whose tracery is in the form of a rose.

Rustication: Masonry employing massive blocks separated by deep grooves or joints.

Sanctuary: See **Chancel.**

Sfumato: The technique used by Leonardo da Vinci to express in painting the delicately gradating tones from light to dark. As an Italian word it means to disperse like mist. Leonardo refers to it in his writing, saying that light and dark should blend "without lines or borders, in the manner of smoke."

Shafts: The portion of a column between the base and the capital comprising most of the height of the column. (See diagram, Greek Orders.)

Spandrel: A curving triangular arch between arches.

Spire: A tall pyramidal form placed over a tower.

Surrealism (first half of the twentieth century):   In painting, a movement that depicts the world of secret desires that issue spontaneously from the unconscious. Artists concentrated on a surreality that depended less on nature than on the human imagination that interprets it; that is, "the depiction of thought completely uncontrolled by reason and independent of all aesthetic or moral preoccupation," according to André Breton, the French poet and critic.

Tempera: A technique of painting on a plaster-covered wooden panel in which egg yolk, rather than oil, was used as a binder for the pigments; popular until the fifteenth century.

Terra-cotta: An Italian word meaning "baked earth;" a process where architectural and sculptural forms are molded in clay and can be colored and glazed before baking.

Tracery: The ornamental stonework in the upper part of a Gothic window. It can also be on walls, screens, vaults, etc.

Transepts: The cross-arm of a cruciform church, normally running northsouth. (See diagram, Latin-Cross Plan.)

Tribune: A gallery, usually located at the upper level of the nave or transept of a church.

Triforium: The story above the nave arcade of a church, enclosed by the roof of a side aisle. In cathedrals it is often occupied by pierced arcading. (See diagram, Gothic Cathedral.)

Triglyph: A group of vertical fluted panels placed between metopes in the frieze of the Doric order. (See diagram, Gothic Cathedral.)

Triptych: A painting, usually of a religious subject, with three panels; the side panels are often one half the size of the larger central panel and hinged to it so that they may be folded over it like doors.

Trompe l'oeil: A visual deception in painting in which objects are rendered in fine detail creating the realistic illusion of tactile and spatial qualities.

Trumeau: A post supporting a tympanum within an arch and dividing a doorway into two doors.

Tudor Design (sixteenth century): A phase of the English Gothic style; actually a decorative late version of the Perpendicular style. (See also **Perpendicular Style.**)

Tympanum: The space between the lintel and the arch of a doorway, often filled with relief sculpture.

Vault: Any form of arched roofing over a building. It may be of stone, brick, or wood.

Voussoirs: The wedge-shaped stones of an arch or vault.

Index

INDEX OF ARTISTS AND CITIES, PLUS ART WORKS LISTED
UNDER: ANTIQUE SCULPTURE AND REMAINS (GREEK,
ETRUSCAN, ROMAN), MANUSCRIPTS, MEDIEVAL SCULPTURE,
MEDIEVAL TAPESTRIES, AND MOSAICS.

Asterisks (*) refer to general information about artists.

The Author

David Lawrence Morton was born in New York City and was graduated from New York University where he earned bachelor and graduate degrees. He has been an executive in the travel industry, and has traveled widely in Europe. With this, his first book, he has combined his two lifelong loves: art and travel. He lives in New York with his wife and two children.